Leaving Paradise

The publication of this book was made possible through sponsorship of the Native Hawaiian Center of Excellence, John A. Burns School of Medicine, University of Hawai'i at Mānoa. Partial funding for this publication was provided by the Department of Health and Human Services, Health Resources Services Administration, Bureau of Health Professions, Division of Health Careers, Diversity and Development.

Leaving Paradise

INDIGENOUS HAWAIIANS *in the*

PACIFIC NORTHWEST,

1787–1898

Jean Barman *and*
Bruce McIntyre Watson

UNIVERSITY OF HAWAI'I PRESS
HONOLULU

Printed in the United States of America

11 10 09 08 07 06   6 5 4 3 2 1

Library of Congress Cataloging-in-Publication Data
Barman, Jean, 1939–
Leaving paradise : indigenous Hawaiians in the Pacific
Northwest, 1787–1898 / Jean Barman and Bruce McIntyre
Watson.
    p. cm.
Includes index.
ISBN-13: 978-0-8248-2943-8 (cloth : alk. paper)
ISBN-10: 0-8248-2943-3 (cloth : alk. paper)
    1. Hawaiians—Northwest, Pacific. 2. Polynesians—
Northwest, Pacific. 3. Hawaiians—Employment—Northwest,
Pacific. 4. Polynesians—Employment—Northwest, Pacific.
5. National characteristics, Hawaiian. 6. Frontier and pioneer
life—Northwest, Pacific. 7. Fur trade—Northwest, Pacific—
History. 8. Northwest, Pacific—History—18th century. 9.
Northwest, Pacific—History—19th century. I. Watson, Bruce
McIntyre. II. Title.
    F855.2.H3B37 2006.
    979.50049'942—dc22
                                          2005037659

University of Hawai'i Press books are printed on acid-free
paper and meet the guidelines for permanence and durability
of the Council on Library Resources.

Designed by Liz Demeter

Printed by The Maple-Vail Book Manufacturing Group

Contents

PREFACE

HAWAIIANS LEAVING paradise are not easy to track down. Nor did we begin our research with that goal in mind. We have each worked with Pacific Northwest history for some time, Jean writing about British Columbia and Bruce interrogating the fur trade. Our discussions over the years with Hawaiian descendants across the Pacific Northwest raised more questions than they gave answers. Their inability to trace their families back to the Islands intrigued us, as did the silence about them in Hawaiian sources.[1] Over the years we looked further, being encouraged to do so by descendants seeking to understand their history.

Much of what we would like to know still escapes us. We will never know the total number of Hawaiians in the Pacific Northwest between 1787, when the first of them arrived, and 1898, when the Islands were incorporated into the United States. Some of the earliest went out of curiosity. Others were recruited as seamen. Many more were hired for the fur trade. Yet others came on their own, in search of a better life. No one kept score, but by the end of the nineteenth century, over a thousand had done so. Most were sojourners, but some decided to stay. They became settlers. Their descendants remain a lively, self-confident, and self-conscious presence in the American and Canadian Pacific Northwest.

While many of the Hawaiians who crossed the Pacific Ocean were not recorded by name, we have tracked some 850 in the Pacific Northwest between 1787 and 1898. Their stories and those of their countrymen comprise the first half of this book, their biographies the second half. Each of these men and women left paradise for their own reasons. Among them were the great changes taking place in their homeland. The history of Hawaiians in the Pacific Northwest is also the history of the Hawaiian Islands.

Neither we nor descendants have been able to trace individuals back to their families in the Hawaiian Islands with certainty. The same questions are asked time and again: "Do we have family on Hawaiian Islands today? If so, who are they and how do we connect with them?"[2] We have located

vii

sparse information about from where in the Islands or elsewhere in Polynesia persons came. For the most part we know only where they boarded ship, usually Honolulu from the early nineteenth century. With a few exceptions, we do not know what happened to individuals on their return.

Three reasons give the explanation. First, the hierarchical nature of Hawaiian society made genealogy the prerogative of chiefs and rulers. Their rights to the land came through inheritance, which meant they had to remember and be able to recite their lineages. Ordinary people found their identity within kindred groups linked by access to land and resources. Compared with the ruling groups, less impetus existed for everyday Hawaiians to pass on their biological inheritance through the generations.[3]

For only a handful of early arrivals to the Pacific Northwest, identified as chiefs, does information survive about familial origins. Ordinary men and women, as were most of those leaving paradise, found genealogy most useful for attaching themselves to their chiefs or rulers. It is these stories that come down through time. According to the son of a longtime Hudson's Bay employee at Fort Langley, "Peon Peon [Peeopeeoh] was a relative of the Kamehamehas (Kings of the S.I.) and came to Ft Vancouver Wash in the Early Twenties [1820s] as a guardian of the Sandwich Islanders Employed by the Hudsons Bay Co." The Kalama family of Washington State has speculated about a relationship to "Queen Kalama, wife of Kamehameha III." A member of the Nahu family of North Vancouver was described on his death in 1957 as "a grandson of Miyu, Hawaiian prince, who was expelled by his brother, King Kamehameha, after attempting to gain the throne." According to local lore that has come down through descendants in British Columbia, the Mahoi family descended from one of "the Royal twins, part of the family that long ruled Hawaii," *mahoe* meaning twins in Hawaiian.[4]

The second reason is the scarcity of sources in the Hawaiian Islands. It was only after the arrival of missionaries in 1820 that the Hawaiian language was written down. It took another couple of decades for the kinds of information that permit family reconstruction to begin to be collected. A legal requirement existed from 1842 to record births, marriages, and deaths, but, as many Hawaiians have discovered in attempting to retrieve their inheritance, even information that might once have existed has not necessarily survived. Communications scholar Rona Tamiko Halualani eloquently documented what she terms "the structured impossibility of substantiating one's Hawaiianness."[5]

The third, even greater difficulty to tracing Hawaiians in the Pacific Northwest back to the Islands has to do with naming practices. As Houston Wood cautions in *Displacing Natives*, "Hawaiian personal names did not indicate gender, place children in genealogies of patrilineal descent, or require women at marriage to become wards of their husbands." In *Hawaiian Names, English Names,* Eileen Root describes how Hawaiian names sometimes refer to qualities or things, or are part of a larger means of self-identification. Persons were known by first names, family names, diminutives, and nicknames. Orphans might adopt the name of the island or place on the island from where they came. Robert Stauffer explains how names could be variously spelled, by, for instance, adding the prefix *Ka* or *Na, the* in Hawaiian. Other possible variations have to do with *nui* for large, *lili* for small, or *opio* for firstborn being tacked on the end. Persons might well change their name. A missionary in the Islands from 1835 into the early 1880s described how Hawaiians "often take new names."[6]

The names we employ here are those that were written down, most often as they were spoken by the person to whom they belonged and as best we can make out the spelling in documents upwards to two centuries old. Record keepers in the Pacific Northwest drew on an English alphabet of twenty-six characters to mimic the sounds they heard, whereas its Hawaiian counterpart, as devised by the first missionaries, contains just twelve letters, the five vowels and *h, k, l, m, n, p,* and *w.* Many names were recorded differently than they would have been at home. The Tahitian *t* sometimes replaced the Hawaiian *k,* and *b* replaced *p* depending on the clerk who wrote the name (Tahitian *taboo* versus Hawaiian *kapu*), which means some names appear Tahitian and may well have been so. Other names appear to be Samoan or Maori or even Rapa Nui from Easter Island. The nominative marker *Ko-* is common in Rapa Nui family names. These same names might also be Hawaiian. Traveling through the Islands in 1823, missionary William Ellis was perturbed by "the great variety of methods adopted by different voyagers to represent the same word." He spelled the island of Molokaʻi "Morokai," Honolulu "Honoruru." Visiting four decades later, American writer Mark Twain considered "*k* and *t* are the same in the Kanaka alphabet, and so are *l* and *r.*"[7]

Many Hawaiians coming to the Pacific Northwest used a single name. They did so even after 1860, when newcomers in the Islands pushed through legislation intended to force indigenous Hawaiians to adopt patrilineal naming practices. Sometimes a Christian first name preceded or replaced a Hawaiian name, hence the multiple Bens, Bills, Charleys, Johns, and Peters in Pacific Northwest records. Others were described by some version of *Kanaka,* meaning human being in Polynesian languages, or *owyhee,* after the island of Hawaiʻi, hence Pahapale Whyhee, Charles Kanack, and Honololo (Canac). The parents of a child baptized in British Columbia as late as 1893 were given in the official register as "John and Cecilia (Canakas)."[8]

Some recorders made no attempt to replicate what they heard and gave names serendipitously. The U.S. scientific exploring expedition of the late 1830s and early 1840s spent considerable time in both the Hawaiian Islands and Pacific Northwest, and employed Hawaiians as crew. The head observed about them that "their Hawaiian names were too difficult for the sailors to adopt, and they very soon had others given them, that arose from personal peculiarities, or from some whim of the sailors with whom they messed; and they were consequently seldom called by their real names, except at muster." A passenger's observation about a Hawaiian taken aboard in the Islands at mid-century is similar. "His name, 'Hameha,' was tattooed on his arm, but we christened him 'Jacky.'"[9] A man called America spent two decades in the fur trade, Ebony fifteen years, Captain Cole a decade. Spunyarn and Ropeyarn, referring to hair texture, and John Bull, indicating an affinity with Britain, were commonplace nicknames for Hawaiians far beyond the Pacific Northwest.

The complexities of names and naming extend from individuals to groups. Hawaiians in the Pacific Northwest were most often called Kanakas, an adaptation of *Kanaka, Kānaka* in the plural. This means of identification was used more generally, not just in the Hawaiian Islands but to describe contract laborers recruited to work Queensland sugar fields from across the South Pacific in the second half of the nineteenth century. In Australia and elsewhere, *Kanaka* became pejorative. Descendants in the Pacific Northwest have urged it not be used to name them or their families. By the mid-nineteenth century newcomer offspring born in the Islands were using "Hawaiian" to refer to themselves, making that term inadequate on its own. The alternative of "Native Hawaiian" is confusing, given its legal definition in the Islands as "any descendant of not less than one-half part of the blood of the races inhabiting the Hawaiian Islands previous to 1778."[10] Hawaiian scholars Kekuni Blaisdell, Jonathan Kay Kamakawiwoʻole Osorio, and Noenoe Silva have reclaimed the term *Kānaka Maoli,* which in translation means true, real, genuine, original, indigenous Hawaiians.[11] We employ the adjective *indigenous,* which has the added advantage of being used by persons around the world to distinguish themselves from colonizers usurping their land and resources.

Our principal sources of written information come from the Pacific Northwest. We took advantage of ships' logs, except for those of whaling vessels, which did not usually stop in the Pacific Northwest and which are examined in historian David Chappell's *Double Ghosts* and on the Bishop Museum's website.[12] Journals and memoirs of the Pacific Fur Company and North West Company throw light on the years up to 1821. The most detailed records come from the Hudson's Bay Company, which thereafter dominated the Pacific Northwest fur trade. By extracting information from its accounts, district reports, post journals, and correspondence, we were able to piece together the work lives of some 400 indigenous Hawaiian employees. Other sources include vital statistics, manuscript censuses, voters' lists, newspapers, diaries and journals, and personal accounts. Harriet Munnick's transcription of Catholic vital statistics from the American Pacific Northwest has been invaluable, as have comparable records for British Columbia.[13]

We located far fewer sources in the Hawaiian Islands. The most important are passenger manifests, lists of seamen and contract laborers, and consular and other government records held in the Hawai'i State Archives, the earliest of which date from the 1840s. Correspondence in the Mission Children's Society Library in Honolulu helped us to understand relationships between missionaries in the Islands and in the Pacific Northwest. Another important source are the writings of nineteenth-century indigenous Hawaiian scholars. David Malo born around 1795, John Papa Ii in 1800, Samuel Manaiākalani Kamakau in 1815, and Kepelino about 1830 each reflected critically on the changes they experienced over their lifetimes. We have also benefited from the scholarship of a new generation of Hawaiian scholars, including Kekuni Blaisdell, Rona Tamiko Halualani, Lilikalā Kame'eleihiwa, George Hu'eu Sanford Kanahele, Jonathan Kay Kamakawiwo'ole Osorio, Noenoe K. Silva, and Haunani-Kay Trask.

Many institutions have opened their doors to us. For their time and attention, we are grateful to the librarians and archivists at the Archivo de Indias, Seville, Spain; Bancroft Library, University of California, Berkeley; Bishop Museum, Honolulu, Hawai'i; British Columbia Archives, Victoria, British Columbia; California Historical Society, San Francisco, California; City of Vancouver Archives, Vancouver, British Columbia; Columbia River Maritime Museum, Astoria, Oregon; Detroit Library, Detroit, Michigan; Fort Nisqually Historic Site Archives, Tacoma, Washington; Fort Vancouver National Historic Site Archives, Vancouver, Washington; Harvard University Library, Houghton Library, Cambridge, Massachusetts; Hawai'i State Archives, Honolulu, Hawai'i; Hawaiian Historical Society, Honolulu, Hawai'i; Hawaiian Mission Children's Society Library, Honolulu, Hawai'i; Hudson's Bay Company Archives, Winnipeg, Manitoba; Huntington Library, San Marino, California; Massachusetts Historical Society, Boston, Massachusetts; Mystic Seaport Museum, Mystic, Connecticut; Library and Archives Canada, Ottawa, Ontario, and Regional Depository, Burnaby, British Columbia; North Vancouver Museum and Archives, North Vancouver, British Columbia; Oblate House, Vancouver, British Columbia; Old Dartmouth Historical Society and Whaling Museum, New Bedford, Massachusetts; Oregon Historical Society, Portland, Oregon; Peabody Essex Museum, Salem, Massachusetts; Puget Sound Regional Archives, Bellevue,

Washington; Rosenbach Library, Philadelphia, Pennsylvania; St. Edward's Church, Duncan, British Columbia; Royal Ontario Museum, Toronto, Ontario; St. Elizabeth's Church, Sidney, British Columbia; Salt Spring Archives, Ganges, British Columbia; San Juan Library, Friday Harbor, Washington; Sisters of St. Ann Archives, Victoria, British Columbia; South Oregon Historical Society, Medford, Oregon; University of British Columbia Library, Special Collections, Vancouver, British Columbia; University of Hawai'i at Mānoa, Hamilton Library, Honolulu, Hawai'i; University of Western Washington, Center for Pacific Studies, Bellingham, Washington; Vancouver Public Library, Special Collections, Vancouver, British Columbia; Vancouver School of Theology, United Church Archives, Vancouver, British Columbia; and Beinecke Rare Book and Manuscript Library, Yale University, New Haven, Connecticut.

There would be no book except for the many descendants across the Pacific Northwest who have made us welcome in their homes and in their lives. We are extraordinarily grateful for the oral histories, documents, and photographs they have shared with us. Carey Myers not only provided invaluable information about "the Hawaiian," as he calls his great-grandfather George Kamano, but took us to meet his wonderful Aunty Vi Johnston, who at the age of ninety stuffed us with sandwiches while taking us through her scrapbooks. Larry Bell introduced us to the difficulties of securing public acknowledgment of Hawaiians' contribution to the making of the Pacific Northwest. Others embracing our research include Lonnie Bate, Violet Bell, Anna Chapman, Cecile Clare, Laura Nahanee Cole, Mel, Rick, and Rod Couvelier, Eliola Cox, Jon Davis, Rachel Day, Theresa Dow, Lynda Farrington, Ronald Fisher, Anne Fowler, Nora Fuller, Susan Garcia, Gladys Gardiner, Gilbert Garrison, Joan Graves, Ray and Duncan Harpur, Stanley Harris, Jan Hastings, Pauline Hillaire, Carol and Christopher Jensen, Leila Johnston, Lloyd Kendrick, Karey Litton, Bill Lumley, Norman and Daniel McPhee, Elizabeth Maurer, Donna Miranda, James and Jerry Nahanee, Olive O'Connor, Roree Oehlman, Tricia O'Leary, Muriel Parker, Mary and Terry Picard, Harry Roberts, Carolynne Sacht, Marion Schick, Josephine and Ken Seeley, Vina Segalerba, Duke and Jill Shepard, Victor Smith, Josephine Steinbach, Donna Stewart, Sophie Tahouney, Hugh Taylor, Ruth Ulrich, and Rose Unger. Thanks also go to Bob Akerman, Louis Cordocedo, Eb Giescke, Carol Harbison-Samuelson, Pauline Harris, Joan Ingram, Tom Koppel, David Lewis, Richard Mackie, Brad Morrison, Shirley Morrison, Myrtle Roberts, Laura Roland, Dale Seeley, and Beatrice Shepard. Chris Hanna is unique for his ability to coax information from the British Columbia Archives. Rod Barman gave valuable technical assistance.

It is not only in the Pacific Northwest where we were helped along the way. Kamuela Ka'ahanui sorted out possible spellings of names and their origins. Over a beer on Rapa Nui, Grant McCall pointed out the possibility of Easter Islanders being part of the story. David Chappell, Malcolm Naea Chun, and Rodney Otanu gave support at critical junctures. Susan Lebo introduced us to the Bishop Museum's project to record the names of Hawaiians who joined whaling vessels. Barbara Dunn of the Hawaiian Historical Society, Lanihuli Freidenburg of the Lahaina Restoration Foundation, Noelani Keliikipi of the Moloka'i Museum and Cultural Center, and Roslyn Lightfoot of the Maui Historical Society patiently answered questions and shared insights. Jason Achiu of the Hawai'i State Archives and Jennifer Leilani Basham of the University of Hawai'i translated materials from Hawaiian to English. David Hanson at the Fort Vancouver National Historic Site tracked down an illusive image of Kanaka Village. At the University of Hawai'i Press, Masako Ikeda has been a supportive editor. Two manuscript assessors were helpful and perceptive. The Native Hawaiian Center of Excellence at the University of Hawai'i generously supported publication.

The goal of this book is to return home indigenous Hawaiians in the Pacific Northwest. They were each born into families that were diminished by their departures. Those who went back were changed by their time away, as were those around them by virtue of their return. As just one example, we know that a few of the men brought wives with them to the Pacific Northwest, but can only speculate whether anyone took home the indigenous women with whom they lived in the Pacific Northwest or children born to them. We are hopeful that descendants in the Hawaiian Islands will be able to link the biographies to their own families and that examination of additional sources, including Hawaiian-language newspapers published from the 1850s onward, will uncover links that have eluded us.[14] Whether it is possible to do so, we, as outsiders, are not equipped to answer.

We also seek to return Hawaiians home in another sense. The great changes occurring between the arrival of the first outsiders in 1778 and the Hawaiian Islands' annexation by the United States in 1898 decimated the indigenous population, both numerically and culturally. Hawaiians' resourcefulness in the Pacific Northwest during these same years argues that they could also at home, if given the opportunity, deal with the larger world much more on their own terms. Their experiences allow us to glimpse what might have been in the Islands themselves.

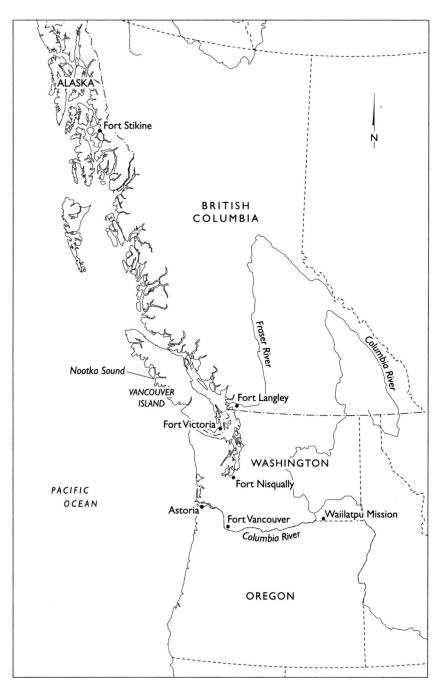

Pacific Northwest where Hawaiians arrived and settled. Map by William L. Nelson.

Chapter 1

LEAVING PARADISE

⟲ CAPTAIN JAMES COOK dropped anchor at Waimea Harbor in the Hawaiian island of Kauaʻi on January 20, 1778. Two months later he reached Nootka Sound on the Northwest Coast of North America and thereby became the first European to visit both the Islands, which he named the Sandwich Islands, and the Pacific Northwest. Less than a decade later Hawaiians began traveling from the Islands to the Northwest Coast. Among the first non-Europeans to do so, they tell a different story about the post-contact years in the Hawaiian Islands than do the usual histories. These men and women repeatedly acted to the benefit of themselves and others in ways that testify, time and again, to their resourcefulness and resilience.

The long prevailing line of reasoning depicts the Hawaiian people as unable to cope with the changes emanating from contact. Their decline in numbers from about 300,000, by a conservative estimate, at the time of Captain Cook's arrival to 80,000 by the mid-nineteenth century and to just 30,000 by century's end gives the plot line for a morality tale in which indigenous ways of life are found wanting.[1] In this view, Hawaiians must have done something wrong to merit their virtual demise. As a newcomer opined in the mid-1830s, "this people is in a deplorable condition—so much of sin, oppression and degradation that they are evidently decreasing very fast."[2] Hawaiians are, in effect, held responsible for the actions of others. In this version of events, the ruling groups did what they could to maintain control, but eventually the United States was compelled to rescue the Islands by taking them into its fold.

The Hawaiian Islands and the Pacific Northwest were intertwined from the moment of contact. The impetus for Hawaiians' departure lay with Cook's voyage. Sea otter pelts acquired on the Northwest Coast fetched such a high price in Asia, where the Chinese used them to trim garments, as to unleash a mad dash for furs. The Islands became a stopover point for merchant vessels in search of pelts. While there, they picked up local men as crew. Sought out for their facility with water, Hawaiians were also distinguished by their physical appearance. According to Cook, "these people were of a brown colour, and though of the common size, were stoutly made."[3]

By the time the fur trade became land based in the Pacific Northwest in the early nineteenth century, Hawaiians had established their reputation as dependable workers and were hired almost as a matter of course. Fort Astoria, the principal American initiative west of the Rocky Mountains, relied on Hawaiians. So did its successors out of Montreal and London, the North West Company and the Hudson's Bay Company. Hawaiians also sustained the early missionaries, worked in the sawmills that sprang up on both sides of the boundary fixed in 1846 between Britain and the United States, and participated in the gold rushes of mid-century. A few came for diversion, as with future kings Lot Kamehameha and David Kalākaua, who visited in 1860. Over a thousand Hawaiians made the crossing to the Pacific Northwest up to the American annexation of the Islands in 1898, some more than once.

By following these Hawaiians to and from the Pacific Northwest, we gain another perspective on the Islands during the late eighteenth and nineteenth centuries. At the time of Captain Cook's arrival in 1787, the eight inhabited islands—from northwest to southeast, Ni'ihau, Kaua'i, O'ahu, Moloka'i, Lana'i, Maui, Kaho'olawe, and Hawai'i—shared a hierarchical way of life based in subsistence agriculture and fishing. Authority over the land and its resources rested with chiefs, or *ali'i,* who gave permission for its occupancy and use, as well as protection, to extended family units. These kindred networks, known as *'ohana,* were comprised of commoners or *maka'āinana,* a word that means, literally, "people living on the land." Writing in 1868, indigenous Hawaiian historian Samuel Kamakau explained how

the Hawaiians were in old days a strong and hard-working people. . . . Cultivation of the land was their main industry. With their hands alone, assisted by tools made of hard wood from the mountains and by stone adzes, they tilled large fields and raised taro, sweet potatoes, yams, bananas, sugar cane, and 'awa [kava, a medicinal plant]; and bartered their product or used it at home. . . . The land was fertile, and the principal crop on Kaua'i, Oahu, and Molokai was wet-land taro. . . . On Maui and Hawaii where there was less wet land, dry-land taro was cultivated.[4]

The *maka'āinana* repaid the *ali'i* with their labor and part of their crop to be used, as explained by political scientist Elizabeth Buck, "for ritual obligations, for maintaining their chiefly apparatus, for redistribution to their supporting *ali'i,* for status (evidence of *kapu* and *mana*) and for warfare." Chiefs had the power to appropriate, channel, or transform *mana,* which was power emanating from the *akua,* or gods. Chiefs organized social relations, eating and dressing habits, the use of material resources, and social and personal order through the *kapu,* or taboo system. The prescriptions and prohibitions of *kapu* not only determined what was sacred and forbidden but helped sustain Islanders in a very effective system of cleanliness and health. Kamakau described his countrymen "prior to the coming of foreigners" as "hospitable, kindly, giving a welcome to strangers, affectionate, generous, givers."[5]

The first outsiders in the Islands were more curious than censorious. Mostly seamen briefly on shore, they were captivated by the salubrious climate and physical beauty of what appeared to many of them a veritable paradise. They were aware of differences, but not interested in effecting change. Much as was happening elsewhere around the world, they differentiated the indigenous population by gender. Women they found pleasurable for sexual purposes, men useful for their labor.

Hawaiian Islanders developed their own strategies for dealing with newcomers so that, as historian I. C. Campbell points out, "for the first few decades after contact, Polynesians went about their affairs as if the coming of Europeans did not represent a turning point in their history." New diseases caused deaths that would otherwise not have occurred, but overall Hawaiians coped. By the early nineteenth century power in the Islands had coalesced around a single ruling chief or king, Kamehameha I, and in 1819 the *kapu* system was abandoned. A Frenchman who visited that year described new tools, familiarity with firearms, and a penchant for European dress, "but that is the extent of the influence that the civilized world has had on the activities and customs of the Sandwich Islanders: the natives have made no changes in the way they build their houses nor in the way they live their lives." Ethnographer Juri Mykkänen concludes that "the society was still largely intact as far as the trajectories of commoner life."[6]

Hawaiian Islanders' resourcefulness during the first decades of contact comes through vividly in the stories told about the first men and women leaving paradise for the Pacific Northwest. Both the handful who were of chiefly status and the far greater number of modest background demonstrated a spirit of inquiry and a facility for dealing with new experiences that cut across the hierarchical way of life they shared at home. Be it the maritime fur trade on the Northwest Coast of North America from 1787 into the 1820s or its land-based counterpart at Fort Astoria in today's Oregon between 1810 and 1814, described in chapters 2 and 3, Hawaiians proved themselves to be hardworking, capable, and dependable. Their tenacity argues that the unification of the Islands around Kamehameha in 1810, with its capital at Honolulu on the island of O'ahu, might well have initiated a time of well-being and prosperity.

Fundamental change was, however, on the way. It arrived in 1820 in the form of Protestant missionaries dispatched from Boston by the American Board of Commissioners of Foreign Missions. The newcomers were entirely different from their predecessors in the Islands. Formed in the Puritan tradition associated with New England, they believed utterly in the superiority of their way of life. Their duty, as they saw it, was to convert Hawaiians to their outlook, but there was a hitch. The missionaries could not abide the *maka'āinana*, or common people, and very soon concentrated their efforts on the small group at the top. Missionaries' actions served to turn chiefs'

VIEW of the ISLAND of WOAHOO the PACIFIC VISITED by C. E. BENSELL in 1821.

A view of the island of Hawai'i, 1821, by C. E. Bensell. Courtesy of Mystic Seaport, 1956. 2111.

attention away from their charges. Ordinary Hawaiians' way of life was disrupted without another to replace it.

From the moment the first missionaries landed in 1820, they made clear their disdain for the *maka'āinana*. Their leader Hiram Bingham described his group's feelings in language devoid of romanticism and fired with the zeal of moral certitude. "The appearance of destitution, degradation, and barbarism, among the chattering, and almost naked savages, whose heads and feet, and much of their sunburnt swarthy skins, were bare, was appalling." According to another arrival, "those wretched creatures" gave "the appearance of being half man and half beast." The first history of the Hawaiian Islands, published in 1843 and reprinted into the twentieth century, asserted that, up to the missionaries' arrival, "the Hawaiians were . . . low, naked, filthy, vile and sensual; covered with every abomination, stained with blood and black with crime." In her perceptive study of missionary wives, historian Patricia Grimshaw characterizes the "response to ordinary, nonchiefly Hawaiians" as "frankly condemnatory."[7]

To the extent missionaries found any Hawaiians up to their standards, it was the ruling groups. As put by Grimshaw and attested by Mykkänen, "the missionaries ardently wished to view the chiefs as players in the mission drama." Ideologically, this attitude was contradictory. As one missionary wife acknowledged about the Islands' system of rule, "I should scarcely have thought I could have become so desirous of any government so different from that in my own land." A visitor about this time pointed up the great status differential that divided the tiny minority from what he termed "the common people," comprising 149,000 of a population he estimated at 150,000. "The greatest wealth they can boast consists of a mat on which to sleep;—a few folds of tapa [bark cloth] to cover them;—one calabash of water, and another for poe [basic foodstuff made from taro];—a rude implement or two for the cultivation of the ground; and the instruments used in their simple manufactures."[8]

Other factors took precedence over Americans' commitment at home to the well-being of all the people in common and to a republican form of government. The Calvinist theology to which missionaries subscribed interpreted worldly success as an indication of God's approval. It was laudable, indeed, the duty, of God's elect to have charge of political and economic as well as spiritual life. So assured, missionaries concentrated their efforts on the favored few. As early as 1823 one of the missionaries took pride "that our warmest friends are among the highest chiefs," adding, "this, I think, makes our future prospects very flattering."[9]

Missionaries needed ordinary Hawaiians for two purposes: as objects for conversion and as a source of labor. In order for the "wretched creatures" of the missionaries' imagination to become docile Christians, which alone justified the newcomers' presence in the Islands, they had to be reformed. Not surprisingly, according to legal ethnographer Sally Engle Merry, "it was Massachusetts prototypes that formed the basis of Hawaiian criminal law."[10] Proclamations from the mid-1820s onward banned sexuality outside of monogamous missionary-ritualized marriage and forbade such key Hawaiian cultural expressions as hula dancing and surfing.

The missionaries' boldest initiative was to make everyone literate so as to be able to read the Bible. The creation of a written alphabet of the Hawaiian language was one of the most positive consequences of missionaries' presence. At its height in the early 1830s, about 50,000 Hawaiians, mostly adults, were enrolled in some 1,100 schools under missionary aegis. Missionaries were unable to follow through, due to their inability to accept ordinary Hawaiians as capable of sanctity. The total admitted into church membership reached a thousand only in 1837, over a decade and a half after the first missionaries arrived.[11] By then almost ninety American Board missionaries and support workers were scattered across seventeen locations.

The *maka'āinana* were primarily useful for their bodies, as when Bingham, in the words of his great-grandson, "cajoled the chiefs into providing a thousand laborers" to build a majestic church of 14,000 coral blocks that still survives in the center of Honolulu. A visitor in the summer of 1837 described how the *maka'āinana* "cannot cultivate their land, because their labour is demanded for the church, the missionaries having obtained the necessary edict which compels the natives to labour on the reefs, to procure blocks of stone for the purpose of building a new church." It is an indication of missionaries' priorities that Hawaiians were excused from church attendance were they "to cut a block of compact coral limestone from the reef, about three feet long, two wide, and one deep, at low water, and transport it to the shore—say half a mile."[12] Churches were constructed through similar means across the Islands.

Contemporary observers with no love for the Americans were convinced that everyday conditions of life were worsening. For all of the bias that underlay their critiques, they are instructive for, unlike the missionaries, these newcomers took plain people's circumstances seriously. A French ship's captain described in 1828 how "ever since the Protestants have gained a measure of influence on these islands, the old agricultural life of the people has deteriorated and rapidly declined." The missionaries' insistence that everyone immediately become literate and labor on their behalf was "leaving their fields untilled" and "their traditional plantations . . . devoured by noxious weeds." He described how "the small ponds where taro was grown are totally dried and barren."[13]

Englishman Richard Charlton, writing four years later, was far harsher. He attributed depopulation of what he termed "an earthly paradise" to missionary excess. Charlton made four points, the first of which echoed his French counterpart. "The bulk of the people are in a state bordering on starvation because the adults are taken away from their enclosures of taro and potatoes to learn to read and spell." Second, persons who wanted to procreate were compelled first to marry in the church, which required money they did not have, and so there were fewer children. Third, "the missionaries have prohibited Fishing, Bathing, Jew's Harps, and the Surf Board, and every other description of amusement among the native population" so that "their spirit is broken." Charlton's fourth point had to do with disease, the most general explanation for population decline. Its calamitous effects he linked to the missionaries "prohibiting bathing, which in that climate is almost as essential to existence as fresh air." Water's importance to good health is confirmed by a traveler who, a decade and a half earlier, had termed Hawaiians "the cleanest people I ever saw, both in their person and habitation." An English visitor in 1839 asserted that "if the missionaries had not caused the discontinuance of *cleanliness,* of *ablution,* constant *sea-bathing,* and proper exercise, in men and women, as their natural habits pointed out," they would have been less adversely affected by disease. The consequence was, as a Frenchman lamented, "this people, which early navigators represented as so happy in their nakedness, seemed to us to be miserable, under the rags which civilization has covered them."[14]

As possibilities diminished at home for Hawaiians to pursue their ways of life, opportunities expanded elsewhere. In 1821 the fur trade west of the Rocky Mountains was consolidated under the Hudson's Bay Company, which shortly thereafter opened up an office in Honolulu which, as detailed in chapters 4 and 5, actively recruited workers from the Islands. Other indigenous Hawaiians were employed by missionaries who from the mid-1830s, as chapter 6 explains, echoed their Islands counterparts in pursuing indigenous souls in the Pacific Northwest.

Back home, Hawaiians' ties steadily weakened to their chiefs and rulers, who increasingly identified themselves in terms of missionaries' aspirations for them. Hawaiian Studies scholar Lilikalā Kameʻeleihiwa attributes the shift to Christian gods being perceived as more promising than the *akua* in keeping Hawaiians from dying. A well-educated indigenous Hawaiian was less generous. According to David Malo writing in 1839, "in former times, before Kamehehameha, the chiefs took great care of their people," but now

"their attention has been turned more to themselves and their own aggran-
dizement."[15] Two of the principal means of alienation were the Chiefs'
Children's School and the Ka Māhele.

The Chiefs' Children's School, which operated in Honolulu from 1839
to 1850, was, according to missionary leader Hiram Bingham, "the teacher
. . . of the kings and queens of the Sandwich Islands." Students were the
Island's last five monarchs, 1854–1893, and eleven offspring of chiefs. Much
as occurred in similar boarding schools for chiefly children on Maui and
elsewhere, they were educated into others' aspirations for them. However
understanding the missionary couple in charge may have been, Amos and
Juliette Cooke inculcated in the top layer of the ruling groups a way of life
totally at odds with what had gone on before. As diplomatically stated about
the student who became Hawai'i's last queen, Liliuokalani, in *American
National Biography*, "her moral values were shaped by the influence of the
missionaries."[16] Taught in English rather than Hawaiian, which was used
in the early missionary schools, this select handful was instructed to prefer
outsiders' ways, including acquisition of their material goods. Ruling groups'
schooling separated them more than ever from the common people and
their obligations toward them.

The other, very important means of dissociating ruling groups from
their charges was the Ka Māhele of the 1840s, a legal division of the Islands'
land that established private property in line with the priorities of missionaries and their newcomer allies. The significance of the shift cannot be overestimated. According to linguist and political scientist Noenoe Silva, "land
tenure was the central feature" of a reciprocal system of "political and social
relationships based on obligations as well as bonds of affection." Previously,
as explained by cultural anthropologist Marion Kelly, "Hawaiians lived in a
subsistence economy based on a communal land tenure system. Although
the land was controlled by the chiefs *(ali'i)*, who expropriated food and labor
from the cultivators of the soil, the commoners *(maka'āinana)*, everyone
had rights of access and use to the resources of the land and the sea." Kamakau emphasized Hawaiians' "inherent love of the land of one's birth inherited from one's ancestor" so that, while not owned, "the land belonged to
the common people" by virtue of their having mostly "lived on the same
land from very ancient times." Beginning in 1845, all Islands land was
divided into individually owned parcels consistent with outsiders' preference for private property in accord with American practice. As summed up
by Kelly: "Traditional Hawaiian culture and society was destroyed as the
capitalist concept of private property replaced communal use of the land
with individual ownership."[17]

The *maka'āinana* lost out twice over. The Ka Māhele removed commoners' obligation to labor on behalf of their chiefs and hence the mutual benefits that ensued. Ordinary Hawaiians were meant to acquire their own land, as were ruling groups and the government, but, as historian Robert Stauffer explains in his detailed examination of "how the land was lost" at Kahana on the island of O'ahu, the six-stage process was so complex and so costly as to deter almost any ordinary Hawaiian who did not receive missionary assistance from making a claim. Not only that, Lilikalā Kame'eleihiwa observes, "some *maka'āinana* may have been reluctant to claim *'Āina* [land] that heretofore had been controlled by the *Ali'i Nui* [highest chiefs], as traditionally that would have been very rude and inappropriate behavior." Despite all of the changes that beset the *maka'āinana*, in the words of Kamakau writing in 1869, "the Hawaiian nation loves its king and chiefs."[18]

According to Marion Kelly, less than one-third of adult male commoners got any land at all, even the smallest plot, whereas the principal chiefs acquired thousands of acres each and the king and government large hunks. Overall, "the *maka'ainana* received less than 1 percent of the land although they comprised 99 percent of the Hawaiian population." An observer lamented in 1849 "the thousands of acres of taro land now laying waste, on all the islands." A decade later a Russian ship's officer described "the native *kanakas*" as being "free but landless." The clusters of "affluent subsistence farmers who were self-sufficient in terms of nearly all the essentials of life" at the time of Captain Cook's arrival were transformed by the mid-nineteenth century, historian Carolyn Ralston explains, into "a class of unskilled and predominantly landless peasants."[19]

Ordinary Hawaiians also lost out as the ruling groups, deprived of their traditional labor pool, very soon sold off virtually all their newly got gains to get the cash needed to mimic newcomers. Kamakau explained how "the chiefs were selling their land to foreigners and to those who had no grants." The "bond of mutual dependence" and "spirit of mutual goodwill" that had characterized the Islands' social structure gave way, in Ralston's words, to ruling groups' "buying sprees with little concern for the people's well being." Anthropologists Patrick Kirch and Marshall Sahlins term the result "a subtropical caricature of European royalty." As summed up by Kamakau, writing in 1869, "the greater benefits of the law went to the foreigners who thus secured the right to live on the land even though they were not of the land."[20]

The *maka'āinana* had every reason to feel abandoned. Ralston contends that "in no other Polynesian societies were the ordinary people forced to confront their chiefs and recognize that they were not protecting the people's own interests." Even Sally Engle Merry, for all of her determination to view the ruling groups' actions sympathetically "as part of a struggle for sovereignty: an attempt to purchase independence with the coin of civilization," is forced to acknowledge, based on her close examination of court cases from the town of Hilo on the island of Hawai'i, that their actions "appeared to Hawaiian commoners to be a betrayal." Noenoe Silva has documented the *maka'āinana*'s resistance to the *ali'i*'s sale of land to outsiders.[21]

Missionaries, together with their children and outsiders mostly allied to them, took charge. It was "under the patronage of American missionaries," according to eminent Islands historian Ralph Kuykendall, that the first sugarcane plantations began operation in the mid-1830s, initiating the rush for economic gain. Missionary teacher turned entrepreneur Amos Cooke observed in 1850 that "while the natives stand confounded and amazed . . . the foreigners are creeping in among them, getting their largest and best lands, water privileges, building lots, etc. etc." He and the others considered they were forwarding the Islands', but very conveniently also their own, best interests by becoming the ruling group's political advisors, as well as entrepreneurs in their own right. As Gavan Daws puts it in his general history of the Islands, "for the foreigners, certainly, it was the beginning of a new era; but for the Hawaiian commoners it was the beginning of the end."[22]

Missionaries viewed their actions as confirming their status and also that of their children as among God's elect. Much as in Puritan New England, whence their outlook originated, economic gain was deemed admirable. Missionaries were encouraged to act as they did by the American Board that had dispatched them to the Islands. Cooke described how the Board advised that "all of their Missionaries at these Islands get free from them as soon as convenient, settle here, with their children, adopt the country as their own, and thus do all that is possible to sustain the country, and Government, whatever the latter may be," very possibly "Republican" within "a few years." This perspective fit conveniently into the conviction among persons whom Daws terms "Manifest Destiny men" that the Islands were American turf.[23]

Missionaries and other newcomers rationalized their actions by continuing to portray indigenous Hawaiians as doomed to disappear and, in the interim, too indolent to act for themselves. "It is a matter of no great surprise that the natives should be, as they really are, a lazy people," Cooke opined in 1850. "Like other savage nations, they are averse to any more labor than is absolutely necessary," a leading official of the American Board of Commissioners of Foreign Missions asserted a few years later. In the view of a missionary wife, the Hawaiian "lacks *stamina,* that reliability of character which distinguishes the people of England, old and new." Labor historian Edward Beechert explains outsiders' self-serving logic: "New Englanders, although vigorously opposed to racial slavery, nonetheless held firmly to the notion of racial superiority. Since 'idleness' was a defect of character found in the 'heathen,' it became necessary as part of the conversion process to 'save the Hawaiians' by introducing them to the discipline of work—the opposite of sin as evidenced in idleness."[24]

Newcomers hoped indigenous Hawaiians would work for minimal wages on the sugar plantations being established on newly got land. Their disinclination to do so seemingly demonstrated the rightness of outsiders' intrusions. "They lack the elements necessary to perpetuate their existence," pontificated the American in charge of the legal system who was also a major planter. "Living without exertion, & contented with enough to eat and drink, they give themselves no care for the future, and mope away life, without spirit, ambition, or hope. . . . I consider the doom of this nation as sealed." This attitude explains Cooke's willingness to go into business and, more generally, his "contemplation of doing something for a future Anglo-Saxon race [in the Islands], provided God, in His wise purposes, should allow this people [Hawaiians] as He has done the aborigines [in other colonized areas of the world to give way to] foreigners."[25] Sugar took off as an export crop after the United States removed import duties in 1876. Until then Hawaiians provided the bulk of the labor, being supplanted by contract workers brought from China beginning in 1852 and Japan in 1868.

A way of life that had sustained Islanders for generations was destroyed. Noenoe Silva reminds us how not just the Chief's Children's School and the Ka Māhele but each and every change fit into a larger agenda working against the interests of the Hawaiian people. "The banning of hula had as much or more to do with establishing colonial capitalism, and thus with establishing control over the labor of the Kanaka Maoli [indigenous Hawaiians], as with religion and the repression of sexuality." In analyzing what he terms "the twisted nature of nineteenth-century colonialism in the Pacific," Hawaiian Studies scholar Jonathan Kay Kamakawiwoʻole Osorio describes "a slow, insinuating invasion of people, ideas, and institutions" that "were not physical only, but also psychological and spiritual." As Osorio perceptively observes, "death came not only through infection and disease, but through racial and legal discourse that crippled the will, confidence, and trust of the Kānaka Maoli as surely as leprosy and smallpox claimed their limbs and lives." As summed up by Hawaiian Studies scholar Haunani-Kay Trask, the missionaries "introduced a religious imperialism that was as devastating a scourge as any venereal pox."[26]

The United States annexed the Hawaiian Islands in 1898. By then new-comers far outstripped the indigenous population. About 30,000 Islanders were wholly indigenous, another 9,000 partially so, compared to 100,000 newcomers, many of them recently arrived contract workers. Thereafter, as communications scholar Rona Tamiko Halualani puts it, indigenous Hawaiians "were surveilled by blood quantum technology and policies and articulated as 'strange,' nonadaptive, unproductive, unfit, and in need of rehabilitation, thereby maintaining the whiteness of the territory."[27] Apart from greater racial, ethnic, and cultural diversity in the nonindigenous population, little has changed to the present day.

Ordinary Hawaiians had to make their own way. While it is impossible to know with certainty the extent to which deteriorating circumstances at home were responsible for individuals leaving paradise, as early as 1839 David Malo tied the two together with considerable specificity.

> On account of this want on the part of the chiefs for the people, some of the people are losing their attachment to the land of their birth; they forsake their places of residence, their kindred, and live here and there where they can find a place. Some, however, follow after the chiefs, . . . but many stand aloof; . . . and living without land, they are without food, and of these, some are induced to go to foreign countries to obtain a subsistence. This, therefore, becomes a means of decrease in the population; of the many that sail to foreign countries, some become sailors by profession and do not return as inhabitants of the islands, being satisfied with the wages for their labor and the food they receive. Some dwell permanently in the countries to which they go, and some upon other islands in the Pacific; because they find themselves comfortable in the places to which they have gone, they return no more. [28]

Some Hawaiians first migrated from their homes to port towns, congregating in what Ralston terms "beach communities." There men were more easily recruited for the fur trade and, in even greater numbers, into whaling. At its height in the 1840s and 1850s about three hundred to five hundred vessels a year stopped at Honolulu or at Lahaina on the island of Maui to pick up supplies and crew before heading off to hunt animals for their oil. During these years, as many as one in five Hawaiians between the ages of fifteen and thirty may have been so employed. Part of the reason lay in men's willingness to work hard, another part in their capacity to do the job. A Hawaiian missionary account of 1844 makes the case. "I have never heard the captain of a vessel who did not speak highly of the native seamen whom he had employed. They are eminently subordinate, docile, good natured and trustworthy; and with proper training they become good efficient seamen."[29]

From about 1860 another option was to harvest guano, the waste material of seabirds, for fertilizer on small isolated islands under American control in the South Pacific. Again, it was missionaries who sought to profit from Hawaiians' labor. In 1859 missionary leader turned Islands politician Gerritt Parmele Judd became the Hawaiian agent for an American guano company. Shortly thereafter he arranged for his son, who a couple of years earlier had participated in raising the American flag on one of the guano islands, to transport the first crew of Hawaiian laborers there to begin harvesting.[30] Thousands more followed in their wake.

In comparison with the fur trade, whaling and guano harvesting were characterized by harsher and sometimes dangerous conditions of work, by greater isolation from outside influences, and by more certainty men would be returned home. In reality, the jobs may not have been that different from those then available at home, as described by Kamakau in 1869:

> Today the working man labors like a cart-hauling ox that gets a kick in the buttocks. He shivers in the cold and the dew-laden wind, or broils in the sun with no rest from his toil. Whether he lives or dies it is all alike. He gets a bit of money for his toil; in the house where he labors there are no blood kin, no parents, no relatives-in-law, just a little corner for himself.

In the view of Kamakau, far too many of his contemporaries, however "learned they may be, are mere stone-carriers and lime-mixers."[31]

Hawaiians who headed to the Pacific Northwest were to a greater extent left to their own resources than had they stayed home. The missionary rhetoric seeking to contain indigenous people around the world took longer to make its way there than to the Islands. Their labor was wanted, be it for the fur trade or some other enterprise, but employers felt no need to control their souls. The men were valued for who they were, not disparaged for what they were not. Generally illiterate in English, the Hawaiians left no records of their own, but contemporary accounts testify to their tenacity. These references were almost always made in passing, which gives them a particular honesty. Even when condescending in tone, comments were in general approving. Indigenous Hawaiians in the Pacific Northwest were described very differently from the stereotypes used in the Islands to justify newcomers' intrusion and usurpation.

Very importantly, Hawaiians who left for the Pacific Northwest did not depart in order to escape traditional ways of life. Rather, they integrated key elements from their upbringing that ensured success in their new venture. When housing was needed urgently, they constructed the thatched huts of their childhoods. Familiar social practices continued both privately and in larger settings. The men took pride in their dances, chanting, and other pleasures. Patterns of obedience to their chiefs that they had internalized when young served them well in their work lives.

At the same time, men adapted. Some may have been persuaded to leave by chiefs and rulers avid for the cash advances their departing subjects turned over to them, but no one could compel men to stay once their initial contract came to an end. Men turned the duty they had shown their chiefs into a similar sense of obligation to their employers. Indigenous Hawaiians were hard workers who repeatedly demonstrated their loyalty in tense conditions, as well as in the tedium of everyday tasks.

It is impossible to know why some Hawaiians soon returned home while others remained in the Pacific Northwest through several terms of employment or for a lifetime. Some men did not measure up to expectations for them, or the jobs into which they were hired disappeared. Family likely drew many men back. A gentler climate in the Islands may also have done so. Others simply wanted to go home. A common pattern was to return at the end of a term of employment, but then go back to the Northwest Coast, perhaps because anticipated opportunities in the Islands were no longer to be had.

However long Hawaiians remained in the Pacific Northwest, common indigenous origins did not bind them to their counterparts there. Only rarely did men and women indigenous to the Northwest Coast travel to the Islands, so there was no common body of lore to share. While many Hawaiians cohabited with Indian women, they did not become Indians. Just as with their fellow fur trade workers, and perhaps because of their influence, they distinguished sharply between local women and their men folk. The first they accepted as sexual partners, much as newcomers did in the Islands. Indian men they held at a distance as alien and potentially dangerous.

The denigration Hawaiians experienced at home eventually caught up with them in the Pacific Northwest. As explained in chapter 7, the international boundary settlement of 1846 was a watershed. Arrivals into the Oregon Territory from the United States found Hawaiians an alien presence they lumped together with blacks, not wanted in any shape or form. The men in charge quickly enacted legislation depriving Hawaiians, and also blacks and Indians, of the rights they accorded themselves. Over time almost all of the Hawaiians who remained south of the border merged into the indigenous people of North America, making their lives on reservations. In sharp contrast, Hawaiians north of the 49th parallel in British territory, the future Canadian province of British Columbia, were accorded the same civil rights enjoyed by members of the dominant society. Chapter 8 describes how they

Thatched huts on the Hawaiian Islands, 1819. From Jacques Arago, *Narrative of a Voyage Around the World* (London: Treuttel and Wurtz, 1823).

Hawaiian male dancers, 1816. From Louis Choris, *Voyage pittoresque au tour du monde* (Paris: Firmin Didot, 1822).

could take up land, vote, and live with dignity. Across the generations descendants on both sides of the border have been subject to discrimination based on physical appearance, but they have all the same, as summed up in chapter 9, continued to make a place for themselves across the Pacific Northwest.

Indigenous Hawaiians in the Pacific Northwest have been largely written out of the history of the Islands. One of the few contemporaries recording their absence was Samuel Kamakau, who from the 1860s had a regular column in the independent Hawaiian-language newspaper *Ka Nupepa Ka'o-ko'a*. In January 1868 he claimed "thousands of Hawaiians have gone away to foreign lands and remained there." A year and a half later Kamakau described how "the Hawaiian race live like wanderers on the earth and dwell in all lands surrounded by the sea." He estimated there were "in Oregon, 500," as well as smaller numbers living in Tahiti and other Pacific Islands, Peru (digging guano), East Coast American ports (after whaling), and "the bush ranges of California [where they went in search of gold]." Apart from Kamakau, reflections such as that in old age by John Papa Ii, an indigenous Hawaiian born in 1800, that "Hawaiians still live on those shores," by which he meant the Pacific Northwest, are rare. As put astutely by Lilikalā Kame'eleihiwa, "we have not yet begun to count all of the Hawaiians elsewhere in the world."[32]

The initiative shown by men and women leaving paradise for the Pacific Northwest in no way accords with the commonplace assertions about indigenous Hawaiians as characterized, so a Swedish visitor described in the mid-nineteenth century, by "born indifference and aversion to all kinds of labor." Such claims, repeated over and over again, came to be believed, even by the individuals themselves. Hawaiian writer George Hu'eu Sanford Kanahele has reflected how "one of the great tragedies in our history lies in the fact that many postcontact Hawaiians believed in their racial and personal inferiority and therefore were ashamed of their ancestors' practices and ideas."[33] Hawaiians in the Pacific Northwest did not write about their experiences, with one or two exceptions, but the testimonies of others indicate the strength of Hawaiian values, retained across time and space. They stood tall, as would have their contemporaries at home, had they been given the opportunity to do so.

Chapter 2

MARITIME SOJOURNERS

~♪ WITHIN A DECADE of Captain James Cook's arrival early in 1778, Hawaiians were expressing a desire to sail to the Northwest Coast of North America as maritime sojourners. Their ability to do so lay with the nature of the trade resulting from his voyage. The rush for sea otter pelts along the Northwest Coast gave the principal impetus to Hawaiians' departure.

Initially Britain dominated the maritime fur trade, but, because of restrictions enforced by its debilitating mercantile system, Americans soon took charge. According to the meticulous lists compiled by historian F. W. Howay, 36 British ships made a total of 74 visits to the Northwest Coast of North America between the trade's beginning in 1785 and 1799, compared with just 16 visits in 1800–1825, only 9 of them by new vessels entering the trade. Twenty-nine American ships, mostly based in Boston, made 55 visits prior to 1800, compared with 222 visits thereafter. This total included both ships already in the trade and 82 new vessels.[1] By the 1820s the sea otter was in decline, and the trade tapering off.

The usual departure time for a trading vessel was late summer or early autumn. After rounding Cape Horn, most ships stopped in the Hawaiian Islands to renew provisions and rest up. Sometimes crew members had taken ill or died, so a need arose for more hands. The earliest instruction directing a ship heading to the Pacific Northwest to "procure a hardy willing fellow from the Isles to embark with you to increase your strength" comes from 1788, a decade after Cook's visits to both places and three years after the first trading vessels made it to the Northwest Coast.[2] Ships' captains were assisted in doing so by a handful of newcomer men who early on threw in their fortunes with the Hawaiian Islands. Translators were available to effect arrangements, which often went through the local chief. Vessels spent the summer, and perhaps a second year if needed, on the coast acquiring sea otter furs from local people for the lucrative China market. Their trading area extended from the northern edge of today's British Columbia south to the mouth of the Columbia River. China was the final stop before either going home or beginning another cycle.

Most maritime sojourners were anonymous. Where they turn up in the records, it is usually in passing references in a ship's log to some activity being performed. Among the exceptions are seven named Hawaiians who were among the first to make the trip to the Northwest Coast. They all traveled in the late 1780s and early 1790s, at the very beginning of the international commerce in sea otter pelts. Their status as curiosities helps to explain the survival of their Hawaiian names and considerable detail about their experiences. Three—Winee, Teheeopea, and Tahomeeraoo—were women. The four men whose stories have come down through time are Kaiana, John Mataturay, Jack Attoo, and Kalehua.

These seven men and women traveled for a variety of reasons. There was the adventure, if sometimes mixed with an element of coercion, but also a desire to acquire newcomers' ways and goods. As Rona Tamiko Halualani explains, "within the extant, ideologically bound hierarchy, Western goods represented new means to elevate one's social position and *mana*."[3] Travelers left paradise with every intention of returning home. At the same time, by virtue of leaving, they placed themselves outside of the established order, which generated uncertainties as to their reception on arriving back. One of the ways they sought to secure a welcome was to come back with goods, usable both to acquire status and to confer it on others through gift giving.

The first indigenous Hawaiian known to encounter the Northwest Coast of North America was a woman. Her visit was a double feat, for Winee, whose name is likely a variant of *wahine*, the Hawaiian word for woman, came as a servant to the first European woman to visit both the Hawaiian Islands and Pacific Northwest. Frances Barkley was a sixteen-year-old bride who accompanied her English sea captain husband on one of the earliest ships to engage in the sea otter trade. *Imperial Eagle*, a British merchant vessel flying the Austrian flag, stopped for supplies on the island of Hawai'i in the spring of 1787. The ship's log noted on May 24, "One of the natives remained on board, signifying an inclination to go in the ship." An account a few years later explained how Frances Barkley "was so pleased with the amiable manners of poor Winee, that she felt a desire to take her to Europe;

Wynee, a Native of Owyhee?
One of the Sandwich Islands.

Winee, the first Hawaiian known to have visited the Pacific Northwest. From John Meares, *Voyages Made in the Years 1788 and 1789, from China to the North West Coast of America* (London: Topographic Press, 1790).

and for that purpose took her, with the consent of her friends, under her own particular care and protection."[4]

Unfortunately, the portion of the *Imperial Eagle*'s log relating to North America has disappeared, as has the diary in which Frances Barkley described the trip. A newspaper article based on her diary indicates that the ship reached Nootka Sound in June 1787. There the two women undoubtedly strolled along the circular sandy shore of Friendly Cove. At summer's end, *Imperial Eagle* set sail to dispose of the pelts it had acquired. By this time Winee was both ill and homesick. So, during a stop at Macao in November 1787 to sell the pelts, she was disembarked, along with the personal items accumulated while with the Barkleys. These included "a gown, a hoop, a petticoat, and a cap," as well as gifts for her parents.[5]

While in Macao awaiting a ship home, Winee almost certainly met up with Kaiana, described by a contemporary as a Kaua'i "chief of illustrious birth and high rank." Then in his early thirties, he was said to be 6 feet, 5 inches and "Herculean" in "the muscular form of his limbs."[6] In the summer of 1787, Kaiana, also known as Tianna, had gone onboard the British merchant vessel *Nootka* when it stopped at the Islands on the way from the Northwest Coast to Asia.

The *Nootka*'s captain, English adventurer John Meares, was taken by Tianna's status, being "the brother of the sovereign of that island," and also by his "amiable" character. Meares explained in his memoir published five years later how Tianna had left his wife and child "in order to return with the knowledge that might instruct" his native island. Tianna had gone ashore from the *Nootka* at Macao, and Meares recorded how, during the Hawaiian's three months there and in Canton, he learned to wear "the dress of Europe with the habitual ease of its inhabitants" and acquired the "most minute practice of personal cleanliness and decorum." While in Macao celebrated Chinese artist Spoilum painted his portrait in a traditional Hawaiian feathered cape and helmet he had brought with him. A chiefly Hawaiian born about 1830 described the cape and helmet as "royal coverings."[7] The garments signaled Tianna's status as an *ali'i*, who were the only persons permitted to wear the regalia.

Both Winee and Kaiana/Tianna embarked when Meares's new vessel, *Felice Adventurer*, left Macao in January 1788. Winee did not make it home. She died at sea on February 5. The captain recorded how "the poor, unfortunate woman justified our fears concerning her, that she would never again see her friends or native land." Shortly before her demise, Winee bequeathed part of her possessions to Tianna, including "a plate looking-glass and a basin and bottle of the finest China," items that would have, Meares

Tianna, a Prince of Atooi,
One of the Sandwich Islands.

Publish'd Aug.16.1790.by J.Walter,N.169. Piccadilly.

Kaiana, the first Hawaiian man known to have visited the Pacific Northwest. From John Meares, *Voyages Made in the Years 1788 and 1789, from China to the North West Coast of America* (London: Topographic Press, 1790).

reflected, "given her a very flattering importance, had she lived to have taken them to her native island."[8] The rest she put in Tianna's care to deliver to her parents. A contemporary sketch of Winee has become, like that of Tianna, the mythic image of an indigenous Hawaiian person.

Tianna followed in Winee's steps by visiting the Northwest Coast, if by accident. Hoping to get home as soon as possible, at a stop at the Philippines he transferred to the *Felice Adventurer*'s sister vessel *Iphigenia*, heading to the Islands. The necessity for repairs caused the *Iphigenia* to change its course and sail directly to Nootka Sound. Without intending to do so, Tianna became the second named Hawaiian to reach the Pacific Northwest.

Clothing signals the challenges that faced these early Hawaiian sojourners. Tianna had toyed with Western dress in Macao. Once again he played with local wear. He is said long to have continued to wear the "fur cap and other warm cloathing [*sic*], with which he had clad himself during the cold season." At the same time, according to Meares, who encountered Tianna at Nootka Sound, he "held the customs of Nootka in detestation."[9]

Tianna made it home in December 1788. As would numerous others, he had some trepidation as to how he would be received. "He was uncertain whether the treasures he possessed would be employed to elevate him into consequence, or to purchase his safety." Iron was the most valuable commodity, and his acquisitions consisted of "saws of different kinds, gimblets, hatchets, adzes, knives and choppers, cloth of various fabrics, carpets of several colours, a considerable quantity of China-ware, and ten bars of iron."[10]

Meares got to the Islands before Tianna and tried to prepare the way for his protégé, only to discover that "an inhuman proscription had been published, threatening him with instant death, if he should return."[11] Tianna averted this taboo, or prohibition, by aligning himself with the future king, then Chief Kamehameha of the big island of Hawai'i. By 1795, the relationship had soured, and Tianna was killed in a battle against him on O'ahu.

In 1788 another ranking Hawaiian reached the Pacific Northwest. Son of a chief on the island of Ni'ihau, John Mataturay joined the British merchant vessel *Princess Royal* on its way to the Northwest Coast. The ship was under the general authority of James Colnett, who explained how its captain, "at the isle of Oneehow [Ni'ihau], in my presence and with my approbation receiv'd the Indian from his father, a second Rank Chief in that Island." Mataturay transferred at the end of the year to the *Argonaut*, which Colnett captained. Even though "doing all the duties of a Servant" to Colnett, he also displayed his versatility. When the *Argonaut* began taking on water, "the Sandwich Isle Indian went overboard and discovered the leak."[12]

Nootka Sound in 1788. From John Meares, *Voyages Made in the Years 1788 and 1789, from China to the North West Coast of America* (London: Topographic Press, 1790).

Shortly after the *Argonaut's* arrival on the Northwest Coast in 1789, the vessel was seized by the Spaniards and everyone taken south to San Blas on the west coast of today's Mexico. There Mataturay, whom the Spanish called Mariano Modetroy, was singled out from the rest of the prisoners by virtue of not being on a regular contract. The Spanish considered he must have been taken from the Islands against his will and so should remain when the *Argonaut* and its crew were released. His captors sought his conversion to Catholicism, as well as to learn from him to further their goal of colonizing the Hawaiian Islands. One of his captors copied down among his diary observations ten pages of Hawaiian words with Spanish equivalents, hinting at Modetroy's teaching ability. "The natives of these islands use very few letters of the alphabet. Its pronunciation is easy, . . . they do not trill the r nor use the l or several other letters of the alphabet." [13]

The exchange of correspondence between Colnett and Spanish authorities gives unusual insight into one Hawaiian's state of mind. Modetroy shared his views on conversion with Colnett, who knew enough of the Hawaiian language. Colnett then relayed them to the Spanish: "How is it Possible when the Padres told him that his own Countrymen, as well as the English, when they died went to the wicked gods to be burnt and what was the service of his going to the good god where no one was he knew. For his Part, be where it would, he should like to be with the English, and his Country men." Modetroy also had a more immediate objection. "What kind of Religion was it they were going to Cram down his throat, that he must not have a wife in this world or the next and starve two or three days a week." He wanted to return home. Colnett explained to Spanish authorities how, "as for the Indian of the Sandwich Islands, he has pledged his word to his parents, his wives, and his king and he can not fail to appear before them on his return without dishonouring himself and his nation." [14]

Colnett proposed that Modetroy be permitted to make his own decision and gave Spanish authorities a Hawaiian translation of what he might be asked:

Oe Noho Noho Padree or [*sic*] Tehuna? [Will you stay with the padres, namely the priests?]

or

Ae Howee Haree Tenenony or [*sic*] Capitan? [Will you return to the house of the ship's captain?]

Modetroy is said to have "answered in Spanish, I will go with Captain Colnett, to my Father, my Mother, my Wife, and my Children." [15]

Modetroy was released and that night taken by Colnett to see a play. The Hawaiian's personality comes through in his response to the imagined events taking place in front of him on the stage. "In one Scene an Armour was carrying on by a Young Lady, and he [Modetroy] called to her on the Stage, in such Manner as to draw the Attention of the Vice Roy, and the whole Audience—indeed his Observations were such as Kept Myself and all around Him in a continued Laughter." [16]

Mataturay/Modetroy was on the *Argonaut* for its return to the Northwest Coast in early July 1790, to die there of unstated causes in December of the same year. *Argonaut*'s log reads: "On the 3rd, Modetroy, the Sandwich Isle Indian Died. Prior to his Death he sent for me to thank me for all the Good I had done him, and meant to do him, desired to be remembered to his father, Mother, and family, Captain [Charles] Duncan [of *Princess Royal*], and Mr. [Richard] Etches [vessel's owner]; and in the Night died without a Groan." [17] Mataturay had thrice visited the Pacific Northwest.

In the summer of 1789 another high-ranking Hawaiian male, Jack Attoo or Ottoo, and a countryman of more modest background named Kalehua left the shores of Ni'ihau on the *Columbia Rediviva,* one of the first two American vessels to enter the maritime fur trade. On the way to Asia to dispose of pelts, its captain Robert Gray took on Attoo as a cabin boy. His chief mate Joseph Ingraham hired Kalehua, whom he called Opye. The *Columbia Rediviva* proceeded to Canton, then home to Boston. Arriving in August 1790, it received an enthusiastic reception as the first American vessel to circumnavigate the world.

Like Kaiana/Tianna, Attoo brought with him a feathered helmet and cape to signify his chiefly status. These he wore to meet the Massachusetts governor and listen to his oratory espousing friendship with the Hawaiian Islands. A contemporary description was highly evocative: "Captain Gray walked arm in arm with the Hawaiian chief Attoo—the first of his race ever seen in Boston. He was a fine-looking youth and wore a helmet of gay feathers, which glittered in the sunlight, and an exquisite cloak of the same yellow and scarlet plumage." [18]

Neither Jack Attoo nor Kalehua/Opye had yet reached the Pacific Northwest and would do so in quite different ways. Attoo stuck with Gray on the *Columbia Rediviva,* which departed in October 1790, a few months after getting to Boston. By the time Attoo got to Nootka Sound the next June, he was tired of ship life and deserted. A relative of the local chief was held hostage to prompt his return. The ship's clerk recorded the sequence of events: "Ottoo, our Sandwich island boy, found means to leave the ship and go among the natives. Captain Gray therefore determined to take the first Chief that came along." After "Captain Gray told him, he was his prisoner, and unless Ottoo was immediately delivered up, he would carry him to sea," the chief had Attoo returned to the ship, where he was flogged as an example to others.[19]

The *Columbia Rediviva* was still on the coast the next February trading for sea otter skins when Attoo redeemed himself by alerting Gray to a plot "to take the ship and murder us all" in retaliation for the previous summer's events. The chief earlier taken captive had asked Attoo to wet the muskets in preparation for an attack two nights hence. In exchange, "if they succeeded he should be made a great Chief and they would give him plenty of skins."[20] The language of the conversation is not indicated, but its complexity suggests Attoo's linguistic sophistication. The incident points up how Attoo, like Tianna before him and most Hawaiians after him, found little in common with indigenous peoples of the Pacific Northwest.

When Attoo finally made it back home to Ni'ihau in November 1892, he refused to go ashore despite his family's warm welcome. One of the seamen onboard ship recorded the encounter: "Vast many canoes off, in one of which was the Father and other relations of our Sandwich Island Lad. they came on board and the meeting was very affectionate, but still our Lad refused to go on shore and Capt. Gray did not think proper for to force him."[21] Attoo continued on to Canton, where he disappears from the historical record.

Kalehua/Opye stuck with Ingraham, who was given command of the brigantine *Hope,* which sailed from Boston in September 1790 and made a brief six-week stop on the Northwest Coast before heading to the Islands. By this time Ingraham had grown fond of his charge, whom he considered "more like a friend" than a servant. Despite attempts "to dissuade him," Opye disembarked in the Islands in late May 1791, taking with him the "clothes, a musket, an American Jack [flag], and many other things" that Ingraham had lavished on him.[22]

Within the year Kalehua/Opye was restless. So he approached Captain George Vancouver in the *Discovery* during a stop at the Islands on his way to affirm Britain's claims to the Northwest Coast. According to Vancouver, who knew Kalehua as Tareehooa, the Hawaiian took the initiative. "As we stood along shore with a light breeze, we were in the evening greatly surprized on being hailed from a large canoe, which was meeting us, in broken English, demanding who we were, and to what country we belonged, and very civilly requesting to be admitted on board." Vancouver not only accepted the Hawaiian onboard, with the consent of his chief, but raised his status. "Tareehooa, who preferred the name of Jack, had been with Mr.

Ingra[ha]m in the capacity of a servant; but was now promoted to the office of interpreter."[23]

According to Vancouver, the new hire proved his worth even before the *Discovery* left the Islands. "Our new ship-mate Jack became very useful; he took upon himself to represent us in the most formidable point of view to all his countrymen; magnifying our powers, and augmenting our numbers, and proclaiming that we were not traders, such as they had been accustomed to see; but that we were belonging to King George, and were all mighty warriors."[24] Kalehua / Jack realized the advantages of allying himself with outsiders, whose authority could then be exaggerated to his own gain. He spent the summer of 1792 on the *Discovery* as it explored around Vancouver Island and then headed north to the Queen Charlotte Islands, located west of present-day Prince Rupert, British Columbia.

As the *Discovery* was leaving the Northwest Coast in October 1792, Jack became a companion to two Niʻihau women who had arrived at Nootka five days earlier on the English schooner *Jenny* and wanted to return home. Teheeopea, age fourteen, and Tahomeeraoo, a relative a few years older, described "their seduction and detention on board" against their will the previous May.[25]

The two young women's presence on the *Jenny* was not unique. John Papa Ii, a well-connected indigenous Hawaiian born at the beginning of the nineteenth century, explained how "many Hawaiian women boarded the ships coming to port" with the permission of their families. They thought they were being strategic. "The husbands and parents, not knowing that it would bring trouble [in the form of venereal disease], permitted such association with foreign men because of a desire for clothing, mirrors, scissors, knives, iron hoops from which to fashion fishhooks, and nails." This time visiting crewmen proved unwilling to abandon their pleasure simply because their ship was departing. George Vancouver described how Teheeopea and Tahomeeraoo "had been brought, not only contrary to their wishes and inclinations, but totally without the knowledge or consent of their friends and relations."[26] The ease with which men on ships enticed local women aboard had been pushed one step too far.

Shortly after George Vancouver took Teheeopea and Tahomeeraoo onboard, the *Discovery* made a lengthy stop down the coast in Spanish California. The journals that he and the expedition's naturalist Archibald Menzies kept speak to the young women's resilience and also to their respectful treatment onboard the British vessel, if to some extent as novelties. Vancouver invited them to participate in "all the civilities and diversions which our Spanish friends so obligingly offered and provided."[27]

The first social event offered to the *Discovery*'s officers was a visit to the Catholic Mission of San Francisco in mid-November 1792. Here Menzies found that the women took to riding horses "without showing the least sign of fear or timidity," as if they had ridden horses all their lives. That evening the local commander received the visitors in his residence. Invited to join the "Spanish ladies" who were "squatted down on their Heels upon a Mat," the two young Hawaiians caused "some little tittering & looks of surprise" when, "being unacquainted with the etiquette of the Mat, instead of folding their Legs in under them they stretched them out at full length." Later, at Monterey, at a dance at the governor's residence, "the two Sandwish [*sic*] Island women at the request of Captain Vancouver exhibited their manner of singing & dancing, which did not appear to afford much entertainment to the Spanish Ladies."[28]

Vancouver was taken by the young women's ability to accommodate to their circumstances. "They seemed much pleased with the European fashions, and in conforming to this new system of manners, they conducted themselves in company with a degree of propriety beyond all expectations." Searching out appropriate garments for them to wear aboard ship, Vancouver selected riding habits. He considered them "best calculated for their situation," making it possible for them to go up and down the ship's ladders without exposing their ankles, as if "educated by the most rigid governess." As to what difference these adventures made to Teheeopea and Tahomeeraoo, according to Vancouver, "they were surprised at the social manner in which both sexes live, according to the custom of most civilized nations; differing so very materially from that of their own."[29]

The trio returned to the Islands in February 1793. Vancouver was impressed by the warm welcome given Kalehua / Tareehooa / Jack by the local chief as the *Discovery* pulled into Kawaihae Bay on the island of Hawai'i. "A present of a hog and some vegetables was in the canoe for Tarehooa; whose gratitude for such a mark of remembrance was instantly testified, by the tears that flowed on his receiving the message."[30] All the same, he remained onboard for the *Discovery*'s second voyage to the Northwest Coast during the summer of 1793. Back home the next March, he decided to stay there for good.

The two women were a different proposition. Vancouver was aware that their adventures greatly offended Hawaiian taboos, particularly given they were "of some consequence" in terms of their social standing. "Their having eaten at mine and other tables in the company of men was an offence of so heinous a nature against their laws as to subject them both to the punishment of death." Vancouver sought to ensure the women were both securely resettled and permitted to retain the items they had accumulated during their adventures. These Menzies described as "Knives Scissors looking Glasses Beads Buttons Ear rings Needles Tapes Nails Axes Fish hooks pieces of iron files rasps & a variety of other tools."[31] Ni'ihau having been abandoned due to a drought, Vancouver returned the two young women to the nearby island of Kaua'i in March 1793. Promised by local chiefs that the two women would be protected, Vancouver acquired houses and land for them.

A final glimpse of Teheeopea and Tahomeeraoo comes from a year later. Vancouver and Menzies saw the pair again on their return voyage to the Islands. In the interim the two young women had each become one of the wives of chiefs, but Vancouver and Menzies "were both very apprehensive that, on our finally quitting these seas, the attentive behaviour they had hitherto experienced would be discontinued."[32]

These seven Hawaiian adventurers were on the one hand curiosities, but on the other role models informing subsequent attitudes. Their initiative distinguished them from the attitudes already forming of indigenous North Americans. In Meares's view, "there was no comparison to be made between the inhabitants and customs of the Sandwich Islands and those among whom we now resided, or of any part of the continent of America." Writing in August 1788 from the Northwest Coast, he explained how "the former are their superiors in every thing that regards what we should call the comforts of life, and their approach to civilization." Meares commended the Hawaiians' behavior.

> They attend to a circumstance which particularly distinguishes polished from savage life, and that is cleanliness:—they are not only clean to an extreme in their food, but also in their persons and houses the same happy disposition prevails:—while the North Western Americans are nasty to a degree that rivals the most filthy brutes, and, of course, prohibits any description from us. Indeed, the very disgusting nature of their food is not diminished by the manner in which it is eaten, or rather devoured.

To the extent Meares saw hope in the indigenous populations he encountered in his adventures, it was in that of the Islands. "We trust it will not prove a vain hope, that these amiable people may soon be taught to abandon even their religious inhumanity; and that near half a million of human beings, inhabiting the Sandwich Islands, may one day be ranked among the civilized subjects of the British Empire."[33]

The details that survive about these seven early maritime sojourners, and about attitudes toward them, contrast sharply with those about their counterparts of much more modest rank. Some were taken against their will. In

1795, a number of unnamed men were kidnapped from Kaua'i by the American trading vessel *Mercury* when the desertion of the crew jeopardized the expedition. They were held below deck until the vessel was out of sight of land and, at the end of the season, returned with letters of recommendation by the captain. The adventure did not sour the men on foreigners. When the *Ruby* arrived at Ni'ihau shortly thereafter, its captain recorded: "Those Islanders I had seen on board the *Mercury* at Nootka came off, and seemed happy to see us, bringing Presents of Matts and Yams."[34]

The abductions carried out by a few unethical ship captains cannot be taken as a template for all the Hawaiians in the maritime fur trade. A young man named Omi probably voluntarily joined the American ship *Atahualpa,* which traded on the Northwest Coast in both 1801 and 1802. He enters the historical record by virtue of being asked to dive for the occasional object, such as a blunderbuss, which fell overboard and in his free time making a cape for King Kamehameha out of local bird feathers.[35]

Some men had first names likely arbitrarily bestowed. Harry Owhyeeman, in effect Harry Hawai'i Man, joined the *Atahualpa* for the next two-year trading season, probably on its stopover in 1803 on its way to the Pacific Northwest, where it began trading the next January. The following spring the vessel was attacked by local men two days after they had been ushered from the decks. The captain and eight of the crew were killed. Harry was stabbed. Six days later fears were expressed in the ship's log that gangrene was going to set in. However, there was no record of Harry dying, and he likely was relieved to disembark in the Islands.

A Hawaiian recorded as Jack joined the Boston trader *Margaret* in early 1791 on its way to the Pacific Northwest. He was among a group of seamen left behind at Nootka Sound at the end of the summer to construct a tender while the ship headed to Canton to sell its furs. The tender was completed by the time the *Margaret* returned in April 1793, but Jack had become ill with scurvy, due to lack of fresh fruit and vegetables, and died two months later. A man named as Samuel was among the crew of twenty-one on the British brig *Sea Otter* on the coast in 1796 and 1797.

Other maritime sojourners went onboard in groups. Without a death, their presence could go entirely unrecorded. The American brig *Otter* acquired four seamen in 1809, two of whose names survive by virtue of dying on the coast. Tohoies was buried ashore, Woahii later in 1810 at sea. Very unusually, eleven Hawaiians, or possibly Polynesians, were named as crew on the Boston brig *Convoy* in the mid-1820s. It is not known whether Ben, John Bull, Caesar Fisher, Harry, John, Moa, Richard, Robert, Samuel, and Spunyarn, likely so-called because of his hair texture, returned home at the end of 1825 or continued to sail on the *Convoy*. If they departed, others likely took their place. A secondhand comment from later in the decade had the *Convoy*'s Boston owners giving it "instructions to call at the Friendly or Society Islands for Islanders to make up numbers as they are less expensive than American Seamen."[36] Three men, named as Perry Jarvis, Jack Rope-yarn, and Tamaree, sailed on the American brig *Owhyhee* in 1827.

Most glimmers are of anonymous men. The log of the *Pearl* noted on March 12, 1805, as it was departing the Islands: "Took on board four Sandwich Island men to go to the coast to strengthen the ship's company." The *New Hazard* sailed from Boston directly to the Northwest Coast, arriving there in March 1811. Having spent the summer trading off the Queen Charlotte Islands, she made a quick autumnal trip to the Islands for supplies and additional men. The useful role played by the six unnamed Hawaiians added to the crew is revealed in passing references in the ship's log amid primary attention to trading activities, again mostly off the Queen Charlottes.

18 APRIL 1811. Kanakas got a gang of water.

8 MAY. Mr. Hall [third mate], James [seaman], and I, with two Kanakas, went ashore and cut two trees; one for a boat's chalks; one for plank.

22 MAY. James, Bump [seaman], with two Kanakas with our northwest passenger [a local Indian] and I went after water.

25 MAY. We have three seamen, one light hand, and five Kanakas sick.

10 JUNE. Boat with boys and Kanakas went after wood.

10 JULY. Kanakas cutting wood.

19 JULY. [Indians trying to take tools from men working ashore] The boat with four men, three Kanakas with [second mate] Mr. Gale went ashore and took the armourer and [seaman] John off. They held daggers to their breasts and said they would cockshuttle [kill] them if they did not give them cartridge box, etc., but they saved all.

21 AUGUST. [First mate] Mr. Hewes struck one of the Kanakas with a large rope over the head so that he fainted, or rather a fit!!

27 SEPTEMBER [nearing island of Hawai'i]. A number of canoes came off, but going quick through the water could not get on board . . . the Kanakas gave them a rope.[37]

Other ships' logs contain similar glimpses. The *Owhyhee* made another voyage to the coast in 1829, again in search of sea otter pelts. While on the Columbia River, the vessel took on five unnamed "Kanakas" from the *Convoy*, a sister ship owned by the same Boston company. The *Owhyhee* sailed up the coast toward Russian America, the future Alaska, where "one

Kanacker boy from Capt. Taylor [of the *Volunteer*] came on board as steward." The captain of the *Volunteer,* also out of Boston, received, apparently in exchange, "9 bales blankets and one case of Calico." The still unnamed Hawaiian steward returned to the *Owhyhee*'s log in February 1830 when, back south on the Columbia River, a seaman together with "the Kanaka boy went ashore without liberty," as a consequence of which, "Put both of them in irons and chained them together till morning." By August the *Owhyhee* had acquired enough skins to depart the Northwest Coast for the Hawaiian Islands and Asia. So, on again meeting the *Convoy* still chasing down furs, the *Owhyhee* gave up two of the "Kanakas" it had onboard.[38] Hawaiians were just as much items of exchange as were the skins that were the object of being there in the first place. The return voyages of the *Convoy* and *Owhyhee* in 1829 would be the last of the American maritime trading expeditions to the Northwest Coast, the sea otter having been virtually exterminated through excessive hunting.

The total number of maritime sojourners, either named or numbered in ships' logs, is impossible to determine. The U.S. secretary of state expressed concern in 1821 over stranded American seamen, discharged on trivial pretexts so that much preferred Hawaiians could be taken on. Hawaiians' considerable presence is suggested by the instructions given to the captain of the *Ann* on leaving Boston for the Northwest Coast via the Islands in 1818 to "take as many stout Islanders as will increase your crew to 21 or 22 . . . and when you return from the [north] coast discharge and pay them off in such articles of trade as you have left." A year later a Frenchman visiting the Islands observed that "so many natives have undergone this apprenticeship that they man Taméaméa's [Kamehameha's] navy."[39]

It is unclear how Hawaiians were remunerated for their services. Some, as indicated by the instructions given to the *Ann*'s captain, were paid with goods they could then take home to the envy of their countrymen. Money in the form of coins was long restricted to chiefs, who hoarded whatever foreign currency came into their possession. Through the 1820s ordinary Hawaiians, particularly in outlying districts, were still not familiar with money as a medium of exchange.[40]

It is even more difficult to know how many Hawaiian women followed in the path of Teheeopea and Tahomeeraoo. There are only hints. On February 9, 1809, American sea captain Joseph O'Cain and his Hawaiian mistress perished when they went through the ice off Sarak Island in Russian America. In April 1811, while sailing along the coast of the future Alaska, the *New Hazard* encountered the American ship *Hamilton* captained by Lemuel Porter. The *New Hazard* log recorded how "Porter and his Sandwich Island

Lady (with her big belly) [came] on board us."[41] The *Hamilton* had stopped in the Islands in October 1809, returning at the end of September 1811, so the unnamed woman may have been onboard for some time and had a range of experiences on the Northwest Coast. In November 1838, the half-Hawaiian wife of ship's captain John Bancroft was wounded by rebellious crew off the coast of California, when she threw herself on the body of her dying husband. Mary Bancroft rode the vessel back home and died shortly after.

Maritime sojourners traveled to the Pacific Northwest for different reasons, including the adventure and the goods to be got. A Frenchman who visited the Islands in 1819 observed that "it is a point of honor among young Hawaiian men to make more than one sea voyage: every trading ship headed to the coast counts natives among its crew."[42] It is impossible to know what happened to them on their return home and, more particularly, their role in encouraging others to leave for the land-based fur trade fast overtaking its maritime counterpart.

Chapter 3

THE ASTORIA ADVENTURE

‿‿⟩THE EXPERIENCES of maritime sojourners likely eased Hawaiians' entry into the land-based fur trade. Their stories of adventure on the Northwest Coast of North America had two decades to travel the Islands by the time of the Astoria adventure.

The fur trade post of Astoria on the Columbia River in today's Oregon originated with the ambition of a single individual. John Jacob Astor left Germany for the United States in 1784 at the age of twenty-one on a ship containing a number of fur traders. This experience may have encouraged him, as he rose in prominence as a merchant, to look to the profits to be made from animal pelts. The area west of the Rocky Mountains was coveted by several countries, principally Britain and the United States, but was under the absolute control of none. The loosely organized North West Company (NWC), a partnership out of Montreal, operated a handful of trading posts west of the Rockies, but that was about the entirety of newcomer incursions on land.

The best-known site was the mouth of the Columbia River, brought to American attention through the overland expedition led by Meriwether Lewis and William Clark that arrived there in the fall of 1805 and returned east to popular acclaim the next spring. The first attempt to follow up with a land-based American presence failed miserably. The three Winship brothers of Boston got the idea of establishing a trading settlement to compete with Russian America with food. Setting out in July 1809, the *Albatross* made the customary stop at the Hawaiian Islands. There the Winships took on two dozen men as crew and laborers, three of whose names survive as Corrina, Richard, and William.

In early June 1810 the Winships selected a location 40 miles up the Columbia. For four days the Hawaiians felled trees. Then it began to rain. The site was under water. No sooner was the project moved to higher ground, when local men made clear the newcomers were not wanted. Within ten days of arriving, the *Albatross* with its half Hawaiian complement headed south in search of furs. On July 23, shortly after leaving the Columbia, Corrina was sent up to heave the main, fell to the deck, and died of his injuries. The ship's log described him as "the best man out of the twenty four on board belonging to the islands."[1] Corrina's body was wrapped and his remains committed to the deep.

Astor had a much more sophisticated plan for establishing the first land base on the Columbia River. Together with three Montreal Scots formerly affiliated with the NWC, he formed a competing partnership in March 1810, known as the Pacific Fur Company (PFC). Astor turned to NWC men for workers. As James Ronda, the historian of Astor's namesake trading post, explains, "success in any western enterprise depended on having the services of experienced Canadian traders and voyageurs."[2] *Canadian* as used in the fur trade referred to French speakers from Quebec, or Lower Canada, as it was known then. Some, particularly men who worked as hunters, were Mohawk Iroquois from the Montreal region. The principal exception was Astor's deputy on the ground, an American named Wilson Price Hunt who sought to have as many of his countrymen employed as possible.

Astor oversaw a three-pronged advance intended both to make money and to strengthen American claims to the area. The earliest group, led by Hunt and composed principally of Americans, set out overland from Lachine, Quebec, in July 1810, to set up a post to be named Astoria near the mouth of the Columbia River. The second party headed off from New York in September on the newly purchased *Tonquin* with trade goods and building materials. The third, much smaller group left a year later, in September 1811, on the *Beaver* with more trade goods. The *Tonquin* got there first, arriving in late March 1811, the overland party in February 1812, and the *Beaver* in May 1812.

It was this adventure that first put Hawaiians on the Northwest Coast for sustained periods of time. They themselves left no record of their experiences but, quite remarkably, six firsthand accounts survive by partners or clerks, who were expected to record events. Even though the Hawaiians were, at the best of times, at the edge of writers' consciousness, the accounts read together reveal a great deal about their contribution to the Astoria adventure.

Three of the accounts originate with the *Tonquin*. One of the partners, Duncan McDougall, wrote from the perspective of the man in charge of the post. Gabriel Franchère was a twenty-five-year-old French Canadian clerk from Montreal who adapted his journal kept during his four years at Astoria into a book published in French in 1820 and in English in 1854. Scots clerk Alexander Ross published a narrative in 1849. Alfred Seton, a New York merchant's son, and Irishman Ross Cox were both eighteen-year-old clerks who arrived a year later on the *Beaver*. Cox's account, based largely on memory, tends to be overstated and self-serving. The sixth account is by NWC partner Alexander Henry, who arrived overland in November 1813. A seventh version that drew on, and at times paraphrased, these and other sources was penned in 1836 by established writer Washington Irving at Astor's request.

The *Tonquin* and the *Beaver* each took on a number of Hawaiians while in the Islands. By now their nautical skills, as well as general capacity, were common knowledge. As Franchère explained, they "are excellent swimmers." Ross concurred. "They are like ducks in the water."[3] He considered "it is next to impossible for a person to get drowned if one or more of them are near at hand."[4]

The acquisition of men had the approval of Kamehameha, by now firmly in charge. Civil war ended in 1810 when the last holdout, the island of Kaua'i, became tributary to him. While, according to Franchère, Kamehameha used captured foreign vessels, foreign advisors, and foreign arms to bolster his forces, just a handful of outsiders had thrown in their lot with the Hawaiians. Franchère counted "about 30 of all nations" on the island of O'ahu, which in 1820 became the center of what was an indigenous kingdom with Lahaina as its capital. Ross found the result to his liking. "All the islands of this group, excepting one, have acknowledged Tammeatameah as their king, and the jarring interests and feuds of the different islands have at last sunk into a system of union which, if we may judge from appearance, renders this country, under its present government, an earthly paradise, and the inhabitants thereof as free from care, and perhaps as happy, as any in the globe."[5]

The *Tonquin* stopped at O'ahu in February 1811. The men in charge of the PFC sought, according to Washington Irving, "to take thirty or forty with them to the Columbia, to be employed in the service of the company," only to have the ship's captain object "that there was not room in his vessel for the accommodation of such a number." Franchère explained the compromise that ensued. "For the service of the Establishment [at Astoria] we engaged twelve Islanders, the term of their contract being three years, during which time we undertook to feed and clothe them and at the expiration of their contract, to give them goods to the value of one hundred *piastres* [Spanish or Mexican silver dollars then in common use on the Islands]. The Captain took on another 12 for the work of the ship."[6]

The number that departed became magnified over time. John Papa Ii, born in 1800, described in old age the "Scotch people, the first ever seen in these islands," who arrived in 1811 on "a certain English ship." In response to "their need for men to work in the great river region in Oregon," Kamehameha arranged that "100 men were sent back on the ship." Ii was quite right in observing that "this was the first time that Hawaiians went to Oregon to kill animals for their fur."[7]

Ii explained how "the ship to carry the laborers came twice," probably referring also to the *Beaver.* Stopping there a year later, the vessel similarly acquired Hawaiians "for the Company's service at the Columbia" and "to assist in working the ship (several of the crew being indifferent sailors)." Writing in retrospect, Ross Cox described the recruitment process in some detail. The first step was to get King Kamehameha's permission.

> On the intelligence being announced [that permission was granted], the vessel was crowded with numbers, all offering to "take on." With the assistance of the above gentlemen [two local residents who had served on the Northwest Coast and had become recruiting agents, American Oliver Holmes and Spaniard Francisco Paula de Marin] we selected twenty-six of the most able-bodied of these volunteers; sixteen for the Company's service, and ten for the ship's. We agreed to pay each man ten dollars a month, and a suit of clothes annually.[8]

Ross Cox noted how women as well as men came forward. "Several of the females also volunteered to accompany us, but we were obliged to decline their kind offers."[9] There was one exception: a Hawaiian woman accompanying an American seaman hired in the Islands who accepted employment only on that condition. This unnamed woman was a flitting presence at Astoria, returning to the ship when it headed up the coast in early June 1812.

The Hawaiians spoke their own language, which, from Ross's perspective, was "very difficult to be obtained by the whites." As to the reason, "these people speak with a quickness which almost baffles imitation; and in very many instances, the same word is repeated twice." Cox explained how communication was to be managed. "An old experienced islander, who was called Boatswain Tom, and who had made several voyages both to Europe and America, was engaged to command them. He got fifteen dollars a month, and was to have the sole control of his countrymen." Cox recalled the process. "When any number of the natives were wanted to perform a particular duty, word was passed to Bos'n Tom; who, to do him justice, betrayed none of the softer feelings of national partiality to his countrymen. The moment he gave 'the dreadful word' it was followed by a horrid yell; and with a rope's end he laid on the back and shoulders of every poor devil who did not happen to be as alert as he wished, accompanied by a laughable *mélange* of curses in broken English, and imprecations in his own language."[10]

Ii described a parallel process occurring with both the *Tonquin* and the *Beaver*. "On each trip a man belonging to the retinue of the heir of the kingdom accompanied the ship on its return voyage." He explained how "the first to go was Nanamake, and the second was Uluhua." According to Ii, the process was not unique, and "other chiefs did likewise because they desired clothing and other goods," in particular, foreign clothing.[11] It may be that Ii was referring to the various chiefly Hawaiians who had taken passage on trading vessels over the past quarter century.

One of the dozen Hawaiians who arrived on the Northwest Coast in early 1811 on the *Tonquin* never made it ashore. Not yet there, he gave his life to the fur trade. The *Tonquin* reached the mouth of the Columbia River on March 22. Duncan McDougall, who would have charge of the new post of Astoria, recalled how, in the process of maneuvering the ship past a bar in the channel, "two Sandwich Islanders, Harry & Peter," and three others were sent ahead in a small boat to make soundings.[12]

Even the Hawaiians' facility with water could not avert catastrophe. The boat was engulfed by a wave, whereupon the two Hawaiians took the lead. One of the other men recalled: "As soon as I got above the surface of the water, I kept tossing about at the mercy of the waves. While in this state I saw the two Sandwich Islanders struggling through the surf to get hold of the boat, and being expert swimmers they succeeded. After long struggles they got her turned upon her keel, bailed out some of the water, and recovered one of the oars."[13]

Harry and Peter then turned their attention to their companion. "The poor fellows tried to haul me into the boat, but their strength failed them. At last, taking hold of my clothes in their teeth, they fortunately succeeded." The water temperature worked to the Hawaiians' disadvantage, for "they were so paralysed with cold" they could not row. "About midnight, Peter, one of the Sandwich Islanders, died in the Boat," whereupon "the other threw himself on the body of his comrade and I could not tear him away."[14] Harry survived, although two weeks later he was still so crippled he was kept on the vessel when the others went ashore to construct the new post.[15]

Peter's fellow Islanders ensured he would be honored in death in a fashion consistent with their religious practices and, in doing so, helped to create a sense of community among themselves. Young Franchère witnessed the ceremony that took place on the evening of March 26, 1811. "Each [of the six Islanders who took part] before leaving the ship had taken an offering of biscuit, pork or tobacco. They put the biscuit under the arm of the deceased, the pork under the chin and the tobacco under the testicles or genital organs. Then they put the body in the grave and after covering it with sand and gravel they formed a double line, with their faces turned eastwards. One officiating as a priest went to fetch water in his hat and having sprinkled the two rows of Islanders, began a prayer to which the others responded. Then they rose and departed and made their way towards the ship without looking back."[16]

The dozen Hawaiians left onboard the *Tonquin* as seamen also soon lost their lives. At the beginning of June the ship left Astoria to trade off of Vancouver Island. Insulted by the low prices offered for their furs and the newcomers' overbearing treatment of them, local people attacked the *Tonquin* in mid-July, killing everyone onboard.

The eleven Hawaiians who disembarked from the *Tonquin* on April 12 and their sixteen counterparts who arrived a year later on the *Beaver* became part of an adventure that was star-crossed from its inception. The post named for Astor's ambition had a short and unhappy life. The plan was ill conceived. The mixture of employees almost guaranteed antipathies once international politics intervened. War broke out between Britain and the United States in 1812, not directly over the Northwest Coast but with consequences for the area, which was put into active dispute between the two countries.

In the interim the Hawaiians benefited from others' perception of them as a group. Within traditional Hawaiian society, ordinary people, as these men almost certainly were, held possessions in common and worked in groups. The post journal generally described Hawaiians as an entity as opposed to giving them discrete names, as it did with the other men. A typical entry ran, as on September 30, 1812: "In the afternoon the Dolly [a small boat constructed at Astoria for the coastal trade] took her departure on a voyage up the River. G. Franchere, Benjamin Clapp, John Little, Joseph

Gervais, Alosy, [Moses] Flanagan & three Sandwich Islanders on board." A week later on October 5: "John Day, Ignace, Thomas McKay with two S. Islanders started this morning a hunting."

To the extent any of the Hawaiians got a name, it was always members of the first group who had arrived on the *Tonquin,* whose integral role in getting Astoria established bequeathed them their individuality. The names given them combined a Christian first name with what was likely a version of their actual name, as heard by the clerk or other person who put it down on paper. More formal first names, such as Robert, Richard, or Thomas, would often be shortened to the more familiar Bob, Dick, or Tom.

This tendency emphasized the Hawaiians' distinctiveness. They existed between two very different ways of life. They were not "white," which is how every journal writer described himself and others of similar skin tones. Neither were they Indians, who were generally feared and, even more so, disliked and disparaged. The sole reference linking the Hawaiians to North American indigenous people was by the American Alfred Seton, who in one of his rare mentions of a group that for the most part he ignored in his journal termed them "Owyhee Indians."[17] For the others, they were "Sandwich Islanders," although from October 1811 McDougall, who was in charge at Astoria, used some variant of *Kanaka* as a general means of identification. No other explanation exists for his doing so but that he picked up the word from the Hawaiians themselves, who by this time must have been acquiring facility in the English language. McDougall's willingness to change his terminology to the Hawaiians' definition of themselves hints at growing respect.

The 2 partners, 10 clerks, 12 "white" employees, and 11 Hawaiians who disembarked from the *Tonquin* in the spring of 1811 had 3 principal tasks: they needed to sustain themselves, construct a post, and establish trading relations to obtain the furs that were the object of the exercise. Hawaiians, along with mostly French Canadians, provided the physical labor necessary to get the jobs done. As did the others, the Hawaiians quickly settled into work routines imposed on them, but also reflecting the talents they appeared to demonstrate.

As entries in the post journal indicate, the Hawaiians played a central role in sustaining the 35 men. The *Tonquin* brought 2 sheep, 2 goats, and 3 pigs, whose tending fell to 2 of the Hawaiians, Edward Cox and James Keemo. The charge of the all-important post garden also fell to the Hawaiians. On April 24, just a dozen days after landing, 4 of them began "to prepare a piece of ground in which we intend to sow some Indian corn, a few garden seeds & about 30 or 40 Potatoes we have brought safe from New York out of near half a bushel we put up very carefully." A year later, May 21, 1812, much the same process ensued: "Kanakers hoeing and sowing the garden."

As food became scarce in the autumn, it was Hawaiians who foraged for edibles. On October 25, 1811, "two S. Islanders were sent across the River to try the Nets" together with two other men. Three days later "our Iroquois hunter and family left the fort to live in Youngs Bay, it being as he thinks good hunting ground. Bob [Pookarakara], a Sandwich Islander, was sent with him." The same day "4 S. Islanders were sent off" with two other men on an unsuccessful attempt to "procure provisions, Fish and hunt etc." A local Native man consented, on November 3, to teach three of the Hawaiians to use a "scoop Net to fish salmon after the Indian fashion." On December 5 "George [Naaco] & Peter [Pahia] (two Sandwich Islanders)" went out hunting along with five others. On December 24 one other man and "William [Karimou] (Sandwich Isldr) who had been out hunting with him arrived with 9 Swan, 2 Geese, & 2 ducks." Five days later, one other man, "our Iroquois Hunter & 3 Sandwich Islanders were sent up the River to hunt." They returned only on January 18, but "with the meat of 6 elk, having gone as far as the entrance of the Cowlitsk [Cowlitz] River."

All the first winter the Hawaiians came and went from hunting and fishing expeditions. Their importance is attested by the entry on February 24: "3 Kanakers who were comming [*sic*] down the river with a canoe load of 11 Sturgeon were unfortunately upset in a ripple opposite tongue point, and narrowly escaped with their lives. Those are disagreeable news as we are very short of provisions and a great many people about us." Still the Hawaiians set out, sometimes with marked success. April 10, "in the morning sent out 3 Kanackers up the river after Sturgeon & Hoop poles," and five days later, "three Kanakers [arrived] also with 12 Sturgeon & a load of Hoops." Three days later, a French Canadian laborer "returned with Wm Karimou & Powrowie, but brought no sturgeon, as they had not caught any since 12th instant."

The Hawaiians also participated in post construction and maintenance. On June 10, 1811, they were recorded as clearing the point of land; two days later, "the Sandwich Islanders hewing & rolling logs off the point." The beginning of the next month they carried out "small timber" for constructing a dwelling house and putting up a fence around the garden, likely to keep out small animals. The post entry of July 3 ran, "Sandwich Islanders clearing the ground between the Fort & the River." On July 22 and again on

August 26, they were "carrying stones" for the men making the chimney of the dwelling house. Demands varied. August 5, "all hands Cutting & Carrying out Pickets," and August 12, "a party of the Sandwich Islanders bringing Pitch, Tar, Resin, Turpentine & Varnish up from the shallop [small boat], & another party rolling logs & clearing about the Fort, etc." The post journal noted on October 14 how "the Sandwich Islanders making a drain from the upper cellar." On December 23 and into early January, "4 Sandwich Islanders clearing a road to haul out timber."

The Hawaiians' third principal role stemmed from the impetus to their employment in the first place, mastery of the water. "Two Sandwich Islanders (Cox & Bob)" formed part of a twin expedition that headed inland by water on July 22, 1811. The group, which included Bob Pookarakara, set off to the Okanagan River in present-day central Washington to establish a trading outpost. The second group was headed by North West Company partner David Thompson, who was returning east after traveling the Columbia River from its source, being the first newcomer to do so. While resting up for a week at Astoria, Thompson traded one of his men, knowledgeable in the local language, for Cox, "a bold and trustworthy fellow" who, according to Alexander Ross, caught Thompson's fancy "as a prodigy of wit and

Fort Astoria. From Gabriel Franchère, *Narrative of a Voyage to the Northwest Coast of America in the Years 1811, 1812, 1813, and 1814* (New York: Redfield, 1854).

humour."[18] Cox, whose first name now changed from Edward to John, was older and more experienced than most of the Hawaiians at Astoria.

While "Bob (the Sandwich Islander)" returned to Astoria as one of half a dozen manning a canoe from the new "establishment on the Okannaakken River," Cox's travels were more extensive. David Thompson enumerated the men who accompanied him as he departed Astoria in July 1811 as "two Iroquois Indians, four Canadians, with Coxe, seven Men." Thompson described John Cox as "a powerful well made Sandwich Islander" who "spoke some English, and was anxious to acquire our language, and would act as Interpreter on our Ship [when it returns] from England to this [Columbia] River."[19]

Cox turns up in Thompson's memoir six days after their departure during a confrontation with local men while proceeding along the Columbia. Thompson asked his men to take aim at them and was pleased how, "on casting my eye on Cox, the Sandwich Islander, he had marked out his man with his large Pistol, which he held as steady as if it had been in a Vice." By this time, the Hawaiian had clearly been trained in using firearms and had been issued one of his own. And on September 6 Thompson notes: "Coxe very ill & most of us a little so."[20]

Later in the month snow fell, which consternated Cox, so Thompson recalled: "The cold increased, and the first shower of snow, he was for some time catching in his hand, and before he could satisfy his curiosity it was melted: and the next morning the ice was formed, which he closely examined in his hand, but like the Snow it also melted into water, and he was puzzled how the Snow and ice could become water."[21] David Thompson settled down on reaching Montreal. Shortly thereafter Cox was put on a sailing vessel headed back to the West Coast, with a stop at London on the way.

The arrival of the *Beaver* in June 1812 not only brought additional goods and personnel to Fort Astoria, including sixteen more Hawaiians, it fired ambitions. Trade had begun along the Okanagan and Thompson rivers. Nine of the Hawaiians were among the three groups that at the end of June headed, respectively, southeast to the junction of the Columbia and Snake rivers near today's Pasco, Washington; south down the Willamette River near present-day Salem, Oregon; and east beyond Fort Okanagan toward the future Spokane.

The Hawaiians, both the original dozen who had been reduced to ten with Peter's death and Cox's departure and the sixteen who arrived in the spring of 1812, continued to participate fully in the range of activities ongoing since Astoria's foundation. The garden was a yearly event, as on April

26, 1813—"S. Islanders hoeing the garden"—and on May 3—"3 S. Islanders working in the Garden planting Potatoes etc." The next day, "4 S. Islanders digging out a large Stump in the garden." The Hawaiians were also involved in chimney building, as on September 3, 1812: "A number of Sandwich Islanders bringing Sand in a canoe from a little distance above, preparing to finish the chimneys in our old house, and build that in the new one." Two weeks later, "[Joseph] St. Amant with the assistance of Two Islanders repairing the old chimney in the men's part of the building."

The Hawaiians repeatedly found themselves dispatched by canoe to go hunting and fishing and to retrieve animals shot for meat. A typical entry was recorded on September 16, 1812: "John Day & Thomas McKay [hunter and clerk] with the S. Islanders arrived from hunting, bringing the meat of an Elk . . . Sent two Islanders in a Canoe to bring home [Iroquois hunter] Ignace & family from hunting, who all arrived in the evening." Two months later, on November 19, "Four Sandwich Islanders with a canoe were dispatched early this morning accompanied by Watatkum [local Indian] for the meat of the Elk he had killed. Returned at evening." January 4, 1813, after a Native man reported killing an elk: "One of the Sawyers with four Sandwich Islanders was therefore dispatched with him in a canoe for it, and returned successfully at evening." Nine days later the exercise was repeated: "[Laborer Alexis] Macon [Masçon], with four Sandwich Islanders, were dispatched in a Canoe with the meat with which they returned at evening, furnishing us with a reasonable supply." Just two days later: "[hunter William] Cannon with the two Sandwich Islanders started again this morning for hunting in another direction."

Fishing, which became feasible by February, was largely provisioned by Hawaiians. On the 10th, ten men "including 4 Sandwich Islanders in two Canoes, having every necessary to commence fishing, a small supply of provisions for immediate use, and a few articles of Goods, such as gurrahs [earthen jars] & Tobacco, for the purpose of purchasing more in case they do not meet with success." Four days later one of the Hawaiians and one other man returned, "bringing 7 Sturgeon and a considerable quantity of Uthlecans [oolichans]." On February 18, McDougall "dispatched the large canoes" with "3 Sandwich Islanders" and two others "to the fishing place." Eight days later "4 S. Islanders" and seven others departed "for the fishing place in the large Canoe." Five men returned on the morning of March 8 in a small canoe with two sturgeon, having "left the large Canoe and 4 S. Islanders behind on the way down with 10 Sturgeon more," who then "arrived in the afternoon." The very next day "2 S. Islanders [were sent] in the small canoe up to the fishing place." The men returned eight days later:

"About breakfast time 3 S. Islanders in a small canoe arrived from the Chelwits with 8 Sturgeon, a timely supply."

The Hawaiians' growing sophistication with the English language is indicated in the next sentence of this post entry: "They brought information that two of our lines had been taken by the Cathlamet Indians, and they had beat one of our fisherman, Aswalacks, who found them in the act of stealing." On April 7: "About 9 a.m. our small canoe came down from the fishing place with William [Karimou] & Peter [Pahia], 2 S. Islanders, bringing all the implements which had been in use, and the necessary account of fish received."

Another of the Hawaiians' ongoing activities was turning wood into charcoal for use as fuel. July 30, 1812: "Two Sandwich Islanders sent to assist the three men already at the Coal Pits, cutting & piling Wood etc." The next day, "three Sandwich Islanders sent in addition to the number Yesterday to the Coal Pits. Raised the platform on one side and nearly completed the flooring." On December 18: "Sandwich Islanders bringing coal for the Blacksmiths." And the next year on April 9: "In the afternoon sent 2 S. Islanders to cut wood at the Coal Pit."

While the Hawaiians were often put under the supervision of others, they also worked on their own, mostly at ongoing maintenance around the post. November 3, 1812: "Two Sandwich Islanders filling with earth beneath the floor of the new house." And December 14: "The Sandwich Islanders employed to keeping things about the place in order." March 16, 1813: "Two S. Islanders cleaning about the buildings and getting fire Wood." Some entries were more general, as on February 17: "Sandwich Islanders cleaning & putting the place in order." Specific circumstances varied the routine, as on March 4: "S. Islanders employed most of the day cutting & clearing away Logs that had drifted round the wharf, which hindered hauling up Canoes at the usual place."

Hawaiians may have fared the best among the men at Astoria. The *Tonquin*'s stop of three weeks at the Hawaiian Islands on the way to the Northwest Coast in February 1811 gave young Franchère enough time for him to feel comfortable speculating on the reasons why the men might have been so willing to join in the adventure. He was writing almost a decade before the first missionaries' arrival. "Although Nature has showered her bounties on these Islanders, who enjoy a healthful climate and can live almost without working, they are nonetheless unhappy. The dependence in which they are kept by their chiefs, who make them work without any hope of reward, the limitations even in the choice of food, would be unbearable to anyone unaccustomed to slavish obedience."[22] The commitment made to the

Hawaiians of food, clothing, and a wage that varied between $10 per month and $100 annually, depending on which account is to be believed, was not that different from what other fur trade laborers received.

Hawaiians had their own accommodations. The additional men who arrived on the *Beaver* necessitated new arrangements. November 26, 1812: "Carpenters etc. removed from the new house, in one end of which was placed the furs, where also the Mechanics will mess during the winter, the other part being occupied by the Sandwich Islanders." December 19: "[John] Patterson [carpenter] employed fixing Births [*sic*] for the Sandwich Islanders in their part of the house."

By rights the Hawaiians should have crumpled. As well as handing over their bodies for labor, they surrendered control over the two most basic elements of sustenance—food and clothing. These were not men hired on to ships who moved between climates, but men on land whose circumstances would remain roughly constant for several years. Both foodstuffs and dress in the Hawaiian Islands related to their tropical character. As the *Tonquin* approached, Franchère described how "the Islanders came out in their canoes, bringing us cabbages, yams, bananas, taro, watermelons, poultry &c." The land was "covered with coconut and banana palms, among which may be seen the huts of the Islanders." The *Tonquin* continued on to the island of O'ahu. "Behind the village [that would become Honolulu] are grown sugar cane, *taro,* bananas and bread fruit, thus named because of its taste, which is like bread."[23] As Franchère explained, the basic foodstuffs consisted of taro, coconuts, bananas, breadfruit, sweet potatoes, and yams, together with fish and pork. Taro was a sweet tuberous root that was boiled, ground, and pounded into a paste to become poi, a thin porridge eaten with the fingers that was the principal item of food along with fish.

After several weeks in the Islands, Franchère felt comfortable enough to make some generalizations about dress. "The men on the whole are well built, tall and wearing no other garment than the *maro* (in the language of the country) or strip of bark-cloth about 2 yards long and one foot wide that they wrap around their waists, fastening both ends at the hip. At first I thought their bodies were painted red but I soon saw that it was the natural colour of their skins." According to Alexander Ross, who also visited in 1811, "the climate here is so mild and warm that the natives seldom wear any clothing." When they do, "the common dress of the men consists of a piece of this tappa, about ten inches broad and nine feet long, like a belt, called maro. The maro is thrown carelessly round the loins, then passed between the thighs, and tied on the left side."[24]

Unfamiliar food and clothing appear to have been a minor inconvenience. The only comment related to clothing comes from a stop on the way to establish outlying posts in the summer of 1812, in which nine Hawaiians participated. "Owing to the extreme heat, the Sandwich Islanders had thrown off their jackets and shirts during the day, and their swarthy bodies, decorated with buff belts, seemed to excite the particular attention of the Indians, who repeatedly pointed towards them, and then spoke to each other with considerable animation."[25] The impression that lingers is of the Hawaiians, however much they appreciated the opportunity to wear traditional garb, otherwise being comfortably dressed much like everyone else.

The Hawaiians had the least difficulty of all of the men at Astoria with food. Franchère recalled how "the supplies we received from the ship soon gave out and from the month of July [1811] on we had to accustom ourselves to a diet of fish," principally salmon, whose oiliness "made some of us ill," but not the Hawaiians. "Those who adapted themselves best to our new diet were the Islanders," who thought it "delicious." Ross Cox made a similar observation anecdotally: "I observed a quantity of small fish; but had no means of catching any, or I should have made a Sandwich Island meal."[26]

Certainly, the Hawaiians suffered as did others from food shortages. Scurvy, caused by lack of fresh fruit and vegetables, made its appearance in mid-February 1813 and soon also affected the Hawaiians. The entry for March 10 ran: "One of the S. Islanders (Peter [Pahia]) ill with symptoms of the scurvy." On May 2: "Dick [Paow], the S. Islander very ill with the scurvy. Two S. Islanders (Boys) still attending the sick." By May 24, perhaps because food options grew wider, "Dick recovered of the Scurvy & resumed his occupation."

The tremendous differences in climate between the Hawaiian Islands and the Pacific Northwest did exact a toll. Even though the ships arrived in the springtime, numerous Hawaiians soon became ill. Writing in early July 1811, Alexander Ross graphically depicted the growing strain.

> The people suffered greatly from the humidity of the climate. The Sandwich Islanders, used to a dry, pure atmosphere, sank under its influence; damp fogs and sleet were frequent, and every other day was a day of rain. Such is the climate of Columbia at this season of the year, and all this time we were without tents or shelter; add to this the bad quality of our food, consisting solely of boiled fish and wild roots, without even salt, and we had to depend at all times on the success or good-will of the natives for our daily supply, which was far from being regular.[27]

Duncan McDougall, who had charge of the post, had a primary obligation for ensuring that men were usefully employed and so kept careful note in his daily log of those unable to do so. July 23, 1811: "Three Sandwich Islanders laid up with sore Backs, Bellies, & limbs." On April 22, 1813: "4 S. Islanders laid up with Colds."

Winter was the worst, as McDougall noted on January 11, 1812: "The sudden change from frost to rain has affected the most of our people in a very serious manner, particularly the Sandwich Islanders." The onset of winter a year later was little different, both for the newcomers and for the more seasoned Hawaiians. November 9: "Nearly all the Sandwich Islanders are laid up on account of the continual Wet & damp weather that now prevails." And the next day: "All the Sandwich Islanders off duty except three." On November 23: "As yesterday Rainy. . . . The few Sandwich Islanders fit for duty employed about the buildings at different Jobs." A week later, there were "few Sandwich Islanders fit for duty."

Alexander Ross, who arrived in 1811 on the *Tonquin*, reflected later in life on the importance of climate to the Hawaiians. "The contrast is great between them here and in their own country where they are all life, all activity, for when I saw them there I thought them the most active people I had ever seen." On the Northwest Coast they became, from Ross's perspective, dull and submissive. "This difference in their habits I am inclined to attribute to the difference of climate, their own being favourable to them in a high degree. When we consider the salubrity of the Sandwich Islands it is hardly to be wondered that the unhappy native, when transplanted to the snows and cold of the Rocky Mountains should experience decay of energies."[28]

As well as being exposed to an unfamiliar climate, Hawaiians suffered from scurvy and from the other great scourge of the day, venereal disease, which spread through sexual relations. Men on ships were prone to use local women whenever possible, which meant venereal disease leaped across indigenous populations. The absence of a trained medical doctor at Astoria exacerbated these and other difficulties. One of the Hawaiians, Thomas Tuana, was already ill with venereal disease at the time of his arrival on the *Tonquin* in the spring of 1811. The respect accorded the Hawaiians is indicated by the concern repeatedly expressed for his condition in the post journal and by the attempts to find a cure for his condition.[29] Nothing worked, and he was most often on the sick list. On July 20, 1812, after a good year of efforts, the post journal referred to "Tuana the S. Islander, who has been a long time laid up (with the Venereal) with little prospect at present of recovering entirely." November 1, he was described, almost affectionately, as "Tuanna, the old invalid." On November 24, desperate measures were applied in line with the limited medical knowledge of the day. "All hands were assembled and the party detained untill [*sic*] afternoon to Witness an experiment performed on our unfortunate Sandwich Islander Tuanna. Having learned that by killing an animal & placing him immediately in the body of it while warm, would effect a cure, one of our horses was brought and the experiment tryed [*sic*]."

The next entries in the post journal were determinedly optimistic. December 17: "The experiment performed on our invalid Tuanna some time since, together with the unremitted attentions of Doctor [Paul] Jeremy [a clerk] has evidently a good effect." A week later: "Tuanna only on the sick list, who is getting much better." The last day of 1812: "Tuana only sick, who appears now to be getting better." And on January 11, 1813: "Jeremy sent in pursuit of Roots, being still attending on Tuana who appears getting better." The hopes for his recovery were such that, on May 7, "set Tuanna at work with [Alexis] Macon in the garden, as he appears now active & strong, much better than he has ever been here." The optimism was short lived, so that on July 9: "J[oseph] Lapierre & Tuanna laid up with the Venereal, both making use of Mercury. One other S. Islander also slightly affected with the same disease, making 3 men sick." However, on August 9, "Tuanna kept employed," and a week later, "Tuanna at work with others."

The Hawaiians garnered a measure of respect from the other men. Days and weeks of hard labor were relieved through several means. Many of the men expected a regular ration of liquor, which sometimes led to fights as well as intoxication. Only glimpses survive of the extent to which the Hawaiians were part of these activities. The post entry for June 4, 1811, hints at their presence. "One of the Sandwich Islanders being merry & rather forward, was struck & cut very ill with a bone by Mr. Mumford, who was also Gay & glorious."

The men in charge at Astoria maintained morale by giving out special food and drink on designated holidays. July 4, 1811: "People employed about the buildings, excepting the Sandwich Islanders who are bur[nin]g up what they gathered the day before. . . . This being the anniversary of the independence of the U.S., fired three rounds of Musketry, and treated all hands with grog." On November 1 the men not only got special edibles, but work stopped. "This being all saints' day all hands got a holyday, & as good a feast as the season could afford." December 25, 1811: "This being Christmas, all hands had a holiday & were treated with Grog on the occasion."

New Year's Day was the major holiday. "At sunrise, the Drum beat to arms and the colours were hoisted. Three rounds of small arms & three discharges from the great Guns were fired, after which all the hands were treated with grog, bread, cheese & Butter. A GOOD Dinner & grog were served out to all hands. At sun down 3 big Guns were fired & the colours taken down, after which we had a dance, and retired about 3 A.M." The other holiday was Easter, which in 1812 fell on March 29. "This being Easter Sunday, all hands were treated on the occasion with flour, Grog & Molasses."

Hawaiians participated along with partners, clerks, and other employees. They may have, however, been a bit more circumspect; alternatively, they were in better physical condition and thereby recovered faster from their excesses. December 25, 1812: "A suitable treat was given to all hands in order that they should enjoy themselves as well as circumstances would permit." Three days later: "The people having kept up Christmas at so high a rate that few of them were able to begin work this morning. Blacksmith's, Sawyers & the Sandwich Islanders only busy." On January 17, 1813, following the return of a group of men from outlying posts, "a regal was given to all hands." The post entry for the next day ran: "The people being engaged yesterday in frolic, were unfit for work. Two Blacksmiths and the Sandwich Islanders only on duty."

As well as the expected times of the year, October 27 was celebrated in 1812 as a mark of respect to the twenty-six Hawaiian workers. "At evening a Regale was given to the Sandwich Islanders, the day being their New Year, much celebrated by their countrymen." At this point in time the Hawaiians used both a lunar calendar with 354 days and a solar calendar with 565 days, so that the new year fell differently each time around.[30] The celebration replaced November 1, which went by unnoticed, unlike the attention paid to that date a year earlier. The distinctly Hawaiian celebration seems to have occurred only once, perhaps because numbers were smaller the previous year and general conditions more uncertain a year later.

The Hawaiians' hard work raised their status. June 17, 1812: "Visited by a number of the Natives, one of whom (a young Lad) was detected in the act of stealing from some of our Sandwich Islanders, and for which had him confined in the Cellar of the Store." Three days later: "An Indian Woman of the Chinooks was last night at a late hour detected in stealing from one of our Sandwich Islanders. She was immediately brought in and put in confinement, where she continued to be kept during this day." Theft from one of the Hawaiians, even if during a likely sexual encounter, was taken as seriously as from any of the other men at the post.

All the same, the Hawaiians were largely bystanders in the contentious decisions that culminated in Fort Astoria being turned over to the North West Company in the fall of 1813. Much uncertainty existed over the war declared between the United States and Britain in June 1812, about which men at the post found out the next January. The Hawaiians fretted alongside everyone else over the failure of a hoped-for supply ship to appear. The post entry of January 25, 1813, affirmed that "every arrangement made that we may consume as little as possible untill [sic] spring, when we may know the event which now gives so much anxiety."

In April 1813, eighteen North West Company employees arrived from their posts west of the Rockies to camp just next to Astoria while awaiting a ship due to arrive with supplies. In theory the situation should have been fraught with tension but was in practice congenial since many of the men at Astoria had mixed loyalties. By now they realized that the Montreal company much better understood the fur trade than did its American competitor. The post entry for April 11 reflected this ambivalence: "They are coming here formidable in Opposition, to await the arrival of a Ship from London on account of the N.W. Company, equiped [sic] with everything necessary & adapted to Indian trade, arranged by men possessed of experience & a thorough knowledge of the business."

The North West Company was run by partners who shared in both the risks and the profits. The trading strategy was to go where the furs were, as opposed to expecting local people to bring their wares to large central posts, as with Astoria and also the fur trade giant, the Hudson's Bay Company. Men lived much of the year at outlying posts, where they traded for furs that were then taken overland during the summer to a central point, Fort William on the northwestern shore of Lake Superior. Partners based in Montreal brought supplies and trade goods to the rendezvous, taking back the furs to be marketed. The growing length of supply lines, after the North West Company jumped across the Rocky Mountains early in the decade, made it more expedient to bring in supplies and take out furs by ship, hence the men's arrival to await the hoped-for vessel.

Although no one at Astoria knew it, the North West Company ship *Isaac Todd* was doing its best to get there. Its voyage began in Montreal in late 1812. It made a stop in London to secure the protection of the Royal Navy in crossing the Atlantic to the Northwest Coast. Among persons onboard on leaving Montreal were, according to a North West partner who sailed on it, "a Sandwich Islander" whose task was "to guide us into the river Columbia, where he had been before." This was John Cox, who had gone east from Astoria to Montreal with David Thompson the previous summer. Negotiations were so protracted in London that the *Isaac Todd* and its escort vessels departed there only in March 1813. At a stop in Rio de

Janeiro the North West men and Cox transferred to the British Royal Navy frigate *HMS Racoon* so he could guide it "up the Columbia" in anticipation the vessel would arrive there first.[31]

Having no knowledge of the various machinations, the men in charge of Astoria gave up on the adventure. A kind of lethargy set in, or so it seems from the Hawaiians now being assigned mainly busy work. May 10, 1813: "S. Islanders at sundry jobs." Two days later: "S. Islanders leveling the walk in front of the Picketing, gravelling it, etc." May 19: "Three S. Islanders bring Coals & at other small jobs about the place." Among the few new initiatives were, on May 27, "working at Tobacco, making it in plugs, pressing it, etc." The next day and off and on through July, one or more of the Hawaiians were "working at Tobacco" or "preparing tobacco for manufacturing." On June 7, the post journal read a bit defensively: "S. Islanders variously employed at different jobs. We have indeed full employment of every person in some way or another." The entry of July 21 was more revealing: "Several hands employed as usual at the Coal Pit, being the only work of consequence going forward beside that of the Mechanics."

The war, the lack of supplies, and proximity of the Northwesters all played into the decision made on the ground in late June 1813 for Astor's Pacific Fur Company to abandon Astoria. By then, it was too late in the season for the men to return overland to American territory, so they and the Northwesters, who had by now given up hopes that their anticipated ship would arrive, decided to divide the fur business. Ross Cox caught the unease. "These unlucky and unexpected circumstances, joined to the impossibility of sustaining ourselves for another year in the country without fresh supplies, which, in the then posture of affairs, it would be hopeless to expect, induced our proprietor to enter into negotiations."[32] In practice the Pacific Fur Company and the North West Company were intertwined. Men flowed from one to the other. The post entry for July 24 noted about the principal Northwester at Astoria, "Mr. [Donald] McKenzie with four S. Islanders in a canoe went round to Fort Clatsop, Captns. Lewis & Clarke's wintering place, having never been there." Three days later McKenzie took "4 S. Islanders" together with five others on "a trading and hunting excursion up the river."

The decision to abandon Astoria did not go down well from a distance, and the following months and years would see rancorous discussion and debate on the topic. The Hawaiians felt the tension in several ways. Astor's American field agent Wilson Price Hunt, who had departed after arriving overland in February 1812, finally secured passage back to Astoria on the Winship brothers' *Albatross,* a vessel that he chartered in the Islands. Arriving in August 1813, he was, in Franchère's words, "astonished when he learned of the decision to leave the country."[33]

Hunt's arrival also provided welcome sustenance to the Hawaiians. He brought taro, which the men quickly turned into poi. The post journal noted on September 27: "S. Islanders pounding and grinding Tarro." Whatever the particulars, and they seem to have slipped from view, the gesture must have been very welcome.

Eventually, even Hunt accepted the inevitability of Astoria's evacuation and made plans to get the Hawaiians back home. Alfred Seton explained how, "on his understanding the situation of affairs, it was thought best for him to proceed immediately to the [Sandwich] Islands to purchase a vessel which was there for sale, to embark the Owyhee Indians [Hawaiians] & Beaver in her."[34] With Hunt's departure, the number of Hawaiians needing to be returned home fell by one, for he took with him the luckless Thomas Tuana. All hope had finally been exhausted that he would recover his health.

In anticipation of Hunt's swift return for the pelts and the Hawaiians, an expedition headed off to the interior posts on October 2 "for the purpose of bringing down the packs and Sandwich Islanders" stationed there. The journal noted two weeks later, "Six men with the Sandwich Islanders carrying out timber & laying up a house for themselves to live in during the winter." About the same time, on October 12, 1813, so Duncan McDougall recorded in the post journal, he simply sold the post. "Came to an understanding with Mr. McTavish respecting the disposing of the whole of the Company's goods, Merchandise & Furs to the N.W. Company." Astoria was officially wound up.

Three days later the Hawaiians' tenure with the Pacific Fur Company came to an end, even though Hunt had not yet returned with a vessel to take them home. "Settled with the Sandwich Islands [*sic*] and gave them to understand the business was given up and that Mr. McTavish became responsible for the amount due them, and that they were at liberty to engage with him 'till Spring, when those that wished to return to the Islands, would be sent home in one of the N.W. Co. Ships. Gave to each of them as a present One New Musket, 1 Powder horn, 3 lbs. Powder, 8 lbs. lead, 10 Gun flints, 1 half axe, 1 Tomyhawk, and 3 lbs. Leaf Tobacco." The following month the post journal for Astoria ended.

The Astoria adventure was, however, not yet over. The daily routines that marked the fur trade had little reason to change. The twenty-five Islanders were still in place, as were many of the other personnel who had guided the Pacific Fur Company. Dick Paow, who had earlier suffered from scurvy, became a servant to the new man in charge, Alexander Henry, who arrived overland shortly after the post's sale. Henry noted in his journal on November 26, "The house intended for us [at Point George] being ready, after having undergone some repairs, we moved into it this afternoon—Messrs. S., B., and H. [Stuart, Bethene and Henry], with Dick, a Sandwich Islander, as our Mr. Dimo [major domo]; we are thus in our winter quarters."[35]

Another stage in the drama that was Astoria soon followed. The British naval vessel *HMS Racoon* finally arrived at the end of November 1813, bearing Cox onboard. All that remained was for the British to take formal possession. The British flag was hoisted and Astoria renamed Fort George in honor of the British king. Alexander Henry recorded on December 18 how "the cutter set off, taking D.P. Jeremie, boatbuilder, four Sandwich Islanders with their baggage, and five hogs, large and small."

The twenty-two Hawaiians left at the newly named Fort George soon gained a very different experience. Dispatched to the outlying posts consistent with North West Company practice, they suffered through an inland winter that must have tried all of their resources. A work party that set out on early December 1813 to construct a post on the Willamette River included "6 Sandwich Islanders" among its twenty-nine men.[36] On December 30 "[Hunter Registe] Belair set off for the Willamette, with two Canadians and four Sandwich Islanders, to hunt beaver until May 1st."

A dozen of the Hawaiians wintered on the Willamette, where they enjoyed the utter confidence of the men in charge, who included Alexander Henry. He recorded on January 17, following a confrontation with an Indian: "A guard of four Sandwich Islanders was placed over the prisoner, with muskets and fixed bayonets." The next day: "I kept no watch last night, but was on guard all day with Messrs. D. Stuart and Franchère and 12 Sandwich Islanders."

By the end of January Alexander Henry was back at Fort George, and on February 4, 1814, "At daybreak I set off a wooden canoe with five Sandwich Islanders, 18 sturgeon, and a quantity of ash hop-poles for Fort George." Again, on February 17: "Sent a large Chinook canoe with six Sandwich Islanders up to Oak point for sturgeon." Hawaiians were assigned to guard duty almost as a matter of course, as when, on February 13, the man in charge of the *Dolly* reported being robbed overnight by Indians. "We sent four Sandwich Islanders on board to watch with him, fired a canon to alarm the natives, and heard no more of the matter."

Three other Hawaiians spent the harsh winter of 1813–1814 at the interior post of Okanagan. Joseph McGillivray, a Northwester who came overland to Astoria in the summer of 1813, was in charge, under him "my men, half Canadians and half Sandwich islanders." While the former spent much of their time hunting, the latter were intended to give protection. It was likely for that reason, but perhaps also out of condescension, that he referred to the Hawaiians in writing to a friend as *"Bonaparte!! Washington!! And Caesar!!* Great names, you will say." No information survives as to these men's actual names.

McGillivray was a newcomer to the Pacific Northwest and had limited understanding of the Hawaiians' strengths. "I have not as yet made a pack of beaver. The lazy Indians won't work; and as for the emperor, president, and dictator, they know as much about trapping as the monks of *La Trappe.*" McGillivray felt more than a little sorry for himself. "Here I am, with a shivering guard of poor islanders, buried in snow, sipping molasses, smoking tobacco, and masticating horse-flesh!"

All the same, McGillivray expressed genuine empathy and considerable understanding for the plight in which the Hawaiians found themselves. "The snow is between two and three feet deep, and my trio of Owyhee generals find a sensible difference between such hyperborean weather and the pleasing sunshine of their own tropical paradise. Poor fellows! They are not adapted for these latitudes, and I heartily wish they were at home in their own sweet islands, and sporting in the 'blue summer ocean' that surrounds them."[37]

In early 1814 a decision was made to move Fort George farther up the Columbia River to a location considered safer and healthier. As the Hawaiians had done earlier in the establishment of Astoria, they cleared away the underbrush and generally prepared the site.

The final postscript to Astoria, from the Hawaiians' perspective, should have come in March 1814 with Hunt's return in the *Pedlar,* procured in the Islands and on which he intended to take the Hawaiians home. As Franchère put in wryly, "one may imagine Mr. Hunt's surprise on finding Astoria under the British flag and in foreign hands." The immediate pleasure for the Hawaiians was the "yams, cocoanuts, and sweet potatoes, all in perfection," that Hunt sent ashore on his arrival.[38]

For most of the Hawaiians this precursor of home was not followed by the reality. The original intention had been that Hunt would embark the Hawaiians as well as men signed on with the Pacific Fur Company who chose not to transfer their allegiance to the North West Company. NWC officials were opposed. Alexander Henry recorded on March 4: "It was evident he wished to take away as many men as he could, and, on our part, we were as desirous of keeping them. The Sandwich Islanders wished much to see their own homes. But as this would not answer our purpose, of course we opposed it, and promised them a safe passage on our own ship." Four days later Henry wrote: "We agreed to give up four Sandwich Islanders to Mr. Hunt, who had been desirous of taking them all."

The other eighteen Hawaiians were persuaded to stay. As for the four men who either persisted in leaving or, perhaps, were not considered useful, on April 29 "all the Sandwich Islanders' accounts settled," and four days later, "Pedlar got underway." Later in the spring the NWC's ship *Isaac Todd* finally made it to Fort George. On its departure it embarked "three Sandwich Islanders who were left here by the *Tonquin*."[39] Two of them—James Keemo and Dick Paow—had come on the *Tonquin*, the third unnamed countryman on the *Beaver*.

If we accept the numbers of persons said to have come on the *Tonquin* and *Beaver*, this means that the Astoria adventure left fifteen of the twenty-eight Hawaiians in the Pacific Northwest. Peter had perished during the *Tonquin*'s arrival in the spring of 1811. Thomas Tuana, who had never been employable due to venereal disease, returned on the *Albatross* in August 1813. Four men whose names have not survived traveled on the *HMS Racoon* in December of that year. The next spring four left on the *Pedlar* and three on the *Isaac Todd*. The fate of the others now lay with the North West Company.

Ten of the fifteen Hawaiians remained at Fort George itself. As soon as the *Pedlar* departed in April 1814, the men left there were enumerated. Four of the Islanders on the list—Harry, Peter Pahia, Paul Pooao or Poah, and Jack Powrowie or Paraurriee—had been in the Pacific Northwest since the arrival of the *Tonquin* three years earlier. Five, previously unnamed in post records but now identified as Chester, James Coah, Patrick Oui, Thomas Pakeeknaak, and Isaac Teow, had arrived two years previous on the *Beaver*. The tenth was John Cox, who came on the *Tonquin*, went east with David Thompson, and returned via London and Rio de Janeiro on the *Racoon*.

The five other Hawaiians were among a large group of men that went overland by canoe to the major trading depot of Fort William on the northeast shore of Lake Superior to take out the furs. The Hawaiians were placed one per canoe likely due to their prowess at paddling. William Karimuo or Kariume, George Naaco, and Bob Packanakra or Pookarakara had come on the *Tonquin*, Ben and Joshua on the *Beaver*. The brigade reached Fort William by mid-July, returning west to Astoria later in the summer.

The Astoria adventure was over, but not the Hawaiians' adventure in the Pacific Northwest.

Chapter 4

IN THE SERVICE OF THE HUDSON'S BAY COMPANY

THE ASTORIA ADVENTURE initiated the Pacific Northwest fur trade. The North West Company was already active west of the Rocky Mountains, and its presence grew following the demise of Astoria. The Northwesters' tenure would be relatively brief. In 1821 the NWC was absorbed into the Hudson's Bay Company (HBC), which thereafter controlled the trade across British North America. Indigenous Hawaiians were as integral to the HBC's success as they had been to that of the Pacific Fur Company. Having proven their worth at Astoria, they would be employed in increasing numbers over the next quarter century. Their participation culminated with the Treaty of Washington of 1846, setting an international boundary between the United States and Britain. Hawaiians' willingness to participate was due both to conditions at home and to the opportunities to be had on a distant shore.

Life in the Islands was changing. The relative stability that marked the later years of Kamehameha's reign ended with his death in 1819. He was succeeded by his son Liholiho, who took the title of Kamehameha II. Hawaiians increasingly realized that foreigners did not suffer when they ignored the innumerable restrictions and prohibitions of the *kapu* system. The eating taboo was broken in a feast ordered by Liholiho in 1819 and by his subsequent orders to destroy the temples from one end of the Islands to the other.

The maritime sojourning that brought the first Hawaiians to the Northwest Coast accelerated these changes. Attoo and Kalehua had been the first of a number of Hawaiians arriving in Boston on trading vessels who became objects for conversion by missionaries zealous to bring indigenous peoples around the world to Christianity. The American Board of Foreign Missions, which was supported by the Congregational and Presbyterian churches, took the lead. In the fall of 1819 seven New England missionary couples together with three converted Hawaiians committed themselves to the Hawaiian Islands, where they arrived the next April. The distinguished American historian Samuel Eliot Morison considered that, by the mid-1820s, "Hawai'i had, in fact, become an outpost of New England."[1] These families initiated a colonial process that would see not just widespread conversion but themselves and their children become some of the principal entrepreneurs and would culminate, by century's end, in the Islands' annexation to the United States.

These important shifts were still in embryonic form at the time the Pacific Fur Company withdrew from Astoria. The next years were a time of transition. While impossible to determine actual numbers due to the scarcity of records, it is clear Hawaiians both went and came. The NWC ship *Isaac Todd,* which had touched shore at the renamed Fort George in the spring of 1814 "manned with Sandwich Islanders," left sixteen of its Hawaiian crew at Canton, where they were taken onboard the British trading vessel *Columbia* on its way to the Northwest Coast.[2] Two died en route, but the remainder had a second chance to drop off when the vessel arrived in the Pacific Northwest in 1815, alternatively to head home.

The scarce North West Company accounts that do survive underline the full extent to which the Hawaiians had become integral to the fur trade. For the men at Fort George, life went on much as before. When an unknown ship was spotted on April 22, 1814, "I sent four Sandwich Islanders on board the *Dolly,* to mount guard with Joe during the night." The vessel having been identified as safely British, three days later the post's head Alexander Henry sent "four Sandwich Islanders to assist in bringing over the ship at high water." On May 2 he dispatched four Hawaiians to plant potatoes and five days later to general gardening. Henry's journal ends on May 22, 1814, when he drowned.

Ross Cox's account follows some of the Hawaiians. In mid-November 1814 a brigade headed off from Fort George to winter at outlying posts to trade for furs. "We had fifty-four canoe-men, including six Sandwich Islanders." The Hawaiians were playing one of their now familiar roles. They soon joined in another as well. Encountering some Indians who attempted to take the brigade's trade goods by force, the partner in charge decided on a show of force. Having distributed ammunition, he first explained the situation to the French Canadians. "He next addressed the Sandwich Islanders, and asked them, would they fight the bad people who had attempted to rob us, in case it was necessary? Their answer was laconic: 'Missi Keit[h], we kill every man you bid us.' So all was satisfactory; and after having examined their muskets, and given each man an additional glass of rum, we embarked."[3]

Two of the Hawaiians spent the winter of 1814–1815 at Okanagan; the other four went with Ross Cox and his group to Spokane. The brigade left so late from Fort George that the way to their winter assignments proved an enormous challenge, particularly for the Hawaiians with their still limited experience with cold weather. Cox's journal entries tell the story.

> DEC 13. The cold was intense, and the ground covered with ten to twelve inches of snow. This necessarily impeded our progress, and prevented us from advancing more than twelve miles a day.
>
> DEC 16. . . . it snowed incessantly.
>
> DEC 17. We arose with the first dawn of morning, and prepared to renew our march; but on mustering the horses we found one of them dead, and the two Sandwich Islanders dreadfully frost-bitten.[4]

Hawaiians were integral at both Okanagan and Spokane. Ross Cox spent the winter of 1816–1817 at Okanagan, where he turned to the Hawaiians for protection after finding two horses stolen. "I selected three Canadians and two Sandwich Islanders to accompany me [to find them], and in less than an hour all our warlike arrangements were completed." The man in charge of Spokane the same winter explained how, on an expedition from there, he "took ten Sandwich Islanders, whom I armed and accoutred quite *en militaire.*" As to why it was so effective to do so, "The *Nez-Pérces* did not half relish the aspect of these invincibles."[5] The Hawaiians' physical selves made them more fearful than those with paler skin tones and a smaller size.

The brigade of over eighty men that left Fort George the next spring to take out furs included "nine natives of the Sandwich Islands." Not all of the men went as far as Fort William, and it is unclear how many of the Hawaiians did so. Having arrived there, Ross Cox "ascertained that the aggregate number of the persons in about the establishment was composed of natives" of twelve countries, including "the Sandwich Islands."[6]

The year 1817 marked a turning point in the Pacific Northwest. The 1814 Treaty of Ghent that ended the War of 1812 stipulated that all land seized had to be returned by 1818. The North West Company was concerned to shore up its claims to the former Astoria, which had been symbolically "seized" by a British Royal Navy captain following its purchase by the NWC. It needed men, so, when the *Columbia* again stopped at Fort

George in August 1816, the NWC requested it "to bring as many of the Sandwich Islanders to the Columbia River as we could conveniently accommodate."[7]

According to the *Columbia*'s chief officer, Peter Corney, the vessel returned in mid-June 1817 with "60 natives (being all we could conveniently accommodate)," all of whom were put "on shore." One of their number, Peeopeeoh later claimed to be a relative of Kamehameha sent as the men's overseer or guardian. Unlike Boatswain Tom on the *Beaver*, Peeopeeoh remained rather than returning home. Reflecting popular understandings in the Islands, Hawaiian historian John Papa Ii wrote in old age that "a hundred Hawaiian men were taken to labor in the Northwest at that time, but the payment received by the king for graciously giving these men away is not known."[8] Ii was referring to the advance that some, if not all, men received before leaving the Islands.

John Papa Ii's assertion of large numbers may relate to the departure of other Hawaiians for other parts of the North American West Coast at about the same point in time. A year after Corney delivered the Hawaiians, he joined an expedition put together in the Islands to liberate Spanish America. The ship he commanded counted 30 Hawaiians among its crew of 100, the lead vessel 50 among a total of 260. The first stop was the capital of Spanish California, Monterey, which Teheeopea and Tahomeeraoo had visited a quarter of a century earlier under Captain George Vancouver's protection. At Monterrey the men "beat a charge and rushed up, the Sandwich Islanders in front with pikes." Corney took special pride that "a Sandwich Islander was the first to haul down their colours." The Spanish having fled, the men entered Monterey without opposition. Again, the 80 Hawaiians adapted. "The Sandwich Islanders, who were quite naked when they landed, were soon dressed in the Spanish fashion."[9]

The two vessels headed south. On an island off Mexico, the Hawaiians suffered a disaster. "We found a root resembling the tarrow of the Sandwich Islands; the Islanders cooked some of it in the island fashion, and immediately after they had eaten of it their bodies and faces became swelled and bloated in a terrible manner, some died in a few days, and others lingered in the greatest agony."[10] A dozen Hawaiians succumbed. By the time the two ships reached Valparaiso, Chile, in July 1819, another forty crew members had died and the expedition lost its will. Most of the remaining men, apparently including Hawaiians, joined the Chilean navy.

The Hawaiians Corney brought to the Pacific Northwest in 1817 had their own adventures. When Alexander Ross was dispatched the next July to establish a new interior post to be named Fort Nez Perce, he was allocated

32 Hawaiians along with 38 Iroquois and 25 French Canadians. In October 1818, according to the partner in charge of Fort George, just "twenty-six natives of Owhyhee" and "two Owhyhees absent" were among a "grand total of sixty-six persons" who were "under either written or verbal agreements, as servants of the North-West Company." The next year three of "our Sandwich Islanders" were killed by local Indians while trapping beaver near a river subsequently named Owyhee in their honor.[11]

The North West Company's dominance in the Pacific Northwest was short lived. The Montreal-based company had always been in competition with the Hudson's Bay Company, a chartered company out of London that operated trading posts across much of British North America with the tacit approval of the mother country. Even though Britain possessed little or no political sovereignty over the vast territory west of the Rocky Mountains, the NWC was at a disadvantage. Not only were its supply lines very long, the HBC was increasingly aggressive. Both companies realized the advantages of joining forces. In 1821 the NWC merged into the HBC, which took on the personnel of its competitor, including the indigenous Hawaiians in its employ. Up to this time the HBC had no Hawaiians among its workforce.

The Hudson's Bay Company had no interest in disrupting the delicate diplomatic balance of the Pacific Northwest. Like the North West Company before it, the HBC was out to make money, its potential for doing so enhanced by the British Crown giving the amalgamated company an exclusive license extending for twenty-one years to trade in the territory west of the Rocky Mountains. This license was limited to trade by British nationals and did not extend to Americans, who were protected by a treaty of joint occupation signed in 1818 in anticipation of a boundary settlement at some later date. For the most part Americans lost interest in the fur trade west of the Rockies. The area was just too far away from St. Louis, which played much the same role as Montreal did for the North West Company. It was only after 1825 that the Missouri companies began straddling the continental divide to trade for furs at an annual rendezvous. The HBC did not seek to take advantage of this vacuum. It was not a political entity intent on claiming the territory on which it operated for the home country. Newcomer settlement was not wanted, for it would change the existing dynamic. The HBC wanted Native people to remain much as they were so that they would continue to acquire the furs on which its economic well-being depended.

In contrast to the loosely organized and little-documented NWC, the HBC was a tightly administered record-rich entity. Chartered in 1670, it was hierarchical in the British tradition. The officers in charge, who shared in the profits along with shareholders, were by definition gentlemen, with the requisite education and social standing. So were the clerks, who were in effect officers-in-training. The great bulk of employees, or "servants," were recruited from the remote Orkney Islands off the north coast of Scotland, from French Canada, and from among the Iroquois of the Montreal area. Men were hired on at their points of origin and dispatched between the various posts as needed. Ordinary workers could never hope to rise into profit sharing, but they did enjoy an assured annual income specified in a multiyear contract, as well as housing and a weekly ration of foodstuffs. The HBC kept meticulous records to ensure everyone received their proper wages as befit their place in the hierarchy. Men were not paid directly. The amount due to them was credited to their account, from which the clerk in charge deducted purchases of clothing or other items and paid them any remaining balance at the end of their employment. They received the money after being returned home, the commitment to do so being part of their contract.

The HBC inherited about three dozen Hawaiians, who were quite unlike their usual range of employees. John Cox and Paul Poah were among the dozen arriving at Astoria in the spring of 1811 on the *Tonquin*. James Coah came a year later, Jimo, Frank Kanah or Kanak, and Harry Bell Noah in 1814. The remainder likely came on the *Columbia* in 1817. Having joined the fur trade between their mid-teens and mid-twenties, they were all still fairly young men.

Alexander Ross, at Fort George since 1811, may have reflected the dominant perspective in his lengthy assessment of the Hawaiians' utility. Their mix of attributes suited the everyday needs of the fur trade. "They are submissive to their masters, honest and trustworthy and willingly perform as much duty as lies in their power; but are nevertheless exceedingly awkward in everything they attempt. And although they are somewhat industrious they are not made to lead but to follow, and are useful only to stand as sentinels to eye the natives or go through the drudgery of an establishment." On the water "they are as active and expert as the reverse on dry land." [12]

Posts' remote locations added to Hawaiians' desirability. "They are not wanting in courage; particularly against the Indians, for whom they entertain a very cordial contempt. And if they are let loose against them, they rush upon them like tigers. The principal purpose for which they were useful on Columbia was as an array of numbers in the view of the natives especially in the frequent voyages up and down the communication." Ross concluded on an upbeat note that "on every occasion they testify a fidelity and zeal for their master's welfare and service."[13]

One-third of a century earlier, short months apart, Captain Cook had landed on the Hawaiian Islands and the Northwest Coast of North America. One group of indigenous inhabitants had become allies, the other the enemy. Ross Cox summed up the dominant view: "From Chili to Athabasca, and from Nootka to the Labrador, there is an indescribable coldness about an American savage that checks familiarity. He is a stranger to our hopes, our fears, our joys, or our sorrows." In sharp contrast, about the time the HBC took charge in the Pacific Northwest, a ship's captain well acquainted with the Hawaiian Islands commended "the rapid progress the natives are making towards civilization (unaided by missionaries) by improving themselves, and cultivating an intercourse with other countries."[14]

The Hawaiians employed by the North West Company were seamlessly absorbed into the HBC's workforce, along with NWC partners and others who chose to affiliate with the amalgamated enterprise. From about 1825 Hawaiians appeared on HBC records as a matter of course, even though they did not, like the others, appear to have signed individual contracts.

George Simpson, who headed the HBC in North America, visited its posts west of the Rocky Mountains in 1824. Up to then the area had not turned a profit, either for the HBC or earlier for the Pacific Fur Company or the North West Company. Simpson undertook a very close assessment, focusing on ways to cut costs and improve productivity. The Hawaiians came in for scrutiny, as did all the employees. "There are about 35 of them now on this side the mountain but we can employ 15 more to advantage if the trade is extended and in that case I would beg to recommend their being taken on board as the Vessel intended for the China trade passes Owyhee [Hawai'i] on her passage hither from England."[15]

Simpson's reasons for favoring Hawaiians spoke to their utility and also to his prejudices. "A few Sandwich Islanders among the Canadians and Europeans can be usefully employed here as Guards and for common drudgery about the Establishments." If relegating them to menial tasks, Simpson commended their trustworthiness, considering them to "be depended on in cases of danger from the natives."[16] The Hawaiians might be indigenous persons, but he in no way equated them with their North American counterparts.

Simpson had some sense of fair play. According to the information he received about Hawaiians' wages, which was inaccurate for the Pacific Fur Company but may have applied to the NWC years, "when they first came here until last year their terms were merely food and cloathing [*sic*]." Such a policy would no longer suffice for, as a visitor to the Islands in 1825 discovered, "they begin now to understand the value of money, and are no longer willing to barter for beads or insignificant trinkets."[17]

The HBC's usual rates "did not provide for Sandwich Islanders." So the officer in charge had "advanced theirs to £17 p annum thereby putting them on equality with the Canadian and European Servants which occasioned much dissatisfaction and very naturally so as they are by no means such serviceable people." Simpson effected a compromise. "We have therefore reduced them to £10 p Annum which satisfies all parties."[18] The Hawaiians' wages would subsequently return to £17 a year.

Simpson's 1824 foray gave a new momentum to the trade. In anticipation of the Columbia River becoming the border between Britain and the United States, a post named Fort Vancouver was constructed over the winter of 1824–1825 about 90 miles upriver on the river's north side. "Four Owyhees" manned the *Dolly* from Astoria days, another four an "old scow" used to transport stock and other items to the new post in March 1825.[19] John McLoughlin, who already headed the HBC's Columbia Department, encompassing a dozen posts west of the Rocky Mountains, was also given charge of the principal post of Fort Vancouver. By the time of Simpson's second tour of inspection four years later, a large farm, flour mill, and sawmill had grown up around Fort Vancouver's 400 acres.

Simpson was also cheered in 1828 by the successful establishment of a new post on the Fraser River in the future British Columbia. Three Hawaiians were part of the group dispatched north in mid-November 1824 to scout out the best location. Cawanaia, Moumouto, and Peeopeeoh, all recruited by the NWC in 1817, appear in the expedition journal only once during the six weeks. On November 30, after several days of "weighty rain" with "strong gusts of rain," Cawanaia and a local Indian were sent to take a sick man back as rapidly as possible along the Cowlitz River. In June 1827, the HBC vessel "*Cadboro* Sailed with an Addition to her crew of five half Breeds and Six Owyhees" to construct Fort Langley, as the new post was named.[20] Among the twenty-five men onboard were Peeopeeoh, who had already visited three years earlier, and Como, who had arrived on the Northwest Coast in 1818.

Hawaiians were, in part due to differences in language, very often assigned repetitive tasks. Men's occupations were not given every day in the Fort Langley journal, which survives for its first years. When they were listed, those of the two Hawaiians were virtually always the same as on the previous days and weeks.

MONDAY 6TH [AUGUST 1827]. All Hands busily employed—Como & Peopeoh erecting a Saw Pit.

TUESDAY 7TH. The two Sandwich Islanders sawing.

TUESDAY 14TH. Como & Peopeoh sawing Pickets.

FRIDAY 17TH. Como & Peopeoh sawing.

TUESDAY 21ST. Como & Peopeoh are still sawing.

MONDAY 27TH. Como & Peopeoh at the Saw.

SATURDAY 1ST [SEPTEMBER]. Como & Peopeoh sawing.

MONDAY 3RD. Como & Peopeoh sawing.

MONDAY 10TH. The two Owyhees are making another Sawpit.

TUESDAY 11TH. Como & Peopeoh sawing.

John McLoughlin. British Columbia Archives, no. PDP 291.

So it went. In effect, the two Hawaiians sawed the wood that built Fort Langley. Only illness gave a respite.

> THURSDAY, 13TH [SEPTEMBER 1827]. Peopeoh is this morning on the sick list—he complains of acute pain in his loins, and violent colic. [Joseph] Cornoyer takes his place on the saw.
>
> WEDNESDAY 19TH. Peopeoh is now recovering.
>
> FRIDAY 12TH [OCTOBER]. Como & Peopeoh constantly at the saw.[21]

As soon as the post's core was built, including a "Dwelling House" for the officers and clerks, "the men are beginning to put up one for themselves."[22] Only when all of this construction was finished did the two Hawaiians get some variety in their work life.

> THURSDAY 8TH [NOVEMBER]. Como & Peopeoh were taken from the Saw and sent to assist [James] Baker & [clerk Amable] Arquoitte in clearing the Bank of the River.
>
> MONDAY 12TH. The Two Sandwich Islanders with Baker and [Jean Baptiste] Dubois are Clearing the Bank in front of the Fort.

Peeopeeoh and Como were soon back to a familiar task, one that they diligently pursued so far as weather permitted over Fort Langley's first winter.

> MONDAY 7TH [DECEMBER]. The two Owyhees sawing Logs for the Big House.
>
> THURSDAY 7TH [FEBRUARY 1828]. The two Owyhees sawing.
>
> MONDAY 11TH. The Two Owyhees sawing.
>
> FRIDAY 15TH. The two Owyhees sawing.
>
> MONDAY THE 18TH. The two Owyhees Sawying [*sic*] plank.
>
> WEDNESDAY 27TH. The two Owhyhees Sawing plank.

Fort Langley journal entries testify to the Hawaiians' endurance and dependability, and also to their utility. George Simpson wanted more of them, but it would take several years for his desire to be realized. Their acquisition became bound up in two complementary initiatives intended to maximize profits. The first was to develop a coastal trade with Native peoples, the second to diversify away from furs into two local commodities, timber and salmon. A coastal trade was perforce seasonal, leaving vessels idle over the winter. Simpson therefore proposed, "during the dead Season of the year, say from October until March," to employ them to carry goods "to the

Sandwich Islands, which we have reason to believe, will not only cover their Expenses through the year, but yield a very handsome profit."[23] The Islands were the closest overseas market from the Pacific Northwest. The trip there took three weeks compared with five months to London.

Two trading vessels, *William & Ann* and *Cadboro,* were obtained from England. Shortly after the brig *William & Ann* arrived at Fort Vancouver in the spring of 1825, the head of the Columbia District "gave thirteen Owhy-hees to the Captain to Strengthen this Crew of the Vessel on the intended Voyage" north to test out the possibilities of a coastal trade.[24] Three years later a sawmill was erected on the Columbia River about five miles from Fort Vancouver. Fort Langley was, for its part, charged to cure salmon in barrels for export.

The *Cadboro*'s first trip to the Hawaiian Islands "to ascertain the state of the market" and to acquire more men occurred over the 1828–1829 winter. The British consul appointed in 1825 to the island port of Honolulu acted as intermediary. While there, the schooner's captain met up with the *William & Ann* on its way from England to Fort Vancouver, and "10 Sandwich Islanders he put on board at Woahoo out of 16 engaged there for the Service as he had not accommodation for them in the *Cadboro*."[25] The next March, while crossing the bar in the Columbia River, the *William & Ann* was wrecked. All onboard perished, including the ten Hawaiians. A few days later the *Cadboro* reached Fort Vancouver safely, bringing the first Hawaiians to enter the fur trade since the 1821 amalgamation.

The Hawaiian trade required finessing. In 1824 Kamehameha II and his queen both died of measles, being succeeded by Kauikeaouli or Kamehameha III, who would rule until his death in December 1854. It was during his reign that the American missionary advance became complemented by an economic invasion. The *Cadboro*'s captain "found that a strong feeling existed against the Honble. Compy. among the American residents there." Not only did they want to control "Shipping of [*sic*] the Coast," they attempted to prevent the HBC from "procuring the Servants we required."[26] By the early 1820s the indigenous population had dwindled to half of an estimated 300,000 in 1778. Additional departures would only push numbers down farther. At the same time, the demand for timber was great. More and more newcomers were establishing businesses and building residences at Honolulu and elsewhere. The HBC's solution was to appoint an agent, initially the British consul, to act on its behalf to sell timber and salmon and to find men and cargo to take away.

The HBC's Honolulu agency, which reported to the Columbia Department, was made responsible for recruiting Hawaiians into the fur trade. John

McLoughlin wrote in August 1829 to "request you would by the first vessel of ours consigned to this place which touches at Wahoo next Spring [1830] send us fifteen active Owhyhee young men." If the HBC wanted to expand coastal trading, then even more Hawaiians would be needed, McLoughlin reminded officials in London. "The compliment [*sic*] for a crew of a vessel for the Coast of the size recommended is twenty-five men and officers to which his number might be made up with Sandwich Islanders by the Capt being instructed to procure them" while in Honolulu on the way from England to the Pacific Northwest.[27]

Only scattered information survives on recruitment. In August 1829 McLoughlin requested of the HBC's agent in Honolulu that Hawaiians be acquired "on the same terms as those you procured for Captain [Aemilius] Simpson [of the *Cadboro* in 1828–1829]—and optional with us to send them back next fall if we do not require them." Two letters that the HBC's agent sent in January 1834 directly to Kamehameha III suggest arrangements occurred at a high level. A third party to whom a recruit named Kawero gave his advance of $14, likely to be permitted to leave, attempted to prevent him from doing so after receiving the money. The letter was to "request your Majesty to order the man who is now in the [HBC] Fort [in Honolulu] to be sent on board." The second request was for the king "to order two native seamen known by the names of Jack Henry and George Parker who volunteered for the service of the said Company at Fort Vancouver" but did not turn up "to be sent on board the Brig *Dryad.*"[28] All three men ended up onboard the vessel, but whether it was due to Kamehameha III's intervention is uncertain.

Thirty-five new Hawaiians appeared in HBC records for the first time in 1830, alongside fifteen continuing employees. Some of them had arrived on the *Cadboro* in 1829, others on the HBC's *Isabella* in the spring of 1830. The men were recruited under two sets of conditions. Ten were promised £17 a year, the other 25 fully £30 a year for the first three years, the apparent length of their contracts. Anglican minister Rev. Beaver, who spent two years at Fort Vancouver in the late 1830s, was told it was only "by which tempting offer this simple but amiable people were induced to enter the service." The tradeoff was, the HBC acknowledged, that the goods they bought while in the Pacific Northwest were marked up almost three times as much—140 versus 50 percent—as for men earning the lower wage of £17 a year.[29]

Given the high wages, it is no wonder the head of the Columbia District demanded the right to return men home after a year if no longer wanted. In the event, just three of the 25 £30/yr men were let go in 1831, another three departed in 1832, 5 at the end of 3 years, the same year one of them died. The other half stayed on, even though their annual wages were reduced in 1834 to the usual rate of £17. So did all but one of the 10 men hired at the lower wage. A third of the remaining 22 men departed at the end of a second contract. One was killed by Indians, underlining that the trade was not without its perils.

Fourteen, or 40 percent, of the men hired in 1830 made their career in the fur trade. William returned home in 1840, Belay in 1842, and Tuaha four years later. Others appear to have remained on the coast, as with Mafinoa and Matte, who left the HBC in the late 1830s, Pa-ay-lay and Timeoy in 1849, Toro and Upahee a year later, and George Faito and Wavicareea in the mid-1850s. Four died on the job: Orohuay in 1844, Ta-i and Toovyoora during a measles epidemic in 1848, and Spunyarn in 1853. The lure of the fur trade was sufficient for these men to make it their life's work, as did numerous of their predecessors and successors.

During the early 1830s a kind of ambivalence developed concerning Hawaiians' worth as compared to that of other laborers. This tension is visible on comparing the first draft of the letter John McLoughlin composed in the fall of 1831 with the one he dispatched. In the unsent draft the head of the Columbia Department alerted the HBC agent in Honolulu to disregard any requests for more Hawaiians. "If you are directed by the Govt and Committee to send in any Owhyees It will not be necessary for you [to] do so as we have as many as we at present require." Neither was the agent to permit a new HBC trading vessel to hire crew in the Islands, "as we have a sufficient number of Owhyhees here to strengthen the crews to go up the Coast." He was likely referring to half a dozen Hawaiian seamen engaged in June 1830 specifically for the coastal trade. The sent letter requested yet more Hawaiians. "When you engage any Owhyhees for this place we would prefer if you could that you sent us as many as possible of them." [30]

Three factors combined to change McLoughlin's mind. First, no other group of laborers much surpassed the Hawaiians. Some years later, in 1844, McLoughlin referred to "the poor qualifications of the [French] Canadians sent to this Department since 1824." As to why he "refrained from giving public notice of it, it was because I did not wish to give trouble, and got through the business the best way I could." [31] By comparison the Hawaiians were hardworking, reliable, and agreeable.

The second reason was more immediate. In the fall of 1830, "for the first time since the Trade of this Department was established," intermittent fever appeared at Fort Vancouver. The illness, likely a form of malaria, carried off three-quarters of the Indian population in the area, as well as putting most employees on the sick list.[32] Unlike other components of the workforce, all of the Hawaiians survived, making them all the more appealing. Contrary to the image of them being promoted at home by missionaries and other outsiders, in the Pacific Northwest they were the survivors.

Third, some of the experienced Hawaiians left, making it also a matter of replacements. Five men decided to go home in 1831, along with the three being returned out of the expensive group arrived the year before. Frank Kanah harked back to 1814. Now entering his forties, he had £27.50 owed him on landing at Honolulu and may have wanted to begin life anew in his native land.[33] Two of the others, Marouna and Ottehoh, recruited by the NWC in 1817, likely had similar goals, but their dreams must have soon turned sour, for within a year they both returned to the fur trade. The changing nature of the Hawaiian Islands may have doomed their aspirations for a better life at home. During the decade and a half of their absence, their homeland had been turned upside down, from an essentially indigenous place to an international emporium increasingly controlled by outsiders.

The HBC barque *Ganymede* not only transported the eight Hawaiians home, it returned to Fort Vancouver in the spring of 1832 with replacements onboard. Over the next four years the numbers of Hawaiians employed by the HBC remained relatively stable at just over sixty. Each year about one-third of that number either left or arrived.

For a brief time during the mid-1830s the HBC's Hawaiians were not the only ones in the Pacific Northwest. The company had a rival that similarly relied on Islanders. British dominance rankled the Americans. One of the most influential pieces of writing was published in Boston in 1830. Hall J. Kelley argued for the Pacific Northwest's immediate occupancy by "the active sons of American freedom" to save it "from the disastrous consequences of a foreign and corrupt population." Kelley was exercised both by "the avarice of the English" in the form of the HBC and by "the rapacity of treacherous Indians." Inspired by Kelley's enthusiasm, Boston merchant Nathaniel J. Wyeth headed west overland in 1832 to prospect the possibility of a trade in furs and salmon "on a similar plan to the Hudson Bay."[34]

Two years later Wyeth put his plan for the Columbia Fishing and Trading Company into action. His two-prong approach was reminiscent of that of John Jacob Astor a quarter of a century earlier. Wyeth led a group overland, while the vessel *May Dacre* sailed around the Horn with supplies and, during an Islands stop, "procuring twenty Islanders." In mid-July 1834 Wyeth's party reached the area of today's Pocatello, Idaho, where the men constructed Fort Hall as their center of operations. In September Wyeth met up on the mouth of the Columbia River with the *May Dacre,* which "brot me 20 Sandwich Islanders." Their first task was to site a second post, named Fort William, about 75 miles up the Columbia. One of the party recalled how, in heading up the river, "we had a good crew of fine robust sailors, and the copper-colored islanders,—or *Kanakas,* as they are called,— did their duty with great alacrity and good will."[35] Five of the eight oarsmen were Hawaiian.

The HBC gave support, the two companies agreeing to keep out of each other's trading territory. One of Wyeth's party described how on their arrival at Fort Vancouver in September 1834 McLoughlin "requested us to consider his house our home, provided a separate room for our use, a servant to wait upon us, and furnished us with every convenience." He reflected how "I shall never cease to feel grateful to him for his disinterested kindness to the poor houseless and travel-worn strangers." Departing a year later, his gratitude had only deepened. "Words are inadequate to express my deep sense of the obligations which I feel under to this truly generous and excellent man."[36]

For all of the HBC's cooperation, the enterprise was dogged. In late October most of the men headed overland to Fort Hall. Conditions were daunting, particularly for the Hawaiians, just arrived from a very different climate. A member of the party considered "they had no doubt heard from some of their countrymen, whom they met at the fort, of the difficulties of the route before them." Wyeth's diary tells the tale.

> 24TH [OCTOBER 1834]. After taking breakfast and giving the [sixteen] Kanackas two hours sleep we put up the river with a head wind day raw and chill.
>
> 26TH. Started Capt. [Joseph] Thing [up the Columbia River to Fort Hall] with 12 Kanackas and 6 whites and all the best Horses.
>
> 31ST. Started up the river [with four] Kanackas on foot for want of Horses and goods on miserably poor animals.
>
> 10TH [NOVEMBER]. Got the news that Capt. Things 12 Kanackas had deserted him and that he had gone in search of them on their trail.
>
> 11TH. Went to Capt. Things camp and learned . . . the Kanackas had taken about 2 bales of goods and 12 horses.[37]

Wyeth dispatched the four Hawaiians he had with him—John Bull, Diblo, Dido, and Tommy—to Fort Hall with Thing while he took up the chase. Despite numerous sightings, the men eluded capture over the winter, during which rumors abounded of one or two being killed by Blackfeet

Indians, drowning, or freezing to death. In the new year seven of them made for Fort Vancouver, where Wyeth found them in March ready to go back to work for him.

Wyeth's flank of Hawaiians was buttressed when the *May Dacre* returned at just about the same point in time from a trip to the Islands. According to a member of the expedition who made the trip, the brig brought "thirty Sandwich Islanders, who are to be engaged in the salmon fishing on the Columbia, and six of these have been allowed the unusual privilege of taking their wives with them." Like their predecessors, men were promised $10 a month, with a $10 advance on their departure. Some of them headed to Fort William, still in the process of construction. The expedition member described how, as of May, the men were still living "in tents and temporary huts, but several log houses are constructing which, when finished, will vie in durability and comfort with Vancouver itself." [38]

The next month brought more trouble.

Two evenings since, eight Sandwich Islanders, a white man and an Indian woman, left the cascades in a large canoe laden with salmon, for the brig. The river was as usual rough and tempestuous, the wind blew a heavy gale, the

Camp Life. From Henry James Warre, *Sketches in North America and the Oregon Territory* (London: Dickinson & Co., 1848).

canoe was capsized, and eight out of the ten sank to rise no more. The two who escaped, islanders, have taken refuge among the Indians at the village below, and will probably join us in a few days.

The member recently returned from the Hawaiian Islands reflected, with good reason, how "it really seems that the 'Columbia River Fishing and Trading Company' is devoted to destruction; disasters meet them at every turn, and as yet none of their schemes have prospered."[39]

The Hawaiians, both the returned runaways and the others, remained integral to Wyeth's hopes. A Presbyterian minister who took passage on the *May Dacre* in the fall of 1835 admired the "thatched building, which was constructed by some Kanakas for the accommodation of the May Dacre." Traditional building methods came to good use. The brig being forced to anchor for lack of wind, "I went on shore for exercise, taking with me a Kanaka, that is, a Sandwich islander, for assistance in any danger." Minister and seaman "made a long excursion through woods and over prairies."[40]

Wyeth's venture continued to be star-crossed or poorly organized, probably both. There were no profits to be had. In the spring of 1836 he gave up on the CRFTC and that summer returned east. The records are lost for Fort William but survive for Fort Hall, indicating that, of the Hawaiians then employed there, five returned home, while six apparently transferred to the HBC when it bought the post for $500 in August 1837.[41] It may be some of these men to whom Rev. Beaver was referring when he described several Hawaiians at Fort Vancouver at about this time as having their wives with them. The area west of the Rockies was once again under HBC control.

The HBC consolidated its position so that, by 1838, "our trade now embraces almost every accessible portion of the Coast as far as the Russian line of demarcation." Each node melded into the next so that "we cannot greatly extend the business of one Post without producing, at some other, a corresponding depression."[42]

Fort Vancouver remained the heart of the enterprise. Upwards of 1,200 acres were now under cultivation. An employee described how "an extensive farm was conducted on which from one to two hundred men were employed, mostly French-Canadians and Kanakas."[43] The enterprise was so large that employees had their own accommodation west of the post on the plain of the Columbia River. This conglomeration of cottages became known as Kanaka Village in response to the thirty to fifty Hawaiians employed there during the 1830s.

Apart from furs and agriculture, one of the important activities at Fort Vancouver was sawmilling. A new arrival of 1836 was told the mill "cuts

2,000 to 2,400 feet of lumber daily; employs 28 men, chiefly Sandwich Islanders, and ten yoke of oxen." Two years later the HBC built a new mill able to produce boards, rafters, beams, spars, and masts for the California and Hawai'i markets at twice the capacity of its predecessor. A visitor of 1839 termed it "a scene of constant toil." He detailed in his journal how "thirty or forty Sandwich Islanders are felling the pines and dragging them to the mill; sets of hands are plying two gangs of saws by day and night." An American who visited Fort Vancouver shortly thereafter considered it was Hawaiians who made the running. "Most all of these men I observed were Sandwich Islanders, their ration consists principally of smoked salmon—sea biscuit, and the pay of each 17 pounds per an."[44]

Another important cluster of Hawaiians manned the HBC's trading vessels. It had become the rule, George Simpson observed as early as 1829, that "about half" of vessels' crews were "Sandwich Islanders hired for the season." He was referring to the *Cadboro,* but the remark could have applied to any of the HBC's fleet. "We likewise require two good stout active Sandwich Islanders who have been at Sea, for 1, 2, or 3 Years as they can be got and on the most reasonable terms you can procure them."[45] Unlike their countrymen, the Hawaiian seamen tended to have double names in the HBC records: Tom Colins, John Fight, Jack Harry, George Momuto, George Parker, Joe Ploughboy.

Expansion became the way ahead, and with it came a growing demand

Kanaka Village, about 1850, possibly by George Gibbs. Courtesy of Fort Vancouver National Historic Site.

for labor. Twenty-nine Hawaiians arrived in 1837, nine in 1839, 70 in 1840, 22 in 1841. As to the reasons individual men were lured by the fur trade, we have only hints. A missionary's son wrote a bit dismissively about Hawaiians on O'ahu in 1839, "there was great poverty, although provident natives in good seasons usually had plenty to eat." The head of the U.S. exploring expedition observed during a stop in the Islands a year later how Honolulu "gave evidence of a change being in progress." Despite the predominance of "native houses, with thatched roofs," which he associated with "a semi-civilization," the city bore testimony to the "spirit of enterprise" by his fellow Americans, who "constitute the majority of the foreign residents." [46]

Even as newcomers were taking charge, the indigenous population receded from view. Just over 100,000 remained by the mid-1830s, which translates into 30,000 to 35,000 adult males. An American visitor in 1833 reflected the general view of outsiders in his observation how "these people, like our Indians, are fast slipping away." From his perspective their demise was inevitable. "And so it seems, there must be an eternal round of races to inhabit this, our earth, island and continent. All races have and probably will have their turn." The Hawaiian government became determined that men who went abroad return home. When the U.S. exploring expedition needed to replace crew during its 1840 stopover, it opted to "to take a number of Kanakas" onboard. The articles of agreement signed with authorities "bound the government of the United States to return them home after their services were no longer needed." [47]

The attraction of decent jobs in no way abated, putting the lie to missionaries' claims that indigenous Hawaiians were by nature lazy. Growing numbers of American and British whaling ships—by one account, over 250 in 1836–1839 alone—competed for their labor. A whaler explained their appeal: "They are so docile and obedient that if you put a gang in a boat they would row all day unless told to stop." Fully five hundred responded to a call for crew issued by the U.S. exploring expedition under the authority of the local governor, out of which the expedition's head "chose about fifty, all able-bodied and active young men, in perfect health." [48]

The only surviving HBC labor contract for Hawaiians comes from February 1840 and is very similar in intent. The governor of O'ahu gave the company's agent in Honolulu permission "to take sixty men to the Columbia River, to dwell there three years, and at the end of the said term of three years . . . to return them to the island of O'ahu." The agreement was in line with HBC policy to provide for employees' return to wherever they signed up. The other aspect of the short document, made with the governor of O'ahu, was that the agent would "pay twenty dollars for each man" who "deserted by reason of ill-treatment, or remain for any other cause" beyond the three years.[49] In the event, seventy men were recruited in 1840, some on five-year contracts, and it may well have been the large number that precipitated the written agreement.

Hawaiians' freedom of action is unclear. Rev. Herbert Beaver, who was at Fort Vancouver during the late 1830s, asserted that "each of them before embarkation in their country, received a small advance of money, part of which their chiefs seize as a bonus for permitting them to have it, and for relinquishing all future claim to their services." He also reported hearing, toward the end of the decade, "the king and the chiefs had issued a decree that no more of them should enter the Company's service." The head of the U.S. exploring expedition who visited Fort Vancouver in the summer of 1841 observed that, while the HBC was obliged to send men home at the end of their contracts, it was only "if they desire it" and frequently they did not. A passenger list for a vessel leaving Honolulu "for Columbia River" in April 1846 noted how the "5 natives" on it had "permission of the governor" to travel.[50]

No one quite knew what the HBC's obligations were. In 1850 eight of the Hawaiians hired between 1840 and 1847, whose contracts had expired, requested permission "to depart [the post] at once by any means they chose proper, in fact to be at perfect liberty." The men were stationed at Fort Rupert on northern Vancouver Island, and everyone there scrambled to sort out their conditions of employment. Any contracts that might have existed were lodged elsewhere. Nobody on the ground had any idea of the men's status. One perspective held "these men are obliged to be returned to Whahoo, whether they wish it or not"; if not, the HBC "forfeited a penalty of 300 dollars." Another view considered that "all kanackas engaged by the company at the Sandwich Islands are bound by their engagements to remain at their posts, wherever it may be, until the arrival of the first vessel belonging to the Honble Company after the expiration of their several agreements." A third perspective, to which numerous Hawaiians themselves subscribed, considered "the HBC is under bond to send each & every Kanacka back to the place whence they are taken at the expiration of their contracts, provided he or they express a determination to revisit their native country." A fourth version held that "the kanackas could leave in any vessel" willing to take them wherever they wanted to go.[51]

In practice the ways in which Hawaiians departed the fur trade were idiosyncratic. The majority returned home as a matter of course. They were encouraged to do so not only by the provision of transportation but, more practically, by only receiving any wages owed them at Oʻahu. Of the seventy men who arrived in 1840, 10 returned home in 3 years or less, another 22 within 6 years or by the end of a second contract, and 5 others died on the job within that time period. Six of those going back almost immediately reenlisted. Like others before them, they may have been disillusioned by the changes they encountered at home, alternatively planning to do so all along once they had visited family and friends. The remainder, or almost half, of those arriving in 1840 remained in the Pacific Northwest over the long term.

The need for so many new men in 1840 resulted from the fur trade's expansion. The HBC west of the Rockies had already developed a trade in lumber and salmon, but, as Richard Mackie has chronicled, the initiative was insufficient to offset declining revenues.[52] Diversification went in four directions.

The first was north along the coast, facilitated by an agreement signed with the Russian American Company in 1839 to provision its fur trade posts with agricultural products. In exchange the HBC received a lease to a coastal strip of Russian territory on which Forts Stikine and Taku were built. Late in 1839 the head of the Columbia District promised "50 men from the Sandwich Islands" for Fort Taku.[53] The number was optimistic. All of the Hawaiians in HBC employ were needed elsewhere. Of the 70 men recruited in 1840, 15 were sent to Taku, 10 to Stikine.

The men's transition was not easy. Fort Stikine's post journal emphasizes the great gulf these raw recruits faced in terms of both work and cultural skills. Arriving at what is now Wrangel, Alaska, on June 1840, the ten could "neither work, understand or be understood." Within five days two were on the sick list, "one of them having had his nail smashed off" onboard the *Vancouver* on the way there. The other had his hand bruised in "getting the cannon onto the Bastions."[54] The surrounding Tlingit people were not in a particularly charitable mood, and the accommodations stank.

> JUNE 28TH [1840]. Training our eleven Owyhees how to hold a gun. Not one in the number knew how to cock or uncock if indeed I believe not one of them ever had a gun in their hands before and a miserable helpless green set of men than they are never can be appointed to any place. Some of them would insist on keeping open the left instead of the right eye. God help us from a rumpus with the Indians.
>
> JUNE 29TH. The spare Kanakas mudding the houses.
>
> JUNE 30TH. Kanakas turning the potatoes and mudding houses.
>
> JULY 1ST. Ohyhees mudding, scraping and cleaning smell in the fort and houses, not quite so offensive in the fort and houses.

> **JULY 3RD.** Sent Montrais with the Kanakas to saw. They make very little of it. Our unfortunate Kanakas are laughed at by the Indians and I do not wonder at it for they are most awkward in every respect.

The contract to provide foodstuffs to Russian America caused, second, the creation of the Puget Sound Agricultural Company (PSAC) in 1838. In principle a separate entity, PSAC shares were restricted to HBC stockholders and officers. Intended to provision HBC posts west of the Rockies as well as the Russians, PSAC was given oversight of Fort Nisqually, established in 1833 on Puget Sound, and of Cowlitz farm about 50 miles farther south. The new enterprise solidified an HBC presence north of the Columbia River, which many still hoped would become the international boundary.

The formation of the PSAC increased demand for Hawaiians. By the time of George Simpson's third visit to the Pacific Northwest in 1841, Nisqually boasted 4,500 sheep purchased in Spanish California, 1,000 cattle, and 100 acres of garden. Cowlitz employed "23 servants, principally Sandwich Islanders and Canadians, whose wages are from £17 to £20 per annum."[55] The Hawaiians and others who tended animals and crops at Nisqually, Cowlitz, and their outstations became PSAC as opposed to HBC employees, a distinction that meant little in practice.

Third, the HBC looked to expand to Vancouver Island located north of Puget Sound. Consensus existed that the island would remain British if, as some now feared, the boundary with the United States was set not along the Columbia River but the 49th parallel, where it currently ran east of the Rocky Mountains. In 1842 the HBC decided to construct a new post on Vancouver Island's southern tip. Due to a limited pool of labor and the presence of the HBC coastal steamer *Beaver,* the tradeoff was to abandon the two northern posts. Fort Victoria was built in the summer of 1843.

A fourth direction was unintended and unwanted. The HBC increasingly found itself trading with newcomers, of which Wyeth was an important precursor. His CRFTC may have failed, but his vision inspired others. The HBC was well aware of the "troublesome and injurious" character of what became by the end of the decade a "mania for emigration to the Columbia." Over the short term the company might benefit by supplying what the head of the Columbia District termed "their little wants." In McLoughlin's view, "the trade will be taken up by other Merchants, if we do not anticipate them."[56] Over the long term, the fur trade was irreconcilable with the growing numbers of arrivals into what Americans called the Oregon Territory.

At the same time as new opportunities opened up, the HBC's two principal sources of labor, French Canada and the Orkneys, dried up due to several factors. Wages remained stagnant. A newcomer to Oregon in the early 1840s recalled "the wages that the common laborers usually received" as "nineteen pounds a year sterling money," whereas skilled tradesmen like himself got "from twenty-two to thirty pounds sterling a year."[57]

Increasingly, employees left the HBC to settle down nearby. George Simpson expressed his frustration in March 1842 that "the desire throughout the service on both sides of the Mountains, for permission to retire and settle as Agriculturalists on the Shores of the Pacific, amounts at present almost to a mania." He reiterated the HBC policy that no employees should "be released from their engagements in the Columbia," but rather only at their point of departure—Quebec, Orkneys, or the Hawaiian Islands. McLoughlin countered that such a policy deprived workers "of the means of making themselves comfortable in their old age, [made] them disaffected to the Company," and ensured most settlers into Oregon were American.[58] More and more employees walked with their feet.

Even as men lost their incentive to remain past their initial contract, recruitment was stymied by growing criticism of conditions of work. Simpson described in June 1843 how "the service of the west side of the mountains is become so unpopular with Canadians, Orkneymen & halfbreeds, that it is a most difficult matter to get men for that part of the country." Complaints of starvation made by returning French Canadians had direct implications for the Hawaiians, for the food the other men rejected was one of their favorites. The head of the Columbia District, John McLoughlin, reported how in August 1841 men at Fort Vancouver "refused dry salmon." The daily allocation was "3 lbs. salt Salmon, and 1 1/2 lbs. Biscuit," or, when potatoes were available, "1 bushel p. week in place of biscuit." A visitor to the Hawaiian Islands a little earlier in time marveled, "Give a Sandwich Islander plenty of poe, with a raw fish or two, at each meal, and he asks for nothing more."[59]

Fundamental disagreement developed over how to meet the HBC's labor shortage. By this time the number of Hawaiians employed in the fur trade had reached its largest total to date at around 150. The numbers were even larger in the imagination. When Oblate missionary priest Jean Baptiste Bolduc stopped in the Hawaiian Islands in the summer of 1842 on his way to the Pacific Northwest, he was informed that "more than 500 Sandwich Islanders are there [in the Columbia] in the service of the [Hudson's Bay] company." A Honolulu missionary newspaper asserted two years later that "there are from 300 to 400 Kanakas employed in the Columbia River, in the service and vessels of the *Hon. Hudson's Bay Co.* on that coast." The article explained how "they are generally engaged for a period of three years, and gain $10 per month."[60] Contemporaries had no way of knowing how many men were in the service of the HBC, but clearly their absence from the Islands was felt.

George Simpson, still in charge of the HBC in North America, was opposed to hiring more Hawaiians. In early 1842 he visited the Islands for the first time. There he witnessed what he summed up as "the slow but sure victory of the highest civilization over the lowest barbarism." Simpson absorbed the perspective of many of his Islands contemporaries in seeing population decline as an inevitable consequence of colonialism. "The population of the islands, like every other barbarous population with whom whites have come in contact, is dwindling away very fast." Simpson estimated numbers were "decreasing at the rate of 5 per cent per annum, so that if the mortality continues in the same ration, the native population will have become extinct in very few years."[61]

Socializing almost completely with missionaries and other outsiders of similar conviction, Simpson absorbed their justifications for two decades of interference with indigenous ways of life in the interests of imposing their own brand of morality. He considered "there are two causes which still continue, though in very unequal proportions, to poison the sources of national life; a spirit, or at least a practice, of emigration among the men, and the depravity of the women." Simpson was informed "about a thousand males in the very prime of life" were annually enticed away on whaling vessels, to the Columbia, or elsewhere. "A considerable proportion of them are said to be permanently lost to their country, either dying during their engagements, or settling in other parts of the world."[62]

Simpson did not want to be responsible for the accelerating population decline, however much he applauded Hawaiians' "habit, if not a love, of labour." He summarily informed John McLoughlin, in charge of the Columbia District, in March 1842 that "of Sandwich Islanders we already have too many in the Service." His solution was to retain the current workforce, "unless worthless or useless," and to retrench, undertaking "no new Expedition, Trading Post, or other branch of business."[63] Simpson did not acknowledge, and perhaps did not realize, that working conditions in the fur trade were as healthy—or more so—than had the men remained at home. Between 1821 and 1843 just twenty deaths were recorded, while employed, among the 240 Hawaiians the HBC either inherited from the North West Company or hired on its own.

McLoughlin was more pragmatic. In November 1843 he went over Simpson's head to HBC headquarters in London to make the opposite case. "I must send to the Sandwich Islands for Islanders to make up the numbers of hands we require, or else we cannot go on with our work." He essentially challenged others to stop him. "I will therefore order the men we require from the Sandwich Islands, and will act as I have hitherto done, though this year I feel I am limited, and trust to Your Honors and the Governor & Councils candid indulgence." A month later McLoughlin requested "fifty Sandwich Islanders from Woahoo by the *Columbia*." As he emphasized to HBC headquarters, "this number will barely, if it does, replace the retiring Servants next year, and the other Vacancies in the Department, caused by deaths, and the Sandwich Islanders, who have been sent by the *Vancouver & Columbia* this fall to Woahoo, say fourteen." Three months later the head of the Columbia District justified his decision to Simpson by emphasizing how he required "to carry on the business on a proper scale 120 men at the lowest calculation" whereas he had only been sent ten men.[64]

McLoughlin acquired 48 more Hawaiians in 1844, likely on the *Columbia,* which arrived at the beginning of May. He got another 42 in 1845, bringing the total number then in the HBC's employ to just over 200. It was the Hawaiians who made it possible for the HBC to carry on its routines. A man who was at Fort Vancouver during the 1840s recalled the "many Kanakas working for the company between 1841 and 1848."[65] Numbers peaked at 174 in 1845–1856, when Hawaiians formed almost one-third of the total number of servants, which were just under 400, employed west of the Rocky Mountains. Whatever the time period, the majority worked at Fort Vancouver. These would be the last of the large annual groups to arrive from the Islands, being succeeded by about 60 additional men spread out over the next decade. Fourteen of them were short-term employees hired in Honolulu in February 1850 to replace crew members who had deserted there so the HBC's barque *Cowlitz* could continue on to Vancouver Island.

The ongoing decline of the Islands' indigenous population was speeded up by epidemics. It was estimated that, in 1848 alone, fully 10,000 "pure Polynesians," or one in ten, fell victim to whooping cough, measles, and influenza. At least one contemporary was convinced the end was in sight: "The measles have decimated the Hawaiian race within the last year and we fear more epidemics will complete its ruin. Alas! for the poor Hawaiian. My heart bleeds at the thought of his approaching destiny!" A census taken in 1850 counted 78,854 "Natives" alongside 1,787 "foreigners" on the Islands. The same year regulations were tightened for shipping and discharging indigenous seamen at the principal port of Honolulu. As well as ensuring returned men were paid off and, where they died, property went to relatives, they were to be advised, while abroad, "not to spend their money in drink, gambling or riding horses, but to take care of it, and to be kind to their mother, wives, or families."[66]

It is impossible to know how many men sent money home from the Pacific Northwest. Clearly, some did so. Fort Nisqually's longtime head recalled how, "sometime in the forties," three of the Hawaiians employed there—Cowie, Keave'haccow, and Joe Tapou—each sent two to three months' wages to their fathers or mothers. Reflecting the prejudices of the day, he explained how the initiative "proves these poor, ignorant Kanakas had a feeling of love for their parents."[67]

The principal reason for the HBC acquiring so few additional Hawaiians had to do not with new regulations but with the fur trade's contraction. The new British fashion of silk hats replaced beaver headgear and the boundary settlement of 1846 put territory south of the 49th parallel into American hands. By 1850 the number of Hawaiians in the HBC's employ had almost halved from just five years earlier. Just under one-third of them were at Fort Vancouver, which would finally close in 1860. Others were at the HBC's new headquarters of Fort Victoria, from 1849 capital of the new British colony of Vancouver Island, or at nearby Fort Langley. The remainder was dispersed among the other posts. By the time a gold rush to the future British Columbia doomed the fur trade in 1858, just twenty Hawaiians were employed. Their presence was still valued, as when, in 1864, the HBC was "enquiring for Kanackas to go to Fort Simpson [on the north coast near today's Prince Rupert] but as yet without success owing to the high rate of wages now ruling here."[68] At such remote north coast locations, the fur trade continued for some time after it collapsed farther south.

Hawaiians were integral to the fur trade in the Pacific Northwest. Astoria set the pattern. The Pacific Fur Company treated Hawaiians with dignity. Much of the work that they, like the other employees performed, was fairly menial. At the same time the men in charge respected Hawaiians' skills, particularly in the water, and trusted them to provide protection. The North West Company and then the Hudson's Bay Company for the most part followed the pattern set by their predecessors.

Hired from choice and out of necessity, the Hawaiians contributed over three thousand man years of labor to the Hudson's Bay Company alone. The company inherited about three dozen and hired another four hundred on its own volition. Each and every one of them had to prove his worth, or he would not be kept on for years and very often decades on end. Well over one-third of the Hawaiians who began work prior to the 1846 boundary settlement remained past their second three-year contract. These men were not part of some anonymous whole, but rather individual persons who contributed each in a distinctive way with their labor in exchange for room, board, and £17 or about $75 a year, the most common wage. Along with Scots and Englishmen, French Canadians, Iroquois, and mixed-race men with paternal origins in French Canada, the Hawaiians sustained an enterprise that played a fundamental role in the transition to newcomer settlement across the Pacific Northwest.

Chapter 5

MAKING A LIFE IN THE FUR TRADE

EMPLOYMENT IN THE FUR TRADE was more than a job. Hawaiians and their counterparts from elsewhere came as young men, between their mid-teens and mid-twenties, when thoughts turned to making a life for themselves. They might consider themselves sojourners, but they nonetheless wanted to get on with their adulthoods. They retained the hopes and fears that we all possess from youth to death. The Hawaiians themselves did not, so far as can be determined, write about their experiences in the fur trade, but other sources give tantalizing hints, often from moments of crisis.

The fur trade was distinctive in the constraints it put on life outside of work. The placement of posts at remote locations ensured employees were at a distance from kin and also from the amenities of the everyday life from whence they had come. They had to rely on each other and on local Native people to satisfy their bodily and spiritual needs. The Hawaiians faced other barriers. As well as being near the bottom of the fur trade hierarchy, they were distinguished from other employees by language and appearance.

Whatever the length of time indigenous Hawaiians remained in the Pacific Northwest, whether they came as maritime sojourners or fur trade laborers, from their arrival they engaged in a reciprocal process of adaptation and co-optation. Sometimes all that survives of the ways in which they did so are glimpses, as with the Kaua'i chief Kaiana, who fancied Western dress, and the two young women, Teheeopea and Tahomeeraoo, who socialized as Captain George Vancouver's guests in Spanish California. These early sojourners adapted but at the same time educated their hosts into greater understanding of persons like themselves. Vancouver took the two young women with him in part as curiosities, but also because they behaved in ways that did honor to him as their protector. John Meares did not have to put into print, short years after the events, his admiration for Hawaiians, both in comparison with their North American indigenous counterparts and on their own terms. When the head at Astoria set aside the Hawaiian New Year as a holiday, he did not do so lightly. The Hawaiians, for their part, learned not just the languages of the fur trade but also its ways of behavior, so much so that they were increasingly employed for guard duty.

The likelihood that ships bringing men to the Northwest Coast would stop at the Islands affected perceptions of Hawaiians and so eased their lot in the Pacific Northwest. One of the most intellectually curious fur trade officers was William Fraser Tolmie, who shortly after completing his medical training in Glasgow was recruited by the HBC for what would be a lifetime career. The twenty-one-year-old used a month's stop in the Islands in early 1833 to search out botanical specimens, which got him beyond a limited range of missionary and other newcomer stereotypes. "The natives seem a good natured race—they are generally above the middle size & some of them very muscular—their features, broad & flat & heads large."[1] In his daily journal they quickly became "Kanakas," indicating the term's common usage without a pejorative connotation.

Tolmie's attitude toward indigenous Hawaiians was formed favorably before he ever set foot in North America and put him at ease with the Islanders he found there. Within two days of arriving at Fort Vancouver in early May 1833, he was supplied with both a dispensary and an "attendant" in the person of "a Sandwich Island boy named Namahama," who had arrived three years earlier. Despite mixed feelings, Tolmie was on the whole optimistic. "He is slow in his motions as a sloth but quiet & docile & will improve."[2]

Taking a trip two weeks later by canoe, Tolmie related how "our crew consisted of four Kanakas, stout fellows, who paddled lustily." One of the men was Mafinoa, who by now had a nickname as well as a variant of his earlier name. Stopping to camp, he readily "left a man, called Mafaroni or more commonly Rosie, a native of Society Islands to arrange camp, kindle fire, & cook." The four men played multiple roles. When some Indians came too close for comfort, Tolmie was "sufficiently alarmed to tell them by Rosie to keep" their distance. "With Rosie's & Kekane's assistance to dry papers, [Tolmie] sat up till the 'noon of the night' changing plant papers" on the specimens he had collected so far. Another time he noted approvingly how "one of the men, a tall athletic Owyhee," scared off "a half starved wolf dog" that came from "a deserted Indian village." Tolmie "had a very refreshing bath in Cowlitz [River], Hiria being on the lookout as the water was very deep & current strong."[3]

The full extent to which Tolmie accepted "the Owhyees" as his equals comes through in a journal entry written on a lazy Sunday afternoon: "Kekane, Rosie & an indian are lolling in the shade & I am reclining in tent—sunset—southern margin of Cowlitz prairie."[4] Rosie had, despite his considerable proficiency in languages, worked in the trade for just three years. His presence testifies to men being recruited more generally across the Pacific or, more likely, his having made his own way to Honolulu, which was increasingly attracting ambitious young men seeking a better life. Keekanah and Hereea each had fifteen years' experience in the Pacific Northwest. The other man was not named in Tolmie's journal.

The glimpses that survive suggest that the Hawaiians occupied an in-between space. No established HBC category existed in which to place them. References sometimes grouped them just below French Canadians, other times on a par with persons of mixed newcomer and Native descent. "On the 24th June [1827] the *Cadboro* Sailed with an Addition to her crew of five half Breeds and Six Owhyees; she has on board the Outfit for Fort Langley and the coasting trade," John McLoughlin wrote in 1827. The taint that persons of mixed French Canadian descent acquired by virtue of their Aboriginal ancestry caused some longtime fur traders like Alexander Ross to rank them below Hawaiians.

> Half-breeds or, as they are generally styled, brulés, from the peculiar colour of their skin, being of a swarthy hue, as if sunburnt, as they grow up resemble, almost in every respect, the pure Indians. With this difference that they are more designing, more daring, and more dissolute. They are indolent, thoughtless, and improvident, licentious in their habits, unbounded in their desires, sullen in their disposition.

Other times Hawaiians were understood to be superior Indians. The head of the Columbia District attributed the difficulties of using force against antagonistic local Natives to HBC expeditions being, at least in part, "composed as they are of Canadian Iroquois a few Europeans Owhyees and native Indians." An HBC official recently arrived from England termed Hawaiians "Kanacka Indians."[5]

Individual Hawaiians were often unnamed. Due in part to their liminal status, in part to their distinctive physical appearance and language, in part to several men often working on the same activity, they tended to be grouped together as Sandwich Islanders, Islanders, *owyhees,* Kanakas, or *kānaka,* but not distinguished as separate human beings. Sometimes, it is only by combining sources that it becomes possible to give personalities to the men who made their lives in the fur trade. The former NWC post of Fort George continued in operation under the HBC as the entryway to the Columbia River and the much larger Fort Vancouver. The journal of the officer in charge in 1846 thrice referred to its two Hawaiian employees:

> T[UESDAY] MARCH THE 5TH [1846] two Islanders empl[oye]d variously one cooking the other procuring wood.

> F[RIDAY] MARCH THE 6TH Islanders empl[oy]d as yesterday only a few hours putting up the Fences.

> MONDAY MAY THE 11TH went Assisted by Mr. Pisk Kippling and a Sn Islander surveyed and marked distinctly Mr [Peter Skene] Ogden's [land] Claim[6]

These men are named in employee records as Jones and Rattine, who were among a dozen men signing on with the HBC in Oʻahu in 1843. Both were immediately sent to Fort George on arrival and would briefly serve elsewhere before dying in 1847 or 1848, still young men, in a measles epidemic.

However long Hawaiians might serve the fur trade, and however much men like Tolmie might be sympathetic toward them, they remained just a little alien to its goals, as comprehended by the men in charge. A clerk at a Nisqually outlying farm recalled "settling a very bad quarrel between five or six Kanakas and some Englishmen." He added, almost as an afterthought, how "few men could have equalled my management of this crowd of strange beings." In November 1844 a forest fire in the vicinity of Fort Vancouver threatened to destroy the post itself. A hundred Hawaiians were employed there, but what caused comment was not their fire fighting but rather "two Sandwich Islanders, who in the confusion broke into the Store, stole Rum and got drunk."[7] The HBC as a policy provided liquor only on special occasions, which made it a more desirable commodity than would otherwise be the case. In general Hawaiians were far less often implicated in such offenses than other employees. Islanders at Wyatt's Fort Hall in the mid-1830s almost never purchased rum or other alcohol, post records attest, unlike some fellow employees quite willing to shell out $3 for a pint.

The Hawaiians also set themselves apart. Be it Fort Hall or Nisqually, they tended to purchase routine items such as plug or twist tobacco at the same time, suggesting they clubbed together. When contracts expired at Fort Rupert in 1850, the Hawaiians argued as a single group of eight for being allowed to leave on their own. During the resulting confusion over their terms of employment, they repeatedly complained about being "detained against their will" and then "bought a canoe to proceed down the straits to Nisqually" on their own.[8]

Language was one of the most fundamental bases of separation. It was only during the later years of the fur trade, as missionaries and other Americans implanted themselves in the Islands, that some men were able to communicate in English at the time they left home. They might well be literate in Hawaiian. According to Rev. Beaver, at Fort Vancouver in 1836–1838, those "who have been more than ten or twelve years in the service, are totally uninstructed; while those, who have entered it at later periods, have been, for the most part, instructed by the missionaries in their native land previous to leaving it, and many of them can read in their own language." The most general circumstance was, so the head of the Columbia District described Hawaiians, and also Iroquois and local Indians, they spoke a "language we do not understand nor they ours."[9]

Even when Hawaiians arrived with a basic fluency in English, they soon came to realize that it was not the language of the fur trade. They had two more languages to learn. The exploring expedition's head Charles Wilkes expressed mild surprise how "Canadian French is generally spoken to the servants: even those who come out from England after a while adopt it, and it is not a little amusing to hear the words they use, and the manner in which they pronounce them." Wilkes added that French was spoken also "at all the other posts of the Company." Equally important for everyday communication, particularly with Native people, was the Chinook jargon. A mixture of English, French, Chinook, and other Native tongues, the pidgin comprised between two hundred and six hundred words and a lot of hand gestures. "The general communication is," one newcomer concluded, "maintained chiefly by means of the Jargon, which may be said to be the prevailing idiom."[10]

An ethnographer with the U.S. expedition counted five languages at Fort Vancouver. Despite hearing English, Canadian French, Chinook, Cree, and Hawaiian, Horatio Hale quickly realized "there are very few who understand more than two languages, and many who speak only their own." He explained how "the Hawaiian is in use among about a hundred natives of the Sandwich Islands who are employed as labourers about the fort." Among the crew of ten who manned George Simpson's boat on his departure from Fort Vancouver on his third trip west of the Rocky Mountains in 1841 were "Sandwich Islanders, who jabbered a medley of Chinook, English, &c., and their own vernacular jargon."[11]

A major moment of crisis, the murder of the officer in charge at Fort

Stikine on the night of April 20–21, 1842, reveals the ways in which language did, and did not, maintain the Hawaiians as a group apart. Nine of the Islanders dispatched there in 1840 were still working at Stikine, alongside a dozen others, on the fatal night when John McLoughlin Jr., the namesake son of the head of the Columbia District, was killed. As workers were emerging from the drudgery of their winter duties, he lost control over his twenty-two men, half of them Hawaiians, the others a mixture of French Canadians and Iroquois. According to their later depositions, everyone signed an agreement to kill him, including all of the Hawaiians except Pouhow.

An unusual degree of detail survives due to depositions and an acrimonious exchange of letters between a protective father and the North American HBC head, George Simpson, who considered the killing to be justifiable homicide. Anahi, Captain Cole, Kakape, Kanackanui, Kahaloukulu, Joe Lamb, Nahoua, Okaia, and Pouhow all testified about the sequence of events. The extent of their understanding of what was happening, let alone their signatures, is in doubt. The victim's father repeatedly emphasized how "the Owhyhees—understand English very little and speak very few words." Young McLoughlin "could communicate with the Canacas only in a few Broken words of Indian as the Kanacas at Stikine speak no Language but their own which my Son could not speak."[12] However, Kakapi or Kakape, Captain Cole, and Ohaia or Okaia could read and write Hawaiian, likely having attended American missionary schools in the Islands.

It was to the Hawaiians that young McLoughlin had turned in his night of crisis, telling them "he would want them By and Bye that he suspected a Plot." He called Kanackanui and several other Hawaiians to take up arms to protect him. According to his father, "the Owhyhees say, the deceased called on them, to fire on the Canadians, as they wanted to kill him."[13] Kanackanui, Ohaia, Anahi, Kakapi, and others grabbed their guns and rushed outside, where a French Canadian wrested Kanackanui's gun from him. In an effort to draw his opponents from the building, McLoughlin yelled "Fire! Fire!" to the Hawaiians. Four shots rang out, the fatal one, probably from the French Canadian's gun, entering McLoughlin's shoulder blades and exiting his throat.

Although the Hawaiians were unable to protect the chief trader, they provided the voice of calm, reason, and stability. On their own initiative, the Hawaiians took the body inside, washed, and dried it. One of the French Canadians came in, removed McLoughlin's ring, and threw the body on the floor. Kanackanui promptly threw him out, but not before Pouhow was able to retrieve the ring. A coffin was built and the corpse removed from the main house to the bath house. On the third day, the corpse was carried to an open grave by some Hawaiians along with three French Canadians.

Language was critical to the subsequent investigation. The senior McLoughlin wanted an interpreter present. "As to the Sandwich Islanders there was no Person there who could speak their language sufficiently well to get a Detailed Statement of the unfortunate affair." To learn what happened precisely, McLoughlin sent "the *Cadboro* with William Spencer, who speaks the Sandwich Island Language fluently enough to Examine the Sandwich Islanders." Spencer had just returned from two years' service at the HBC agency in Honolulu. Simpson gave a slightly different version of how their testimony was obtained. "The Sandwich Islanders, Cole and Kekepe, gave their evidence through another Sandwich Islander, one of the Sailors on board the Cowlitz, who spoke English sufficiently well to act as interpreter." [14]

John McLoughlin first tried, unsuccessfully, to get the employee who killed his son tried at Sitka in Russian America. Then he sent the accused, along with fourteen others as witnesses, to York Factory in eastern Canada. The number included "Captain Cole (Sandwich Islander who saw [the accused, Urbain] Heroux stand with his foot on my son's neck writhing in the agonies of death)" and "Kakepé (another Sandwich Islander who saw Heroux fire the fatal shot and heard my son fall)." Traveling with the group was "William Spencer to act as Interpreter to the Sandwich Islanders." [15]

Despite language difficulties, the head of the Columbia Department considered the Hawaiians to be the heroes, to the extent there were heroes, in his son's death. While he wanted all the employees punished, he made an exception for the Hawaiians who, in his view, had exonerated themselves by their behavior. "The Owhyhees are on duty, as though they had been tampered with by the Canadians, and Iroquois, they did not join with them, though from ignorance, they seem not to have informed their master." A close observer of the fur trade took pride in the role played by the Hawaiians. "It is worthy of note that at the last the young man seems to have relied upon his Owhyhees (Hawaiians) to make a stand against the whites." [16]

As for the nine Hawaiians, Anahi, Kahaloukulu, Kakepe, Joe Lamb, and Pouhow all returned to Oʻahu and vanished into obscurity. Captain Cole went back in 1844 but rejoined in 1847 for three years, at which time he died of tuberculosis at a HBC post. Kanackanui, presumably a large man, eventually succumbed to tuberculosis at another HBC post. Okaia died at Fort Victoria in 1854. Nahoua raised a family in the Victoria area and may have died there.

It is impossible to know the full extent to which Hawaiians built on their distinctive language to maintain their ways of life. A meteor shower occurring on a trapping expedition in 1833 was remembered less for its brilliant appearance than for Hawaiians' frantic response to it. The men were so convinced "some mighty kapu had been broken for the gods to carry on so" that everyone else had their hands full trying to calm them down. "The Hawaiians were brave enough when faced with whitewater rivers, raging surf, or surging rapids. But heavenly pyrotechnics were beyond their ken and they trembled, frantic with fear, as they prayed to Pele and other deities."[17]

It is the asides that speak most clearly to Hawaiians' determination to continue their cultural practices, despite others' amusement. An English visitor of 1825 described how Hawaiians "are in the habit of disfiguring their mouths by extracting four or five of their front teeth, as commemorating the death of any deceased hero." He was pleased by how "this barbarous custom has been fast disappearing." George Simpson similarly observed in 1842 how they would "knock out with a mallet as many front teeth as the ranks of the deceased may demand." He recalled how, "some time ago, we had one of these mutilated veterans on the Columbia, who, as if the honor fully atoned to him for the loss, used to boast of having sacrificed his teeth in the service of so renowned a conqueror as Kamehameha the Great."[18]

Canadian painter Paul Kane, who joined the outward brigade from Fort Vancouver in July 1847, recorded how, in the evening, the eight Hawaiians among the paddlers "afforded great amusement by a sort of pantomimic dance, accompanied by singing." These men were engaged in a form of traditional dancing, but for Kane and the others the unfamiliar was to be ridiculed. "The whole thing was exceedingly grotesque and ridiculous, and elicited peals of laughter from the audience."[19]

Similarly, a clerk at Fort Nisqually described how, at the usual fur trade dances, "the Indian women and halfbreed women and girls were passionately fond of dancing" a kind of "jig" with which they "keep time to music by simply bobbing or jumping up and down." His description of the Hawaiians' contribution to such festivities makes clear that the men's crossing the ocean did not equate with their losing contact with traditional practices. "We had in our employ at that time about ten Kanakas. To vary the entertainment I would persuade these men to dance some of their native dances. They would cheerfully comply, and standing in a row would begin a wild and monotonous chant, keeping time by moving their bodies with great exactitude and twisting about, in which I could see no dancing, but merely posturing and sometimes it seemed to me to be an unseemly performance in the presence of the ladies."[20] Chanting was, along with the hula, at the heart of cultural practices. Chants were considered to be infused with *mana,* or spiritual power.

Reciprocity sometimes existed. The head of Fort Nisqually during the 1850s recalled: "Aloha is a Kanaka word for greeting, 'good morning' or 'how are you' &c. I think it ought to be spelt 'Arihoa.' At one time I employed here eight or ten Kanakas, and I have frequently used the term and heard them use it, when greeting them at any time, the same as the Chinook term of 'how are you,' or 'good morning' [which is] Klahowya."[21]

The Hawaiians also accommodated. Despite the limitations of language, common sociability went on much as it began at Astoria. New Year 1835 at Fort Simpson saw an evening celebration in which the French Canadians sang "several paddling songs. Our two Iroquois danced the war dance with the great spirit of their tribe & the S. Islanders sung Rule Britannia tolerably well." The next day the men "received each an allowance of a Pint of Rum," which may explain, a day later, "a boxing match between an Iroquois & Islander—the latter floored his opponent neatly & came off victor."[22]

Not only were hours long, most jobs were physically exhausting and corporal punishment for alleged misbehavior was commonplace. According to depositions in the murder of John McLoughlin Jr. at Fort Stikine in 1842, his drinking and violent streaks became increasingly pronounced and, in drunken stupors, he would pummel employees with his fists and whip them until the blood ran. His father sought to demonstrate that his son had not maltreated the men under him but only inflicted punishment with cause and gave as an example "Joe Lamb for Giving away meat out of the Kitchen." A witness testified how "Capt Cole (a Kanaca so called) was flogged twice for sleeping on his watch when the safety of the Establishment depended on his Vigilance."[23] Given that the Hawaiians provided the only defense for young McLoughlin at the time of his murder, they clearly accepted the punishments as consistent with the protocols of the fur trade.

Assertions of noncompliance manifested themselves in the fur trade mainly through desertion, a military term used for quitting while under contract, and occasional theft. The numerous instances of desertion started with Jack Attoo in 1791 who, tiring of his voyage on the American trading ship *Columbia,* deserted off the coast of Vancouver Island. He was brought back to be flogged by Captain Robert Gray. Alexander Ross described how in 1816 a renegade blacksmith persuaded "eighteen of his deluded followers, chiefly Owhyhees," to climb Fort George's 20-feet-high palisades "one dark night" and "set off for California" in the conviction their fortunes would be made. Tracked by the post interpreter, "the fugitive islanders wheeled about, and accompanying the interpreter, returned again to the establishment on the third day."[24]

Two decades later a dozen Hawaiians deserted Nathanial Wyeth's expedition. Much as had their predecessors, they soon discovered the Pacific Northwest outside of the fur trade was not a comfortable place. Their only practical option, Wyeth mused, would have been to head to Spanish California. Local Indians seemed much more willing to report sightings in the hopes of being rewarded than to welcome their fellow indigenous people. Wyeth's journal is revealing of attitudes.

> 13TH [NOVEMBER 1834]. At night dispatched 4 men after two Kanackas that have been seen by the Indians about 15 miles below Walla Walla on the main river.
>
> 16TH. An Indian brot in one shod Horse which had been taken by the Kanackas he found it at the Utalla River and brot word that they saw two of the scamps had bot a canoe and gone down.
>
> 25TH. Today I hear that one of the two Kanackas who went down the river in a canoe as per former report has been killed for killing horses by the Indians other reports say a Kanacka has killed an Indian. I also hear that 6 of the runaways are on the heads of John Days River the whole of which storys I take to be lies invented to tell me in the hopes of a small present of tobacco.
>
> 26TH. We hear such contardictory [*sic*] and impossible accounts from the Indians of the Kanackas that I do not know what to believe.
>
> 31ST. There is here a small village of Inds. from which I understand by signs that the two Kanackas who de[s]cended the river stole horses here or killed Horses, and in some wrangle with the chief concerning it one of the Kanackas shot him.
>
> 4TH [DECEMBER]. We hear that the two Kanackas have been followed by the Indians and killed in revenge for killing one of them and their Horses.[25]

All of the Hawaiians who survived a winter on their own gratefully returned to work on being located by Wyeth.

Hawaiians on HBC trading vessels possessed more freedom of action than did their counterparts stuck on land. In the fall of 1840 a Hawaiian was among five seamen on the HBC barque *Columbia* who "deserted in California." Punishments could be severe. Rev. Beaver, who had no love for the HBC and may well have exaggerated, claimed that a Hawaiian was, for some unrevealed crime, "flogged and put in irons" for "five months and four days."[26]

Hawaiians who stuck with the fur trade came to accept that they had to persevere even when their labor did not receive the praise it might have merited. During his visits in 1824 and 1828 George Simpson approved several initiatives involving Hawaiians that were intended to maximize profits. The North West Company had systematically trapped beaver along the south side of the Columbia River, and Simpson ordered these annual expeditions to continue. The Snake parties, so named after the area of eastern Oregon in which they mostly occurred between 1824 and the boundary settlement of 1846, netted the HBC £30,000, or fully $135,000.

The first two expeditions, both in 1826, were meant to explore the coast south of the Columbia River, as well as to trap beaver. The group, sent in mid-May 1826 with orders to return by late August, included three Hawaiians among its twenty members. Traveling by horse, the men stopped periodically to trap and trade for beaver skins. The officer in charge almost inherently doubted the Hawaiians' utility. Twelve days away, he named everyone without judgment, excepting for "Toureawanhie, Dick, and America, Labourers, but of very inferior capacity." The trio searched out beaver sites, arranged for canoes from local people, and set traps that then became their individual responsibility to monitor. America, who had been "unwell of a Breast Complaint since leaving Fort Vancouver," was by the beginning of July unable to tend his traps. The journal entry three weeks later groused that even the "Indians" were "more usefull [*sic*] generally speaking, than the Owyhees we have who have been two thirds of the time disabled for duty and even now two of them have the greatest difficulty to walk from disease." The Hawaiians were soon back at work, but with middling success, causing the expedition's head to assert that "the want of Industry is more the cause of their ill luck than the actual scarcity of Beaver."[27] However, when the expedition returned in mid-August with just 285 skins, one-third of them obtained from trade, the head attributed the small number to the few beaver along the coast.

A follow-up expedition set out a month later, taking a different route and utilizing a combination of horses and canoes. Despite the same officer being in charge, the number of Hawaiians was increased to five, or one-quarter of the total. Alongside the maligned Toureawanhie, Dick, and America were Keekanah and Tawai. The group did not endear themselves when, a month into the expedition, "Touocoahina lost his horse with his traps and other property." A few weeks later the Hawaiians redeemed themselves. "Our party of Owyhees are beholden to their agility in swimming for the recovery of their traps and property that went to the bottom at a very deep place, in a gale of wind the canoe filled and turned over." Even then, the head found cause for complaint. "They lost a day to recover their things, two beavers however were lost."[28] The party arrived back at Fort Vancouver in mid-March 1827.

Four of the Hawaiians who participated in these two expeditions had arrived on the *Columbia* in 1817 and by now, almost a decade later, had developed a strong sense of camaraderie and self-worth. They must have come to terms with the foibles of the fur trade, given they would each, despite the repeated criticism, make it the focal point of their careers. America, who came in 1822, would return home in 1832 but soon be back to the coast, whereas the others would all continue through the mid-1840s, if not longer. Despite the grumbles by the men in charge, men like these were the effective backbone on which the HBC depended.

For most Hawaiians making their life in the fur trade, their routine was much more ordinary than on the Snake expeditions. Charles Wilkes of the U.S. exploring expedition described an average day, as it operated at Fort Vancouver in 1841.

> At early dawn the bell is rung for the working parties, who soon after go to work: the sound of the hammers, click of the anvils, the rumbling of the carts, with tinkling of bells, render it difficult to sleep after this hour. The bell rings again at eight, for breakfast; at nine they resume their work, which continues till one; then an hour is allowed for dinner, after which they work till six, when the labours of the day close.

Within that routine Hawaiians performed a range of jobs, as millers, watchmen, woodcutters, cooper's assistants, personal servants, porters, general laborers, house builders, cow, sheep and pig herders, and gardeners. According to an arrival there in 1847, "the Canadian Frenchmen and Kanakas were what might be called the understrappers for the company, hauling wood, water and other drudgery, packing pelts and moving pelts and moving goods from the ships to the store."[29]

As Como and Peeopeeoh found out in the late 1820s, endlessly sawing wood at Fort Langley, most jobs in the fur trade were by their nature repetitive and tedious. A decade later a fifteen-year-old countryman who shared the name of John Bull with his Fort Hall contemporary arrived at Fort Nisqually. The only Hawaiian there, he was without doubt lonely as well as alone. The post journal during his first year identified him more often by difference than by individuality.

MONDAY 23RD [JULY 1838]. The Owhyhee is dept at watching our potato field.

SATURDAY 18TH (AUGUST). The Owhyhee daily employed at watching the sheep with two young In[dia]n lads, besides looking at our potato field.

MONDAY 20TH. The Owhyhee and two young Indian lads watching the sheep and Potatoes.

TUESDAY 11TH [SEPTEMBER]. The Owhyhee watching our potatoes.

TUESDAY 18TH. The Owhyhee watching the potatoes.

FRIDAY 28TH. John Bull watching our potatoes field.

FRIDAY 5TH [OCTOBER]. The Owhyhee chopping firewood.

FRIDAY 12TH. The Owhyhee still chopping firewood.

MONDAY 29TH. The Owhyhee was [employed] at putting dung in our garden.

WEDNESDAY 7TH [NOVEMBER]. The Owhyhee was busy at spreading dung in the garden.

FRIDAY 1ST [FEBRUARY 1839]. Bull still employed at sundry jobs about the place.

MONDAY 4TH [MARCH]. John Bull in the garden.

MONDAY 18TH. John Bull with seven Indians were employed at dunging the drills for the potatoes.

MONDAY 27TH [MAY]. The Owhyhee employed in the garden.[30]

John Bull became a valued employee. For men like Bull, Como, and Peeopeeoh who expressed some willingness to adapt, in part by learning some French or English, the monotony that marked much of fur trade labor gradually gave way to more interesting employment. They might begin as "raw Islanders," as put by the head of Fort Langley, but they were just as capable as others of learning on the job. The post journal noted in 1830 how Como and Peeopeeoh were, along with several others, "re-engaged 2 yrs."[31] Como would remain at Fort Langley until 1839 and then work at Fort Vancouver until his death there in 1850. Peeopeeoh would be employed at Fort Langley until 1852, when he retired in the vicinity. John Bull would spend the next eight years in the Fort Nisqually area, part of the time as a shepherd. He returned home, but very soon was back in the Pacific Northwest, where he remained until his death in about 1865.

It is impossible to know how much Hawaiians affected the terms of their employment as opposed to their being dictated by the officers in charge. Men were routinely moved about as need arose. In the fall of 1829 the head of the Columbia District added as a brief postscript to an officer at an outlying post that "I send Kikarrow and Peter to remain with you." The first was Kaharrow, a Hawaiian of a dozen years' employment at Forts Vancouver and Nez Perce, the second likely a Native person. "I will send you two Owhyhees and a Canadian," ran a postscript to a letter of autumn

1831 to the head of Fort Colvile, located in eastern Washington. The two new men, Corriacca and Spunyarn, were among the 1830 arrivals. They would each remain at the inland post until mid-decade, when Corriacca would be killed by Blackfeet Indians and Spunyarn incorporated into the annual Snake expeditions. Similarly, in August 1831, as the *Cadboro* was about to depart north, the head of the Columbia District informed Peter Ogden, who was in charge of constructing the post, that "you will Receive four Owhyees who will replace any you will have to send Back."[32]

Longtime employees acquired the most independence of movement and individuality. They were named in the correspondence, as with the head of the Columbia District deciding in early spring 1831 not only to leave Heveea as the only Hawaiian at Fort Colvile but to consider the decision sufficiently important to highlight it in a letter. A couple of months later Heveea was again named, by virtue of his now being designated one of the "Vancouver Men."[33] Heveea, or Hereea, had worked in the trade since 1817, at Fort Colvile off and on for the past four years, and would remain there, at Fort Vancouver, and at Fort Langley until his death in 1837.

An incident at Fort Langley in 1830 hints at Hawaiians' ways of life. The post's mandate to cure salmon for the Hawai'i trade made more hands necessary. Among the Hawaiians who arrived in the Pacific Northwest that spring on the *Isabella,* three were assigned to Fort Langley. Just a month later, "one of our new Owhyees" at the end of the work day "signified to his companions that he was going to wash himself." When Maniso "did not return immediately nor has he appeared Since," an all-out search of land and water was launched to no success.[34] Its vigorous quality testifies to the Hawaiians' worth as employees, but also as human beings, from the perspective of the men in charge.

The attempt to ferret out an explanation for Maniso's disappearance is telling on several accounts. It indicates some Hawaiians who signed on with the HBC may have shared common experiences in the Islands that softened the transition from one society to the other. The attempt also demonstrates Hawaiians' accommodation, with earlier arrivals like Como acting as interpreters for their countrymen. The only hope for Maniso's survival appeared to be, the post journal recorded, "a fit of mental derangement, for the Islanders Say that he was Subject to fits in his own Country and often wandered about for days—Como further Says that in the passage from the Islands to Columbia he understood he threatened to throw himself overboard & Peeopeeoh adds that he was very melancholy of late—ate little or nothing & that yesterday afternoon in particular he Complained of being fatigued." Archibald McDonald, the head of Fort Langley, added, on a protective note, that "we never had occasion to use a harsh word with him." To find out more, he queried the *Isabella*'s captain: "Pray have you any knowledge of any of the [Sandwich] Islanders falling into fits on board your vessel coming to the Columbia; if so please let us know the particulars."[35]

The next act in this little human drama played out two weeks later when a Kwantlen Indian reported how he "found our dead man on the beach" nearby, "all naked his head Split in two Several Arrow wounds in his body —and his right Side rupt'd open with the Knife." The post journal recorded how the account "of Course whetted our rage against Indians that we before but suspected." McDonald informed the captain of an HBC schooner docked nearby of "our determination to punish them if possible as soon as the vessel is here or rather on her way up when abreast of the village" near where the body was reportedly found.[36]

Revenge that, as Fort Langley's head put it, "might have ended in the total ruin or abandonment of the Establishment" was only narrowly averted. As "the plans of attack" were being finalized, "we Saw this Same Said dead man walk in to the Fort in the dusk of the evening in his Shirt a perfect Skelton!!!" The story Maniso told speaks to the Hawaiians' dress and sensibilities. It turned out he had indeed wandered off "as it were blind and insensible," lost his "pea doublet & Trowsers" en route, been afraid to eat berries for fear of "poisoning himself," and only made it back after hearing the post's "Bugle Horn."[37]

The drama played itself out in two ways. Two days after Maniso returned, three Native men, hoping for a reward, "Came up with the Owhyhee's Clothing perfectly entire & in the State in which he threw it off." A week later, Maniso "was provided a passage to the doctors." McDonald explained how "Maniso, the poor Islander that caused us so much anxiety lately, goes back on the vessel [*Vancouver* arrived with supplies] & in his room I keep one of those on board to make up the complement of 13 men."[38] The "3 raw Owhyhees" assigned Fort Langley together with Como and Peeopeeoh, one of them Maniso's replacement, were Ta-i, Toro, and Wavicareea. The trio would, like their two countrymen, make a career in the fur trade.

Whatever their tenure, Hawaiians received a fairly similar annual wage, accommodation, and weekly allotment of food. The amount long stuck at £17 as it did for other employees. An American who arrived at Fort Vancouver in late 1844 was told "that the wages of Sandwich Islanders, of whom the Hudson's Bay Company had a considerable number, were $5 per month [£13–14 a year], and salmon and potatoes furnished for food."[39]

Most men spent most of their wages. According to Rev. Beaver, by the time Hawaiians arrived in the colder climate of the Pacific Northwest, they were destitute and had to borrow against their first year's wages to purchase adequate clothing. A member of the U.S. exploring expedition, which visited Fort Vancouver in the summer of 1841, reported how "many of the servants complained" that, out of their £17 per annum, "they have to furnish themselves with clothes." The result was that "when their time expires they find themselves in debt, and are obliged to serve an extra time to pay it."[40] The fifty or so Hawaiians hired by Nathaniel Wyeth in 1834–1835 received $10 a month, but were expected to buy at least some of their clothing and food. The Fort Hall account books indicate they were among the most frugal of the post's employees, limiting their routine purchases to plug tobacco and coffee at $1.50 and rice at 75¢ a pound, iron spoons and porringers at $1 each, large knives $1.25, shaving soap 50¢ a cake, and needed items of clothing. A red flannel shirt went for $4, leather pants $5, shoes $5, moccasins $1, flannel drawers $3, frock coat $3, and a green capote or great coat $20.

HBC employees received a weekly allotment of food, one that suited the Hawaiians more than it did the others. Food may also have been one of their strongest everyday ties to relatives back home. Just as fish comforted Hawaiians at Astoria during a general shortage of provisions, salmon was enjoyed by both men in the Pacific Northwest and their counterparts in the Islands. In March 1829, the Fort Langley post journal recorded how "ten of our best here," including the two Hawaiians, "are preparing for a Start tomorrow the length of Cowlitz Portage—they are served with 10 days provisions in potatoes & Salted Salmon." From about 1830 preserved, or pickled, salmon was sent to the Islands in barrels from the Northwest Coast. A missionary wife in Honolulu took pleasure in the fall of 1839 how "we have now some salmon from the Columbia River which relishes very well."[41]

The dish known as lomilomi salmon, which came into fashion in the Hawaiian Islands, was likely a cause for nostalgia among men returned home. Salmon arriving in brine in barrels from the Pacific Northwest was first soaked for a time to remove some of the salt, the meat was taken off the bones, and onions and tomatoes added to offset any rotten taste acquired along the way. Little changed from its nineteenth-century original, lomilomi salmon remains a favored Islands food.

The cherished missing item for men in the Pacific Northwest was, of course, poi. A contemporary described how "the Islanders at the Columbia" once attempted a remedy. "The poor Kanakas tried their utmost to manufacture a sort of poe—sweet potatoes, Irish potatoes, and even wappatoos [lily bulb eaten by local Natives], were operated upon, but all to no purpose." He explained how, when his brig left the Columbia on a visit to the Islands in late 1834, "their farewells to us were mingled with desires loudly expressed, that on our return, we would bring them each a calabash of poe."[42]

Descriptions of the weekly rations dispensed at the different fur trade posts across time are very similar. One official account gave the standard daily options "west of the Mountains" as (1) 3 pounds salt fish and 2 pounds potatoes, (2) 3 pounds salt fish and 1 1/2 pounds flour, (3) 6 pounds fresh salmon or codfish and 2 pounds potatoes, (4) 4 dried salmon, (5) 10 pounds fresh salmon or codfish, or (6) 8 pounds fresh venison. A member of the U.S. exploring expedition described how in 1841 the allocation for the Hawaiians operating the sawmill near Fort Vancouver "consists principally of smoked salmon." The same year HBC governor George Simpson was told that "weekly rations are usually twenty-one pounds of salted salmon and one bushel of potatoes, for each man; and, in addition to fish, there are also venison and wild fowl, with occasionally a little beef and pork." At the Cowlitz farm, where a dozen or so Hawaiians worked, Simpson found "the servants being principally fed on grain, fish and potatoes."[43]

The weekly distribution of food signaled the transition from work to private life. An 1841 visitor to Fort Vancouver witnessed how, "at five o'clock on Saturday afternoon the work is stopped, when the servants receive their weekly rations."[44] According to an employee from the beginning of the 1830s, once "men got their rations on the saturday," they "cooked, and lived" according to their own devices.[45]

Men's material conditions varied from post to post. They very often constructed their own quarters as part of their work obligation shortly after a post came into being. Where enough Hawaiians were employed in a single location, they might have their own building or site. According to a long-time employee, while men at Fort Vancouver "lived outside the Fort—in dangerous parts of the country the men were hutted inside the Forts." At Fort Nisqually the Hawaiians lived on a hillside across the creek that ran in front of the post; at Fort Langley, a ways down the Fraser River. The locations accorded the Hawaiians were not necessarily the best. A worker at Fort Rupert on northern Vancouver Island described "the Kanakas house" as "a place with the smell hardly fit for a pig to go in," not because of anything they did but rather its location next to the post's drain.[46]

Accommodations were most organized at Fort Vancouver, due to the large numbers employed there. A Presbyterian minister who arrived in the mid-1830s described "eight substantial buildings within the enclosure, and a great number of small ones without, making quite a village appearance." Another visitor about the same time referred to "thirty or forty log huts . . . placed in rows, with broad lanes and streets between them" that "looks like a very neat and beautiful village." An American sent by the U.S. president to get accurate information on Oregon counted thirty-four buildings within the post "enclosed by a picket forming an area of 750 by 450 feet," while "outside and very near the fort there are forty-nine cabins for laborers and mechanics." A man at Fort Vancouver during the 1840s retained all his life a very vivid impression of the "little cabins outside the fort built for the Hudsons Bay Company servants" at "any place around."[47]

The "little houses outside the fort," as an American characterized them in 1832, comprised Kanaka Village, so named because of the many Hawaiians employed at Fort Vancouver. Hawaiians' proportion of the workforce increased steadily, to a majority during the mid-1840s. A man who had arrived just after the border settlement of 1846 recollected "a lot of Kanakas and Canadian Frenchmen who lived in at least twenty houses in Kanaka Town." He explained how it was "where the employees of the Hudsons Bay had houses," persons he described as "Kanakas, half-breeds, Canadian Frenchmen."[48]

Employees essentially had their own community. A visitor of 1834 was admiring. "The most fastidious cleanliness appears to be observed; the women may be seen sweeping the streets and scrubbing the door-sills as regularly as in our own proverbially cleanly city." Paul Kane, who arrived at the end of 1846, described how "the men, with their Indian wives, live in log huts near the margin of the river, forming a little village—quite a Babel of languages, as the inhabitants are a mixture of English, French, Iroquois, Sandwich Islanders, Crees and Chinooks." Another visitor about the same time was struck by the prevalence of the trading jargon of Chinook. Many employees "can only converse with their wives in this speech,—and it is the fact, strange as it may seem, that many young children are growing up to whom this fictitious language is really the mother tongue, and who speak it with more readiness and perfection than any other."[49]

The houses varied in construction. The HBC tinsmith hired in 1837 recalled the houses as "all made of slabs, put up with posts in the ground, notched in the posts and the slabs inserted in the notches and covered with cedar bark." So far as construction was concerned, "each one of us erected our own buildings." A visitor shortly thereafter described the buildings as made of "wood, generally hewn logs, like the universal log House of Canada."[50]

These cottages and their counterparts at other posts provided the material base for Hawaiians' lives in the fur trade. The decisions of Como, Peeo-peeoh, John Bull, Heveea, and others to persevere for years and decades on end related not just to manageable work conditions, but to opportunities to get on with their lives. The location of the trade meant that, when they did so at the emotional level, they turned to local women similarly indigenous to themselves. It is impossible to know Hawaiians' attitude toward Indian women, but the insight of Hawaiian sociologist Romanzo Adams about early nineteenth-century Islanders may be instructive: "The Hawaiians did not think in terms of biological heredity. They were wholly unaware of the theory or doctrine that the people of some race were born with innate traits superior to those of another race, and so they neither accepted nor rejected it."[51]

From the earliest days of the fur trade, both officers and employees of all backgrounds sought out Indian women. The short-term goal was sexual satisfaction. An employee from the early 1830s onward recalled how "all the Co's ships admitted any number of the Indian women on board, the canoes returned for them and no troubles come in this way." John McLoughlin observed, following his son's death in April 1842, that he was the only head of an outlying post who "would not allow the men to bring women from the Indian camp for the night into the Fort." It was this policy that "the men considered the greatest grievance, because they had more indulgence at the other places." One of them explained at the subsequent investigation how it was, as a consequence of young McLoughlin "not allowing the men to take Indian wives or bring Indian women into the Fort," that they acted.[52]

Longer-term relationships were sometimes fraught with uncertainty. Officers in charge used various means to restrict or prohibit them, but over time increasingly focused on regulation as opposed to censure. Even George Simpson, who considered the practice an unwanted distraction, was forced to acknowledge during his 1824–1825 visit to the Pacific Northwest that "nearly all the Gentlemen & Servants have families altho' Marriage ceremonies are unknown in the Country." In his view, "it would be all in vain to attempt breaking through this uncivilized custom."[53]

For the most part ordinary employees lived their private lives beyond the scrutiny of the men in charge, the Hawaiians even more so, making it difficult to tease them out. Their nature surfaces most often in moments of crisis. One such episode had to do with blankets and beads intended for the coastal trade that went missing from the HBC brig *William & Ann* in 1825. America, three years on the coast, essentially squealed on seven of his countrymen. Having been in the Pacific Northwest eight to fourteen years, they had developed a sense of community from which America may have felt excluded. The officer in charge searched the accused men's belongings. Finding "not the slightest shadow of suspicion," he confronted them. Several admitted that, yes, they had taken items but not for their own use. Rather, it was to curry favor with the Native women with whom they were living. "Morrouna admits his having helped himself to a Blanket at the time Harry [Bell Noah] took his . . . the plain matter of fact is that they and the women they kept while allowed to live in the hold [of the *William & Ann*] with the property must have taken the deficiency [uncovered] in the Outfit." James Canton or Coah, Kakarrow or Kaharrow, and Tourawhyheene pleaded extenuating circumstances. Two others, including John Cox who had a dozen years in the fur trade, maintained their innocence. "Cox positively denies having given Blankets to his own wife. . . . Towai [Tawai] positively denied having taken the beads."[54] The offenses were clearly forgiven, for all of the men, including America, made the fur trade their life's work. America would return home in 1841 after twenty years away, Tawai in 1845 and Tourawhyheene two years later after thirty years each. James Canton or Coah, Kaharrow, Harry Bell Noah, Marouna, and John Cox all died at Fort Vancouver, between 1828 and 1850.

Personal lives sometimes surface in post journals, as in that for Fort Langley in 1829. In February the head allowed a French Canadian employee "to take a woman from the Camp & each man had a half pint liquor on the occasion in the evening." Two days later, "another of our men . . . is permitted to take a wife." The fortunate spouse was made well aware that his behavior was being approved and monitored at the same time. The reasons were, moreover, strategic, so the post journal explained: "Heretofore, it was thought desirable to have no connection of this kind," but to realize that, "to reconcile the bucks to Fort Langley without Some indulgence of this nature is utterly out of the question."[55]

The two Hawaiians then at Fort Langley, Como and Peeopeeoh, were willing participants in this condoned cohabitation. The post journal recorded short days after the new policy was proclaimed in 1829 how "Como—an Owhyhee, & one of our best men here is married to the Sister of Nicameus—the Quaitline [Kwantlen] Chief—all hands had a half pint & a hop on the occasion." A year later the head noted how "all our Men have taken Women," which "has had the effect of reconciling them to the place and of removing the inconvenience and indeed the great uncertainty of being able to get them year after year replaced from the Columbia." A dozen years later, in 1841, Oblate missionary Modeste Demers made his first visit to Fort Langley. He reported that "about twenty men are employed there at agricultural activities, of whom eight are Canadians, one an Iroquois, and the others Kanakas, inhabitants of the Sandwich Islands; all having wives and children after the fashion of the country."[56]

A social hierarchy developed at Fort Langley, as it likely did at other posts. French Canadian employee Jason Allard remembered a Christmas afternoon, likely in the 1840s, when one-third or more of the servants were Hawaiians. After being invited for treats in the fort's big hall, the "women who were married to white men," who were "related to the chiefs" and clearly considered themselves superior, got into a fight with "the wives of the Kanakas." Each of these women was determined to protect her status. "From one imaginary insult or slight the fight was on. There was no prancing and sparring. It was run and grab for the hair of the head. A regular tug-of-war ensued. Finally they were separated by their husbands and all was peace and quietness."[57] Apart from such a holiday afternoon, Hawaiians were not permitted to bring their wives into the post.

A handful of Hawaiians may have, in the model permitted by Wyeth, brought wives from home. Rev. Beaver, at Fort Vancouver in 1836–1838, considered "the few women who come with them, [as] having been selected from the lowest grade" and therefore "more than commonly depraved." He argued to HBC authorities that any more women should possess a certificate "of marriage with the men, whom they accompany." The post journal

Fort Langley, 1862, by William Henry Newton. British Columbia Archives, PDP 29.

for Cowlitz farm in December 1847 during a measles epidemic referred to "the Owhyhees—there are 3 of them 2 men & 1 woman quite unable to do the least thing for themselves." Similarly, an arrival at Fort Vancouver in 1853 felt comfortable asserting that "the Frenchmen were generally married to Indian women and the Kanakas lived with Kanaka women." He described how other men "left their wives at home," which did not, however, prevent short-term relationships with local women.[58] No records name Hawaiian women connected with the fur trade. It is possible that they were the daughters of earlier Hawaiian employees and local women.

Most relationships, whatever their composition, were fairly pragmatic with benefits to both partners. Men's everyday lives were made more pleasurable, whereas women and their families got the advantages to be had from the goods newcomers had at their disposal. At Fort Hall the most common luxury items Hawaiians purchased were almost certainly intended to maintain local women, as well as wives brought from home—wooden combs at $1.75, mirrors up to $2.25, Jew's harps 50¢, vermilion dye 75¢ a packet, and trade beads from 50¢ to $6 a bunch, depending on the size and quality.

Initially relationships were confirmed by traditional means. According to descendants, Kalama found himself a Nisqually chief's daughter named Mary Martin, who lived in a big longhouse near Fort Nisqually's outlying Muck farm, for whose hand he gave her family blankets, beads, and clothing. It cost fellow Nisqually employee Ehoo four blankets, a tin kettle, and tobacco "to purchase a wife." The arrival of missionaries added a new complexity. A Presbyterian minister who came in 1835 was very critical of men "living with their families without being married." He was particularly condemnatory of how "they do not call the women with whom they live, their wives, but their *women*."[59] Surviving records indicate a growing number of Hawaiians, as well as other HBC employees, engaging in a Christian marriage ceremony.

Post entries reveal that children born to Hawaiians were acknowledged and valued, not just by parents but by persons in charge. Visiting Kanaka Village in 1841, George Simpson was, he wrote, almost overrun by "the swarms of children at the little village." The entry for the Fort Nisqually agricultural outstation of Tlithlow for March 27, 1851, ran poignantly: "The Kanaka Sam [Koemi] lost his young son aged 15 mths. died of Influenza. S. had it taken to the Fort [Nisqually] and buried there, a coffin having been by Cowie made."[60] Sam Koemi had been recruited at Oʻahu four years earlier to be sent to Nisqually as a shepherd. His countryman Cowie was by comparison an old hand with a decade of employment, mainly at Nisqually and its outstations, both as a shepherd and as a general laborer. The respect paid to the dead child is evident from the clerk in charge both giving Cowie time off to make the coffin and the grieving father time off to have his son properly buried.

Numerous Hawaiians, as well as other workers, went to great lengths to avoid separation from their wives and children. The head of the 1841 U.S. exploring expedition described employees' circumstances. "Not infrequently, at the expiration of their engagement, they have become attached, or married, to some Indian woman of half-breed, and have children on which account they find themselves unable to leave, and continue attached to the Company's service, and in all respects under the same engagement as before."[61] Many Hawaiians, as well as other employees, remained for very long time periods at the same post, which must have at least in part responded to their preferences.

Other Hawaiians moved into a kind of semi-employment. They headed out on their own, but not quite. As caught by the head of the U.S. expedition, men's departure from a formal contract with the HBC did not end their relationship with the company, for they "are still dependent on the Company for many of the necessaries of life, clothing, &c."[62] HBC accounts are filled with the names of Hawaiians who for years following the formal end of their contract continued to draw on amounts still owed them.

At the same time, many men likely anticipated from the time they entered into a relationship it would have a transient quality and may have departed with few regrets. They had come to the Pacific Northwest to improve their lot and, as with Wyeth's Hawaiians, went back in better material circumstances than when they had left. John Bull earned $360 for three years' labor at Fort Hall, just over two-thirds of which went to ongoing expenses, another $50 to outfitting himself for his return, leaving $53.93 due him in Oʻahu. Bull was determined to be well dressed, his predeparture purchases consisting of cord, cloth, and duffel trousers, three cotton shirts, two pairs of socks and shoes, a waterproof hat, and black silk handkerchief. Unlike several of his returning countrymen from Fort Hall, he did not indulge in either cotton braces or a vest. The beads and other little luxuries some of the men purchased prior to departure may have been bought for wives and sisters back home. The archaeological dig undertaken by Patrick Kirch and Marshall Sahlins in the 1970s–1980s in an Oʻahu rural hinterland turned up a variety of foreign goods they link to whaling, if not directly then through acquisition of dollars making their purchase possible locally.[63]

Other Hawaiians abandoned their families through no fault of their own. Men did not just live on the Northwest Coast, they died there. The damp and cold weather that beset Hawaiians at Astoria continued to take its toll. The new HBC physician who arrived in the Pacific Northwest in 1833 described the next January how "several of the Polynesians have today complained of Chilblains, some of which are of an aggravated character." As to the reason: "The fellows have been very careless in not properly wrapping their toes during the late intensely cold weather & now that it has become milder they suffer from their former negligence."[64]

Few Hawaiians actually died of the cold. "We were amazed at how well the inhabitants of the Torrid Zone can bear the cold and hardship of navigating off the Northwest Coast of America without damaging their health," a Frenchman commented in 1819.[65] Only one of the dozen runaway Hawaiians who eluded Wyeth's grasp over the winter fell victim to the weather.

The principal causes of death were the various illnesses that swept through the fur trade, beginning with intermittent fever around Fort Vancouver during the early 1830s. Among its victims was Harry Bell Noah in September 1831, by now almost two decades in the Pacific Northwest. Arrived at Astoria on the *Beaver* in the spring of 1812, still in his mid-teens, he had passed his adulthood in the fur trade. Three years after his death his family, likely in the Fort George area, was still purchasing goods out of the monies remaining in his HBC account.

The measles epidemic of the late 1840s was the most devastating. The head of Cowlitz farm wrote worriedly in his journal on December 16, 1847: "11 of the farm servants, Owhyhees and Indians, have all been seriously indisposed since Sunday last & it now appears they have all got the measles." The next day came news that "this disease in its worse form is raging at Vancouver."[66] Measles accounted for at least nine Hawaiian deaths at Fort Vancouver and nearby Fort George over the winter of 1847–1848. Charley and Jem Mamuka lived long enough to be baptized by Catholic priests as Paul Cali and Joseph Finmanut, intended to ease their way into a Christian afterlife. Kahela, Kaneoukai, Korhooa, Napoua, Tayapapa, Toovyoora, and Jones had no such good fortune and slipped away under their own names.

Twenty-nine Hawaiians died of measles and other diseases across the Pacific Northwest between 1847 and 1850, or about 15 percent of those employed in the fur trade during these years. The head at Cowlitz explained how "the Owhyhee part of the crew being laid up with the measles," it was impossible to move boats with goods. At the end of December 1847 he recorded: "A batteux with 6 Owyhees arrived at Plomondons landing from Vancouver to resume their duty on the f[a]rm. They have all happily got over the measles but have been two whole months absent." Almost a year later the head of Fort Victoria blamed a poor crop on "measles having fallen upon this place in seed time, and prostrated two thirds of the people of this establishment who are chiefly Hawaiians."[67]

The response of men in charge to ill Hawaiians speaks to the Islanders' value to the fur trade. Their accidents and maladies were taken seriously, as with John Horapapa, who may have, like Thomas Tuana at Astoria, been ill with venereal disease at the time he joined the fur trade. Horapapa was one of a dozen Hawaiians at Fort Simpson on the north coast in 1835. Just a year after being hired in O'ahu, he became incapacitated. Dr. Tolmie tried to cure the sores on his leg, but with little success. It was decided to send Horapapa back to Fort Vancouver. "I leave one Man, Portelanu, in place of an Islander, Horapapa, who is represented as in a very bad state of health and otherwise unfit for the place," read the journal of John Work, the officer in charge of the coastal trade.[68]

The HBC brig *Lama* took the Hawaiian onboard on September 12. As the ship made its way down the east coast of Vancouver Island Horapapa's condition grew worse and he began to cough up blood. Medicines had no effect and on September 22 Horapapa died somewhere in the vicinity of Cape Flattery. That day John Work recorded in his journal: "It was wished to bury him on shore, but as we could not get to land, and it being uncertain when we could, and as he could not be properly kept for any time on board, we were constrained to give him a sailor's burial and comit him to the deep. The funeral service was read. What little cloths [*sic*] he had were nailed up in his chest to go on to the Columbia."[69] It was not just during illness but also in death that Hawaiians were respected.

The Hawaiians who died in the Pacific Northwest left their bones there. The burial ground at Fort Vancouver was described in the spring of 1833 as located "in a fertile upland meadow greatly beautified by wild flowers & trees in flower," but not enclosed. "Some of the graves are surrounded with palisades but the great number are merely covered with stones & logs of wood." Five years later it had "a rough fence around it" that was "partly picket and partly rail." This man recalled "fifteen or twenty graves in it in 1839, some of them marked with crosses, some only had head boards." A Catholic intermittently at Fort Vancouver during the 1840s remembered "all kinds of people buried there," including "the wives and children of employees and persons who had been in the employment of the Hudsons Bay Company." An arrival of 1847 described the "graveyard where the whites, the Kanakas and everybody else buried." A woman who came in 1848 recalled how "the only burying ground there was for everybody." She "saw some

Catholic crosses there over the graves," but "other graves were marked by head boards without crosses."[70]

Not only did men enter into the service of the HBC at a critical stage in the life cycle, many of them remained for considerable periods of time. Most often they took local women as wives and very often had families. However long Hawaiians remained, they continued both to set themselves apart through drawing on each other and through being set apart by others. They made a life in the fur trade in good part on their own terms.

Chapter 6

HAWAIIANS IN THE
MISSIONARY ADVANCE

∿ THE CONTINUITY IN WORK ROUTINES that characterized the fur trade masked important shifts taking place in the Pacific Northwest. By the mid-1830s life was changing. Isolation from outside influences gave way to newcomers with a purpose. As had occurred in the Hawaiian Islands, missionaries were the forward flank. Their goal of conversion obscured the broader intent of sweeping indigenous people aside to make way for newcomers and their ways of life.

From the perspective of the early missionaries heading to the Pacific Northwest, the Islands gave a powerful example of what could be accomplished. Among the adventurous Hawaiians who hopped aboard trading vessels in the early nineteenth century was a young man immortalized as Obookiah. On arriving in New England, he became such an exemplary convert to Christianity that he inspired the American Board of Commissioners for Foreign Missions to make the Islands a prime target.[1] The same Boston group that opened up the Islands spurred the Pacific Northwest initiative. It was stories circulating in Honolulu, via trading vessels going back and forth, about the large numbers of indigenous peoples that turned attention in that direction. An Islands missionary who visited the Pacific Northwest in 1829 was absolutely convinced "that a mission to the North-West coast will soon be expedient, and that whenever it is expedient, it had better be attempted, probably, by some of the missionaries from the Sandwich Islands." In his view "the mission on the N.W. coast might be regarded as a branch of the Sandwich Island mission."[2]

Missionaries who headed to the Pacific Northwest maintained close contact with Hiram Bingham and the other missionaries in the Islands. Not only the Honolulu congregation but also Kamehameha III and his sisters contributed financially to the new venture. Even where missionaries came overland to the Pacific Northwest instead of via the Islands, they were comforted by how, as one of the earliest wives put it, "we are so near the Sandwich Island [*sic*] and can hear so often and directly from our missionaries there that we feel to be near neighbors to them." The feeling was mutual, an Islands missionary telling "our nearest neighbors" how "you seem to us like brethren."[3]

These early Protestant missionaries, sent by the American Board to convert what one contemporary termed "the wild Indians," were followed by other groups.[4] The HBC brought out an Anglican, or Episcopal, cleric in 1836 to tend principally to the officers and others of British background, and encouraged Oblates to preach to its French Canadian employees and, along the way, convert their Native wives and families. That left the Hawaiians, and the HBC eventually secured a missionary from Honolulu to provide them with similar services.

This first generation of missionaries did not much like, or trust, the indigenous peoples they had come to convert. It was Hawaiians who repeatedly navigated the missionaries' canoes, both literally and figuratively. A Presbyterian minister who visited Fort Vancouver in the autumn of 1835 was furnished with a canoe "propelled by Sandwich islanders, of whom there are many in this country, who have come here as sailors and laborers." Another missionary recorded as a matter of course having in the early 1840s "obtained two Indian canoes, and one white man, three Indians, and a Hawaiian to navigate them."[5] Just as Hawaiians sustained the maritime and land-based fur trades, they supported the missionaries with their labor.

American Board missionaries to the Pacific Northwest did not seek to convert the Hawaiians as a group. Individual missionaries might target persons in their employ, but there was never any large-scale effort comparable to that transforming the Islands. The exception was a visit by an Islands missionary, who in the spring of 1839 preached "in Hawaiʻian to some 8 or 10 in the Co. service." The event was not memorable. Asked a half century later if he could "recollect of any preaching to the Kanakas by any one," a Fort Vancouver employee responded, "Not as I know of."[6]

The first American Board missionary designated for the Oregon Territory was Methodist Jason Lee, who went west overland with Nathaniel Wyeth in 1834. He was, like the others who followed in his wake, sustained materially, emotionally, and spiritually by his Islands counterparts. With

HBC assistance, Lee established himself on the banks of the Willamette River about 10 miles from present-day Salem and secured the services of a dozen Hawaiians. Most of them were contracted directly from the Islands through the HBC's Honolulu agency at the going rate of travel expenses plus $10 a month in wages, board, and food. Some of their names survive as Mafinoa hired in 1835, Moo, Namaurooa, and Tooa in 1837, Bill Mahoy and Rora in 1838, and Long Jack in 1841. Often working in small groups, these men sustained the Methodist mission. They did everything from construction to kitchen work to blacksmithing to farm work to harvesting. A Hawaiian nicknamed George, possibly one of the men above, was described as "very useful in helping us" build the mission, as were the other men. In March 1838 George, then serving as the cook, was "building him[self] a house [a thatched hut] in the Sandwich Islands fashion, and has got one side covered with grass."[7] Much as occurred with Wyeth's Hawaiians, George used his ingenuity to maintain familiar ways.

In the fall of 1834 Jason Lee began a school, eventually enrolling three dozen Native pupils and also three Japanese shipwrecked along the coast. The mission record book recorded the next March 5: "J. Lee returned in health and safety from Vancouver, bringing with him Chas. Cohana a half breed youth, (who is now *admitted* [sic] into the family)."[8] The new arrival was almost certainly the seventeen-year-old son of longtime Fort Vancouver laborer Cawanaia, who arrived from the Islands in 1817.

Also attending school was "half breed" Thomas Pakee, the seven-year-old son of a disabled Hawaiian laborer who may have settled down nearby with a Chinook woman. Lee took particular pride in how Pakee was "received into the mission house" along with nine other "natives." Soon thereafter young Thomas grew ill from "a painful scrofulous disease," a form of tuberculosis. Missionary attention turned, not so much to a cure, as to signs of conversion. "In the latter part of his 'suffering time' his reason was partially lost; but his mind would dwell on religion, and he would often . . . desire to kneel at his knees and pray." From the missionary's perspective, Thomas Pakee "died in peace" in August 1839.[9] The next year, perhaps because of his death, his two younger siblings were baptized not Methodist but Catholic.

As did young Pakee, the Hawaiians in Lee's employ became surrogates for the local people he and the others found much more difficult to bend to their will. The attitude is caught in the diary entry of one of his missionary assistants:

> NOV. 21ST [1839]. Rora, the Hawaiian, a faithful servant of the mission, died in full assurance of a home in heaven. During the revival of religion last win-

ter he said to me, on referring to the happiness of the converted Indian boys, by-and-bye all do like that up there, pointing to the skies and smiling as he spoke. Pleasing reflection that Rora, the brown Islander, is now praising God in heaven with as favorable acceptance as the delicate European.

Two years later it was still "some whites and several Owyhees" who had to substitute during "a blessed revival" for the Native people whom missionaries like Lee were sent to convert.[10]

Like Nathaniel Wyeth, Jason Lee left an ambivalent legacy. When Charles Wilkes, head of the U.S. exploring expedition, visited Lee's mission in the spring of 1841, he was not impressed. "One of the first sights that caught my eye was a patent threshing machine in the middle of the road, that seemed to have been there for a length of time totally neglected." Wilkes recorded "an evident want of the attention required to keep things in repair, and an absence of neatness that I regretted much to witness." Informed the Methodists ran a school enrolling twenty, he encountered supposed students who "were nearly grown up, ragged and half-clothed, lounging about under the trees" whose "appearance was any thing but pleasing." Wilkes reflected how "I was greatly disappointed."[11]

Fellow Methodist missionary Gustavus Hines, who arrived in Oregon in 1840, put the blame on Jason Lee's reliance on the Hawaiians. Three years later he called attention to Lee's "numerous gang of 'Kanakas' whose labour does not pay their board, but who are paid ten dollars per month whether sick or well." Nor were they obliging as surrogate objects for conversion. Of 49 people Hines counted on the Methodist mission's books in 1843, 26 were "Whites," 19 Indian children, and just 4 Hawaiians, of whom one was "in full connexion," the other 3 "on trial." A missionary who was part of Lee's venture contended that "facilities have been furnished" in which the Hawaiians were free to meet "their own people for public worship as often as every sabbath."[12]

Hines's negative attitude toward the Hawaiians did not keep him from wanting one of his own. Jason Lee was recalled in 1843, amid questions about what he had accomplished for an expenditure of $100,000. He and Hines headed off to justify the mission, but Hines only got as far as the Islands before turning back for lack of passage to the United States. While in Honolulu Hines was one of the three men signing contracts with King Kamehameha III to acquire their own servants. Like the others, Hines agreed "to take care of him in sickness and in health, to provide him with suitable food and lodgings, according to the climate, and to observe in good faith the obligations which devolve on him as master." Unfortunately for

Hines, Kane decided he did not want to go home at the end of his contract. As the vessel was about to depart Oregon for the Islands in the summer of 1845, "the Boy Kane deserted from the Boat." Like the others, Hines had agreed to an indemnity of $200 should he not return his Hawaiian "unless Providentially prevented," but managed to avoid payment, not being considered culpable for Kane's action.[13] Kane has not been traced further.

Jason Lee's Hawaiians were successfully returned home through the good offices of the HBC, but with a hitch. His successor, who was mandated to make drastic cutbacks, found a huge unpaid bill for their services. "I supposed the Sandwich Islanders who were returned to Hudson Bay Company in June and July, 1844, were nearly paid, whereas for their labor and their return to the Islands, the mission has had to pay more than fifteen hundred dollars." Even though "supposed[ly] paid off" by Lee, his successor discovered "only one or two were settled with; there are ten or eleven to be settled with." Lee's wage of $10 a month he considered excessive, given Hawaiians "may be had for six." Not only that, the men had to be paid "for their service from the time they left Oahu." The financial situation got so desperate the wife of the missionary teacher was ordered "to let her Sandwich Islander go, but she replies that nothing would induce her to let him go except to save [her] life."[14] Given Jason Lee's shortcomings, the Hawaiians were likely the most solid aspect of his enterprise.

Other Protestant missionaries were not far behind the Methodists in arriving in Oregon Territory. Marcus and Narcissa Whitman, Henry and Eliza Spalding, and prospective missionary Henry Gray traveled to Oregon in 1836 under the auspices of the American Board. The Whitmans established themselves at Waiilatpu near the HBC's Fort Walla Walla, Henry and Eliza Spalding about 125 miles farther east at Lapwai in present-day Idaho. Among a second group arriving in 1838 were Gray returned with a bride and Asa and Sarah Smith, who after a short time at Waiilatpu established their own mission at Kamiah southeast of Lapwai. The Grays were assigned to the Lapwai mission. All of these couples relied on Hawaiians.

Having trekked overland from the United States for months on end, the missionaries stopped at Fort Vancouver to get their bearings. As Narcissa Whitman penned in her journal, "no person could have received a more hearty welcome, or be treated with greater kindness than we have been since our arrival." She reported home how "the means of sustenance and comfort" received from "the Gentlemen of the Hudsons Bay Company" was "so much beyond our expectations when we left home" as to call "for the most sincere praise and gratitude to God." Writing several years later, Henry Spalding echoed Narcissa's observation. "We have ever found the gentlemen of the Co. ready to favor us with supplies from their stores & by their means of conveyances. We could not expect more favors from a father than we have received from Doct McLoughlin & the same can be said of all the gentlemen of the Co. with whom we have had acquaintance."[15]

The HBC's assistance included advice on acquiring workers. Its appreciation of the Hawaiians in its employ meshed well with the Whitmans' understanding of the marvelous changes being wrought in the Islands by their fellow missionaries also under the American Board of Commissioners for Foreign Missions. One of them described at about the same time "the native churches," in which Hiram Bingham and a colleague "preached two sermons every sabbath in the Hawaiian language to immense congregations of natives." Marcus Whitman explained to a colleague: "We intend to send to Rev. Mr. Bingham of the Sandwich Islands for islanders, as laborers. Dr. McLoughlin offers to bring them for us."[16]

Whitman, Spalding, and Gray penned a joint letter to Bingham, explaining how "we find it difficult to obtain labourers here, & Doct McLoughlin advises us to send you for the Natives of the Sandwich Islands." The request was rather like an order for merchandise from a catalogue. "We contemplate two stations & on that account would like 6 men with their families. We want you to do us the favour to procure that number of good faithful men & send them by the first opportunity, probably in March." Not only was the order precisely stated, it added a second item as important as the first. The letter continued. "We would like them to bring families if possible that is their wives. We are anxious to obtain sheep & Doct McLoughlin proposes that we obtain as many as can be sent from the Islands, & wishes to share with us. Any number from 50 to 200 would be acceptable." The men assured Bingham that "Doct McLoughlin will write their Agent in Oahu to favor us with anything their ships can contain."[17]

On the Whitmans' departure from Fort Vancouver toward the end of 1836, they took with them "two Owyhees from Vancouver" as "labourers" to assist in putting their mission in order.[18] As with Jason Lee, the Whitmans would be responsible for their wages per the HBC's arrangement. The two men, recorded in HBC records as Nemanē and Jack Ropeyarn, undertook both outdoor and household tasks. As Narcissa explained to her family: "They make excellent cooks and house servants. Our men do their own cooking, and sometimes cook for me." The men also had other responsibilities. Going to visit the Spaldings, the Whitmans "took one man an Hawaiian to assist us" and left the other "to take care" of Waiilaptu in their absence.[19]

Narcissa Whitman was able to accommodate to her new circumstances in good part because of the Hawaiians' presence. She was somewhat ambivalent. After their first winter at Waiilatpu, she confided to her family: "Those two Owyhees will remain with us we know not how long. Here we are lost again, because they speak a different language."[20]

The birth of a daughter in March 1837 put greater household responsibilities on Narcissa. Her first reason for trusting Jack and Nina, as she called Nemanē, was because they had become indispensable. "They are the best for labor of any people this side of the mountains," for "the Indians do not love to work well enough for us to place any dependence upon them." She described herself as "a mother in heathen lands, among savages."[21] If similarly indigenous, the Hawaiians were for Narcissa and the other American missionaries an entirely different proposition.

Narcissa Whitman's second reason for trusting the Hawaiians was equally important. Like others of her generation, she was inspired by the story of Obookiah. "I find a peculiar tender feeling in my heart for these Islanders in consequence of my acquaintance with Obokiah's History." Viewing the Hawaiians through a far more romantic lens than she ever did the Cayuse that she and the others were there to convert, Narcissa Whitman identified them with her aspirations for the mission life. "They have kind and tender feelings, and their attachments are strong." Writing to her family in May 1837, she made a special request for the two men in the household: "Hope you will remember them especially in your prayers that they may learn a knowledge of the ways of salvation."[22] In another of her letters Narcissa found Jack Ropeyarn particularly praiseworthy for abandoning tobacco, changing his appearance, and giving his heart to God.

The comfort the Hawaiians gave the Whitmans may have been responsible for the head of Fort Vancouver placing young Mungo Marouna in their care in the fall of 1837. Ostensibly the ten-year-old was sent "for Medical aid," Marcus being trained as a doctor, but McLoughlin likely had broader motives. Mungo was in need of a family, and the Whitmans proved able and willing to take on the responsibility, so much so that Marcus decided "to build larger than we otherwise would" in order to accommodate him.[23] Mungo's situation echoed that of young Thomas Pakee. His mother was a Native woman, his father Marouna a Hawaiian recruited by the North West Company in 1817 who had spent the past two decades at or near Fort Vancouver. He was one of the men caught swiping blankets from the HBC vessel *William & Ann* for his wife in 1825. Whether or not he was already ill or incapacitated, Marouna would die at Fort Vancouver a year later.

Narcissa took special pleasure how young Mungo Mevway, as she called him, "gives pleasing evidence of a change of heart." She must have been reminded of Obookiah as she listened to "the lispings of his desires to God in prayer." After a year with the Whitmans, Mungo knew enough English to be able to communicate in what Narcissa termed "the first prattlings of an infant child." Whether or not she projected some wish fulfillment on him, Narcissa was genuinely saddened when news arrived of Marouna's death. "He has recently heard that his father is dead, which makes him feel very bad, and he cries; then he goes to Jesus and prays, and feels comforted."[24]

However much the Whitmans benefited from Mungo and the two men in their employ, they longed for more reputable Hawaiians. Marcus explained about Nemanē and Jack Ropeyarn how "I had some trouble with them on account of the Indian women, [they] having left their wives at home." According to Marcus, "The Indians are constantly asking them to take some of their women, & one asked liberty of me to do so a few days since," to which "I replied he had a wife at home & for that reason must not take one here." All the same, the Whitmans did not want to chance fate. Their solution was to request "two more from the Islands with their wives" to assist in "domestic labours."[25]

In October 1837 Marcus requested Bingham to send "two men & their wives by first opportunity." By this time the Whitmans were sufficiently experienced to realize that "if they understand English a little it would be desirable." A couple, "both members of Mr. Bingham's native church," arrived in June 1838. Marcus Whitman recorded in his accounts £12.10 for the "passage of an Hawaiian & wife from the Sandwich Isl." He considered he got good value for money, so he reported to Honolulu a few months later about the symbolically named Joseph and Maria Maki. "The man & wife you spoke of also came safely & in health & good spirits. They are likely to be very useful to us & their example good among the Indians. The health of the woman is much improved as you thought it might & she is now quite useful." The Makis did much of the rough work around the mission, Joseph "laying the floors, making the doors, etc." of the mission house.[26] Maria Keawea Maki acted as cook.

As well as being good workers, the Makis lived up to their religious billing. Marcus Whitman reported to the American Board how "the whole deportment of Mahai & wife has been eminently Christian amiable & devoted to the good of the Indians & the cause of Missions." He emphasized how "the patient & undeviating care of every trust would do honour in the performance of every duty." Hearing the Makis pray, Narcissa rhapsodized: "You cannot imagine how it strengthened our hearts . . . notwithstanding we could not understand a single word."[27]

In August 1838 the Whitmans and Spaldings organized the first Presbyterian church in Oregon at Waiilatpu. They admitted the Makis as the first two members. Spalding recorded the event for posterity:

> The following persons immediately presented letters & were admitted to our numbers viz
> Joseph Maki from the church in Honolulu, Oahu, Rev. Hiram Bingham, Missionary of the ABC.F.M., pastor . . .
> And Maria Keawea Maki wife of the above.[28]

According to Narcissa, the organizational meeting had a ripple effect. "Mungo continues to appear well & will be received to our little number when he is sufficiently instructed." Jack Ropeyarn had apparently undergone conversion. Narcissa described how "Jack, the Hawaiian" and one other "during the meeting think they have made a surrender of their hearts to God." As did thousands of missionaries across time, including their counterparts in the Islands, she wrestled with her inability to have certainty about Jack Ropeyarn's state of mind. He was just a little too alien for comfort. "There is a great change in his appearance. He has given up the use of tobacco. We are unable to understand him or make him understand us. He knows so little of our language & we can judge only from his outward appearance."[29]

A newly arriving missionary described the Whitmans' household at Waiilaptu as containing sixteen persons over the winter of 1838–1839. The missionaries, wives, and children made up eleven of these, Hawaiians there to serve them the remainder. "Five natives of the Sandwich Islands [were] then in the employ of Dr. Whitman, Joseph and his wife Maria, Jack, Mungo, and Havia [Nemanē]." As did the Whitmans, he took note of the Makis' special status as "members of the Sandwich Island church."[30]

It was young Marouna/Mevway who a year later helped search for the Whitmans' two-year-old daughter after she, according to her mother, "went to the river with two cups to get some water for the table." Narcissa explained how "I began to get alarmed for Mungo had just been in and said there were two cups in the river."[31] Her worst fears that her only child had drowned were confirmed shortly thereafter.

The Whitmans soon had another disappointment. Marcus lamented how "my labor was excessive last fall, after the death of our dear Joseph" in August 1840. "We had done but little towards cutting our wheat when he was taken ill." As had happened before, Joseph Maki took some medicine, likely prescribed by Marcus, and appeared to recover. Then, "from some reason perhaps eating unripe melons he was taken again with inflammation of the bowels, which proved rapid & incurable." Marcus described at some length how his dying "Brother and fellow labourer" wanted Bingham to know how "he came here to live & die for the good of the Indians, & it was good to *die here.*"[32]

Narcissa eulogized Joseph Maki at length, indicating the great extent to which she and Marcus had relied on the couple emotionally as well as practically to get their mission up and running. "Our loss is very great. He was so faithful and kind—always ready and anxious to relieve us of every care. . . . He died as a faithful Christian missionary dies—happy to work in the field—rejoiced that he was permitted to come and labor for the good of the Indians." She was equally concerned about Maria: "His wife is just as faithful, but she is a feeble person. I know not how I could do without her."[33] Maria Keawea Maki returned home the next year.

Mungo Marouna/Mevway left the Whitmans' household to work for the HBC about the same time Maria Maki departed in the fall of 1841. Part of the reason may be what Narcissa termed "his bad conduct." Marcus explained how "the boy whom we brought up, but who is now under engagement [with the HBC], has gone with Mr. [Cushing] Eells to assist at that station so that Mrs W & myself are alone with two small girls (half-breeds)."[34] The two, ages three and six, had been left in their care by their American frontiersmen fathers Jo Meek and Jim Bridger. Cushing Eells was an American Board missionary who came overland with his wife at the same time as the Smiths and Grays in 1838. The next spring the Eells established a mission among the Spokane Indians about 25 miles from present-day Spokane.

It is unclear whether the Whitmans had other Hawaiians in their employ. One of the principal activities at Waiilatpu intended to model suitable agricultural activities was to build up a large flock of sheep. The first sheep arrived from the Hawaiian Islands in the summer of 1838. Their tending caused the Whitmans to turn once again to Hiram Bingham, who this time proved unable to assist. The head of Fort Vancouver noted in the fall of 1840 how he had also written on the Whitmans' behalf to the Islands. "Mr. Bingham having failed in obtaining the Sandwich Islanders applied for by the Missions in the Columbia I engaged Seven men at Woahoo to assist in the management of Sheep."[35]

Mungo Marouna/Mevway continued to turn up from time to time in Narcissa's letters. A year after his departure she expressed relief that "Mungo appears quite humble—says he is sorry for his bad conduct." Mungo was being pragmatic. He had found himself a Native wife and, Narcissa wrote, "wants I should teach his wife to write or rather have her work for me."

According to Narcissa, Mungo had got her from a Native man who "had the first claim on her" at a cost of "4 horses, 1 gun, 1 coat, vest, pantaloons, leggings, 2 shorts and 100 loads of ammunition and a blanket."[36]

Whatever his past misdeeds, Narcissa considered Mungo to be a trusted friend and confidant. He arrived with his new wife the morning after she was terrified by a nighttime intruder while alone in Marcus's absence. "I told him about the Indian coming into my room—the first I spoke of it to any one." Mungo had an errand at Fort Walla Walla and, almost as a matter of course, left his wife with Narcissa. While at the HBC post, "Mungo told them of my fright," an initiative of which Narcissa heartily approved. The next Sunday Narcissa held "a Bible class in English" for Mungo and two others. Mungo and his wife continued to have close relations with the Whitmans, Marcus in 1845 sending dispatches with "Mungo & wife" to other missionaries.[37]

Narcissa Whitman depended far more than she publicly acknowledged on Hawaiians for both physical and emotional support, particularly during the first years when newcomer women like herself were a lone presence in a distant land. Nemanē and Jack Ropeyarn, the Makis, and Mungo Marouna legitimized for her the goal of indigenous conversion for which she and her husband had crossed a continent. She never accommodated to the Cayuse. The agonized phrases that crept into her letters home—"the greatest trial to a woman's feeling is to have her cooking and eating room always filled with four or five or more Indians," "they are so filthy they make a great deal of cleaning"—were not written out of malice but from recognition of a great gulf she was simply unable to cross.[38] The Hawaiians became surrogate Indians, aspirations for their conversion giving the fulfillment that made it possible for her to bear a difficult situation for years on end.

Mungo and his wife had a daughter Elizabeth, who in March 1848, three months after the Whitmans were massacred by the Cayuse along with several other members of their household, was baptized a Catholic. The act was almost certainly due to a serious illness, for young Elizabeth died a week later.[39] Clearly, the exposure to Christianity that Narcissa had given the young Mungo stuck if not the denominational specifics.

Much the same dependence on Hawaiians occurred with the Spaldings and Grays. Henry and Eliza Spalding, who came overland with the Whitmans, borrowed Jack Ropeyarn for a time during the winter of 1836–1837, but found him unsatisfactory. Established at their own mission of Lapwai, they decided, like the Whitmans, to seek out a more malleable Hawaiian directly from Bingham's Honolulu flock. In June 1838, the same time the Makis arrived to assist the Whitmans, Henry Spalding got an unnamed

Hawaiian directly from the Islands. At first Spalding did not put much trust in his new acquisition. He was so afraid to leave his few precious sheep with him when going to visit the Whitmans later the same summer that he drove his small flock with him to Waiilatpu.[40]

The Spaldings' "Hawaiian hired man" emerges from obscurity by virtue of rescuing him in the summer of 1840 after Spalding got into a scuffle with a young Indian. The unidentified Hawaiian "seized the Indian by the hair & handled him roughly when Mr. Sp. made his escape from him." The incident points up, once again, the distance that separated the Hawaiians from local Indians. Spalding sought at evening prayers "to get the chiefs to say that the Indian should be whipped." Not only did they disagree, they considered "that the Hawaiian should be whipped for pulling the Indian's hair."[41] For missionaries convinced they were wanted, yet untrusting of the persons they had come to convert, the Hawaiians were an integral middle force, in effect the only allies they had in this strange place apart from each other.

Henry Gray and his wife proved even less able to deal with the Hawaiians they acquired. They wanted a couple like the Makis, and in February 1840 Hiram Bingham informed the head of Fort Vancouver that "two natives of the Sandwich Islands, hopefully pious, *Iakobo* [Jacob] and his wife *Hamua,* have come from a district 30 miles distant, and offered themselves to go and render assistance to the mission in the Oregon, and at my request they take passage in the *Vancouver,* to be conveyed to Mr. Gray of the Oregon Mission, at his expense." Bingham "aided them in completing an outfit of clothing &c supposed to be sufficient for the voyage & journey," but that was all.[42] By this time the Honolulu mission was getting tired of the seemingly endless requests for assistance being put to them by their Oregon colleagues and determined they would not be out of pocket by them.

The young couple seemed an excellent find. "They offer their services freely, as assistants in diffusing the blessings of the gospel, and are not expecting monthly wages, but a comfortable support, instruction in the domestic arts, &c. unless it shall appear more agreeable to their wishes after they become settled to fix on a sum which shall be reasonable." At first the going was agreeable, but by the fall of 1842 Iakobo and Hamua wanted to return home and Gray arranged a passage in an HBC vessel only to have them decide to stay if paid a regular wage. Gray agreed on a three-year term at $10 per month, "the price usually paid for Hawaiians in this country."[43]

Nonetheless, the relationship deteriorated. By virtue of paying Iakobo and Hamua a salary, Gray expected more from them. He described in July 1843 how "they have had several stubborn fits, & two days since they told me they are going home, I suppose they will go for I shall not detain them, although we need some domestics in our family, & it puts us to considerable inconvenience at this time." Clearly far more was happening than Gray was willing to let on. It seems possible Iakobo and Hamua were intending to set out on their own, for "they have taken the liberty to sell and give away their clothes to Indians for horses & things they had no use for so that they will be quite destitute of clothing." Gray proposed to "pay what is coming to them for their passage home and allow them to dispose of the horses and things they have on hand, as they please," but to do nothing else for them.[44] Presumably, the couple returned home, although they may have stayed in the area.

Just as did the others, Asa and Sarah Smith drew on the good offices of the HBC to acquire a Hawaiian. In April 1839 they obtained Long Jack, who had previously assisted Catholic missionaries and would also work for Jason Lee, with the proviso that he be paid at the usual rate. Asa felt compelled to give the American Board a detailed justification for his actions. "In future I shall have in my employment one Owyhee who receives seventeen pounds per annum. This will be all that I shall need. It is necessary to have some assistance & Indians are not to be depended upon." As well as working around the mission, Jack accompanied the Smiths to the annual missionary meeting at Lapwai that fall.[45]

A little over a year later, Long Jack left. His reason for doing so underlines the importance of community to the Hawaiians spread across the Pacific Northwest. "In June [1840] the Hawaiian who had worked for me left, principally on account of his being alone, having none of his countrymen with him to converse with." Asa Smith's concern makes clear the full extent to which Jack was a servant, pure and simple. "During the summer we have worn our clothes without ironing." Smith looked for a solution to his Islands counterparts. "The trials connected with domestic assistance are by no means small. One Hawaiian is not contented alone. We must have two, or a man & his wife. I have accordingly written to the Islands for a Christian man & his wife to be sent out."[46]

In his lament over Long Jack's departure, Asa Smith described at length the place in the social order he considered the Hawaiians occupied. They existed in between the comfortable world he had left behind and the alien Native world to which he had come to minister.

> It is better to have Hawaiian help than to depend on Indians. It requires no small sum in the course of a year for Indian goods to pay for their work & when we get it, it amounts to but little. As we usually pay Indians, it is about half what the wages of a Hawaiian are, & yet all things considered, 4 Indians would

not be worth so much as one Hawaiian, & the Hawaiians are poor help compared with what can be had in the States. They are slow & awkward & at the best we have a great deal to do ourselves. One good faithful American I am sure would be worth more than 4 Hawaiians, & 4 Hawaiians would require more food than 8 Americans.[47]

The Smiths soon got Long Jack back. The HBC engaged him for another two years and once again subcontracted him. Asa was ambivalent, for Jack had never been as docile as he would prefer household help to be. "Tho' we need his help so much, we really felt some regret at his return. He had been so stubborn & so insolent to Mrs. S. at many times that we found he would be a great trial to us." Not only that, "he has come back an awful smoker." Asa effected a compromise whereby Jack would not "smoke in the house" or "with the Indians on my premises."[48]

Long Jack proved his worth. The Nez Perces the Smiths were attempting to convert were not only ungrateful, they wanted the Smiths off their land. Jack became a critical support. Asa recounted how, in October 1840, a few days after Jack's return, the Nez Perces "ordered me in the most absolute terms to leave on the morrow." Asa Smith's diary entry captures the drama of the event. "Mrs. S. was very much frightened at their rage & ran out to call Jack. He came but one of them tried to prevent his coming in. I seized the latch & Jack forced himself in." Repeated threats over the next twenty-four hours made Sarah Smith even more frightened. "Mrs. S. is in great fear & is nearly sick in consequence of it. Jack slept in the kitchen last night & does tonight. Today he has been sharpening his knife & tonight laid it by his side ready for an attack if they should break into the place."[49] The Smiths could not withstand the pressure and within a few months decided to leave Kamiah, whereupon Jack slips from view. The Smiths departed in the fall of 1841, taking Maria Maki with them as far as their Honolulu stop on the way back to the United States.

The other American Board missionaries followed in the model of the Whitmans, Spaldings, Grays, and Smiths. Or they tried to. A missionary who in August 1843 requested "a Hawaiian and wife to come and assist us in our domestic affairs" was turned down, likely due to the difficulties with the other two couples who had been sent. In lamenting the rejection, he acknowledged that "there has been too much disregard of the spiritual interests of the Hawaiians in this country."[50] Others were more successful. By arrangement with the head of Fort Vancouver, Cushing Eells and his wife Myra borrowed Mungo Marouna from the HBC for years on end. In 1847, by then married with a young family, twenty-year-old Marouna decided to fend for himself. Drawing on the English skills acquired from his upbringing by the Whitmans and service with the Eells, Marouna established himself as an interpreter and guide based in the Willamette Valley.

Despite the contribution of Hawaiians to the American missionary advance, it did not achieve its stated objectives. The Jason Lee financial debacle and then the murder of the Whitmans were far less decisive than were structural factors. George Simpson observed during his third visit to the Pacific Northwest in 1841 how "the American missionaries are making more rapid progress in the extension of their establishment and in the improvement of their farms, than in the ostensible object of their residence in this country."[51] The next year the American Board of Commissioners for Foreign Missions decided to close its principal Oregon stations, and it was only the determination of Marcus Whitman that prevented their decision being enacted. His murder and that of his wife Narcissa and the others six years later doomed the enterprise.

It was the Hawaiians who prevented a greater debacle. By virtue of serving as surrogates for the real thing, they kept missionaries from having to confront their general dislike of the Native peoples they had come to convert. The early missionaries made little attempt to understand local peoples' ways of life or to meet them part way, as did the HBC, if for very different purposes. On the other hand, missionaries like Jason Lee and the Whitmans, Spaldings, and Smiths were enormously important for marking out the Oregon Territory as an American possession.

The arrival of an Anglican, or Episcopalian, presence at Fort Vancouver corresponded almost to the day with that of the Whitmans and Spaldings in September 1836. The impetus was, however, very different. The HBC was an English enterprise, and England was officially an Anglican country, so it was inevitable that sooner or later an Anglican, or Episcopalian, minister would be dispatched to Fort Vancouver. The attitude of superiority that Rev. Herbert Beaver and his wife Jane displayed toward the American missionaries foretold their inability to condone difference of any kind, much less the difference that the Hawaiians represented. The head of Fort Vancouver and of the Columbia District, John McLoughlin, requested Narcissa Whitman and Eliza Spalding to mentor his daughter Maria while at the post on their arrival. They were pleased to do so, only to have Beaver summarily inform them that they "will refrain from teaching, in any respect, the children," since the HBC in London had given him sole charge of their welfare.[52]

Rev. Beaver almost immediately fell out with the head of the Columbia Department, and, for that matter, with almost everyone he met. Beaver expected a proper church at the ready for him, symbolizing the authority he considered he possessed over the lives of the fur traders. McLoughlin and the others were comfortable in their existing ways of life, including their de facto unions with Native or mixed-race women. Short months after his arrival Beaver raged to HBC authorities in London: "No legal marriage, no regular Baptism, no accustomed rites of Burial; Men, for the most part, not practicing, and women totally ignorant of the duties of religion."[53] Despite the HBC's expectation that Beaver would also minister to Native people, he deemed it beneath his dignity to do so.

The thirty to thirty-five Hawaiians at work at Fort Vancouver did not figure into Beaver's terms of reference, except when useful to exert his authority. Despite the couple's demand for a servant or two, they rejected "a decent, active, married Sandwich Islander and his wife" offered to them. Beaver considered that, "as his residence here would be short, the trouble of teaching them would not be compensated by their subsequent utility."[54]

Beaver had absolutely no interest in preaching to the Hawaiians. Only in his final letter home, after two years of wrangling, did he acknowledge their presence and then to his own ends. In his view, "the little Christianity, which they brought with them, becomes speedily forgotten and lost, and their former good, but unstable, principles are quickly undermined by the inroads of surrounding corruption." Beaver later went further, asserting that not only did "they soon lose the Christian instruction which has been imparted on them by their excellent missionaries at home; they revert to the abdominal practices of their idolatrous times, and form connexions with the Indians, to whose level they speedily sink."[55]

Rev. Beaver was, in his correspondence, far more outwardly racist toward the Hawaiians than were his American missionary counterparts. "Removed from the eyes of their Pastors [in the Islands], these half-reclaimed savages have, in several cases, reverted to certain abominable practices of their idolatrous times." Beaver was particularly outraged at being expected to read "our burial office" for "a Sandwich Islander of old standing." He considered it "highly important that the Heathen around us should not behold the rights of Christianity administered to persons, who are not Christians." It was young Mungo's father Marouna who had died. Beaver was even more outraged that, after his refusal to hold a service for Marouna, an HBC officer did so as "a tribute of respect to the departed."[56]

Beaver offered two suggestions concerning the Hawaiians, neither of which required any effort on his part. The first was for the HBC's agent in Honolulu "to institute minute enquiries into the characters of the Kanakas, who may be shipped for the Columbia River, whither none would be allowed to proceed, on whose steadfastness in well-doing a reasonably grounded reliance cannot be placed by the missionaries, who should be consulted, and from whom they should all bring to your Chaplain a certificate of Baptism." The second suggestion was "the introduction among them, with his wife, of one of their more than ordinarily respectable countrymen, who might act as a kind of overseer over them, and preside over their religious exercises, for which a small building, should be set apart." Despite during his two years at Fort Vancouver having demanded a high level of comfort for himself and his wife, Beaver emphasized that such a person should not "require a greater rate of wages, than that usually given."[57]

Rev. Herbert Beaver's vendetta did not end with his departure. He did his best to undermine "the Hudson's Bay Company's settlements on the River Columbia." Four years after departing the Pacific Northwest, he wrote a long letter to the Aborigines' Protection Society of London. Having listed every possible HBC transgression against the very same Native people about whom he cared nothing when there, Beaver turned his attention to the Hawaiians. In his retrospective view, "their condition is little better than that of slavery, being subject to all the imperious treatment which their employers may think fit to lay on them, whether by flogging, imprisonment, or otherwise, without a possibility of obtaining redress." He described a Hawaiian being "severely flogged" for "making a trifling mistake" due to "his ignorance of the language in which they were conveyed." Two others were meant to have died of ill treatment, one on the way to the Pacific Northwest from "a flogging he had received for stealing a pig," the second "of a wound inflicted on his head by the commander of one of the Company's vessels," which was put down to apoplexy.[58] It is difficult not to conclude that Beaver was subject to overstatement and, more important, that his charges concerning the Hawaiians were simply one more means to get at the HBC itself, including its officers and employees who dared to consort with their Indian inferiors.

One of the reasons behind the HBC's antipathy toward Rev. Beaver, apart from his unpleasant character, was his religious affiliation. The head of the Columbia District considered that the HBC's far greater need was for a Catholic priest, given that, as Narcissa Whitman soon appreciated, "most of the people here are Roman Catholics." Not just McLoughlin himself but most employees were Catholic. Narcissa was told, while at Fort Vancouver at the time of Beaver's arrival in the autumn of 1836, "they have been expecting a Roman Catholic priest this fall from Canada, but he does not come; none can be found who will come is the excuse."[59]

Catholic missionaries were not far behind their Protestant counterparts. Jason Lee's arrival in the Willamette Valley caused French Canadians settling nearby to request a Catholic priest, an action met with disdain by the Methodists. "I pity from my heart the catholic Canadian French they are so ignorant" for preferring "the agents of antichrist," one of the Methodist missionaries intoned to his counterpart in the Islands.[60] Oblate fathers François Blanchet and Modeste Demers arrived in 1838 and, with the assistance of the Hawaiian Long Jack, fanned out across the HBC posts to minister to Catholic employees. Unlike the other missionaries, the Catholics itinerated to wherever potential converts were to be found.

Nothing testifies more forcefully to the Catholics' capacity than the venom expressed toward them by other missionaries. Even while acknowledging their standards for religious conversion effectively precluded Native people—to quote Henry Spalding, "although I have not admitted any to the church as yet, many give pleasing evidence of being born again"—they lambasted the Catholics for daring to try where they had failed.[61] Narcissa Whitman expressed the dominant sentiment in writing four years after the first Oblates' arrival: "Romanism stalks abroad on our right hand and on our left, and with daring effrontery. . . . The zeal and energy of the priests are without a parallel, and many, both white men and Indians, wander after the beasts." [62]

Much like the Presbyterians, the Oblates used their contacts in the Islands to get needed help. In March 1842 a Catholic missionary in the Islands sent Demers three unnamed Hawaiians. Common wisdom among Catholics in Honolulu had some five hundred Hawaiians, "all pagans," or three times the actual number, at work in the fur trade in the Pacific Northwest, making it very attractive to have assistants able to speak their language and so convert their countrymen to Catholicism.[63] The missionary who dispatched the Hawaiian trio ran a school in Honolulu enrolling over two hundred pupils, and they may have been drawn from its numbers. The published correspondence of the Oblate missionaries contains no subsequent references to these three men, nor does it indicate any significant interest in the conversion of Hawaiians. The Catholics' immediate attention was on Native people, French Canadians, and other "white" newcomers.

All of these missionary efforts were not lost on the Hawaiians. A man some two decades in the Pacific Northwest attempted to persuade Indians not to pay any attention to the Catholic newcomers. An HBC clerk reported in April 1839 how "the Old Chief See-yah-sa-soot's Clicat-tat son arrived from Vancouver where he was told by an Owhyhee, Como, that the Catholic Priests were no Chief but bad men from the infernal regions to disturb the Indians in the good faith."[64] Como nonetheless permitted his children by a local woman named Nancy to be baptized Catholic, even though he did not himself believe. The priest obligingly described the parents as "both infidels."[65] Men like Como and the Whitman's Mungo Marouna/Mevway were taking no chances. Baptism functioned as an insurance policy just in case the priests' notions of the afterlife were correct.

Whereas most Hawaiians did not themselves attend the Catholic church, some of them came under its influence through their wives. A Catholic at Fort Vancouver in the summer of 1844 recalled how "the people coming and going from that church" were "Canadians" and "their wives," in contrast to which the post's "Sandwich Islanders, Scotchmen, and a few Englishmen, they did not go to the church."[66] A Scot Presbyterian employee with a Native wife explained how "the Indian women who were married to the servants of the Hudsons Bay Company belonged to the Catholic Church."[67] To encourage their presence, recalled another employee, "the preaching was in French and [Chinook] Jargon."[68] Children like Jeanne born in 1832 and Philomena in 1840 were baptized Catholic, very likely at their mothers' instigation, their fathers identified only as a "Owyhee" or "Kanaka."[69]

The insurance policy of baptism was easier to acquire than was marriage. According to the tinsmith at Fort Vancouver during the late 1830s, the priest did not marry everyone who was living together as soon as he "got in, late in the fall of 1838." In his recollection: "It took the priests some three or four months before they could instruct these [Indian] women as to what marriage meant and what baptism meant. He baptized them before marriage. They did not allow them to live together as man and wife while they were being instructed."[70]

It was mostly long-term employees who took advantage of the priests to have their children baptized, or perhaps it was their wives who took the initiative. Dick had worked in the fur trade for over two decades at the time his sons Richard and James were baptized Catholic in 1838, Ta-i and Wavacareea a dozen years each on their sons' baptisms in 1841. George Borabora was with the HBC for over a dozen years at the time his daughter Catherine was baptized in 1849, Kamakeha and Ohia each a dozen years on their offsprings' baptism in 1852. Like Mungo Marouna, both Cawanaia and Keekanah opted for a double dose. Their daughters Angelique and Cecilia were baptized by Rev. Beaver and, on his departure, as Catholics. A few men had their marriages formalized in the church, including John Bull and Keavé in 1849 and Kaluaikai on his deathbed in 1853. Each time Spunyarn had a child baptized at Fort Vancouver, he was recorded as Spaniard or

L'Espagnol, which was how the Catholic priest heard his name. These men's initiatives signaled their principal loyalty had transferred to the Pacific Northwest.

The growing number of missionaries of all denominations caused the head of the Columbia Department to reflect on Beaver's suggestion of a Hawaiian counterpart to take charge of the Hawaiians' spiritual and educational welfare. McLoughlin may well have been influenced by the missionaries' occasional observations that "the condition of the Hawaiians in this country is deplorable." One of them lamented to his Hawaiian counterpart in 1842 how "they work as busily on Sabbath as on any other day," clearly unaware that that was the only time for HBC employees to attend to familial obligations. The exception was "those among us [who] have meetings among themselves every Sabbath, some of them are no doubt pious, but they all need books, etc." He requested "some Hawaiian Bibles, testament hymns, tracts, etc." but at the same time considered himself unable to make much use of them. "I have thought seriously of attempting to learn their language," but was fully occupied.[71]

So the HBC acted. In the summer of 1844 McLoughlin requested the Honolulu agency "to search out a trusty educated Hawaiian of good character to read the scriptures and assemble his people for public worship." Even though McLoughlin expected the individual to serve as teacher, religious instructor, and interpreter, he was niggardly on wages. "You may give him £10 per annum," which was a little over half the usual wage.[72] In the event McLoughlin paid him £40, twice the wage of his countrymen.

Gerritt Parmele Judd, a leading missionary to the Honolulu congregation, persuaded William Kaulehelehe to accept the position, lauding him as having "a good character and high recommendation as a faithful, industrious Skillful Teacher and in regular standing as a member of the church." As an added advantage, this proposed "Chaplain to the Hawaiians in the Columbia" would be accompanied by his wife Mary S. Kaai, who "is highly recommended to me."[73] William, and perhaps also his wife, was highly literate in Hawaiian.

The couple was allocated the school house at Fort Vancouver for Sunday services, which soon became known as the Owyhee Church. The head of the post reported in January 1845 that Kanaka William, as he became known, was both satisfied and giving satisfaction, apart from his ignorance of English. He "seems to exercise a salutary influence on the minds of his countrymen."[74] The next June the Kaulehelehes set up residence in Kanaka Village.

The easy optimism was soon dispelled. The Hawaiians were comfortable with their lifestyle. Even though almost all of them had left the Islands after the missionaries' arrival and their major effort at mass literacy, they did not view acceptance of the precepts of missionary Christianity as part of their job description. William Kaulehelehe described how "during the days we were living with the Hawaiians there was much abuse, malicious speaking, a very few people loved us." As to the reason, "we wanted them to observe the Sabbath," but "on that day they did their carpentering, horse riding, agriculturing and the like." The situation became so tense that the couple had to be taken back into "the enclosure."

William Kaulehelehe and his wife Mary on a visiting card made after moving to Victoria in the early 1860s. British Columbia Archives, no. 56784.

William Kaulehelehe found himself in an impossible situation. To the extent he was welcomed by his countrymen, it was as someone who could resolve their grievances. The Hawaiians increasingly found themselves objects of discrimination by newcomers. Here there was, they thought, someone sent from their homeland, and from their king, who had their best interests at heart. "The Hawaiians have repeatedly and daily asked me to see about their trouble of being repeatedly abused by the white people without any cause." The difficulty was that the newcomer had no authority to interfere. "They thought I had come as an officer to settle their difficulties. I said no. I did not come to do these things. I had no instructions from the king and ministers of the government of Hawaii to do these things." The explanation did nothing to mollify the men. "They were not satisfied," William Kaulehelehe explained to his Hawaiian protector.

A Congregational missionary newly arrived at Fort Vancouver in 1848 was very impressed by how "a converted heathen has left his country and become a Christian missionary to his countrymen abroad." At the same time George Atkinson could not resist a few barbs reflecting his assumptions about right behavior. "Has not been ordained. Has no church and few members. Has from twenty to forty hearers, every Sabbath. Has much difficulty to keep them from drinking." For Atkinson, alcohol was particularly sinful. As to its source, he was forced to acknowledge about his own countrymen, "some Americans bring it over and sell it clandestinely just below the fort to all classes." According to Atkinson, Kaulehelehe's obligation extended to "a weekly report on those who drank on the week or Saturday previous."[75]

William Kaulehelehe made small gains. "There is a little order on Sundays now, not like former times when there was much disturbance," he reported back to Honolulu. He also, according to a contemporary, "preached to the Kanakas in their camp among their houses."[76] Over time he learned to compromise and also to justify his compromises. "Men and women have attended the two meetings on each Sunday. But on account of daily labor we have not found time to conduct school and meeting. We thought of conducting a school at night but can't because the nights are short."

Not so much as converts but more generally as intermediaries, the Hawaiians played an important role during the missionary thrust into Oregon Territory. The Native people who were the goal of the exercise did not respond nearly as obligingly as hoped. "They appear to feel that their customs are of equal authority with the commands of God," one of the missionaries despaired to a counterpart in Honolulu.[77] A visitor in 1846, with one possible exception, "could hear of no attempts going on to educate or convert the aborigines of the country by Americans."[78] It is not surprising that, repeatedly, the Hawaiians became the missionaries' protectors against the very people they were there to save. With the exception of the Makis and possibly Iakobo and Hamua, they did so not as converts but out of concern for their fellow human beings, be they missionaries or not. The Hawaiians' service cannot be overestimated.

Chapter 7

BOUNDARY MAKING

〜⁀〉 THE CRITICAL MARKER for Hawaiians in the Pacific Northwest was 1846. That year Britain and the United States agreed on an international boundary. The Treaty of Washington extended the border west along the 49th parallel and then south around Vancouver Island. The agreement respected property belonging to the Hudson's Bay Company, its Puget Sound Agricultural Company subsidiary, and British subjects. No one noticed or perhaps cared about the two hundred Hawaiians then employed by the HBC.

The boundary settlement did not occur in a vacuum. Its origins harked back to the War of 1812, after which the Pacific Northwest existed in a kind of political limbo. The immediate basis to the 1846 agreement lay with changing demographics. The hopes once held by the HBC that the international border would run along the Columbia River were dashed by growing American settlement. The Oregon Territory, comprising the future states of Oregon, Washington, and Idaho, already existed in practice and would be formalized two years later in 1848.

The missionaries had been the forward flank. They may not have saved that many Native souls, but they brought the Pacific Northwest into the American orbit. Their arrival in the 1830s, in the wake of Nathaniel J. Wyeth, caught the popular imagination. Their actions inspired growing numbers of Americans to make their way west by what became known as the Oregon Trail. In the spring of 1840, Narcissa Whitman recorded how "a tide of immigration appears to be moving this way rapidly." Three years later she was convinced that "Oregon will be occupied by American citizens." The head of the Columbia District reported in the fall of 1844 how "the immigrants on the way to this place are said to amount to twelve hundred persons." Four years later a missionary a dozen years in the Pacific Northwest explained with pride to a new arrival how "its population has doubled every year since then, 5 families in 1836, 10 in 1837, making at the end of 1848 20,000."[1]

Settlement did not originate only with Americans coming overland. By 1838, according to an HBC estimate, the settlement at Willamette contained twenty-three "Canadians formerly in the service," eighteen Americans, and ten persons attached to the Methodist mission. There was, HBC officer James Douglas wrote that year, "a restless desire, in the Company's servants, to escape from our service to the Colony." Men wanted a more ordinary life, what most of them had experienced growing up in the Orkneys, in French Canada, or elsewhere. The American naval officer examining Oregon in 1846 recorded how "almost every one, upon the expiration of his five years' service, fixed himself upon a piece of land and became a cultivator."[2]

The men in charge of the fur trade were very aware of the implications of the changes going on around them. They could only watch as the very bases for the trade slipped away. Not only was it more difficult to maintain a workforce, Native people were acquiring options other than trading in pelts. James Douglas, in charge of Fort Vancouver in McLoughlin's absence, reflected in 1838: "The interests of the Colony, and the Fur Trade will never harmonize, the former can flourish, only, through the protection of equal laws, the influence of free trade, the accession of respectable inhabitants; in short by establishing a new order of things, while the fur Trade, must suffer by each innovation."[3]

All the same, it is important to record, the HBC did not hinder newcomers but rather, as with Wyeth and the missionaries, sustained them as a matter of course. A member of the U.S. exploring expedition that visited Fort Vancouver in 1841 expressed surprise how "American missionaries had frequently stopped here for weeks & months with their wives partaking of the Company's hospitality and attended by the Company's servants gratis." A family reaching the post in December 1844 was given a place "to lodge, and a good supper." The American naval officer sent two years later to examine the situation in the Oregon Territory found his "wants of every kind were immediately supplied by the Hudson's Bay Company." He ended up more than a little perturbed by how "the amount of debt due the company by Americans exceeded eighty thousand dollars." There was "so little disposition" to pay up the HBC was forced "to refuse any further credits."[4]

The HBC's policy did little to change the attitudes of Americans determined to fold the Oregon Territory, as it was becoming known, into the United States. The HBC's generosity was not always reciprocated. In November 1839 McLoughlin wrote to the company's agent in Honolulu on behalf of an American who had settled in the Willamette Valley. Ewing Young sought two Hawaiians, promising travel and the going rate of $10 per month. At least one of them ended up being abandoned. A visitor a few months after Young's death in early 1841 found his enterprise vacant except for "a sick man, a native of the Sandwich Islands, lying in a bunk." A mechanic arrived with the first missionary couples recalled over sixty years later "having considerable prejudice as an American citizen, against the Hudson's Bay Company and its influences here." Time had not softened his views. "I consider the company the vilest of the vile."[5]

Men in the fur trade were very aware of the political, as well as economic, consequences of settlement. Douglas felt "oppressive anxiety" over "the yearly increasing difficulties which, every one, acquainted with our affairs, must anticipate from the collision of the foreign and independent interests, growing up on every side, around us." He had good reason to be concerned. As early as 1838, a bill was introduced into the U.S. Congress authorizing the president to occupy the Oregon Territory. To the extent the Hawaiians were acknowledged, the congressional committee appointed to investigate the area's prospects noted that the Fort Vancouver "sawmill cuts 2,000 to 2,400 feet of lumber daily; employs 28 men, chiefly Sandwich Islanders."[6]

Hawaiians lost out several times over with the boundary settlement. Even though they came as sojourners, as contract workers for the HBC, they did so at a time in the life span when they were looking to the future. A commitment to family life encouraged their continued residence in the Pacific Northwest. Boundary making caused a very different society to come into being in the American Pacific Northwest than that familiar to the Hawaiians by virtue of their employment by the Hudson's Bay and Puget Sound Agricultural companies. The attributes that made them attractive workers were not valued by newcomers to the Oregon Territory.

Two generally held attitudes impinged mightily on the Hawaiians. The first was strong American antipathy toward Britain, harking back to the struggle for independence from the former mother country, still in living memory. An early missionary to Oregon penned nostalgically in his journal on July 4, 1835: "Four years since the death of my father & 59 since the declaration of independence of the United States." The Hudson's Bay Company was emblematic of the yoke that the United States had overthrown. Missionaries and settlers might be individually grateful for the sustenance they received, but it made them no less antagonistic toward an enterprise that they considered an imposition on land manifestly destined to be theirs. As a young HBC clerk recalled, "Britishers were looked upon as intruders, without a particle of right to be there."[7] By virtue of their employment, the Hawaiians were identified with the HBC and thereby just as unwanted as was the company itself.

Far more critical to the Hawaiians' future were attitudes toward race. Newcomers could not help but be struck by Hawaiians' physical appearance. Persons whose vessels stopped in the Islands on the way to the Pacific Northwest were somewhat prepared, but those who came by land, as was increasingly the case, were not. An American arrived overland from the United States in 1832 put in words what many others felt. "Stopped over night at a sawmill of the [Hudson's Bay] company on a creek, and saw there, two strange looking men, saw at once that could be neither Caucasian, Indian or African. And so it proved, they were Kanakas, Sandwich Islanders, in the employ of the traders."[8]

Even HBC head George Simpson was not quite prepared, on visiting the Islands in 1842, to experience indigenous Hawaiians close up. Skin tones were the critical marker. "In complexion, the natives look like a connecting link between the red man and the negro, being darker than the former, though still removed many degrees from the sooty hue of the latter." Next to pigment, hair mattered. "They occupy the same intermediate position: in all of them it is black; curling, or rather waving and undulating in general."[9]

Many newcomers' attitudes went beyond surprise into ridicule and discrimination. The two groups with which the Hawaiians were most often compared, blacks and Native peoples, were both vigorously disliked. The dominant attitude toward Indians is captured in Wyeth's comparison of "the Hideous squaw with the polished white woman, the faithless savage with the upright and busy white man." Missionaries were, if anything, even more disparaging about the persons to whom they had come to minister. Narcissa Whitman lamented to her mother how "they are an exceedingly proud, haughty and insolent people." A Methodist missionary who arrived in 1840 described local Indians three years later as "perishing heathen" and "a stupid and melancholy doomed race of men."[10] Missionaries' response presaged, and legitimized, a much more broadly based set of attitudes that would cause Native peoples to be treated abominably across the American Pacific Northwest.

Not just Hawaiians' indigenous origins, but the relationships that they, like other men in the fur trade, formed with Native women worked to their disadvantage. When the various missionaries met for their annual meeting in February 1839, Marcus Whitman was reproved for daring to marry a nearby French Canadian settler to a Nez Perce woman, even though the groom was one of the charter members of the Presbyterian church on its formation the previous August. About the same time the head of a nearby fur trade post sought to engage his mixed-race daughter to a young Presbyterian missionary. Narcissa Whitman "did not consider her worthy of him" by virtue of being a "half breed" as well as a Catholic, and thwarted the union. The missionaries led the way to what became a more general attitude. John McLoughlin reported in March 1845 how "some of the Immigrants last come have said that every man who has an Indian wife ought to be driven out of the Country, and that the half breeds should not be allowed to hold lands."[11]

If Native people were actively disliked, persons perceived to be black in skin color were abhorred. The Oregon Provisional Government established in 1848 enacted legislation to keep out not just slaves but freed and free blacks. "Be it enacted by the Legislative Committee of Oregon . . . that when any free Negro or Mulatto shall have come to Oregon he or she, as the case may be, if of the age of eighteen or upwards shall remove from and leave the country within the term of two years for males and three for females." Any person who did not do so "shall receive upon his or her bare back not less than twenty nor more than thirty stripes" and every six months thereafter until "he or she shall quit the Country."[12]

A number of Hawaiians were nonetheless determined to acquire the rights accorded newcomers to the Oregon Territory. A missionary visiting from the Islands described how "some Hawaiians presented themselves before the proper officers, and desired to become American citizens, and be allowed to vote in the coming election on the lst of June [1849], but the Governor did not feel authorized by the existing laws of the U.S. to allow them to do it." The governor referred the issue to the supreme judge of the territory, and the Hawaiians were excluded on the basis of federal legislation limiting naturalized citizenship to white males. The 1849 Oregon Census, entitled "an enumeration of the inhabitants and qualified voters," did not bother to count Hawaiians. The best men could hope for was, as in the U.S. Census the next year, to be called "dark Hawaiian," as were Nisqually employees Kahannui, Kalama, and Kupahi, better yet "dark Hawaiian, not black," as was Joe Tapou.[13]

The same year, 1850, the U.S. Congress passed a land grant act for the Oregon Territory. Through the determination of the territorial delegate, Samuel R. Thurston, Hawaiians were excluded from applying for land grants and from ownership of lands already occupied. Thurston's argument, reflecting local sentiment, linked racial prejudice with the general dislike of the HBC. He spoke out against a proposed amendment to the bill on the grounds that "it would give land to every servant of the Hudson's Bay Company, including some hundreds of Canakers, or Sandwich Islanders, who are a race of men as black as your negroes of the South, and a race, too, that we do not desire to settle in Oregon." [14]

Thurston subsequently moderated his position toward the HBC, making clear that race was the fundamental issue. "Those foreigners in Oregon, who have left the company, or shall leave it, and prove their love of our country by completing their final oath of love and allegiance, should have an appropriation, and be taken into the fold of American citizenship—aye, sir, should have a donation of land; but I am not for giving land to Sandwich Islanders or negroes. I have no fears of defining my position here." Noting recent Oregon territorial legislation excluding free blacks from the territory, Thurston pronounced that "the Canakers and negroes, if allowed to come there, will commingle with our Indians, a mixed-race will ensue, and the result will be wars and bloodshed in Oregon." [15] The final wording of the Donation Land Act of 1850 provided for land grants to "every white male settler or occupant of the public lands, American half breeds included," but not Hawaiians. [16]

Hawaiians were given repeated signals that they did not belong in the Oregon Territory and, after it became separate in 1853, in Washington Territory. Not only were Hawaiians in Oregon unable to acquire a land grant or be naturalized or vote, they also could not purchase liquor or testify against whites in the courts. In 1858 Washington Territory made it a crime to sell liquor to "Kanakas." Legislation passed in Oregon in 1862 decreed that "each and every negro, chinaman, kanaka, and mulatto, residing within the limits of this state, shall pay an annual poll-tax of five dollars," or be subject to "forced labor for the state" until the tax was paid along with "the expenses of arrest." Oregon also made it illegal for any white person to intermarry with any "Negro, Chinese, or any person having one-quarter or more Negro, Chinese, or Kanaka blood, or any person having more than one-half Indian blood." The penalty for engaging in or performing such a ceremony was imprisonment up to a year. The ban would stay on the books until 1951. [17] Washington's similar prohibition did not extend to Hawaiians, being less visible there.

For a time Hawaiians continued to have, at least, secure jobs. The boundary settlement did not immediately doom the fur trade south of the border. As well as protecting existing rights, the 1846 boundary agreement gave the Hudson's Bay Company a considerable period of time for winding down operations. A lengthy dispute over what constituted adequate compensation for property encouraged the HBC and PSAC to continue operations as long as possible in the hopes of securing the highest possible value. The United States was just as determined to secure its presence and established military posts close to HBC posts, including Fort Vancouver near the fur trade post of the same name and Fort Steilacoom close to Nisqually.

At the time of the boundary settlement in 1846, Fort Vancouver was a very large operation, employing some two hundred men, over half of them Hawaiians. A woman there from 1846 to 1848 recalled "principally Kanakas and Canadian French and some Scotchmen" in the HBC employ. She described how "they were farming, sometimes making hay, taking care of sheep, hogs and farming." A visitor in June 1848 reported 15,000 to 20,000 sheep in three different flocks. "We saw them shearing sheep, Indians, Kanakas, Scotch, &c." As operations wound down, numbers of Hawaiians declined. According to a Catholic priest at Fort Vancouver, by 1848 "the village contained perhaps fifty buildings, occupied by whites, half-breeds and Kanakas."[18] The order in which employees were listed had shifted, Hawaiians coming third. The number working there fell from a high of 119 at the time of the boundary settlement to 71 by 1848 and 34 two years later.

Among the Hawaiians who continued to make their livelihoods at Fort Vancouver was John Cox, among the very first group of Hawaiians to arrive at Astoria. A swineherd, he made his everyday livelihood on grazing land just south of the post called in his honor Cox's Plain or Coxland. A missionary visiting from the Islands in the spring of 1849 first ran into William Kaulehelehe, who lamented how he was "laboring under serious hindrances" in consequence of so many of his countrymen "becoming *palaka* (indifferent to religion)." He took the newcomer to meet John Cox, who informed him, probably in Hawaiian, that he was "three tens and nine years" away from the Islands. Cox proudly explained how he had come on the *Tonquin* and once visited England. He told another visitor a year earlier that he did "not wish to go to the Islands," and also, likely because Kaulehelehe was not present this time, that he did not "care to attend" his services.[19] The venerable John Cox, whom Paul Kane painted as "Old Cox" at about this time, died in Kanaka Village on a warm sunny day in February 1850.

Two of the 1817 arrivals, Dick and Moumouto, were among those raising their families by Native women in Kanaka Village. However, by the beginning of the 1850s, when the U.S. Army was taking control of the Vancouver area, the condition of the village buildings deteriorated and Hawaiians who wanted to remain in the area were left to their own devices. Mou-mouto may have drifted to his wife's village, whereas Dick held on there as a pensioner. On his death on a cold winter's day in December 1855, he was probably buried in the graveyard north of the fort near to John Cox. William Kaulehelehe also remained at Fort Vancouver. In 1845, a year before the Washington Treaty, he and his wife Mary had returned to live in Kanaka Village.

The most sustained operations south of the border were the Puget Sound Agricultural Company farms managed from Fort Nisqually. Because their journals have survived, we know quite a lot about the Hawaiians who worked at them. At any one time between the early 1840s and 1870, when the post finally closed, almost half of the ten to twenty regular employees were Hawaiians. Generally raw recruits on their arrival, they were soon incorporated into the seasonal round. Sheep were sheared in the spring, after which the wool was compressed into bales of 80 to 90 pounds each to be sent out by brigade for shipment to England. A large garden, fruit trees,

John Cox, painted by Paul Kane in 1849. Royal Ontario Museum, no. 946-271.

and wheat and oat fields were cultivated. Furs were collected year around, pressed, and dispatched.

Sam Arioha, Cowie, Kahannui, Kalama, Keave'haccow, Sam Koemi, Kupahi, Aleck Napahay, and Joe Tapou provided the critical core. The nine Hawaiians contributed 160 man years of labor to Nisqually and its outstations. As put by the post's last head, "they were good, steady men." In 1850 alone, Cowie put down flooring, made swing gates, shingled and reguttered the store, and built a new slaughter house as well as tending the garden, cutting oats, and binding and cradling wheat. The next winter he had charge of a largely Indian gang that cut a new road and then rebuilt the post's kitchen and constructed new stables. Having completed these tasks, Cowie was in March sent with an Indian crew to Tlithlow farm about 5 miles away, where over the next three months he oversaw construction of a residence suitable for an English couple being dispatched to head its operation. It was only when it came to the finishing touches that he was considered to be inadequate to the task. "An Englishman sent out first of the week to assist Cowie in fitting up interior of house, and have at this time finished fitting window frames, glass is almost done all the partitions of the rooms."[20] Cowie had other talents. When a clerk's wife died, he took the lead in making first a coffin and then an enclosure around her grave.

The growth of settlement tempted men to strike out on their own and

Fort Nisqually, 1867, by Edwin Augustus Porcher. Yale Collection of Western Americana, Beinecke Rare Book and Manuscript Library, no. 2004453.

encouraged a more equitable work relationship. Traditional Christmas and New Years holidays were scrupulously kept, including special food, common celebration, and excessive drinking.

> THURSDAY 19TH [DECEMBER 1850]. Gave out to the plain people [men working at outlying locations] the "Regal" for Christmas day as follows: To the white men and Kanakas, each 4 lbs. flour, 1 1/2 lbs. sugar, 1 lb. coffee, 1 lb. hogslard & 6 lbs. pork.

> THURSDAY 26TH. Canadians & Indians employed as on Tuesday, the Englishmen Edwards & Kanakas (Borabora excepted) not at their duties in consequence of having over exerted themselves at the Ball, on the previous night.

> TUESDAY 31ST. Rather a bad day for work in consequence of serving out a Regal for tomorrow, provisions served out the same as for Christmas day last.

The next year an element of distinction was visible:

> WEDNESDAY 24TH [DECEMBER 1851]. Served out Regal to the people the same as given last year. . . . A pint of American brandy purchased at Olympia [Washington] was served out to each whiteman.

> WEDNESDAY 31ST. Served out a Regal to people, the same as on Christmas Day.

PSAC soon realized that discrimination was not in its own best interests, hence the change in holiday policy the next year.

> FRIDAY 24TH [DECEMBER 1852]. Afternoon served out a regal to the white men and Kanakas: 5 lbs. flour, 3 lbs. sugar, 1 lb. coffee, 1/4 gal. molasses, 1 lb. tallow, 5 lbs. pork and 1/4 gal. Am[erican] brandy. To the Indians: 3 lbs. flour, 1/4 gal. molasses, 2 lbs. sugar, and 1 lb. tallow.

> SATURDAY 25TH. Men enjoying themselves dancing and singing in one of the Stores, previously cleared of goods.

> FRIDAY 31ST. Serviced out a regal to the men, the same as on Christmas day.

> SATURDAY 1ST [JANUARY 1853]. Raining all day. Men enjoying themselves dancing.

Much the same happened in subsequent years.

> MONDAY 2ND [JANUARY 1854]. Gave a dinner to all the whitemen and Kanakas. A ball in the evening in the new House. All passed off very pleasantly.

> MONDAY 1ST [JANUARY 1855]. Gave a dinner to all the white men and Kanakas, a Ball in the evening in the Shearing house, all passed off pleasantly.

PSAC used a variety of means to cajole men to stick with Nisqually. When a contract came up for renewal, negotiations now ensued. Thirty-year-old Keave'haccow had worked for two years at Fort Vancouver after arriving in the Pacific Northwest in 1844. Several countrymen coming at the same time were still employed there, and he wanted to visit them. The post journal recorded the exchange.

> TUESDAY 24TH [JULY 1849]. Keava'haccow by permission left for Fort Van-couver to see his friends, before leaving he made an engagement for further term of two years from 1st Nov., wages £17 per annum.

The Hawaiians bargained upward toward parity with better-paid French Canadians.

> TUESDAY 4TH [JANUARY 1853]. Cowie & Koemi whose former engagements have expired have reengaged. Cowie for two years at £25 yr commission & Koemi for one year at £20.

Hawaiians at Nisqually balanced the advantages afforded by steady employment with a personal life. Acquisition of a Native wife from the neighborhood was an incentive to stick around, even though such relationships could be fraught with difficulty. A clerk recorded:

> MONDAY, MARCH 1, 1847. About 9 at night, when I was turning in, [a] thoroughly tired Sandwich Islander from the Fort came to tell me that his Indian wife had run away from him, stealing all his property, and was supposed to have gone to her friends here. Went with him to the different [Indian] lodges and turned them all out, creating no small confusion amongst them, but could nowhere find her.[21]

The departure may have been for good, alternatively intended to demonstrate one wife's unwillingness to be taken for granted. Most relationships acquired a reciprocal character, as indicated by husbands spending their wages not just to clothe themselves but also on their families. Shawls, bonnets, "lambswool frocks," lengths of calico and gingham, thread and thimbles, women's stockings and shoes were frequent purchases, as were children's boots and hose as temperatures fell in the autumn, variously sized kettles and pots, eating utensils, and such food items as rice, molasses, syrup, sugar, salt, yeast, and tea.

The realization that men had other options caused their transgressions to be treated more gently than would have been the case a few years earlier. On a November weekend in 1849 "the three Sandwich Islanders Cowie, Kalama and Keave'haccow went on board the INEZ yesterday, with their women, after the anchor had been raised, and they have not returned." Kalama, described by a contemporary as "a big burly Kanaka," was the most experienced of the trio, having been in the service for a dozen years.[22] The clerk in charge had noted a week earlier, on November 19, how "Sandwich Islanders occasionally drunk, and often trafficking in one way or another with the crew of the American ship INEZ to the neglect of their work," but he had no suspicion anything untoward was about to happen. The adventure turned out to be a lark, the group dropping off four days later at the vessel's next stop. They returned to no apparent punishment, but rather a sigh of relief. The very next day "Cowie assisted by Kalama and Keava'haccow (who is henceforth to be employed about the Fort) making a new cart wheel, and repairing another which will serve as its partner."

Four months later the three Hawaiians were again footloose.

> SATURDAY 16TH [MARCH 1850]. Cowie, Sandwich Islander, declined taking rations today, saying that he meant to leave the service. He removed his things into a mat lodge outside the Fort.
>
> SUNDAY 17TH. Kalama and Keava [Keave'haccow] removed their things today, intending to leave.
>
> MONDAY 18TH. The three Sandwich Islanders did not go to duty today.

Officially, the three men were deserters for leaving before their contracts were up. However, the HBC and PSAC were so hard up for workers they gratefully accepted each of them back, as he discovered it was more difficult than anticipated to make his own way. Cowie was the first to return. As recorded in the Fort Nisqually journal, his arrival more resembled a joyful reunion than a time for denunciation.

> MONDAY 16TH [SEPTEMBER 1850]. The Kanaka Cowie, one of the late runaways here today beginning again to be taken into the employ of the Company.

Both Keave'haccow and Kalama headed to Fort Vancouver, where Keave'haccow joined the HBC. Kalama returned to the Nisqually area in March 1851 to employment nearby. Eighteen months later he decided to contract with PSAC for another two years' service, but soon drifted away to work for a former HBC carpenter settled not far away. Keave'haccow came back in September 1851, but remained restless. The post journal recorded a month later, on October 16: "Cowie, Koeme & Keave'haccow making ready for a pleasure trip to the Columbia. They promise to return in a fortnight." The trip did not satisfy Keave'haccow's wanderlust. In March 1852 and again in August 1854 he "left off working for the Comp[any]" in favor of employ-ment by nearby settlers. The first time he stayed away for three months, the second time two months, before returning to a familiar routine. Kahannui also repeatedly attempted to break away. The post journal recorded on May 23, 1853, "The Kanaka Kahannui after being told he was too in debt has deserted." Kahannui had overrun the amount due to him in wages. Having discovered he could do no better on his own, he returned three months later to no apparent punishment. The repercussions may have played out, however, at the level of family life, for on November 29, 1853, the clerk in charge of the post journal sadly recorded, "Kahannui's Indian wife hung herself whilst in a fit of passion this morning." Kahannui left again the next summer, being recruited back as a shepherd in November 1855. Kahannui's reasons for returning to work were bluntly economic, his very first action being to buy himself a shirt and vest, stockings, and shoes.

As Kahannui, Cowie, Keave'haccow, Kalama, and the others soon learned, options on their own were not as rosy as they might have originally considered. They were illiterate in English and likely also in Hawaiian: Keave'haccow could just sign his name as "Ke a re hociu."[23] Life in the PSAC and HBC gave opportunities for mutual support that were not eas-ily cast aside. When Kalama had his face slashed at Fort Nisqually on August 14, 1853, he was first attended to by a steward at the U.S. Military Hospital in Steilacoom. Two days later he was brought back to the Nisqually post so "he could be attended by his Kanaka friends." The day before Christmas in 1862 Cowie and Keave'haccow clubbed together to buy a pig for $4; Kalama paid $3 for one of his own, likely because of a larger family. It is impossible to know, but tempting to speculate, the traditional Hawaiian feast known as a *lū'au* was in the offing.

Families were recognized and men given time off, as at Cowlitz, to con-struct accommodations for them. The Cowlitz farm journal recorded:

WEDNESDAY 24TH [NOVEMBER 1847]. Took down the Kanakas house & removed beyond the stream—not before it was time.

THURSDAY 25TH. Employed putting up the Kanakas' house and the shep-herds'.

THURSDAY 9TH [DECEMBER]. The owhyhees putting up a house for them-selves.

WEDNESDAY 2 [FEBRUARY 1848]. 2 of the Owhyhees getting a house made habitable for themselves.

MONDAY 7TH [FEBRUARY 1848]. Shifting Mowies house to the other side of the rivulet.[24]

Much the same occurred at Nisqually itself.

> FRIDAY 14TH [OCTOBER 1853]. Kanakas putting up a dwelling house for themselves.
>
> MONDAY 24TH. Cowie putting up a dwelling house for himself.

The men's wives were an accepted part of post life, as seen at Nisqually and Muck:

> TUESDAY 15TH [JANUARY 1850]. Mrs. Kalama delivered of a stout boy.
>
> MONDAY 9TH [AUGUST 1858]. Myself & wife, Kalama, Keheva [Keave'haccow], and wives and several other Indians all harvest hands and com-[menced]. cutting oats.[25]

Men's wives, and also their mothers-in-law, were employed on a seasonal basis. In exchange for a credit to be spent for goods of their choice, Mrs. Sam [Arioha], Mrs. Napahay, Mrs. Cowie, and Mrs. Kalama, so they were recorded, weeded potatoes, thinned turnips, and helped in sheep shearing. The favored items obtained were cloth and thread, shawls, soap, and, once in a while, a looking glass.

Men sometimes took time off from work, with the days deducted from their accounts, to care for their families.

> FRIDAY 29TH [JUNE 1849]. Kalama off on leave to look for his wife.
>
> MONDAY 19TH [JULY 1852]. Kanakas with permission out working at their potato patches.
>
> THURSDAY 3RD [NOVEMBER 1853]. Tapou attending to his sick child.

Cowie in particular was devoted to his family, as indicated by frequent purchases of such items as boys' boots and shoes, pilot bread and crackers, and soup plates. His son's illness was all the more upsetting.

> FRIDAY AUGUST 14TH 1868. Coure not at work today.
>
> MONDAY 24TH. Coure not at work, being engaged in attending a sick child.
>
> WEDNESDAY 26TH. "Coure's" boy is lying at the point of death also.
>
> FRIDAY 28TH. Coure's child died and was buried today. Coure quit work for a time, and gone down [Puget] Sound.
>
> MONDAY 31ST. Afternoon. Coure com[d] work by cutting green oats for Hay.

The Hawaiians at Fort Nisqually engaged in a gradual settling-down process, exemplified by Keave'haccow simplifying his name to Keheva. When HBC employee James Goudie decided in the early 1850s to take his family to Fort Victoria, he stopped along the way at Fort Nisqually. There he traded his roan race horse to "a Kanaka named Cowie, a man well up in years," in exchange for "seven or eight, perhaps ten inferior (principally breeding mares)." An official of the U.S. Indian Department based at the nearby American military post of Steilacoom complained to the head of Nisqually in 1857 how an Indian "says that he sold a horse to one of your kanackas and he did not pay him but half at the time and he wishes to get the balance now." The letter continued: "If you please you will also tell all of those kanackas that if they do not stop selling whiskey to indians that I shall send them to the guard house at the station they have been selling whisky to the Indians some time I have told them several times but they take no notice."[26] Resourcefulness came in many forms.

The Hawaiians used various strategies to nourish their families, as indicated by their repeated purchases of guns, powder, shot, fishing hooks, and lines. Many if not all had their own horses and so ready transportation. Their families tended large vegetable gardens and grew crops, as attested by purchases of a half bushel or bushel of wheat or oats in the early spring and cash advances in late summer to pay for the crops to be milled. As early as 1845 Joe Tapou planted wheat and had his own horse. In 1854 he twice traded poultry his family had raised to the company store for yard goods and children's clothing. Several times a year Tapou bought dressed sheep and deer skins and sinews, used by his wife to make moccasins, which she then traded to the post for purchase by the shepherds. Eight pair got her a fringed shawl. From the early 1850s Tapou was buying seed beads, possibly to trim moccasins. At least a couple of the men seem to have somehow acquired property. In 1857 Cowie had to pay "cash 84 cents tax on your property," suggesting land in his own name.[27] Keaveʻhaccow was assessed 13¢ tax on his property in 1856, 21¢ a year later.[28] Men's pride in ownership is suggested by Keaveʻhaccow purchasing three 7-by-9-inch panes of window glass, hinges, and a stock lock.

Not all of the Hawaiians responded as PSAC hoped. In May 1853, a fairly recent arrival named Tamaree was discharged for selling liquor to Indians and his countryman Kupahi reprimanded "on account of being lazy." Like the footloose Kalama and Keaveʻhaccow, they went to work for nearby settlers, but also engaged in a mini crime spree at first blamed on the Indians.

> MONDAY 19TH [SEPTEMBER 1853]. The Store at the beach has been broken in (it is suspected by Indians, and 18 blankets & two sacks of brown sugar taken therefrom).

It was Kalama, perhaps to curry favor with his former employer, who implicated the pair.

TUESDAY 3RD [JANUARY 1854] The Kanaka Kalama came this evening and charged the Kanakas Tamaree and Kupahi with having stolen the 18 blankets 3 & 2 pts and two sacks of sugar that were missed out of the beach Store on the 19th of September last, he also says that at the same time they took 50 Green Blankets & 50 Scarlet ditto. Tamaree took 50 blankets with him to the Kikatat Country to trade for horses and the rest he divided amongst the Kanakas in the employ here.

Kalama was not guiltless. He acknowledged stealing three sheep together with Tamaree, whom he accused of killing a dozen PSAC cattle and selling the meat to settlers. The post journal recorded two days later how "Kupahi confessed to having assisted Tamaree in stealing the blakts, etc." and "the other Kanakas also own having received blakts from Tamaree." The Hawaiians agreed, the post journal recorded on January 6, to give the company each a horse for their share in the villainy. PSAC needed their labor, as it did that of Kupahi and Kalama, who were reemployed once they realized they were not going to fulfill their aspirations in the larger society of the Oregon Territory. Having been cast the villain, Tamaree was tried at nearby Steilacoom later in the year.

The numerous Hawaiians who left only to come back did so out of necessity, as indicated by their purchase of basic clothing for themselves and their families immediately on their return. The very day Kupahi restarted in February 1856, he bought himself a shirt and two pairs of trousers, shoes and socks, a handkerchief, comb, and soap. A month later he splurged on a wooden shaving box and razor, brown felt hat, and Jew's harp. Within the month he had borrowed against future earnings to acquire another shirt and pair of trousers, boots, "gent's tweed shooting coat," a figured satin vest, and India rubber braces, as well as scissors and thread, matches, blanket, chest lock, shawl and "ladies' cloth topped boots."[29]

The boundary settlement made inevitable the HBC's and PSAC's eventual withdrawal from south of the border. The population defined by the Census as "white" reached almost 12,000 in Washington Territory by 1860. The men in charge at Nisqually acknowledged the distinction through their designation, from about this time, of settlers buying goods from them as "Whiteman" instead of by name. However useful such newcomers might find Nisqually in the short term, they did not want it on what they considered to be their territory. Once local Indians were subdued by force in the American Pacific Northwest during the mid-1850s, the way ahead seemed predestined, and to a large extent it was. The men in charge at Nisqually found themselves increasingly isolated. The post journal recorded on October 11, 1867: "Discharged Sam the Shepherd in consequence of the number of sheep he is constantly losing." Within the year Sam Arioha was back at work. Apart from local Indians, PSAC had no one else to hire.

The comfort that the fairly closed nature of Fort Nisqually gave meant that many of those who had left formal employment remained close at hand. Similar to men's wives, they were hired back on a short-term basis as need arose. The post journal noted on June 16, 1856, how "5 Kanakas" were "washing sheep at $2 per day," as were "5 women." The group went through three flocks of upwards to 500 sheep each before, two days later, "Cowie's flock of sheep brought in to be washed tomorrow." On September 23, 1861: "2 [regularly employed] Kanakas commenced working out Road Tax [assessed Fort Nisqually]. Engaged 5 Kanakas to work along with them." The additional men hired in 1861 were probably drawn from Kahannui, Kalikeeney, Kamehemeha, Kelocha, Koemi, Kupahi, and Napahay, all of whom had worked at Nisqually and were now on their own. Since leaving regular employment in 1851 due to paralysis, Aleck Napahay and his wife were the most frequently hired for specific jobs.

As the fur trade wound down south of the border, Hawaiians were forced to consider their options. A considerable proportion had already returned home, particularly during the 1840s, when men's activities were being monitored from the Islands through the vehicle of the HBC agency in Honolulu and also when ships were regularly plying the Pacific. Even during these years, some men tarried.

Several reasons explain why Hawaiians considered staying on in the Pacific Northwest. Visiting seamen likely brought news of deteriorating conditions at home, where indigenous Hawaiians were losing their autonomy and self-respect in the face of exploitation by outsiders. The Ka Māhele or land division initiated in 1846 meant that some men no longer had a home to return to. Hawaiian historian Samuel Kamakau described a quarter of a century later how, despite attempts to investigate "the land claims of the common people, . . . those who were grasping took the land of the ignorant and entered it under their own names, while others got the land by lying and flattery."[30]

Not only did the regulations give a fairly short time period, until February 1848, for ordinary Hawaiians to make a claim to a parcel of land, the claim had to be based on continuous occupation and cultivation as attested by others. Writing in 1869, Kamakau directly linked both the Ka Māhele, and also the Chiefs' Children's School, to Hawaiians' disinclination to return home. He asked rhetorically,

Why have they wandered to strange land and other kingdoms on earth? They say because they were burdened by the law of the land. The time when all these people went away was that in which the chiefs took up learning letters, and made the law for governing the land which is called the missionary law. . . . The foreigners have benefited and they have stayed here because they like new lands, but the people of Hawaii waited for the benefits of the government under the law from strange lands.

Men who had headed off to the Pacific Northwest with the intention of improving their family's well-being missed out. HBC employee William Naukana told of returning home sometime in the 1850s only to find that family land had been turned into a sugar plantation, and so he came back again to the Pacific Northwest. As summed up by Kamakau in 1864 about Hawaiians abroad, "many wail there and never return. . . . What a pity!"[31]

Other men no longer had family left. By 1849 the indigenous Hawaiian population had fallen to a quarter of the 300,000 conservatively estimated to be living there at the time Captain Cook had arrived two-thirds of a century earlier. Almost 8,000 deaths were recorded over the past year alone compared with just 1,500 births. Kamakau lamented two decades later how, "with the coming of strangers, there came contagious diseases which destroyed the native sons of the land." Adherence to outsiders' priorities had been counterproductive to indigenous Hawaiians like himself. "We build churches, labor day and night, give offerings to charity and the Sabbath dues, but the land is become empty; the old villages lie silent in a tangle of bushes and vines, haunted by ghosts."[32]

Men who returned home may have discovered they were not much wanted. George Simpson, whose views were colored by missionaries during his 1842 visit, disparaged "those who have at once enlarged their notions, and saved a little money abroad." In his view, in line with British notions of social order, they had risen above their station in life, no longer deferring to the missionaries' admonitions intended to encourage humility. "These fellows, so long as their cash lasts, lounge and saunter all day in the sunshine," fitted out as dandies. His observations echo the outfits of clothing Wyeth's Hawaiians bought in preparation for returning home. Simpson seemed almost pleased by how, "in the process of time, these bucks relapse, as a matter of course, through all the stages of worse-for-the-wearishness, shabbiness, and dilapidation, down to the *malo* [loincloth], with perhaps a garland on the head and a *kapa* [bark cloth] on the shoulders." Echoing missionaries' perspective, Simpson maligned this customary practice, considering the "wreath of flowers and leaves" worn by "one sex as well as by the other" to be "a piece of effeminacy."[33]

Some accounts of returning men are more sympathetic. The observation made in a Hawaiian newspaper in 1844 about seamen on whalers and other vessels likely applied as well to those who gave their labor to the Pacific Northwest. "All these traveled Kanakas are readily distinguished amongst the population, by their superior cleanliness, dress and assimilation to foreigners in their manners and habits." Aspirations on return were not necessarily that great, as indicated by a man newly back to the island of Hawai'i in 1855. "Like many other Hawaiians he had gone with the whale fishers some years before and he had now returned to his heart's desire, his wife, his village and his hut. . . . In the evening various neighbors came to hear the stories of the widely traveled person. They boiled goat's milk, in a kettle, brought out calabashes with milk and poi, and partook of a meal . . . , after which they smoked, sang and gossiped." Returned Hawaiians were particularly desirable as exemplars or scapegoats. A missionary at Hilo on the island of Hawai'i explained: "Our young men often shipped for whaling voyages. Noting these cases, I would watch for their return, and then visit them, inquiring whether they chased whales on the Lord's day, used intoxicants, or violated other Christian rules of morality; and I dealt with them as each case demanded."[34]

The paths taken by Hawaiians who decided, for one reason or the other, to remain in the Pacific Northwest testify to their resilience and determination as they struggled to find a middle way. As settlement grew south of the border, sudden departures became more feasible. Artist Paul Kane described how on the outward brigade from Fort Vancouver in July 1847 "two of our Sandwich Islanders deserted." Men about to go on brigade "received 10£ sterling each in goods as their outfit." The two Hawaiians, "in passing the Cascades, had hid their bags in the woods, and hoped to get them back again to the coast with their booty." They visited a nearby Indian camp, perhaps to acquire supplies, only to be surrounded. "The Islanders, thinking they were going to be killed, surrendered and begged for mercy." The Indians were well aware of their best option. In exchange for returning the two men to the HBC, they were given "four blankets and four shirts." Kane was not sympathetic to the Hawaiians. While their punishment of being kicked and knocked down "until they could not get up any more" might appear "savage and severe to persons in civilized life," Kane considered "it is only treatment of this kind that will keep this sort of men in order."[35]

Like other fur trade employees, Hawaiians were dazzled by gold. The rushes that broke out across the North American west at mid-century gave promise of a way of life largely denied them within settler society. The discovery of gold in California in 1848, shortly after the Americans acquired it from Mexico, was unprecedented. Virtually one-third of the 150 Hawaiians then in HBC employ deserted in 1849–1851, as did large numbers across the workforce. A visitor to Fort Vancouver in May 1849 described William Kaulehelehe's consternation at "so many of his countrymen leaving for the mines."[36] Two-thirds of the sixty or so Hawaiians then in the post's workforce, almost all of them arrivals during the 1840s, slipped away, often in small groups. Only three longtime employees did so, Timeoy who arrived in 1830, Joe Ploughboy a year later, and Tatooa in 1837. Loyalty may have played a role in keeping older employees, but so did the need for physical vigor to make the trek south.

Just one in five of the Hawaiians who skipped out returned to HBC employ, the remainder disappearing into the California gold rush. Other Hawaiians were already there. Adventurer John Sutter, who would be linked to gold's discovery in California, visited Oregon in 1838, which may have introduced him to the Hawaiians' utility as workers. Arriving in California from Honolulu a year later with "eight Kanakas, all experienced seamen," and two of their wives in tow, he persuaded the governor of Mexico to sell him a large hunk of land on the American River. The Hawaiians were paid $10 a month on three-year terms to work his property. He later recalled: "I could not have settled the country without the aid of these Kanakas. They were always faithful and loyal to me." As did their counterparts in the Pacific Northwest, the men used traditional ways in difficult moments, as in erecting "two grass houses after the manner of the houses on the Sandwich Islands."[37] Thatched huts provided the earliest accommodation for Sutter and his party.

Countrymen soon followed. By June 1847 forty Hawaiians were working as boatmen and servants in the San Francisco area. These men were among the first to mine discoveries of gold on Sutter's property that set off the great rush. Several hundred more Hawaiians soon joined them, both from Oregon and directly from the Islands. Some were seamen deserting vessels docking in San Francisco. Many more came as passengers, named on lists that survive in the Hawai'i State Archives. Among their number were two of Henry Obookiah's compatriots at mission school in New England, men who had accompanied the first missionaries to the Islands in 1820 and now sought another adventure. Missionary teacher turned entrepreneur Amos Cooke lamented "the influence of California" causing "our native farmers [to] leave their potatoes and onions to rot in the ground."[38]

Some Hawaiians did well. Their prowess with water came to their aid, as they dived for gold on river bottoms. In July 1849 a missionary from the Islands visited an encampment of about seventy-five Hawaiians digging on a fork of the American River, many of whom he already knew. He took pride in how they "regularly assembled upon the Sabbath for Divine Service, which was conducted by two of their number." The visiting clergyman took about twenty letters sent by the men with him back home, also "small quantities of gold dust to their families and friends at the islands."[39]

Hawaiians' initiative worked to their detriment both at home and in California. In 1850 the Hawaiian government under Kamehameha III enacted a law "to prohibit natives from leaving the Islands." As well as ongoing population decline, the act emphasized in its preamble how "the want of labor is severely felt, by Planters and other agriculturalists." Newcomers' priorities took preference. They wanted cheap labor and, to the extent they could keep the indigenous population at home, the wages they offered were exploitative. Unskilled laborers got $2 to $3 a month, rising briefly to a high of $6 a month during the height of the California gold rush, plus a grass hut and taro patch. Out of their wages, workers were charged $1 to $1.50 a month for food supplied by their employer while at work.[40] By comparison, wages in the Pacific Northwest fur trade ranged from £17 to, by mid-century, £20 a year plus accommodation and food, which equated to $6.50 to $8 a month. Men hired by missionaries and settlers received, in the pattern established by Wyeth, $10 a month plus room and board. It is no wonder men had to be legislated to stay home.

The new law passed in 1850 stipulated that "no native subject to the King shall be allowed to emigrate to California or other foreign country unless for some urgent necessity." Again, in the interest of newcomers, departing newcomer families were permitted "to take with them such native nurse or domestic servants as they may urgently require," giving a bond to return them as was also the case with seamen. Indigenous Hawaiians could in effect only leave under the oversight of someone deemed to be their moral and racial superior. As a Hawaiian-language newspaper described two decades later, they were effectively imprisoned in their own country. "People who are trying to keep them back . . . wish to work them like oxen. They receive their grass and water but poverty remains forever theirs, for the pay received is very small on sugar plantations."[41]

Hawaiians' success worked to their disadvantage in California as well. One of the missionaries visiting in the summer of 1849 cautioned "the Hawaiians to be upon their guard and not to give offence to Americans." Their ambivalent status is signaled in the passing reference in the first paragraph of short-story writer Bret Harte's gold rush classic "The Luck of Roaring Camp," published in 1868, to "the day that French Pete and Kanaka Joe shot each other to death."[42] Hawaiians' darker skin tones stereotyped them just as did French Canadians' accents and national origins. Miners who perceived themselves as superior by virtue of being "white" and American managed to have a tax of $20 a month levied from 1850 on all "foreigners," including Hawaiians and the far greater numbers of Chinese. Hawaiians were deprived of standing in the courts by virtue of being classified with Chinese and Indians, and could not legally defend themselves against claim jumpers and others wanting to benefit from their hard work.

All the same, numerous men and a handful of women held on. Following Sutter's departure, his Hawaiians and others, who mostly had families by local Indian women, settled near Fremont in a community they called Puu Hawai'i, or Hawaiian Haven. From there they supplied fish and foodstuff to nearby boomtowns and to Sacramento. An Islands missionary who visited California in 1858 heard of about a hundred indigenous Hawaiians living between the various gold diggings. Those he met had come from almost every part of the Islands between 1849 and 1857. "I inquired of them when they would return to the land of their birth *('aina hanau)*. They replied they did not know. . . . It is my feeling that they will not return to Hawai'i." A fellow missionary who visited in 1868 acknowledged they were "doing well so far as this world is concerned." As had his predecessor, he sought their return to keep them from "living just like the *haoles,*" or white persons, to be politely but firmly informed "they did not wish to return home."[43]

Other Hawaiians pursued other rushes. Gold finds moved steadily north, and excitement reigned from the early 1850s on the Rogue River in southern Oregon. Such locations as Kanaka Flat recall the Hawaiians' presence. So does the restrictive legislation passed in Oregon in 1859, compelling Hawaiians as well as Chinese to pay $2 per month for mining gold, $50 per month for engaging in any kind of trade or barter.[44]

Again, numerous men persevered. According to a contemporary account, the Hawaiians "used big wooden bowls, the same as the Mexicans and Spanish used." The 1860 Census for Jackson County, where most of the mining camps were located, enumerated forty men it identified only as "Kanacka," all of them miners. They were living in six clusters, in cabins or shacks of two to four men each. A mining register recorded claims being sold in 1862 "to Kanaka Jo for the sum of Thirty Dollars." Four years later, "Keleikipi (Kanaka) and Co." registered a new claim "about twenty yards from the house now occupied by us."[45]

Kanaka Flat was a typical mining camp with a saloon and a dance hall. The Jacksonville newspaper recorded a "row" in April 1867 "among the squaws on Kanaka Flat" instigated by two women going "to the house of a

Kanaka named Bottles, to get a shawl which was claimed by Lilly." Other Hawaiians were a moderating influence, attributed to their having already "heard from the missionaries the words of the gospel." According to a fellow miner at Kanaka Flat, "these brown, or coppercolored Argonauts brought with them a glowing faith in the saving grace of a righteous Redeemer." He described them in some detail. "The Kanakas were invited to the little [Methodist] church in town and were received with the right hand of Christian fellowship. And it was one of the pathetic incidents of the time to hear those recent escapees from heathendom and cannibalism testifying in class-meeting—some in tolerably good English and others in their own tongue—to the truth of the faith they cherished."[46]

One of the men who settled down at Kanaka Flat was George Maio, recorded as a native of the Sandwich Islands on wedding Susan, a "Squaw" of the Rogue River tribe of Indians, in October 1861. Half a dozen years later, in March 1867, "Kanaka George," likely the same person, was twice assessed road taxes of $4. The 1880 Census for Jacksonville lists fifty-year-old George Mayo as a sawyer who was by "race" a "K" for Kanaka. His then Indian wife, named as Evaline, was ten years his junior and they had three children. The family was sufficiently integrated into the community for the local newspaper to record eight years later how "Kanaka George and wife have returned from Siskiyou County, California, after an absence of several years." Located near the Oregon boundary, Siskiyou had, according to tradition, "maybe a hundred or so [Hawaiians] scattered along the creeks where they worked the placer mines," including Kanaka Mine, during the mid-1880s.[47]

As the rush for gold moved even farther north during the mid-nineteenth century, it became easier for Hawaiians and others to take a chance on sudden riches without giving up the small achievements they had made in their work and personal lives. Some were inadvertent participants. Tamaree, who would get into trouble at Fort Nisqually a couple of years later, was the cook on the sloop *Georgiana,* on which some two dozen adventurers set out from Olympia in November 1851 in response to news of discoveries on the Queen Charlotte Islands on the north coast. Soon after the men arrived, a gale wrecked the sloop. Tamaree was sent "to take a rope on shore," and everyone disembarked. The local Haida Indians were waiting. They stripped both the ship and the men before taking them captive. Eighteen days later one of the passengers was permitted to travel to the nearby HBC post of Fort Simpson to attempt to arrange their release. Among the three men he considered strategic to accompany him was "Tamoree the Kanaka cook."[48] It would take another month for the men to be ransomed.

Longtime employees Kalama and Keave'haccow at Fort Nisqually were among those entranced by gold. At the time news of finds on the mainland of the future British Columbia became known in the spring of 1858, they were both working at Muck farm, where about two thousand sheep were overseen in good part by Hawaiians. The Nisqually post journal recorded:

> THURSDAY 8TH [APRIL 1858]. Kalama and Keave'haccow in from Muck for a settlement of their account, they intend going to Thompson's River gold digging.

The adventure was short lived, and they were soon back at familiar pursuits at Muck.

> MONDAY 7TH [JUNE 1858]. The Kanackas Keheva & Kalama arrived from the Thompson River gold mines, I think they have not much gold.
>
> WEDNESDAY 9TH. The Kanakas, Kalama & Kehava, seem to desire work again.
>
> SATURDAY 12TH. Kalama & Keheva commenced work on the 9th. Inst.
>
> FRIDAY 18TH. Kalama & Keheva making a gate for back of garden.

Part of the reason men like Kalama returned was the personal lives they had constructed for themselves. Numerous Hawaiians looked for opportunities near the posts where they worked. By the early 1840s, according to a contemporary, "a large number" of them "lived in and around Oregon City and worked on the river boats." The town had only recently been established on the Willamette River. A young man who arrived there in 1846 recalled finding a mill job. "'Many a day,' he says, 'I worked alongside the Kanakas.'" He considered them "good workmen" who were "especially useful in work about the water." The newcomer's respect for the Hawaiians as workers did not extend into sociability, or perhaps separation was mutually desired. "They had their own quarters, which they kept themselves, and provided their own sustenance quite independently."[49]

At the beginning of 1846 John McLoughlin left the HBC to settle in Oregon City. An American naval officer who visited him explained how he "devotes himself to the operation of a fine flour and saw mill which he has built at the falls." Traces survive about some of the Hawaiians who worked for him. In November 1844, while still employed as head of Fort Vancouver, McLoughlin took over the contract of Mikapako, brought from the Islands earlier in the year by a medical doctor leaving to join the military. McLoughlin signed a bond that, "at the end of his Engagement" in 1848, "I promise to send [him] Back to Oahu—Desertion and Death Excepted." In June 1846 McLoughlin subcontracted a Hawaiian from the HBC, being "Charged with Tom's Wages from 1st June 1846 to 1st June 1847."

When Tom, who might have been any one of a number of employees, left, McLoughlin requested "another Sandwich Islander" from the HBC, explaining he also expected "an Islander or two from the Islands." By the time the new Hawaiian was obtained from the HBC a month later, McLoughlin did not need him, for "I fell in with a Kanacka who came with Mr. Cooper [on the HBC brig *Mary Dare* on June 26] and Engaged him for a Month or two." So McLoughlin returned the other Hawaiian back to the HBC. "I send you your Kanacka with Many Thanks."[50]

So many Hawaiians worked around Oregon City that a private school "only for Hawaiians" opened in the home of a just arrived Congregational missionary from the Islands. The school, which lasted a few years at most, was said to be "of a religious character, but reading and writing in the English language was also taught." A number of Hawaiians remained in the vicinity. In June 1860 the local Catholic priest baptized the children of three Hawaiians and Indian women living in Oregon City—William Anounou's daughter Baptistine age 3 months, Kio Kaoulipe's offspring Pierre age 4 and Marie age 1, and William Smith's sons Paul age 3 and Andre age 1.[51]

Hawaiians also turn up in other Oregon towns. In 1844 a sawmill owner about 30 miles east of Astoria, who was likely selling lumber to the Islands, contracted for five men "from King Kamehameha at $5 a month plus board consisting of salmon and potatoes." The same year three men on their way to the Pacific Northwest arranged with "the King of the Hawaiian Islands" for servants to whom they promised passage both ways, food and lodging, and $72 to $100 a year in exchange for two years' service. One of these was Mikapako, whose contract McLoughlin took over later in 1844. Newcomers realized that even if to be disparaged in terms of their skin color, Hawaiians were useful as cooks and house servants, as well as outdoors. A fellow employee arrived from the United States found them "willing, cheerful workers."[52]

In the years and decades following the boundary settlement of 1846, the best the Hawaiians could hope for in the American Pacific Northwest was to be inconspicuous. Newcomers did not want to acknowledge their presence and so, to some extent at least, simply did not see them. A visitor of 1846, who spent considerable time at Fort Vancouver, estimated there were only sixty "Kanakas or Sandwich Islanders" in the Oregon Territory. Almost three times that number were then in the HBC's employ south of the border, a considerable number of others making their lives independent of the company. At least a couple of longtime Hawaiian employees at the PSAC properties centered at Fort Nisqually had long lived nearby with their families, but when the last clerk there compiled a list of "the first settlers" in the vicinity, Hawaiians were nowhere present. The first federal Census taken of Oregon Territory, in 1850, counted just fifty Hawaiians resident there. It took particular moments to render Hawaiians visible. A resident of Port Townsend in Washington Territory noted in 1859 how "a couple of Kanakas arrived from Smith Island," about 6 miles offshore, with a message concerning some belligerent Indians.[53] Numbers in Siskiyou County in northern California were sufficiently large that, when one part of the area was organized in 1890, it was called Honolulu in honor of men who had come to mine but were now farmers or laborers.

Not only did some men remain, others arrived. Indigenous Hawaiians losing out at home had three principal options elsewhere. They could whale, they could dig guano, or they could work in sawmills springing up across the Pacific Northwest. In each case, a man would contract, usually in Honolulu, for a specified time period and wage of $10 to $15 per month, receiving a month or two's advance that might go to their family or chief and a commitment to be returned home. Whaling in the North Pacific and digging guano in the South Pacific employed many thousands of men. Although totals do not survive, in terms of numbers employed, Pacific Northwest sawmilling lagged far behind.

The mill most systematically recruiting Hawaiians was operated from 1853 by the Puget Mill Company at the site Native people called Teekalet, later named Port Gamble, on Puget Sound in northwest Washington. Three businessmen shipping lumber from Maine to California during the gold rush needed a better supply and so headed north up the coast. They brought machinery and the first workers from Maine, but ongoing staffing was difficult in this area not yet attracting newcomers. About the time a second mill started operation in 1858, Hawaiians began to be recruited on year contracts at $15 per month with a month's advance, reduced in 1862 to $10 per month but with a two months' advance as an inducement. At least some, if not all, of the Hawaiians were hired through the agent for native seamen at the Port of Honolulu, who for a commission recruited men and arranged for their dispatch and return consistent with government regulations.

Labor and passenger lists in the Hawai'i State Archives record thirty men traveling back and forth in the years 1858–1867 in the same ships carrying lumber from the Puget Mill Company several times a year to the Islands. Thereafter records do not survive. At least two vessels, the brig *Consort* in 1860 and the Hawaiian barque *Mauna Kea* in 1867, were wrecked on the way, with two of the Hawaiians on the first and all on the second being rescued.[54] The latter group, which included one female Hawaiian, was given assistance to reach Port Gamble, the cost subsequently repaid by the mill owners. Another four men were contracted in October 1860 for a year by nearby Port Madison Mill Company.

Men working for the Puget Sound Mill Company followed a routine not unlike the fur trade. The mill whistle woke them at 6:20, giving them 20 minutes to get to breakfast provided for them and then another 20 minutes to report for an 11 1/2 hour day. The Hawaiians had their own quarters, as did the local Natives sometimes employed there and Chinese who began to be hired in the 1860s.[55] The work was hard, and most Hawaiians remained only through a single contract. None was there at the time of the 1860 Census, even though at least eight were recorded as having departed Honolulu but not yet returning. It may be the enumerator did not consider them worth writing down. A decade later, two dozen Hawaiians, identified as "Kanakas," were working in the Port Gamble sawmill. Two of them had wives and families born in the Islands. Nine men were there in 1880, all but two in their mid-teens. As had their predecessors they almost certainly came for the short term to make a bit of money.

The sociability Port Gamble spawned is indicated by a letter written home in Hawaiian describing a *lū'au* held there in August 1865. The hosts were John Kau, almost certainly a longtime HBC employee who had moved there on retirement, and his wife Mary Pau. The guest of honor was their six-year-old son Pilipo, Philip in English. The occasion was so auspicious that taro for poi was brought from home. "Foods of every variety were prepared, such as *kalo poi* from Honolulu, pork and fish, and *haole* foods also, tea and coffee, bread, and many other foreign dishes." Joe Kuaawa, a likely mill employee, opened the event with a prayer to *Ka mea Hemolele o ka lani,* the "Perfect one of the heavens," or God. There were two sittings on the family's *lanai,* or porch. The first was for a "large group" of Hawaiians, the second for *haole*s, or whites. The letter, printed in the newspaper *Ka Nupepa Kuokoa,* claimed "this is the first time that the Hawaiians have accomplished such a good deed in this place."[56]

It is impossible to know how many Hawaiians already in the Pacific Northwest were employed in sawmilling on Puget Sound. When Sam Arioha was discharged in October 1867 "for frequently losing sheep in consequence of careless herding," PSAC made arrangements for him to be given a job in the Port Madison mill. The Nisqually operation was the last to close south of the border. By the time it did so in 1870, its longtime Hawaiian employees had essentially settled down. Nisqually's last head remembered some of the men, including Joe Tapou, heading a few miles north to the new city of Tacoma, where they got jobs in a sawmill. The recollection is consistent with, according to an early local historian, "quite a number of Kanakas in Old Tacoma, at least in 1877," including nine among the hundred of school age. A directory published the next year described Puget Sound sawmill workers as "white, Chinamen, Indians and Kanackas."[57]

Other Hawaiians arrived in the Pacific Northwest on their own volition. Some dropped off trading vessels. As late as 1846, it was "customary for them to procure a reinforcement of Kanakas in passing the Sandwich Islands." By law the owners of Hawaiian vessels were bound to return seamen home and had to give bonds to that effect, making desertion the means to remain. A "Hawaiian seaman named Pualoka" did precisely that in 1866. The practice continued. Two decades later the Hawaiian consul at Port Townsend "found a Hawaiian, a native of Honolulu, on the street here, and, on questioning him, I ascertained that he had come here as a stowaway."[58]

Even as some arrived, others returned home. From the mid-nineteenth century to the time of the Islands' annexation by the United States in 1898, the government maintained consular offices abroad, not just at Port Townsend but at Victoria on Vancouver Island and elsewhere across the Pacific Northwest. Hawaiians turned to them in times of crisis, as with "a Kanaka who claims to be a half brother of His Majesty" after being charged with horse stealing in the Oregon countryside in the summer of 1879. Kapaukau, who had changed his name to Tidahore Parkaer, wanted to "go home," a request to which the Hawaiian minister of foreign affairs acquiesced so long as any possible connection to the royal family was avoided.[59] The consul in Portland was optimistic a pardon could be secured.

In similar fashion, in 1886 the consul at Port Townsend requested passage for a man named Nūheana who had originally arrived at Victoria during the 1858 gold rush at the age of fifteen and a year later slipped across the border. Kanaka Jack, as he became known, worked as a baker and, for a time after his hands were crushed in a cracker machine, continued to support himself. Eventually he was taken into the county hospital, where he gained "the friendship and sympathy of the entire community," but now wanted "to see his native land once more." Faced with an alternative of being billed 95¢ a day for his care, the Hawaiian government agreed to cover the costs of his return.[60]

The 1893 worldwide depression hit Hawaiians in the Pacific Northwest hard. The next spring the consul at Seattle asked "if anything can be done to alleviate the suffering of pure blooded natives living upon the shores of Puget Sound who are now out of employment, and in many cases destitute." Some fifteen persons, "who in many cases left the Islands, so they inform me, under misapprehension as to their possibilities to earn their living in this country," were now "very anxious to return" to what the consul termed the "land of sunshine and plenty." The situation was complicated by a number of them having "married half Indian wives, and they may wish their wives sent back with them." By this time the Hawaiian legislature regularly appropriated funds for the "Relief and Return of Indigent Hawaiians," and the Seattle consul was informed that "it would be allowable to pay for the passage of half-Indian wives of native Hawaiians who are indigent and who desire to return home."[61] No information survives as to who or where these persons were or whether any of them took up the offer.

Most of the Hawaiians who remained south of the border became invisible, even when present. Sometimes only a nickname survives. Among residents of Siskiyou County in northern California at the turn of the century was "Old Kanaka Mary," recalled for wearing "a big long necklace made of nuggets" and on her own raising a dozen or so homeless children. Near her house was another element of times past in the form of a "small Kanaka Cemetery, fenced and marked."[62] On its grave markers still there today are names with a distinctive Hawaiian ring—Jim and Mary Jan Alpia, Mayo and his likely wife Lucy Mayo.

So far as mainstream society in the United States was concerned, Hawaiians did not really exist. A writer in 1909 on the Oregon gold rush mused over "what ultimately became of the Kanakas." In his view, "some of them no doubt fell by the wayside; but let us hope that the rest of them found their [way] back to that salubrious clime from which they were unwittingly enticed." A decade and a half later a historian pointed out in the *Oregon Historical Quarterly* how "the Hawaiian strain seems to have vanished quickly and to have left no appreciable reminder behind." From the author's perspective, Hawaiians and Indians comprised "two barbarian peoples." The "barbarian islander" of his imagination almost inherently had no role to play in the Oregon that was by now firmly in place. According to American historian Janice Duncan, "by 1900 most Kanakas resident on the mainland had recognized the futility of seeking homes, security, and equality in the United States and retreated to their homeland where their abilities were respected and where the benefit of their experiences was eagerly sought."[63] They certainly did so in the imagination, whatever the reality.

Chapter 8

NORTH OF THE
49TH PARALLEL

THE MARITIME and land-based fur trades formed the lives of most of the Hawaiians making their way to the Pacific Northwest. To survive men only had to do what they were told, although, of course, they did much more in their personal lives. The fur trade's decline forced them to find their own resources. Many returned home, but others did not. For the most part Hawaiians north of the 49th parallel found themselves in a more congenial setting than did their countrymen to the south.

The boundary agreement of 1846 did not just create the Oregon Territory, it defined an area to the north under British control. The Hudson's Bay Company's center of operations in the Pacific Northwest became Fort Victoria on Vancouver Island, which remained in British hands. Hawaiians were part of the move north. In 1849 Fort Victoria's new head James Douglas traveled with his family, together with "636 lbs. of Gold dust, and 20 packs of Otters, worth altogether about £30,000," by canoe from Fort Vancouver to take charge of the post. The party was accompanied by a single Hawaiian as well as an invalid seaman. The unidentified Hawaiian served both to man the canoe and for protection, for the party carried, as Douglas put it, "a noble prize for a gang of thieves." At HBC posts, the evening meal for officers and their guests was a formal affair. Douglas had at Victoria a Hawaiian cook and another who acted as his servant, ensuring guests were provided with "tobacco and long clay pipes."[1]

Vancouver Island was made a British colony in 1849. The Colonial Office dispatched a governor from London to take charge. Richard Blanshard arrived to find the HBC did not have accommodations ready for him. Among the eleven men set to the task were half a dozen Hawaiians. A Hudson's Bay official who arrived about the same time recalled, perhaps a bit condescendingly, how wood for his house "was cut by Kanakas in a sawpit—so it was not very regular in thickness." The Hawaiians were so central to building the new governor's house that he vigorously protested to Douglas when several of them were needed elsewhere. Douglas, who coveted the position of governor for himself, had little charity toward the newcomer. "I am sorry that you should consider it necessary to remark on the removal of the three Kanaccas," since they were not "permanently attached to the party employed at the Cottage." The men still at work were named as Kenoha, Kenome, and Karehua.[2] Indicative of the various ways names were spelled to reflect how they were heard, the three are listed in HBC records as Konea, Kanomé, and Kuawaa.

Other Hawaiians worked at Fort Langley, at Fort Rupert, founded in 1849 to exploit coal deposits for use by Royal Navy steamships plying the West Coast, and at the coalmining community of Nanaimo. John Sebastian Helmcken, who acted as magistrate at Fort Rupert, recalled "a great deal more of French and Kanaka spoken than other languages." The dozen Hawaiians were "all old hands," two-thirds of them previously up the coast at Fort Stikine. The men proved resilient when nine of their contracts expired in 1850 and they demanded to leave on their own. They were eventually persuaded to remain, being, in Helmcken's admiring words, "ever found faithful."[3] The Fort Rupert coal workings were abandoned in 1852, but the HBC maintained the site as a trading post manned by a handful of Hawaiians and others.

The discovery of higher-quality coal farther south at a site named Nanaimo caused several Hawaiians to be dispatched there. According to the HBC head there, the overseer "prefers good Sandwich Islanders as being the most manageable." An English miner described Kahua as "a stout, good-tempered Kanaka, willing at all times, in fair or foul weather, day or night, to do as he was bidden by those in authority to direct him." He was particularly impressed by how Kahua "was nearly as much at home in the water as a duck," so that "if a loaded lighter got sunk in the harbor, as was the case more than once, Kahua was the man to dive and place a rope or chain underneath so that it could be lifted."[4] Jim Kimo acted as night watchman, firing off a gun at midnight, at the same time beating his drum and calling out "All's Well."

The British colony of Vancouver Island and the HBC became interwoven after James Douglas replaced the unhappy Blanshard as governor in

1851. The discovery of gold on the adjacent mainland seven years later brought a second British colony, named British Columbia, into being, also headed by Douglas. Declining revenues as the gold rush ran its course caused the two colonies to be joined under the latter name in 1866. Five years later British Columbia became a province of the new Canadian Dominion.

Numerous Hawaiians ended their fur trade careers on the British side of the border, where they possessed, as a matter of course, the same civil rights as did other newcomer males. Their identification with the HBC almost automatically gave Hawaiians credibility, not surprising given many leading Victoria residents were retired HBC officers. So far as can be determined, restrictions were never discussed. Hawaiians slid into the edges of the dominant society and were permitted to vote and preempt land. All that was necessary was to naturalize as a British subject, which was a simple process. As passed down to a grandson, with a touch of exaggeration: "Well our first elections here in B.C., the Hawaiians all voted. Because, when they came out to vote in them days, there were very few whites around you see. Well there was just as many Hawaiians that voted as were white people. Those that stayed in this country see, well they got their vote."⁵

The reason for Hawaiians' acceptance may well have been, as this grandson explained, British Columbia's tiny newcomer population. Compared with Oregon and Washington, it was very small indeed. British Columbia counted 8,500 "whites" in 1870, compared to 87,000 in Oregon and 22,000 in Washington. Another 1,500 had come from China either directly or via California compared with 3,500 south of the border. About 500 were "colored," being blacks arrived from California to escape discrimination. Oregon and Washington had an equal number who persisted in remaining despite the discriminatory legislation against them. It was far easier south of the border for newcomers to impose their prejudices than in British Columbia.

At the same time, there is no question but that, as in Oregon and Washington, inequities existed north of the 49th parallel. In 1850 James Douglas got approval for small allotments near Fort Victoria to HBC employees with the goal of "forming Villages in the vicinity of the Company's large agricultural establishments."⁶ No consideration was given to including Hawaiians, perhaps because they were meant to return home at the end of their employment.

The reality was that Hawaiians continued to be mobile north as well as south of the border. They both came and went, just as they had done for over half a century. In 1859 the Hawaiian government opened a consular office in Victoria. While chiefly concerned with trade, the consul, a Victoria businessman who had lived in the Islands and knew the language, repeatedly dealt with local Hawaiians, just as did his counterparts to the south. In 1879 he sought advice on "applications from two native Hawaiians for their passage home by steamer."[7] The unnamed men, one of whom was destitute, considered the government was under an obligation to get them there.

One of the principal events encouraging new arrivals was the British Columbia gold rush. Much as in California, seamen deserted. Three of the six seamen the *Emma Rooke* took on at Honolulu in August 1860 slipped away when the schooner arrived in Victoria. Other men arrived licitly. An exchange in the Hawai'i State Archives indicates that at least some of them did so with official blessing. In May 1858 the governor of O'ahu wrote Hawaiian Minister of Foreign Affairs Robert Wyllie to grant permission for half a dozen men to depart, along with four of their wives. Wyllie so informed the Hawaiian consul at Olympia and Puget Sound, appointed two years previous. "His Excellency the Governor of Oahu requests me to recommend to your kind care the King's native subjects, Kimo, Ulu, Keoki, Kanakaole, Paku and Manoa, who are proceeding to the gold diggings in Oregon, Washington Territory, and on the tributaries of Fraser River. Therefore, I recommend that when they or any others of the King's subjects apply to you, you will protect them with your advice and assistance."[8] Not only did the Hawaiian government not realize how great were distances in the Pacific Northwest, the consul, a local appointee, was otherwise occupied and rather, summarily, turned the request over to the HBC at Fort Vancouver.

These men, their wives, and some fifteen other Hawaiians who came as paying passengers on vessels to British Columbia in 1858 were largely left to their own devices, as were the others who arrived less visibly and the three dozen, many unnamed, who followed them on passenger lists over the next four years. A few can be traced as returning home, but most simply disappear into the Pacific Northwest. Their presence survives most vividly in a place name, Kanaka Bar, named for the presence of Hawaiians, including some from Fort Langley, being among the first wave of men hoping to get rich from gold to be found in the Fraser River.

Sawmilling was another draw, especially for men who wanted security of tenure, an assured wage, and the promise of returning home. In the pattern of its Puget Sound counterparts, the Alberni Mill Company hired sixteen men in 1863–1864 directly from Honolulu to work in a mill it operated on central Vancouver Island. By then most nearby trees had been cut, and it is possible the Hawaiians' employment was an economy measure, for operations soon wound down. All but four returned home at the end of their year contract.

Victoria's prominence as the gateway to the gold fields was responsible for a week's visit by Hawaiian royalty in September 1860. The king's brother Prince Lot Kamehameha and David Kalākaua, both educated at the Chiefs' Children's School and future rulers, were on the way to California. Victoria reminded the prince "very strongly of San Francisco at the time of his visit in 1849." So far as the public record goes, the group limited their contacts to local worthies.[9] Consul Henry Rhodes, who oversaw their visit, was well aware of the many ordinary Hawaiians living in Victoria and vicinity, but so far as can be determined, the entourage had no contact with them. Much as at home, the visitors demonstrated no sense of obligation toward the common people.

The precise number settling down north of the border is impossible to calculate, just as it is to the south. In some cases only a name survives, in others a number of sources come together. As one example, several Tamarees flit through the historical record so frequently but so ephemerally as to cause consternation without resolution. The best guess is that about a hundred Hawaiians stayed. They were both former HBC employees and newcomers. Some of the latter may have earlier worked in the fur trade but, because they changed their names, cannot be matched up.

As occurred in Oregon and Washington, almost all of the Hawaiians who can be traced produced families by a Native woman or, possibly, the half-Native daughter of a fellow Hawaiian. This pattern was in no way unique, paralleling the course taken by many settlers of the first generation in response to British Columbia's longtime shortage of newcomer women. Unlike the American Pacific Northwest, where intact families arrived from the 1830s, newcomers north of the 49th parallel were principally men on their own who had been enticed there by gold, earlier by the fur trade. The pattern took a long time to be broken. To the end of the nineteenth century three times as many newcomer men as women lived in the province. It was not only Hawaiians but British Columbians of diverse backgrounds who during these years had families by local indigenous women.

Just as is the case in Oregon and Washington, descendants have found it extremely difficult to trace these women of the first generation. Written records are sparse, apart from the odd church marriage or death registration, and oral recollections scanty. Personal glimpses such as that from the Christmas party at Fort Langley are extremely rare. One woman's comment has repeated itself time and again: "We don't know anything about it, we don't know who the woman was, we don't know where she was from except we think she was a Salish Indian. But we don't know, there is nothing there that we can go by. There are no records."[10]

In general Hawaiians north of the 49th parallel stuck together, seeking to retain so far as possible a familiar way of life. Their ways of doing so echo the *'ohana* or kindred network with which they would have been familiar from the Islands. The clusters they formed are also reminiscent of the coastal beach communities described by Caroline Ralston.[11] Two principal clusters emerged in the aftermath of the fur trade, as well as a number of smaller ones. Whatever the grouping, Hawaiians were resourceful in ways their brothers, sisters, and cousins could have been back home if given the opportunity.

The first major cluster developed around Fort Langley. The grouping took on the characteristic of an *'ohana* following the decision the Hawaiians made in 1840 when Fort Langley was moved upriver a couple of miles to better farming land. The men and their families opted to continue to live near the old post, commuting to work each day. The cluster encompassed longtime employee Peeopeeoh, his two sons Joseph Maayo and Henry Peeopeeoh, and fellow workers Ohia, Peter Ohule, and Wavicareea, who had a son Robert also at work at the post. Both Peeopeeoh and Wavicareea retired in 1852–1853 and, as the younger men's contracts came up for renewal, some of them also chose to go off on their own. So many Hawaiians did so that by 1857 enough "free Kanakas" were living around Fort Langley for the HBC to request that the "seven able men among their number" help transport an especially large load of goods.[12]

The gold rush threatened for a time to disrupt these Hawaiians' way of life. The land on which they lived with their families was surveyed in the fall of 1858 and then auctioned off for a town site promoted as the capital of the new British colony of British Columbia. A government official who stopped by in January 1859 found there "a large body of Kanakas—a mixed-race half Indian half Sandwich Islanders." He praised them as "a very steady people." When the head of the Royal Engineers, sent to British Columbia to maintain order and build infrastructure, visited two months later, Peeopeeoh confronted him. "I was waited upon by a Kanaka named 'Pio-Pio,' who states that prior to the new town of Langley being surveyed, he had cleared and had been in occupation of a piece of land there, from which he was ejected when the site of the town, of which it formed a part, was decided upon." Peeopeeoh had already made his case once. "He informed me that he had preferred some claim for compensation to which he had, up to that time, received no reply." Peeopeeoh wanted Governor James Douglas to intervene. "He requested me to bring his case under Your Excellency's notice, before the season should be too far advanced for his agricultural operations."[13]

Without a commitment, the Hawaiians were unwilling to move from what a newspaper termed their "Kanaka ranch." Peeopeeoh was strategic. If he could not undo the past, he could secure the future for the cluster he headed. "On enquiring of him the nature of the compensation he wished for, he replied that he desired an equivalent in land to that from which he was removed, and that he had selected the site of the old Katsie Village— from which the Indians have removed to the opposite side of the river, and which lies on the north bank of the Fraser about three or four miles below Langley—as the spot upon which he would prefer to settle."[14] The head of the Royal Engineers was impressed by Peeopeeoh, now age sixty, or he would not have taken the time to put on paper as much detail as he did.

The Hawaiians soon acquired a recourse responding to their demands. As of January 1860 it became possible to preempt 160 acres of land before it was surveyed, and they were among the first to do so just across the Fraser River from where they were being dispossessed. Within weeks Peeopeeoh, his son Joseph, and also Peter Ohule and Ohia, who were now his sons-in-law, claimed adjacent parcels of 160 acres each along what would become known as Kanaka Creek. Wavicareea's son Robert soon joined them at what became this cluster's longtime home. The extended family network adapted to private landholding without giving up the essence of their way of life.

The second principal cluster had its origins at Fort Victoria and nearby San Juan Island. The international boundary jogged south through the "main channel" around Vancouver Island. Both the United States and Britain claimed San Juan as lying on their side of the channel and did all they could to assert possession. In December 1853 the Puget Sound Agricultural Company established Belle Vue farm on the south end that employed Hawaiians as shepherds. Americans began taking up land that overlapped with the farm and also attempted to collect taxes on all residents. Tempers repeatedly flared. A local history describes how at one point twenty Hawaiians armed with knives faced off against Americans with guns. The Hawaiians also had to face off, from time to time, against north coast Indian raiding parties, one of which killed three unnamed Hawaiians as well as "a white man" on nearby Orcas Island in 1858.[15] In 1859 open military confrontation between Britain and the United States was narrowly averted, whereupon the two countries agreed to refer the island's ownership to international arbitration.

The Hawaiians who called San Juan home were as much settlers as they were employees, recalled a woman who arrived in "that wild country" as a young girl in 1864. "We ran carefree all through the woods and over the hills." Lily Firth, daughter of an early settler, would frequently "meet a big kinky haired black-faced Kanaka." It "seemed to me the woods were quite full of them going and coming, hither & thither, through the little trails in the woods." Over time she got to know her neighbors well.

> Another old Kanaka with his family, & a number of his friends, moved out to a point near our home, I would guess about 1 1/2 miles from our place. There was a great long point of land that went out into the Strait of Juan de Fuca. After this colony settled in there, the settlers named it Kanaka Point. Out near the end of this Point on the north side there was quite a sheltered bay where boats could lie in anchor in any kind of bad storms, which are quite severe on the Strait at times, that was also named Kanaka Bay.[16]

A sense of community grew up among the cluster living around Kanaka Bay, near to Belle Vue farm. According to a local history, the men were each allocated 20 acres to farm. If so, the policy echoed that at Fort Victoria. Half a dozen were recent arrivals in the Pacific Northwest. Ten others, including John Bull, Peter Friday, and William Naukana, were longtime employees of a decade or more. Bull, who arrived at Fort Nisqually in 1838 still in his teens, tended sheep off and on for eight years before returning home. Like so many others he was soon back in the Pacific Northwest. In 1849 he wed a Clallum woman in a Catholic ceremony in Victoria. The couple had a sizable family before John Bull's death in the early 1860s, whereupon his widow Mary married countryman John Kahana.

Peter Friday started at Cowlitz farm in the early 1840s, working in a variety of positions before being sent to San Juan. Along the way he acquired a son, Joe, born in about 1844, who like his father became a shepherd. The elder Friday returned home at least twice before settling down at what became known as Friday Harbor and was initially a sheep station managed out of Belle Vue farm. The Fridays were great supporters of community, in 1864 subscribing to a fund to start the first school, which Friday children attended. William Naukana, who also used the surname of Lagamine, joined the HBC in 1845 and was stationed variously prior to Belle Vue farm in 1857. Lily Firth recalled how her mother, who taught the school, "hired a Kanaka girl to stay at our home & take care of us." This companion, whom all her life Lila remembered "so well, her name was Mary Lagamine," was likely one of Naukana's daughters.[17]

The San Juan cluster maintained close ties with their countrymen at Fort Victoria, a short canoe ride away. Some twenty Hawaiians capped their fur trade years at the post, only three of whom are on record as returning home. Most of them had spent a decade or more in the Pacific Northwest and were keen to settle down. So many did so, the principal street along the water was dubbed Kanaka Row. A young Englishman who came out with his parents in PSAC service in 1851 decried on his arrival at Victoria "no Town or any approach to civilization but the H. Bay Fort wherein all was centered approaching to a Colony except a few log shanties occupied by half breed Iroquois, French Canadians and Kanacks who risked their lives outside relying upon the woman influence most of them living with Native women."[18]

Other Hawaiians opted for a harbor on the Saanich peninsula north of the fort. According to his son, when John Kahana jumped ship at Fort Victoria's nearby port of Esquimalt sometime in the mid-1850s, "he fled to Gold Harbor in the Saanich Arm where other Hawaiians were living,

John Kahana and Mary Bull with her young son Robert Bull, early 1860s. Center for Pacific Northwest Studies, Western Washington University, Howard Buswell Collection, no. 583.

employees or former employees of the HBC," and hid out there "until the ship had left and it was safe to appear in Victoria."[19] Sometime thereafter he hopped across to San Juan Island, where he met up with John Bull's widow.

The two longest employees of the men at Fort Victoria were George Borabora, who was probably Tahitian, and John Kau. Borabora started at Fort Vancouver in 1835 and spent almost two decades between Forts McLoughlin, Nisqually, and Langley before capping his career at Fort Victoria. His family turns up on Catholic records from Fort Langley, but whether he stayed or went back home is unknown. John Kau, who arrived in 1834 already in his thirties, spent a decade at Fort McLoughlin before relocating to Victoria. Returning home in 1849, he was soon back in the Pacific Northwest.

Like their countrymen on San Juan, the Hawaiians at Fort Victoria contributed to a community in the making. The post's new status from 1849 as capital of the British colony of Vancouver Island did not bring with it any means to keep order. A small militia, the Victoria Voltigeurs, was formed primarily of fur trade employees, including at least four Hawaiians. Pakee was a ten-year veteran in the fur trade, Ebony and Tom Keavé each had seven at the time they joined the Voltigeurs in 1851. Balau, who arrived in the Pacific Northwest in 1845, followed them into its ranks a couple of years later.

The gold rush beginning in 1858 not only spelled the end to the Voltigeurs, it transformed Fort Victoria into a boomtown. City fathers did their best to live up to their heady new status. One of their initiatives was, in September 1858, officially to change Kanaka Row to "the name of the great *savant* and traveler [Alexander von] Humboldt." In practice the informal name was long held in recognition of the Hawaiians who lived there, by now an amalgam of retired fur trade workers and newcomers lured by gold. In 1864 the Victoria consul observed to the Hawaiian minister of foreign affairs how "I have been able, in many instances, to render efficient services to natives of the Hawaiian Islands, of whom there are a large number here, by protecting them, in an unofficial way, in their transactions with others, and also in several instances by procuring them, when in sickness, admission to the hospital."[20]

Hawaiians came to Victoria not only by choice. Longtime HBC chaplain William Kaulehelehe and his wife were forced north. As the land around Fort Vancouver was gradually taken over by the U.S. Army, a standoff developed. Kanaka William, who now lived in Kanaka Village, continued to hold services at his Owhyhee Church until it was torn down sometime in the late

1850s. Military authorities were determined to remove all vestiges of the despised HBC, including Kaulehelehe and his wife. The HBC officer in charge protested early in 1860 that "one of the Company's oldest and most faithful servants" should not be forced out of his longtime home. It was only after the Americans removed the windows and doors that Kaulehelehe capitulated. The next day, March 20, 1860, Kaulehelehe watched as the general in charge burned his home to the ground. The only concession was to permit the elderly couple to occupy an old house near the Catholic church "while the Company is closing up its affairs at this place."[21] William Kaulehelehe retreated with his wife Mary Kaai or Kaaipoop to Fort Victoria, where he was naturalized as a British subject and worked as a clerk in the HBC store and as an interpreter. Somewhere along the way the couple adopted a young girl named Mary Opie, which means "firstborn" in Hawaiian. Born about 1849, she was likely the child of a fellow Hawaiian and a Native woman.

The men, women, and children of Kanaka Row and elsewhere in Victoria were in no way anonymous to each other. The assessment roles of 1862–1864 listed Thomas Keavē and Louis Keavē as owning property, valued at $1,200 and $1,500, respectively, next door to each other at 209 and 210 Humboldt Street. Their proximity suggests that the two men, who

Kanaka Row in about 1859. The two Keavē properties are the two large houses on the right, the Nahoua property the small cottage on the center left; the house on the left may also have been owned by a Hawaiian. British Columbia Archives, H-1492.

joined the Hudson's Bay Company in 1844 and 1840, were related, possibly brothers. Nahoua, who also arrived in 1840, lived just down the street.

Neither were Victoria families anonymous to their families back home. William Kaulehelehe regularly sent to Honolulu for copies of two Hawaiian-language newspapers, *Kū'oko'a* and *Au 'Oka'a,* which he shared with friends. When Kahaleiwi, who arrived in 1858 with the gold rush, died in Victoria three years later, it was two of the men who traveled with him there, Nahi-ana and Kapoi, who administered his estate, and Kaulehelehe who got in touch with the Hawaiian consul to ensure relatives back home in Honolulu received the residue of $39. Similarly, a Hawaiian seaman who was rescued and taken to Victoria after the whaler he was on had to be abandoned in the Bering Strait in 1866 decided to remain "with a brother of his who was residing here." The complexities of naming are evident in Keewele, so he termed himself on reaching Victoria, explaining to the Hawaiian consul he had shipped out in Honolulu under the name of Joe Silver.[22] However difficult it may be in retrospect to link these men back to the Islands, they themselves knew who they were and how they were related.

Whatever their contributions and however respectable they might be, Hawaiians living on Kanaka Row or elsewhere stood out. Supposed transgressions of the law were the stuff of newspaper headlines. The Victoria *Colonist* reported in 1860 on a fight there in which "Palew, a Kanaka, became enraged at one of his countryman" and smashed all the windows in his house.[23] Three decades later a Thomas Pellew, perhaps the same man, also known as Palloo, possibly a son, was working as a molder at the Albion Iron Works.

Morals charges particularly delighted the press. Between 1859 and 1862 Nahoua, now a restaurant worker, was repeatedly charged. In 1859 he was fined £2 for selling liquor to the Indians. A year later he was accused of "keeping a house of ill fame" in his Kanaka Row/Humboldt Street property, basically because he and his Tsimshian wife could not control their adolescent daughters. The police officer who instigated the charge testified: "Every time I pass the house I see five or six half breed women and Indian women and there are some half breed boys and Kanakas in the same room together. I have seen both the squaws and Kanakas drunk and disorderly on several occasions." A newcomer father and son described how a young woman at the house had called out to them in Chinook, "Cla-hoy-a," hello, when they passed.[24] The situation became more complex after Nahoua's wife Kat-e-kah accused a Victoria police officer of promising her husband's release in exchange for sexual favors. In 1862 Nahoua was again convicted, this time imprisoned for two weeks.

The sudden death of William Kaulehelehe and Mary Kaaipoop's fifteen-year-old adopted daughter Mary Opio in late June 1864 set off another tizzy. A Victoria newspaper claimed that "Kanaka Mary," as it termed her, "was three months gone in the family way" and "there are grounds for suspicion that her death has resulted from the employment of means for the purpose of procuring abortion." At the inquest, Kaulehelehe described Mary's death at four in the afternoon, whereupon the coroner testified she "had never been impregnated" and probably died from pneumonia. Despite the evidence and the inquest's determination of "death from natural causes" the press continued to refer to her as "the noted cyprian," or prostitute.[25]

One of the most serious threats to Hawaiians' hardwon respectability occurred farther north on Vancouver Island. Following employment by the HBC at Fort Rupert through much of the 1850s, Peter Kakua migrated to Nanaimo's coal mines. On a fateful evening in December 1868, Kakua hacked his wife, daughter, and in-laws to death. The close nature of the Hawaiian community is indicated by his next action, as given in testimony at his trial by a countryman named Thomas Tamaree. "I know Peter. Peter come to my house. Tell me kill his wife, his girl, her father, her mother. He told me he was going away to the Sound. Peter said that he, Peter, wanted to go to town to buy some stuff. I & two other Kanakas went & *looked* & saw the bodies in Peter's house."[26]

At the trial, at which William Kaulehelehe acted as court interpreter, there was no question but that Peter Kakua would be found guilty. Despite the jury recommending "mercy on the ground that Kanakas are not Xtians [Christians] & killing men may not be such an offence in their eyes," he was sentenced to death. Interviewing him in the Hawaiian language, the Hawaiian consul discovered mitigating circumstances. Kakua had acted only after finding his Native wife Qu-en in bed with her father in what he perceived as "the act of adultery."[27] Rhodes's petition for mercy was signed by many of the leading men of Vancouver Island, but it changed no minds and Kakua was hanged the next March.

The accommodation to changing ways that marked Victoria area families is illustrated in two marriages at Victoria's St. Andrew's Catholic Church. None of the participants in the first, in September 1867, can be identified as to their means of arrival. A thirty-three-year-old Tahitian Noah Kamo married fourteen-year-old Mary Ann Pelai, described as the daughter of "the Hawaiian Pelai" and of a Native woman from the Fort Langley area. The witnesses were two Hawaiians named Pierre Puhelard and John Halim.[28] Puhelard was in the Pacific Northwest at least from 1864, when he fathered a daughter by a Native woman named Christina Walla Walla. According to oral accounts, John Halim was enticed from the Islands by the British Columbia gold rush. The first of his several children by a Lummi woman was born in 1864. Like so many others who flit through the records of the second half of the nineteenth century, becoming visible through marriage or death, hospital treatment, or some transgression of the law, these four men are historical enigmas.

The second was a double marriage on December 20, 1870, that similarly illustrates the tendency to cluster together. Kama Kamai, who worked at Victoria in 1854 and then moved to San Juan Island, was renamed Andrew Kamai on his baptism the same day. He already had four sons and two daughters by a Songhees woman named Mary Ann he now legally wed. In the other ceremony Kamai's eldest daughter Mary from an earlier union married Alexander Kānē, the baptized name of a man known as Korney or Kearney who had worked on the Belle Vue farm since 1860. The two men witnessed each other's marriage. Their countryman and San Juan neighbor Joe Friday served as the second witness at both ceremonies.[29]

Shortly thereafter the Hawaiians' way of life on San Juan Island came to an abrupt halt. A year after British Columbia joined Canada in 1871, the international arbitrator awarded the island to the United States. The decision made its Hawaiian contingent subject to the legalized discrimination experienced by their countrymen in Oregon and Washington. An American who lived on San Juan Island explained how, "when the island became the possession of the United States, the Kanakas were not allowed to become citizens."[30]

Just as families were pondering whether or not to pull up stakes, a crisis erupted that may have hastened decisions in the making. Among Lily Firth's neighbors were the Nuanas, who had two sons just a little older than she was. "Nuana, his wife was an Indian, they had a family. The 2 older boys we came to know quite well. The eldest was named Joe, the second Kye. Quite often these 2 boys would stroll up our way, & as my 2 older brothers were about their age, they would stop & play around our Pond, with my brothers."[31] The boys' father may have been William Newanna, who joined the HBC from Oʻahu in 1843 and worked at Fort Vancouver until he deserted for the California gold fields. Returned a wiser man, he settled on San Juan to mind sheep and settle down.

One day in the spring of 1873, when Lily was eight, Joe Nuana asked her brother Henry, who was 12, to borrow his gun to hunt pigeons. That evening Joe returned it to Lily in haste with "no game that I could see." Two days later a nearby settler and his pregnant wife were found murdered. Even as Lily's mother began to wonder if Joe was implicated, he was arrested in

Kanaka Row in Victoria, to which his family had retreated. Clearly erratic in his behavior, Joe confessed, was tried, and was hung a year and a half later.[32]

Most San Juan Hawaiians who decided to leave looked north to the Gulf Islands, lying between the British Columbia mainland and Vancouver Island. Lily Firth recalled how "most of them went back to the British side to an Island called Salt Spring Island. The few that stayed on San Juan were those that had married Indian women, & had families." The most prominent family to remain was the Fridays. "One in particular I remember quite well was old man Friday & his family, he had settled away out on the Island somewhere in early days perhaps what is now called Friday Harbor & later moved back in the Island. Anyway, I have already heard that Friday Harbor was named after that old Kanaka by some hook-crook-or-other."[33]

Joe Nuana while in custody, 1873. British Columbia Archives, I-77614.

While the Hawaiians who moved to Salt Spring and nearby islands did not leave any records of their own, William Naukana related their story to a neighbor whose daughter ensured it would survive through time. Bea Hamilton, who wrote the first history of Salt Spring Island, explained how "this old Kanaka found that he didn't care for the United States rule. They lost their flag, they lost their Queen and their King, they were used to being ruled under a Queen, so they came over here and they felt that they would be a little happier in this community, in British Columbia because it was under the Queen's rule, in those days, Queen Victoria." According to Hamilton's sister, they "came across in a big canoe." Naukana's grandson explained that "the reason they settled on the Gulf Islands, well it reminded them of their home."[34]

By now mostly middle aged, the Hawaiians started all over. According to members of the Hamilton family, who settled on the south end of Salt Spring Island near Fulford Harbour in 1897: "From there down to Isabella Point this land was owned and lived on by the Kanakas. About 18 of these Kanakas came over from, actually they came from the San Juan Islands. They were led by an old Kanaka called William Naukana, his people actually called him Lickaman." Numbers were sufficiently large for a visitor of 1885 to label that part of Salt Spring "a Kanaka or Sandwich Islander settlement."[35]

Salt Spring's appeal gained by virtue of several compatriots already there. The first to preempt land was Kiavihow, who a few years earlier had done the same outside of Victoria. Taking up 160 acres at Isabella Point on the west side of Fulford Harbour in February 1869, he put all his energy into creating a new way of life for his family. By 1875, according to the Hawaiian consul in Victoria, "Ke-awe-houw Sandich Isdr" had "all fenced 7 ft. high, cleared 6 acres, has a good house cost $150, a wife & family."[36]

Among Kiavihow's neighbors was William Haumea. According to Bea Hamilton, "the Kanaka wasn't very big; he was bald-headed except for a fringe of dark hair that circled his head, giving him a wild look which gave credence to the circulated story" during her childhood that he was a cannibal.[37] As with so many others, it is unclear how Haumea got to the Pacific Northwest, but clearly he was resourceful, for he was the only Hawaiian to make it on the first voters' list compiled after British Columbia's entry into Confederation in 1871. He first lived on Fulford Harbour on the south end of Salt Spring, as did John Kahana who had wed John Bull's widow. In 1886, Haumea acquired 40-acre Russell Island just to the south. Together with his Native wife Mary and namesake daughter, Haumea developed fine fruit orchards first on Salt Spring and then on Russell Island.

One of the first of the San Juan families to take up land on Salt Spring was William Newanna, who settled west of Isabella Point in January 1874, two months before young Joe Nuana was hung. Once again the Hawaiian consul gave assistance, in this case getting drawn the map that accompanied the preemption request. Whether or not it was because of the tragedy, a son later changed his surname to Tahouney.

Other men opted for their own small island. Hamilton explained how "these chaps came over and they preempted land on Portland Island just across a few miles out from Saltspring."[38] William Naukana and his good friend Johnny Pallao, who had wed one of his daughters, were likely already living there when in August 1875 the first officially preempted lot 1, the second lot 2. The two men lost no time in following Haumea and Newanna

William Naukana. Courtesy of Rose Unger.

onto the second voter's list, compiled the same year. An elderly Hawaiian named Thomas Tamaree, who worked for them on Portland, soon joined them on the list. He was likely the same Tamaree who earlier lived on San Juan. Also on the voter's list was John Kahana, another San Juan migrant.

Although the move north meant beginning again, the Hawaiians had their families with them, their wits about them, and, in the case of Portland, a talisman of the life they had given up. "When Grandpa Naukana moved from San Juan Islands into Canada, he brought his white rose bush with him." As explained by Naukana's grandson: "They had just all oxen in them days. My grandfather raised heavy stock and bull calves, of course they castrated the bull calves to make the ox teams." Relying on stories told to her father, Bea Hamilton described Portland Island's way of life. "William Nau-

John Pallao, who married William Naukana's daughter Sophie. Courtesy of Rose Unger.

kana grew all his own vegetables you know. Once he got his seeds from someone, he saved his own. He only had to buy them once, he saved them every year and he made his own tobacco." Hamilton explained the process in detail.

> He would cut a round off a log and he bore a hole right down through the middle of it and he would crush the tobacco leaves and put the leaves down in the bottom, pour a little molasses on it and a tod of rum, more tobacco leaves and right up until he had got it crammed full. I suppose that would have to set for a little. He would split the log open and he would have his long tobacco stick which they cut and smoked when they needed a smoke.[39]

Kama Kamai, his son-in-law Alexander Kānē, and their families also moved north, opting for Coal Island not far from Portland. In early October 1873 Kamai swore out his naturalization as a British subject, making it possible for him, a month later, to preempt the western half of the island. Kānē took up the other half. Kamai and his Native wife Mary had at least nine children, the Kānēs five or more.

Several smaller clusters of Hawaiians dotted coastal British Columbia, some longer-lasting than others. In May 1861 Peter Ohule and Kalehua Kamalii preempted land near Victoria, and in September 1862 "3 Kanakas," two of them named as John Adams and Kalle Kopane, preempted land farther north in the Cowichan Valley. Apart from Ohule, a longtime HBC employee, the men's identities are obscure, possibly because they refashioned their fur trade names. Indeed, a newly minted "John Adams" signed himself "Koema Filoma," which the official stated on the form was his "Kanaka" name.[40]

Some Fort Langley men headed down the Fraser to the lumber mills that sprang up on Burrard Inlet in the early 1860s. "Kanaka Road where some Indians and Kanakas lived" consisted of houses on pilings near to Moodyville mill on the Inlet's north side. Kanaka Road's south shore counterpart was Kanaka Ranch, at the foot of today's Denman Street in downtown Vancouver, from where men trekked to Hastings mill. Three of its residents, Eihu, Nahanee, and Nahu, are said to have come with the fur trade, whereas the family of Keamo Keana, who took the name of James Keamo, takes pride in his arriving "on a sailing ship; he just came for the trip, and stayed here." A young girl who lived nearby recalled how "there were a lot of Kanakas about, not just one or two, and they would talk in their language; it was queer to hear them."[41] Men not only worked in the sawmill itself, they loaded the large sailing ships that took its spars and other lumber products south to Valparaiso, Chile, west to the Hawaiian Islands, and elsewhere.

The mainland colonial capital of New Westminster attracted a number of recent arrivals, mostly single men likely arrived on passing vessels who may or may not have remained to raise families in British Columbia. The area hospital admitted eight men born in the Sandwich Islands for a range of complaints between 1865 and 1878, some of whom were pronounced "cured" and others who died. Their identities survive as New Westminster baker James Anahi, cook Charley Mahoy, and packer Levi Mahoosh; Langley laborer John Ellum or Halim and farmer Mayar; Burrard Inlet wood cutter Joe Kanaka and sailor Charles Mahoosh; and Puget Sound millhand Joseph Lons.[42]

Farther north in the Georgia Strait dividing Vancouver Island from the mainland, George Kamano also found himself his own island. According to oral tradition, he was shanghaied at O'ahu at age fourteen, jumped ship in Victoria, and retained a lifelong fear of being caught. In reality he most likely joined the HBC on the Islands. Kamano worked for the HBC at Fort Rupert and may have been taught to read and write at the Oblate mission established nearby in 1863. Six years later Kamano left the HBC to follow St. Michael's mission on its relocation to nearby Harbledown Island, which was his wife's home territory. He was periodically in charge prior to its closure in 1874. The same year he naturalized and decided to remain at the site with his growing family, which eventually reached ten children.

The Kamanos developed a large garden and orchard with several different varieties of apples, selling produce to the local Natives. Kamano gained such a fine reputation as a farmer as to be one of the few coastal British Columbians making it into an 1883–1884 *Pacific Coast Directory* published in San Francisco. Kamano retained pride in his heritage, as indicated by a visiting German who was collecting Native artifacts along the coast. He described Kamano as "a native of the Sandwich Islands who deserted his ship and was a castaway there."[43] When Kamano's daughter Harriet wed in 1899, he ensured she was given what is recalled in the family as "a Hawaiian wedding," complete with a bridal *lei,* or necklace of fresh flowers. Responding to a Census enumerator two years later, Kamano stated that his first language was Hawaiian and he still spoke it. The family's way of life combined Kamano's Hawaiian origins with that of his wife, who is remembered for holding potlatches, Aboriginal gift giving ceremonies to mark events in the lifespan, of upwards to a week in length.

The cluster originating on San Juan Island and at Fort Victoria and centered on southern Salt Spring, with extensions to nearby Russell, Portland, and Coal islands, most closely resembled an *'ohana.* Bea Hamilton vividly described how "they built log houses all along [the shore] because that is how they lived, some of them were large, some of them were small."⁴⁴ Subsistence farming was combined with fishing and some logging or other paid employment in order to acquire the necessary cash to purchase necessities like sugar and flour from the local store.

One of the means for creating community had a spiritual component. Men working in the HBC were not known for their piety, as William Kaulehelehe had learned to his dismay. More particularly, they did not appreciate his brand of Protestantism instilled by Hawaiian Islands missionaries. At the same time, a descendant has reflected, quite accurately, British Columbian "Hawaiians were mostly Catholic" and "quite religious."⁴⁵ It was the energetic and sustained Oblate activity that had found a response, assisted by Native wives possibly first converted. All but three of the more than two

George Kamano. Courtesy of Carey Meyers.

hundred Hawaiians by birth or descent located in the British Columbia manuscript Censuses of 1881, 1891, and 1901 gave their religion as Catholic, the three exceptions being daughters married to Protestant newcomers.

Hawaiian families were fundamental to the construction of St. Paul's Catholic Church on southern Salt Spring in the early 1880s. "Our church up here in Fulford Harbour see, it was known as an Hawaiian church among the real old Kanakas because the Hawaiians, they built it," a grandson explained. It took a good five years of voluntary labor to build the church, which physically resembled the small mission churches dotting the Hawaiian Islands. The inaugural event was the baptism in late December 1885 of grandsons of William Naukana and of a fellow Hawaiian named Mahoi. A hand-drawn map of St. Paul's cemetery, done by Naukana's youngest daughter Matilda in the early 1930s before many stones were lost or moved in the course of road widening, contains the names of forty members of the Haumea, Kamai, Mahoi, Naukana, Newanna, Pallao, and other Hawaiian families. Hawaiian religiosity likely underlies the advice William Naukana is said to have passed down to a grandson, "Don't feel bad when I go, I'm going to heaven. It is you folks that is going to be left with all the problems of the sicknesses, the politics and all this and that."[46]

St. Paul's Catholic Church and its congregation, including many Hawaiian families, 1885. British Columbia Archives, F-8627.

Families also built community through maintaining traditions brought from home. According to the Hamiltons, the Hawaiians who settled nearby "brought their own flag with them over here I believe, the Hawaiian flag." They also brought a love of music and delight in playing stringed instruments. "They all brought their guitars with them. I think that you could have called this a little Hawaii along here."[47]

The Gulf Islands cluster celebrated each autumn's harvest with a *lū'au*-style party, where food was roasted in a fire pit dug in the beach. Families moved virtually intact from island to island. William Naukana and Johnny Pallao would throw a *lū'au* on Portland. After a week or so, the celebrants would go on to the Newannas on Salt Spring and then to the Kamais on Coal Island and so on. A grandson recalled the parties, as the story passed down in his family: "The Hawaiians all go to Coal Island, that is off of Sidney [on nearby Vancouver Island], they would sing and they would dance there for a week. They sang and they danced, mom said that they had such big crowds there, some danced all day and some slept all day. The ones that slept all day, they danced all night and the ones that danced all day, slept all night." In what may have been an overstatement, two of Naukana's grandsons reminisced: "Well they sang and danced all winter until the time came to put in their crops."[48]

Even while embracing tradition, families were concerned that their children be able to cope in the setting that was British Columbia and Canada. Although members of the first generation, both the men and their Native wives, were mostly illiterate, offspring, so far as geography permitted, attended local schools alongside neighbors' children, as occurred on San Juan Island with the Fridays. Sometimes considerable effort was necessary for them to do so. William Naukana's youngest daughter Matilda, born in July 1874 on Portland Island, began school at Beaver Point on southern Salt Spring in 1883. At first she rowed across each day, but bad weather kept her away. So she boarded with the Ruckle family who farmed near the school and as a consequence "learned to knit and crochet from Mrs. Ruckle, who was Swedish." Naukana left Portland Island for Kiavihow's one-time property at Isabella Point so Matilda could attend school more easily.[49] Kiavihow had died in 1883 and, despite his widow's best efforts, she was unable to maintain ownership for their young son Frank.

Other families turned to Catholic private schools. St. Ann's Convent School in the Cowichan Valley, on Vancouver Island just across from Salt Spring, was intended to educate mixed-race daughters away from their Native mothers' way of life toward that of their newcomer fathers. Emma Pallao was sent there from Portland in 1874 at the tender age of four, her sister Lucy three years later. Mary, Maggie, and Amanda Kānē and Catherine Kamai arrived from Coal Island in the early 1880s. Other children, as also occurred with the Kalama family of Washington, were pushed into residential schools intended for Native children. James Keamo's daughters Emma and Josephine were cajoled into a Methodist residential school in the Fraser Valley to make up enrollments, even though their father was, as acknowledged in its register, "a Kanaka."[50]

Whatever its form, schooling was prized. A treasured photo of 1905 celebrated the presentation of the Roll of Honor to Johnny Pallao's fifteen-year-old grandson Willie.[51] He stands proudly next to his teacher in the local public school on Salt Spring. Nearby are a combination of fellow students and community leaders. The latter include a very elderly Newanna, his daughter Sophie and her husband, and William Naukana's son-in-law, the husband of his beloved youngest daughter Matilda.

Presentation of Roll of Honor to Willie Pallao, 1905. Willie Pallao stands on the far left, Newanna sits just to the right; his daughter Mary on the far right, next to her, William Naukana's youngest daughter Matilda, both of whose husbands and families are around them. Salt Spring Archives, Salt Spring Island, British Columbia.

For all of their accomplishments, the Hawaiians were repeatedly scrutinized, particularly as the character of British Columbia changed following the completion of a transcontinental railroad in the 1880s. An Anglican missionary on nearby Kuper Island during the 1880s recorded several encounters in his diary.

> SEPTEMBER 20, 1882. A Kanaka Canoe passed us, paddling & sailing. I hailed them "Kaw mika klatawa" [Chinook—"Where you go?"] Answer "Coal Island" "Kaw mika Chahko," [Chinook—"Where you come?"] "Victoria."
>
> JULY 22, 1885. At 1/2 past 8 o.C. we anchored in the little cove on the East side of Portland Island—From the Kanakas on "Portland" he [son Percy] bought a small quarter of Lamb.
>
> AUGUST 7, 1886. Indians camped on the beach, viz. Joe the Constable, Joe fr[om] Comiaken, wife & 2 child[re]n . . . the wife is 1/2 Kanaka 1/2 Indian.[52]

Some newcomers, like their counterparts in the American Pacific Northwest, brought with them their prejudices. Many arrivals had little, if any, consciousness of the historical legitimacy of the Hawaiians' presence or any reason to feel empathy with them. Whether or not the shift was so related, the new voters' list compiled in 1881 added "(Kanaka)" after each of the Hawaiians listed on it, a practice that held for a decade and a half. An Englishman who visited Coal Island in 1883 "found that its present occupants are Honolulu Indians, who have been imported with six wives a-piece."[53]

Most newcomers' boundaries of acceptability did not extend beyond persons of pale skin tones similar to themselves. Physicality mattered. A child of the late nineteenth century recalled in old age how "Eihu was a Kanaka, looked Hawaiian, and talked that Language."[54] The province was home to very few persons of similar skin tones. Some of the several hundred blacks who had arrived during the gold rush years continued to make their lives between Victoria and nearby Salt Spring Island, but most returned to the United States following the American Civil War.

The most difficult path for many Hawaiians to walk related to their wives and in-laws. The relationship men in the fur trade were expected to have with Native peoples was ambivalent at best. Common indigenous origins did not translate into any sense of community. Very little information survives as to how Hawaiians dealt with their in-laws or with Native people generally. One of the rare exceptions comes from a Native gathering sponsored by the Catholic Church in the Fraser Valley in 1877. A "medicine man" turned up despite a ban by the bishop, and a battle seemed certain after Native men struck the bishop. According to a contemporary account, "immediately out of the crowd appeared a Kanaka (a native of the Sandwich Islands), who hoisted the Medicine Man on his back and took him in his canoe."[55] The unnamed hero essentially diffused a potentially disastrous situation, but whether he did so out of fraternity with Native people or to shield the Catholic Church is unknown.

Hawaiians continued to do what they could to accommodate to the changes occurring in their new homeland. Numerous men changed the spellings of their surnames and even their first names. On being naturalized a British subject in 1862, Koemi Filoma changed his name to John Adams.[56] Palua changed his to Pellao and then Palow and Pellow. Newanna's son opted for Tahouney. Keamo Keana's namesake son James Keamo became James Campbell as he rose in status to foreman on the Vancouver waterfront. The

James Keamo on his marriage to Anne Cummings,
daughter of a Scot and Native woman, in 1908.
Courtesy of Ruth O'Connor Ulrich.

(Top)

James Keamo *(center front)* in charge of his longshoring gang. Courtesy of Olive Keamo O'Connor.

(Left)

James and Anne Keamo's children, Elmer, Jimmy, Olive, and Mona, in about 1918. Courtesy of Olive Keamo O'Connor.

studio portraits and informal photographs that survive of these families, carefully posed and neatly dressed in the current fashion, underline the importance given to respectability and to correct behavior.[57]

Hawaiians not only voted, they participated in civic affairs. In 1879 Peter Ohule's son George Apnaut was elected to the city council of Maple Ridge, the newcomer community that had grown up around the Hawaiians' pre-emptions on the north side of the Fraser River in 1860. In July 1895 "we, the undersigned, residents of Salt Spring Island" requested an improvement in their mail service. Among the eighty-five signatories were ten who were Hawaiians, their sons, or sons-in-law.[58]

Given the opportunity to be their own persons, Hawaiians in British Columbia adapted even as they retained practices brought from home. They were a lively, self-conscious presence in late nineteenth-century British Columbia. Their story exists in snatches, not surprisingly so given the everyday position that most of them occupied within the social structure. Their physical features caused them to stand out, but for the most part their behavior was ordinary, not much distinguished from that of numerous other newcomers during these years.

Elmer Keamo in adulthood. Courtesy of Ruth O'Connor Ulrich.

These Hawaiians and their counterparts south of the 49th parallel put a lie to the inherent lack-of-capacity argument still being used to demean their counterparts at home. The numbers of "pure Hawaiians" fell to forty thousand by the mid-1880s, down to thirty thousand by the end of the century. Missionaries still sought to blame them for their fate. Among their "sad frailties" were, according to one of them writing in 1889, drunkenness, disease, sorcery, and idolatry, but most of all promiscuity. He asserted males suffered from "extensive loss of procreative power," attributed to "early sexual excess during puberty."[59] In fact, venereal disease introduced by newcomers had serious consequences for both men and women in terms of fecundity.

It was not only missionaries who persisted in such racialized thinking. "A study in social evolution" published in 1899 by a Yale University professor took for granted "the simple Hawaiian mind." William Fremont Blackman accepted without qualification the racial inferiority argument embedded in the missionary rhetoric. "The Kanaka" he put "at the level of the negro in the southern United States; and together they present impressive proof of the almost insuperable difficulty of establishing and maintaining in purity the monogamous family in colored races not far removed from the state of nature." In his view, "decay of native population" was inevitable on "contact with civilization."[60]

For two generations and more, missionaries' close association with ruling groups dealt ordinary Hawaiians a double blow. Not only were their ways of life systematically discredited, they were largely ignored yet blamed for changes over which they had no control. The Hawaiians who made it to the Pacific Northwest walked with their feet. Whether or not they intentionally sought to escape a climate of demoralization we cannot know, but it is undeniable that, so long as they remained in the Islands, they were caught. Indigenous Hawaiians in both the American and Canadian Pacific Northwest possessed opportunities denied them at home. They held jobs, they married and had large families, they took the initiative time and again. Their experiences point up their resourcefulness and, more generally, what might have been in the Hawaiian Islands themselves.

Chapter 9

MOVING ACROSS THE
GENERATIONS

◡ MOVING ACROSS THE GENERATIONS is not easy. The lives of Hawaiians by descent survive in glimpses. They turn up in religious records only for the minority of parents who acquiesced to church rituals. Manuscript Censuses, beginning with the Oregon Territory in 1850, enumerate some families and offspring. Oral recollections and images are indispensable to understanding their experiences through time and place.

Offspring fared less well than they would have if they more closely resembled the dominant societies coming into being across the Pacific Northwest. The first generation of Hawaiian men who had families did so with local indigenous women or perhaps the half-indigenous daughters of countrymen. Offspring were half, possibly three-quarters, indigenous Hawaiian by descent, half or one-quarter indigenous North American. Both Hawaiians and Indians in the Oregon Territory were explicitly excluded from the dominant society. From the mid-1860s onward, neither they nor their offspring were legally permitted to marry into the dominant society. North of the 49th parallel Hawaiians were spared legalized discrimination, but not necessarily its informal counterpart in the form of race prejudice.

Despite a similar inheritance, sons and daughters fared differently. So long as the fur trade remained intact, sons might make a place for themselves in its bottom ranks. The Hudson's Bay Company regularly hired employees' sons by Native women. The extent to which it took responsibility depended in good part on the relationship with the father. Young Mungo Marouna and Thomas Pakee were, as examples, both placed with missionaries when their fathers, respectively, became ill or returned home.

Concern was most evident with long-term employees, as with Marouna, Como, Tawai, and Peeopeeoh. All four were recruited by the North West Company in 1817–1818 and became HBC mainstays. Thomas Como and William Tawai spent their childhoods at Fort Vancouver, where their fathers worked. Como, who had at least three children by a Native woman named Nancy, remained there until his death in 1850, at which time he was a cook. In 1849, age fourteen, Thomas Como was apprenticed to his father's countryman Spunyarn, a cooper at Fort Vancouver for the past half dozen years. Tawai returned home in 1841, but, dissatisfied, was back within a couple of years. His son William became a shepherd at Fort Nisqually, following in the footsteps of his father who was for a time a pigherd at Fort Vancouver. Peeopeeoh's son Joseph, who took the surname of Maayo, was apprenticed at his father's post of Fort Langley in 1847, when he was twenty or twenty-one. By 1853 he was working in the cooperage, much as his countryman Thomas Como was doing at Fort Vancouver. Joseph Maayo's brother Henry likely worked at Fort Langley from time to time, but on an informal basis. Also part of the post's workforce was Robert Wavikareea, whose father joined the HBC from O'ahu in 1830 and spent his entire work career at Fort Langley.

Young men coped variously with the fur trade's decline in the decade following the border settlement of 1846. Mungo Marouna, who lost an important emotional support with the Whitmans' deaths in 1847, built on the English-language skills Narcissa gave him to become an interpreter and guide. Like so many others, Thomas Como skipped out to California in 1849, but was back at work at Fort Vancouver within the year. In 1856 he volunteered for the U.S. Army to fight the Indians and in July was "dangerously wounded." [1] Both men sought to create a space for themselves where they could find some measure of dignity in the emerging dominant society.

The desire for adventure that marked Mungo Marouna's and Thomas Como's early adulthoods became exaggerated with William Tawai, as it also did for young Joe Nuana on San Juan Island. Tawai returned home permanently in 1845, which may have set his son adrift. The clerk in charge of Nisqually remembered William Tawai as "a half breed Kanaka & Indian" and was clearly less trusting of him than if he were a "Kanaka" or "Sandwich Islander," the two terms being used interchangeably in the post journal. [2] He was repeatedly given charge of a group of Indian laborers to cultivate the post's large garden, harvest crops, and clear land. He was also spinning out of control.

FRIDAY 25TH [JUNE 1852]. Tawai of late behaving shamefully, getting drunk with the Indians & staying out in the camp all night.

MONDAY 14TH [FEBRUARY 1853]. Tapou, Keave'haccow & Tawai drunk & disorderly.

MONDAY 11TH [APRIL]. Tawai drunk & quarreling.

Somewhere along the way this "very stout, strong man" lost an arm. The injury did not prevent William Tawai from becoming "a terror" and, "when drunk, a veritable fiend." According to the clerk, "with his one arm he could wield an axe with as much force as any of the two handed men about the place." The situation got so bad that "the other men and the Indians greatly feared him, for when in liquor he was a dangerous man." William Tawai had "an Indian wife of whom he was very jealous," and "he ill-used the woman brutally." The clerk and Tawai almost inevitably got into a direct confrontation.

> During one of his drunken fits, he stood in the fort yard, 'twas in the afternoon, and commenced abusing—in terribly profane language—some of the other men, and then he commenced to abuse Dr. Tolmie [head of Fort Nisqually] and myself (we were in the trade shop) and receiving no notice from us, he came to the shop door and into the shop, and abused the doctor shamefully. This gave me an opportunity I had long looked for, and after threatening to assault us both, I jumped over the counter, took him by the neckerchief, and as big and heavy (upwards of 200 lbs.) [as he was] I dragged him through the fort yard and dumped him upon a pile of refuse.

The matter did not end there. "After a little while he came to the door with a gun, and dared me to come out," which the clerk did somewhat foolishly, although he managed to get "near enough to snatch the gun from him."[3]

The clerk added with a verbal sigh of relief that shortly thereafter William Tawai "left the place, very much to the peace of mind of all in it." As to his destination, "he went to BC, and during the Fraser River mining excitement, I think I heard that he was drowned in the rapid Frasers River."[4] The security that William Tawai's job gave him may have postponed but could not prevent his anger from surfacing time and again. He was never able to find himself a space that gave him any sense of satisfaction. Whether he would have in other circumstances than the American Pacific Northwest of the 1850s, it is impossible to know.

William Tawai's counterparts north of the border were more likely to grow up within an extended family or clan not dissimilar to that their fathers had experienced at home. This advantage was at best relative, once the fur trade ran its course. Whichever side of the 49th parallel they came of age, sons found it difficult to be accepted within the dominant society. The jobs available to them tended to be menial. Joe Nahanee's son William and Keamo's son James worked on the Vancouver waterfront. Kama Kamai's son Louis was a baker in Victoria. John Pallao's namesake son was in 1901 working as a laborer near Victoria to support his growing family.

The difficult path sons walked becomes visible in an Anglican priest's baptism of two children of Peeopeeoh's son Henry by a local Native woman named Margaret in 1860. Not only did the priest arbitrarily anglicize Henry's surname of Peeopeeoh to Pound, he ridiculed the young couple on paper, if not also to their face.

> I had to baptize two children of a Kanákkar (Sandwich-islander), named Henry, who was a Christian, but lived at a little settlement of Kanákkers with his father, Peeopeeoh, very much like the Indians as to domestic habits. When the babe was presented for baptism the mother held it out by the toes, as though it was a petrifaction; the stiffness resulting from its being swaddled, like the Indian babies upon a board.

The cleric went on to disparage the cluster around Peeopeeoh in more general terms. "Very unsatisfactory was the state into which many of the Hudson's Bay employés had degenerated: living insulated, from boyhood often to grey hairs, amongst debased savages, they had married squaws, and their half-bred offspring but too often were mere degraded savages like the mother."[5] If not institutionalized, racism could be just as vicious in British Columbia as south of the border.

British Columbia sons had two options when it came to marriage. As did Henry Peeopeeoh/Pound, some found Native women. George, Carey, and Michael Kamano from Harbledown Island all did so, as did Charles Kamai from Coal Island and William Nahanee from Kanaka Ranch. Others, including young Johnny Pallao from Portland Island and Joe Newanna from Salt Spring, sought out the mixed-race daughters of nearby settlers.

The right to live on an Indian reserve, or reservation, was limited in Canada to persons with status, which descended only through the male line. The offspring of Hawaiian men had no right to be there, even if married to a Native woman. The law had to be finessed, with missionaries sometimes acting as intermediaries. In about 1910 William Nahanee moved his large family by a Squamish chief's daughter onto her reserve on the north shore of Burrard Inlet. His grandson James explained that the two trade-offs were to embrace Catholicism and downplay their non-Native descent. "He did not mention his Hawaiian ancestry."[6] Among descendants taking a similar path was the Wavicareea family in the Fraser Valley, who changed their surname to their father's first name of Robert. Members of the Kamai and Friday families moved onto the Songhees and Saanich reserves near Victoria.[7]

Sons south of the border were, in sharp contrast, encouraged onto reservations. Charles Cawanaia, Peter Kalama, and Charley Kahana were among those doing so. Charles Cawanaia, born shortly after his father Cawanaia arrived in 1817 and for some time a pupil in Jason Lee's missionary school, spent much of his life farming near Fort Vancouver. Despite marrying three mixed-race women in succession and fighting the Cayuse following the Whitman massacre, he and his family had by the time of the 1870 Census become "Ind." Peter Kalama, born in 1864 to longtime fur trade employee Kalama and his Nisqually wife Mary, attended the Chemawa Indian School near Salem, Oregon, from 1880 to 1886, ranking first in his graduating class. The Dawes Allotment Act of 1887 consolidated the process whereby persons claiming Native descent through either parent could take up land on reservations. Peter Kalama settled down on the Klamath Falls Reservation where, by his third wife Alice, a Puyallup Indian, he had a dozen children,

Nahanee clan, 1906, celebrating the ninth birthday of his son Edward, sitting in the center of the front row. William Nahanee is on the far left in the top row, his sister Lucy is next to him and his half-sister Maggie Eihu is four persons to the right. Most of the others are also Hawaiian by descent. Courtesy of James Nahanee.

many of whose descendants live on the Nisqually Reservation near Yelm, Washington.[8]

Charley Kahana, who in old age talked at length about his life experiences, was typical of many sons as to the process by which they became Indian.[9] His ship jumper father had settled down with the widow of longtime HBC employee John Bull on San Juan Island, where Charley was born in 1865. After the boundary settlement, his father "sold out" and "went up to Salt Spring Island on the British side," but Charley preferred "the American side." He placed far less value in adulthood on maintaining his Hawaiian identity by remaining among his father's countrymen than on returning to the familiar world of his childhood. Later, by asserting his mother as Lummi as well as Clallum, he settled onto 9 acres on the Lummi Reservation at the mouth of the Nooksack River in northwest Washington.

To make ends meet, Charley Kahana did a bit of everything—fishing, driving horses, captaining a schooner on the Victoria–San Juan run—but it was music that became his passion. As a child he was transfixed at a dance by how "two half-breed French" men "made that fiddle talk." Returning home, he took two cedar shingles, which his father split to sell in Victoria, added "a little block" for the head, "put keys on it, got horsetail for the bow." In order to acquire his first real violin Charley traded his small dugout canoe with an Indian on Salt Spring. "I've been fiddling since 1876," he recalled proudly. Charley made his public debut two years later. Two French Canadians were set to play at a dance on Orcas Island, where he and his childhood friend Johnny Pallao were staying with his older half brother Joe Bull. When the two fiddlers became too drunk to perform, Joe told the host, "Well, that boy can scratch a fiddle a little bit." Charley explained how "I got a hold of the fiddle, me and Johnny, the two of us crashed the fiddle you know, and they danced all right." Charley took satisfaction in old age that "this was my first quadrille, and I have been playing for dances ever since." As well as fiddling at every Pacific Northwest "old time dance hall" and spending several seasons entertaining "boatloads of passengers between Seattle and Tacoma" for $25 a round trip "on a good day," he made a bit of money by winning prizes at fiddling contests.

For Charley Kahana, it was a good life, one that gave him a sense of accomplishment that eclipsed his racial origins. From the perspective of outsiders, his was an occupation compatible with Indian identity, much like the mixed-race fiddlers who inspired him as a youth. A newcomer who proudly described himself as a member of the "Second White Family to Settle in the Lynden District" on the Nooksack River, arriving in 1872, published a memoir in old age that was surprisingly understanding of Native people. Among

Charley Kahana with his girl friend Mary
Ann Brown in Everett in 1896 *(above)*
and in mid-life *(right)*. Center for Pacific
Northwest Studies, Western Washington
University, Howard Buswell Collection,
nos. 175, 173.

those he included were both Charley's older half sister, noted as the "Indian wife" of a local settler, and Charley himself. "I rustled a fiddle and with the help of an Indian boy by the name of Charley, we gave them a good time for a couple of hours. . . . He attained quite a good deal of prominence playing at picnics and over the radio; and won several prizes in Old Fiddlers' contests." [10]

Daughters were perforce destined for the marriage market, and here the workings of gender gave them options not available to their brothers. The longtime scarcity of non-Native women, in British Columbia in particular, combined with women's inferior position generally to make them acceptable wives to newcomers of modest means. Women were in any case expected to merge their identity into that of their husband. So long as newcomer women were in short supply, Hawaiian daughters offered an attractive alternative north of the 49th parallel, to a lesser extent to the south.

During the late 1850s and 1860s, an illusive Hawaiian recalled only as Haley fathered several daughters by a woman born, according to oral tradition, of a French Canadian and an American Indian. Growing up at Burrard Inlet, where their father likely worked in a lumber mill, Margaret, Fisabee, and Mary Haley were much in demand. Still in her teens, Maggie was caught by a respectable middle-aged American living in Moodyville, the future North Vancouver. Family stories have her holding court in "a large house with Chinese servants, lots of money, a big house on a hill." On Maggie's death from tuberculosis in the late 1880s, Philander Swet dispatched their two daughters to St. Ann's Convent School in the Cowichan Valley before heading south across the border to make his fortune. As soon as Sarah and Agnes Swet came of age, they are said to have "bought a horse and buggy and traveled by carriage down the west coast to California" to make their lives there.

Fisabee Haley opted for a French Canadian hotelier, Maximilian Michaud, and then a Scots logger, Duncan McDonald. An early Vancouver historian rhapsodized about Fisabee in her prime: "In the hotel the beautiful Frisadie from the Kanaka rancherie presides. In years to come Frisadie will become a legend on the inlet, and grizzled pioneers will sigh regretfully when they recall her golden-skinned loveliness." [11] Maggie and Fisabee's younger sister Mary had sons by newcomer laborers before settling into a long-term relationship with a second-generation Hawaiian. She and North Vancouver longshoring foreman Leon Nahu had five children whose descendants were long prominent in the industry.

The Haley sisters' adventures point up the difficult line daughters had to walk, even in British Columbia. While gender worked to their advantage, their physicality raised suspicions, as it had about Nahoua's daughters and William Kaulehelehe and Mary Kaaipoop's adopted daughter. A mill manager's daughter who arrived at Burrard Inlet in 1872 recalled in old age "what a fine good woman Mrs. Swet was," but cautioned in the same breath that she was "an Indian wife." According to a contemporary, Fisabee was in reality only part of the merchandise attracting customers to the hotel's weekly dances, "where 'the boys' took their lady friends and morganic wives—no white ladies attend—only squaws and half-breed women (a few only of the latter)." The early Vancouver historian who was caught up by Fisabee's charms cautioned that the congenial hotelier and "the dark, sultry, mercurial 'Mrs' Michaud who charms all sojourners" were "not exactly married." [12] Michaud was free to leave when it pleased him, as indeed he did, using a trip home to Quebec to acquire a proper wife. The gender imbalance meant, at the same time, that women like Fisabee and her sister Mary rebounded. Even so, Fisabee's Scots logger only married her legally a week before she died of cancer, likely to ensure their children's legitimacy.

It is not surprising then that, given the choice, so many daughters, as did Mary Haley, settled down with countrymen. Catholic records routinely distinguished Hawaiians of the second generation as "half breed Kanakas," "semi-Kanakas," or just "Kanakas." [13] Kaluaikai joined the HBC in 1845 in his late teens. On his deathbed with smallpox at Fort Vancouver in May

Philander Swet, typical of the older men who sought out attractive young part-Hawaiian daughters like Maggie Haley. North Vancouver Museum and Archives, no. 8814.

1853, he was baptized a Catholic with the name of Pierre Kalawataye and then married to "Marguerite métisse Kanac." Marguerite, whose parentage is unknown, was the mother of his four-month-old daughter Julie. In similar fashion, Maggie Haley was named as "Marguerite Kanaka" on her daughter Sarah Swet's baptism.

Peeopeeoh's daughters Paiva or Aglae and Sophie both found husbands from among their father's and brothers' fellow workers at Fort Langley. Ohia worked at Fort Vancouver and on the HBC steamer *Beaver* for five years before being dispatched to Langley in 1845, where he had a couple of children by a Kwantlen woman before falling under Aglae's spell in the mid-1850s. It was very likely the family's spell, given that Ohia worked as a cooper making kegs, barrels, and vats for salt salmon, possibly destined for the Hawaiian Islands, alongside Aglae's brother Joseph. They had at least two children together by the time her sister Sophia had a son George by a similarly longtime Fort Langley employee Peter Ohule, or Apnaut, also from the Islands.

Other daughters acted similarly. The double marriage of Kama Kamai and his daughter in Victoria in December 1870 is indicative. So are those of three of William Naukana's daughters. At the time the family was still living on San Juan Island, Sophie had wed her father's contemporary John Pallao, or Palua, by whom she had a dozen children. Her sisters Annie partnered with Kahananui, and Cecilia with a Hawaiian named George Napoleon Parker who may have been part of the Parker family romanticized for sailing their own craft across the Pacific to British Columbia. The Kahananuis and Parkers settled on Salt Spring on what thereby became known as Kanaka Road. In like fashion, William Newanna's daughter Sophie found herself a partner in one of the Port Gamble mill workers, Louis Kallai, and on his death wed Hawaiian Henry Mundon. William Haumea's daughter Mary got together with a Hawaiian named John Peavine Kahou, whose background, like that of so many others, is an enigma.

Another option for daughters was, as with the Haley sisters, a newcomer man. Whereas Kamano sons found Native women, their sisters partnered with Norwegian, Scots, American, and Nova Scotian loggers, farmers, and jacks of all trades. Following the death of her Hawaiian husband, Peeopeeoh's daughter Sophie found herself a local farmer. In July 1867 Sophie Mary Magdalene Apnatih, described as a "Halfbreed Kanaka, widow of the late Apnatih," married Maritimer William Nelson in the Catholic church at New Westminster. Their daughter Annie wed Hawaiian James Keamo. Several Gulf Islands daughters followed suit. Mary Newanna had one newcomer partner after the other. By the second, Englishman William Lumley, she produced ten children that added to the two she already had. A contemporary descended from Hawaiians described the young Lumleys as "the most beautiful children, beautiful, their sons were handsome and the girls were all beautiful."[14] Other daughters married mixed-race persons like themselves. William Naukana's daughter Julia, for instance, opted for the son of a nearby American sawmill owner and a Native woman.

British Columbia daughters were, like the Kamano and Newanna sisters, extraordinarily tough and resourceful women who very often co-opted the men catching their eye into their existing way of life. Sophie Newanna's

Cecilia Naukana with her husband George Napoleon Parker and family. Courtesy of Rose Unger.

two Hawaiian husbands in succession lived with her family in Salt Spring. Eihu's daughter Maggie brought two newcomer husbands in succession home with her to Kanaka Ranch located on the Vancouver shoreline, where they became part of a multigenerational cluster with a Hawaiian base that continued into the 1920s. The first was a gold miner who, in deference to his religious sensibilities, she wed in a Methodist ceremony, the second a Scots longshoreman. Joe Nahanee's daughter Lucy, who also grew up at Kanaka Ranch, followed her husband, a German steamboat engineer, to his places of work. All the same, Lucy remained, in the words of a neighbor across the street who knew her in her old age, "Hawaiian and they call them Kanakas."[15]

Annie Naukana with her children and second husband, recalled only as Mr. Vermet. Courtesy of Rose Unger.

Maria Mahoi or Mahoy, whose father labored in the fur trade, had a similar trajectory. Living first on Salt Spring and then on nearby Russell Island, she had seven children by a sea captain from Maine via California and then another half dozen by the son of an establishment Englishman and Cowichan woman. The pride she took all her life in her Hawaiian heritage caused others to refer to her by her birth name. In her history of Salt Spring Island, neighbor Bea Hamilton described her as "Maria Mahoi," later on in the text to "Mrs. George Fisher, who was a Kanaka known as Maria Mahoi." [16]

As for the other Naukana daughters, Mary Ann landed a Danish fisherman whom she took home with her to Portland Island. The other two had

Julia Naukana with her husband George Shepard. Courtesy of Rose Unger.

Maria Mahoi as a young woman
(above) and in middle age *(right)*.
Courtesy of Violet and Larry Bell
and Salt Spring Archives, Salt
Spring Island, British Columbia.

husbands whose fathers were newcomers and mothers Native women. Julia wed the son of an American who owned a sawmill on Vancouver Island, and the couple similarly settled down on Portland. The youngest, Matilda, partnered in succession with two mixed-race men sharing the same Native mother and different newcomer fathers, by whom she had a total of sixteen children. Asked to describe Matilda, a daughter-in-law responded: "She was very stout and jolly and she sure ruled the roost. When she said fix the fire, you got up and you fixed the fire, that was it, there was no argument."[17]

After Matilda Naukana settled down, her father bequeathed her his Isabella Point property, where descendants continue to live. He retired to a small cottage near to his longtime companion Johnny Pallao, who died in 1907, Naukana two years later, said to be ages ninety and ninety-five, respectively. They were buried near each other in St. Paul's churchyard under the names of John Pallow and Noukin, where their memorial stones face, in the very far distance, their longtime home of Portland Island and beyond that San Juan Island.

William Naukana's gravestone, St. Paul's Catholic Church, Salt Spring Island, where he was buried with the surname of Noukin. Courtesy of Bryan Jackson.

Numerous daughters south of the border similarly found newcomer husbands. John Bull's daughter Catherine married a Scot, with whom she settled down near Belle Vue farm on San Juan Island. Thomas Como's sister Marguerite wed a stone mason from New York. The priest observed he was thereby legitimizing a "natural marriage."[18]

Among others following a similar path were daughters of Cawanaia and Mackaina, part of the North West Company cohort at Fort Vancouver. As did Marguerite Como, both Angelique Cawanaia and Therese Mackaina sufficiently submerged themselves into their husbands' identities to find a measure of acceptance in the dominant society. Following Cawanaia's death in 1839, Angelique wed a French Canadian who arrived about the same time he had. A widower with a young son, Jean Baptiste Bouchard had worked alongside the Hawaiians as a boatman, which may account for the acquaintanceship. The couple put down roots in the Cowlitz Valley. Shortly after Mackaina left the fur trade in 1837 to settle nearby, his daughter Therese by a Chehalis woman married Joseph Plouf in a Catholic ceremony at Fort Vancouver. From Montreal, Plouf was a blacksmith. The couple lived in the Willamette Valley, near to where a number of French Canadian families farmed. They had seven children when he was killed by a musket ball in 1849. Within the year Therese found herself a second French Canadian husband.

The daughter of Thomas Tamaree, who testified at the murder trial of Peter Kakua in Nanaimo in 1869, found herself a newcomer husband in Juneau, Alaska. Jenny Tamaree had attended St. Ann's Convent School in the Cowichan Valley for at least two years when her father died and her Tlingit mother took her home with her to Wrangell. At age nineteen, Jenny wed an Irishman twenty-five years her senior, whereas her older brother Tom, who settled in Victoria, married a Squamish woman.

Gender more than any other factor took descendants in different directions. The same assumptions that put newcomer men at the head of society constrained Hawaiian men in the second and subsequent generations. These assumptions kept their sisters in the shadows and thereby, somewhat ironically, gave them more marital options. To the extent families have overcome this structural factor, it has been through intermarriage.

Offspring of the two principal clusters, centered in the Fraser Valley and on the southern Gulf Islands, were most likely to find a middle way. Proximity encouraged acquaintanceships. As put by one descendant, "they all married and intermarried." Another has observed how "a lot of families married and separated and remarried." Perhaps not surprisingly, only at the end of a long afternoon of conversation in 1990 in Victoria did two longtime friends realize they shared common great-grandparents of mixed Hawaiian and Native descent.[19]

Whatever the familial circumstances, it has not been easy for descendants to retain a sense of Hawaiian identity. Place names have assisted. Kanaka Row in Victoria, Kanaka Road in Moodyville, now North Vancouver, and Kanaka Ranch in downtown Vancouver may no longer officially exist, but other sites survive. Owyhee River, named for three Hawaiians in the employ of the North West Company who lost their lives there in 1819, is a popular recreation spot in eastern Oregon. Kanaka Bay and Kanaka Point are still

Jenny Tamaree on her marriage to Thomas Mulcahy, Wrangell. 1885. Courtesy of Theresa Dow.

on San Juan Island maps. The site where Peeopeeoh and the other Hawaiians settled across the Fraser River from Fort Langley, in present-day Maple Ridge, is remembered as Kanaka Creek. The spot on the Fraser Canyon where Hawaiians searched for gold became, and remains, Kanaka Bar. A number of nearby Native people living nearby have adopted Kanaka as a surname.

Onetime places of residence remain for descendants a talisman of times past. St. Paul's Catholic Church still stands watch over Salt Spring Island descendants. Naukana's grandson recalled about nearby Portland Island, long since sold to others: "I was over there last year where my grandfather cleared. They had about eighty or one hundred acres cleared on Portland Island at one time. It is amazing to walk through there and see a little old apple tree in a big tree say three feet in diameter going straight in the air. It is the same all over Salt Spring you can run into these old apple orchards that are grown over." [20] An autumnal walk through Portland Island, now part of Canada's Gulf Islands National Park, still turns up apple trees long since gone wild, the tangy flavor of their fruit harking back a century and more.

Some memories hark back to actual events. Five years married in Juneau, Jenny Tamaree queried her much older brother, resident in British Columbia, what he recalled about their father, the Tom Tamaree who testified at Peter Kakua's murder trial: "Have [you] ever known whether papa owned any property in Honolulu, or have you ever heard that his father owned land, cattle, and fruit and do you remember when papa used to get a box of fruit from his home and letters telling that those came from his own property left to him from his father do you remember anything from it." [21] If Tom Tamaree responded, the letter has, sadly, long since disappeared.

Memories have passed down by various means. Vi Johnston, who in 2005 celebrated her hundredth birthday, was thirteen when her grandfather George Kamano died in 1918. Not surprisingly, given the family's Harbledown Island home was principally populated by Native people, "I always thought Hawaiians were another brand of Indians." She recalled only a single moment of sharing that harked back to his homeland. "I remember my grandfather saying he used to climb up on trees like a monkey just to eat coconut." [22]

Men like William Naukana kept stories alive by sharing them with others, in his case Bea Hamilton's father. In old age Naukana claimed his father was a grandson of Hawaiian royalty who by virtue of marrying a commoner lost his place in the hierarchy. He detailed, as his father had to him as a child, Captain James Cook's death in 1779, three decades before Naukana's birth. In Naukana's version, Cook returned at a taboo time when no woman was allowed to go onboard ship, but, after crew were permitted ashore to mend a broken mast, they broke the *kapu*. From the perspective of Naukana's father, Cook would not have been killed if the *ali'i* had been home to keep order.[23]

Captain Cook long remained a living presence on the Gulf Islands. His murder was part of the collective memory. The stories became even more real in 1890 when an Irishman named Alfred Cooke arrived to teach at Salt Spring's Isabella Point school. Naukana's son-in-law Johnny Pallao had by this time moved his family to the hill behind Isabella Point and offered to board the new teacher. An elderly, reclusive Hawaiian nicknamed Kea lived

St. Paul's Catholic Church, Fulford Harbour, Salt Spring Island, in 2003. Courtesy of Bryan Jackson.

in a shack hidden away in the bushes near the water. Every day Kea would trek up the hill to pass the time seated in a corner of Pallao's kitchen. Once the teacher arrived, he kept away until he heard Cooke had gone to Victoria. He arrived to discover the teacher had changed his mind about the trip. Johnny Pallao introduced the two whereupon Kea stammered, "No-no-be not angry, I no kill your grandfather and no eat him." It took a long exchange in Hawaiian for Pallao to determine Kea thought the new teacher was a descendant of Cook, with whose murder his family was complicit. Having learned the teacher was not related, Kea returned to his daily perch. Cooke was unfazed and remained at the school a decade.[24]

Over time, much of what men of the first generation identified with their homeland dropped by the way. Language was an early casualty, as families accommodated to their settings. Most families spoke English in combination with Chinook, the trading jargon long used across the Pacific Northwest. According to a granddaughter, "the wife of Grandpa Naukana spoke Indian and Chinook but he wanted children to speak only English and Chinook, not Native Indian and not Hawaiian." Naukana's neighbor William Haumea, according to a man who grew up nearby, "didn't talk much English," so he and his wife Mary "spoke to each other in Chinook." Neighbor Nick Stevens recalled Haumea coming over to his house to borrow some thread, but, not knowing the word in English, told his parents that "my wife wants some rope to sew with."[25]

The most that survived of the Hawaiian language, as explained by a Salt Spring granddaughter-in-law, were words and phrases. There were "a lot of the Hawaiian words that we used everyday, just in our general conversations." She explained: "We always used to use these phrases, we didn't know the meaning of them and we didn't even know if we were saying them right. When we went to Hawai'i on our first trip, we heard these words and began to put meaning to them." Their origin lay with this woman's mother-in-law, William Naukana's youngest daughter Matilda. "They came down from her father. He taught her I suppose. She picked it up from him and then she used to use them and then her children did likewise and used them."[26]

Even where men made an effort to teach their children Hawaiian, the inheritance could be snatched away from them. A woman born on the American side of the border early in the twentieth century treasured the Hawaiian grandfather she both knew and did not know. "I was told as a little girl that my grandfather was shanghaied on a sailing vessel. He jumped ship in Tacoma." Perhaps for that reason this "grand old man with white hair who was never in a temper" traded in his Hawaiian name for the surname of Samuel. All the same, he was determined to give his children the gift of the Hawaiian language, but his granddaughter lost the inheritance on being sent to residential school. "The U.S. government allowed nothing but English" at Chemawa Indian School. What could not be taken away was a treasured food item, poi, which was in her recollection "a mixture of flour and water allowed to sour at the back of the cook stove" and "eaten with the fingers." She mused over how, even in a bastardized form, "it was a feast and never mind tomorrow." [27]

The prohibitions enacted in the American Pacific Northwest took their toll. In the popular view, the few who remained in the Oregon Territory "married into various Indian tribes and disappeared from local records." Historian Momilani Naughton contends that by the mid-twentieth century "many descendants of the early Hawaiians had lost the awareness that they were part Hawaiian." An Oregon descendant of longtime fur trade employee Mackaina recalled "hearing the word 'Oywhee' often in her childhood, but at the time had no idea what it meant." Another Oregon woman was always "told that her grandfather, Charles J. Cowaniah [Cawanaia], was an Indian," but the family could never quite figure out "his tribal connections." [28]

Some descendants north of the 49th parallel nourished their sense of self across the generations through contact with visitors from the Hawaiian Islands. Members of a clan living across the Fraser River from New Westminster still remember "Hawaiians coming from the Islands to bring gifts to grandmother, they came on boats to Westminster, every time they came they would bring gifts." A descendant explained in 2004 how her sister, a small child at the time, "looked out and saw dark people coming and hid until they left, she would not come out until they left." [29] The Keamo/Campbell family of Vancouver had a special link through James's sister Emma having wed Hawaiian entertainer Sol Bright. The family cherishes photos of the Brights' daughter Wanda playing the ukulele and of visiting Hawaiian musicians, including Hilo Hattie, obligingly posing time and again.

Sometimes it is only the genes that endure. The first Songhees chief, who ruled over the Fort Victoria area until his death in 1864, was nicknamed Freezy for his frizzled hair. Long after the name of his Hawaiian seaman or fur trade father disappeared from memory, if it was ever known, the body retained the consequences of contact. An observer at about the time Fort Victoria was constructed recalled how he "was nicknamed 'Freezy' in adaptation of the French word 'frizer' to curl, in reference to his mop of closely frizzled hair, an inheritance of his Kanaka progenitor." [30]

The bond created by physical appearance cannot be overestimated. Such distinguishing features as dark skin tones, firm build, and wavy hair have appeared and reappeared in Pacific Northwest families generation after generation. Members of the Lummi tribe in northwest Washington still take pride in the waviness of their hair. Physical features have sometimes caused consternation, as with the 1901 Canadian Census when everyone had to identify themselves by color, the choices being white, black, yellow, or red. Most Hawaiians and their descendants termed themselves, perhaps with enumerators' assistance, black. William Naukana, however, described himself as yellow, as did his daughter Matilda and her children.[31] U.S. Censuses were similar except that some enumerators in Oregon and Washington put down *K* for *Kanaka,* seemingly on their own initiative. Where bureaucrats overwrote the designation, they replaced the *K* with *B* for black.

Physical distinctiveness has had varied consequences. A member of a Kwakiutl chiefly family on Vancouver Island recalled in his memoir, pub-

Wanda Bright. Courtesy of Ruth O'Connor Ulrich.

lished in 1941, the difficulties associated with his sister-in-law's Hawaiian inheritance. Even though she "was a strong woman and could do all the work that a chief's wife should do in housekeeping and cooking," she was not accepted. "The people thought that she was not fit for a chief's wife; she was low down." Charles James Nowell shared in the general view, and would tell her she "is not fit to be the wife of my brother, that she was the

Hilo Hattie *(center front)* with James Keamo/Campbell to the left and members of his family. Courtesy of Ruth O'Connor Ulrich.

child of a man from Honolulu or some place, and he was dark brown—
almost black." Her paternal inheritance betrayed her, as did the status associated with it. "Only her mother was the part of her that was Indian."[32]

Although descendants' physicality has been cause for prejudice, it has
also served as a bond uniting families and clans. The son of a Vancouver
Island man with "dark skin" who was born with "eyes that go from dark
green to gray" mused approvingly that it might come from the Hawaiian
link. Describing her husband, a Hawaiian of the third generation, a wife
recalled, "He looked like an Hawaiian. He had the complexion, the features, the whole bit. When we went to Hawai'i the men folks down there
would say, 'Hi bra, what island you from?'" A Hawaiian of the fourth generation told of finding a long-lost relative whose father had married into the
Tsimshian people of the north coast. "You can see that they are part Hawaiian because they have really curly wavy hair and that you know."[33] There
was no need to say more.

Even in extreme old age, at the end of the twentieth century, Lloyd
Kendrick retained the wavy hair and forceful build characteristic of his for-
bears. Not only his body but his memory went back almost two centuries in
time to his great-great-grandfather Peeopeeoh. He was raised on the Apnaut
family property, part of the Hawaiian enclave across the Fraser River from
Fort Langley. His great-grandmother was Sophie Peeopeeoh Ohule/Apnaut
Nelson. She lived with Lloyd's family in old age and would comfort him as
a small child with "stories that were just beyond me." He explained: "I
couldn't visualize that those stories she told me about Hawai'i were true.
She told me that the sun shone every day, and I just couldn't believe it. And
the fruit, papayas, bananas, and all sorts of things which I just couldn't
comprehend." Sophie, who died when Lloyd was six, was sharing with him
the stories her father Peeopeeoh told her about the islands when he grew up
there before the missionaries' arrival. In his memory it was a veritable paradise. "She would sit with us and tell us stories about Hawaii—it was all
sunshine."[34]

In the later twentieth century, numerous descendants in both the American and Canadian Pacific Northwest sought to recover their Hawaiian heritage. One of the events rekindling interest was accidental in its inception.
During British Columbia's centennial in 1971 the provincial government
sponsored a foreign press tour, one of whose members was from the Islands.
Sailing past Salt Spring Island, Mary Cooke's Canadian host pointed out "a
place called Kanaka Row." During a subsequent conversation with one of
William Naukana's grandsons, Cooke was unnerved by how, "except for the
[slight British] accent, his manner of communicating was unmistakably

Hawaiian" and "his plump hands gestured in the easy, graceful way of the Polynesian." When she told him the Hawaiian flag still flew in the Islands, Paul Roland mused how "we had a Hawaiian flag on Salt Spring Island once."[35]

Mary Cooke was overcome. "So Hawaiian—yet they knew so little about Hawai'i." They retained just five words of the Hawaiian language— *aloha* [love or hello], *auwe* [woe or alas], *puaa* [pig or pork], *lua* [bathroom], and *haole* [outsider]. The Honolulu newspaper for which Mary worked was intrigued and sent a part-indigenous Hawaiian reporter to find out more. Visiting with Nuakana and Newanna descendants, Sally Jo Moon found these "old-time Hawaiians" reminiscent of "my own *hapa-haole* [part Hawaiian] aunts and uncles." Later in the year Mary Cooke arranged for several Naukana and Newanna descendants to visit the homeland their grandfathers had left a century and a quarter earlier. They were welcomed by Hawaiians sharing the surname of Naukana and by a variety of entertainers and celebrities.[36]

Beaver Point School on southern Salt Spring Island in the early 1930s. All are Hawaiian descendants except for, in the back row, the teacher and the students first and third from left, in the middle row fifth and sixth from left, and in the front row, first from left. Courtesy of Duke and Beatrice Shepard.

The visit revived interest in Hawaiian traditions. Much as in the Islands themselves, where by 1930 more persons were of partial than wholly indigenous Hawaiian descent, descendants in the Pacific Northwest came to recognize that consciousness matters as much as, or more than, genetics in determining identity.[37] The *lū'au*-style feasts of the late nineteenth century began again on Salt Spring. They have become an annual gathering on the Naukana family holding. The prohibitions once placed on the Nahanee clan of the Squamish Nation gave way to pride in ancestry, exemplified by a leading family member's personalized license plate reading "Kanaka." The Nahanees, totaling five hundred or more, have repeatedly hosted visiting

Tamara Dart, descendant of the Naukana and Newanna families, 1991, on being crowned Miss Surrey, a Vancouver suburb with a then population exceeding 200,000. *The Leader* (Surrey), March 16, 1991.

groups of indigenous Hawaiians, including outrigger teams. The family was instrumental in beginning a competitive outrigger canoe club that represents the Squamish Nation in international events.

The difficulties of establishing precise biological links have not kept descendants from forging mutually rewarding ties with Island families sharing a surname and possibly a common inheritance. The Kalamas have sustained contact with Kalamas living on the island of Moloka'i, a member of which represented them at a Kalama family reunion in Washington State. A Haley descendant moved from Washington State to the island of Hawai'i to track her origins. Many descendants have repeatedly visited the Islands in search of connections.

The growing consciousness of Hawaiian identity was helped along by a somewhat spontaneous event that occurred in 1992. A descendant of Kanaka Ranch's Eihu organized a first general reunion entitled "The Hawaiian Connection" at Fort Langley in conjunction with celebrations marking Canada's 125th anniversary. Although news of the event spread informally, over two hundred persons turned up representing virtually the entire British Columbia socioeconomic spectrum from Native leaders to a former provincial cabinet minister to ordinary men, women, and families. A number of persons arrived from Washington and Oregon. Most had never met before, but many discovered they shared the same stories and in some cases common ancestry. Dominant physical features created a special bond. One man quipped that, while looking for a parking space, he had seen his uncle nine times over even though he was long since dead. An elderly man who grew up in Victoria as white told of the shame he felt as a boy whenever his visibly Hawaiian grandmother came to visit and how he wished he had not denied her a place in his childhood. The editor of the province's principal Native newspaper, a Nahanee descendant, summed up the event as "a re-affirmation of ourselves."[38]

The 1992 reunion and its successors have also attracted more recent, ethnically diverse migrants to the American Pacific Northwest from the Hawaiian Islands.[39] In the 2001 Canadian Census 1,325 British Columbians identified themselves as Hawaiian by ethnic origin, all but 60 as one component of a composite origin. Almost all of them descend from the nineteenth century. The American Pacific Northwest, as part of the United States, has attracted more recent arrivals. In 2000 4,883 persons in Washington and 2,244 in Oregon described themselves as "Native Hawaiian," many more as partially so. By getting to know others across the Pacific Northwest whose grandfathers, great-grandfathers, and great-great-grandfathers left paradise a century and more before them, some of these men and women have also gained a stronger sense of their identity as Hawaiian than they had before. It was a Hawaiian newcomer to the Pacific Northwest who in August 2004 took the initiative to honor a granddaughter of Leon Nahu and Mary Haley with the name of Lei-aloha in a ceremony reminiscent of "ancient tradition" attended by over two hundred Hawaiian descendants.[40]

Indigenous Hawaiians have contributed in many and important ways to the making of the Pacific Northwest. Their role extends far beyond early seafaring and the fur trade. The first nonwhite group of sojourners, they also became some of the earliest nonwhite settlers. Repeatedly, indigenous Hawaiians acted in the best interests of themselves and of the distant shore that gave them opportunities not available at home. They demonstrated through their persistence and tenacity what might have been in the Islands themselves, had outsiders been less intent on imposing their will. Hawaiians in the Pacific Northwest belie the myth that the history of their homeland was inevitable.

Hawaiians and Other Polynesians in the Pacific Northwest

ABBREVIATIONS

CRFTC   Columbia River Fishing and Trading Company
fl.   flourished in Pacific Northwest
HBC   Hudson's Bay Company
NWC   North West Company
PFC   Pacific Fur Company
PPS   Published Primary Sources
PS   Primary Sources
PSAC   Puget Sound Agricultural Company
SS   Secondary Sources

Note: See also bracketed codes in Sources.

Adams (fl. 1853)

HBC employee, associated with:

ship *Pekin* (1853) seaman
ship *Mary Catherine* (1853) seaman

Adams shipped aboard the HBC chartered vessel *Pekin* in Honolulu probably in the summer of 1853, sailed to the Northwest Coast, and arrived back September 27, 1853, on the *Mary Catherine.* He was given the final balance of his wages on his return.

PS: HBCA SandIsLonIC3

Adams, George (fl. 1834–1840)

CRFTC/HBC employee, associated with:

ship *May Dacre* (1834) passenger
CRFTC brigade (1834) member
HBC Snake party (1835) member
Forts William and Hall (1835–1837)
Snake party (1837–1840) middleman

George Adams was one of twenty Hawaiians recruited for Nathaniel J. Wyeth's CRFTC in 1834 and among the dozen who deserted in November of the same year on the way to Fort Hall. On March 12, 1835, Wyeth found seven of his runaway Hawaiians, including George, at Fort Vancouver. George first worked at Fort William and then at Fort Hall.

By October 10, 1837, George Adams had joined the HBC and was trapping on the Snake River. He was discharged at the end of his three-year contract and sent to Oʻahu on November 15, 1840. He, like others with similar names, could possibly be of mixed descent, inheriting his European surname through his father and being given a Christian name.

PS: HBCA FtVanSA 4–6, YFDS 8, 11, YFSA 19–20, OHS FtHallAB, CRFTCCB; *SS:* Beidleman, "Fort Hall," 238

Adams, Jack [variations: **Kaanana, Kaananai**] (fl. 1849–1853)

HBC employee, possibly of mixed descent, d. 1853 at Fort Vancouver, associated with:

barque *Columbia* (1849) passenger or seaman
barque *Cowlitz* (1850) seaman
Fort Vancouver (1850–1851, 1853)

Jack Adams joined the HBC in Oʻahu sometime before 1849, probably as a seaman, but can only be tracked when he arrived back in Oʻahu in December 1849 aboard the HBC barque *Columbia.* He reenlisted and began to receive wages on January 6, 1850, sailing to the coast on the barque *Cowlitz* but deserting the vessel at Fort Victoria along with **Kaina.** He probably made his way to Fort Vancouver, where he worked for a short period as a laborer, and on June 11, 1851, he again deserted. He died two years later at Fort Vancouver.

PS: HBCA SandIsAB 10, YFSA 30–32, FtVanSA 9–11, YFDS 21–22

Adams, John [variations: **Keomi Filoma, Konie Filama**] (fl. 1862)

Occupation unknown, associated with:

probably Victoria (1862)

Little is known of John Adams other than he was sworn in as a British subject probably in Victoria, on August 11, 1862. Below his name on the document an official wrote "'Konie Filama' in Kanaka," and he signed his name "Keomi filoma" at the bottom of the attestation. That same day, **Keava Kamu** and **Kalle Kopane** received their naturalization papers. The following day **William R. Kaulehelehe** received his, indicating a possible friendship among the four.

A month later John Adams preempted land in the Cowichan District of Vancouver Island. This was probably his reason for becoming naturalized. So did Kalle Kopane and a third "Kanaka" not named on the certificate, who might have been Kamu.

PS: BCA GR-Naturalization, Crt-Naturalization, GR-Preemption

Adamson, John [variations: **Kaananai, Kaanana, John Adams**] (fl. 1853)

HBC employee, possibly of mixed descent, d. 1853 at Fort Vancouver, associated with:

Fort Vancouver (1853) laborer

John Adamson joined the HBC in Oʻahu in 1853 and died the same year, most likely at Fort Vancouver and from smallpox, which was in the area at the time.

PS: HBCA SandIsAB 7, YFSA 30–32, FtVanSA 9–11, YFDS 21–22

Aganey (fl. 1837–1844)

HBC employee, associated with:

Fort Vancouver (1837–1842) middleman, (1842–1844) laborer

Aganey signed on with the HBC in Oʻahu in July 1837, beginning his work at Fort Vancouver on August 10, 1837. He appears to have remained there until November 23, 1844, at which point he left for Oʻahu.

PS: HBCA SandIsAB 1, FtVanSA 4–8, YFDS 8, YFSA 19–20, 24

Ahao (fl. 1841–1844)

HBC employee, d. June 19, 1844, on barque *Columbia* at Fort Victoria, associated with:

Fort Vancouver (1841–1842) middleman, (1842–1843) laborer
barque *Columbia* (1843–1844) laborer

Ahao signed on with the HBC from Oʻahu in 1841 on a three-year contract, beginning work at Fort Vancouver on July 4, 1841. He completed his first contract and, just as he was about to begin a new one as a laborer on the barque *Columbia,* he died while his vessel was anchored at Fort Victoria. He may have been buried at the first Fort Victoria cemetery.

PS: HBCA FVASA 6–8, YFDS 12, 15, YFSA 24

Ahulau (fl. 1862)

Laborer, associated with:

Port Gamble (1862) sawmill worker

Ahulau and six other men were contracted in Honolulu on February 14, 1862, by the agent of Puget Mill Co. to work at its sawmill for $10 per month with a $20 advance. It is uncertain how long he did so or whether he was native Hawaiian. His name suggests he may have been Chinese.

PS: HSA Seamen

Aikanai (fl. 1860)

Seaman, associated with:

schooner *Emma Rooke* (1860) seaman

Aikanai was among five Hawaiians contracted by the schooner *Emma Rooke* when it sailed from Honolulu to Victoria on August 29, 1860. The men were paid $15 per month with a $15 advance. He deserted, very possibly at Victoria.

PS: HSA Seamen

Aikane [variations: **Aikani, Aikana**] (fl. 1845–1849)

HBC employee, associated with:

Willamette (1845–1846) laborer
Fort Vancouver (1846–1847) laborer, Indian trade (1847–1849) laborer, farm (1849) laborer

Aikani joined the HBC in Oʻahu in 1845 on a three-year contract and spent the next four years as a laborer in the area immediately surrounding Fort Vancouver. On September 10, 1849, he deserted, probably for the gold fields of California.

PS: HBCA YFSA 25–29, YFDS 15–16

Alaala (fl. 1864)

Laborer, associated with:

Port Gamble (1864) sawmill worker

Alaala and five other men were contracted in Honolulu on February 5, 1864, by the agent of Puget Mill Co. to work at its sawmill for $10 per month with a $20 advance. It is uncertain how long he did so or whether he was native Hawaiian. His name suggests he may have been Chinese.

PS: HSA Seamen

Alani (fl. 1850)

HBC employee, associated with:

brigantine *Mary Dare* (1850) passenger

Alani hired on with the HBC in Oʻahu in 1850 and sailed to the coast on the *Mary Dare.* It is uncertain where he worked or for how long.

PS: HBCA SandIsAB 10

Alauka (fl. 1844–1849)

HBC employee, associated with:

Fort Vancouver (1844–1849) laborer

Alauka joined the HBC from Honolulu in 1844 and spent the next five years at Fort Vancouver. On October 10, 1849, he deserted, probably for the gold fields of California.

PS: HBCA YFSA 25–29, YFDS 20

Alchockwē (fl. 1847)

Occupation unknown, associated with:

Fort Vancouver area (1847)

A Hawaiian with the unusual name of Alchockwē was living in the Fort Vancouver area, probably at Kanaka Village, in 1847 with a Chinook woman. They had a child, Lucine (1847–?).

PPS: Munnick, *Vancouver,* vol. 2

Aliao (fl. 1844)

HBC employee, associated with:

Fort Vancouver (1844) laborer

Aliao joined the HBC from Oʻahu in 1844. After sailing to the coast, he worked at Fort Vancouver as a laborer until November 12, 1844, at which point he returned to Oʻahu.

PS: HBCA YFSA 24, YFDS 15

Alioa [variation: **Kamus Alvoi**] (fl. 1841–1850)

HBC employee, b. ca. 1825, associated with:

Fort Vancouver (1841–1842) middleman
Fort George [Astoria] (1842–1845) middleman
Fort Vancouver (1845–1850) laborer

Alioa joined the HBC from Oʻahu on July 4, 1841, age about sixteen. He spent the next eight years at forts on the Columbia River. In August 1845, he transferred some money to his mother in Hawaiʻi. On September 25, 1849, he deserted, most likely for the gold fields of California. He must have soon returned, for a man named Kamus Alvoi, likely him, was in 1850 living in the Kanaka Village area of Fort Vancouver.

PS: HBCA FtVanSA 7–8, YFDS 12, 20, SandIsAB 5, YFSA 24–29, 1850 U.S. Census, Oregon, Clark Co.

America (fl. 1822–1841)

HBC employee, associated with:

Columbia Department (1822–1823)
Fort George [Astoria] (1823–1825) laborer
Columbia Department (1825–1826) laborer
Umpqua Snake expeditions (1826–1827) laborer
Fort Vancouver (1827–1830) middleman, (1830–1831) middleman/laborer
barque *Ganymede* (1831) passenger
barque *Cowlitz* (1841) passenger or seaman

America, from Oʻahu, joined the HBC in 1822. He is mentioned frequently in the journal account of the 1826–1827 southern expedition to the Umpqua. On Sunday, July 2, 1826, for example, "one of our Owhyheeʻs (America) is very unwell of a Breast Complaint since leaving Fort Vancouver." He was ill through August. America continued to be employed, as a middleman or Indian trader, until November 1, 1831, when he was discharged and sent to Oʻahu on the *Ganymede*. He must have returned to the coast, for, on May 21, 1841, he or possibly another Hawaiian named America boarded the *Cowlitz* at Fort Vancouver to work his passage back to Oʻahu.

PS: HBCA FtGeoAB 10–12, YFSA 3–9, 11, FtVanAB 10, FtVanSA 1–2, PJ 2, YFDS 2a, 3a–3b, 4b, Log of *Cowlitz* 1

Anahi [variation: **Onaha**] (fl. 1840–1846)

HBC employee, associated with:

Fort Stikine (1840–1843) middleman, (1843–1846) laborer

Anahi joined the HBC from Oʻahu in 1840, arriving at Fort Vancouver in April of that year. He was sent on the steamer *Beaver* to Fort Stikine, arriving on June 13 to work as a laborer. Not being used to the cold, on December 19, 1840, he froze three toes on each foot although he had been told to warm himself if he felt cold. Three other Hawaiian Islanders froze that same night, none as seriously. He was present at Fort Stikine during the murder of the post manager, John McLoughlin Jr., but likely did not participate in the event. He worked at Stikine until November 30, 1846, at which point he returned to Oʻahu.

PS: HBCA YFSA 20, 24–26, FtVanSA 6, 8, YFDS 17, FtStikPJ 1; PPS: McLoughlin, *Fort Vancouver*, vol. 2: 358

Anahi, James (fl. 1868)

Baker, b. ca. 1817, d. May 13, 1868, in New Westminster, associated with:

New Westminster (1868) baker

Described as born in the Sandwich Islands, James Anahi was unsuccessfully treated in the Royal Columbian Hospital in New Westminster in May 1868 for an abscess of the liver. James Anahi was married.

PS: BCA PR-RoyalCol

Ananu, Joseph (fl. 1870)

Laborer, b. ca. 1831, associated with:

Port Gamble (1870) sawmill worker

At the time of the 1870 Census, Joseph Ananu was one of twenty-two Hawaiians working at Puget Mill at Port Gamble.

PS: 1870 U.S. Census, Washington Territory, Kitsap Co., Port Gamble

Anounou, William (fl. 1859–1860)

Occupation unknown, associated with:

Oregon Territory (1859–1860)

Nothing is known about William Anounou, a Hawaiian in the Oregon Territory whose daughter by an unnamed Native woman, Baptistine (1860–?), was baptized by an itinerant Catholic priest in 1860.

PSP: Munnick, *Oregon City*

Apike (fl. 1843)

HBC employee, associated with:

Columbia Department general charges (1843) laborer

Apike joined the HBC in Oʻahu as a laborer likely in 1843. He appeared to work in the Columbia Department from June 1 of that year but was discharged to Oʻahu on November 15. No reason was given for his short period of employment.

PS: HBCA FtVanSA 8, YFSA 23, YFDS 14

Arioha, Sam (fl. 1854–1870)

PSAC employee, associated with:

Fort Nisqually and outstations (1854–1870) shepherd, cook

Arioha spent most of his time watching over sheep at the PSAC Fort Nisqually outstations. Nicknamed Sam, he also worked as a cook from time to time. On October 11, 1867, the Nisqually journal noted, "Discharged Sam the Shepherd in consequence of the number of sheep he is constantly losing." Likely due to a general labor shortage, he was rehired the next spring and remained until the post closed in the spring of 1870.

Arioha had an Indian wife who was hired, along with her mother, for such seasonal tasks as weeding turnips. His purchases indicate a son and perhaps other children. He has not been traced after 1870.

PS: HL FtNisPJ 10–11, FtNisSA 9–15, IB 3–4, FtNisB 8–9, 11–12, FtNisMFJ

Attoo, Jack [variations: **Ottoo, Atu**] (fl. 1791–1792)

Maritime fur trade green hand, b. in Niʻihau, associated with:

ship *Columbia Rediviva* (1789–1792) green hand, cabin boy

Jack Attoo, a high-ranking young Hawaiian born in Niʻihau, was an unintentional ambassador from Hawaiʻi in Boston. He joined the ship *Columbia* in the summer of 1789 when it was passing through the Hawaiian Islands. In Canton, a short time later on November 16, 1789, he was listed as a member of the crew for its return journey to Boston. After reaching there in 1790, he dressed in his feathered helmet and cloak, met the governor, and listened to his oratory on future friendship with Hawaiʻi.

From Boston, Jack Attoo traveled to the Northwest Coast in 1791 and in June, in Clayoquot Sound, no doubt tired of the long journey, he tried to desert. Tootiscoosettle, the eldest brother of the local chief, was held hostage to prompt the return of Attoo. When the vessel returned to the same area in February 1792, Attoo informed the *Columbia*'s captain Robert Gray of a plot by the local chiefs to take the ship and murder all aboard, an act of revenge related to the previous year's encounter. Attoo was taken back to Niʻihau, where his family came off shore and warmly greeted him. Attoo, however, refused to go ashore and continued on to Canton. His fate beyond that point is unknown. He has not been tracked through any other maritime fur trade records.

PPS: Howay, *Voyages,* 150–151, 185–186, 271–273, 310–311, 387–389, 418–419; *SS:* Chappell, *Double Ghosts,* 132

Aupu (fl. 1840–1845)

HBC employee, associated with:

Fort Vancouver (1840–1841) middleman
Snake party (1841–1845) middleman, (1845) goer and comer

Aupu joined the HBC in 1840 in Oʻahu and served with the Snake party as a middleman. He worked until December 10, 1845, at which point he returned to Oʻahu, where he was paid his final HBC wages.

PS: HBCA YFSA 20, 24–25, FtVanSA 6–8, YFDS 16, SandIsAB 5

Awana (fl. 1845–1848)

HBC employee, associated with:

Willamette (1845–1847) laborer
Willamette Falls (1847–1848) laborer

Awana, a laborer from Oʻahu, joined the HBC in 1845 on a three-year contract. He was very near the end of his contract on September 1, 1848, when he deserted, possibly for the California gold fields.

PS: HBCA YFSA 25–28, YFDS 19

Bahia (fl. 1845–1850)

HBC employee, associated with:

Fort Vancouver (1845–1846) laborer
barque *Columbia* (1846) laborer
Fort Victoria (1847–1849) laborer
brigantine *Mary Dare* (1849) laborer
Fort Victoria? (1849–1850) laborer

Bahia joined the HBC in Oʻahu on May 7, 1845, and worked as a laborer at coastal posts and on coastal shipping for the next five years. He returned to Hawaiʻi in December 1849 and, shortly after, reenlisted for a further two years. Bahia has not been traced beyond 1850.

PS: HBCA YFSA 25–32, Log of *Columbia* 9, SandIsAB 3, 10

Baker, Joe [variation: **Joseph Baker**] (fl. 1836–1841)

HBC employee, associated with:

steamer *Beaver* (1836) passenger
Fort Vancouver general charges (1836–1840) middleman and Indian trader
Fort Taku (1840–1841) middleman
barque *Columbia* (1841) passenger

Joe Baker signed on with the HBC in January 1836 in Oʻahu as a middleman and came to the coast on the *Beaver*'s maiden voyage. Once there, he worked as an Indian trader. Baker was unusual in that he had his Hawaiian wife with him. He worked with the company until November 20, 1841, and then returned to Oʻahu with his wife.

PS: HBCA SandIsLonIC 1, YFSA 15, 19–21, YFDS 6–7, 12, FtVanSA 3–7, Log of *Columbia* 4

Balau (fl. 1845–1858)

HBC employee, associated with:

Fort Vancouver (1845–1847) laborer
New Caledonia (1847–1850) laborer
Fort Rupert (1850–1854) laborer
Victoria (1854–1858)

Balau joined the HBC in Oʻahu on May 7, 1845, and worked as a laborer at various posts until 1854, when he joined the Victoria Voltigeurs, a militia group, where he was last recorded in 1858. From that point he has not been traced.

PS: HBCA YFSA 25–32, SandIsAB 3, FtVicSA 1–3; *SS:* Koppel, *Kanaka,* 70

Balia, J. (fl. 1860)

Cook, b. ca. 1820, associated with:

Fort Vancouver area (1860) cook

J. Balia, along with fellow Hawaiian **Jack Powhoken,** worked as a cook in 1860 for an HBC officer, three clerks, and a few other HBC employees remaining at the nearly abandoned Fort Vancouver. He wasn't a contracted employee and may have been working casually.

PS: 1860 U.S. Census, Washington Territory, Clark Co.

Bancroft, Mary Holmes (fl. 1837–1838)

Wife, of mixed descent b. to Oliver Holmes and Hawaiian chiefess Mahi, d. 1839, associated with:

brigantine *Lama* (1837–1838) passenger

The daughter of seaman Oliver Holmes and Hawaiian chiefess Mahi, Mary married English fur trader John Bancroft on November 22, 1836, and was on the Pacific Coast with him on the *Lama,* recently purchased from the HBC. Using Kaigani Haida hunters, the ship headed to California. There, in November 1838, a combination of heat, food that was given out sparingly when the hunt was poor, and Bancroft's insulting complaints on behalf of his wife to the Kaigani about the offensive smell of fish oil and dried fish, as well as his own drinking and abuse of the Kaiganis, led to his downfall. A quarrel took place between the captain and the hunters, and having thought he settled it, Bancroft retired for dinner. When he returned to the deck, the argument began again and, realizing that the Natives passed almost all their firearms up from their canoes onto the deck, Bancroft ordered the first mate to stop the transfer. This done, Bancroft went to the forecastle where the Natives were gathered and invited the Kaigani Haidas to fire. They took him up on his invitation, and the captain fell mortally wounded.

Mary Bancroft threw herself between the Natives and her husband and was herself shot in the foot and thigh. The Kaiganis took control of the ship and ordered the first mate to take them up the coast to their home on Dall and Prince of Wales islands in the southern Alaska panhandle. When the group arrived on December 26, 1838, the Kaiganis took most of the furs and some other ship's property ashore with them. The vessel didn't stop to anchor but sailed with Mary Bancroft back to Honolulu, arriving there on January 13, 1839. She died two weeks later.

PS: MHS *Margaret,* HHS Reynolds, biographical information from Barbara Dunn, Howay, HBCA FtSimp[N]PJ 4, FtVanCB 8, 15, SandIsLonIC 2; *PPS: Sandwich Island Gazette,* February 2, 1839: 4; *SS:* HSA newspaper article in Cartwright; "List"; Ogden, *Sea Otter Trade,* 128–130, 179; Bancroft, *History of the Northwest Coast,* vol. I: 341–342, vol. II: 604–606; Meilleur, *Pour of Rain,* 147–148; Pierce, *Russian America,* 18–19

Barlow, Kion (fl. 1870)

Farmer, b. ca. 1836, associated with:

San Juan Island (1870) farmer

It is not known when Kion Barlow reached the Pacific Northwest but, by 1870, the thirty-four-year-old Hawaiian was living alone on his own land on San Juan Island. He was illiterate and owned $1,000 in real estate, another $300 in personal property.

PS: 1870 U.S. Census, Washington Territory, San Juan Island

Belay (fl. 1829–1842)

HBC employee, b. ca. 1806 in Oʻahu, associated with:

Fort Vancouver general charges (1829–1831) middleman or laborer
Fort Vancouver (1831–1833) middleman/laborer
Fort Colvile (1833–1834) middleman or laborer
Fort Vancouver (1834–1837) middleman or laborer, (1837–1838) middleman, general charges (1838–1840) middleman
Snake party (1840–1842) middleman
Fort Vancouver (1842) middleman or laborer

Oʻahu-born Belay joined the HBC in 1829, in his early twenties, and spent the majority of his time in the southern Columbia area. He is on record as having deserted during outfit 1832–1833. He reenlisted and worked until June 4, 1842, whereupon he departed for Oʻahu.

PS: HBCA FtVanSA 2–8, YFDS 4a–7, 13, YFSA 10–15, 19–20, 22

Ben [1] (fl. 1812–1814)

PFC/NWC employee, associated with:

ship *Beaver* (1812) passenger
Astoria [Fort George] (1812–1814) laborer
overland brigade (1814) canoeman

Ben came to the Northwest Coast as an employee for the PFC probably aboard the *Beaver* in May 1812. After Astor's company was taken over by the NWC, Ben joined the Canadian company and became part of the overland expedition to Fort William in 1814. From that point, he may have gone on to London and, possibly, taken a NWC vessel back to the Pacific. Alternatively, he may have returned west overland, then to Hawaiʻi.

PS: RosL *Astoria;* PPS: Henry, *Journal,* 711

Ben [2] (fl. 1825)

Maritime fur trade seaman, associated with:

brig *Convoy* (1825) seaman

Ben shipped aboard the brig *Convoy* at Oʻahu after it arrived at that island on March 16, 1825, to unload cargo and take on supplies for the Northwest Coast. After sailing April 1 as a laborer, Ben and the vessel traded for a season, returning to Honolulu November 2. It is not known whether he continued to sail with the *Convoy.*

PS: BCA PR-*Convoy; SS:* Howay, "List"

Ben [3] (fl. 1845–1864)

HBC employee, associated with:

Fort Vancouver (1845–1846) laborer

Thompson River (1846–1851) laborer
Fort Victoria (1851–1854)
San Juan (1854–1857) laborer
Fort Victoria (1857–1860) laborer
Fort Simpson (1863–1864) laborer

Ben, from Oʻahu, joined the HBC in 1845. He spent most of his twenty-year career as a laborer at coastal posts and appeared to finish his work in 1864 at Fort Simpson, after which his accounts showed no further movement, indicating he may have left the area or died.

While Ben was working on San Juan, he raised a family. His wife may have been from the Point Roberts area. A son (?–1854) was taken to Victoria to be buried.

PS: HBCA YFSA 25–32, FtVicSA 1–10, 12–16, BelleVuePJ 1

Benjy (fl. 1853)

HBC employee, associated with:

ship *Pekin* (1853) seaman
ship *Mary Catherine* (1853) seaman

Little is known of Benjy who shipped aboard the HBC chartered vessel *Pekin* in Honolulu probably in the summer of 1853, sailed to the Northwest Coast, and arrived back in Honolulu September 27, 1853, on the *Mary Catherine*. He was given the final balance of his wages on his return.

PS: HBCA SandIsLonIC 3

Betty (fl. 1860)

Occupation unknown, b. ca. 1830, associated with:

Fort Vancouver area (1860)

Betty was one of the few named Hawaiian women living in the Pacific Northwest. In 1860, she was in the same household as **John Kie** in the Kanaka Village area and may have been his wife.

PS: 1860 U.S. Census, Washington Territory, Clark Co.

Bill [1] (fl. 1825)

Maritime fur trade seaman, associated with:

brig *Convoy* (1825) laborer

Bill shipped aboard the brig *Convoy* at Oʻahu after it arrived on March 16, 1825, to unload cargo and take on supplies for the Northwest Coast. After sailing April 1 as a laborer, Bill and the vessel traded for a season, returning to Honolulu November 2. It is not known whether he continued to sail with the *Convoy* and he has not been subsequently traced.

PS: BCA PR-*Convoy; SS:* Howay, "List"

Bill [2] (fl. 1843–1846)

PSAC employee, associated with:

Cowlitz farm (1843–1846) laborer

Bill probably joined the HBC in 1843. He worked at the Cowlitz farm until November 30, 1846, the end of his contract, at which point he returned to Oʻahu.

PS: HBCA FtVanSA 8, YFSA 24–26, YFDS 17

Bill [3] (fl. 1853)

HBC employee, associated with:

ship *Pekin* (1853) seaman
ship *Mary Catherine* (1853) seaman

Bill [2] and [3] may be the same. This Bill shipped aboard the HBC chartered vessel *Pekin* in Honolulu probably in the summer of 1853, sailed to the Northwest Coast, and arrived back in Honolulu September 27, 1853, on the *Mary Catherine*. He was given the final balance of his wages when he arrived back.

PS: HBCA SandIsLonIC 3

Bill [4] (fl. 1864)

Occupation unknown, b. ca. 1829, associated with:

Victoria area (1864)

A Hawaiian identified as Bill left Victoria for Honolulu on the *Domitila,* arriving November 12, 1864. He may have acquired the nickname while in the Pacific Northwest, arriving under a different name. Alternatively he is the same person as Bill [3].

PS: HSA Passenger

Bill, Big (fl. 1834–1835)

CRFTC employee, d. ca. November 1835 in Liberty, Missouri, associated with:

ship *May Dacre* (1834) passenger
CRFTC brigade (1834–1835) member
Fort William (1835) laborer

Big Bill was one of twenty Hawaiians recruited for Nathaniel J. Wyeth's CRFTC in 1834 and among the dozen who deserted in November of the same year on the way to Fort Hall. On March 12, 1835, Wyeth found seven of his runaways, including Big Bill, at Fort Vancouver. Big Bill returned to work, likely at Fort William. Heading overland as part of his employment, he died in Liberty, Missouri, in November 1835.

PS: OHS FtHallAB, CRFTCCB

Billy (fl. 1844–1849)

HBC employee, associated with:

Fort Vancouver (1844–1847) laborer, (1847–1849) laborer and carpenter

Billy, from Oʻahu, appeared in the Columbia in outfit 1844–1845 as a laborer with the HBC. He worked at Fort Vancouver until March 1, 1849, at which point he went to California, likely to take part in the gold rush there. His fate after that is unknown.

PS: HBCA YFSA 24–28, YFDS 19

Bingham (fl. 1837–1839)

HBC employee, associated with:

Fort Vancouver (1837–1839) laborer, (1839) middleman

Bingham, probably named after missionary Hiram Bingham who arrived at the Hawaiian Islands in 1820, signed on with the HBC in July 1837 in Oʻahu and began work at Fort Vancouver on August 10. He appears to have worked for two years and was discharged in 1839, when he likely returned to the Islands.

PS: HBCA SandIsAB 1, FtVanSA 4–6, YFDS 8, YFSA 19–20

Block [variation: **Taoukee**] (fl. 1843–1849)

HBC employee, associated with:

Fort Vancouver (1843–1849) laborer

Block, from Oʻahu, appears to have joined the HBC in 1843, for his first contract ended in 1846. He worked until August 6, 1846, at which point he returned to Oʻahu. He reenlisted and went back to his job in Fort Vancouver. On February 1, 1849, he deserted, possibly lured by the gold of California.

PS: HBCA FtVanSA 8, YFSA 24–26, 28, YFDS 17, 19

Boki [variation: **Bokee**] (fl. 1832–1838)

HBC employee, associated with:

brig *Lama* (1832) seaman
Fort Simpson naval service (1832–1834) seaman
brig *Eagle* (1834) seaman and passenger
Columbia Department (1834–1836)
barque *Nereide* (1838) seaman

Unlike his famous namesake, the governor of Oʻahu, who disappeared into oblivion in 1829, this Boki was engaged in Oʻahu by the HBC on September 6, 1832, and worked for two years on HBC ships before being discharged at Fort Vancouver and sailing back to Oʻahu on the *Eagle* as a passenger. He appears to have been engaged on and off, mainly on HBC vessels, until he was last found sailing to Fort Langley on the *Nereide* in 1838. After that he disappears from the records and probably returned to the Islands that year.

PS: HBCA SMP 14, YFSA 12–15, 17, YFDS 5a–5c, Misc.; *SS:* Bradley, *American Frontier*

Bole, John [variation: **Boli**] (fl. 1844–1857)

HBC employee, associated with:

Fort Victoria (1844–1852) laborer

John Bole joined the HBC from Oʻahu in 1844 and spent the next eight years at Fort Victoria as a laborer. Although he finished working for the HBC in 1852, he appears to have stayed in the area for another five years. Just what happened to him after that has not been ascertained, nor has any family been traced.

PS: HBCA YFSA 24–28, 30–32, FtVicSA 1, 4–7, 9

Bolster, Henry Kanahele (fl. 1894)

Seaman, associated with:

Seattle (1894)

Henry Kanahele Bolster was a disabled seaman put off from a Hawaiian vessel in Seattle in the spring of 1894. Using funds the Hawaiian government earmarked for the "Relief and Return of Indigent Hawaiians," he was given steerage passage home via Victoria.

PS: HSA Victoria

Borabora, George (fl. 1835–1855) [variation: George Budabud]

HBC employee, probably Tahitian, b. ca. 1788 possibly in Tahiti, associated with:

Fort Vancouver (1835–1836) middleman or laborer
Fort McLoughlin (1836–1841) middleman
Fort Langley (1841–1849) middleman, (1849–1850) laborer

Fort Nisqually (1850–1851) laborer
Fort Langley (1851–1852) laborer
Columbia Department (1853–1854) laborer
Fort Victoria (1854–1855) laborer

George Borabora signed on with the HBC in Oʻahu and began work in the Columbia on November 1, 1835. In the 1850 U.S. Census, he appeared as George Budabud, living in the same household as Napic (**Aleck Napahay**) and **Joe Tapou**. In the fall of 1850, an ill Borabora went to Nisqually from Fort Victoria for treatment under Chief Trader Dr. William F. Tolmie. While recovering he worked in the garden, mended fences, and so on. By January 1851, he was sufficiently recovered that he returned to work at Langley. He is last on record in 1855.

George had one daughter, Catherine (1848–1849), who was baptized a Catholic on June 17, 1849. The name of his wife is unknown. By process of elimination, he was likely the father of Louis Bin (?–bap. 1852–?), baptized Catholic at Fort Langley on February 8, 1852.

PS: HBCA YFSA 15, 19–20, 24–31, YFDS 6–7, FtVanSA 3–8, FtVicSA 1–5, HL FtNisPJ 7, BCA VS-StAndC, 1850 U.S. Census, Oregon Territory, Lewis Co.

Bottles (fl. 1867)

Miner, associated with:

Rogue River Valley, Oregon (1867) miner

A Hawaiian identified only as Bottles was mining gold at Kanaka Flat in the Rogue River Valley of Oregon in April 1867, when a fight erupted at his house.

SS: "Killed," *Oregon Sentinel,* April 6, 1867

Boy, John (fl. 1870)

Laborer, b. ca. 1843, associated with:

Port Gamble (1870) sawmill worker

At the time of the 1870 Census, John Boy was one of twenty-two Hawaiians working at Puget Mill at Port Gamble.

PS: 1870 U.S. Census, Washington Territory, Kitsap Co., Port Gamble

Bull, John [1] (fl. 1825)

Maritime fur trade seaman, associated with:

brig *Convoy* (1825) seaman

Possibly from Oʻahu, John Bull shipped onto the brig *Convoy* after it landed in Honolulu in 1825, discharged cargo, and loaded supplies for the Northwest Coast. The brig sailed April 1, traded that season, and returned November 2, 1825. John Bull has not been subsequently traced.

PS: BCA PR-*Convoy; SS:* Howay, "List"

Bull, John [2] (fl. 1834–1837)

CRFTC employee, associated with:

ship *May Dacre* (1834) passenger
CRFTC brigade (1834) member
Fort Hall (1834–1837) laborer

John Bull was among twenty men recruited for Nathaniel J. Wyeth's CRFTC in 1834. He along with **Diblo, Dido,** and **Tommy** went straight to Fort Hall, where he stayed until November 1837. John Bull received the remaining amount due him at Oʻahu at the end of the year.

PS: OHS FtHallAB; *PPS:* Beidleman, "Fort Hall," 238

Bull, John [3] [variation: **Stephano**] (fl. 1838–ca. 1860)

HBC/PSAC employee, b. ca. 1823, d. ca. 1860, associated with:

Fort Nisqually (1838–1844) middleman
Cowlitz farm (1844–1845) laborer
San Juan Island (1849–ca. 1860) farmer and PSAC shepherd

Signing on with the HBC in Oʻahu in 1838 at about age fifteen, John Bull, also known as Stephano, appears to have spent most of his time as a farm laborer around Fort Nisqually. He worked until December 10, 1845, at which point he returned to Oʻahu, but made his way back to the Victoria area, most likely to San Juan Island. There he and his family lived in close proximity to his friend, **Peter Friday.** In 1858 he went to work for the PSAC and is last on record in 1860. He probably died not long after, for his widow was remarried by 1865.

John Bull had one wife and several children. On August 29, 1849, he married Marie Hoihosiuk (ca. 1830–?), a Clallam woman. Their children were Jean Auguste (?–bap. 1850–?), Catherine (?–bap. 1853–?), Sophie (?–bap. 1857–?), Joe (?–?), and at least one other daughter. The family was Catholic. Sophie married a Scot, August McDonald, in 1865 and settled on San Juan Island. Another daughter married Joe Emerly and lived on the Nooksack River near the future Lynden, Washington. The Emerlys' son Joe raised a family at Bellingham, Washington.

PS: HBCA FtVanSA 5–8, YFSA 19–20, 24–25, SandIsAB 5, LondIC 3, HL FtNisPJ 4, FtNisSA env, 2, FtNisB 2, 6, 8, FtNisIB 2–3, BCA VS-StAndC, CCC

Bull, Tom (fl. 1834–1835)

CRFTC/HBC employee, drowned 1835 in Columbia River, associated with:

ship *May Dacre* (1834) passenger
CRFTC brigade (1834) member
HBC Snake party (1835) member

Tom Bull was one of twenty men recruited for Nathaniel J. Wyeth's CTFTC in 1834 and one of a dozen who deserted in November of the same year on the way to Fort Hall. Tom Bull reportedly joined Thomas McKay's HBC Snake party and was spotted on the Snake River February 12, 1835. Sometime thereafter, he drowned in the Columbia River.

PS: OHS FtHallAB, CRFTCCB; *PPS:* Wyeth, *Correspondence,* 250

Caesar [variations: **Casar, Cesar**] (fl. 1845–1849)

HBC employee, associated with:

Fort Vancouver (1845–1849) laborer
Fort Victoria (1849) laborer
barque *Columbia* (1849) passenger

Caesar, from Oʻahu, joined the HBC in 1845. He worked mainly at Fort Vancouver as a laborer until October 31, 1849, at which point he returned to Oʻahu aboard the barque *Columbia* and received his last HBC wages in Honolulu.

PS: HBCA YFSA 25–29, YFDS 19, SandIsAB 10

Cakaeo (fl. 1844–1851)

HBC employee, associated with:

Willamette (1844–1846) laborer
Fort Vancouver (1846–1849) laborer
Fort Langley (1849–1851) laborer

Cakaeo joined the HBC in 1844 and worked as a laborer at coastal trading posts until 1851. He likely returned to the Hawaiian Islands.

PS: HBCA YFSA 24–32, FtVicSA 1–2

Calay (fl. 1850)

Raftsman, b. ca. 1820, associated with:

Oregon City (1850) raftsman

Calay, a raftsman living in Oregon City in 1850, may have been Chinese from Hawai'i. However, according to the U.S. Census of that year, he was born on the Islands. Nothing else is known of him.

PS: 1850 U.S. Census, Oregon, Clackamas Co.

Calefu, Bire (fl. 1880)

Laborer, b. ca. 1862, associated with:

Port Gamble (1880) laborer

At the time of the 1880 Census, Bire Calefu was one of nine "Kanakas" working in Port Gamble, almost certainly at the sawmill. He was illiterate.

PS: 1880 U.S. Census, Washington Territory, Kitsap Co., Port Gamble

Canot [variation: **Canoe**] (fl. 1821–1834)

HBC employee, b. ca. 1802, died May 13, 1834, at Fort Alexandria, associated with:

New Caledonia (1821–1824) middleman or laborer
Fort St. James (1824–1825) middleman
Fort Babine [Kilmaurs] (1825) laborer
New Caledonia (1825–1828) middleman
Fort St. James (1828–1829) middleman
Chilcotin (1829–1830) middleman
New Caledonia (1830–1834) middleman
Fort Alexandria (1834) middleman

Canot, whose unusual non-Polynesian name may have come about because of his ability with small boats, appears to have joined the HBC in 1821 at the age of nineteen. His otherwise competent career was not without danger. In April 1828, he was traveling with an HBC interpreter Duncan Livingston from Fort Babine when, in an attempt to get some food to replace that stolen from their cache, they happened upon a Native village. Livingston, suspecting that something was amiss, sent Canot off; Canot was pursued but managed to avoid being caught. As he was running, the Sandwich Islander heard two shots that killed Livingston so Canot made his way to Babine to report the news there. On May 7, 1834, while working at Fort Alexandria, he took sick. He died seven days later and was buried the following evening.

Canot left a family, but their names have not been traced.

PS: HBCA YFSA 1–2, 4–9, 11-14, YFDS 1a, 3a–4a, 5a–5c, FtStJmsLS, RD, CB, FtVanSA 1–2, FtAlexPJ 1, AB

Caru, Thomas (fl. 1865)

Occupation unknown, b. ca. 1833, associated with:

Victoria area (1865)

Thomas Caru, possibly a variant of Karhooa, appeared only once on record and that was in the Victoria jail records on July 16, 1865, when the 5 foot, 7 inch Protestant Hawaiian was sentenced to serve six hours for being drunk and disorderly. He did not have a trade and may have been a wandering laborer or seaman.

PS: BCA Crt-Gaols

Cawanaia [variations: **Cowannie, Okanaya**] (fl. 1817–1839)

NWC/HBC employee, b. ca. 1798, d. November 30, 1839, likely in Fort Vancouver, associated with:

Fort George [Astoria] (1817–1825) sawyer?
Columbia Department (1825–1826) sawyer
Fort Vancouver (1826–1830) sawyer, Indian trade (1830–31)
Fort Vancouver (1831–1835) sawyer, (1835–1839) middleman or laborer

Cawanaia began his employment with the fur trade in 1817 and spent most of his career as a sawyer at Fort Vancouver. In outfit 1834–1835, he was disabled and received only partial wages. He died on November 30, 1839, likely at Fort Vancouver.

Cawanaia had a son **Charles** (ca. 1817–1883) born shortly after his arrival in the Pacific Northwest, who was baptized Methodist by missionary Jason Lee in December 1834, and a daughter Angelique (ca. 1825–?), baptized by Anglican Reverend Herbert Beaver on July 22, 1838, at Fort Vancouver. She was rebaptized June 7, 1842, at Fort Vancouver by Catholic priest Modeste Demers with the more Catholic name of Marie Angelique. Angelique wed a French Canadian boatman, Jean Baptiste Bouchard, who arrived the same time as her father.

PS: HBCA FtGeor[Ast]AB 10–12, YFSA 2–9, 11–15, 19, YFDS 2a, 3b–4a, 5a–7, FtVanSA 1–5, BCA VS-CCC, Jackson; *PPS:* Munnick, *Vancouver,* vol. 1

Cawanaia, Charles [variations: **Cohana, Charles Oawhy, Kawiniha, Canire, Coweniat, Cowaniah**] (ca. 1817–1883)

Farmer, of mixed descent, b. ca. 1817 likely at Fort George [Astoria], d. 1883 in Oregon, associated with:

Fort George [Astoria] (1817–1825) child
Fort Vancouver (1826–1830) child
Portland area (1840s–1883) farmer

Charles Cawanaia was born shortly after his father **Cawanaia**'s arrival in the Pacific Northwest in 1817. He is likely "Chas. Cohana a half breed youth," whom missionary Jason Lee baptized Methodist in December 1834 and took into his school in the Willamette Valley in March 1836. Later Cawanaia farmed south of Portland. In 1844 he reported owning horses worth $100. During the Cayuse Indian War of 1848, which followed the massacre of missionaries Marcus and Narcissa Whitman, Charles Cawanaia served as a private in a French Canadian Company. In the 1870 Census Cawanaia and his family were identified as Indians.

Charles Cawanaia had at least sixteen children by three mixed-race women in succession: Margaret Flett (–?–), whom he wed in 1846; Catherine (ca. 1838–?), born at Red River with whom he was living at the time of the 1850 Census; and Amelia Johnson (1844–1934), the daughter of an HBC employee from England and a Grand Ronde woman whom he wed in 1862. Charles Cawanaia was recorded as Charles Oawhy when he and Melie or Amelia, with whom he was already living, had their child, Pascal (1852–?), baptized by the Catholic archbishop of Oregon City on June 10, 1854. Other children, many of whom died young from tuberculosis, included William (1846–?), Eliza (ca. 1848–?), Charles (1852–?), Johnson (ca. 1853–?), Samuel (ca. 1866–?), Thomas (ca. 1868–?), Laura (1870–?), and Angeline (?–1948).

PS: 1850 and 1870 U.S. Census, Oregon, Washington Co., Jackson; *PPS:* Munnick, *Vancouver,* vol. 2; Carey, "Mission Record Book"

Charley [1] (fl. 1834–1837)

CRFTC/HBC employee, associated with:

ship *May Dacre* (1834) passenger
CRFTC brigade (1834) member
Forts William and Hall (1835–1837) laborer
Columbia Department (1837) laborer

Charley was one of twenty men recruited for Nathaniel J. Wyeth's CRFTC in 1834. He was among the dozen who deserted in November of the same year on the way to Fort Hall. On March 12, 1835, Wyeth found seven of his runaways, including Charley, at Fort Vancouver. Charley returned to work at Forts William and Hall until August 15, 1837, when his account was settled by the HBC. He may have gone to work for the HBC, possibly under a different name.

PS: OHS FtHallAB, CRFTCCB; *PPS:* Wyeth, *Correspondence,* 250

Charley [2] [variations: **Paul Cali, Charles Kanack**] (fl. 1843–1847)

HBC employee, b. ca. 1822, d. December 19, 1847, at Fort Vancouver, associated with:

Fort McLoughlin (1843–1844) laborer
Fort Vancouver (1844–1847) laborer

In 1843, at the age of twenty-one, Charley joined the HBC from Oʻahu as a laborer. After spending the first outfit at Fort McLoughlin, he worked the next four outfits at Fort Vancouver. In August 1845, he transferred some of his salary to his father. At Fort Vancouver, in December 1847, he caught the measles and on December 18, in danger of death, was baptized by the Catholic priests under the name Paul Cali. He died a day later, the same day as **Jem Mamuka**, and was buried on December 21.

Charley may have had one wife, Nancy (?–?) presumably Native, and one recorded child. The child, son of Charles Kanack, was Andre (?–bap. 1843–?).

PS: HBCA FtVanSA 8, YFSA 24–27, SandIsAB 5, YFDS 18, BCA PR-Lowe; *PPS:* Munnick, *Vancouver,* vol. 2

Charley [3] (fl. 1853)

HBC employee, associated with:

ship *Pekin* (1853) seaman
ship *Mary Catherine* (1853) seaman

Little is known of this Charley who shipped aboard the HBC chartered vessel *Pekin* in Honolulu, probably in the summer of 1853, for the Northwest Coast and arrived back September 27, 1853, on the *Mary Catherine.* He was given the final balance of his wages in Honolulu.

PS: HBCA SandIsLonIC 3

Charley [4] (fl. 1871)

Occupation unknown, b. ca. 1839, associated with:

Victoria area (1871)

On October 29, 1871, a 5 foot, 4 inch thirty-two-year-old Hawaiian named Charley appeared on the Victoria police records as being fined $100 and sentenced to six months in prison for selling spirits to the Indians. He was noted as being Roman Catholic by religion and not having a trade.

PS: BCA Crt-Gaols

Charley, W. B. (fl. 1880)

Laborer, b. ca. 1863, associated with:

Port Gamble (1880) laborer

At the time of the 1880 Census, W. B. Charley was one of nine "Kanakas" working in Port Gamble, almost certainly at the sawmill. Unlike the others, he was literate.

PS: 1880 U.S. Census, Washington Territory, Kitsap Co., Port Gamble

Cheer (fl. 1850–1862)

Occupation unknown, associated with:

Fraser Valley

In 1891 a widowed woman named Katherine Cheer (ca. 1831–?), identified in the Census as Native, lived at Maple Ridge across the Fraser River from Fort Langley in an extended household containing three sons, whose father was born in the Hawaiian Islands. His identity is a mystery. Her sons Daniel (ca. 1851–?), Joseph (ca. 1860–?), and Thomas Cheer (ca. 1862–?) were fishermen. Also living in the household were Daniel's Native wife Mary and their five children. By 1901 Daniel and Joseph Cheer were living on the Whonnock Indian reserve and identifying themselves as Indians, as family members have continued to do. Descendants long continued to take pride in their Hawaiian descent with its origins in the fur trade.

PS: 1891 Canada Census, British Columbia, Maple Ridge, 1901 Canada Census, British Columbia, Matsqui: *SS:* Lugrin, *Pioneer Women,* 107; Miller, *Valley of the Stave,* 28–29; Morton, *Fort Langley,* 288

Chester (fl. 1812–1814)

PFC/NWC employee, associated with:

ship *Beaver* (1812) passenger
Fort George [Astoria] (1812–1814) laborer

Chester was brought to Astoria, probably in May 1812 on the *Beaver,* as an employee of the PFC. On April 4, 1814, he agreed to stay on with the NWC through the summer. He has not been traced further and likely returned to Hawai'i.

PS: RosL *Astoria; PPS:* Henry, *Journal,* 711

Cho (fl. 1850)

Raftsman, b. ca. 1820, associated with:

Oregon City (1850) raftsman

Cho, a raftsman living in Oregon City in 1850, was born in the Sandwich Islands, according to the U.S. Census of that year but, since those inhabiting the house had Chinesesounding names (Moolah, Calan, etc.), he may have been Chinese from Hawai'i. Nothing else is known of him.

PS: 1850 U.S. Census, Oregon, Clackamas Co.

Coah, James [variation: **James Canton**] (fl. 1812–1828)

PFC / NWC / HBC employee, b. ca. 1796, d. April 17, 1828, at Fort Vancouver, associated with:

ship *Beaver* (1812) passenger
Fort George [Astoria] (1814–1825) laborer
Columbia Department (1825–1826) laborer
Fort Vancouver (1826–1828) laborer

Sixteen-year-old James Coah was brought to Astoria as a PFC laborer probably on the *Beaver* in 1812, although later records appear to exclude his PFC service. Two years later he joined the NWC and in 1821, at the time of amalgamation, transferred to the HBC. He spent most of his time at the Fort George store. On October 9, 1825, he together with **Harry Bell Noah, Kaharrow, Tourawhyheine,** and **Marrouna** confessed to having stolen blankets from the trade goods of the *William & Ann.* After his death at Fort Vancouver in 1828, his name was carried on the books for three years, indicating that a surviving family may have been drawing on his account.

PS: RosL *Astoria,* HBCA FtGeoAB 4, 10–12, YFSA 1–11, 17, YFDS 2a, 3a, FtVanSA 1, 3–4, AB 19; PSS: Henry, *Journal,* 711; McDonald, *Blessed Wilderness,* 29

Coayyvay [variation: **Coayeeray**] (fl. 1830–1833)

HBC employee, associated with:

Fort Vancouver general charges (1830–1831)
Fort Simpson (1831–1833) laborer
Fort Vancouver (1833) laborer

Coayyvay joined the HBC in 1830. He worked at Fort Simpson and Fort Vancouver and departed the Columbia for O'ahu on November 1, 1833.

PS: HBCA FtVanSA 2, YFDS 4a–5b, YFSA 11–13

Cole, Captain (fl. 1840–1850)

HBC employee, d. March 12, 1850, at Fort Rupert, associated with:

Fort Stikine (1840–1844) middleman
Fort Victoria (1847–1849) laborer
Fort Rupert (1849–1850) laborer

Captain Cole may have come from the O'ahu Charity School of which Captain George W. Cole was an officer in the 1830s. Cole joined the HBC in 1840 and was witness to the murder of John McLoughlin Jr., the son of chief factor John McLoughlin in April 1842 at Fort Stikine. According to McLoughlin, Cole witnessed the accused murderer "stand with his foot on my son's neck writhing in the agonies of death." Consequently, Cole was among the witnesses sent to York Factory to testify. He worked until November 23, 1844, at which point he returned to O'ahu and received his final wages at the end of that year in Honolulu. He reenlisted for three more years and began work on August 19, 1847. He was at coastal forts until his death from tuberculosis on March 12, 1850. He was buried the same day in the Fort Rupert graveyard.

PS: HBCA YFSA 20, 24, 27–32, FtVanSA 6–8, CB 31, YFDS 15, SandIsAB 3, FtRupPJ; *SS:* Bradley, *American Frontier,* 382n

Colins, Tom [variation: **Collins**] (fl. 1831–1833)

HBC seaman, associated with:

schooner *Cadboro* (1831) seaman
Naval Department (1831–1832) seaman
Fort Simpson naval service (1832–1833) seaman

Tom Colins, described as a "Sandwich Islander," was engaged by the HBC on June 16, 1831, in Oʻahu, as a seaman for the Columbia Department. He worked in coastal shipping servicing the various posts until November 1, 1833, when he returned to Oʻahu.

PS: HBCA SMP 14, YFDS 4b–5b, YFSA 11–13

Com (fl. 1840–1848)

HBC employee, d. 1848 at Fort Vancouver, associated with:

Fort Vancouver (1840–1841) middleman
Snake party (1841–1843) middleman
Fort Vancouver (1843–1844) middleman/laborer
Snake party (1844–1848) laborer
Fort Vancouver (1848) laborer

Com joined the HBC from Oʻahu in 1840. He went back on November 15, 1843, but he returned to the coast, again alternating between Fort Vancouver and the Snake River country. He died in 1848 at Fort Vancouver, and the salary owed him was paid to his relatives in Hawaiʻi.

PS: HBAC YFSA 20, 23–29, FtVanSA 6–8, YFDS 14, SandIsAB 7

Como [variation: **Henry Comeau**] (fl. 1818–1850)

NWC/HBC employee, b. ca. 1794, d. September 18, 1850, at Fort Vancouver, associated with:

Pacific slopes (1818–1821) middleman
New Caledonia (1821–1824) middleman or laborer
Fort St. James (1824–1825) middleman
Columbia Department (1825–1826) middleman
Fort Vancouver (1826–1827) middleman or laborer
Fort Langley (1827–1839) middleman
Fort Vancouver general charges (1839–1842) middleman
Fort Vancouver (1842–1844) middleman, (1844–1847) laborer, (1847–1848)
    middleman, (1848–1849) laborer, (1849–1850) cook

Como, who joined the NWC as a middleman in 1818, became one of the longest-serving Islanders in the fur trade. His thirty-two years were spent working in New Caledonia, Fort Langley, and Fort Vancouver. No explanation was given when Como and a Mr. Johnstone, while trading fish at the Cascades on July 26, 1846, were tied up and left on the beach by the Natives. Both had to be rescued by personnel from Fort Vancouver. Como, also known as Henry Comeau, died of unstated causes at Fort Vancouver on September 18, 1850. He was likely buried in the fort's graveyard even though his children were associated with the Vancouver [Washington] Catholic church and the St. Paul Catholic Church on French Prairie [Willamette Valley, Oregon].

Como had one wife, Nancy (?–?), a Native woman. Their three recorded children were Marguerite (ca. 1829–?), who married John Collis in 1853, Marie (1833–?), and **Thomas** (ca. 1835–?)

PS: HBCA YFSA 1–9, 11–12, 14–15, 20, 24–31, YFDS 1a–2a, 3a–3b, 5a–7, 21, FtStJmsLS, FtVanAB 10, SA 1–9, BCA PR-Lowe; *PPS:* Munnick, *Vancouver,* vols. 1–2, *St. Paul,* vol. 1

Como, Thomas [variation: **Toma Coma**] (1835–1850s)

HBC apprentice cooper, of mixed descent, b. ca. 1835 likely in Fort Langley, possibly d. 1856 at Grande Ronde, associated with:

Fort Vancouver (1849–1851) apprentice, (1851–1852) apprentice cooper
U.S. Army (1856) soldier

Thomas Como, the son of **Como** and a Native woman, Nancy, followed the typical career path of someone born into the fur trade. Likely born at Fort Langley, he probably went with his father to Fort Vancouver at the age of four and was raised there. At the age of fourteen, he became an apprentice cooper on a contract that ended in 1854. He did not fulfill his contract, for in outfit 1849–1850 he left for California. He did not strike gold and returned shortly after, for in the following outfit he was back at work. However, his employment did not last long, and he was discharged in 1852. In 1856 he volunteered for the U.S. Army and in July was "dangerously wounded" in an expedition against Indians in the Grand Ronde area of Oregon. Whether he survived and, if so, what he did after the volunteers were disbanded in October 1856 is unknown.

PS: HBCA YFSA 2932, FtVanSA 9, 1850 U.S. Census, Oregon, Clark Co.; *PPS: History of the Pacific Northwest,* 589

Corriacca (fl. 1830–1835)

HBC employee, died August 1835, associated with:

Fort Vancouver general charges (1830–1831)
Fort Colvile (1831–1835) middleman or laborer

Corriacca joined the HBC from Hawai'i some time in 1830. He was killed by the Blackfeet Indians, probably in the Flathead area, in August 1835.

PS: HBCA FtVanSA 2–3, YFDS 4a–6, YFSA 11, 13–15

Corrina (fl. 1810)

Maritime fur trade seaman, b. ca. 1780, d. July 23, 1810, aboard the *Albatross,* associated with:

brig *Albatross* (1810) seaman

Corrina is one of the few Hawaiian Islanders in the maritime fur trade who was named. In 1810, thirty-year-old Corrina was one of two dozen Sandwich Islanders engaged by the brig *Albatross* to crew the vessel on its voyage to, on, and from the Northwest Coast. Unfortunately for Corrina, on or around July 23, 1810, after he was sent up to heave the main, he fell to the deck and died of his injuries. Log keeper William Gale said that Corrina was "the best man out of twenty four on board belonging to the Islands." Corrina's body was wrapped and his remains committed to the deep.

PS: Private MS *Albatross*

Cowelitz (fl. 1845–1846)

HBC employee, associated with:

Fort Vancouver (1845–1846) laborer

Cowelitz, from O'ahu, joined the HBC in 1845 on a three-year contract and for unstated reasons was given the name of the Cowlitz Native nation. He worked only until August 6, 1846, when he returned to O'ahu.

PS: HBCA YFSA 25–26, YFDS 17

Cowie [variation: **Kaui, Coure**] (fl. 1841–1870)

HBC/PSAC employee, b. to Ke-a-view and unknown mother, associated with:

Fort Vancouver (1841–1842) laborer
Fort Nisqually (1842–1870) laborer and shepherd

Cowie joined the HBC from Oʻahu in 1841 and began receiving wages on July 1 of that year. In August 1845 he transferred two and a half months' salary to his father Ke-a-view, who lived in "Wyeʻti" in Honolulu. Cowie spent his thirty-year fur trade career at Fort Nisqually working for the HBC affiliated PSAC as a laborer, carpenter, and shepherd, both at the post itself and at the outstations of Tlithlow and Muck. Repeatedly, Cowie had charge of an Indian crew or held other supervisory positions, which explains his 1854 wage of $120 a year whereas the other Hawaiians there received $96. Cowie took several impromptu breaks from employment. On one of these, March 17, 1850, Cowie, **Keave-ʻhaccow**, and **Kalama** suddenly announced they were "leaving the service." Whatever Cowie did in the interim, he was welcomed back "into the employ of the Company" six months later. After Fort Nisqually closed in 1870, Cowie and his countrymen Keaveʻhaccow and **Joe Tapou** reportedly worked, at least for a time, at a nearby sawmill.

Cowie had a wife by November 1849 when he, Kalama, and Keaveʻhaccow went with "their women" for a three-day spontaneous holiday aboard a departing vessel. In October 1853 Cowie built a separate "dwelling house for himself" at Fort Nisqually, which may indicate he had a family by that time. He certainly did so by 1855 when he purchased two pairs of children's shoes. In 1857 Cowie was assessed property tax, indicating he had land in his own name. A son died in August 1868.

PS: HBCA FtVanSA 6–14, YFDS 12, YFSA 24–32, SandIsAB 5, FtNis Huggins HL FtNisPJ 5–15, FtNisSA 2–3, 5–15, env, FtNisIB 3–4, FtNisTB 1–2, FtNis IA 5, FtNisB, 8–12, env, FtNisTJ, FtNisMFJ, FNNisbox 6

Cox, John [variations: **Edward Cox, Coxe**] (fl. 1811–1850)

PFC/NWC/HBC employee, b. ca. 1779, d. February 2, 1850, at Fort Vancouver, associated with:

ship *Tonquin* (1811) passenger
Fort Astoria (1811) laborer
with David Thompson (1811) laborer
Fort George [Astoria] (1814) NWC laborer, (1821–1825) HBC middleman
Columbia Department (1825–1826) middleman
Fort Vancouver (1826–1835) middleman and pigherd, (1835–1837)
Fort Vancouver (1840–1842) middleman, (1842–1843) pigherd
Columbia Department (1843–1850) freeman

John Cox joined the crew of the *Tonquin* as a laborer around February 21, 1811, when the vessel being operated by the PFC stopped at Oʻahu and took on a complement of twenty Hawaiian Islanders. One month later, on March 22, the *Tonquin* arrived at the mouth of the Columbia and, on April 12, Cox was noted as helping to unload the vessel. A few months later Cox went east with explorer David Thompson, traveling via London on his way back to the north coast. His entire career appears to have been spent in the Fort George [Astoria] and Fort Vancouver area, leaving almost nothing in the form of a paper trail. In 1824–1825, he was attached to the Fort George store. In October 1825 he was part of a group of Hawaiians accused of having stolen blankets from the trade goods of the *William & Ann,* but denied any involvement. He appears to have retired in 1843–1844 and likely continued to live in Kanaka Village at Fort Vancouver. There, on a warm, sunny February 2, 1850, he died at somewhere between the ages of seventy-one and eighty-four.

A painting of John Cox by traveler Paul Kane hangs in the Royal Ontario Museum in Toronto.

John Cox had a wife in 1825. He also appears to have had a Native slave, Marie (1831–1845) whom he likely inherited through a previous Native wife.

PS: RosL *Astoria,* HBCA NWCAB 9, YFSA 1–9, 11–15, 19–20, FtGeo[Ast]AB 4, 10–12, YFDS 2a, 3a–3b, 4b–7, FtVanAB 10, SA 1–8, CB 9, BCA PR-Lowe; *PPS:* Henry, *Journal,* 711; Munnick, *Vancouver,* vol. 2; McDonald, *Blessed Wilderness,* 29; Atkinson, "Diary," 185

Crownriver [variation: Crowener] (fl. 1850–1853)

HBC employee, b. ca. 1827, associated with:

Fort Vancouver (1850–1851) laborer
Snake Country (1853) laborer

Crownriver appeared to join the HBC around 1850 but deserted on June 29, 1851. He was in the Snake Country in 1853–1854 with a notation indicating that he had already "left," having received partial wages. He may have reenlisted and deserted again in 1853, but this cannot be substantiated.

PS: HBCA YFSA 30–31, YFDS 22, FtVanSA 9–10, 1850 U.S. Census, Oregon, Clark Co.

Davis (fl. 1853)

HBC employee, associated with:

ship *Pekin* (1853) seaman
ship *Mary Catherine* (1853) seaman

Little is known of Davis, who shipped aboard the HBC chartered vessel *Pekin* in Honolulu probably in the summer of 1853 during the height of the smallpox epidemic, sailed to the Northwest Coast, and arrived back in Honolulu September 27, 1853, on the *Mary Catherine.* He was given the balance of his wages when he arrived back.

PS: HBCA SandIsLonIC 3

Davis, Jim (fl. 1865)

Occupation unknown, b. ca. 1827, associated with:

Victoria area (1865)

The thirty-eight-year-old 5 foot, 6 inch Honolulu-born Jim Davis, according to the colonial jail records, was "tattooed on both arms" and a "Kanaka." Literate, a Protestant by religion, but possessing no trade, Davis was sentenced to three months for "R. & V." in Victoria on May 9, 1865.

PS: BCA Crt-Gaols

Davis, Tim (fl. 1865)

Occupation unknown, b. ca. 1840, associated with:

Victoria area (1865)

Even though **Jim** and Tim Davis were in the area the same year and there is a similarity of names, this 5 foot, 8 inch twenty-five-year-old Davis could neither read nor write, had no religion, and in 1865 was sentenced to $10 or one month in jail for assault in the Victoria area. Nothing else is known about him.

PS: BCA Crt-Gaols

Diblo (fl. 1834–1837)

CRFTC/HBC employee, associated with:

ship *May Dacre* (1834) passenger
CRFTC brigade (1834) member
Forts Hall and William (1834–1836) laborer
Columbia Department (1836–1837) part-time HBC employee

Diblo was one of twenty men recruited for Nathaniel J. Wyeth's CRFTC in 1834. He along with **John Bull, Dido,** and **Tommy** reached Fort Hall just before Christmas and remained there or at Fort William until the beginning of 1836. Diblo did part-time work for the HBC in 1836–1837 and then disappears from the records.

PS: OHS FtHallAB, HBCA FtVanSA 3–4, YFDS 7, YFSA 16–17; *PPS:* Beidleman, "Fort Hall," 238

Dick [1] [variations: **Loolon, Dick Owhyhee**] (fl. 1817–1855)

NWC/HBC employee, b. ca. 1800, d. December 18, 1855, at Fort Vancouver, associated with:

Columbia River area (1817–1822) laborer
Fort George [Astoria] (1822–1825) laborer
Columbia Department (1825–1826) laborer
Umpqua Snake expeditions (1826–1827) laborer
Fort Vancouver (1827–1854) middleman or laborer

Dick joined the NWC from Oʻahu around 1817 at about the age of seventeen and worked in the fur trade for over a third of a century. At the time of amalgamation, he continued working with the HBC in the Fort Vancouver area, possibly at the sawmill, and lived in Kanaka Village. By the beginning of the 1850s, the U.S. Army was assuming control of the Vancouver area. The condition of the village buildings deteriorated and those Hawaiians, such as the now fifty-year-old Dick and his family, who were not deployed to Fort Victoria with the company, were left to their own devices. According to the 1850 Census, which put his birth date at an unlikely 1818, he was then working as a steward for the remaining people at the fort. He last appeared with the HBC in 1854 as a pensioner at Fort Vancouver, and subsequently died and was buried on December 18, 1855, probably in the graveyard north of the fort.

Dick had a wife and four children. With his wife, a native Chinook, he was the father of Richard (?–bap. 1838–?), James (?–bap. 1838–?), baptized Anglican, Therese (1840–?), and Luce (1843–1844), baptized Catholic.

PS: HBCA FtGeo[Ast]AB 10–12, YFSA 2–9, 11–15, 19–20, 24–32, YFDS 2a, 3a, 4a–7, FtVanSA 1–10, CB 9, 1850 U.S. Census, Oregon Territory, Clark Co., BCA CCC; *PPS:* Munnick, *Vancouver,* vols. 1–2

Dick [2] (fl. 1834–1837)

CRFTC/HBC employee, associated with:

ship *May Dacre* (1834) passenger
CRFTC brigade (1834) member
Forts William and Hall (1835–1837) laborer
Columbia Department (1837) laborer

Dick was one of twenty men recruited for Nathaniel J. Wyeth's CRFTC in 1834 and among the dozen who deserted in November of the same year on the way to Fort Hall. He was later found by Wyeth at Fort Vancouver and taken to Fort William and then Fort

Hall, where he worked until October 1837, when his account was settled by the HBC. At that point, Dick apparently went his own way. Because of the name's similarity to **Dick** [1], there is a possibility that some of the baptized children may be his.

PS: OHS FtHallAB; *PPS:* Wyeth, *Journal,* 250; *SS:* Beidleman, "Fort Hall," 238

Dido (fl. 1834–1836)

CRFTC employee, d. ca. June 23, 1836, at Liberty, Missouri, associated with;

ship *May Dacre* (1834) passenger
CRFTC brigade (1834) member
Fort Hall (1834–1836) laborer
Expedition east (1836) member

Dido was one of twenty men recruited for Nathaniel J. Wyeth's CRFTC in 1834. He along with **John Bull, Diblo**, and **Tommy** went straight to Fort Hall, where he probably went out on various trapping expeditions, often with his friend Diblo. While there, Dido made shirts and smoked tobacco for use or further trade. Having become acclimatized, in 1836 he joined the overland expedition east after the company collapsed, and died en route with $100 yet owed to him. The amount may have been paid to one or more relatives back home.

PS: OHS FtHallAB, CRFTCCB; *SS:* Beidleman, "Fort Hall," 238

Dwarty, Joe (fl. 1881)

Laborer, b. ca. 1841, associated with:

Victoria area (1881) laborer

Joe Dwarty liked his alcohol for, on November 6, 1881, the 5 foot, 7 inch forty-year-old Hawaiian laborer had just wracked up his eleventh conviction for being drunk and disorderly in the Victoria area. He paid his fine and has not been traced further. He was Roman Catholic by faith and could neither read nor write.

PS: BCA Crt-Gaols

Ebony (fl. 1844–1859)

HBC employee, associated with:

Fort Vancouver (1844–1845) laborer
barque *Vancouver* (1845) seaman
Fort Vancouver (1845–1846) laborer
barque *Columbia* (1846) seaman
Fort Victoria (1846–1849) laborer
schooner *Cadboro* (1849–1850) seaman
Fort Victoria (1850–1851) laborer
steamer *Otter* (1858) stoker
Craigflower farm (1859) woodcutter

Ebony joined the HBC in 1844 and served on several company ships as a seaman. Like most, he did a variety of jobs. For example, on November 23, 1849, he was sent ashore from the *Cadboro* for three days at Fort Nisqually to make candles. He appeared to stop work in 1851 and join the Victoria colonial militia, the Voltigeurs. In June 1858, after the Voltigeurs were disbanded, he worked as a stoker on the steamer *Otter* and was in the Victoria area cutting wood in 1859.

PS: HBCA YFSA 24–32, Logs of *Vancouver* [2] 2, *Columbia* [2] 9, *Cadboro* 6, *Otter,* YFDS 22, FtVicSA 1, PSACAB 38

Ehoo (fl. 1841–1847)

PSAC employee, associated with:

Cowlitz farm (1841–1843) shepherd, laborer
Fort Nisqually outstation (1843–1847) shepherd

Ehoo joined the HBC from Oʻahu in 1841 and began to receive wages on July 9 of that year. He spent the majority of his career in the Fort Nisqually area, where he worked as a shepherd until November 10, 1847, at which point he returned to the Sandwich Islands. In January 1845 Ehoo acquired goods from PSAC in order "to purchase a wife."

PS: HBCA FtVanSA 6–8, YFDS 12, 18, YFSA 24–27, Bio, HL FtNisSA 2–3, 5, env, FNNisB env, FtNisbox 6; *PPS:* Anderson, *Physical Structure,* 166–171

Ehu (fl. 1858)

Occupation unknown, associated with:

Vancouver Island (1858)

Ehu was one of fourteen Hawaiians departing Honolulu for Victoria on the schooner *Alice* on June 22, 1858, enticed by the euphoria of the gold rush.

PS: HSA Passenger

Eihu [variations: **Ehiu, Ehu, Na Enoka Ehu, Enid Ehu**] (fl. 1845–1886)

PSAC/HBC employee, died ca. 1886 at Coal Harbour, Burrard Inlet, associated with:

Cowlitz farm (1845–1847) laborer
Vancouver (1847–1850) laborer
Burrard Inlet (1860s–1886) millman

The records of Eihu, whose name denotes one of traditionally low rank in Hawaiian society, are not entirely clear. According to oral tradition, Eihu had a good education at a mission school and, in fact, trained to be a teacher. He joined the HBC on May 7, 1845, from Oʻahu and worked until 1850, when he returned to Hawaiʻi. Oral accounts claim that, after his return to the Sandwich Islands in 1850–1851, Eihu had three children. As transactions were carried on his account until 1853, he may have been using up £20 of credit and running a debt of £4 by 1852–1853 in Oʻahu or was back in the Columbia. A clue may be in the 1849–1850 district statements that said that "his advances charged settlers Tariff." He is said to have returned to British North America around 1856 and may have gone to the Langley area, where he became a Native teacher. Apparently, he then moved to Burrard Inlet, where he was employed at the Hastings sawmill.

In 1869, Eihu and his family settled on 3 acres on Coal Harbor, built a cottage, and planted fruit trees; **Nahanee, Keamo,** and perhaps others joined them to form an enclave known as Kanaka Ranch. In August 1871, no doubt to secure his land rights, Eihu took out naturalization papers in New Westminster. He continued to live in the Coal Harbour area until his death in about 1886, being buried on nearby Deadman's Island. Eihu's Hawaiian-language bible, printed in 1872 and one of the first bibles to reach the area, now rests in the Vancouver Archives.

Eihu appears to have had two successive wives. According to his descendants, his first wife was an unnamed Hawaiian woman ("Wahine Ehu") by which he had in Oʻahu Ioane (?–bap. 1851–?), Samuela Ulumeheihei (?–bap. 1852–?), and Noa Pikao (?–bap. 1857–?). When he returned to the West Coast, he married Mary See-em-ia (?–?), likely a Squamish woman, with whom he had Margaret (ca. 1857–1925). Margaret had two newcomer husbands, first Ben McCord and then Daniel McPhee.

PS: HBCA YFSA 24–32, FtVAnASA 9, YFDS 20, SandIsAB 3, Bio

Eleahoy (fl. 1837–1845)

HBC employee, associated with:

Fort Vancouver (1837–1840) middleman
Snake party (1840–1841) middleman
Fort Vancouver (1841–1843) middleman
Fort McLoughlin (1843–1844) middleman
Willamette (1844–1845) laborer

Eleahoy joined the HBC in July 1837 at the Honolulu office and began work at Fort Vancouver on August 10 of that year. He was at various locations and helped to transport people in and out of the Snake Country. He worked until June 24, 1842, at which point he returned to Oʻahu. However, he was soon reengaged. He retired again on July 18, 1845, and returned to Oʻahu. On his final return he received an extra gratuity, for he had gone almost blind.

PS: HBCA SandIsAB 1, 5, FtVanSA 4–8, YFDS 11, 13, YFSA 19–22, 24–25

Elene (fl. 1852)

Occupation unknown, associated with:

Victoria area (1852)

Nothing is known of Elene, except that his daughter Louise (?–bap. 1852–?) was baptized Catholic in Victoria on April 25, 1852.

PS: BCA VS-StAndC

Emene (fl. 1870)

Laborer, b. ca. 1829, associated with:

Port Gamble (1870) sawmill worker

At the time of the 1870 Census, Emene was one of twenty-two Hawaiians working at Puget Mill at Port Gamble.

PS: 1870 U.S. Census, Washington Territory, Kitsap Co., Port Gamble

Faito, George (fl. 1830–1856)

HBC employee, associated with:

Fort Vancouver general charges (1830–1831) middleman
Fort Simpson (1831–1833) middleman
Fort Vancouver (1833–1837) middleman or laborer, (1837–1844) middleman,
  (1844–1847) laborer, (1847–1849) laborer and sawyer
Fort Victoria (1849–1851) sawyer, (1851–1853)
Colwood farm (1856) laborer
Belle Vue sheep farm (1856) laborer

George Faito joined the HBC from Hawaiʻi in April 1830 and spent much of his career in the fur trade at Fort Vancouver. After nineteen years he moved to Fort Victoria, where he worked as a sawyer and, later, a laborer at nearby farms. He appears to be the George F. of the Catholic Church records. If this is the case, his wife was Josephine (1824–1849).

PS: HBCA FtVanSA 2–8, YFSA 11–15, 19–20, 24–32, YFDS 4a–7, SMP 14, FtVicSA 1–3, PSACMis, BCA VS-StAndC

Fight, John (fl. 1831–1834)

HBC employee, associated with:

schooner *Cadboro* (1831) seaman
Naval Department (1831–1832) seaman
Fort Vancouver (1832–1833) middleman, Indian trade (1833–1834)
brig *Eagle* (1834) passenger

John Fight was engaged by the HBC on June 13, 1831, at Oʻahu as a seaman in the Columbia. He worked largely in the Vancouver area until December 1, 1834, when he returned to Oʻahu aboard the brig *Eagle*.

PS: HBCA SMP 14, YFSA 11–15, YFDS 4b–5c, SandIsM

Fisher, Caesar (fl. 1825)

Maritime fur trade seaman, associated with:

brig *Convoy* (1825) seaman

Caesar Fisher shipped aboard the brig *Convoy* at Oʻahu after it arrived at that island on March 16, 1825, to unload cargo and take on supplies for the Northwest Coast. After sailing April 1 as a laborer, Fisher and the vessel traded for a season, returning to Honolulu November 2. It is not known whether he continued to sail with the *Convoy*.

PS: BCA PR-*Convoy; SS:* Howay, "List"

Fooina [variations: Fo-o-ina, Foina] (fl. 1830–1836)

HBC employee, d. 1836–1837 in the Columbia area, associated with:

Fort Vancouver general charges (1830–1831)
Fort Vancouver (1831–1835) middleman or laborer
Fort Vancouver general charges (1836) laborer
Columbia Department (1836–1837) laborer

Fooina, who was originally engaged from Oʻahu in 1830, spent part of his time working at the Fort Vancouver sawmill. In 1835 he returned to Oʻahu but was reengaged late that year or in January 1836. He died sometime in the 1836–1837 outfit but, as no wages were credited to his name, died early in the outfit or was too ill to work.

PS: HBCA FtVanSA 2, CB 9, YFDS 4a–6, YFSA 11–16

Freezy [variation: **Chee-ah-thluk**] (?–1864)

Songhees chief, of mixed descent, d. 1864 in Victoria, associated with:

Victoria area (?–1864)

Chee-ah-thluk, a mid-nineteenth-century chief of the Songhees near Victoria, British Columbia, was nicknamed "Freezy" for his frizzled hair, an inheritance of his unnamed Hawaiian father. His maternal inheritance resulted in what a contemporary termed "a most remarkably flattened head." Freezy died in 1864.

Freezy and his Native wife were the parents of Charley (?–bap. 1863–?) and Joanna (?–1877). The Catholic record at his son's baptism described him as "King Freezy, king of the Songhees."

PS: BCA VS-StAndC, PR-Anderson; *PPS:* Helmcken, *Reminiscences,* 284, Fawcett, *Recollections,* 285

Friday, Joe (1844–1895)

Laborer, of mixed descent, b. ca. 1844 in Pacific Northwest to Peter Friday and an unknown Native woman, d. April 14, 1895, at sea off the coast of Alaska, associated with:

San Juan Island (1860s) shepherd
San Juan Island (1860s–1890s)
Victoria (1895) sealer

Born in the Pacific Northwest, Joe Friday worked as shepherd for the HBC on San Juan Island prior to its being awarded to the United States in 1872. His close relationship to the other Hawaiians living there is attested by his being a witness to the weddings of **Kāne** and **Kamai** in Victoria on December 20, 1870. Unlike the two others who took their families north to British Columbia, Friday remained on San Juan Island, likely because his father continued to live there. He was employed as an "Indian cook" on a sealing schooner that capsized off the coast of Alaska in a gale and snowstorm in April 1895, with loss of all hands aboard. His widow, then living on the Songhees reserve outside of Victoria, received his remaining wages.

Considerable confusion exists as to which events are associated with Joe Friday and which with his father **Peter Friday**. Joe Friday's signature is on the 1864 request to establish a school on San Juan Island. He also signed a petition of 1872, along with numerous British residents, requesting the British to continue to watch over their affairs.

PS: BCA VS-StAndC

Friday, Peter [variations: **Polaie, Poalima**] (fl. 1841–1894)

PSAC/HBC employee, d. ca. April 11, 1894, possibly on San Juan Island, associated with:

Cowlitz farm (1841–1843) middleman
Fort Victoria (1843–1844) laborer
Columbia Department general charges (1844–1845) laborer
barque *Cowlitz* (1845) passenger
Fort Victoria (1845–1849) laborer
ship *Mary Dare* (1849) laborer
Fort Rupert (1850–1852) laborer
San Juan Island (1852–1857) farmer
Belle Vue sheep farm (1857–1860) laborer
San Juan Island (1860–1870s) farmer, (1870s–1894) retired

Just what motivated this Sandwich Islander, then probably in his early twenties, to join the HBC in 1841 is unknown, although family tradition has him floating ashore in the Pacific Northwest on a chicken coop after the ship he was on sank. His Hawaiian name may have been Poalima, alternatively the Hawaiian for Friday may have been transcribed as Polaie. Friday, as he was known on HBC records, began work on July 9 of that year and spent the next eleven years working at coastal posts, going home at the finish of each contract. He first returned on January 10, 1845, and was reengaged on May 7, sailing from Honolulu in September on the *Cowlitz*. He worked until October 5, 1848, when he returned to Oʻahu for the second time, but again came back to the Pacific slopes. In the early 1850s, Friday, who along the way acquired a first name of Peter, moved to San Juan Island. He established a farm in an area now known as Friday Harbor and raised a family, but he was not without trouble. On May 20, 1859, his house was ransacked by marauding Haida and in November of that year he lost sheep to the same group. In the spring of 1860, he left PSAC and began farming on his own. By the time of the 1880 Census Peter Friday was unable to work. He had "no use of one leg" due to syphilis. He died in April 1894 and was buried on April 11.

On December 19, 1870, Friday formalized his marriage in a Catholic ceremony to Mary (ca. 1834–1926), who was Songhees. Their children were Mary (1860–1912), Lazare

(1866–1883), John (1872–1902), and Emma (1875–1906). **Joseph Friday** (ca. 1844–1895) was an older son of Peter Friday and an unknown Native woman. In 1864, the Friday family subscribed to a fund to establish the first school on San Juan Island, and the Friday children were subsequently enrolled there.

PS: HBCA FtVanSA 6–8, YFDS 12, 15, 19, YFSA 24, 26–28, 30–32, SandIsAB 3, 9, FtVicSA 1, BCA-VS-RossBayCem, StAndC, StElizC, HSA Passenger, U.S. 1880 Census, San Juan Island; *SS:* McDonald, *Making History,* 67; Wood, *San Juan Island,* 94

George [1] (fl. 1837–1838)

Cook, associated with:

Willamette mission (1837–1838) cook

George was working as a cook at the Willamette mission in 1837–1838, when he built himself "a house in the Sandwich Islands fashion." He may be the same person as **Moo, Namaurooa,** or **Tooa,** George being a nickname given him by the missionaries.

PS: Boyd, *People of the Dalles,* 227–228

George [2] (fl. 1843–1845)

HBC employee, associated with:

Fort Vancouver (1843–1845) laborer

George joined the HBC from Oʻahu around 1843 on a contact that ended in 1846. He worked at Fort Vancouver until July 18, 1845, at which point he returned to Oʻahu. It is possible he was George [1].

George had one wife and one recorded child. He and an unnamed Chehalis woman had Louis Mari (1844–1844).

PS: HBCA FtVanSA 8, YFSA 24–25, YFDS 16, SandIsAB 5; *PPS:* Munnick, *Vancouver,* vol. 2

George [3] (fl. 1853)

HBC employee, associated with:

ship *Pekin* (1853) seaman
ship *Mary Catherine* (1853) seaman

This George, who could possibly be George [1] and/or [2], shipped aboard the HBC chartered vessel *Pekin* in Honolulu probably in the summer of 1853, sailed to the Northwest Coast, and arrived back in Honolulu September 27, 1853, on the *Mary Catherine.* He was given the final balance of his wages when he arrived back.

PS: HBCA SandIsLonIC 3

George [4] (fl. 1859)

Laborer, associated with:

Port Gamble (1859) sawmill worker

On March 21, 1859, George returned to Honolulu from Teekalet in Puget Sound on the barque *Jenny Ford.* George is likely a nickname, making it unclear how long he worked at the sawmill.

PS: HSA Passenger

George [5] (fl. 1860)

Laborer, b. ca. 1830, associated with:

Fort Vancouver area (1860) laborer

George was living in the Kanaka Village area in 1860 with a large group of Hawaiians and their families and probably worked on a casual basis for what remained of the HBC interests in the area.

PS: 1860 U.S. Census, Washington Territory, Clark Co.

Gerfe (fl. 1850)

Occupation unknown, b. ca. 1826, associated with:

Fort Vancouver area (1850)

A Hawaiian with the improbable name of Gerfe was living in the Kanaka Village near Fort Vancouver in 1850. Nothing else is known of him.

PS: 1850 U.S. Census, Oregon, Clark Co.

Grego, Lonalem (fl. 1869–1870)

Occupation unknown, associated with:

Victoria/San Juan area (1869–1870)

Nothing is known about Lonalem Grego except for his marriage on December 19, 1870, to a Songhees woman named Mary (?–?). The witnesses were Cahouna, who was **William Newanna**, and Lagamin, who was **William Naukana**. Given they both lived on San Juan Island, it is likely Lonalem Grego also did so. He and Mary had Helen (?–bap. 1870–?)

PS: BCA VS-StAndC

Haihā (fl. 1870)

Laborer, b. ca. 1829, associated with:

Port Gamble (1870) sawmill worker

At the time of the 1870 Census, Haihā was one of twenty-two Hawaiians working at Puget Mill at Port Gamble.

PS: 1870 U.S. Census, Washington Territory, Kitsap Co., Port Gamble

Halelea, Levi [variation: **Haalelea**] (fl. 1860)

Member of Royal Hawaiian household, b. 1822 in Lahaina, Maui, to governor of Moloka'i and Kipa, d. October 3, 1864, in Honolulu, associated with:

schooner *Emma Rooke* (1860) passenger
Victoria (September 18–24, 1860) visitor

When Levi Halelea came to Victoria aboard the *Emma Rooke* in 1860 accompanying Prince **Lot**, he was a member of the house of nobles and the king's privy council. He was also the private secretary and land agent for Kekauonohi (governess of Kaua'i and widow of Prince Kealiiahonu). Halelea married Kekauonohi soon after the death of Kealiiahonu. His reactions to his week-long visit to Victoria have not been recorded. He continued with the schooner to San Francisco and then back to Hawai'i.

PS: HSA Passenger Manifests, 82, Victoria; *SS: Pacific Commercial Advertiser,* October 8, 1864; *Colonist,* September 19–25, 1860; Kuykendall, *Hawaiian Kingdom,* vol. 2

Haley (fl. 1856–1867)

Occupation unknown, associated with:

Burrard Inlet (1856–1867)

While Haley himself cannot be traced, a Hawaiian-born man using that surname fathered four daughters and a son, according to oral tradition by a woman whose father was Hawaiian and whose mother was French and Indian. Margaret (ca. 1857–ca. 1888), Fisabee (ca. 1858–1897), Mary Agnes (ca. 1867–1904), Annie (ca. 1869–?), and William (?–?) made their lives on Burrard Inlet, the future Vancouver. Maggie had two daughters by American lumberman Philander Swet; Fisabee had two children by French Canadian hotelier Maximilian Michaud, another six by Scots logger Duncan McDonald; Mary had sons by two newcomer men before beginning a family of five with a second-generation Hawaiian, Leon Nahu; Annie may have died young. William worked as a deckhand and steamboat engineer on ships going between the Pacific Northwest and the Hawaiian Islands.

PS: Family recollections, 1881, 1891, 1901 Canadian Censuses

Halim, John [variations: **Hallam, Haley, Ellum**] (1858–1880s)

Laborer, associated with:

Fraser River (ca. 1858) gold miner
Moodyville (1860s) sawmill worker

According to oral accounts, John Hallam left Hawai'i as a young man for the British Columbia gold rush and, after an unsuccessful spell in the gold fields, drifted to the lumber mill at Moodyville on the north shore of the Burrard Inlet and then settled in the Fraser Valley. John Halim is likely the man called John Ellum who was treated in the Royal Columbian Hospital in New Westminster on October 13, 1865, for rheumatism and pronounced cured.

John Halim "of the Sandwich Isles" appeared in the Victoria Catholic records on May 28, 1868, when he and his Lummi wife Mary (?–?) had their son John (ca. 1864–?) baptized. By the time of the 1881 Census they were also the parents of Abraham (ca. 1872–?) and Naghou (ca. 1878–?). A son James (ca. 1869–1956) by a Katzie chief's daughter named Falmok or Philamenia changed his surname to Adams. In the 1920s James Adams became chief of the Katzie tribe in the Fraser Valley.

PS: BCA VS-StAndC, PR-RoyalCol, 1881 Canada Census, British Columbia, New Westminster North; *SS:* Ed Moyer, "Fraser Valley Chief Guards A Dwindling Tribe," *Vancouver Sun Magazine,* January 3, 1948

Ham (fl. 1845–1851)

HBC employee, d. ca. 1851 likely at Fort Vancouver, associated with:

Fort Vancouver (1845–1850) laborer

Ham joined the HBC from O'ahu in 1845. His contract ended in 1850 and in outfit 1850–1851 he did not receive wages, carrying a £5.9.8 credit into the outfit. He carried a £4.7.9 debt into the following outfit where it was noted that he died, likely at Fort Vancouver, where he worked as a laborer.

PS: HBCA YFSA 25–32

Hamua (fl. 1840–1843)

Laborer, associated with:

vessel *Vancouver* (1840) passenger
Gray's mission (1840–1843) laborer

Hamua and her husband **Iakobo**, from 30 miles outside of Honolulu, responded to a call put out by Hiram Bingham to assist Protestant missionary Henry Gray in Oregon and, in February 1840, the young couple headed there on the HBC's vessel *Vancouver.* By the summer of 1843 their relationship had deteriorated with Gray, who proposed to send them home. Presumably, they went.

PS: HMCS OrMission

Handy, Jim [variation: **Keon Handy**] (fl. 1855–1870)

Farmer, b. ca. 1835, associated with:

San Juan Island (1855–1870)

Jim or Keon Handy may be the same as **William Naukana,** also known as Lygamen and by several other names. By 1870, he was a farmer, on San Juan Island, who had $800 in real estate and $500 in personal assets and a growing family.

Jim Handy had one wife, Cecilia (ca. 1840–?), a Native born in Washington Territory [formerly Oregon Territory]. Although she could neither read nor write, she attended school within that year. Their children were given as Juliana (ca. 1856–?), Anna (ca. 1859–?), Mary (ca. 1861–?), and Jane (1870–?).

PS: 1870 U.S. Census, Washington Territory, San Juan Island

Hanerere (fl. 1860)

Seaman, associated with:

schooner *Emma Rooke* (1860) seaman

Hanerere was among five Hawaiians contracted by the schooner *Emma Rooke* when it sailed from Honolulu to Victoria on August 29, 1860. The men received $15 per month with a $15 advance. He was discharged on November 2.

PS: HSA Seamen

Hanihowa (fl. 1822)

HBC employee, associated with:

Columbia Department (1822) employee

Hanihowa worked for the HBC in the Columbia Department until the summer of 1822, when he returned to the Sandwich Islands.

PS: HBCA FtGeo[Ast]AB 10, YFSA 2

Haona [variation: **Houna**] (fl. 1845–1847)

HBC employee, d. April 24, 1847, at Fort Hall, associated with:

Fort Vancouver (1845–1846) laborer
Snake party (1846–1847) laborer
Fort Hall (1847) laborer

Haona joined the HBC from Oʻahu on May 7, 1845, for three years. He died two years later at Fort Hall.

PS: HBCA YFSA 25–26, YFDS 18, SandIsAB 3

Harris, Harry (fl. 1832–1834)

HBC seaman, possibly Hawaiian or of mixed descent, associated with:

brig *Lama* (1832–1834) seaman
brig *Eagle* (1834) passenger

Harry Harris, who may have been a Hawaiian or of mixed descent, was engaged by the HBC in Oʻahu on September 5, 1832, and appears to have come to the Northwest Coast aboard the *Lama*. He worked as a seaman on coastal shipping until November 1834, when he was sent back to Oʻahu on the *Eagle*.

PS: HBCA SMP 14, YFSA 12–14, YFDS 5a–5c, SanIsAB 1

Harry [1] (fl. 1811–1814)

PFC/NWC employee, associated with:

> ship *Tonquin* (1811) passenger
> Fort Astoria (1811–1813) employee
> Fort George [Astoria] (1814) laborer

Harry was one of twelve locals the *Tonquin* picked up in February 1811 at Hawaiʻi to work for the PFC. After arriving at the mouth of the Columbia on March 22, 1811, and after two days of efforts to establish a safe passage across the bar, the captain sent out Harry, fellow Sandwich Islander **Peter**, Stephen Weeks, Job, Aiken, and John Coles in the pinnace (small boat) to take soundings. When the pinnace filled with water, Aiken and Coles were lost but Weeks, Harry, and Peter stripped off their shirts and managed to right the pinnace, bailing it out with their hands. After Peter succumbed, Harry threw himself on his body, probably as much in grief as to get what body heat he could. Weeks and Harry were rescued. Harry took some time to recover and appears to have still been working at Fort Astoria during the takeover by the NWC in 1814. He was on record on April 4, 1814, as being prepared to work for the NWC through the summer at Fort George [formerly Astoria], but has not been traced further.

PS: RosL *Astoria;* *PPS:* Franchère, *Journal,* 73–74; Henry, *Journal,* 711

Harry [2] (fl. 1825)

Maritime fur trade seaman, associated with:

> brig *Convoy* (1825) seaman

Harry shipped aboard the brig *Convoy* at Oʻahu after it arrived at that island on March 16, 1825, to unload cargo and take on supplies for the Northwest Coast. After sailing April 1 as a laborer, Harry and the vessel traded for a season, returning to Honolulu November 2. It is not known whether he continued to sail with the *Convoy*.

PS: BCA PR-*Convoy;* *SS:* Howay, "List"

Harry [3] (fl. 1853)

HBC employee, associated with:

> ship *Pekin* (1853) seaman
> ship *Mary Catherine* (1853) seaman

Harry shipped aboard the HBC chartered vessel *Pekin* in Honolulu probably in the summer of 1853 during the height of the smallpox epidemic, sailed to the Northwest Coast, and arrived back in Honolulu September 27, 1853, on the *Mary Catherine*. He was given the final balance of his wages on his return.

PS: HBCA SandIsLonIC 3

Harry [4] (fl. 1860)

Laborer, b. ca. 1835, associated with:

> Fort Vancouver area (1860) laborer

Harry was living with a group of Hawaiians and their families in the Kanaka Village area of Fort Vancouver in 1860. He, like the others, probably worked for what remained of HBC interests in the area.

PS: 1860 U.S. Census, Washington Territory, Clark Co.

Harry, Jack [variation: Jack Henry] (fl. 1831–1835)

HBC seaman, associated with:

brig *Cadboro* (1831) seaman
Naval Department (1831–1832) seaman
brig *Dryad* (1832–1834) seaman
Fort Vancouver (1834–1835) laborer
barque *Ganymede* (1835) seaman

Jack Harry was engaged by the HBC on June 16, 1831, in Oʻahu as a seaman to work in Columbia shipping. When he was back in Oʻahu in January 1834, he took a few days off, without liberty, to stay ashore, probably to visit friends or relatives. It took the intervention of King Kamehameha III to get him onboard. He returned to the Northwest Coast and worked on coastal shipping as a seaman and landsman until October 3, 1835, when he embarked on the barque *Ganymede* for his final return voyage to Oʻahu, where he was paid his final HBC wage.

PS: HBCA SMP 14, YFSA 11, YFDS 4b, 5b–6, FtVanSA 3, SandIsLonIC 1, HSA 402-3-47

Haumea, William, [variation: **Hamea**] (fl. 1874–1902)

Farmer and orchardist, d. September 1902 on Russell Island, British Columbia, associated with:

Salt Spring Island (1874–1886) farmer
Russell Island (1886–1902) farmer

William Haumea appeared on British Columbia's earliest voting list, in 1874, as a farmer at Fulford Harbour on southern Salt Spring Island, and continued to do so. Ambitious to expand his farm and orchard, in 1886 Haumea purchased nearby Russell Island. In 1901 he gave his income from farming over the past year as $300. He died a year later.

William Haumea and an Indian woman named Mary (?–?) had a namesake daughter.

PS: 1881, 1891, and 1901 Canada Census, British Columbia, Salt Spring; *PPS:* British Columbia, *Sessional Papers,* voting lists

Hawaapai (fl. 1850)

HBC seaman, associated with:

barque *Cowlitz* (1850) seaman

Hawaapai served on the HBC vessel *Cowlitz* from February 3 to September 17, 1850, from Oʻahu to the Northwest Coast and back again. On August 27, at Honolulu he and the other Hawaiian crewmen refused to work, claiming their contract was up, but nonetheless returned to work for another month while the ship was in harbor. After that he has not been traced.

PS: HBCA SandIsAB 10, 11, Log of *Cowlitz* 8

Hawaii (fl. 1841–1843)

HBC employee, associated with:

Fort Vancouver (1841–1842) middleman and laborer
Columbia Department general charges (1842–1843)

Hawaii joined the HBC from Oʻahu in 1841 and began receiving wages on July 9 of that year. He spent the next two outfits likely at Fort Vancouver, where he worked until October 31, 1843. At that point he returned to Oʻahu.

PS: HBCA FtVanSA 6–8, YFDS 12–14, YFSA 23

Henry, John [1] (fl. 1834)

CRFTC employee, d. ca. December 1834 at Walla Walla [Washington], associated with:

ship *May Dacre* (1834) passenger
CRFTC brigade (1834) member

John Henry was among twenty men recruited for Nathaniel J. Wyeth's CRFTC in 1834 and one of the dozen who deserted in November of the same year on the way to Fort Hall. Not long after, he was reported drowned in the Columbia River.

PS: OHS FtHallAB, CRFTCCB; *PPS:* Wyeth, *Correspondence*, 250

Henry, John [2] (fl. 1870)

Laborer, b. ca. 1840, associated with:

Oregon City (1870) huckster

At the time of the 1870 Census, John Henry worked as a huckster in Oregon City. He was illiterate and owned $400 in real estate and $250 in personal goods. John Henry had a wife, Nancy (ca. 1850–?), born in Oregon but also described as "black" and therefore very possibly the daughter of another Hawaiian. They were the parents of Louis (ca. 1860–?) and Ella (ca. 1862–?).

PS: 1870 U.S. Census, Oregon, Oregon City

Hereea [variations: **Hareea, Haarea, Heveea, Hiria, Haario**] (fl. 1817–1837)

NWC/HBC employee, b. ca. 1798, d. September 1837, likely at Fort Vancouver, associated with:

Columbia River area (1817–1822) laborer
Fort George [Astoria] (1822–1825) laborer
Fort Vancouver (1826–1827) middleman
Fort Colvile (1827–1830) middleman, Indian trade (1830–1831) middleman
Fort Colvile (1831–1832) middleman or laborer
Fort Vancouver (1832–1833) laborer or middleman
Fort Langley (1833–1837) laborer or middleman

Hereea joined the fur trade around 1817 from Oʻahu about age nineteen, working on the Pacific slopes for the NWC until the merger with the HBC compelled him to join the latter. He worked largely in the Columbia River area in various capacities including at the Fort Vancouver sawmill, and is recorded as dying at Fort Vancouver in September 1837. He may have returned to Oʻahu for a short visit earlier in 1837 when a man named Haario engaged with the company there in July 1837 and sailed to Fort Vancouver.

PS: HBCA FtGeo[Ast]AB 10–12, YFSA 2–9, 11–15, 19, YFDS 2a, 3a–7, FtVanAB 10, SA 1–4, CB 9, SandIsAB 1; *PPS:* Tolmie, *Journals*, 191

Hipa, James (fl. 1880)

Laborer, b. ca. 1863, associated with:

Port Gamble (1880) laborer

At the time of the 1880 Census, James Hipa was one of nine "Kanakas" working in Port Gamble, almost certainly at the sawmill. He was literate.

PS: 1880 U.S. Census, Washington Territory, Kitsap Co., Port Gamble

Honno (fl. 1844–1848)

HBC employee, d. 1848 at Fort Langley, associated with:

Fort Vancouver (1844–1848) laborer

Honno probably joined the HBC from Oʻahu in 1844. He spent almost four years as a laborer at Fort Vancouver and died in 1848, apparently at Fort Langley. In 1846, one barrel of salmon was purchased in his name, possibly as a gift to his family back home in the Hawaiian Islands.

PS: HBCA YFSA 24–27, 29, SandIsAB 5

Honnu (fl. 1837–1841)

HBC employee, associated with:

Fort Vancouver (1837–1839) middleman
Fort Nisqually (1839–1841) middleman

Honnu joined the HBC in July 1837 from Oʻahu and began work at Fort Vancouver as a middleman on August 10 of that year. He appears to have served one contract, as he was discharged in Oʻahu in outfit 1841–1842 and did not receive wages for that outfit.

PS: HBCA SandIsAB 1, FtVanSA 4–6, YFDS 8, YFSA 19–21, HL FtNisB 2

Honolulu [variation: Henry Honolulu] (fl. 1845–1851)

HBC/PSAC employee, b. ca. 1825, associated with:

Fort Vancouver (1845–1848) laborer
Cowlitz farm (1848–1850) laborer
Fort Vancouver (1850–1851) laborer

In 1845, at age twenty, Honolulu joined the HBC from Oʻahu as a laborer on a three-year contract. He stopped working for the company in 1851 but showed transactions on his account until 1852, whereupon he disappeared from the records. He appears in the 1850 U.S. Census of Clark County as Henry Honolulu.
    Honolulu had an unnamed Native wife and a son Pierre (1851–?).

PS: HBCA YFSA 25–32, 1850 U.S. Census, Oregon, Clark Co.; *PPS:* Munnick, *Vancouver,* vol. 2

Hoolapa [variation: Hoolapu] (fl. 1837–1850)

HBC employee, died April 6, 1850, at or near Fort Vancouver, associated with:

Snake party (1837–1841) middleman
Fort Vancouver (1843–1848) laborer
Cowlitz farm (1848–1850) laborer

Hoolapa entered the service of the HBC from Oʻahu in 1837 and began his work on July 31 of that year in the Snake Country. Nothing was recorded of his personality or work habits when he acted as a goer and comer, transporting trappers in and out from Fort Vancouver. On November 20, 1841, he returned to Oʻahu but reentered the service. Back in the Columbia he spent the next five years at Fort Vancouver and his last two years as a laborer on the Cowlitz farm. On April 6, 1850, while in the vicinity of Fort Vancouver, Hoolapa became involved in a scuffle between a well-known claim jumper, Amos Short, and a Mr. Gardiner. Both Gardiner and Hoolapa were shot and killed by Short and Short's son-in-law. The following day an inquest was held and likely Hoolapa was buried that day or the next in the Fort Vancouver cemetery.
    Nothing is known of Hoolapa's family in the Columbia but he may have been married, as there was movement on his account after his death.

PS: HBCA FtVanSA 4–8, YFDS 8, 12, YFSA 19–21, 23–32, HL FtNisCFJ, BCA PR-Lowe

Hoolio (fl. 1841–1846)

PSAC employee, associated with:

Cowlitz farm (1841–1843) laborer
Fort Nisqually (1843–1844) laborer
Cowlitz farm (1844–1847) laborer

Hoolio joined the HBC from Oʻahu in 1841 and began to receive wages on July 9 of that year. He spent the majority of his time as a laborer on the Cowlitz farm, where he worked until November 30, 1846, when he returned to Oʻahu.

PS: HBCA FtVanSA 6–8, YFDS 12, 17, YFSA 24–26, HL FtNisB env, FtNisSA 2, env, FTNisbox 6

Hopoa (fl. 1815)

Maritime fur trade seaman, associated with:

schooner *Columbia* (1815) apprentice seaman

Hopoa was an apprentice seaman on the NWC schooner *Columbia* in 1815 when it was on the Northwest Coast. Nothing else is known about him.

PS: HBCA NWCAB 5

Horapapa, John (fl. 1834–1835)

HBC employee, d. September 22, 1835, aboard the brig *Lama,* associated with:

Fort McLoughlin (1834–1835) laborer
brig *Lama* (1835) passenger

John Horapapa, who signed on with the HBC in 1834 in Oʻahu, should not have joined the fur trade, as he was in an advanced state of venereal disease. By 1835 he was working at Fort McLoughlin, where Dr. Tolmie tried to cure sores on his leg but with only partial success. By September 12 of that year the sores returned, and he was replaced at the fort and taken aboard the brig *Lama.* As the ship steamed down the east coast of Vancouver Island, Horapapa's condition grew worse and he began to cough up blood. Medicines had no effect, and on September 22 he died somewhere in the vicinity of Cape Flattery. As they couldn't bury him on shore, he was given a seaman's burial at sea and what little clothes he had were nailed up in his chest to go on to the Columbia River.

PS: FtSimp[N]PJ 3, HBCA YFSA 14–15, YFDS 5c–6, FtVanSA 3; *PPS:* Work, *Journal,* 81–82

Houmare, Nahua (fl. 1858)

Occupation unknown, associated with:

Victoria (1858)

On May 18, 1858, in Victoria a man recorded as Nahua Houmare charged another man with assault. He was likely one of the persons named as **Tamaree** or **Nahoua**.

PS: BCA Crt-Petty

Iakobo (fl. 1840–1843)

Laborer, associated with:

vessel *Vancouver* (1840) passenger
Gray's mission (1840–1843) laborer

Iakobo, or Jacob, and his wife **Hamua**, from 30 miles outside of Honolulu, responded to a call put out by Hiram Bingham to assist Protestant missionary Henry Gray in Oregon and, in February 1840, the young couple headed there on the HBC vessel *Vancouver*. By the summer of 1843 their relationship had deteriorated with Gray, who proposed to send them home. Presumably, they went.

PS: HMCS OrMission

Iaukeo [variations: Ioukeo, W. Iaukeo] (fl. 1845–1855)

HBC employee, associated with:

Fort Vancouver (1845–1846) laborer
Snake party (1846–1847) laborer
Snake Country (1847–1851) laborer, (1853–1855) laborer

Iaukeo joined the HBC from Oʻahu on May 7, 1845, for three years. He retired on July 20, 1851, remaining in the area of Fort Vancouver, and then reenlisted, retiring once again in 1855. By 1850–1851, he had acquired an initial "W" and so may have used an additional name.

PS: HBCA SandIsAB 3, YFSA 25–32, YFDS 22, FtVanSA 9–12

Iokepa (fl. 1861)

Occupation unknown, associated with:

Victoria (1861)

Iokepa and two other Hawaiians left Victoria for Honolulu on the *Constitution*, arriving October 3, 1861. No information was located on how he got to the Pacific Northwest.

PS: HSA Passenger

Isaac (fl. 1834–1839)

CRFTC/HBC employee, associated with:

ship *May Dacre* (1834) passenger
Fort Hall (1834–1837) laborer
Snake party (1837–1839) middleman
barque *Nereide* (1839) passenger

Isaac was one of twenty men recruited for Nathaniel J. Wyeth's CRFTC in 1834 and among the dozen who deserted in November of the same year on the way to Fort Hall. Found, he remained with the company through 1835. Isaac subsequently joined the HBC and was working in the Snake party by October 20, 1837. He worked probably at Fort Hall, acquired by the HBC, for two more outfits and left for Oʻahu on the *Nereide* on January 1, 1839.

PS: HBCA FtVanSA 4–5, YFDS 8, YFSA 18, SMP 14, OHS FtHallAB; *PPS:* Beidleman, "Fort Hall," 238

Itati (fl. 1840–1845)

HBC employee, associated with:

Fort Nez Perces (1840–1842) middleman, (1842–1843) laborer
Fort Vancouver general charges (1843–1844) laborer
steamer *Beaver* (1844–1845) stoker
Fort Vancouver (1845) laborer

Itati joined the HBC from Oʻahu in 1940. He worked at Forts Nez Perces and Vancouver and also as a stoker on the HBC steamer *Beaver* until December 31, 1845, when he returned to Hawaiʻi, where he was paid off.

PS: HBCA YFSA 20–21, 24, 25, FtVanSA 6–8, SandIsAB 5

Jack [1] (fl. 1792–1793)

Maritime fur trade seaman, d. June 17, 1793, on Northwest Coast, associated with:

ship *Margaret* (1791–1793) seaman

Jack joined the ship Margaret during a stop on the Hawaiian Islands. The *Margaret* departed Boston on October 24, 1791, and after an Islands stop arrived at the Queen Charlotte Islands on April 24, 1792. The vessel traded a season, then sailed to the Sandwich Islands and Canton, where the furs were sold. A group of men, including Jack, were left behind at Nootka to build a tender and, when the *Margaret* arrived back in April 1793, the tender was complete. However, Jack contacted scurvy while working on the tender and died on the Northwest Coast on June 17, 1793.

PS: MHS *Margaret; SS:* Howay, "List"

Jack [2] (fl. 1833)

HBC employee, associated with:

Fort Vancouver (1833) sawmill worker

Little is known of Jack, a sawmill worker at Fort Vancouver in 1833. He could possibly be **John Jack** or **Long Jack**.

PS: HBCA FtVanCB 9

Jack, John (fl. 1836–1837)

HBC employee, associated with:

steamer *Beaver* (1836) passenger
Fort Vancouver (1836–1837) middleman
brig *Lama* (1837) middleman

John Jack had a very short career with the HBC, signing on in Oʻahu in 1836 and taking the *Beaver* on its maiden outward voyage to the Columbia River. He worked only for a year before being discharged in Oʻahu again on July 16, 1837. The reasons are unknown.

PS: HBCA SandIsLonIC 1, FtVanSA 3–4, YFDS 7–8, YFSA 17

Jack, Long (fl. 1837–1843)

HBC employee, associated with:

Fort Vancouver (1837–1838) middleman
Catholic mission (1838–1839) laborer
Kamiah mission (1839–1841) laborer
Willamette mission (1841–1843) laborer

Long Jack signed on with the HBC in Oʻahu in July 1837, beginning his work at Fort Vancouver on August 10 of that year. In outfit 1838–1839, he worked with the newly arrived Catholic missionaries Fathers Blanchet and Demers. From April 1839 to early 1841, Jack worked for the Asa Smith Presbyterian mission at Kamiah. In June 1840 he ran away from the mission to the HBC at Fort Vancouver because as he didn't have anyone to talk to in Hawaiian. However, the HBC convinced him to return and, in October 1840, he defended the Smiths against the Nez Perces who ordered them to leave immediately for being on their land. The Smiths could not stand the pressure and soon left. Consequently, in 1841–1842, Jack was transferred to Jason Lee's Methodist mission in the Willamette Valley. He continued to work until 1843, when he likely returned to the Sandwich Islands.

PS: HBCA SandIsAB 1, FtVanSA 4–7, YFDS 8–9, 12; *PPS:* Drury, *Diaries,* 97–98, 132, 151–152, 192, 196–197

Jackson, Andrew (fl. 1880)

Laborer, b. ca. 1856, associated with:

Vashon Island (1880) sawmill worker

Given in the Census as born on the Islands, Andrew Jackson was in 1880 working in a sawmill on Vashon Island, Washington. He had an Indian wife Christine (ca. 1861–?) and son Charles (ca. 1878–?).

PS: 1880 U.S. Census, Washington Territory, Skamania

Jarvis, Perry (fl. 1827)

Maritime fur trade seaman, associated with:

brig *Owhyhee* (1827) seaman

Perry Jarvis appears to have worked as a seaman on the brig *Owhyhee* when it traded on the Northwest Coast in 1827. In fact, this person may be two people, Perry and Jarvis, given the lack of commas inserted by the record-keeper. When the vessel returned to O'ahu in July 1827, he was (they were) discharged.

PS: CHS *Owhyhee; SS:* Howay, "List"

Jerry (fl. 1853)

Occupation unknown, b. ca. 1813, associated with:

Fort Vancouver (1853) prisoner

Nothing is known about Jerry, who was being held a prisoner at Fort Vancouver in June 1853, when he was baptized, in danger of death.

PPS: Munnick, *Vancouver,* vol. 2

Jim [1] (fl. 1837–1838)

HBC employee, associated with:

Fort Vancouver (1837–1838) middleman

Jim joined the HBC in O'ahu in July 1837 and began to work at Fort Vancouver on August 10. He appears to have worked only one year, for he returned to O'ahu on November 1, 1838, as a passenger on the *Columbia* along with Swiss-American frontiersman Captain John Augustus Sutter and his servant, heading for Honolulu, and with the Anglican minister from Fort Vancouver and his wife, Herbert and Jane Beaver, heading for London.

PS: HBCA SandIsAB 1, FtVanSA 4–5, YFDS 8, YFSA 18, SMP 13

Jim [2] (fl. 1853)

HBC employee, associated with:

ship *Pekin* (1853) seaman
ship *Mary Catherine* (1853) seaman

Jim shipped aboard the HBC chartered vessel *Pekin* in Honolulu probably in the summer of 1853 during the height of the smallpox epidemic, sailed to the Northwest Coast, and arrived back in Honolulu September 27, 1853, on the *Mary Catherine.* He was given the final balance of his wages when he arrived back.

PS: HBCA SandIsLonIC 3

Jimo (fl. 1814–1827)

NWC/HBC employee, b. ca. 1798, d. April 11, 1827, at Fort Vancouver, associated with:

Pacific slopes (1814–1821) middleman
Columbia Department (1821–1822) employee
Fort George [Astoria] (1822–1823) employee
Columbia Department (1823–1824) employee, (1824–1826) cook
Fort Vancouver (1826–1827) cook

Jimo appears to have joined the fur trade in 1814 at the age of sixteen and worked in the Columbia District. At the time of amalgamation, he transferred to the HBC and was soon being employed as a cook. He died suddenly on April 11, 1827, at Fort Vancouver. Ten years later his family, at an unknown location, was still receiving an annuity.

PS: HBCA NWCAAB 9, YFSA 1–8, 17, FtGeo[Ast]AB 10, YFDS 2a, FtVanAB 10, SA 1

Jo, Kanaka (fl. 1862)

Miner, associated with:

Jackson Co., Oregon (1862) miner

On November 21, 1862, Kanaka Jo purchased a gold mining claim in Jackson County, Oregon, for $30. Nothing else is known of him.

SS: Blue, "Mining Laws," 139

Joe (fl. 1884–1885)

Stowaway, associated with:

Port Townsend (1884–1885)

The Hawaiian consul at Port Townsend reported in October 1884 about a young native of Honolulu who gave his name only as Joe. Joe claimed to have secreted himself on a vessel leaving Honolulu for the Pacific Northwest until it was too late to get off and now wanted to go home. The consul wanted to treat him as a stowaway who thereby did not have to be assisted. The outcome is not in the consular correspondence.

PS: HSA Victoria

Joe, Jim (fl. 1880)

Laborer, b. ca. 1850, associated with:

Port Gamble (1880) laborer

At the time of the 1880 Census, Jim Joe was one of nine "Kanakas" working in Port Gamble, almost certainly at the sawmill. He was illiterate.

PS: 1880 U.S. Census, Washington Territory, Kitsap Co., Port Gamble

John [1] (fl. 1815)

Maritime fur trade seaman, associated with:

schooner *Columbia* (1815) apprentice seaman

John was an apprentice seaman on the NWC schooner *Columbia* when it was on the Northwest Coast in 1815. Nothing else is known about him.

PS: HBCA NWCAB 5

John [2] (fl. 1825)

Maritime fur trade seaman, associated with:

brig *Convoy* (1825) seaman

John shipped aboard the brig *Convoy* at Oʻahu after it arrived at that island on March 16, 1825, to unload cargo and take on supplies for the Northwest Coast. After sailing April 1 as a laborer, John and the vessel traded for a season, returning to Honolulu on November 2. It is not known whether he continued to sail with the *Convoy*.

PS: BCA PR-*Convoy; SS:* Howay, "List"

John [3] (fl. 1840–1843)

HBC employee, associated with:

Fort Vancouver (1840–1843) middleman and laborer
Whitman mission (1842) laborer

John joined the HBC from Oʻahu in 1840 and spent the next three years working as a middleman at Fort Vancouver. He labored there until December 9, 1843, near the end of his contract, when he returned to Oʻahu. He is almost certainly the same John who was working at the Whitman mission in 1842 when Narcissa was almost attacked in her bedroom by a Native man. She called out to John, who rescued her.

PS: HBCA YFSA 20, 23, FtVanSA 6–7, YFDS 9; *PPS:* Whitman, *Letters,* 143

John [4] (fl. 1860)

Laborer, b. ca. 1835, associated with:

Fort Vancouver area (1860) laborer

John was living in the Kanaka Village area in 1860 with a large group of Hawaiians and probably worked on a casual basis for what remained of the HBC interests in the area.

PS: 1860 U.S. Census, Washington Territory, Clark Co.

John [5] (fl. 1863–1864)

Laborer, associated with:

Alberni (1863–1864) sawmill worker

John and six other men were contracted in Honolulu on September 23, 1863, by the agent of Alberni Mill Co. to work for $10 per month with a $20 advance. They left for Victoria on the *Alberni* on the same day. On December 22, 1864, all of the men, except for **Kealili,** who ran away, arrived back in Honolulu from Alberni on the ship *Buena Vista.*

PS: HSA Seamen, Passenger

Johnny (fl. 1869)

Seaman, b. ca. 1841, associated with:

Victoria area (1869)

Johnny, a twenty-eight-year-old 5 foot, 7 inch "Kanaka," deserted his ship in the Victoria area in 1869. He was discharged and has not been followed beyond that point.

PS: BCA Crt-Gaols

Johnny, Owhyhee (fl. 1829–1831)

HBC employee, associated with:

Fort Vancouver general charges (1829–1831)
barque *Ganymede* (1831) passenger

Owhyhee Johnny probably joined the HBC in 1829. He worked in the Columbia District but was discharged to Oʻahu on November 1, 1831, sailing on the *Ganymede*.

PS: HBCA FtVanSA 2, YFDS 4a–4b, YFSA 11

Johnson, Cohill (fl. 1880)

Laborer, b. ca. 1865, associated with:

Port Gamble (1880) laborer

At the time of the 1880 Census, Cohill Johnson was one of nine "Kanakas" working in Port Gamble, almost certainly at the sawmill. He was illiterate.

PS: 1880 U.S. Census, Washington Territory, Kitsap Co., Port Gamble

Jomanno [variations: Iomanno, Jomano] (fl. 1845–1852)

HBC employee, b. ca. 1826, associated with:

Fort Vancouver (1845–1847) laborer
Cowlitz farm (1847–1850) laborer
Fort Vancouver (1850–1851) laborer
Cowlitz farm (1851–1852) laborer

Jomanno joined the HBC from Oʻahu on May 7, 1845, for three years. For the next seven years, he split his time laboring at Fort Vancouver or on the Cowlitz farm. At the time of the 1850 U.S. Census he was living in Fort Vancouver's Kanaka Village with five other Hawaiians. He deserted from the Cowlitz farm on August 21, 1852, and has not been traced after that.

PS: HBCA YFSA 25–32, YFDS 23, FtVanSA 9, 1850 U.S. Census, Oregon, Clark Co.

Jones (fl. 1843–1848)

HBC employee, d. January 31, 1848, at Cape Disappointment, associated with:

Fort George [Astoria] (1843–1847) laborer
Cape Disappointment (1848) laborer

The Hawaiian recorded as Jones signed on with the HBC from Oʻahu in 1843. He spent his entire career as a laborer at Fort George at the mouth of the Columbia. On January 31, 1848, he died at Cape Disappointment, likely from the measles epidemic at the time.

PS: HBCA FtVanSA 8, YFSA 24–27, YFDS 16–18

Joseph [1] (fl. 1853)

Prisoner, b. ca. 1813, d. June 2 or 3, 1853, at Fort Vancouver, associated with

Fort Vancouver (1853) prisoner

In 1853 a forty-year-old Hawaiian was, for untraced reasons, in prison at Fort Vancouver when he caught smallpox. On May 23, in danger of death, he was given the Christian name of Joseph and baptized by the secular Catholic priest J.B.A. Brouillet then at Fort Vancouver. He died a few days later and was buried in the cemetery of the mission.

PPS: Munnick, *Vancouver,* vol. 2

Joseph [2] (fl. 1860)

Laborer, b. ca. 1840, associated with:

Fort Vancouver area (1860) laborer

Joseph was living in the Kanaka Village area of Fort Vancouver in 1860 along with a large group of Hawaiians and their families. He probably worked on a casual basis for what remained of the nearby HBC post.

PS: 1860 U.S. Census, Washington Territory, Clark Co.

Joshua (fl. 1812–1814)

PFC/NWC employee, associated with:

ship *Beaver* (1812) passenger
Fort George [Astoria] (1812–1814) laborer
overland brigade (1814)

Joshua was brought to Astoria, probably in May 1812 on the *Beaver,* as an employee of the PFC. On April 4, 1814, he was on the list of men going overland from Fort George [Astoria] and may have reached as far as Fort William on the Great Lakes.

PS: RosL *Astoria; PPS:* Henry, *Journal,* 771

Junion, James (fl. 1815)

Maritime fur trade seaman, possibly Polynesian, associated with:

schooner *Columbia* (1815) seaman

James Junion is listed as a crew member of the NWC schooner *Columbia* in 1815 when it was on the Northwest Coast. Nothing else is known about him.

PS: HBCA NWCAB 5

Kaahami, William (fl. 1870)

Laborer, b. ca. 1837, associated with:

Port Gamble (1870) sawmill worker

At the time of the 1870 Census, William Kaahami was one of twenty-two Hawaiians working at Puget Mill at Port Gamble.

PS: 1870 U.S. Census, Washington Territory, Kitsap Co., Port Gamble

Kaai (fl. 1863–1864)

Laborer, associated with:

Port Gamble (1863–1864) sawmill worker

Kaai and five others were contracted in Honolulu on December 4, 1863, by the agent of Puget Mill Co. for $10 per month with a $20 advance. The next day he left for Teekalet on the barque *N.S. Perkins.* It is unclear how long he worked at the sawmill there.

PS: HSA Seamen, Passenger

Kaai, Mary S. [variation: **Mary Kaaipoop**] (fl. 1845–1865)

Wife, b. ca. 1822, d. December 31, 1865, in Victoria, associated with:

Fort Vancouver (1845–1860)
Fort Victoria (1860–1865)

Mary Kaai arrived at Fort Vancouver on June 23, 1845, with her husband **William R. Kaulehelehe,** who came to act as chaplain and teacher to the Hawaiians working there for the HBC. The couple first lived in the Kanaka Village and then in the post itself. Later they moved to Fort Victoria, where Mary Kaaipoop died on December 31, 1865, age forty-three. They had an adopted daughter Mary Opio (ca. 1849–1864).

PS: BCA VS-CCC; *SS:* Klan, "Kanaka William"

Kaaihawela (fl. 1864)

Laborer, associated with:

Port Gamble (1864) sawmill worker

Kaaihawela and five others were contracted in Honolulu on February 5, 1864, by the agent of Puget Mill Co. to work at its sawmill for $10 per month with a $20 advance. It is uncertain how long he did so.

PS: HSA Seamen

Kaailanok (fl. 1865)

Occupation unknown, b. ca. 1845, d. April 23, 1865, in Victoria area associated with:

Victoria area (1865)

Nothing is known of Kaailanok except for his death as an Anglican in the Victoria area in 1865.

PS: BCA VS-CCC

Kaanaan (fl. 1870)

Laborer, b. ca. 1847, associated with:

Port Gamble (1870) sawmill worker

At the time of the 1870 Census, Kaanaan was one of twenty-two Hawaiians working at Puget Mill at Port Gamble.

PS: 1870 U.S. Census, Washington Territory, Kitsap Co., Port Gamble

Kaehetou (fl. 1844–1849)

HBC employee, associated with:

Fort Vancouver (1844–1849) laborer

Kaehetou, from Oʻahu, appeared in the Columbia in outfit 1844–1845 on an HBC contract that ended in 1847. He worked as a laborer at Fort Vancouver and deserted in 1849, presumably for the gold fields of California.

PS: HBCA YFSA 24–29

Kaeuhe (fl. 1850)

Laborer, b. ca. 1826, associated with:

Fort Vancouver area (1850)

Little is known of Kaeuhe other than he was living in Kanaka Village, near Fort Vancouver, with five other Hawaiians in 1850.

PS: 1850 U.S. Census, Oregon, Clark Co.

Kahaleiwi (fl. 1858–1862)

Laborer, d. 1862 in Victoria, associated with:

Victoria (1858–1862) gardener

Kahaleiwi was one of fourteen Hawaiians who left his hometown of Honolulu for Victoria on the schooner *Alice* on June 22, 1858, enticed by the euphoria of the gold rush. He ended up working in Victoria as a gardener and "outdoor boy." On his death in early 1862, his countrymen **Nahiana** and **Kapoi** administered the estate, and **William Kaulehelehe** took charge of ensuring relatives back home would receive the residue of $39.

Kahaleiwi had a wife (?–1862) who probably came with him and died a few weeks after he did.

PS: HSA Passenger, Victoria

Kahalia (fl. 1881)

Farmer, b. ca. 1835, associated with:

Salt Spring Island (1881)

Described as a "Kanaka" born in the Sandwich Islands, Kahalia was in 1881 farming on Salt Spring Island. He was living with a Native woman recorded as Mary (ca. 1848–?). Nothing else is known about him.

PS: 1881 Canada Census, British Columbia, Cowichan

Kahaliopa [variations: **Kahaliopeea, Kalahaliopuha**] (fl. 1859–1860)

PSAC employee, associated with:

Belle Vue sheep farm (1859–1860) shepherd

It is not known how or when Kahaliopa came to the Pacific Northwest, but on April 30, 1859, he, **Peter Friday, Friday's son Joe, John Bull** [3], and **Tamaree** [4] were all engaged for one year as shepherds on San Juan Island. At the finish of his contract, he went to Victoria and disappears from the records.

PS: HBCA FtVicSA 7, 8, Belle VuePJ 2

Kahaloukulu [variations: **Kililukulu, Keakelukulu**] (fl. 1840–1845)

HBC employee, associated with:

Fort Stikine (1840–1843) middleman
Fort Victoria (1843–1844) middleman
steamer *Beaver* (1844–1845) laborer

Kahaloukulu joined the HBC from Oʻahu in 1840, arriving in April at Fort Vancouver. His first assignment was as a watchman at Fort Stikine, which he reached on June 13 on the steamer *Beaver*. During his three years there, he also appeared to do duty as a miller.

The competent Sandwich Islander was at Fort Stikine during the trying spring of 1842, when discipline broke down, the liquor flowed freely, and John McLoughlin Jr., who was in charge, was not only drinking too much alcohol but also brutally flogging the servants, likely including Kahaloukulu. A plot was hatched, and McLoughlin was murdered, but Kahaloukulu appeared to be innocent of any complicity and stayed on at the fort until 1843. He testified at the investigation that he had seen McLoughlin drunk only a couple of times before the event. After leaving Stikine, he worked at Fort Victoria and spent his last outfit on the steamer *Beaver* until January 10, 1845, at which point he returned to Oʻahu.

PS: HBCA YFSA 20, 24–25, FtVanSA 6–8, CB 31, YFDS 15, FtStikPJ 1–3, SandIsAB 3

Kahana, John [variations: **John Hallum Kahano, Kanahan, Alum Kioni**] (fl. 1855–1901)

Laborer, b. ca. 1835 on Oʻahu, associated with:

Victoria area (mid-1850s) occupation unknown
Whatcom/Bellingham, Washington (1858–1860?) coal miner
San Juan Island (1865–1870s) farmer and laborer
Salt Spring Island (1870s–1901) farmer

From Oʻahu, John Kahana deserted at Esquimalt just outside of Victoria, probably in the mid-1850s. According to his son, he took refuge at Gold Harbour on southern Vancouver Island, where a group of Hawaiians was living, until the ship had left. He worked as a coal miner at Whatcom, the future Bellingham, Washington, where he met his wife Mary Skqalup. The widow of his countryman **John Bull** [3], Mary had held on to his homestead on San Juan Island, and they moved there. In 1865 Kahana signed a petition by San Juan settlers to get a school built. He worked as a laborer for other farmers and made shakes he sold at Victoria for a reported $2 a thousand. At the time of the 1871 Census Kahana was working as a laborer.

Sometime after the boundary settlement of 1872, Kahana moved to Salt Spring Island. He appeared on British Columbia's voting list from 1879 as a farmer at Fulford Harbor. At the time of the 1901 Census, he was fishing on the Fraser River and described himself as literate.

John Kahana married John Bull's widow Mary (ca. 1830–?), who was Clallum and possibly also Lummi. Their son Charles (1865–?) was baptized at the Catholic cathedral in Victoria on March 28, 1866. Kionitow (ca. 1867–?) followed two years later, Isaac William (ca. 1875–?) somewhat later in time. They may have had other children.

PS: BCA GR-Naturalization, VS StAndC, UWW Jeffcott, Buswell, 1870 U.S. Census, Washington Territory, San Juan Island, 1901 Canada Census, British Columbia, Richmond; *PPS:* British Columbia, *Sessional Papers,* voting lists

Kahananui [1] (fl. 1858)

Occupation unknown, associated with:

Vancouver Island (1858)

Kahananui was one of fourteen Hawaiians departing Honolulu for Victoria on the schooner *Alice* on June 22, 1858, enticed by the euphoria of the gold rush.

PS: HSA Passenger

Kahananui [2] (fl. 1864–1865)

Laborer, b. ca. 1837, associated with:

Alberni (1864–1865) sawmill worker

Kahananui and three others were contracted in Honolulu on June 23, 1864, by the agent of Alberni Mill Co. to work for $10 per month with a $20 advance. Two days later they departed Honolulu for Alberni on the schooner *Alberni.* They returned to Honolulu on February 7, 1865, on the *Egoria.*

PS: HSA Seamen, Passenger

Kahananui [3] (fl. 1864–?)

Occupation unknown, associated with:

Salt Spring Island

Kanahanui, said to be from the United States, married **William Naukana**'s daughter Annie. They lived for a time on Salt Spring Island near to Annie's sister Cecilia and her family at a location that became known as Kanaka Row. They had at least one daughter, Jennie (ca. 1865–1945).

SS: Family recollections

Kahannui (fl. 1844–1860)

HBC/PSAC employee, b. ca. 1815, associated with:

Fort Vancouver (1844–1846) laborer
Fort Nisqually and outstations (1846–1860) laborer and shepherd

Kahannui joined the HBC in 1844 at the age of twenty-nine from O'ahu. For the next fifteen years he worked as a laborer at Fort Vancouver and the HBC subsidiary, PSAC, at Fort Nisqually. In the 1850 U.S. Census, he lived in the same household as **Koemi** and **Kupahi**, all three described as "dark Hawaiian." Although Kahannui was employed mainly as a shepherd working at the outstations, he also sometimes worked at the fort in the garden, and with wood, doing such things as making carts, splitting shingles, and making fences. As a shepherd he was involved in castrating, shearing, washing the sheep, and bringing large flocks into the post. On May 23, 1853, after being told he was too far in debt, he quit temporarily but soon returned to work at the outstations. The next spring he again deserted, to be rehired a year later. He was last on record in June 1860, when he was paid the outstanding balance due him.

Kahannui had a Native wife at least by 1848 who hanged herself "in a fit of passion" on November 29, 1853. They had one or more unnamed children. He is possibly the same as **Kahananui** who married a daughter of **William Naukana**.

PS: HBCA YFSA 24–32, FtVanSA 9–11, HL FtNisPJ 6, 8–9, 12, FtNisSA 2–3, 5–14, env, FtNisB 6, 8, FNNisTB 1, FtNisIB 3–4, FtNisTJ, FTNisMFJ, 1850 U.S. Census, Oregon, Lewis Co., *SS:* Anderson, *Physical Structure*

Kahaowno, William (fl. 1880)

Laborer, b. ca. 1853, associated with:

Vashon Island (1880) sawmill worker

William Kahaowno was in 1880 working in a sawmill on Vashon Island, Washington. He had an Indian wife Susan (ca. 1856–?) but no children.

PS: 1880 U.S. Census, Washington Territory, Skamania

Kaharro (fl. 1847–1850)

Occupation unknown, associated with:

Fort Vancouver area (1847–1850)

Kaharro was living in the Fort Vancouver area from 1848. He took as a wife a Grand Dalles Native woman and had children Marie (1848–1848) and Jean (1849–?).

PPS: Munnick, *Vancouver,* vol. 2

Kaharrow [variations: **Kakarrow, Kikarrow**] (fl. 1817–1830)

NWC/HBC employee, b. ca. 1796, d. June 20, 1830, at Fort Vancouver, associated with:

ship *Columbia* (1817) passenger
Columbia Department (1817–1822) laborer
Fort George [Astoria] (1822–1825) laborer
Columbia Department (1825–1826) laborer
Fort Vancouver (1826–1827) laborer
Fort Nez Perces (1827–1828) middleman
Fort Vancouver (1828–1830) middleman

Kaharrow joined the fur trade around 1817 from O'ahu and spent his career in the Columbia District. Early on, he was attached to the Fort George store. On October 9, 1825, he together with **Harry Bell Noah, James Coah, Tourawhyheine,** and **Marrouna** confessed to having stolen blankets from the trade goods of the *William & Ann.* Kaharrow must have redeemed himself, for in March 1828 he was part of the fur trade brigade heading out from Fort Vancouver. He died at Fort Vancouver in 1830. The cause may have been an unnamed disease that was brought in by vessels at the time.

It was likely Kaharrow's son William who was baptized Methodist by missionary Jason Lee in December 1834, although it could have been Kaharrow himself.

PS: HBCA FtGeo[Ast]AB 10–12, YFSA 2–9, YFDS 2a, 3a–3a, FtVanAB 10, 28, SA 1–4; *PPS:* McDonald, *Blessed Wilderness,* 29; Ermatinger, "York Factory," 113

Kahela [variation: **Kahile**] (fl. 1845–1848)

HBC employee, d. 1848 at Fort Vancouver, associated with:

Fort Vancouver (1845–1848) laborer

Kahela joined the HBC from O'ahu on May 7, 1845, on a two-year obligation. He died in 1848 at Fort Vancouver, probably from the effects of measles.

PS: HBCA YFSA 24–27, 29, SandIsAB 3

Kahelekulu (fl. 1869)

Child, b. ca. 1863, associated with:

Port Gamble (1869)

On September 2, 1869, six-year-old Kahelekulu (ca. 1863–?) left Honolulu for Teekalet on the barque *Camden.* He was almost certainly going with, or to join, a father employed in the sawmill there.

PS: HSA Passenger

Kaheli (fl. 1863)

Laborer, associated with:

Port Gamble (1863) sawmill worker

Kaheli and four other men were contracted in Honolulu on March 18, 1863, by the agent of Puget Mill Co. to work at its sawmill for $10 per month with a $20 advance. It is uncertain how long he did so.

PS: HSA Seamen

Kahemehou [variation: **Kahemehau**] (fl. 1840–1843)

HBC employee, associated with:

Fort Vancouver (1840–1843) middleman

Kahemehou joined the HBC in 1840 from O'ahu. He worked at Fort Vancouver until November 15, 1843, at which time he returned to O'ahu.

PS: HBCA YFSA 20, 23, FtVanSA 6–8, YFDS 14

Kahetapou (fl. 1840–1844)

HBC employee, associated with:

Fort Vancouver (1840–1844) middleman

Kahetapou joined the HBC from O'ahu in 1840 as a middleman on a five-year contract. He worked at Fort Vancouver until November 12, 1844, at which point he returned to O'ahu. His contract was to have ended a year later, and no information has been located as to why he went back earlier.

PS: HBCA YFSA 20, 24, FtVanSA 6–8, YFDS 15

Kahili (fl. 1849)

PSAC employee, associated with:

Fort Nisqually outstation (1849) shepherd

Kahili is a difficult person to follow. It is not exactly clear when he came to the Northwest Coast, but by May 31, 1849, he was working at a Nisqually outstation when he was ordered to go to Victoria. From that point he has not been followed.

PS: HL FtNisPJ 6, *SS:* Anderson, *Physical Structure*

Kahinamia (fl. 1850)

HBC seaman, associated with:

    barque *Cowlitz* (1850) seaman

Kahinamia shipped onboard the HBC vessel *Cowlitz* in February 1850 at Honolulu and sailed to the coast on a voyage on which the captain was unhappy with the performance of the Hawaiians. Kahinamia likely returned to O'ahu on the same or another vessel, as he has not been traced on further records.

PS: HBCA SandIsAB 10, Log of *Cowlitz* 8

Kahoolanou [variation: Kahoolainou] (fl. 1844–1849)

HBC employee, associated with:

    Fort Vancouver (1844–1845) laborer
    Snake party (1845–1845) laborer, (1845–1846) goer and comer
    Fort Vancouver (1846–1847) laborer
    Snake Country (1847–1849) laborer
    Fort Vancouver (1849) laborer

Kahoolanou joined the HBC from O'ahu in 1844. Based at Fort Vancouver, he also worked in the Snake Country. On July 20, 1849, he deserted, presumably for the gold fields of California. He has not been traced after that.

PS: HBCA YFSA 24–29, YFDS 16, 20

Kahoomano [variation: Kalevomano] (fl. 1863–1864)

Laborer, associated with:

    Port Gamble (1863–1864) sawmill worker

Kahoomano and five others were contracted in Honolulu on December 4, 1863, by the agent of Puget Mill Co. to work at its sawmill for $10 per month with a $20 advance. The next day he left for Teekalet on the barque *N.S. Perkins*. It is unclear how long he worked there.

PS: HSA Seamen, Passenger

Kahoonana, Joe (fl. 1870)

Laborer, b. ca. 1842, associated with:

    Oregon City (1870) huckster

At the time of the 1870 Census, Joe Kahoonana was working as a huckster in Oregon City. He was illiterate.

PS: 1870 U.S. Census, Oregon, Oregon City

Kahoree [variations: Kahoore, Kahoorie, Kahoure, Kahourie, Kahouree] (fl. 1837–1848)

HBC employee, associated with:

    Fort Umpqua (1837–1839) middleman
    Fort Vancouver (1839–1841) middleman
    California estate (1843–1845) laborer
    Fort Victoria (1845–1848) laborer

Kahoree joined the HBC in July 1837 from Oʻahu and began work at Fort Umpqua around August 10 of that year. He worked until November 20, 1841, at which point he returned to Oʻahu. He appears to have reentered the service in outfit 1843–1844, when he was employed by the HBC in its California estate in San Francisco. In 1845 he was transferred to newly constructed Fort Victoria as a laborer. His contract ended in 1848 and around mid-November 1848 he again returned to Oʻahu.

PS: HBCA SandIsAB 1, YFSA 19–22, 24–28, YFDS 8, 12, 19, FtVanSA 4–8

Kahou, John Peavine (fl. 1883–1893)

Farmer, associated with:

Salt Spring Island (1883–1893) farmer

John Peavine Kahou was a farmer at Beaver Point on Salt Spring Island during the early 1890s. On the voters' list, 1890–1893, he was described as a "Kanaka." In the Census Kahou described himself as able to read and write.

Kahou and Mary (1858–1892), said to have been the daughter of **William Haumea,** were the parents of Isaac William (ca. 1884–?) and infant twins. According to oral tradition, Kahou had a temper and beat his pregnant wife so severely that she and the twins died in childbirth.

PS: 1891 Canada Census, British Columbia, Salt Spring; *PPS: Gulf Islands Cemeteries,* 42; British Columbia, *Sessional Papers,* voters' lists

Kahua [variations: Kahooa, Tahooa] (fl. 1856–1859)

Laborer, associated with:

Nanaimo (1856–1859) sawmill worker

Kahua beat and dried furs, manned canoes, and worked in the sawmill at Nanaimo from at least 1856 up to 1859, when he left for the British Columbia mainland. Kahua was particularly adept in the water, diving to put a rope or chain around vessels that had sunk so they could be lifted to the surface.

PS: BCA Nanaimo; *PPS:* Bate, "Reminiscences"

Kahue (fl. 1862)

Laborer, associated with:

Port Gamble (1862) sawmill worker

On December 15, 1862, Kahue arrived back in Honolulu from Teekalet on the barque *Jenny Ford.* It is unclear how long he had worked at the sawmill there.

PS: HSA Passenger

Kahue, Sam (fl. 1873)

Seaman, b. ca. 1847, associated with:

Victoria area (1873)

Some time during his life, the 5 foot, 7 1/2 inch twenty-six-year-old Hawaiian seaman Sam Kahue contacted smallpox for, as the Victoria area records noted, he was marked with it. On September 27, 1873, while at Victoria, he was penalized for being drunk and disorderly by having the choice of paying a fine or spending six hours in jail.

PS: BCA Crt-Gaols

Kai (fl. 1837–1846)

HBC/PSAC employee, d. October 10, 1846, at Fort Vancouver, associated with:

Fort Vancouver (1837–1838) middleman
barque *Nereide* (1838) seaman
Fort Vancouver (1838–1841) middleman
Cowlitz farm (1841–1843) middleman
California estate (1843–1845) laborer
Columbia Department general charges (1845–1846)
Fort Vancouver (1846) laborer

Kai signed on with the HBC in Oʻahu in July 1837 and began work at Fort Vancouver on August 10 of that year. He worked there, on the barque *Nereide* as a seaman, and at the Cowlitz farm until June 24, 1842, at which point he returned to Oʻahu, but soon reengaged on a contract that ended in 1846. He was sent to the California estate, then back north to the Columbia. He was engaged on a contract that would have ended in 1848. He died, after nine years of service, on October 10, 1846, at Fort Vancouver.

PS: HBCA SandIsAB 1, FtVanSA 4–8, SMP 14, YFSA 19–20, 22, 24–26, YFDS 13

Kai, William (fl. 1886)

Occupation unknown, associated with:

Salt Spring Island (1886)

Nothing is known of Kai, except that on January 1, 1886, on Salt Spring Island he married Catherine. He might be **William Newanna**'s son Kai.

PS: StEdC

Kaia [variation: **Kiaa**] (fl. 1864–1865)

Laborer, associated with:

Alberni (1864–1865) sawmill worker

Kaia was among five men contracted in Honolulu on August 24, 1864, by the agent of Alberni Mill Co. to work for $10 per month with a $20 advance. They departed Honolulu on September 1 on the *Alberni*. Four of them, including Kaia, arrived back in Honolulu on February 7, 1865, on the *Egoria*.

PS: HSA Seamen, Passenger

Kaialu (fl. 1859)

Seaman, associated with:

vessel *Koloa* (1859) seaman

Kaialu was one of five Hawaiians the Puget Mill Co. hired to man the *Koloa* leaving Honolulu for Puget Sound on April 13, 1859. The men returned on November 29, 1859, and were discharged February 11, 1860.

PS: HSA Seamen

Kaiana [variation: **Tianna**] (fl. 1788)

Kauaʻi chief, b. ca. 1755 probably in Kauaʻi, died May 1795, at battle of Nuuanu Pali on Oʻahu, associated with:

snow *Nootka* (1787) passenger
snow *Felice Adventurer* (1788) passenger
snow *Iphigenia Nubiana* (1788) passenger

Kaiana, a popular and larger than life "Prince of Atooi" [Kauaʻi], visited China and the Northwest Coast in the late eighteenth century. Eventually, however, his overzealous actions drew suspicion and hostility that led to his death. The tall, handsome Kaiana first came to light when he is said to have greeted and offered hospitality to Captain James Cook.

Nine years later, in the summer of 1787, when the *Nootka,* captained by John Meares, reached Kaua'i, and because Kaiana wanted to visit the Britain he had often heard about, he hopped onboard and on September 5, 1787, sailed to China. In Macao and Canton, which he was disappointed to find was not Britain, Kaiana walked the streets in his feathered cap, cape, and spear. As iron nails were valuable to him, Kaiana tried unsuccessfully to barter for food with them. Kaiana decided he didn't like the Chinese, as they hid their women from sight. In Canton he befriended merchant John Henry Cox, who lavished him with gifts and, according to Kaiana, guns and ammunition. Anxious to return to his wife and children in the Hawaiian Islands, the gift-laden Kaiana, along with an ailing fellow Sandwich Islander **Winee,** joined the *Felice Adventurer* to sail on January 20, 1788. Because the accompanying vessel *Iphigenia Nubiana* intended on going directly to the Sandwich Islands, Kaiana transferred to it at the Philippines, where it was being repaired.

Due to delays and the lateness of the season, the *Iphigenia* sailed north to Cook Inlet and down the coast to Nootka Sound where, on August 17, 1788, it met the *Felice Adventurer,* whose crew was overjoyed at seeing their Sandwich Island friend once again. As Kaiana had been almost a year away from his home, the novelty of foreign cultures had begun to wear off and he expressed disgust at such things as the level of cleanliness and the habits of the Northwest Coast Natives. Nonetheless, he was overjoyed at being on the newly built vessel, *North West America,* when it slid into the waters of Nootka.

Kaiana eventually reached Maui in December 1788 amid political strife and, rather than immediately disembarking, chose to stay under the protection of the *Iphegenia* the first few weeks while he reacquainted himself with key figures on the Islands. Weighing his odds, he along with his wife and children remained with Kamehameha on the big island of Hawai'i, becoming his trusted lieutenant. Feelings began to change, however, as early as 1790 when Kaiana, who was overruled by Kamehameha, proposed seizing the American trader *Eleanora* for its guns and ammunition.

Between 1792 and 1795 Captain George Vancouver met Kaiana several times but grew to distrust his sincerity and intentions. As early as 1792 he suspected Kaiana of wanting to seize both his vessels for their guns, arms, and ammunition. In 1793 Vancouver observed that there had clearly been a falling out between Kaiana and Kamehameha. By 1795, Kaiana had split with Kamehameha and joined the forces of Kalanikupule, chief of O'ahu. In May of that year in the battle of Nuuanu Pali against Kamehameha, the "Prince of Atooi" lost his life.

PPS: Meares, *Voyages,* 6–8, 210; Portlock, *Voyage,* 359–363; Vancouver, *Voyage,* 448, 813–814, 826–827; *SS:* Nokes, *Almost a Hero,* 116–117; Miller, "Ka'iana"

Kaihi [variation: **Kaihé**] (fl. 1845–1851)

HBC employee, associated with:

Fort Vancouver (1845–1849) laborer, (1849–1851) blacksmith

Kaihi joined the HBC in O'ahu on May 7, 1845. He worked up to March 1, 1851, as a blacksmith and laborer at Fort Vancouver, and then disappeared from the records. He may have returned to O'ahu.

PS: HBCA SandIsAB 3, YFSA 26–31, YFDS 21

Kaihuolua (fl. 1858)

Occupation unknown, associated with:

Vancouver Island (1858)

Kaihuolua was one of fourteen Hawaiians departing Honolulu for Victoria on the schooner *Alice* on June 22, 1858, enticed by the euphoria of the gold rush.

PS: HSA Passenger

Kaikuanna (fl. 1843–1846)

HBC employee, associated with:

Fort Vancouver (1843–1846) laborer

Kaikuanna signed on with the HBC in Oʻahu in 1843 as a laborer. As his contract ended in 1846, he worked until August 6 of that year and then returned to Oʻahu.

PS: HBCA FtVanSA 8, YFSA 24–26, YFDS 17

Kaikuauhinē [variations: Kaikuawhinē, Kaikuawahinē] (fl. 1844–1850)

HBC employee, associated with:

Willamette (1844–1846) laborer
Fort Vancouver (1846–1847) laborer, Indian trade (1847–1849)
Fort George (1849–1850) laborer

Kaikuahinē, from Oʻahu, appeared in the Columbia in outfit 1844–1845 after joining the HBC as a laborer. He ceased working in 1850 but movement on his account indicates that he or his family was making use of the account, possibly in the area.

PS: HBCA YFSA 24–32

Kaikumakau (fl. 1844–1845)

HBC employee, associated with:

Snake party (1844–1845) laborer

Kaikumakau joined the HBC in 1844 from Oʻahu on a three-year contract. He was employed in the Snake party as a laborer, and likely returned to the Hawaiian Islands at the end of his term.

PS: HBCA YFSA 24

Kailelemauli (fl. 1858)

Occupation unknown, associated with:

Vancouver Island (1858)

Kailelemauli was one of fourteen Hawaiians departing Honolulu for Victoria on the schooner *Alice* on June 22, 1858, enticed by the euphoria of the gold rush.

PS: HSA Passenger

Kailiana (fl. 1860–1862)

Laborer, associated with:

Port Gamble (1860–1862) sawmill worker

Kailiana and three others were contracted in Honolulu on November 1, 1860, by the agent of Puget Mill Co. to work at its sawmill for $15 per month with a $15 advance. The same man, or possibly another man by the same name, was contracted in Honolulu on February 14, 1862, to work there for $10 per month with a $20 advance. It is uncertain how long he did so.

PS: HSA Seamen

Kailimai [variation: **Kuilimai**] (fl. 1845–1846)

HBC employee, d. October 31, 1846, probably at Fort Langley, associated with:

Fort Vancouver (1845–1846) laborer
Fort Langley (1846) laborer

Kailimai joined the HBC in Oʻahu on May 7, 1845, for three years. He died October 31, 1846, probably at Fort Langley, his place of work, and was likely buried in the fort grave-yard.

PS: HBCA YFSA 25–26

Kailoohe (fl. 1863)

Laborer, associated with:

Port Gamble (1863) sawmill worker

Kailoohe and four others were contracted in Honolulu on July 8, 1863, by the agent of Puget Mill Co. to work at its sawmill for $10 per month with a $20 advance. It is uncertain how long he did so.

PS: HSA Seamen

Kaimaina (fl. 1844–1847)

HBC employee, associated with:

Fort Vancouver (1844–1846) laborer
New Caledonia (1846–1847) laborer
Fort Vancouver (1847) laborer

Kaimaina, from Oʻahu, joined the HBC in 1844 on a three-year contract. He split his time as a laborer between Fort Vancouver and New Caledonia, working until July 1, 1847, at which point he returned to Oʻahu.

PS: HBCA YFSA 24–27, YFDS 18

Kaina [1] (fl. 1850–1853)

HBC employee, d. ca. 1853, likely at Fort Vancouver, associated with:

barque *Cowlitz* (1850) seaman
Fort Vancouver (1853) laborer

Kaina joined the HBC in Honolulu in February 1850 as a seaman aboard the *Cowlitz*. As the ship's captain was unhappy with the performance of the Hawaiians at shipboard tasks, Kaina and **Jack Adams** jumped ship at Fort Victoria in April. Kaina may have made his way to Fort Vancouver, for he is on its records as having died in outfit 1853–1854, during the time of a smallpox epidemic.

PS: HBCA SandIsAB 10, FtVanSA 9

Kaina [2] (fl. 1859)

Seaman, associated with:

vessel *Koloa* (1859) seaman

Kaina was one of five Hawaiians the Puget Mill Co. hired to man the *Koloa* leaving Honolulu for Puget Sound on April 13, 1859. He returned on November 29, 1859, and was discharged February 11, 1860.

PS: HSA Seamen

Kainoalau [variations: **Kainoalue, Kaimoalau**] (fl. 1845–1854)

HBC employee, associated with:

Fort Vancouver (1845–1846) laborer
New Caledonia (1846–1848) laborer
Fort Langley (1848–1850) laborer
Fort Rupert (1850–1852) laborer
schooner *Cadboro* (1852–1853)
Columbia Department (1853–1854) laborer

Kainoalau joined the HBC in 1845 from O'ahu on a three-year contract. Although he worked mainly at coastal posts until about 1854, his account showed transactions for another two years, indicating that he may have remained in the area.

PS: HBCA YFSA 25–32, FtVicSA 1–3

Kaioe (fl. 1858)

Occupation unknown, associated with:

Vancouver Island (1858)

Kaioe was one of fourteen Hawaiians departing Honolulu for Victoria on the schooner *Alice* on June 22, 1858, enticed by the euphoria of the gold rush.

PS: HSA Passenger

Kaipumakau [variation: **Kapumaku**] (fl. 1844–1853)

HBC employee, d. 1853 at Fort Vancouver, associated with:

Snake party (1844–1847) laborer
Snake Country (1847–1851) laborer
Fort Vancouver (1853) laborer

Kaipumakau joined the HBC in O'ahu in 1844 on a three-year contract. He spent almost his entire career working within the Snake River country and retired on August 15, 1851. He remained in the Fort Vancouver area, probably living in the Kanaka Village located near the post, which, by the 1850s, was beginning to deteriorate. He died in 1853 at the post.

PS: HBCA YFSA 24–32, YFDS 22, FtVanSA 9–10

Kaivā (fl. 1862)

Laborer, associated with:

Port Gamble (1862) sawmill worker

On December 15, 1862, Kaivā arrived back in Honolulu from Teekalet on the barque *Jenny Ford.* It is unclear how long he worked at the sawmill there.

PS: HSA Passenger

Kaiwaiwai (fl. 1845–1850)

HBC employee, associated with:

Fort Stikine (1845–1849) laborer
Fort Rupert (1849–1850) laborer

Kaiwaiwai joined the HBC in O'ahu on May 7, 1845. He worked as a laborer at the northern posts of Stikine and Rupert until 1850 but movement on his company account for the next three years indicates that he may have stayed in the area although he cannot be traced further.

PS: HBCA SandIsAB 3, YFSA 25–32

Kakaio [variation: **Kaikaio**] (fl. 1850)

HBC seaman, associated with:

barque *Cowlitz* (1850) seaman

Kakaio shipped onboard the HBC vessel *Cowlitz* on February 3, 1850, at Honolulu and sailed to the Northwest Coast on a voyage on which the captain was unhappy with the performance of the Hawaiians. The "Kanaka" crew rebelled on August 27 in Honolulu harbor, but most returned to the vessel on September 20 to finish their work. Beyond that, Kakaio has not been traced.

PS: HBCA SandIsAB 10–11, Log of *Cowlitz* 8

Kakepe [variations: **Kakapi, Kekepe, Kakepē, Kakape**] (fl. 1840–1844)

HBC employee, associated with:

Fort Stikine (1840–1844) laborer
Columbia Department general charges (1844)

Kakepe, who learned to read and write from American missionary instructors at Oʻahu, joined the HBC from Oʻahu in 1840. He spent his entire fur trading career at the northern post of Fort Stikine. It was there, on April 20, 1842, that he was called to arms by its head, John McLoughlin Jr., to protect him, but it was for naught when McLoughlin received a bullet through the chest. Kakepe was among the witnesses sent to York Factory to testify about the event. He was employed until November 23, 1844, at which point he returned to Oʻahu and has not been traced beyond receiving his wages at the end of that year.

PS: HBCA YFSA 20, 24, FtVanSA 6–8, CB 30, 31, YFDS 15, SandIsAB 3, 5; *PPS:* McLoughlin, *Fort Vancouver Letters, 1839–44*, 358

Kakua, Peter (fl. 1853–1869)

HBC employee, b. in Honolulu, executed May 19, 1869, in Nanaimo, British Columbia, associated with:

Fort Vancouver (1853–1854) laborer
Fort Victoria (1854) laborer
Fort Rupert (1854–1859) laborer
Fort Victoria (1859–1863) laborer
steamer *Labouchere* (1864) seaman
Nanaimo (1864–1868) coal miner

In 1853 Peter Kakua traveled from Honolulu to Fort Vancouver and then to Victoria, where he was hired by the HBC to work at Fort Rupert. In 1859 he returned to Victoria and, by his own account, worked for Governor James Douglas for a year and then for several others. After nine months on a steamer, he got a job with the Vancouver Coal Company in Nanaimo.

Alcohol and violence proved the downfall of Peter Kakua. In 1862 this 5 foot, 8 inch well-built Hawaiian took as a wife a Native woman, Mary/Que-en. He first appeared on record on August 8, 1865, when he was charged with assault and sentenced to three months in prison. By 1868, his marital relationship had soured, and Peter's wife sent a message via her brother that she and their six-month-old daughter were going to live elsewhere. Peter reacted by drinking for several days. On December 3, 1868, when he returned to his house, he was met by Shil-at-nord and Squash-e-lek, his father- and mother-in-law, as well as his wife who had all come to collect her belongings. Peter reacted by leaving and drinking more whiskey.

When Peter returned at midnight, he discovered his wife, so he thought, "in the act of committing adultery with her own Father." He tried to drag his father-in-law out of his bed and house. A fight ensued in which Peter killed his father-in-law, mother-in-law, wife, and daughter with an axe. Remorseful, he told fellow Hawaiian **Thomas Tamaree** [4] what he had done and then tried to persuade a "coloured man" to take him to the mainland in his canoe but they made it only as far as Newcastle Island, where they were captured.

With **William Kaulehelehe** as interpreter, a jury of twelve men found Kakua guilty of willful murder but "with a recommend[ation] to mercy on the ground that Kanakas are not Xtians [Christians] & killing men may not be such an offence in their eyes." The Hawaiian consul in Victoria, **Henry Rhodes,** did his best to secure counsel for Kakua, since he was "perfectly destitute," and then to represent his interests, but to no avail. Peter Kakua was hanged in May 1869 and buried on Newcastle Island in unconsecrated ground.

PS: BCA Crt-Gaols, Kakua, HSA Victoria; *PPS:* Illberbrun, "Kanaka Pete"

Kalaau (fl. 1864–1865)

Laborer, associated with:

Alberni (1864–1865) sawmill worker

Kalaau was among five men contracted in Honolulu on August 24, 1864, by the agent of Alberni Mill Co. to work for $10 per month with a $20 advance. They departed Honolulu on September 1 on the *Alberni,* and four of them including Kalaau arrived back in Honolulu on February 7, 1865, on the *Egoria.*

PS: HSA Seamen, Manifests

Kalaielua (fl. 1863)

Laborer, associated with:

Port Gamble (1863) sawmill worker

Kalaielua was one of five men contracted in Honolulu on March 18, 1863, by the agent of Puget Mill Co. to work at its sawmill for $10 per month with a $20 advance. It is uncertain how long he did so.

PS: HSA Seamen

Kalaikini (fl. 1858–1860)

Laborer, associated with:

Vancouver Island (1858)
Port Gamble (1860) possibly sawmill worker

Kalaikini was one of fourteen Hawaiians departing Honolulu for Victoria on the schooner *Alice* on June 22, 1858, enticed by the euphoria of the gold rush. On May 29, 1860, Kalaikini arrived back in Honolulu from Teekalet on the barque *Jenny Ford.* It is unclear whether he worked at the sawmill there.

PS: HSA Passenger

Kalākaua, David [variations: **David Lonoikamaka Keola Kalakaua, King Kalākaua**] (fl. 1860)

Hawaiian royal court official, b. November 16, 1836, in Honolulu to Caesar Kaluaiku Kapaʻakea and Analea Keohokōlole, d. January 20, 1891, in San Francisco, associated with:

schooner *Emma Rooke* (1860) passenger
Victoria (September 18–24, 1860) visitor

David Kalākaua was a twenty-four-year-old member of the house of nobles and the king's privy council when he visited Victoria for seven days in 1860 as part of Prince **Lot Kamehameha**'s entourage. Like Lot, he had been educated at the American missionary-run Chiefs' Children's School. His impressions of Victoria have not been traced.

Fourteen years after the visit, Kalākaua assumed the throne upon the death of the elected King Lunalilo. Supporters for the succession of the widow of Kamehameha IV, Queen Emma, rioted when David was chosen and he had to call in marines from British ships anchored at Honolulu. The same year Kalākaua went to Washington to garner support for a reciprocal trade treaty that eventually brought American money and businessmen into Hawaiʻi. Even though he worked to revive Hawaiian culture (he himself was an accomplished poet and musician), his lavish spending habits such as world travels, a penchant for royal pageantry, and public luaus incurred huge debts and eventual public disfavor. Kalākaua was forced to accept a new constitution and his powers were reduced to that of a figurehead. Near the end of his life, he sailed to San Francisco to attempt to regain his health but died in a hotel there in 1891.

David Kalākaua had one wife, Esther Kapiolani II (1834–1899). They had no children.

PS: HSA Passenger, Victoria; *SS: Pacific Commercial Advertiser,* January 30, 1891; *Colonist,* September 19–25, 1860; Kuykendall, *Hawaiian Kingdom,* vol. 1, 2; *Royal Lineage*

Kalama [variation: **John Kalama**] (fl. 1837–1870)

HBC/PSAC employee, b. ca. 1819, associated with:

Fort Nez Perces (1837–1840) middleman
Snake party (1840–1841) middleman
Fort Nisqually (1841–1842) middleman
Fort Vancouver (1843–1844) middleman or laborer, (1844–1847) laborer
Cowlitz farm (1847–1849) laborer
Fort Nisqually (1849–1850, 1852–1854, 1856–1860, 1862–1863, 1865–1866, 1868–1870)

"Big burly" and a "stout man," 6 foot Sandwich Islander Kalama nearly lost an eye and a nose to the fur trade. Kalama joined the HBC in July 1837 from Oʻahu and on August 10 began work at Fort Nez Perces and the Snake Country. In outfit 1840–1841 he helped transport people and goods in and out of the Snake Country. He returned to Oʻahu on November 10, 1842, but reengaged again. Good at any type of rough work, he did farming and carpentry tasks until March 17, 1850, when he along with **Cowie** and **Keaveʻhaccow** walked off the job. Just where Kalama spent all of the next couple of years is uncertain, but it is known that he worked for a time for a settler in the Nisqually area. In December 1852 he reengaged for two years.

However, at an August 14, 1853 party where too much alcohol flowed, a fight ensued and the Hawaiians squared off against the Natives. Kalama was attacked by Gukynun (Cut-face Charlie). Kalama's face was badly slashed, his nose and one eye almost cut out, and his forehead badly injured. Dr. William Fraser Tolmie or a Steilacoom Military Hospital steward sewed his nose back on, stitched his face, and sent him to the Steilacoom Military Hospital for two days before he was brought back to Fort Nisqually for recovery.

The experience must have unnerved Kalama, for he drifted away from the fort and worked at Muck, an outpost of Fort Nisqually, until January 3, 1854, when he returned to the fort and turned in fellow Hawaiians **Tamaree** [3] and **Kupahi** for their robbery of the Fort Nisqually store three months previous. Kalama, by the same token, admitted that he had stolen three sheep. Kalama was taken back on as an employee, perhaps in exchange for turning state's evidence against Tamaree and Kupahi. For the next six months, he did a variety of jobs around the fort, mainly in carpentry, until June 14, 1854, when he deserted once again.

The disfigured Sandwich Islander disappeared from the records for the next two years. In April 1856, he returned to PSAC employment. He got itchy feet a year later when, along with fellow Hawaiian Keave'haccow, he settled his account and set out to dig for gold at Thompson River. Both returned in June with little gold and began work again. Over the next dozen years Kalama moved in and out of employment at Fort Nisqually.

Kalama had one or more wives and several children. He repeatedly bought very large quantities of basic food items, indicating he was either supporting a large family or reselling goods. An unnamed wife had a baby boy on January 15, 1850, at Fort Nisqually. From 1860 on he purchased children's shoes and hose in multiple quantities.. According to family genealogy, Kalama had a son Peter (1864–1947) by Mary Martin (ca. 1840–?), the daughter of a Nisqually chief. After attending Chemawa Indian School (1880–1886), Peter became the progenitor of the large Kalama family in today's Washington State.

PS: HBCA SandIsAB 1, FtVanSA 4–8, YFDS 8, 11, 13, YFSA 19–20, 22, 224–232, 1850 U.S. Census, Oregon, Lewis Co., HL FTNisPJ 6–10, 12, 15, FtNisSA 7–9, 11–14, env, FtNisB 8–9, 11–12, FtNisbox 4, 6, FtNis MFJ; *PPS:* Huggins, "Reminiscences"; Roberts, "Round Hand"

Kalape (fl. 1863)

Laborer, associated with:

Port Gamble (1863) sawmill worker

Kalape and four others were contracted in Honolulu on July 8, 1863, by the agent of Puget Mill Co. to work at its sawmill for $10 per month with a $20 advance. It is uncertain how long he did so.

PS: HSA Seamen

Kalapuni (fl. 1860)

Laborer, associated with:

Port Gamble (1860) sawmill worker

Kalapuni was one of four men contracted in Honolulu on November 1, 1860, by the agent of Puget Mill Co. to work at its sawmill for $15 per month with a $15 advance. It is uncertain how long he did so.

PS: HSA Seamen

Kalauhala (fl. 1859)

Seaman, associated with:

vessel *Koloa* (1859) seaman

Kalauhala was one of five Hawaiians the Puget Mill Co. hired to man the *Koloa* leaving Honolulu for Puget Sound on April 13, 1859. The men returned on November 29, 1859, and were discharged February 11, 1860.

PS: HSA Seamen

Kalawaianui (fl. 1880)

Miner, b. ca. 1829, associated with:

Jacksonville, Oregon (1880)

Kalawaianui was mining in Jacksonville, Oregon, in 1880. He was single. No other references to him have been located.

PS: 1880 U.S. Census, Oregon, Jacksonville

Kalehua [variations: **John or Jack Ingram, Tareehooa, Opye, Opey, Opie**] (fl. 1792)

Seaman, b. ca. 1773, associated with:

HMS *Discovery* (1792–1793) seaman

A native of the island of Kaua'i, Kalehua was a true adventurer. One indication was the many names by which he was known, including John or Jack Ingram, Tarehooa, and Opye.

In 1789–1790, Kalehua, then in his teens, first traveled from Hawai'i to China and Boston aboard John Gray's Boston trading vessel, the *Columbia Rediviva,* with Joseph Ingraham as chief mate. It was possibly here that he acquired the name John or Jack Ingram. After spending six weeks in North America, Kalehua returned to Hawai'i on another Boston trading vessel, *Hope,* this time with Joseph Ingraham in charge, arriving home on May 20, 1791. Here, he was referred to as Opey or Opie. Kalehua was not satisfied with circumnavigating the globe only once, so when English explorer George Vancouver arrived on the *Discovery,* Kalehua, as he was known to Vancouver, seized the opportunity by paddling out to the vessel and asking Vancouver if he could travel with them. As a result, on March 5, 1792 , the affable Kalehua joined the *Discovery,* spending between April and October 1792 on the Northwest Coast around Vancouver Island and north to Queen Charlotte Sound.

On October 12, 1792, just as the *Discovery* was about to leave Nootka for Hawai'i, Kalehua took on the additional role of chaperone and companion for two Ni'ihau girls, **Teheeopea** and **Tahomeeraoo,** who had been brought to Nootka five days before on the three-masted Bristol schooner *Jenny,* and now wished to return to the Sandwich Islands.

On February 14, 1793, when the *Discovery* pulled into Kawaihae Bay on the island of Hawai'i, Chief Keeaumoku sent a canoe out with a gift of a hog and some vegetables to meet the *Discovery* to see if his "favourite servant" might be onboard. An overwhelmed Kalehua broke into tears when he saw the reception. Sometime before February 20, Kalehua had taken a bull and a cow as a gift to King Kamehameha I, but the cow died on the passage to the island. On that day he accompanied Kamehameha onboard the *Discovery,* where the king was royally entertained.

Kalehua continued to remain part of the crew, for between May and October 1793 he was on the coast opposite the Queen Charlotte Islands and in the southern Alaskan panhandle. He stayed with the *Discovery* until the end of its last visit to the island of Hawai'i and on March 2, 1794, was left back home in the protection of King Kamehameha.

PS: DetL Hope; *PPS:* Vancouver, *Voyage*

Kalemaku [variation: **Kalemaka**] (fl. 1845–1848)

HBC employee, d. 1848, probably at Fort Langley, associated with:

Fort Vancouver (1845–1846) laborer
New Caledonia (1846–1848) laborer
Fort Langley (1848) laborer

Kalemaku joined the HBC from Oʻahu on May 7, 1845, for three years and renewed for two more years. He worked as a laborer in several locations until his death in 1848, probably at Fort Langley.

PS: HBCA YFSA 25–29, SandIsAB 3

Kalenopale (fl. 1844)

HBC employee, associated with:

Fort Vancouver (1844) laborer

Kalenopale was likely hired on by the HBC from Oʻahu in 1844. After arriving on the coast, he worked at Fort Vancouver until November 12, 1844, at which point he returned to Oʻahu.

PS: HBCA YFSA 24, YFDS 15

Kaliai (fl. 1860)

Seaman, associated with:

schooner *Emma Rooke* (1860) seaman

Kaliai was among five Hawaiians contracted by the schooner *Emma Rooke* when it sailed from Honolulu to Victoria on August 29, 1860. The men received $15 per month with a $15 advance. He was discharged on November 2.

PS: HSA Seamen

Kalikeeney [variation: Kanaka Jack] (fl. 1859–1860)

PSAC employee, associated with:

Fort Nisqually outstation (1859–1860) shepherd

Little is known of Kalikeeney, who began work as a shepherd at a Fort Nisqually outstation along with **Kelocha** in July 1859. The pair departed the next February.

PS: HL FNPJ 12–13, FtNisSA 14; *SS:* Anderson, *Physical Structure,* 185

Kalili [variation: Kealili] (fl. 1863–1864)

Laborer, associated with:

Alberni (1863–1864) sawmill worker

Kalilu was one of seven men contracted in Honolulu on September 23, 1863, by the agent of Alberni Mill Co. to work for $10 per month with a $20 advance. The same day they left for Victoria on the *Alberni.* On December 22, 1864, all of the men, except for Kalili, arrived back in Honolulu from Alberni on the ship *Buena Vista.* A notation states he "ran away."

PS: HSA Seamen, Passenger

Kallai, Louis [variations: Kalai, Kaline, John Carline, John Kelly] (fl. 1875–1881)

Laborer, b. 1840 to Jacob Kaline and Koakow in Honolulu, d. June 16, 1881, on Salt Spring, associated with:

Victoria area (1875)
Port Gamble (1875–1879)
Salt Spring Island (1881)

Louis Kallai's activities spanned both sides of the border. On March 8, 1875, Hawaiian Louis Kaline married **William Newanna**'s daughter Sophia (1858–?). They were living in

Port Gamble when their son George (1875–?) was born on December 10 of the same year, followed by Daniel (ca. 1877–1936) and Lena (ca. 1879–1956). Louis Kallai died in 1881 on Salt Spring Island, where the family was then living.

PS: BCA VS-StAndC, SSA

Kaloha (fl. 1858–1860)

Occupation unknown, associated with:

> Vancouver Island (1858)
> Port Townsend (1860)

Kaloha was one of fourteen Hawaiians departing Honolulu for Victoria on the schooner *Alice* on June 22, 1858, enticed by the euphoria of the gold rush. He is almost certainly the Kaloha who returned to Honolulu from Port Townsend on the barque *Jenny Ford,* arriving February 25, 1860.

PS: HSA Passenger

Kalpu, Joseph (fl. 1848–1860)

Laborer, b. ca. 1820, associated with:

> Fort Vancouver area (1860) laborer

Joseph Kalpu was living in the Kanaka Village area in 1860. He did not appear to be a regular contracted employee and may have worked casually for the HBC.

Joseph had a Native wife, Mary (ca. 1829–?), and son Karney (ca. 1849–?), both born in Washington Territory. The date of birth suggests Kalpu was in the Pacific Northwest for some time.

PS: 1860 U.S. Census, Washington Territory, Clark Co.

Kalua [1] (fl. 1850–1858)

HBC employee, associated with:

> brigantine *Mary Dare* (1850) passenger
> Fort Simpson (1850–1852) middleman, (1852–1855) laborer
> Columbia Department (1856–1857) laborer
> Fort Simpson (1857–1858)

Kalua joined the HBC in Honolulu in 1850 and sailed to the Northwest Coast. His work record over the next eight years at Fort Simpson is unclear, and the intervals of ambiguity imply visits to Hawai'i or just poor bookkeeping. In May 1852 he cut his finger with an axe, dividing the knuckle and resulting in the removal of a piece of bone. There is a possibility that Kalua knew how to read and write for, in 1857, when he was recruited by Anglican missionary William Duncan for his Men's Night School, Kalua was described as unable to read and write in English, implying that he could in Hawaiian. Kalua has not been traced after 1858.

PS: HBCA SandIsAB 10, YFSA 30–32, FtVicSA 1–2, 4–6, FtSimp[N]PJ 7, UBC Duncan

Kalua [2] (fl. 1863)

Laborer, associated with:

> Port Gamble (1863) sawmill worker

Kalua and four others were contracted in Honolulu on July 8, 1863, by the agent of Puget Mill Co. to work at its sawmill for $10 per month with a $20 advance. It is uncertain how long he did so.

PS: HSA Seamen

Kalua, Maufu (fl. 1880)

Laborer, b. ca. 1863, associated with:

Port Gamble (1880) laborer

At the time of the 1880 Census, Maufu Kalua was one of nine "Kanakas" working in Port Gamble, almost certainly at the sawmill. He was literate. It's possible he was the son of **Kalua** [2].

PS: 1880 U.S. Census, Washington Territory, Kitsap Co., Port Gamble

Kaluaahana (fl. 1863)

Laborer, associated with:

Port Gamble (1863) sawmill worker

Kaluaahana was one of five men contracted in Honolulu on March 18, 1863, by the agent of Puget Mill Co. to work at its sawmill for $10 per month with a $20 advance. It is uncertain how long he did so.

PS: HSA Seamen

Kaluahe [variation: **Kaluahi**] (fl. 1850–1851)

HBC employee, associated with:

brigantine *Mary Dare* (1850) passenger
Fort Rupert (1850–1851) laborer
Fort Simpson (1851) laborer

Kaluahe joined the HBC in Oʻahu early in 1850 to serve two years on the Northwest Coast. He worked as a laborer at the northern posts of Fort Rupert and Fort Simpson, was discharged on September 8, 1851. He may have returned to Oʻahu at that time.

PS: HBCA SandIsAB 10, YFSA 30–31, YFDS 22, FtVicSA 1

Kaluaikai [variations: **Kulaikai, Kalauaikai, Pierre Kalawataye**] (fl. 1845–1853)

HBC employee, b. ca. 1823, d. ca. June 2, 1853, at Fort Vancouver, associated with:

Fort Vancouver (1845–1849) laborer
Snake Country (1849–1850) laborer
Fort Vancouver (1850–1851) steward, (1851–1853) freeman

Kaluaikai joined the HBC from Oʻahu on May 7, 1845, and spent most of his working career at Fort Vancouver. He left the company around February 1851, remaining in the area of the post, where he died of smallpox around June 2, 1853. Smallpox, like other diseases, may have been brought in by the U.S. Army from the Isthmus of Panama and took a large toll in the Fort Vancouver Kanaka Village where Kaluaikai probably lived. He was quite likely buried in the Fort Vancouver graveyard.

On May 31, 1853, while Kaluaikai, whose name was written down as Pierre Kalawataye in the Catholic records, was on his deathbed, he married Marguerite (1835–?), the mixed-descent daughter of another unnamed Hawaiian and a Native woman. Together they had Julie (1853–?) who was four months old at the time of Kaluaikai's death.

PS: HBCA SandIsAB 3, YFSA 25–31, YFDS 21; *PPS:* Munnick, *Vancouver,* vol. 2

Kalui, Thomas (fl. 1883–1884)

Occupation unknown, associated with:

Salt Spring Island (1883–1884)

Nothing is known of Thomas Kalui, except that his child by Mathilda (?–?), who was named Louise (1884–?), was baptized on March 24, 1884, in a Catholic ceremony held at the home of **William Haumea** at Fulford Harbour on Salt Spring Island.

PS: StEdC

Kamai (fl. 1864)

Occupation unknown, associated with:

Port Angeles, Washington (1864)

Kamai and two other Hawaiians left Honolulu for Port Angeles on the *N.S. Perkins* on October 25, 1864. He may be the same person as **Kame**, who was working at the Puget Mill at nearby Port Gamble in 1870.

PS: HSA Passenger

Kamai, Kama [variations: Kama, Kanai, Andrew Kamai, Comai, Kami Kam, Comaii] (fl. 1844–1890)

HBC/PSAC employee, b. ca. 1830, d. June 19, 1890, likely on Coal Island, associated with:

Fort Vancouver (1844–1846) laborer
New Caledonia (1846–1847) laborer
Vancouver (1847–1849) laborer
barque *Columbia* (1849) passenger
brigantine *Mary Dare* (1850) passenger
Fort Victoria (1851–1854) laborer
Belle Vue sheep farm (1854–1855) laborer
San Juan Island (1855–1872) farmer
Coal Island (1873–1890) farmer

Kama Kamai, from Oʻahu, joined the HBC in 1844 at the age of twenty-four and worked as a laborer at a variety of posts throughout the Columbia Department. Although his contract was to have ended in 1851, he left prematurely for Oʻahu on October 20, 1849, but reenlisted in 1850, when he was enumerated in the Census of that year in Lewis County, Washington, possibly on his way to Fort Victoria. After he began working for PSAC on San Juan Island, he accidentally blew off his left hand. He was treated in Victoria, at which time he retired. From 1854 to 1856, he carried on ongoing transactions with the company. Kama, almost certainly Kama Kamai, paid another visit home in 1866. He left Victoria for Honolulu, arriving October 22, 1866. A man named as both Kama and Comaii departed Honolulu for Victoria on December 26, 1866.

The 1870 Census described Kamai as a farmer on San Juan Island with $1,000 in real estate and $300 in personal property. He lived there until 1872, or until the international boundary between the United States and Canada was settled. On October 3, 1873, having just moved north to British Columbia, Kamai swore out his British subject status, which gave him the right to preempt land. He signed with his mark, indicating he was illiterate. A month later Kama Kamai claimed 160 acres, the western half of small Coal Island lying off of Vancouver Island, and he began to farm. His countryman and son-in-law **Alexander Kāne** also moved to the island with his family. Kamai died on June 19, 1890, likely on Coal Island, and was buried in the cemetery of St. Paul's Church at Fulford Harbour on Salt Spring Island.

Andrew Kamai, to use the name with which he was baptized in the Catholic Church at the time of his marriage in 1870, had numerous children. By an unknown woman, he was the father of Mary (ca. 1851–?), who on December 20, 1870, in Victoria married Hawaiian Alexander Kāne. The same day her father Kama Kamai formalized his marriage to Mary Ann (ca. 1846–?), who was Songhees. The Kamais' recorded children were John (ca. 1856–?), Joseph (ca. 1860–?), Mary (ca. 1861–?), Susan (ca. 1861–?), Charles (ca. 1863–1933), Louis (1866–1949), Moses (ca. 1871–?), Catherine (1872–?), Agnes (1875–?), and Louisa (1878–?). Some members of the Kamai family have opted for their maternal identity and identify themselves as Songhees.

PS: HBCA YFSA 24–28, 30–32, FtVicSA 1–3, YFDS 20, SandIsAB 10, BelleVuePJ 1, 1850 U.S. Census, Oregon, Lewis Co., 1870 U.S. Census, Washington Territory, San Juan Island, 1881 Canada Census, British Columbia, Saanich, 1891 Canada Census, British Columbia, Victoria, HSA Passenger, BCA VS-StAndC, Crt-Naturalization, GR-Preemption, StElizC, StEdC

Kamaikaloa [variation: **Kamoalow**] (fl. 1844–1849)

HBC / PSAC employee, associated with:

Fort Vancouver (1844–1846) laborer
Cowlitz farm (1846–1847) laborer
Fort Vancouver Indian trade (1847–1849) laborer

Kamaikaloa joined the HBC in Oʻahu on May 7, 1844, and worked as a laborer at Fort Vancouver and on the Cowlitz farm. In outfit 1849–1850, he deserted, most likely for the gold in California. He probably did so in the spring of 1849, as he received no wages for outfit 1849–1850.

PS: HBCA SandIsAB 3, YFSA 24–29

Kamaka (fl. 1844–1860)

PSAC / HBC employee, associated with:

Cowlitz farm (1844–1850) laborer
Fort Vancouver (1850–1851) laborer
Belle Vue sheep farm (1859–1860) laborer

Kamaka joined the HBC / PSAC in 1844 from Oʻahu on a three-year contract and worked as a laborer on the Cowlitz farm and at Fort Vancouver. His contract ended in 1851, and he deserted on July 1 of that year, possibly heading south for gold. He may have wandered around for eight years for, on May 4, 1859, a man with the same name, and likely the same person, reengaged with PSAC to work on San Juan Island for one year. At the end of his contract in 1860 he went to Victoria and hasn't been traced further.

PS: HBCA YFSA 24–31, YFDS 22, FtVanSA 9, BelleVueAB; *PPS:* Roberts, "Round Hand"

Kamakeha [variation: **Kamackeha**] (fl. 1840–1854)

HBC employee, d. ca. 1854, associated with:

Fort Taku (1840–1841) middleman
Fort McLoughlin (1841–1843) middleman
Fort Victoria (1843–1847) middleman, (1848–1851) laborer

Kamakeha, from Oʻahu, joined the HBC in 1840. He worked at coastal forts until November 10, 1847, at which point he returned to Oʻahu. He reenlisted and began work again on July 15, 1848. In June 1851, he retired once again, this time remaining in the area. He carried on transactions with the HBC until outfit 1854–1855, at which point he was noted as being deceased.

Kamakeha chose an unnamed Native woman as a mate, and together they had a son, Joseph (?–bap. 1852–?), who was baptized Catholic.

PS: HBCA YFSA 20, 24–27, 29–32, FtVanSA 6–8, YFDS 18–19, SandIsAB 7, FtVicSA 1–2, BCA VS-CCC

Kamako (fl. 1850)

HBC seaman, associated with:

barque *Cowlitz* (1850) seaman

Kamako shipped onboard the HBC vessel *Cowlitz* in February 3, 1850, at Honolulu and sailed to the coast on a voyage on which the captain was unhappy with the performance of the Hawaiians. When the vessel returned to Hawai'i that August, the Hawaiian crew rebelled, claiming their contracts were up but they nonetheless returned to work a further month. Beyond that, Kamako has not been traced.

PS: HBCA SandIsAB 10–11, Log of *Cowlitz* 8

Kamalii, Kalehua (fl. 1861)

Occupation unknown, associated with:

Victoria area (1861)

Kalehua Kamalii preempted land in the vicinity of Victoria on May 6, 1861, signing with his mark. He may well be a former HBC employee using a more formal version of his name for this official document.

PS: BCA GR-Preemption

Kamalikadow (fl. 1870)

Laborer, b. ca. 1831, associated with:

San Juan Island (1870)

A thirty-nine-year-old Kamalikadow was living by himself in an area where other Sandwich Islanders lived on San Juan Island in 1870. Nothing else is known about this Hawaiian laborer other than he was illiterate and may be the same person as **Kamailakoa**.

PS: 1870 U.S. Census, Washington Territory, San Juan Island

Kamano, George [variations: Kaumano, Kahoomana, Camano, Kaumana] (fl. 1854–1918)

HBC employee, b. ca. 1835 to Okerry Cahoomana and Nainema, d. May 1, 1918, at Alert Bay, British Columbia, associated with:

Fort Rupert (1854–1868) laborer
Columbia Department (1868–1869) laborer
Harbledown Island (1869–1900s) farmer and rancher
Alert Bay (1900s–1918) retired

According to his British Columbia marriage certificate the oldest son of Okerry Cahoomana and of Nainema, Kamano left the Hawaiian Islands as a young man. He most likely joined the HBC from O'ahu in 1854, although oral tradition persists that he was "shanghaied" in O'ahu and jumped ship in Victoria (or wrecked on a whaling ship), only to be smuggled by Natives to Fort Rupert. Whatever method he used to get there, he worked at Fort Rupert for the next fifteen years to 1869 as a laborer. There, at the Oblate mission, which was established in 1863, he may have learned to write as, at one time, he was left in charge of the Fort Rupert post in the absence of the chief trader.

In 1869 Kamano retired from the HBC and followed the Catholic St. Michael's mission which, by that time, had moved from the Fort Rupert site to New Vancouver, Harbledown Island, about 35 miles south of Fort Rupert, which was his wife's home territory.

There he worked at, and was periodically left in charge of, the mission, which eventually closed down in 1874. Oblate priest Father Foquet explained how "we are leaving all the affairs of the mission in the care of Kamano." The same year Kamano decided to throw in his lot with British Columbia, and was naturalized a British subject.

Required to be self-sufficient, the Kamano family developed on Harbledown Island a garden and orchard of several different varieties of apples, selling their potatoes, carrots, and turnips to the local Natives. Kamano had a lifelong fear of being sent back to the Sandwich Islands, and not wanting to return, developed a solitary posture on Harbledown Island, where he raised a large family. Until the latter twenty years of his life, he worked daily the woods near his island home, returning only to eat and sleep at his house. He did nonetheless command a certain outside respect for, in McKenney's 1883–1884 *Pacific Coast Directory* out of San Francisco, George Kamano was listed among the important men in the vicinity of Alert Bay. While he preferred the solitude of his working environment, his more outgoing wife held potlatches throughout the area, some lasting for as long as a week. In his latter years, after the death of his wife, he lived with his daughter Lillian at Alert Bay and finally died of pneumonia. He was buried on May 4, 1918, behind the Anglican church at Alert Bay along with many other members of his family. Coffin Island of the Karlukwees Indian Reserve, near Harbledown Island, was in 1947 renamed Kamano Island.

Kamano had one wife and ten children. On December 25, 1866, at Fort Rupert, George Kamano formalized his marriage in a Catholic ceremony to Pauline Clahoara (1845–1893) of the Tenaktak/Tanakteuk band of the Kwakuitl people. Their children were George (1864–1895), Louis Charles/Carey (1866–1904), Mary Anne (1868–1904), Lillian (1868–1955), Michael (1870–1956), Joseph (1872–1958), Emma (1874–1907), Maria (1876–1941), Harriet (1880–1904), and Maggie (1882–1902). The children learned Kwagiult as their first language, but could also speak English.

PS: HBCA FtVicSA 2–16, Bio, OblH Alert, Priv-MS Huson, Johnston, Kamano, Myers, 1881 and 1891 Canada Census, British Columbia, Vancouver Island, Burials; *SS:* McKenney, *Directory;* Barbeau, *Totem Poles,* 654; *Pioneer Journal,* May 9, 1956, 4 ; Nicholls, "Kamano," 12

Kame (fl. 1870)

Laborer, b. ca. 1830, associated with:

> Port Gamble (1870) sawmill worker

At the time of the 1870 Census, Kame was one of twenty-two Hawaiians working at Puget Mill at Port Gamble. He may be **Kamai**, who arrived at Port Angeles in 1864.

PS: 1870 U.S. Census, Washington Territory, Kitsap Co., Port Gamble

Kamehameha, Lot [variations: Lot Kapuʻaiwa, King Kamehameha V] (fl. 1860)

Hawaiian Kingdom government minister, king, b. December 11, 1830, to Kinau and Mataio Kekūanaōʻa, d. December 11, 1872, associated with:

> schooner *Emma Rooke* (1860) passenger
> Victoria (September 18–24, 1860) visitor

When Prince Lot Kamehameha visited Victoria in September 1860, he was minister of the interior and minister of finance to his younger brother Kamehameha IV [Alexander Liholiho]. At the time of the visit, Lot was not in the best of health and his physicians had advised him to sail to Victoria and then, if his health permitted, to California. In Victoria, he stayed at the French Hotel, limited his public appearances to colonial government officials, and did not appear to meet the number of Hawaiians living in the area. On the trip, he was accompanied by his father and governor of Oʻahu **Mataio Kekūa-**

naō'a; his aide-de-camp Josiah C. Spalding; **David Kalākaua**, a distant cousin and future king; and **Levi Halelea**, part of his privy council. Afterward, they sailed to California. The prince, who had been educated at the American missionary run Chiefs' Children's School and had traveled with his brother to the United States and Europe, was to be the last of the Kamehameha kings. In 1863, he assumed the throne upon his brother's death and during the nine years of his reign gave himself greater powers under a new constitution, increased foreigners' power in the Hawaiian Islands, and improved the balance of trade. Indeed, the *Emma Rooke* had onboard 15 tons of Hawaiian sugar to be sold at Victoria. Lot never married and had no successors and so the next king had to be chosen by the Hawaiian legislature.

PS: HSA Passenger, Victoria; *PSS: Colonist,* September 19–25, 1860; Kuykendall, *Hawaiian Kingdom,* vol. 1, 2; *Royal Lineage*

Kamehemeha [variation: **Kameheha**] (fl. 1859–1870)

PSAC employee, associated with:

Fort Nisqually (1859–1860, 1869–1870) laborer

Little is known of Kamehemeha, who worked at Fort Nisqually in 1859–1860 and also in 1869–1870.

PS: HL FtNisB 8, 12

Kameu, Kama (fl. 1880)

Laborer, b. ca. 1862, associated with:

Port Gamble (1880) laborer

At the time of the 1880 Census, Kama Kameu was one of nine "Kanakas" working in Port Gamble, almost certainly at the sawmill. He was described as illiterate.

PS: 1880 U.S. Census, Washington Territory, Kitsap Co., Port Gamble

Kamo, Noah [variations: **Noa Kama, Tom Kam**] (fl. 1867–1894)

Occupation unknown, b. ca. 1834 in Noro Kahe, Tahiti; d. April 12, 1894, in Vancouver, associated with:

Victoria area (1867)
Moodyville (1894)

Just how and when Noah Kamo came to the Northwest Coast has not been ascertained but by 1867 the thirty-three-year-old Tahitian was in the Victoria area. There, on September 1, 1867, he married fourteen-year-old Mary Ann Pelai (ca. 1853–?), daughter of the Hawaiian **Pēlāi** and Stathill of the Elsi tribe near Fort Langley. Kamo was a widower living at Moodyville when he died in 1894, leaving an estate of $150 and a son George Kama (?–?) and daughter Matilda Kama (c. 1875–?)

PS: BCA VS-StAndC, BCVS

Kamo, William (fl. 1859–1875)

Farmer, b. ca. 1825, associated with:

San Juan Island (1859–1875)

By 1870 William Kamo was living as a farmer on San Juan Island raising a family. During the 1870 U.S. Census, his wife was absent. Their two boys were Joseph (ca. 1860–?) and Hoeki (ca. 1861–?). Joseph was only baptized Catholic in Victoria on April 10, 1875. William Kamo may have been the same person as **William Newanna.**

PS: 1870 U.S. Census, Washington Territory, San Juan Island, BCA VS-StAndC

Kamohakeha (fl. 1851–1852)

Occupation unknown, associated with:

Victoria area (1851–1852)

The name of Kamohakeha survives only because of the baptism of his son Joseph (?–bap. 1852–?) by a Native woman at Christ Church Anglican Cathedral in Victoria in 1852.

PS: BCA VS-CCC

Kamu, Keava (fl. 1862)

Occupation unknown, associated with:

Victoria (1862)

Keava Kamu was sworn in as a British subject, probably in Victoria, on August 11, 1862. He was sufficiently literate to sign his name. That same day, **John Adams** and **Kalle Kopane** also received their naturalization papers. The following day **William R. Kaulehelehe** received his, indicating a possible friendship among the four.

In late September 1862 Adams and Kopane preempted land adjacent to each other in the Cowichan area of Vancouver Island. The certificate mentions but does not name a third "Kanaka," who might have been Kamu.

PS: BCA GR-Naturalization, Crt-Naturalization, GR-Preemption

Kamua (fl. 1860)

Laborer, associated with:

Port Madison, Washington (1860) sawmill worker

Kamua was one of four men contracted in Honolulu on October 5, 1860, by the Madison Mill Co. to work at its sawmill for $15 per month with a $20 advance. Their term of service of a year began only on arriving in Puget Sound. The records of Kamua and another man had an X after them, but it is unclear what it meant. Perhaps he died while in the Pacific Northwest. Alternatively, he might be **Kamuela**, who in 1863 contracted to work at Puget Mill Co.

PS: HSA Seamen

Kamuela (fl. 1863)

Laborer, associated with:

Port Gamble (1863) sawmill worker

Kamuela and four others were contracted in Honolulu on March 18, 1863, by the agent of Puget Mill Co. to work at its sawmill for $10 per month with a $20 advance. It is uncertain how long he did so or whether he was the same person as **Kamua**.

PS: HSA Seamen

Kanackanui [variation: **Kanakanui**] (fl. 1840–1852)

HBC employee, d. July 8, 1852, at Fort Simpson, associated with:

Fort Stikine (1840–1845) middleman, (1845–1849) laborer
Fort Rupert (1849–1850) laborer
Fort Simpson (1850–1852) laborer

Kanackanui or "big Kanaka" joined the HBC in 1840 from Oʻahu and arrived at Fort Vancouver in April of that year. After noting his arrival at Fort Stikine around June, when it was stated that all the Hawaiians could neither understand nor be understood, he was not mentioned again in the surviving Stikine journals indicating, to his credit, a general competency in his work. Paradoxically, he had been taught to read the scriptures, probably in Hawaiian, by American missionary instructors.

Kanackanui was two years into his service there when, on April 20, 1842, some of the post's employees rebelled against the discipline of manager John McLoughlin Jr., who, late at night, called Kanackanui and several other Hawaiians to arms to protect him. Kanackanui grabbed his gun and rushed outside, but another employee wrested it from him. Nonetheless, Kanackanui followed the rest to the gallery. In spite of a modicum of protection, McLoughlin was killed by his own men, who claimed they did it because McLoughlin was a brutal drunk. In a deposition, Kanackanui testified that he saw McLoughlin only "tipsy once about the Holidays," which countered other servants' stories. Kanackanui probably was one of the Hawaiians who took the body inside, washed and dried it, and threw one of the French Canadian employees out for throwing the body on the floor. During his nine-year stay at Stikine, Kanackanui obviously learned English, probably French, and a few Native dialects as well as the trading jargon of Chinook. When the HBC abandoned Stikine, he went to Beaver Cove on northern Vancouver Island to assist in the construction of a new Fort Rupert. After one outfit there, he went to Fort Simpson where, in the morning of July 8, 1852, he died from the lingering effects of venereal disease, the journal entry of the day stating that he had been a very good servant. His interment was not noted the following day but he was probably buried in the old graveyard on the hill behind the fort.

Kanackanui's family, if any, has not been traced.

PS: HBCA FtStikPJ 1, YFSA 20, 24–32, FtVicSA 1–2, DS, FtVanSA 8, CB 30–31, FtVicASA 1–2, FtSimp[N]PJ 7; *PPS:* McLoughlin, *Fort Vancouver Letters, 1839–44,* 368

Kanackeha (fl. 1853–1854)

HBC employee, associated with:

Columbia Department (1853–1854) laborer

Kanackeha's name appeared on the 1853–1854 Fort Victoria abstracts with no additional information.

PS: HBCA FtVicSA 1

Kanah, Frank [variation: Kanak] (fl. 1814–1831)

NWC/HBC employee, b. ca. 1792, associated with:

Columbia area (1814–1822) laborer
Fort George [Astoria] (1822–1825) laborer
Columbia Department (1825–1826) cowherd
Fort Vancouver (1826–1831) cowherd
barque *Ganymede* (1831) passenger

Frank Kanah joined the fur trade in 1814, at the age of about twenty-two, and is on record as having transferred from the NWC to the HBC in 1821. He worked in the Columbia District, likely spending most of his time at Fort George [formerly Astoria], eventually as a cowherd, before he was discharged to Oʻahu on November 1, 1831, sailing on the *Ganymede.*

PS: HBCA NWCAB 9, YFSA 1–9, 11, FtGeo[Ast]AB 10–12, YFDS 2a, 3b–4b, FtVanSA 1

Kanahoua (fl. 1848–1853)

Occupation unknown, associated with:

Fort Vancouver area (1848–1853)

Little is known of Kanahoua other than he appeared in the Fort Vancouver area in 1853. At that time he had a four-year-old child, Pierre (ca. 1849–?), by an unidentified Native woman.

PPS: Munnick, *Vancouver,* vol. 2

Kanai, Gabriel (fl. 1842–1843)

Occupation unknown, associated with:

Fort Vancouver area (1842–1843)

Little is known of Gabriel Kanai, who was present as witness at two non-Hawaiian Roman Catholic burials in the Fort Vancouver area in 1842–1843. This presence indicates perhaps some relationship with the Church.

PPS: Munnick, *St. Paul,* vol. 1

Kanak, Bill (fl. 1885)

Wood cutter, b. ca. 1860, d. June 1885 in Victoria, associated with:

Victoria (1885) laborer

Described as born in Honolulu, laborer Bill Kanack died of consumption in Royal Hospital in Victoria in June 1885 at age twenty-five.

PS: BCA GR-BCVS

Kanaka [1] (fl. 1859–1860)

HBC employee, associated with:

Columbia Department (1859–1860) laborer

Kanaka worked for the HBC, receiving his 1859–1860 wages on the outstanding balances account. In outfit 1860–1861 he appeared on the sundries account with a credit of £25 carried over from the previous outfit. He likely did casual labor.

PS: HBCA FtVicSA 7

Kanaka [2] (fl. 1880)

Farmer, b. ca. 1851 in Hawaiian Islands, associated with:

Steilacoom City (1880) farmer

Little is known of Kanaka who was born in the Sandwich Islands but in 1880, at the age of twenty-nine, was working as a farmer in the area of Steilacoom, Washington.

PS: 1880 U.S. Census, Washington Territory, Stelacoom, Pierce Co.

Kanaka [3] (fl. 1880)

Laborer, b. ca. 1851, associated with:

Vashon Island (1880) sawmill worker

Kanaka was in 1880 working in a sawmill on Vashon Island, Washington. He was single.

PS: 1880 U.S. Census, Washington Territory, Skamania

Kanaka, Aluda (fl. 1850)

Occupation unknown, b. ca. 1830, associated with:

Oregon City (1850)

Aluda, who may be **Alauka** returned from the gold fields of California, was living in Oregon City in 1850. Other than the fact that he was sharing a residence with **John** and **Tahuis Mowrey** and **John Kanaka**, nothing is known about him.

PS: 1850 U.S. Census, Oregon, Clackamas Co.

Kanaka, Ben (fl. 1880)

Farmer, b. ca. 1843, associated with

Steilacoom City (1881) inmate

Ben Kanaka was, at the age of thirty-eight in 1881, in the insane asylum at Steilacoom City, Pierce Co., Washington. Earlier he appears to have been farming nearby.

PS: 1880 U.S. Census, Washington Territory, Pierce Co.

Kanaka, James (fl. 1850)

Laborer, b. ca. 1820, associated with:

Fort Vancouver (1850) laborer

A Hawaiian named as James Kanaka was working as a laborer at Fort Vancouver in 1850. Nothing else is known of him.

PS: 1850 U.S. Census, Oregon, Clark Co.

Kanaka, Joe [1] (fl. 1868–1893)

Laborer, b. ca. 1825, d. April 1893 in New Westminster, associated with:

New Westminster area (1868–1893) laborer

Described as a woodcutter born in the Sandwich Islands, forty-three-year-old Joe Kanaka was treated in the Royal Columbian Hospital in New Westminster on April 24, 1868, for an ankle fracture. A laborer about sixty-nine years old named Kanaka Joe, who was probably the same person, died in April 1893 in New Westminster after being afflicted with syphilis for a long time and looked after by the local police.

Joe Kanaka was married at the time he was treated in hospital.

PS: BCA VS-BCVS

Kanaka, Joe [2] (fl. 1888–1897)

Laborer, b. ca. 1841, associated with:

Victoria (1888)
New Westminster (1888–1897) prisoner

Described as 5 feet, 7 1/2 inches tall, 184 pounds in weight, and born in the Sandwich Islands, Joe Kanaka was on November 26, 1888, in Victoria sentenced to thirteen years' imprisonment for manslaughter. He was sent to New Westminster Penitentiary, from where he was discharged on June 22, 1897. He was illiterate both when he entered prison and when he was discharged.

Joe Kanaka was married at the time he was imprisoned for manslaughter.

PS: NAC Penitentiary; *PPS:* British Columbia, Superintendent of Police, *Annual Report,* 1894

Kanaka, John (fl. 1850)

Occupation unknown, b. ca. 1822, associated with:

Oregon City (1850)

A twenty-eight-year-old John Kanaka was resident in Oregon City in 1850, living in the same household as fellow Hawaiians **John** and **Tahuis Mowrey** and **Aluda Kanaka**. Nothing else is known of him.

PS: 1850 U.S. Census, Oregon, Clackamas Co.

Kanaka, Muttou (fl. 1850)

Laborer, b. ca. 1825, associated with:

Fort Vancouver area (1850) laborer

A twenty-five-year-old Muttou Kanaka, working as a laborer, was recorded as being in the Kanaka Village area of Fort Vancouver in 1850.

PS: 1850 U.S. Census, Clark Co.

Kanaka, Thomas (fl. 1877–1891)

Laborer, b. ca. 1851 in Samoa, associated with:

New Westminster (1881) mill worker
Vancouver (1891) laborer

A thirty-year-old Thomas Kanaka, who described himself as born on the Samoan Islands, was working as a millman somewhere on Burrard Inlet in 1881. Ten years later he was a general laborer in nearby Vancouver.

By 1891 Thomas Kanaka and an unnamed woman were the parents of Dora (ca. 1878–?), Louisa (ca. 1884–?), and John (ca. 1886–?).

PS: 1881 Canada Census, British Columbia, New Westminster, 1891 Canada Census, British Columbia, Vancouver

Kanakahou (fl. 1844)

Servant, associated with:

Oregon (1844) laborer

On March 28, 1844, in Honolulu, two "native Hawaiians" named Kanakahou and **Kiaimoku** agreed to accompany British subject William T. Bailey to Oregon for two years as servants in exchange for passage both ways, food, lodging, and $100 per year each. Kanakahou signed the agreement with his mark. It is not known what happened subsequently.

PS: HSA 402-10-248

Kanakaole (fl. 1858)

Occupation unknown, associated with:

British Columbia (1858)

Kanakaole was one of six Hawaiians to whom the governor of Oʻahu gave permission in May 1858 to proceed to the British Columbia gold rush. He, and likely also his wife, left Honolulu for Vancouver Island on the schooner *Alice* on June 22, 1858. Kanakaole has not been traced further.

PS: HSA Passenger, Victoria

Kanaki, John (fl. 1870)

Laborer, b. ca. 1805, associated with:

Oregon City (1870) huckster

At the time of the 1870 Census, John Kanaki was working as a huckster in Oregon City. He was illiterate.

PS: 1870 U.S. Census, Oregon, Oregon City

Kanalow [variation: Kanailow] (1854)

PSAC employee, d. July 13, 1854, off Gonzales Point, Victoria, associated with:

Belle Vue sheep farm (1854) personal servant

It is not known when Kanalow came to Vancouver Island from Hawai'i, but by 1854 he was working as a personal servant at the sheep farm on San Juan Island. That same year, on a return trip from Victoria, he and several others drowned when their canoe upset in stormy seas. In total, seventeen people, mostly unnamed Natives, drowned.

PS: HBCA BelleVueAB

Kanē [1] (fl. 1844–1846)

HBC employee, associated with:

Fort Vancouver (1844–1846) laborer

Kanē, from Oʻahu, joined the HBC in 1844 on a three-year contract and worked at Fort Vancouver as a laborer. As his contract ended in 1846, he worked until August 6 of that year, at which point he returned to Oʻahu.

PS: HBCA YFSA 24–26, YFDS 17

Kane [2] (fl. 1844–1845)

Servant, associated with:

Oregon (1844–1845) laborer

On March 28, 1844, in Honolulu, "a native Hawaiian" named Kane agreed to accompany American Methodist missionary Gustavus Hines to Oregon for two years as a servant in exchange for his passage, food, lodging, $72 per year, and passage home. Kane signed the agreement with a sure hand, indicating he was literate. As the pair were about to return to Hawai'i in October 1845, Kane deserted. He has not been traced further.

PS: HSA 402-10-248

Kānē, Alexander [variations: Korney, Kearney] (fl. 1860–1891)

Farmer, b. ca. 1845, associated with:

Belle Vue sheep farm (1860–1873) farmer
Coal Island (1873–1891) farmer

It is unclear how Alexander Kānē, so named on his baptism into Catholicism in Victoria on December 20, 1870, got to the Northwest Coast, but he was working on San Juan Island in 1860. The same day he was baptized, Kānē married his countryman **Kama Kamai**'s daughter Mary (ca. 1859–?). The witnesses were Kamai, married the same day to another Songhees woman, and **Joe Friday**. After San Juan Island was awarded to the United States, Kānē followed his father-in-law north to Coal Island.

The recorded children of Alexander Kānē and Mary Kamai were Mary (ca. 1871–

1888), Nellie (ca. 1872?), Margaret (ca. 1873–?), Amanda (ca. 1875–?), David (1879–1883), Josephine (1881–1882) , Philip (ca. 1884–?), Alexander (1885–?), and David (ca. 1886–?).

PS: BCA VS-StAndC, StElizC

Kane, William [variation: **William Carney**] (fl. 1880–1901)

Laborer, b. 1835, associated with:

Moodyville (1881) sawmill worker
Vancouver (1901) patient

Described as born in the Sandwich Islands and coming to Canada in 1880, William Kane was in 1901 widowed and a hospital patient in Vancouver. He is likely the same person as William Carney, who in 1881 was a widowed mill hand at nearby Moodyville.

PS: 1901 Canada Census, British Columbia, Vancouver

Kanelupu (fl. 1840–1849)

HBC employee, associated with:

Fort Vancouver (1840–1843) middleman
barque *Columbia* (1843–1844) seaman
Fort Vancouver (1844–1845) laborer
barque *Vancouver* (1845–1846) seaman
Fort Vancouver (1846–1847) laborer, (1847–1848) steward
Willamette Falls (1848–1849) laborer

Kanelupu joined the HBC in 1840, beginning his work at Fort Vancouver on July 14 of that year. On September 30, 1849, after working nine years at coastal posts and in shipping, he deserted, presumably for the gold fields of California, and has not subsequently been traced.

PS: HBCA YFSA 20, 24–29, YFDS 11–12, 18, 20, FtVanSA 6–8, Logs of *Columbia* 6, *Vancouver* 7

Kaneoukai (fl. 1840–1848)

HBC/PSAC employee, d. ca. January 2, 1848, likely at Fort Vancouver, associated with:

Fort Vancouver (1840–1842) middleman
Fort Nisqually (1842–1843) middleman
steamer *Beaver* (1843–1844) laborer
Columbia Department general charges and steamer *Beaver* (1844–1845) laborer and woodcutter
Fort Vancouver (1845–1848) laborer

Kaneoukai joined the HBC from Oʻahu in 1840 and began on July 1 of that year, receiving his wages from July 14. For the next seven and a half years, he worked in various locations in the Columbia as a middleman, seaman, and woodcutter. He died on or about January 2, 1848, most certainly from the measles.

PS: HBCA YFSA 20, 24–27, FtVanSA 6–8, YFDS 11, 15, BCA PR-Lowe

Kanikoa (fl. 1864)

Laborer, associated with:

Port Gamble (1863–1864) sawmill worker

Kanikoa was one of six men contracted in Honolulu on December 4, 1863, by the agent of Puget Mill Co. to work at its sawmill for $10 per month with a $20 advance. Three days later he left for Teekalet on the barque *Constitution*. It is unclear how long he worked there.

PS: HSA Seamen, Passenger

Kanno, William (fl. 1835)

CRFTC employee, d. ca. 1835 at the Cascades [Washington], associated with:

ship *May Dacre* (1835) passenger
Fort Hall (1835) laborer

William Kanno was among thirty Hawaiians, six with wives in tow, who joined Nathaniel J. Wyeth's CRFTC in early 1835. He died at the Cascades, likely in 1835.

PS: OHS FtHallAB, CRFTCCB

Kano (fl. 1864–1865)

Laborer, associated with:

Alberni (1864–1865) sawmill worker

Kano and four others were contracted in Honolulu on August 24, 1864, by the agent of Alberni Mill Co. to work for $10 per month with a $20 advance. They departed Honolulu on September 1 on the *Alberni* and four of them, including Kano, arrived back in Honolulu on February 7, 1865, on the *Egoria*.

PS: HSA Seamen, Passenger

Kanoho [variations: **Kanoha, Joseph Kanako**] (fl. 1845–1852)

HBC employee, b. ca. 1825, associated with:

Fort Vancouver (1845–1852) laborer

Kanoho joined the HBC from Oʻahu on May 7, 1845, for three years. He worked at Fort Vancouver as a laborer until he deserted on January 11, 1852. This is probably the same person as the Joseph Kanako in the 1850 U.S. Census.

PS: HBCA SandIsAB 3, YFSA 25–31, FtVanSA 3, 1850 U.S. Census, Oregon, Clark Co.

Kanomē [variations: **Kenome, Kanomi**] (fl. 1847–1852)

HBC employee, associated with:

Columbia Department (1847–1848) middleman
Fort Victoria (1848–1849) laborer
Fort Rupert (1849–1850) laborer
Fort Victoria (1850–1852) laborer

Kanomē joined the HBC in 1847 as a middleman the same time as his friend, **Kealoha**. They appear to have worked together as laborers at Forts Victoria and Rupert until Kealoha died in 1849 and Kanomē inherited all his possessions. He wanted to return to Oʻahu in 1850 but, as an HBC vessel was not readily available, he continued working until around 1852 and may then have returned to Oʻahu.

PS: HBCA YFSA 27–32, FtVicSA 1–2, BCA PR-Helmcken; *PPS:* Helmcken, *Reminiscences,* 108

Kanooe (fl. 1841–1844)

HBC employee, associated with:

Fort Vancouver (1841–1842) middleman
steamer *Beaver* (1842–1843) woodcutter

Fort Vancouver general charges (1843–1844) middleman
Fort Vancouver (1844) laborer

Kanooe joined the HBC from Oʻahu in 1841 and began receiving wages on July 9 of that year. He worked largely at Fort Vancouver until November 12, 1844, at which point he returned to Oʻahu. He received his final wages in Honolulu on December 31.

PS: HBCA FtVanSA 6–8, YFDS 17, YFSA 24, SandIsAB 3

Kanu, William (fl. 1870)

Laborer, b. ca. 1836, associated with:

Port Gamble (1870) sawmill worker

At the time of the 1870 Census, William Kanu was one of twenty-two Hawaiians working at Puget Mill at Port Gamble.

PS: 1870 U.S. Census, Washington Territory, Kitsap Co., Port Gamble

Kanwhil, George (fl. 1870)

Laborer, b. ca. 1843, associated with:

Port Gamble (1870) sawmill worker

At the time of the 1870 Census, George Kanwhil was one of twenty-two Hawaiians working at Puget Mill at Port Gamble. It's possible he was the same person as **Kamu** and/or **Kamuela.**

PS: 1870 U.S. Census, Washington Territory, Kitsap Co., Port Gamble

Kaohimanunu (fl. 1861)

Occupation unknown, associated with:

Victoria (1861)

Kaohimanunu and two other Hawaiians departed Victoria for Honolulu on the *Constitution,* arriving October 3, 1861. It is not known how he got to the Pacific Northwest.

PS: HSA Passenger

Kaoulipe, Kio (fl. 1855–1860)

Occupation unknown, associated with:

Oregon Territory (1855–1860)

Nothing is known about Kio Kaoulipe, whose children by an unnamed Native woman, Pierre (1856–?) and Marie (1859–?), were baptized by an itinerant Catholic priest in 1860.

PPS: Munnick, *Oregon City*

Kapahi (fl. 1864–1865)

Laborer, associated with:

Alberni (1864–1865) sawmill worker

Kapahi and four others were contracted in Honolulu on August 24, 1864, by the agent of Alberni Mill Co. to work for $10 per month with a $20 advance. They departed Honolulu on September 1 on the *Alberni* and four of them, including Kapahi, arrived back in Honolulu on February 7, 1865, on the *Egoria.*

PS: HSA Seamen, Passenger

Kapahu [1] (fl. 1844–1849)

HBC employee, associated with:

Fort Vancouver (1844–1849) laborer

Kapahu, from Oʻahu, joined the HBC in 1844. He worked as a laborer at Fort Vancouver until he deserted, possibly at the beginning of outfit 1849–1850, for he received no wages for that outfit. He likely headed to California.

PS: HBCA YFSA 24–29

Kapahu [2] (fl. 1860)

Seaman, associated with:

schooner *Emma Rooke* (1860) seaman

Kapahu, who may have been the same man as Kapahu [1], was among five Hawaiians contracted by the schooner *Emma Rooke* when it sailed from Honolulu to Victoria on August 29, 1860. The men received $15 per month with a $15 advance. He deserted, probably at Victoria.

PS: HSA Seamen

Kapapa (fl. 1861)

Occupation unknown, associated with:

Victoria (1861)

Kapapa and two other Hawaiians departed Victoria for Honolulu on the *Constitution,* arriving October 3, 1861. No information exists on how he got to the Pacific Northwest.

PS: HSA Passenger

Kapaukau [variation: **Tidahore Parkaer**] (fl. 1879)

Occupation unknown, associated with:

Portland (1879)

On being arrested in July 1879 for horse stealing in the Oregon countryside, "a Kanaka who claims to be a half brother of His Majesty" requested assistance from the Hawaiian consul in Portland to return home. Kapaukau, who styled himself Tidahore Parkaer, sent a very eloquent letter protesting his innocence, to which the Hawaiian minister of foreign affairs responded he should be given passage if a pardon could be secured, but without any reference to a possible connection to the Hawaiian royal family. The outcome is unclear.

PS: HSA Victoria

Kapawa (fl. 1844–1849)

HBC employee, associated with:

Willamette sawmill (1844–1846) laborer
Fort Vancouver (1846–1849) laborer

Kapawa joined the HBC from Oʻahu in 1844 and began work at the Willamette sawmill on July 12, 1844. He deserted on October 10, 1849, and likely headed for the gold fields of California.

PS: HBCA YFSA 24–29, YFDS 15

Kapia (fl. 1847)

Servant, b. ca. 1822, associated with:

Columbia area (1847)

A Hawaiian named as Kapia left Portland on the barque *Toulon* for Honolulu, arriving December 16, 1847. The barque tended to have one or more Hawaiian servants on its trips between the Pacific Northwest and Honolulu.

PS: HSA Passenger

Kapoi [variation: **Kupa**] (fl. 1858–1863)

Occupation unknown, associated with:

Vancouver Island (1858–1863)

Kupa was one of fourteen Hawaiians departing Honolulu for Victoria on the schooner *Alice* on June 22, 1858, enticed by the euphoria of the gold rush. As did several of the others, he settled in Victoria. When his ship companion **Kahaleiwi** died in late 1862, it was Kapoi and **Nahiana** who administered the estate. Kapoi's signature suggests he was just literate, if that.

PS: HSA Passenger, Victoria

Kapoua [variation: **Kapooa**] (fl. 1844–1846)

HBC employee, associated with:

Fort Vancouver (1844–1846) laborer
steamer *Beaver* (1846) woodcutter

Kapoua, from Oʻahu, appeared in the Columbia in outfit 1844–1845 with a contract that ended in 1846. He worked as a laborer at Fort Vancouver and a woodcutter on the steamer *Beaver* until December 10, 1846, at which point he returned to Oʻahu.

PS: HBCA YFSA 24–26, YFDS 17

Kapoula (fl. 1858)

Occupation unknown, associated with:

Vancouver Island (1858)

Kapoula was one of fourteen Hawaiians departing Honolulu for Victoria on the schooner *Alice* on June 22, 1858, enticed by the euphoria of the gold rush. It's possible he was the same person as **Kapoua**, who worked for the HBC a dozen years earlier.

PS: HSA Passenger

Karae (fl. 1840–1845)

HBC employee, associated with:

Fort Vancouver (1840–1843) middleman
steamer *Beaver* (1843–1845) laborer, (1845) stoker

Karae joined the HBC from Oʻahu in 1840. He worked as a middleman at Fort Vancouver and also as a laborer and stoker on the *Beaver*. As his contract ended in 1845, he worked until December 31 of that year, at which point he returned to Oʻahu.

PS: HBCA YFSA 20, 24–25, FtVanSA 6–8, YFDS 16

Karakeha [variation: **Mitery Karakeha**] (fl. 1804–1806)

Maritime fur trade cabin boy, associated with:

ship *Pearl* (1804–1806) cabin boy

Karakeha, who may have had a first name of Mitery, made his way to Boston before he joined the voyage on the ship *Pearl* to the Northwest Coast. The maritime fur trading vessel sailed from Boston harbor on September 2, 1804. After rounding the Horn and laying over in Hawaiʻi from February 26 to March 27, 1805, the *Pearl* reached Newittee on

April 5. From that date, until the following year on August 6, 1806, the *Pearl* traded on the coast between Newittee and Kaiganee. It then departed for the Sandwich Islands. After a layover in Canton between November 1806 and January 1807, the *Pearl* sailed for Boston, arriving May 10, 1807. It is uncertain whether Karakeha sailed the complete voyage back to Boston.

PS: MHS *Pearl*

Karehoua [variation: **Karehina**] (fl. 1840–1852)

HBC employee, associated with:

Taku/Durham (1840–1843) middleman
Fort Stikine (1843–1844) middleman, (1844–1849) laborer
Fort Rupert (1849–1850) laborer
Fort Simpson (1850–1852) laborer

Karehoua signed on with the HBC in Oʻahu in 1840 and worked for the next dozen years at various northern posts. His contract ended in 1850, when he first expressed an interest in returning to Hawaiʻi, but he continued at Fort Simpson until October 1, 1852, when he retired. It is not known whether he returned to Oʻahu.

Karehoua had a family, the names of which are untraced. In September 1849, while he was employed at Fort Rupert, his wife gave birth to a baby girl.

PS: HBCA YFSA 20, 24–32, FtVanSA 6–8, FtVicSA 1–3, DS 1, FtRupPJ, FtSimp[N]PJ 7, BCA PR-Helmcken

Karimou, William [variation: **Kariume**] (fl. 1811–1814)

PFC/NWC employee, associated with:

ship *Tonquin* (1811) passenger
Fort Astoria (1811–1814) laborer
overland brigade (1814) middleman or laborer

William Karimou joined the crew of the *Tonquin* as a laborer around February 21, 1811, when the vessel operated by the PFC stopped at Oʻahu and took on a complement of twenty Sandwich Islanders. One month later, on March 22, the *Tonquin* arrived at the mouth of the Columbia, and on April 12 William Karimou was noted as helping to unload the vessel. The Sandwich Islander stayed on shore, helped to construct the fort and, on October 12 of that year, sailed up the Columbia River on the maiden voyage of the newly constructed vessel *Dolly*. He did a variety of tasks including, for example, smoking deer skins there on May 21, 1813. He was last traced going overland in a brigade of canoes and likely made it as far as Fort William on the Great Lakes.

PS: RosL *Astoria; PPS:* Henry, *Journal,* 711

Karooha (fl. 1840–1854)

HBC employee, associated with:

Fort Vancouver (1840–1842) middleman
Fort Stikine (1842–1843) middleman, (1843–1849) laborer
Fort Rupert (1849–1850) laborer
Fort Simpson (1850) laborer

Karooha, who entered the service of the HBC in 1840, worked at various places along the Northwest Coast before retiring to Oʻahu in outfit 1844–1845. He reenlisted again, and his contract ended in 1850, when he expressed a desire to return to Hawaiʻi. As there was movement on his account until 1854, he may have stayed in the area for at least that period.

PS: HBCA YFSA 20, 24–30, 32, YFDS 11, FtVanSA 6–8, FtVicSA 1, BCA PR-Helmcken

Karreymoure [variation: **Karreymourie**] (fl. 1844–1850)
HBC employee, d. ca. 1850, associated with:
  Fort Vancouver (1844–1850) laborer
Karreymoure joined the HBC in Oʻahu in 1844 and worked as a laborer at Fort Vancouver. His contract was to have ended in 1850, but on September 20, 1849, he deserted, presumably for the gold fields of California. He returned and, in outfit 1850–1851, he worked for four months before dying.
PS: HBCA YFSA 24–28, 30–31, YFDS 20–21

Kasalies, Louis (fl. 1867)
Laborer, associated with:
  Port Gamble (1867) sawmill worker
On May 29, 1867, Louis Kasalies left Honolulu to Teekalet on the barque *Kutusoff.* It is unclear how long he worked at the sawmill there or whether he was an indigenous Hawaiian.
PS: HSA Passenger

Katkamn (fl. 1858)
PSAC employee, associated with:
  Fort Nisqually outstation (1858) shepherd
Little is known of Katkamn, who was in December 1858 herding sheep at Muck farm.
PS: FtNis Muck

Kau, John [variations: **Kaau, Ka-au, Kaoo**] (fl. 1834–1870s)
HBC employee, b. ca. 1800, associated with:
  Fort McLoughlin (1834–1836) middleman or laborer, (1836–1843) middleman
  Fort Victoria (1843–1844) middleman, (1844–1849) laborer
  brigantine *Mary Dare* (1850) passenger
  Fort Victoria (1850–1854) laborer
  Port Gamble (1855?–1875) occupation unknown
John Kau joined the HBC from Oʻahu in 1834 and spent the next twenty years at Forts McLoughlin and Victoria. In 1849, he took a trip to Honolulu and returned the following year for two more years. After his retirement, he had transactions with the HBC for two years before moving to Port Gamble on Puget Sound in Washington Territory. A Hawaiian described in a letter a luau he attended at the Kau residence in 1865 in honor of Kau's son Philip.
  John Kau was a versatile, well-traveled man. On September 2, 1869, by this time appearing to be very old, being described on the passenger list as age 111, he left Honolulu for Teekalet on the barque *Camden.* He may be the same man, given as John, who on January 21, 1875, arrived in Honolulu from Port Gamble on the barque *Powhattan.*
  John Kau and **Mary Pau** (?–?) had a son Pilipo (ca. 1859–?). On August 26, 1869, perhaps to attend school, Philip Kau arrived in Honolulu on the *Camden,* which then took his father back to the Pacific Northwest.
PS: HBCA FtSimp[N]PJ 3, YFSA 14–15, 19–20, 24–32, YFDS 5c–7, FtVanSA 3–8, SandIsAB 10, FtVicSA 1–2, 1850 U.S. Census, Oregon, Clark Co., HSA Passenger; *SS:* Naukana, "News"

Kaua'i (fl. 1847–1848)

HBC employee, b. likely on Kaua'i, d. July 21, 1848, at Fort Victoria, associated with:

Columbia Department (1847–1848) laborer
Fort Langley (1848) laborer

Kaua'i joined the HBC in 1847 but had a short career with the company, as he died at Fort Victoria on July 21, 1848, of unspecified causes.

PS: HBCA YFSA 27–28, FtVicSA 1–2, YFDS 19

Kaueviela (fl. 1864)

Laborer, associated with:

Port Gamble (1863–1864) sawmill worker

Kaueviela was one of six men contracted in Honolulu on December 4, 1863, by the agent of Puget Mill Co. to work at its sawmill for $10 per month with a $20 advance. Three days later he left for Teekalet on the barque *Constitution.* It is unclear how long he worked there.

PS: HSA Seamen, Passenger

Kaukale (fl. 1864)

Laborer, associated with:

Port Gamble (1863–1864) sawmill worker

Kaukale was one of six men contracted in Honolulu on December 4, 1863, by the agent of Puget Mill Co. to work at its sawmill for $10 per month with a $20 advance. The next day he left for Teekalet on the barque *N.S. Perkins.* It is unclear how long he worked there.

PS: HSA Seamen, Passenger

Kaukuhai (fl. 1862)

Laborer, associated with:

Vancouver Island (1862)

Kaukuhai was one of eight laborers who left Honolulu for Victoria on the *Constitution* on May 2, 1862. It is unclear where they were headed.

PS: HSA Passenger

Kaula (fl. 1860–1861)

Seaman or laborer, associated with:

Victoria (1860–1861)

Kaula was one of four Hawaiians on the *Consort,* which was wrecked off northern Vancouver Island in late November 1860 en route from Honolulu to Puget Sound. The men, who got away in an Indian canoe, finally reached Victoria in mid-January, destitute, to be rescued by the Hawaiian consul. Two were seamen and the other two were contracted by a Puget Sound sawmill. The men's subsequent activity is not known.

PS: HSA Victoria

Kaulehelehe, William R. [variation: **Kanaka William**] (fl. 1845–1874)

Teacher, missionary, and HBC employee, b. ca. 1809 in Hawai'i, d. June 22, 1874, in Victoria, associated with:

Fort Vancouver general charges (1845–1847) teacher
Columbia Department (1847–1848) teacher, general charges (1848–1850) teacher
Fort Vancouver (1853–1860) teacher
Western Department (1860–1861) laborer
Fort Victoria (1862–1869) assistant

William R. Kaulehelehe joined the HBC in 1845 on a three-year contract as a teacher, unusual for Hawaiians, who were generally hired for labor only. On the request of the head of Fort Vancouver, Dr. John McLoughlin, Hawaiian American mission physician Dr. G. P. Judd hired Kaulehelehe, then in his mid-thirties, out of the Kawaiahao Church to act as chaplain to his fellow Hawaiians in the Columbia. Arriving at Fort Vancouver with his wife, **Mary S. Kaai**, or Kaiapoop, on June 23, 1845, the couple set up residence in the Kanaka Village. Their presence was somewhat resented, as it was felt that it would tone down the freedoms of the other residents and make them, for example, "observe the Sabbath, because on that day they did their carpentering, horse riding, agriculturing, and the like." To alleviate the tense situation, Kaulehelehe was moved into a house inside the fort, but this move did not help him influence the whites, who reportedly abused the Hawaiians without cause. He was, on the other hand, somewhat successful in getting them to observe the Sabbath although less so in curbing drinking among his fellow Hawaiians, who purchased alcohol from Americans just below the fort. His small congregation was made even smaller in 1849 with the large number of defections to the California gold fields.

Things did not go well for Kaulehelehe. Before 1850, he was moved back to the village outside the fort. The "Owhyhee Church" within the palisade walls was torn down sometime between 1855 and 1858 and was not replaced. As the HBC traditional area was gradually preempted by the U.S. Army following the 1846 boundary settlement, the humble and undoubtedly deteriorated dwelling of Kaulehelehe thrust the Hawaiian chaplain into the international spotlight. Balking at the evacuation orders of the U.S. Army, Kaulehelehe was told by HBC officer John Work to hold his ground. This was to little avail, for, as Yvonne Klan writes in *The Beaver:*

> But William [Kaulehelehe] and Work held fast. On 12 March 1860, William watched the army remove the fences from around the Company's fields. On the 16th he saw the soldiers burn down a vacated house which had been used [to] store hay. On the 19th the soldiers destroyed the Company's old hospital and another house, and then they turned their attention to William's dwelling. When they removed the doors and the windows William finally left. The next day, March 20, the Hawaiian watched helplessly while soldiers set fire to the remains of his old home. (43)

The incident provoked British protests to the U.S. president, who issued an order to cease interference with the employees of the HBC. Kaulehelehe moved to Fort Victoria, where he was naturalized as a British subject on August 12, 1862. He signed with a sure hand. He lived in a house on Humboldt Street, known as Kanaka Row, and worked as a clerk in the HBC store and as an interpreter until about 1868–1869. He died on June 22, 1874, and was buried at the Ross Bay Cemetery.

William Kaulehelehe was married to Mary S. Kaai or Kaiapoop (ca. 1822–1865) and had an adopted daughter Mary Opio (ca. 1849–1864).

PS: HBCA YFSA 25–32, FtVanSA 9–15, FtVicSA 10–16, BCA GR-Naturalization, VS-BCVS, RossBayCem, 1860 U.S. Census, Washington Territory, Clark Co.; *SS:* Klan, "Kanaka William"

Kaulehua (fl. 1864)

Laborer, associated with:

Port Gamble (1864) sawmill worker

Kaulehua and five others were contracted in Honolulu on February 5, 1864, by the agent of Puget Mill Co. to work at its sawmill for $10 per month with a $20 advance. It is uncertain how long he did so.

PS: HSA Seamen

Kaumaia [variation: **Kaumoea**] (fl. 1845–1848)

HBC employee, associated with:

Willamette (1845–1846) laborer
Fort Vancouver (1846–1848) laborer

Kaumaia joined the HBC from Oʻahu on May 7, 1845, for three years and worked in the Columbia District. He returned to Oʻahu in July 1848, where he was paid off.

PS: HBCA YFSA 25–30, SandIsAB 3, 6

Kaumualiʻi, George Prince [variations: **Humehume, Taumuarii, Tamoree**] (fl. 1804)

Child, b. 1798 on Kauaʻi to Kaumualiʻi (1780–1824), king of Kauaʻi and Niʻihau, d. May 3, 1826, in Honolulu, associated with:

Hazard (1804) visitor

George Prince Kaumualiʻi, whose birth name was Humehume, was sent by his father King Kaumualiʻi from Kauaʻi to America in 1804 to get a formal education. The trading vessel carrying him there sailed first to the Northwest Coast and then back to China before arriving in the eastern United States eighteen months later. His claim to fame rests on his enlisting in the U.S. Marines in 1815, the next year being taken under the wing of the American Board of Commissioners of Foreign Missions, and returning to the Islands with the first group of missionaries in 1820. He attempted unsuccessfully to free his home island of Kauaʻi from outside rule prior to his death from influenza in 1826.

George Prince Kaumualiʻi married Betty Davis (1803–?), the half Hawaiian daughter of an English advisor to the first Kamehameha, and then to Kaʻahumanu (?–?).

SS: Warne, "George Prince Kaumualiʻi," 59–71

Kauna [variations: **Karua, Karuna, Karoua**] (fl. 1858–1859)

PSAC employee, associated with:

Belle Vue sheep farm (1858–1859) shepherd

It is not known how or when Kauna came to the Pacific Northwest, but he worked as a shepherd on San Juan Island at least from May 1858 to July 1859.

PS: HBCA FtVicSA 7, 8, BelleVuePJ 2

Kaura (fl. 1843–1844)

Occupation unknown, associated with:

Fort Vancouver area (1843–1844)

It is not known how Kaura came to Vancouver but, by 1844, he was probably living in the village with his wife, a Cowlitz Native woman, with whom he had Marie (1844–?).

PPS: Munnick, *Vancouver,* vol. 2

Kawahiniai (fl. 1850)

HBC seaman, associated with:

barque *Cowlitz* (1850) seaman

Kawahiniai served on the HBC vessel *Cowlitz* from February 3 to September 17, 1850, traveling from Oʻahu to the Northwest Coast and back again. On August 27 at Honolulu, he and the other Hawaiian crewmen refused to work, claiming their contract was up but nonetheless returned to work for another month while the vessel was at anchor. After that he has not been traced.

PS: HBCA SandIsAB 10–11, Log of *Cowlitz* 8

Kawelai, J. (fl. 1880)

Laborer, b. ca. 1863, associated with:

Port Gamble (1880) laborer

At the time of the 1880 Census, Kawelai was one of nine "Kanakas" working in Port Gamble, almost certainly at the sawmill. He was described as able to read but not write.

PS: 1880 U.S. Census, Washington Territory, Kitsap Co., Port Gamble

Kawero [variations: **Tom Kawero, John Keuvero**] (fl. 1834)

HBC employee, associated with:

brig *Eagle* (1834) passenger
Fort Vancouver (1834) laborer
brig *Eagle* (1834) passenger

Kawero worked for the HBC in 1834. He almost did not leave the Islands, for the man to whom he gave his advance of $14 received from the HBC, likely to be permitted to depart, changed his mind and attempted to detain him. It took King Kamehameha's intervention to resolve the matter. Kawero put in a brief appearance in the Columbia, returning to Oʻahu aboard the brig *Eagle* on December 1, 1834.

PS: HBCA YFSA 14, YFDS 5c, SMP 14, Disbursements of brig *Eagle,* August 30, 1834, B.191/2/1, HAS 402-3-47

Kayriow [variations: **Kayriou, Kay-riow**] (fl. 1837–1840)

HBC employee, associated with:

Fort Vancouver (1837–1838) middleman
Fort Simpson (1838–1840) middleman

Kayriow signed on with the HBC in July 1837 in Oʻahu and began work at Fort Vancouver on August 10 of that year. He was later transferred to Fort Simpson, where he appeared to act as a gatekeeper. He was discharged on November 15, 1840, at which time he returned to Oʻahu.

PS: HBCA SandIsAB 1, FtVAnASA 4–6, YFDS 8, 11, YFSA 19–20, FtSimp[N] 4

Keahanelē (fl. 1847–1854)

HBC employee, associated with:

Columbia Department (1847–1848) laborer
New Caledonia (1848–1849) laborer
Fort Langley (1849–1854) laborer

Keahanelē joined the HBC in 1847 on a three-year contract that ended in 1850. He began work as a laborer on August 12, 1847, and appears to have worked until 1854, when he likely returned to the Sandwich Islands.

PS: HBCA YFSA 27–32, FtVicSA 1–3

Keahi [1] (fl. 1840–1846)

HBC employee, associated with:

Fort Vancouver (1840–1842) middleman, (1842–1846) laborer

Keahi appears to have spent his career with the HBC around Fort Vancouver. He joined the company in 1840 from Oʻahu. As his contract ended in 1846 he worked until August 6 of that year, at which point he returned to Oʻahu.

PS: HBCA YFSA 20, 24–26, FtVanSA 6–8, YFDS 17

Keahi [2] (fl. 1864)

Laborer, b. ca. 1849, associated with:

Alberni (1864) sawmill worker

Keahi was one of four men contracted in Honolulu on June 23, 1864, by the agent of Alberni Mill Co. to work for $10 per month with a $20 advance. Two days later he and the others left Honolulu for Alberni on the schooner *Alberni.*

PS: HSA Seamen, Passenger

Keahimaunui (fl. 1862)

Laborer, associated with:

Port Gamble (1862) sawmill worker

Keahimaunui and six others were contracted in Honolulu on February 14, 1862, by the agent of Puget Mill Co. to work at its sawmill for $10 per month with a $20 advance. It is uncertain how long he did so.

PS: HSA Seamen

Keaiia (fl. 1861)

Laborer, associated with:

Port Gamble (1861) sawmill worker

Keiia and five others were contracted in Honolulu on October 5, 1861, by the agent of Puget Mill Co. to work at its sawmill for $15 per month with a $15 advance. It is uncertain how long he did so.

PS: HSA Seamen

Keaini, William (fl. 1870)

Farmer, b. ca. 1849, associated with:

San Juan Island (1870)

William Keaini was one of the many farming Hawaiians living on San Juan Island while it was in dispute. In 1870, the twenty-one-year-old Keanini owned land worth $600 and lived there with his Native wife, Mary (ca. 1853–?), who was born in Washington Territory.

PS: 1870 U.S. Census, Washington Territory, San Juan Island

Keala [1] [variation: **Kehele**] (fl. 1845–1849)

HBC employee, associated with:

Willamette (1845–1846) laborer
Fort Vancouver (1846–1849) laborer

Keala joined the HBC in Oʻahu on May 7, 1845, and worked as a laborer. He deserted in 1849, probably before the beginning of outfit 1849–1850. Like others, he appears to have been smitten with gold fever.

PS: HBCA SandIsAB 3, YFSA 24–29

Keala [2] [variation: **J. Keala**] (fl. 1861–1865)

Laborer, b. ca. 1840, associated with:

Victoria area (1861, 1863–1865)

Keala departed Honolulu for Victoria on the *Constitution* on May 14, 1861. He must have returned home but soon grown restless, for a man with the same name left Honolulu for Victoria on the same vessel on March 5, 1863. A Hawaiian laborer named as J. Keala left Victoria for Honolulu on the *Domitila,* arriving April 17, 1865.

PS: HSA Passenger

Kealene (fl. 1861)

Laborer, associated with:

Port Gamble (1861) sawmill worker

Kealene was one of six men contracted in Honolulu on October 5, 1861, by the agent of Puget Mill Co. to work at its sawmill for $15 per month with a $15 advance. It is uncertain how long he did so.

PS: HSA Seamen

Kealoha [1] (fl. 1847–1849)

HBC employee, d. December 10, 1849, associated with:

Columbia Department (1847–1848) laborer
Fort Victoria (1848–1849) laborer
Fort Rupert (1849) laborer

Although Kealoha joined the HBC in 1847 from Oʻahu on a three-year contract that ended in 1850, he may have worked at the Honolulu compound as early as 1846. He was in on the construction of Fort Rupert in 1849 and by December of that year had become very ill with a complaint of the bowels. He died of pneumonia and, on the same December day, was buried at the Fort Rupert graveyard, where prayers were read in Hawaiian by one of his friends. Kealoha gave all his personal possessions to his friend, **Kanome,** and any money owing was to go to a sister in Oʻahu.

PS: HBCA SandIsAB 6, YFSA 27–32, FtVicSA 1–2, FtRupPJ; *PPS:* Helmcken, *Reminiscences,* 108

Kealoha [2] (fl. 1860, 1864)

Laborer, associated with:

Port Gamble (1860, 1864) sawmill worker

On May 29, 1860, Kealoha arrived back in Honolulu from Teekalet on the barque *Jenny Ford.* The same man, or possibly another man by the same name, was among six men contracted in Honolulu on February 6, 1864, by the Puget Mill Co. to work at its sawmill for $10 per month with a $20 advance. It is uncertain how long he did so.

PS: HSA Passenger, Seamen

Keamo (fl. 1863)

Laborer, b. ca. 1849, associated with:

Port Gamble (1863) sawmill worker

Keamo and four others were contracted in Honolulu on March 18, 1863, by the agent of Puget Mill Co. to work at its sawmill for $10 per month with a $20 advance.

PS: HSA Seamen, 1870 U.S. Census, Washington Territory, Kitsap Co., Port Gamble

Keamo, James [variations: **Keamo Keana, James Campbell**] (fl. 1870s–1905)

Laborer and fisherman, b. 1840 in Honolulu to Keamo Noa and Nono, d. 1905 in New Westminster, associated with:

Burrard Inlet (1870s–1890s) sawmill worker and fisherman

According to oral tradition Keamo was "a full blood Hawaiian from Honolulu" who came "on a sailing ship, just came for the trip, and stayed here." He was employed at a Burrard Inlet sawmill at the time of his marriage in 1876.

Keamo gave his name as Keamo Keana at his marriage to Annie Nelson (ca. 1861–ca. 1911) on July 11, 1876. Annie's father was a Fraser Valley farmer from the Maritimes, her mother Sophie the daughter of Hawaiian **Peeopeeoh** and a Native woman. James and Annie Keamo's children were James Grant (1877–1947), Laura (1879–1917), Philip (ca. 1880–1917), Emma (ca. 1882–?), Josephine (1886–?), Walter (1889–1964), Harold (1893–1919), Alfred (1895–?), and Edith (1903–?). For convenience in securing employment, Keamo and some of his sons sometimes used Campbell as their surname.

PS: BCA VS-BCVS, VanA Keamo

Keanahapa (fl. 1860)

Laborer, associated with:

Port Gamble (1860) sawmill worker

Keanahapa was among four men contracted in Honolulu on November 1, 1860, by the agent of Puget Mill Co. to work at its sawmill for $15 per month with a $15 advance. It is uncertain how long he did so.

PS: HSA Seamen

Keapu (fl. 1860)

Laborer, associated with:

Port Madison, Washington (1860) sawmill worker

Keapu was one of four men contracted in Honolulu on October 5, 1860, by the Madison Mill Co. to work at its sawmill for $15 per month with a $20 advance. Their term of service of a year began only on arriving in Puget Sound. The records of Keapu and another man had an X after them, but it is unclear what it meant.

PS: HSA Seamen

Keavē [1] [variations: **Kiawet, Louis Kiaret**] (fl. 1840–1863)

HBC employee, b. ca. 1824, associated with:

Fort Taku (1840–1842) middleman or laborer, (1842–1843) laborer

Fort Victoria (1843–1848) laborer, (1849–1852) laborer
Victoria area (1852–1863) occupation unknown

Keavē joined the service of the HBC in 1840 when he was about sixteen and worked first in the far north at Fort Taku and then at Fort Victoria. He returned twice to Oʻahu, once in the spring of 1845 and around mid-November 1848. His work appears to have ended around 1852, but he carried on transactions with the company until about 1855. He settled in the Victoria area with a family and owned a property on Kanaka Row/Humboldt Street valued in the early 1860s at $1,500. He lived next door to **Thomas Keavē**, indicating the two may have been related.

Keavē's family life is unclear. He may have been given the first name of Louis when he married Emelie (ca. 1827–?), a Clallam woman, on August 29, 1849, in a Catholic ceremony at Victoria. They had one son, Jean Baptiste (1849–1850). Keavē appears to have had another wife, Ursule (?–?), of unknown origin, and together they had one recorded child, Elizabeth (?–bap. 1863–?).

PS: HBCA YFSA 20, 24–28, 30–32, FtVanSA 6-8, YFDS 19, SandIsAB 3, 9, FtVicSA 1–2, BCA VS-StAndC; *SS: Government Gazette,* 1862, 1864

Keave [2] (fl. 1840–1845)

HBC employee, associated with:

Fort Umpqua (1840–1843) laborer
Fort George [Astoria] (1843–1844) laborer
Fort Vancouver (1844–1845) laborer

Keave joined the HBC from Oʻahu in 1840 and worked in the Columbia District. As his contract ended in 1845, he worked until December 10 of that year, at which point he returned to Oʻahu and was paid his final company wages.

PS: HBCA FtVanSA 7–8, YFSA 22, 24–25, YFDS 16, SandIsAB 5

Keave [3] (fl. 1862–1864)

Laborer, associated with:

Port Gamble (1862–1864) sawmill worker

Keave and six others were contracted in Honolulu on February 14, 1862, by the agent of Puget Mill Co. to work at its sawmill for $10 per month with a $20 advance. The same man, or possibly another man with the same name, was contracted on May 27, 1864, along with five others, at the same rate.

PS: HSA Seamen

Keavē, Thomas [variations: Kiawet, Kiavet] (fl. 1844–1860s)

HBC employee, associated with:

Snake party (1844–1845) laborer
Fort Vancouver (1845–1846) laborer
Snake party (1846–1848) laborer
New Caledonia (1848–1849) laborer
Fort Victoria (1850–1852) laborer
Victoria area (1852–1860s)

Tom Keavē, from Oʻahu, joined the HBC in 1844 on a three-year contract and spent his time between the Snake party and Fort Vancouver. In outfit 1848–1849, when he was based in New Caledonia, he deserted from the Columbia brigade at Fort Langley, possibly intending to head for the gold fields of California. However, he soon returned and appeared to work until 1852 at Fort Victoria, after which, for the next three years, he carried on transactions with the HBC. In 1857–1858 Keavē was a member of the Voltigeurs, a special militia set up in 1851 in the Victoria area. He remained in the Victoria area raising a family and owned a property on Kanaka Row/Humboldt Street valued in the early 1860s at $1,200. He lived next door to **Keavē** [1], indicating the two may have been related.

Tom Keavē's family records are not clear. His first recorded wife was Emelie (?–?), a Saanich woman, whom he married in a Catholic ceremony, likely at Victoria. Their children were Louis (?–bap. 1854–?) and Joseph (?–bap. 1858–?). Emelie must have died, and Tom Keavē's next wife, whom he also married in a Catholic ceremony, was Louise (?–?), a Cowichan woman, with whom he had Helene (1858–?). A third wife was Marie (?–?), another Native woman, with whom he had George (?–bap. 1860–?) and possibly Charles (?–bap. 1865–?).

PS: HBCA YFSA 24–28, 30–32, YFDS 19, FtVicSA 1–2, BCA VS-StAndC; *PPS: Government Gazette,* 1862, 1864; *SS:* Koppel, *Kanaka,* 70

Keave'haccow [variations: **Ke a r hociu, James Kaverharea, Keava, Keheva, Kehava, Keheava**] (fl. 1842–1869)

HBC/PSAC employee, b. ca. 1824 to Kuohi and unknown mother, associated with:

Fort Nisqually (1842–1843) laborer
Fort Vancouver (1844–1845) laborer
Snake party (1845–1846) goer and comer
Fort Nisqually (1846–1848) laborer
Fort Langley (1848–1849) laborer
Fort Nisqually (1849–1850) laborer
Fort Vancouver (1850–1851) laborer
Fort Nisqually (1851–1869) laborer

The life of 5 foot, 8 inch Keave'haccow, who joined the HBC from O'ahu and spent the majority of the next three decades in and around Fort Nisqually, can largely be framed by his appearances in the post journals.

Keave'haccow may have left home as a young man, but he did not separate his new life from his old. Shortly after arriving at Nisqually, Keave'haccow transferred two months' salary to his father Kuohi in Honolulu. He signed his own and his father's names in his own hand as Ke a r hociu and Kue oi, indicating a degree of literacy. With the passage of time, Keave'haccow accommodated to his new setting. In July 1849 he left Fort Nisqually for Fort Vancouver for two weeks to see his friends, but not before signing on for two more years starting from November 1, 1849. On March 17, 1850, he along with **Cowie** and **Kalama** announced they were "leaving the service." Keave'haccow likely headed to Fort Vancouver, where he may have entered the 1850 Census as James Kaverharea.

Keave'haccow went to work at Fort Vancouver on November 1, 1850, but returned to Nisqually the next September and continued on with his agricultural work, doing a variety of jobs until March 8, 1852, when he left the HBC's employ to work for a nearby settler. Keave'haccow reappeared on June 7, erecting a dairy at Tlithlow and working at a variety of jobs, many requiring carpentry skills. Keave'haccow left again in August 1854, this time returning after two months away. Keave'haccow didn't always do carpenter or agriculture duties, for on July 7, 1853, he was out marking the boundaries of the PSAC's claim. The usually affable Keave'haccow had the unpleasant duty on November 10, 1854, in nearby Steilacoom City, of testifying against fellow Sandwich Islander **Tamaree** who stole from the company's beach store. On November 14, 1855, Keave'haccow was sent to

Muck farm and didn't reappear in the Fort Nisqually journals until November 4, 1857. On April 8, 1858, Keave'haccow returned to Nisqually to announce that he and **Kalama** were going to Thompson River to look for gold, an adventure that lasted just two months. He left again in August 1859, signing with his mark for the $18.38 in his account, but in a familiar pattern returned to work within a year.

Keave'haccow appears to have been in general a dedicated, sober, hard worker; however, on February 14, 1853, he was noted as being drunk and disorderly along with **Joe Tapou** and **Tawai.** Similarly, on March 28 of the same year, Keave'haccow and a French Canadian employee Jean Baptiste Chailfoux were drunk and unable to work. On returning from the gold fields, Keave'haccow simplified his name to Keheva, suggesting adaptation to new circumstances. He left the service of the company for the last time in July 1869 and reportedly went to work, along with his countrymen Cowie and Joe Tapou, at a nearby sawmill.

Keave'haccow had an Indian wife at least by 1853 when he purchased women's clothing. From 1855 he bought children's shoes, indicating one or more were old enough to be wearing them. Both Keave'haccow's wife and his mother-in-law worked at Nisqually whenever such short-term jobs as weeding vegetables were to be had.

PS: HBCA YFSA 24–32, YFDS 16, FtVanSA 9–14, HLFtNisPJ 5–6, 8–10, 12–15, FtNisSA 3, 5, 7–15, env, FtNisTB 1–2, FtNisB 8–9, 11–12, FTNisbox 4, 6, FtNisMFJ, 1850 U.S. Census, Oregon, Clark Co.

Kee [variation: **Ki**] (fl. 1845–1856)

HBC employee, associated with:

> Fort Colvile (1845–1848) laborer
> Fort Langley (1848–1849) laborer
> New Caledonia (1849–1850) laborer
> Fort Victoria (1850–1852) laborer
> Columbia Department (1855–1856) laborer

Kee joined the HBC in O'ahu on May 7, 1845, and worked steadily as a laborer at various posts until 1852. He appeared to return to work in 1855–1856, for he is noted as having received wages but in the following 1856–1857 outfit he was described as being at Fort Victoria and not receiving wages. He has not been traced beyond that point.

PS: HBCA YFSA 25–32, FtVicSA 1–5

Keea [variations: **Kia, Kea, G. Keea**] (fl. 1848–1858)

HBC employee, associated with:

> Fort Vancouver (1848–1849) laborer
> Thompson River (1849–1851) laborer
> Fort Langley (1852–1853)
> Columbia Department (1855–1856)
> Fort Victoria (1856–1857) laborer
> Columbia Department (1857–1858) laborer
> steamer *Otter* (1858) steward

Keea signed on in 1848 in O'ahu with the HBC, with whom he worked off and on as a laborer at various posts for ten years. He began work on July 15, 1848, but deserted in outfit 1850–1851; he was back working in outfit 1852–1853 although he appeared to have stopped working in 1853–1854. From 1854 he worked until 1858, when he appeared to retire. By 1858, he had acquired an initial name starting with G. (George?). From that point on, he is not found in the records again.

Keea had an unnamed Kwantlen wife and two recorded children, Basile (?–bap. 1856–?) and Jean (?–bap. 1856–?). Both children were baptized Catholic on June 29, 1856, at Fort Langley.

PS: HBCA SandIsAB 7, YFSA 28–30, 32, YFDS 19, FtVicSA 1–6, Log of *Otter,* BCA VS-StAndC

Keekanah [variations: **Keikanneh, Keekaneh, Keekany, Keekane, Kekane, Tchikané**] (fl. 1817–1846)

NWC/HBC employee, b. ca. 1798, d. August 31, 1846, likely at Fort Vancouver, associated with:

Columbia River area (1817–1822) laborer
Fort George [Astoria] (1822–1826) laborer
Umpqua Snake expedition (1826–1827)
Fort Vancouver (1827–1830) laborer, Indian trade (1830–1831) laborer
Fort Vancouver (1831–1843) middleman or laborer
Fort McLoughlin (1843–1844) middleman
Willamette (1844–1845) laborer
Fort Vancouver (1845–1846) laborer

Keekanah joined the NWC fur trade around 1817, and worked many years in the Columbia Department. Part of that time was spent in the sawmill at Fort Vancouver. In 1835 he retired and returned to Oʻahu on the *Ganymede,* leaving Fort Vancouver on October 3. Upon arrival he was paid his final wage; however, he had a change of mind and returned to the Northwest Coast to work. His contact ended in 1845 and he died August 31, 1846, quite likely at Fort Vancouver.

Keekanah partnered with a Chehalis woman, their child being Cecelia/Cecile (ca. 1828–?), who was first baptized Anglican by the Rev. Herbert Beaver, and then, to ensure a passage to heaven, Catholic by priest F. N. Blanchet.

PS: HBCA FtGeo[Ast]AB 10, 12, YFSA 2–9, 11–15, 19–21, 24–26, FtVanAB 10, SA 1–8, CB 9, YFDS 2a, 3a–7, SandIsLonIC 1, BCA VS-CCC; *PPS:* Munnick, *Vancouver,* vol. 2; Tolmie, *Journals,* 189

Keemo, James (fl. 1811–1814)

PFC/NWC employee, b. probably on Oʻahu, associated with:

ship *Tonquin* (1811) passenger
Fort Astoria (1811–1814) laborer
ship *Isaac Todd* (1814) passenger

James Keemo joined the crew of the *Tonquin* as a laborer around February 21, 1811, when the vessel of the PFC stopped at Oʻahu and took on a complement of twenty Sandwich Islanders. One month later, on March 22, the *Tonquin* arrived at the mouth of the Columbia and, on April 12, James Keemo was noted as helping to unload the vessel. Keemo worked at Astoria until the spring of 1814, when he returned home.

PS: RosL *Astoria*

Keepanui (fl. 1863–1864)

Laborer, associated with:

Alberni (1863–1864) sawmill worker

Keepanui was among seven men contracted in Honolulu on September 23, 1863, by the agent of Alberni Mill Co. to work for $10 per month with a $20 advance. The same day they left for Victoria on the *Alberni*. On December 22, 1864, all of the men, except for **Kealili** who ran away, arrived back in Honolulu from Alberni on the ship *Buena Vista*.

PS: HSA Seamen, Passenger

Keepau (fl. 1870)

Laborer, b. ca. 1832, associated with:

Port Gamble (1870) sawmill worker

At the time of the 1870 Census, Keepau was one of twenty-two Hawaiians working at Puget Mill at Port Gamble.

PS: 1870 U.S. Census, Washington Territory, Kitsap Co., Port Gamble

Keewele [variation: **Joe Silver**] (fl. 1866–1867)

Seaman, associated with:

Victoria (1866–1867)

Keewele was a native Hawaiian seaman in whaling under the name of Joe Silver who ended up in Victoria in April 1867 after his brig was abandoned in Bering Straits, and he was picked up by a passing vessel. He decided to stay since he had a brother living there.

PS: HSA Victoria

Keharoha [variation: **Kehaoroah**] (fl. 1840–1845)

HBC employee, associated with:

Fort Vancouver (1840–1841) middleman
Snake party (1841–1842) middleman
barque *Vancouver* (1842–1843) laborer
Fort McLoughlin (1843–1844) laborer
Willamette (1844–1845) laborer

Keharoha joined the HBC from Oʻahu in 1840 and began working at Fort Vancouver on July 15 of that year. He worked as a goer and comer for the Snake party and subsequently in a variety of locations throughout the Columbia. As his contract ended in 1845, he worked until July 18 of that year, at which point he returned to Oʻahu.

PS: HBCA YFSA 20, 24–25, FtVanSA 6–8, YFDS 11–12, 16

Keharou [variation: **Keharrow**] (fl. 1840–1847)

HBC employee, associated with:

Fort Vancouver (1840–1841) middleman
barque *Columbia* (1841–1842) middleman
Fort Stikine (1843–1846) middleman, (1846–1847) laborer

Keharou joined the HBC from Oʻahu in 1840 and worked at Fort Vancouver and on the barque *Columbia*. He worked until November 10, 1847, when he returned to Oʻahu.

PS: HBCA YFSA 20, 24–25, 27, YFDS 12, 18, FtVanSA 6–8

Keharoua [variations: **Keheroua, Kehoroua**] (fl. 1840–1849)

PSAC/HBC employee, d. July 10, 1849, at Fort Vancouver, associated with:

PSAC (1840–1841) laborer
Cowlitz farm, (1841–1842) middleman, (1842–1843) laborer
Fort Vancouver (1843–1849) laborer

Keharoua joined the HBC from Oʻahu in 1840 as a middleman and worked across the Columbia District. His contract was to have ended in 1851, but he died at Fort Vancouver on July 10, 1849, and was likely buried at the cemetery there.

PS: HBCA YFSA 20, 24–25, 27–29, FtVanSA 6-8, YFDS 20

Kehow [variation: **Kehou**] (fl. 1845–1851)

HBC employee, associated with:

Fort Vancouver (1845–1849) laborer
Fort Victoria (1849–1850) laborer
Fort Vancouver (1850–1851) laborer

Kehow joined the HBC from Oʻahu in 1845 on a three-year contract. He worked at Forts Vancouver and Victoria until he deserted on June 30, 1851. He has not been traced after that. He may be the same person as **Kahua**.

PS: HBCA YFSA 25–31, YFDS 22, FtVanSA 9

Kei (fl. 1846–1847)

HBC employee, associated with:

Fort Vancouver (1846–1847) laborer

Kei joined the HBC from Oʻahu in 1846 on a two-year contract. No further information has been located about him.

PS: HBCA YFSA 26

Kekaa (fl. 1864)

Laborer, associated with:

Port Gamble (1864) sawmill worker

Kekaa was one of six men contracted in Honolulu on February 5, 1864, by the agent of Puget Mill Co. to work at its sawmill for $10 per month with a $20 advance. It is uncertain how long he did so.

PS: HSA Seamen

Kekaaola (fl. 1864)

Laborer, associated with:

Port Gamble (1863–1864) sawmill worker

Kekaaola and five others were contracted in Honolulu on December 4, 1863, by the agent of Puget Mill Co. to work at its sawmill for $10 per month with a $20 advance. Three days later he left for Teekalet on the barque *Constitution*. It is unclear how long he worked there.

PS: HSA Seamen, Passenger

Kekahuna [variation: **Kikuhanna**] (fl. 1845–1848)

HBC employee, associated with:

Willamette (1845–1846) laborer
Fort Vancouver (1846–1848) laborer

Kekahuna joined the HBC from Oʻahu on May 7, 1845, for three years, working in the Fort Vancouver area. He received his final wages in Honolulu in July 1848. He did not receive wages for outfit 1848–1851 although, for unexplained reasons, his name remained on the books.

PS: HBCA SandIsAB 3, 7, YFSA 25–30

Kekko (fl. 1853)

HBC employee, associated with:

ship *Pekin* (1853) seaman
ship *Mary Catherine* (1853) seaman

Kekko shipped aboard the HBC chartered vessel *Pekin* in Honolulu probably in the summer of 1853 during the height of the smallpox epidemic, sailed to the Northwest Coast, and arrived back in Honolulu September 27, 1853, on the *Mary Catherine*. He was given the final balance of his wages when he arrived back.

PS: HBCA SandIsLonIC 3

Kekoa [variation: Kikoa] (fl. 1847–1856)

HBC employee, associated with:

Columbia Department (1847–1848) laborer
Fort Langley (1848–1849) laborer
New Caledonia (1849–1850) laborer
Fort Langley (1850–1855) laborer

Kekoa joined the HBC from Oʻahu as a laborer in 1847 on a three-year contract that ended in 1850. He began work on August 12, 1847, and was mainly employed at Fort Langley. In outfit 1854–1855, he did not receive wages. He may have still been in the area in 1855–1856 but no further information has been located about him.

PS: HBCA YFSA 27–32, FtVicSA 1–3, YFDS 18

Kekone, Dick (fl. 1880)

Laborer, b. ca. 1864, associated with:

Port Gamble (1880) laborer

At the time of the 1880 Census, Dick Kekone was one of nine "Kanakas" working in Port Gamble, almost certainly at the sawmill. He was illiterate.

PS: 1880 U.S. Census, Washington Territory, Kitsap Co., Port Gamble

Kekūanōʻa, Mataio (fl. 1860)

Governor of Oʻahu, b. ca. 1791 to Kiʻilaweau and Inaina, d. November 24, 1868, in Honolulu, associated with:

schooner E*mma Rooke* (1860) passenger
Victoria (September 18–24, 1860) visitor

When Mataio Kekūanōʻa came to Victoria on a week's visit in 1860 he was a member of the house of nobles and the king's privy council. He had served with the Hawaiian royal family for some time. As early as the 1820s, he was an intimate friend of Kamehameha II and sailed to England with the king and queen but avoided the disease to which the monarchs succumbed there. He consolidated his position in the 1820s when he married two of Kamehameha's descendants. After his second wife's death in 1839, he served as governor of Oʻahu, a position that he held when he sailed to Victoria with his son Prince **Lot Kamehameha** in 1860. That same year he was appointed president of the board of education and later defended Hawaiian rather than English as a vehicle of instruction in the schools. Even though he had no legal training, he was appointed judge on Oʻahu and was considered a man of ability, integrity, and good intentions.

Mataio Kekūanōʻa had two wives. In 1825, he married Pauahi (ca. 1797–1826), the granddaughter of Kamehameha I and Kanekapolei. Together they had Ruth Keʻelikolani (1826–1883). Upon the death of Pauahi, he married Kinau (ca. 1806–1839), the daughter of King Kamehameha I and Kalakua, in 1827. Together they had five children: Moses Kekuaiwa (1829–1848), Lot (1830–1874) [Kamehameha V], Alexander Liholiho (1834–1863) [Kamehameha IV], and Victoria Kamamalu (1838–1866).

PS: HSA Passenger Manifests, Victoria; *SS: Pacific Commercial Advertiser,* October 8, 1864; *Colonist,* September 19–25, 1860; Anderson, *History;* Kuykendall, *Hawaiian Kingdom,* vols. 1–2; *Royalty*

Kelape (fl. 1863)

Laborer, associated with:

Port Gamble (1863) sawmill worker

Kelape was among five men contracted in Honolulu on July 8, 1863, by the agent of Puget Mill Co. to work at its sawmill for $10 per month with a $20 advance. It is uncertain how long he did so.

PS: HSA Seamen

Keleikipi (fl. 1866)

Miner, associated with:

Jackson Co., Oregon (1866) miner

On July 31, 1866, "Keleikipi (Kanaka) and Co." made a gold mining claim on Kanaka Flat in Jackson County. Nothing else is known.

SS: Blue, "Mining Laws," 139

Keliaa (fl. 1862)

Laborer, associated with:

Vancouver Island (1862)

Keliaa was one of eight laborers who left for Victoria on the *Constitution* on May 2, 1862. It is unclear where they were headed.

PS: HSA Passenger

Kelie, John (fl. 1881)

Farmer, b. ca. 1850, associated with:

Victoria (1881)

Describing himself as a "Kanaka" born in the Sandwich Islands, John Kelie was in 1881 a married farmer living in a Victoria hotel.

PS: 1881 Canada Census, British Columbia, Victoria

Kelocha [variation: Capt. Cook] (fl. 1859–1860)

PSAC employee, associated with:

Fort Nisqually outstation (1859–1860) shepherd

Kelocha was a shepherd at a Fort Nisqually outstation from July 1859 to February 1860. Engaged on a monthly wage, he departed the same day as his countryman **Kalikeeney.**

PS: HL FTNisPJ 13, FtNisSA 14; *SS:* Anderson, *Physical Structure,* 185

Kema (fl. 1864)

Occupation unknown, associated with:

Port Angeles, Washington (1864)

Kema, his wife, and two other Hawaiian men left for Port Angeles on the *N.S. Perkins* on October 25, 1864. No other information has been located about them.

PS: HSA Passenger

Kemo, Joseph (fl. 1870)

Laborer, b. ca. 1825, associated with:

Port Gamble (1870) sawmill worker

At the time of the 1870 Census, Joseph Kemo was one of twenty-two Hawaiians working at Puget Mill at Port Gamble.

PS: 1870 U.S. Census, Washington Territory, Kitsap Co., Port Gamble

Kemopupuka (fl. 1858)

Occupation unknown, associated with:

Port Gamble (1858)

Kemopupuka left Honolulu for Teekalet on May 8, 1858, on the barque *May Flower.* No other information has been located about him, but presumably he worked for a year or more in the sawmill there.

PS: HSA Passenger

Kemwāami (fl. 1870)

Laborer, b. ca. 1853, associated with:

Port Gamble (1870) likely sawmill worker

At the time of the 1870 Census, Kemwāami was one of twenty-two Hawaiians working at Puget Mill at Port Gamble.

PS: 1870 U.S. Census, Washington Territory, Kitsap Co., Port Gamble

Kenula (fl. 1860)

Laborer, associated with:

Port Madison, Washington (1863) sawmill worker

Kenula and three other men were contracted in Honolulu on October 5, 1860, by the agent of Madison Mill Co. to work at its sawmill for $15 per month with a $20 advance. The term of service of a year began only with their arrival in Puget Sound.

PS: HSA Seamen

Keo (fl. 1843–1849)

HBC employee, associated with:

Fort Vancouver (1843–1849) laborer

Keo was a laborer who most likely joined the HBC from Oʻahu in 1843. He worked his entire career at Fort Vancouver and deserted on October 10, 1849, likely for the gold fields of California. He has not been traced after that.

PS: HBCA FtVanSA 8, YFSA 24–25, 27–29, YFDS 17, 20

Keoki (fl. 1858)

Occupation unknown, associated with:

British Columbia (1858)

Keoki was one of six Hawaiians to whom the governor of O'ahu gave permission in May 1858 to proceed to the British Columbia gold rush. He, and likely also his wife, left Honolulu for Vancouver Island on the schooner *Alice* on May 19, 1858. They had deck passage. Keoki has not been traced further.

PS: HSA Passenger, Victoria

Keomohuli (fl. 1862)

Laborer, associated with:

Vancouver Island (1862)

Keomohuli was one of eight laborers who left for Victoria on the *Constitution* on May 2, 1862. It is unclear where they were headed.

PS: HSA Passenger

Keone (fl. 1867)

Occupation unknown, associated with:

Victoria area (1867)

A Hawaiian identified as Keone left Honolulu for Victoria on January 8, 1867.

PS: HSA Passenger

Keopool (fl. 1870)

Laborer, b. ca. 1846, associated with:

San Juan Island (1870) laborer

A twenty-four-year-old Keopool was, by 1870, living alone on his own land on San Juan Island. He couldn't read or write and worked as a laborer. Nonetheless, he owned $600 in real estate and another $600 in personal property.

PS: 1870 U.S. Census, Washington Territory, San Juan Island

Keoumoumanui (fl. 1861)

Laborer, associated with:

Port Gamble (1861) sawmill worker

Keoumoumanui and five others were contracted in Honolulu on October 5, 1861, by the agent of Puget Mill Co. to work at its sawmill for $15 per month with a $15 advance. It is uncertain how long he did so.

PS: HSA Seamen

Kepupu, John (fl. 1870)

Laborer, b. ca. 1835, associated with:

Port Gamble (1870) sawmill worker

At the time of the 1870 Census, John Kepupu was one of twenty-two Hawaiians working at Puget Mill at Port Gamble.

PS: 1870 U.S. Census, Washington Territory, Kitsap Co., Port Gamble

Keroha (fl. 1840–1843)

HBC employee, associated with:

barque *Columbia* (1840–1841) seaman
Fort Vancouver Indian trade (1841–1842) middleman
Fort George [Astoria] (1842–1843) laborer

Keroha joined the HBC from Oʻahu in 1840. It is uncertain how he came to the Northwest Coast but, by November 28, 1840, he was working as a part-time crew member on the *Columbia* when it sailed to Monterey. After a few months, he worked in the Forts Vancouver/George area until November 15, 1843, at which point he left for Oʻahu.

PS: HBCA SMP 14, YFSA 20, 23, FtVanSA 6–8, YFDS 14

Keupa (fl. 1860–1862)

Laborer, associated with:

Port Gamble (1860–1862) sawmill worker

Keupa and three others were contracted in Honolulu on November 1, 1860, by the agent of Puget Mill Co. to work at its sawmill for $15 per month with a $15 advance. On February 14, 1862, he, or possibly another man by the same name, was contracted in Honolulu to work there for $10 per month with a $20 advance.

PS: HSA Seamen

Kiaimoku (fl. 1844)

Servant, associated with:

Oregon (1844) laborer

On March 28, 1844, in Honolulu, two "native Hawaiians" named Kiaimoku and **Kanakahou** agreed to accompany British subject William T. Bailey to Oregon for two years as servants in exchange for passage both ways, food, lodging, and $100 per year each. Kiaimoku signed the agreement with a sure hand, indicating his literacy. It is not known what happened subsequently.

PS: HSA, 402-10-248.

Kiavihow [variations: **Keave, Kiāve, Chawey, Chowy**] (fl. 1865–1883)

Farmer, b. ca. 1815, d. May 19, 1883, on Salt Spring Island, associated with:

Victoria area (1865) farmer
Salt Spring Island (1869–1883) farmer

In November 1865 a man recorded as Kiavihow, who signed with his mark, preempted 100 acres in the outskirts of Victoria. By 1869 and perhaps earlier he was almost certainly living on Salt Spring Island. In early 1869 a man recorded both as Kiav-how and as Kaive-ou signed with his mark to take up 160 acres of land on the west side of Fulford Harbour. By 1875 he had cleared 6 acres, built a fence 7 feet high, and had "a good house cost $150, a wife & family," Hawaiian consul **Henry Rhodes** attested. That year he applied for title to the still unsurveyed land. During this time, he may have made periodic visits to Victoria for, on September 13, 1871, fifty-year-old Kiavi-ow was found guilty of assault in that city and fined $10 or one month in prison. In 1882 a man named Chawey, born in about 1815, was sentenced to one month's hard labor in a Victoria jail for selling liquor to Indians. Kiavihow died on Salt Spring Island on May 29, 1883, of old age.

The man named as Chawey was married to Mary (?–?) and their children were Lucy (ca. 1867–?) and Frank (1874–?). Two years after Kiavihow's death, William Fraser Tolmie, longtime head at Fort Nisqually, interceded on behalf of his widow, whom he named as "Madame Kiāve." Remarried to a Songhees man, she sought, unsuccessfully, title to "three or four acres, cleared and long cultivated by her deceased husband, a Sandwich Islander, and long an employee of the HBC" on Salt Spring. She wanted the property for "her little boy Frank Kiāve (the only survivor of her children)" against the claims of Lagamine, **William Naukana**, then on Portland Island.

PS: BCA Crt-Gaols, GR-Pre-emption, VS-StAndC, PR-Tolmie, 1881 Canada Census, British Columbia, Cowichan; *PPS:* Tolmie, *Journals;* British Columbia, Superintendent of Police, *Annual Report, 1882*

Kie, John (fl. 1860)

Laborer, b. ca. 1820, associated with:

Fort Vancouver area (1860) laborer

John Kie, along with several Hawaiians and their families, was living in the Kanaka Village area of Fort Vancouver in 1860. As a laborer, he may have worked for what remained of the HBC interests or for the nearby U.S. military post. Living in the same household was **Betty** (ca. 1830–?), also born in the Sandwich Islands. She may have been his wife.

PS: 1860 U.S. Census, Washington Territory, Clark Co.

Kihino, John (fl. 1850)

Laborer, b. ca. 1825, associated with:

Fort Vancouver area (1850)

John Kihino was living in Kanaka Village near Fort Vancouver in 1850. No other records of him have been found.

PS: 1850 U.S. Census, Oregon, Clark Co.

Kikapalalē [variations: Kekapalelē, Kikapalle] (fl. 1845–1854)

HBC employee, associated with:

Fort Vancouver (1845–1847) laborer
New Caledonia (1847–1848) laborer
Fort Langley (1848–1849) laborer
New Caledonia (1849–1850) laborer
Fort Langley (1850–1854)

Kikapalalē joined the HBC from Oʻahu on May 7, 1845. He worked until 1852, possibly 1854, at interior and coastal posts and may have stayed in the area, as transactions appeared on his account until 1855–1856.

PS: HBCA SandIsAB 3, YFSA 25–32, FtVicSA 1–3

Kiko (fl. 1864)

Laborer, associated with:

Port Gamble (1864) sawmill worker

Kiko was one of six men contracted in Honolulu on May 27, 1864, by the agent of Puget Mill Co. to work at its sawmill for $10 per month with a $20 advance. It is unclear how long he worked there.

PS: HSA Seamen

Kilulawahui (fl. 1850)

HBC seaman, associated with:

barque *Cowlitz* (1850) seaman

Kilulawahui shipped onboard the HBC vessel *Cowlitz* on February 3, 1850, at Honolulu and sailed to the coast on a voyage on which the captain was unhappy with the performance of the Hawaiians. The Hawaiian crew rebelled on August 27 in Honolulu harbor but most returned to the vessel on September 20 to finish their work. Beyond that, Kilulawahui has not been traced.

PS: HBCA SandIsAB 10–11, Log of *Cowlitz* 8

Kimo (fl. 1858–1859)

Occupation unknown, associated with:

British Columbia (1858)
Port Gamble (1859) sawmill worker

Kimo was one of six Hawaiians to whom the governor of O'ahu gave permission in May 1858 to proceed to the British Columbia gold rush. Kimo's absence from any passenger lists may indicate he did not go, but it is also possible he was simply not named. On March 21, 1859, Kimo, likely the same man, arrived back in Honolulu from Teekalet on the barque *Jenny Ford*. It is unclear how long, or if, he worked at the sawmill there.

PS: HSA Passenger, Victoria

Kimo, James (fl. 1850–1861)

HBC employee, b. ca. 1821, d. June 16, 1861, at Nanaimo, associated with:

brigantine *Mary Dare* (1850) passenger
Fort Rupert (1850–1853) laborer
Nanaimo (1853–1861) laborer

Kimo was a relatively late arrival in the Pacific Northwest fur trade. He was hired from O'ahu by the HBC on a three-year contract in 1850 and worked at Fort Rupert. In 1853, he may have followed the large exodus to the coal-mining settlement of Nanaimo, where he contentedly lived in a cabin with a cabbage patch and sometimes worked as a fisherman and stonemason. Dressed in a bright red sash and tassel on his cap, he undoubtedly enjoyed his job as night watchman, calling "All's Well" at midnight while he simultaneously fired his gun and struck his drum. His job was abolished in 1860 and, on June 16, 1861, the forty-year-old James Kimo died in Nanaimo.

PS: HBCA SandIsAB 10, YFSA 30–32, FtVicSA 1–2, Bio, BCA VS-StPaul; SS: Bate, "Reminiscences"

King, Bill (fl. 1834–1837)

CRFTC/HBC employee, associated with:

ship *May Dacre* (1834) passenger
CRFTC brigade (1834) member
Forts William and Hall (1835–1837) laborer
Columbia Department (1837) laborer

Bill King was one of twenty men recruited for Nathaniel J. Wyeth's CRFTC in 1834 and among the dozen who deserted in November of the same year on the way to Fort Hall. On March 12, 1835, Wyeth found seven of his runaway Hawaiians, including Bill

King, at Fort Vancouver. King was back at Fort Hall later that year, where he remained until October 1837, when his account was settled by the HBC. He has not been traced further.

PS: OHS FtHallAB, CRFTCCB; SS: Beidleman, "Fort Hall," 238

Kini (fl. 1862)

Laborer, associated with:

Vancouver Island (1862)

Kini was one of eight laborers who left for Victoria on the *Constitution* on May 2, 1862. It is unclear where they were headed.

PS: HSA Passenger

Kiona [variation: Keowna] (fl. 1845–1869)

HBC employee, associated with:

Fort Vancouver (1845–1846) laborer
steamer *Beaver* (1846–1848) stoker
Fort Simpson (1850–1859) laborer
Upper Skeena (1866) laborer
Fort Simpson (1869) laborer

Kiona joined the HBC in Oʻahu on May 7, 1845, on a three-year contract and remained on the Northwest Coast for at least the next quarter century. He worked until December 5, 1848, primarily as a stoker on the *Beaver,* at which point he returned to Oʻahu. He reentered the service and began work at Fort Simpson. On January 4, 1853, he was smitten with love and deserted Fort Simpson to be with his Indian wife in the nearby camp. Two days later he was found in an Indian lodge and brought back. As the wife would not remain in the fort with him and he would live only outside with her, it was felt that he would be useless. However, he continued to be employed.

It is quite possible that Kiona had learned how to read and write Hawaiian because, in 1857, when he was recruited by missionary William Duncan from among the Fort Simpson employees for his Men's Night School, Kiona was described as being unable to read or write in English, implying that he could in Hawaiian. In outfits 1859–1860 and 1861–1862 he appeared on the sundries accounts with no designation or wages, only a £0.8.4 debt carried over from the previous outfit. As a result of a survey by William Manson, "on November 17, 1866, Thomas Hankin was sent up the Skeena on the sloop *Petrel* with one man, James Otely, and a temporary assistant, Kiona," to erect a new post as Hagwilget, a post not far from Fort Simpson that lasted only two years before it was closed down. In September 1869, a Hawaiian named Keowna was working at Fort Simpson.

Kiona's wife and family, if such existed, have not been traced.

PS: HBCA SandIsAB 3, 7, YFSA 25–28, 30–32, FtSimp[N]PJ 7, FtVicSA 1–7, YFDS 19, UBCSC Duncan, BCA PR-Morison; SS: Large, *Skeena River,* 44

Ki-o-ne (fl. 1850)

Raftsman, b. ca. 1826, associated with:

Oregon City (1850) raftsman

Ki-o-ne, a raftsman, was living in Oregon City at the time of the 1850 Census. Nothing else is known of him.

PS: 1850 U.S. Census, Oregon, Clackamas Co., Oregon City

Kioplik (fl. 1870)

Laborer, b. ca. 1850, associated with:

San Juan Island (1870) laborer

In 1870 Kioplik was living in the same household as **Alum Keoni** and working as a laborer. He was illiterate.

PS: 1870 U.S. Census, Washington Territory, San Juan Island

Knowalo, William (fl. 1859–1881)

Laborer, b. ca. 1825, associated with:

Burrard Inlet (1881) sawmill worker

Described as born in the Sandwich Islands, William Knowalo was in 1881 working as a millhand at Moodyville in North Vancouver.

Knowalo and Emma (ca. 1840–?), likely a Native woman, were the parents of Maryanne (ca. 1860–), who by 1881 was married, so he must have been in the area some time, perhaps under another name.

PS: 1881 Canada Census, British Columbia, New Westminster

Koa [1] (fl. 1840–1843)

HBC employee, associated with:

Fort Vancouver (1840–1843) middleman

Koa signed on with the HBC from Oʻahu in 1840. He worked at Fort Vancouver until November 15, 1843, near the end of his contract, at which point he returned to Oʻahu.

PS: HBCA YFSA 29, 23, FtVanSA 6–8, YFDS 14

Koa [2] (fl. 1862)

Seaman, associated with:

Constitution (1862) seaman

Koa worked as a seaman on the *Constitution,* leaving Honolulu for Teekalet in Washington Territory on December 7, 1862. His wage was $30 per month with a $30 advance.

PS: HSA Seamen

Koamanunui (fl. 1862)

Laborer, associated with:

Port Gamble (1862) sawmill worker

On December 15, 1862, Koamanunui arrived back in Honolulu from Teekalet on the barque *Jenny Ford.* It is unclear how long he worked at the sawmill there.

PS: HSA Passenger

Koemi, Sam [variations: **Kanaka Sam, Kaemi, Koeme**] (fl. 1847–1860)

HBC/PSAC employee, b. ca. 1820, associated with:

Fort Nisqually outstations (1847–1860) shepherd

Koemi joined the HBC from Oʻahu as a laborer in 1847 on a three-year contract. He began work on August 9 as a Nisqually outstation shepherd. At the time of the 1850 Census, Koemi lived in the same household as **Kupahi** and **Kahannui**, all three being described as "dark Hawaiian." Koemi continued working as a shepherd until February 1860. He has not been traced further.

At Tlithlow Sam Koemi had a wife and a son (1850–1851) who died of influenza and was buried at Fort Nisqually.

PS: HBCA YFSA 27–32, FtVanSA 9–10, YFDS 13, HL FtNisSA 5–9, 11–14, env, FtNisTB 1, FtNisPJ 8–9, FtNisbox 6, FtNisTJ, 1850 U.S. Census, Oregon, Lewis Co.; *PPS:* Roberts, "Round Hand"; *SS:* Anderson, *Physical Structure*

Kolpa, Harry (fl. 1860)

Laborer, b. ca. 1830, associated with:

Fort Vancouver area (1860) laborer

Harry Kolpa was living in the Kanaka Village area of Fort Vancouver in 1860 and probably worked for what remained of the HBC interests in the area. He did not appear to be employed as a regular contracted employee for the London-based company.

PS: 1860 U.S. Census, Washington Territory, Clark Co.

Komaai (fl. 1864)

Laborer, associated with:

Port Gamble (1864) sawmill worker

Komaai was among six men contracted in Honolulu on May 27, 1864, by the agent of Puget Mill Co. for $10 per month with a $20 advance. It is unclear how long he worked at the sawmill there.

PS: HSA Seamen

Kom-ah-hu (fl. 1861)

PSAC employee, associated with:

Fort Nisqually (1861) shepherd

A Kanaka named as Kom-ah-hu began work as a shepherd at Fort Nisqually in January 1861 on a $15 monthly salary. The same day he bought himself a capot, or great coat, for $8. No other references to him have been located, suggesting he soon departed.

PS: HL FTNisB 8

KomaKau (fl. 1858)

Occupation unknown, associated with:

Oregon City (1858)

Nothing is known about KomaKau, who on November 28, 1858, in Oregon City married Maria Maltwash from the Yamhill reserve in a Catholic ceremony, despite "difference of religion."

PS: Munnick, *Oregon City*

Komakia [variation: Thomokia] (fl. 1849–1859)

Occupation unknown, associated with:

Victoria area (1849–1859)

Komakia appeared in the Victoria area between 1850 and 1859. Two children attributed to him were Adele (?–bap. 1850–?) and Marguerite (?–bap. 1859–?). His wife was not named.

PS: BCA VS-StAndC

Kome (fl. 1856)

PSAC employee, associated with:

Fort Nisqually (1856) laborer

A Sandwich Islander identified as Kome was hired at Fort Nisqually in January 1856. The last entry for him was June 10, whereupon he disappears from the records.

PS: HL FTNisSA 11

Konea [variations: Kenoha, Konia] (fl. 1840–1860)

HBC employee, associated with:

Fort Vancouver Indian trade (1840–1842) middleman
Snake party (1842–1843) middleman
Fort Vancouver (1843–1844) laborer
Fort Victoria (1844–1846) laborer
Cowlitz farm (1847–1849) laborer
Fort Victoria (1850) laborer
Belle Vue sheep farm (1859–1860) laborer

Konea joined the HBC from Oʻahu in 1840. He worked at various locations until December 10, 1845, and returned to Oʻahu. He reenlisted and came back to the Columbia in April 1846, only to desert, most likely with the gold rush in California, in 1849. He likely worked in the Pacific Northwest for a number of years thereafter and in 1859–1860 was a farm laborer on San Juan Island.

Konea had an Indian wife and two recorded daughters, Suzanne (1844–?) and Rosalie (1846–1847).

PS: HBCA YFSA 20, 24–25, 27–29, FtVanSA 6–8, YFDS 16, BelleVuePJ 2, HSA Passenger; *PPS:* Munnick, *Vancouver,* vol. 2; Roberts, "Round Hand"

Koneva [variation: Koniva] (fl. 1840–1846)

PSAC/HBC employee, associated with:

PSAC (1840–1841) middleman
Snake party (1841–1843) middleman
Fort Vancouver (1843–1845) middleman
Snake party (1845–1846) goer and comer
Fort Vancouver (1846) laborer

Koneva joined the HBC from Oʻahu in 1840. He began his work with PSAC, but in the following outfit was a goer and comer with the HBC for the Snake party. He worked until August 6, 1846, at which point he returned to Oʻahu.

PS: HBCA YFSA 20, 24–26, FtVanSA 6–8, YFDS 12, YFSA 16–17

Koniba, Joseph (fl. 1880)

Laborer, b. ca. 1840, associated with:

Vashon Island (1880) sawmill worker

Koniba was in 1880 working in a sawmill on Vashon Island, Washington. In 1880 Koniba had an Indian wife Annie (ca. 1845–?), but no children.

PS: 1880 U.S. Census, Washington Territory, Skamania

Konochourri (fl. 1858–1860)

PSAC employee, associated with:

Fort Nisqually outstation (1858–1860) shepherd

Little is known of Konochourri who was engaged in December 1858 to herd sheep at Muck farm and settled his wages on January 7, 1860, prior to departure.

PS: HL FtNisMFJ, FtNisSA 14

Kooi, John (fl. 1870)

Laborer, b. ca. 1835, associated with:

Port Gamble (1870) sawmill worker

At the time of the 1870 Census, John Kooi was one of twenty-two Hawaiians working at Puget Mill at Port Gamble.

PS: 1870 U.S. Census, Washington Territory, Kitsap Co., Port Gamble

Kopa [variation: Kopalemehou] (fl. 1838–1841)

Seaman, associated with:

Fort Vancouver area (1838–1841)

Although Kopa was never described as Hawaiian in the (Fort) Vancouver Catholic Church records, Harriet D. Munnick, the tireless compiler of the records, felt this seaman to be so entered him as such. Kopa had a Chinook Native wife, by the name of Tepathels (?–?), in port in the Fort Vancouver area. Together, they had Jean (1839–?) and Paul (1839–?). The fact that his children, apparently born in the same year, were baptized five months apart could mean that there were two separate mothers.

PPS: Munnick, *St. Paul,* vol. 1

Kopane, Kalle (fl. 1862)

Occupation unknown, associated with:

Cowichan area (1862)

Kalle Kopane was sworn in as a British subject probably in Victoria, British Columbia, on August 11, 1862. He signed his name with a sure hand. That same day, **John Adams** and **Keava Kamu** also received their naturalization papers. The following day **William R. Kaulehelehe** received his, indicating a possible friendship among the four.

In late September 1862 Adams and Kopane preempted land adjacent to each other in the Cowichan area of Vancouver Island. The certificate mentions but does not name a third "Kanaka," who might have been Keava Kamu.

PS: BCA GR-Naturalization, Crt-Naturalization, GR-Preemption

Korhooa [variations: Karhooa, Kaialohua] (fl. 1840–1848)

HBC employee, d. February 10, 1848, at Fort Vancouver, associated with:

Snake party (1840–1844) middleman
Fort Vancouver (1844–1845) laborer
barque *Cowlitz* (1845) passenger
Fort Vancouver (1845–1848) laborer

Korhooa joined the HBC from Oʻahu in 1840 and in outfit 1843–1844 was transporting trappers in and out of the Snake Country. He worked until January 10, 1845, at which point he returned to Oʻahu. His visit was short, for he was reengaged May 7 and returned in September to the Columbia, where he died at Fort Vancouver on February 10, 1848, most certainly of the measles.

PS: HBCA YFSA 20, 24, 26–27, YFDS 14–15, 18, FtVanSA 6–8, SandIsAB 3, 5, HSA Passenger

Krimi, K (fl. 1870)

Laborer, b. ca. 1826, associated with:

Oregon City (1870) laborer

At the time of the 1870 Census, Krimi was a laborer in Oregon City. He was illiterate.

PS: 1870 U.S. Census, Oregon, Oregon City

Kuaava [variation: **Joe Kuaawa**] (fl. 1864–1865)

Laborer, associated with:

Port Gamble (1864–1865) sawmill worker

Kuaava and five others were contracted in Honolulu on May 27, 1864, by the agent of Puget Mill Co. for $10 per month with a $20 advance. It is unclear how long he worked at the sawmill there. He is likely the Joe Kuaawa who gave prayers at the luau **John Kau** and **Mary Pau** held for their son at Port Gamble in 1865.

PS: HSA Seamen; *SS:* Naukana, "News"

Kuahu (fl. 1864)

Laborer, associated with:

Port Gamble (1864) sawmill worker

Kuahu and five others were contracted in Honolulu on May 27, 1864, by the agent of Puget Mill Co. for $10 per month with a $20 advance. It is unclear how long he worked at the sawmill there.

PS: HSA Seamen

Kuana (fl. 1848–1855)

HBC employee, associated with:

Fort Vancouver (1848–1849) laborer
Fort Victoria (1849–1855) laborer, (1851–1855) laborer

Kuana joined the HBC from Oʻahu in 1848 and began work at Fort Vancouver on July 15. The next year he was transferred to Fort Victoria, where he was a laborer. His contract ended in 1855, at which point he appears to have stopped work with the company.

PS: HBCA SandIsAB 7, YFSA 28–32, YFDS 19, FtVicSA 1–3

Kuawaa [variations: **Karehua, Kuhawaa**] (fl. 1843–1856)

HBC employee, associated with:

Fort Vancouver (1843–1847) laborer
Fort Simpson (1847–1848) laborer
Fort Stikine (1848–1849) laborer
Fort Rupert (1849–1850) laborer
Fort Victoria (1850–1856) laborer

Kuawaa joined the HBC from Oʻahu in 1843 on a three-year contract. Over the next dozen years he worked at various coastal posts. In 1850 he expressed a strong desire to return to Hawaiʻi from the rather gloomy and turbulent Fort Rupert but, instead, continued working at Fort Victoria until 1856. It is unclear whether or not he then went home.

PS: HBCA FtVanSA 8, YFSA 24–32, FtVicSA 1–4, BCA PR-Helmcken

Kukapu (fl. 1864)

Laborer, b. ca. 1839, associated with:

Alberni (1864) sawmill worker

Kukapu was one of four men contracted in Honolulu on June 23, 1864, by the agent of Alberni Mill Co. to work for $10 per month with a $20 advance. Two days later, he and the others left Honolulu for Alberni on the schooner *Alberni*.

PS: HSA Seamen, Passenger

Kula [variation: **Kale**] (fl. 1850)

HBC seaman, associated with:

barque *Cowlitz* (1850) seaman

Kula shipped onboard the HBC vessel *Cowlitz* in February 1850 at Honolulu and sailed to the coast on a voyage on which the captain was unhappy with the performance of the Hawaiians. Consequently, Kula and the other Hawaiians rebelled. Others returned, but Kula and **Paledin** refused to do so and stayed ashore. He has not been traced further.

PS: HBCA SandIsAB 10, Log of *Cowlitz* 8

Kuluailehua (fl. 1844–1849)

HBC employee, associated with:

Willamette (1844–1846) laborer
Fort Vancouver (1846–1849) laborer

Kuluailehua joined the HBC from O'ahu in 1844 and worked in the Columbia district as a laborer. In 1847–1849 he was employed by retired Fort Vancouver head John McLoughlin but paid through the HBC. He retired in 1849 before June 1 of that year, for he received no wages for outfit 1849–1850. He remained in the area.

PS: HBCA YFSA 24–29, YFDS 18–19

Kumano (fl. 1850–1851)

Occupation unknown, associated with:

Fort Vancouver area (1850–1851)

It is not known when Kumano came to the Pacific slopes but, by 1851, he had partnered with a Native woman and had a four-month-old child, Joseph (1850–?).

PPS: Munnick, *Vancouver,* vol. 2

Kupahi [variations: **Kuphai, Ku Kuphi**] (fl. 1847–1869)

HBC/PSAC employee, b. ca. 1825, associated with:

Columbia Department (1847–1848) laborer
Fort Nisqually and outstations (1848–1853, 1856, 1858–1859, 1869) outstation shepherd and laborer

Kupahi joined the HBC from O'ahu as a laborer in 1847 and began work on August 19 of that year. At the time of the 1850 U.S. Census, he lived in the same household as **Koemi** and **Kahannui,** all three described as "dark Hawaiian." Kupahi first worked at a Nisqually outstation farm as a shepherd and then, in August 1852, moved back into the fort itself. At Nisqually, he worked on the house at the beach, brought in lumber, repaired wagons, fixed roofs, and made shingles. He also pressed wool, attended fires in a nearby swamp, and worked in the gardens.

In May 1853 Kupahi was reprimanded "on account of being lazy." On September 19, he and **Tamaree** broke into the company store and stole a considerable number of blankets. Near the end of the following month he went off to tend cattle and shortly after went to work for a farmer who had squatted on PSAC land near the fort. When his countryman **Kalama** revealed the details of the robbery in January 1854, Kupahi was retroactively discharged. He admitted to the theft and was rehired in February 1856. He worked off and on as a shepherd at Muck farm until 1859, when he disappears from the records for a decade. He was briefly reemployed at Nisqually in the spring of 1869.

Kupahi bought women's items in 1856, suggesting he had acquired a wife.

PS: HBCA YFSA 27–28, 30–32, YFDS 18, FtVanSA 9–10, HL FtNisSA 5–8, 11, 13-14, env, FtNisPJ 7–10, 12, FtNisTJ, FtNisB 12, 1850 U.S. Census, Oregon, Lewis Co.

Kupai (fl. 1860)

Seaman, associated with:

schooner *Emma Rooke* (1860) seaman

Kupai was among five Hawaiians contracted by the schooner *Emma Rooke* when it sailed from Honolulu to Victoria on August 29, 1860. The men received $15 per month with a $15 advance. He deserted, probably at Victoria.

PS: HSA Seamen

Kupanihi (fl. 1858)

Occupation unknown, associated with:

Vancouver Island (1858)

Kupanihi was one of fourteen Hawaiians departing Honolulu for Victoria on the schooner *Alice* on June 22, 1858, enticed by the euphoria of the gold rush.

PS: HSA Passenger

Kupehea [variation: **Kupihea**] (fl. 1845–1849)

HBC employee, associated with:

Fort Vancouver (1845–1849) laborer

Kupehea joined the HBC from Oʻahu on May 7 1845, on a three-year contract and worked at Fort Vancouver as a laborer. He deserted in 1849, possibly being lured to the California gold fields.

PS: HBCA SandIsAB 3, YFSA 25–29

Kupo [variation: **Kupuu**] (fl. 1860–1861)

Laborer, associated with:

Washington Territory (1861)

Kupo was one of four men contracted in Honolulu on October 5, 1860, by the Madison Mill Co. to work at its sawmill for $15 per month with a $20 advance. Their term of service of a year was to begin only on arriving in Puget Sound. He was one of four Hawaiians sailing on the *Consort,* which was wrecked off northern Vancouver Island in late November of the same year en route from Honolulu to Puget Sound. The men, who got away in an Indian canoe, reached Victoria in mid-January, destitute and clothesless, to be rescued by the Hawaiian consul. Most probably, Kupo proceeded to the Puget Sound sawmill.

PS: HSA Seamen, Victoria

Laeoitte (fl. 1844–1847)

HBC employee, d. August 10, 1847, at Fort Vancouver, associated with:

Fort Vancouver (1844–1847) laborer

Laeoitte joined the HBC from Oʻahu in 1844 on a three-year contract and, after arriving on the Northwest Coast, worked exclusively at Fort Vancouver as a laborer. He died at Fort Vancouver on August 10, 1847, of unstated causes.

PS: HBCA YFSA 24–27, YFDS 18

Lahaina [1] (fl. 1830–1835)

HBC employee, b. on Maui, associated with:

Fort Vancouver general charges (1830–1831)
Fort Simpson (1831–1832) middleman or laborer
Fort Vancouver (1832–1835) middleman or laborer
barque *Ganymede* (1835) passenger

Lahaina joined the HBC in 1830. From Fort Vancouver, he was taken north, where he was in on the original construction of Fort Simpson at the mouth of the Nass River. He then returned to Fort Vancouver, where he continued to work for the next four years, likely as a laborer. He left Fort Vancouver for Oʻahu on the barque *Ganymede* on October 3, 1835. He was discharged in Oʻahu in 1836 and paid his final HBC wage there.

PS: HBCA FtVanSA 2–3, YFDS 4a–6, YFSA 11–15, SandIsLonIC 1

Lahaina [2] (fl. 1858)

HBC employee, b. on Maui, associated with:

Belle Vue sheep farm (1858) laborer

Lahaina was a young boy when he was found working for the HBC on San Juan Island. On August 15, 1858, he may have been touched with Fraser River gold fever, for he deserted with some Americans. He then disappeared from the records.

PS: HBCA BelleVuePJ2

Lahowbalow [variation: **Lahuhalu**] (fl. 1839–1842)

PSAC/HBC employee, associated with:

Cowlitz farm and Fort Langley (1839–1840) middleman
Fort Simpson (1840–1842) middleman

Lahowbalow joined the HBC from Oʻahu in 1839 on a contract that expired in 1842. He returned to Oʻahu on November 10, 1842.

Lahowbalow and an unnamed Indian woman were the parents of Christine (1840–?).

PS: HBCA YFSA 19–20, 22, YFDS 13, FtVanSA 5–8; *PPS:* Munnick, *Vancouver,* vol. 1

Lamb, Joe (fl. 1840–1846)

HBC employee, associated with:

Fort Stikine (1840–1845) middleman
steamer *Beaver* (1845–1846) middleman, (1846) engineer's servant

Although Joe Lamb's name is identical to the *Atahualpa*'s third mate, who was with the vessel on the Hawaiian Islands twice in 1812–1813, no relationship has been traced. Joe Lamb joined the HBC from Oʻahu in 1840, arriving at Fort Vancouver in April of that year. Joe's first assignment was as a cook at Fort Stikine, where he arrived on the steamer *Beaver* on June 13.

A year later, in the fall of 1841, Joe Lamb was working as a steward and later overheard HBC servant Pierre Kanaguasse talking about murdering Fort Stikine's head, John McLoughlin Jr. Kanaguasse assured Lamb that there would be no punishment if it were done. On April 21, 1842, John McLoughlin Jr. called Joe Lamb and others to arms to protect him but it was to no avail, as McLoughlin was executed by his HBC servants. Lamb himself testified that he had seen McLoughlin tipsy two or three times. The Sandwich Islander, unlike many of the other servants at the fort, was never implicated in the murder by Dr. John McLoughlin Sr. even though he himself had been flogged by McLoughlin Jr. for either giving away meat or stealing meat out of the kitchen, a relatively minor infraction. Lamb left Fort Stikine and worked on the steamer *Beaver* for a little more than a year. As his second contract ended in 1846, he worked as an engineer's servant until December 10, 1846, at which point he returned to O'ahu.

PS: HBCA YFSA 20, 24–26, FtVanSA 6–8, CB 30–31, YFDS 17, FtStikPJ 1–2

Lami (fl. 1870)

Laborer, b. ca. 1849, associated with:

Port Gamble (1870) sawmill worker

At the time of the 1870 Census, Lami was one of twenty-two Hawaiians working at Puget Mill at Port Gamble.

PS: 1870 U.S. Census, Washington Territory, Kitsap Co., Port Gamble

Laowala (fl. 1839–1848)

HBC employee, d. 1848, likely at Fort Langley, associated with:

Fort Langley (1839–1843) middleman, (1843–1844) laborer, (1844–1845) middleman, (1845–1848) laborer

Laowala, who possibly could be **Jack Lawler,** joined the HBC in 1839 from O'ahu and sailed to Fort Langley aboard the *Cadboro* in May of that year. He worked there until the spring of 1848, when he died. He may have gone to Nisqually for treatment by its head, Dr. William Fraser Tolmie; he was there in the winter of 1847–1848.

PS: HBCA SMP 14, YFSA 19–20, 24–29, FtVanSA 6–8, HL FtNisSA 5; *SS:* Anderson, *Physical Structure,* 171

Lassaro (fl. 1873)

Occupation unknown, associated with:

Victoria (1873)

On June 17, 1873, "Lassaro, a Kanaka," was charged in Victoria police court with supplying liquor to Indians and fined $20.

PPS: "Police Court," *Colonist,* June 18, 1873

Lawler, Jack (fl. 1834–1837)

CRFTC employee, associated with:

ship *May Dacre* (1834) passenger
CRFTC brigade (1834) member
Forts William and Hall (1835–1837) laborer
Columbia Department (1837) laborer

Jack Lawler was one of twenty men recruited for Nathaniel J. Wyeth's CRFTC in 1834 and among the dozen who deserted in November of the same year on the way to Fort Hall. On March 12, 1835, Wyeth found seven of his runaway Hawaiians, including Lawler, at

Fort Vancouver. He rejoined Wyeth, spent time at Fort William, and returned to Fort Hall later that year. He worked there until October 1837, when his account was settled by the HBC. What he did next is unknown.

PS: OHS FtHallAB, CRFTCCB; SS: Beidleman, "Fort Hall," 238

Leapelaule (fl. 1859)

Occupation unknown, associated with:

Victoria area (1859)

Nothing is known of Leapelaule other than his burial in Victoria on May 12, 1859.

PS: BCA VS-StAndC

Leno (fl. 1863)

Laborer, associated with:

Port Gamble (1863) sawmill worker

Leno and four others were contracted in Honolulu on July 8, 1863, by the agent of Puget Mill Co. to work at its sawmill for $10 per month with a $20 advance. It is uncertain how long he did so.

PS: HSA Seamen

Levi (fl. 1863)

Laborer, associated with:

Port Gamble (1863) sawmill worker

Levi was one of five men contracted in Honolulu on July 8, 1863, by the agent of Puget Mill Co. to work at its sawmill for $10 per month with a $20 advance. It is uncertain how long he did so.

PS: HSA Seamen

Lewis (fl. 1835)

CRFTC employee, d. June 9, 1835, in Columbia River, associated with:

ship *May Dacre* (1835) passenger
Fort William (1835) laborer

Lewis was among thirty Hawaiians, six with wives in tow, who joined Nathaniel J. Wyeth's CRFTC in early 1835. He drowned on June 9 in the Columbia River.

PS: OHS FtHallAB, CRFTCCB

Lewis, Charles (fl. 1835)

CRFTC employee, d. June 9, 1835, in Columbia River, associated with:

ship *May Dacre* (1835) passenger
Fort William (1835) laborer

Charles Lewis was among thirty Hawaiians, six with wives in tow, who joined Nathaniel J. Wyeth's CRFTC in early 1835. He drowned on June 9 in the Columbia River.

PS: OHS FtHallAB, CRFTCCB

Lewis, James (fl. 1881–1882)

Fisherman, b. ca. 1846, associated with:

New Westminster area (1881–1882) fisherman

Described as a Kanaka born on the Sandwich Islands, James Lewis was twice sent to jail in New Westminster. In 1881 he was sentenced to one month's hard labor for selling liquor to Indians, in 1882 six months of hard labor for the same offense.

PPS: British Columbia, Superintendent of Police, *Annual Report,* 1881, 1882

Likē [variation: **Like Taharnai**] (fl. 1844–1853)

HBC employee, b. ca. 1825, associated with:

Fort Vancouver (1844–1846) laborer
Fort Colvile (1846–1849) laborer, (1849–1850) servant
Fort Vancouver (1850–1851) laborer
Fort Colvile (1851–1853) laborer

Likē joined the HBC from Oʻahu in 1844. He worked mainly in the Fort Vancouver/ Fort Colvile area. In 1846, the cost of one barrel of salmon was deducted in Honolulu, probably meant as a family gift. In the 1850 Clark Co. Census, he acquired the surname of Taharnai and was living with **Joseph Taharnai**, two years older and likely a brother. In outfit 1851–1852, he was off duty three and a half months. He retired in 1853.

PS: HBCA YFSA 24–32, YFDS 20, 22, FtVanSA 9–10, SandIsAB 5, 1850 U.S. Census, Oregon, Clark Co.

Little (fl. 1835)

CRFTC employee. d. ca. 1835 at Fort William, associated with:

ship *May Dacre* (1835) passenger
Fort William (1835) laborer

Little was among thirty Hawaiians, six accompanied by their wives, who joined Nathaniel J. Wyeth's CRFTC in early 1835. He died at Fort William, likely in 1835.

PS: OHS FtHallAB, CRFTCCB

Lohiau (fl. 1840–1842)

HBC employee, d. June 1, 1842, at Fort Vancouver, associated with:

Fort Vancouver (1840–1841) middleman
Fort Vancouver general charges (1841–1842) middleman

Lohiau joined the HBC in Oʻahu in 1840. His contract was to have ended in 1843, but he died at Fort Vancouver, where he worked, on June 1, 1842. His wages were paid to his relatives in Hawaiʻi.

PS: HBCA YFSA 20, 22, FtVanSA 6–7, SandIsAB 3

Long, Ira [variation: **Jo Long**] (fl. 1834)

CRFTC employee, d. November 1834, at Walla Walla, associated with:

ship *May Dacre* (1834) passenger
CRFTC employee (1834) member

Ira Long joined Nathaniel J. Wyeth's CRFTC in Hawaiʻi in 1834. After coming to the Columbia he struck out on a brigade under Joseph Thing toward Fort Hall. In early November, because Long became sick and was suspected of being mentally deranged, he was given tea and other luxuries. On November 23, he disappeared and reportedly died at Walla Walla.

PS: OHS FtHallAB, CRFTCCB; *PPS:* Wyeth, *Correspondence,* 235–239, 249–250

Long, Joseph (fl. 1835–1844)

HBC/PSAC employee, associated with:

Fort Vancouver (1835–1836) laborer
Fort McLoughlin (1836–1840) middleman
PSAC (1840–1841) laborer
Cowlitz farm (1841–1842) middleman, (1842–1844) laborer

Joseph Long joined the HBC from Oʻahu in 1835. He began work in the Columbia on October 12, 1835, and was employed at various coastal forts for the next ten years. He worked until November 12, 1844, at which point he returned to Oʻahu, where he received his final wages on December 31.

PS: HBCA YFSA 15, 19–20, 24, YFDS 6–7, 15, FtVanSA 3–8, SandIsAB 3

Lons, Joseph (fl. 1870s–1878)

Millhand, b. ca. 1839, d. May 19, 1878, in New Westminster, associated with:

Puget Sound (1870s) sawmill worker
Burrard Inlet (1878) sawmill worker

Described as born in the Sandwich Islands, Joseph Lons worked as a millhand on Puget Sound before moving north to Burrard Inlet. He was unsuccessfully treated in the Royal Columbian Hospital in New Westminster on May 15, 1878, for phthisis and died four days later.

PS: BCA PR-RoyalCol

Lowpirani (fl. 1840–1841)

HBC employee, associated with:

Fort Taku (1840–1841) middleman
Fort Vancouver (1841) middleman

Lowpirani joined the HBC from Oʻahu in 1840 and began his career at the lonely northern outpost of Fort Taku, at the end of Taku harbor. He worked there for a little more than one year, until November 20, 1841, when he returned to Oʻahu. He did so early, for his contract was to have ended in 1843.

PS: HBCA YFSA 20–21, FtVanSA 6–7, YFDS 12

Luokaha (fl. 1863–1864)

Laborer, associated with:

Alberni (1863–1864) sawmill worker

Luokaha and six others were contracted in Honolulu on September 23, 1863, by the agent of Alberni Mill Co. to work for $10 per month with a $20 advance. The same day they left for Victoria on the *Alberni*. On December 22, 1864, all of the men, except for **Kealili** who ran away, arrived back in Honolulu from Alberni on the ship *Buena Vista*.

PS: HSA Seamen, Passenger

Maalo [variations: **Marro, Malo**] (fl. 1844–1850)

HBC/PSAC employee, associated with:

Willamette (1844–1847) laborer
Cowlitz farm (1847–1849) laborer
Fort Victoria (1849–1850) laborer

Maalo joined the HBC from Oʻahu in 1844 and began his career in the Willamette area. He spent two outfits on the Cowlitz farm before moving north to Victoria in 1849. He deserted from Fort Victoria in April 1850, and has not been traced after that.

PS: HBCA YFSA 24–30, YFDS 16, FtVanSA 9, HL FtNisPJ 6; *PPS:* Robert, "Round Hand"

Maayo, Joseph [variations: **Mayayo, Maaye, Mayou, Mayo Pupu**] (1826–1915)

HBC employee, of mixed descent, b. ca. 1826 at Fort Langley to Peeopeeoh and Catherine, associated with:

Fort Langley (1847–1849) apprentice laborer
New Caledonia (1849–1851) laborer, (1851–1852) boute
Fort Langley (1853–1856) laborer, (1856–1860) cooper
Various Fraser Valley locations (1860–1915) farmer and laborer

Joseph Maayo, the son of longtime HBC employee **Peeopeeoh**, was born and raised, along with sisters Algace / Paiwa and Sophie and brother **Henry**, at the first site of Fort Langley. He was about twenty-one years old when he signed on with the HBC at Fort Langley on November 1, 1847, and probably worked alongside his father for the next two years. After spending three years in New Caledonia, plus a year unaccounted for, Maayo returned to Fort Langley in 1853, where he worked at the cooperage all year round with Orkneyman William Cromarty and fellow Hawaiians **Ohia** and **Peter Ohule** making kegs, barrels, and vats for salt salmon.

Joseph Maayo retired after 1860. Along with his father and brothers-in-law **Peter Ohule** and **Ohia,** Maayo preempted land across the Fraser River on the north side. He registered the land as a crown grant in 1883. In 1915, Joseph Maayo was apparently living on an Indian reserve in the Fraser Valley and still fishing. The date of his death has not been traced.

Joseph's wife was Mary Nevnartnart (ca. 1843–?), a Native woman from the Fort Langley area. Two children were François (1867–?) and Stephen (1872–?). Other children may have been Nancy (ca. 1865–?), Matilda (ca. 1870–?), Sophia (ca. 1878–?), and Mary (ca. 1881–?).

PS: HBCA YFSA 27–32, YFDS 18, 22, FtVicSA 1–7, OblH Fraser; *SS:* Laing, *Colonial Farm Settlers,* 99; Lugrin, *Pioneer Women,* 107; Morton, *Fort Langley,* 264

Mackaina [variation: **Makaine Owyhee**] (fl. 1817–1837)

NWC / HBC employee, b. ca. 1796, associated with:

Columbia River area (1817–1822) laborer
Columbia Department (1822–1823) laborer
Fort George [Astoria] (1823–1825) laborer
Columbia Department (1825–1826) laborer
Fort Vancouver (1826–1836) laborer

Mackaina joined the fur trade in 1817 and continued on with the HBC after the coalition with the NWC. He worked mainly around Fort Vancouver. At the end of his employment term, he was listed as returning to Oʻahu in 1836 on the barque *Columbia,* but likely returned and stayed in the area, for he was listed as one of those who retired in 1836–1837 but remained in the district.

Mackaina had a wife and one recorded daughter. He and Louise (?–?), a Chehalis or Chinook woman, had Therese (?–?) who married Joseph Plouf and then Baptiste Laroque. Mackaina may have attended the marriage of his daughter, Theresa, on June 17, 1839, at the Fort Vancouver church.

PS: HBCA YFSA 2–9, 11–16, FtGeo[Ast]AB 11–12, YFDS 2a, 3a–3b, 4b–7, FtVanSA 1–2, 4, BCA VS-CCC; *PPS:* Munnick, *Vancouver,* vol. 1; *SS:* Schlesser, "Kanakas," 6

Mafinoa [variation: **Rosie Mafaroni**] (fl. 1830–1839)

HBC employee, b. likely on the Society Islands, associated with:

Fort Vancouver general charges (1830–1831) middleman or laborer
Fort Langley (1831–1833) middleman or laborer
Fort Vancouver (1833–1835) middleman or laborer
attached to Jason Lee (1835–1837) laborer
Willamette mission (1837–1838) middleman
Fort Vancouver (1838–1839) middleman

Mafinoa joined the HBC in April 1830 and, in May 1833, was with William Fraser Tolmie on the Columbia River shortly after the latter's arrival in the area. On the 19th of that month, Mafinoa was left at the campsite on shore to arrange the camp, light a fire, and cook a meal for the group. In outfit 1835–1836 he was transferred to missionary Jason Lee. He returned to Fort Vancouver to work in 1838 and disappears from view a year later. Mafinoa's family, if any, has not been traced.

PS: HBCA FtVanSA 2–5, YFDS 4a–7, YFSA 11–15, 17; *PPS:* Tolmie, *Journals,* 183

Maharoui, Henry (fl. 1850)

Laborer, b. ca. 1825, associated with:

Fort Vancouver area (1850) laborer

Henry Maharoui was living in the Kanaka Village of Fort Vancouver in 1850. He was in a household with two others with the same surname, likely brothers. One of them was an HBC employee known as **Opunui,** and a second brother may have been the same person as HBC employee **Naharou.**

PS: 1850 U.S. Census, Oregon, Clark Co.

Maharoui, Kekaui (fl. 1850)

Laborer, b. ca. 1823, associated with:

Fort Vancouver area (1850) laborer

Kekaui Maharoui was living in the Kanaka Village of Fort Vancouver in 1850 in a household with two others with the same surname, likely being brothers. One of them was in HBC records as **Opunui,** and a second brother may have been the same person as HBC employee **Naharou.**

PS: 1850 U.S. Census, Oregon, Clark Co.

Mahavius (fl. 1842–1843)

HBC employee, associated with:

Fort Vancouver general charges (1842–1843) laborer

Mahavius joined the HBC from O'ahu in 1842 and worked as a laborer at Fort Vancouver. His contract ended in 1843.

PS: HBCA FtVanSA 7

Mahoe [1] (fl. 1859)

Seaman, associated with:

vessel *Koloa* (1859) seaman

Mahoe was one of five Hawaiians the Puget Mill Co. hired to man the *Koloa* leaving Honolulu for Puget Sound on April 13, 1859. The men returned on November 29, 1859, and were discharged February 11, 1860.

PS: HSA Seamen

Mahoē [2] [variations: **Mahoy, Mahoi**] (fl. 1845)

HBC employee, associated with:

   Columbia Department general charges (1845) laborer

Mahoē joined the HBC from Oʻahu on May 7, 1845, and worked until July 18 of that year, at which point he returned to Oʻahu.

PS: HBCA SandIsAB 3, 6, YFSA 25, YFDS 16, Bio

Mahoi, G. [variation: **Gabriel Maggai**] (fl. 1864–1881)

Occupation unknown, possibly d. 1881 on Salt Spring Island, associated with:

   New Westminster (1864–1866)
   Salt Spring Island (1880–1881)

A Hawaiian named as G. Mahoi was twice arrested and jailed in the gold rush boom-town of New Westminster for "selling liquor to Indians" between 1864 and 1866. He may be **Mahoy** [2] and the same person named as Gabriel Maggai who was on Salt Spring Island at least from 1880 and died there in 1881.

PS: BCA Crt-NewWest, StEdC

Mahoosh, Charles (fl. 1869)

Seaman, b. ca. 1835, associated with:

   New Westminster (1869) seaman

Described as born in the Sandwich Islands, Charles Mahoosh, or Mahusia, was treated in the Royal Columbian Hospital in New Westminster on February 26, 1869, for an inflamed knee. He was pronounced cured. He has not been subsequently traced.

PS: BCA PR-RoyalCol

Mahoosh, Levi (fl. 1866)

Laborer, b. ca. 1841, associated with:

   New Westminster (1866) packer

Described as born in the Sandwich Islands, Levi Mahoosh was treated in the Royal Columbian Hospital in New Westminster on September 4, 1866. He was pronounced cured. He has not been subsequently traced.

   Levi Mahoosh was single at the time he was treated in hospital.

PS: BCA PR-RoyalCol

Mahoui, Richard (fl. 1850)

Laborer, b. ca. 1805, associated with:

   Fort Vancouver area (1850) laborer

A forty-five-year-old Richard Mahoui (possibly a variant of Mahoy) was living in Kanaka Village near Fort Vancouver in a house with five other Hawaiians in 1850.

PS: 1850 U.S. Census, Oregon, Clark Co.

Mahow [variation: **Mahou**] (fl. 1844–1851)

HBC employee, associated with:

Willamette (1844–1846) laborer
Fort Vancouver (1846–1847) laborer
New Caledonia (1847–1849) laborer
schooner *Cadboro* (1849–1851) laborer

Mahow joined the HBC from Oʻahu in 1844 and worked at various locations over the next half dozen years. On March 1, 1848, he was mentioned in the Fort Alexandria journal: "Mahow, the Owhyhee, who is always ailing and useless for any active employment, occupied repairing saddles for the brigade." He appeared to finish working in 1851 and may have been in the area, for there was movement on his account for the next year.

PS: HBCA YFSA 24–32, FtAlex PJ 7

Mahoy [1] (fl. 1840–1844)

PSAC/HBC employee, d. November 12, 1844, likely at Cowlitz farm, associated with:

PSAC (1840–1841) laborer
Fort Vancouver (1841–1842) middleman, (1842–1844) laborer
Cowlitz farm (1844) laborer

Mahoy joined the HBC from Oʻahu in 1840 or 1841 and spent his time in the lower Columbia area as a laborer. He died in 1844 while he was working at the Cowlitz farm, probably about the time he was ready to retire to Oʻahu.

PS: HBCA YFSA 20, 23–24, FtVanSA 6–8, YFDS 17

Mahoy [2] (fl. 1848–1859)

HBC/PSAC employee, associated with:

Columbia Department general charges (1848) laborer
Fort Rupert (1849–1853) laborer
Colwood farm (1856) laborer
Victoria area PSAC farms (1856–1859) laborer

Mahoy entered the service of the HBC from Oʻahu in 1848 and began receiving his wages on July 15. He spent most of his career at Fort Rupert. He appears to have left Fort Rupert around 1853 and worked at PSAC farms in the Victoria area until at least 1859. He may be the same person as **G. Mahoi.**

Mahoy may have been the father, by a local Native woman, of Maria (ca. 1855–1937), who was, according to oral tradition, born in the vicinity of Victoria. Maria, who lived on Salt Spring and Russell islands, married first Abel Douglas (ca. 1841–1908) and then George Fisher (1865–1948).

PS: HBCA SandIsAB 7, YFSA 28–32, FtVicSA 1, YFDS 19, PSACAB 38, Bio; *SS:* Kardas, "People," 175–176; Barman, *Maria Mahoi*

Mahoy, Charley (fl. 1876–1881)

Laborer, b. ca. 1838, associated with:

New Westminster area (1876) cook
Victoria area (1878) occupation unknown
New Westminster area (1881) cook

Charley Mahoy was working as a cook in New Westminster when, on February 26, 1876, he was treated in Royal Columbian Hospital for an ulcerated leg. Mahoy had some difficulty staying out of trouble. He was discharged from his job on April 28 of the same year for an infraction of rules. In the spring of 1878, the 5 foot, 4 inch, forty-year-old Hawaiian laborer was imprisoned for one month (with home leave) for stealing and was released on June 6. No sooner was he out of jail, than he was convicted on July 12 for selling spirits to the Indians and was released in October. Charley, illiterate and a member of the Church of England, at first appeared to mend his ways, for he again got a job in New Westminster as a cook. However, in 1881 he was sentenced to three months hard labor for larceny. He has not been traced subsequently.

PS: BCA Crt-Gaols, PR-RoyalCol; *PPS:* British Columbia, Superintendent of Police, *Annual Report,* 1881

Mahoy, Jemmy [variation: **Jimmy Mahoy**] (fl. 1832–1839)

HBC employee, d. July 8, 1839, at Fort Vancouver, associated with:

Fort Vancouver (1832–1833) laborer
Fort Simpson (1833–1835) laborer
Fort Vancouver (1835–1836) laborer
Fort George [Astoria] (1836–1838) middleman or laborer
Fort Vancouver (1838–1839) middleman

Jemmy Mahoy joined the HBC in O'ahu on September 5, 1832. In outfit 1834–1835 he was disabled but nonetheless paid a relatively high wage. He worked largely at Fort Vancouver, likely as a laborer or middleman, and died there on July 8, 1839.

PS: HBCA YFSA 12–14, 19, YFDS 5a–7, 10, FtVanSA 3–5

Mahoy, William [variation: **Bill Mahoy**] (fl. 1837–1846)

HBC employee, associated with:

Fort Vancouver (1837–1838) middleman
Willamette mission (1838–1839) laborer
Fort Vancouver (1839–1841) middleman
Fort Vancouver sawmill (1842–1844) laborer
Willamette (1844–1846) laborer
Vancouver (1846) laborer

William Mahoy joined the HBC from O'ahu in July 1837 and began work at Fort Vancouver on August 10 of that year. He worked as a laborer around the Fort Vancouver area until August 6, 1846, when he returned to O'ahu.

PS: HBCA SandIsAB 1, FtVanSA 4–8, YFDS 8–9, YFSA 19–20, 22–26, Bio

Maiai, Ka Wahini [variation: **Kaivalionemakiai**] (fl. 1864)

Laborer, b. ca. 1846, associated with:

Alberni (1864) sawmill worker

Ka Wahini Maiai and three others were contracted in Honolulu on June 23, 1864, by the agent of Alberni Mill Co. to work for $10 per month with a $20 advance. Two days later, the men left Honolulu for Alberni on the schooner *Alberni.*

PS: HSA Seamen, Passenger

Maikai (fl. 1844–1849)

HBC employee, associated with:

Fort Vancouver (1844–1845) laborer
Snake party (1845–1846) goer and comer, (1846–1847) laborer
Snake Country (1847–1849) laborer

Maikai joined the HBC from Oʻahu in 1844 and worked principally with the Snake party. He deserted in 1849, likely for California and probably in the first half of the year, as he received no wages for outfit 1849–1850.

PS: HBCA YFSA 24–29, YFDS 16

Maikalua (fl. 1862)

Laborer, associated with:

> *Constitution* (1862) passenger
> Vancouver Island (1862)

Maikalua was one of eight laborers who left for Victoria on the *Constitution* on May 2, 1862. It is unclear where they were headed.

PS: HSA Passenger

Maiknihi (fl. 1870)

Laborer, b. ca. 1837, associated with:

> Port Gamble (1870) sawmill worker

At the time of the 1870 Census, Maiknihi was one of twenty-two Hawaiians working at Puget Mill at Port Gamble.

PS: 1870 U.S. Census, Washington Territory, Kitsap Co., Port Gamble

Maio, George [variation: Kanaka George] (fl. 1861–1888)

Miner, associated with:

> Rogue River Valley, Oregon (1861–1880s) miner and likely farmer
> California (1880s) occupation unknown
> Rogue River Valley, Oregon (1888) occupation unknown

George Maio, a native of the Sandwich Islands and almost certainly a gold miner, wed Susan (?–?), described as a "Squaw" of the Rogue River Tribe, in Jackson County in October 1861. The couple settled down in the area. In March 1867 "Kanaka George" was twice assessed road taxes in Jacksonville. The local newspaper recorded in May 1888 how "Kanaka George and wife have returned from Siskiyou County, California, after an absence of several years."

PS: SOHS Marriage RT, "Here and There," *Democratic Times,* May 11, 1888

Mak-ai, John H. [variation: McKay] (fl. 1881)

Laborer, b. ca. 1853, associated with:

> New Westminster area (1881) laborer

Described as born on the Sandwich Islands, John H. Mak-ai must have spent most of 1881 in the New Westminster jail. He was sentenced five times within the single year. He got 3 days for selling liquor to Indians, 3 days for being drunk and disorderly, 2 months hard labor for selling liquor to Indians, 2 months hard labor for assault, and then 14 days hard labor for assault.

PPS: British Columbia, Superintendent of Police, *Annual Report,* 1881

Makaopiopio (fl. 1858)

Occupation unknown, associated with:

> Vancouver Island (1858)

Makaopiopio was one of fourteen Hawaiians departing Honolulu for Victoria on the schooner *Alice* on June 22, 1858, enticed by the euphoria of the gold rush.

PS: HSA Passenger

Makaoura [variation: **Makouroa**] (fl. 1841–1845)

HBC employee, associated with:

Fort Vancouver (1841–1843) middleman or laborer, (1843–1844) laborer
Willamette (1844–1845) laborer
Columbia Department general charges (1845) laborer

Makaoura joined the HBC from O'ahu as a middleman in 1841 and began receiving wages on August 1 of that year. His contract ended in 1843, but he worked until July 18, 1845, when he returned to O'ahu.

PS: HBCA FtVanSA 6–7, YFDS 12, 16, YFSA 22–25

Maki, Joseph (fl. 1838–1840)

Laborer, d. August 8, 1840, associated with:

Whitman's mission (1838–1840) laborer

Members of Hiram Bingham's Honolulu congregation, Joseph Maki and his wife **Maria** were sent to assist the Whitman mission at Waiilatpu. They arrived in June 1838, after which Joseph helped to build the mission house. When the Whitmans organized the first Presbyterian church in Oregon at Waiilatpu in August 1838, the Makis were admitted as the first two members. Joseph Maki died of illness at the mission in 1840.

PS: HMCS OrMission; *SS:* Drury, *Whitman,* 208; Drury, *Spalding,* 188; Eells, *Whitman,* 118–120

Maki, Maria Keawea (fl. 1838–1841)

Laborer, associated with:

Whitman's mission (1838–1841) cook

Maria Maki came with her husband **Joseph** to the Whitman mission at Waiilatpu in June 1838. There Maria worked as a cook. When the Whitmans organized the first Presbyterian church in Oregon at Waiilatpu in August 1838, the Makis were admitted as the first two members. Maria returned home in 1841 following her husband's death.

PS: HMCS OrMission; *SS:* Drury, *Whitman,* 208; Drury, *Spalding,* 188; Eells, *Whitman,* 118–120

Makoa (fl. 1859)

Laborer, associated with:

Port Gamble (1859) sawmill worker

On November 28, 1859, Makoa arrived back in Honolulu from Teekalet on the barque *Jenny Ford.* It is unclear how long he worked at the sawmill there or how he got there.

PS: HSA Passenger

Maluae (fl. 1864)

Laborer, associated with:

Port Gamble (1864) sawmill worker

Maluae was among six men contracted in Honolulu on February 5, 1864, by the agent of Puget Mill Co. to work at its sawmill for $10 per month with a $20 advance. It is uncertain how long he did so.

PS: HSA Seamen

Mamala (fl. 1841–1845)

PSAC employee, associated with:

Cowlitz farm (1841–1842) middleman, (1842–1845) laborer

Mamala joined the PSAC from Oʻahu in 1841 on a three-year obligation and began to receive wages on July 9 of that year. He worked as a farm laborer at Cowlitz until November 12, 1844, when he returned to Oʻahu. He reenlisted again on May 7, 1845, and worked until December 10, at which point he returned to Oʻahu, where he was paid his final HBC wages.

PS: HBCA FtVanSA 6–7, YFDS 12, 17–18, YFSA 22–24, SandIsAB 3, 5

Mamuka, Jem [variations: Jim Manuka, Joseph Finmanut] (fl. 1832–1847)

HBC employee, b. ca. 1807, d. December 19, 1847, at Fort Vancouver, associated with:

Fort Simpson naval service (1832–1834) seaman
Fort Simpson (1834–1835) middleman or laborer
Fort Vancouver (1835–1836) laborer or middleman
South party (1836–1842) middleman or laborer
Snake party (1842–1843) middleman
Fort Vancouver (1843–1846) laborer
Fort George [Astoria] (1846–1847) laborer, (1847–1847) Indian trade

Jem Mamuka joined the HBC in Oʻahu on September 5, 1832, about age twenty-five, and left for the Columbia, where he was to remain for the next fifteen years. He worked at the original Nass River site of Fort Simpson and assisted in the move to the new site on December 1, 1834. During outfit 1834–1835, he was disabled but soon back at work in the Fort Vancouver area. Some time in December 1847, while he was working there, he caught the measles and on December 18 was baptized. He died the next day and was buried under the name Joseph Finmanut by the Catholic priests, no doubt to pave his way into the Christian afterlife.

PS: HBCA YFDS 5a–7, 17–18, YFSA 12–15, 19–20, 23–26, FtSimp[N]PJ 3, FtVanSA 3–7, BCA PR-Lowe; *PPS:* Munnick, *Vancouver,* vol. 2

Mana (fl. 1847)

Servant, b. ca. 1834, associated with:

Columbia area (1847)

A young Hawaiian named as Mana left Portland on the barque *Toulon* for Honolulu, arriving December 16, 1847. The barque tended to have one or more Hawaiian servants on its trips between the Pacific Northwest and Honolulu.

PS: HSA Passenger

Manenē (fl. 1845–1849)

HBC employee, associated with:

Fort Vancouver (1845–1849) laborer

Manenē joined the HBC in Oʻahu in 1845 and worked at Fort Vancouver as a laborer. His contract was to have ended in 1850, but he deserted on July 20, 1849, likely for the gold fields of California.

PS: HBCA YFSA 25–29, YFDS 20

Manero (fl. 1830–1833)

HBC employee, associated with:

Fort Vancouver general charges (1830–1831) laborer, (1831–1833) laborer

Manero joined the HBC in April 1830. He spent his entire time at Fort Vancouver and left for his return voyage to Oʻahu on November 1, 1833.

PS: HBCA FtVanSA 2, YFDS 4a–5a, YFSA 11–14

Maniela [variation: **Maniala**] (fl. 1841–1844)

PSAC employee, associated with:

Cowlitz farm (1841–1844) middleman

Maniela joined the PSAC in 1841 and worked at the Cowlitz farm as a middleman. His contract ended in 1844.

PS: HBCA FtVanSA 6–7

Maniso (fl. 1830)

HBC employee, associated with:

brig *Isabella* (1830) passenger
Fort Langley (1830) laborer
schooner *Vancouver* (1830) passenger

Maniso, who was subject to seizures and wandering, was unfit for the fur trade due to his potential to destabilize relations with the Native peoples. Consequently, he had to return to the Hawaiian Islands soon after his arrival. He signed on with a large group of Hawaiians that came on the *Isabella.* After going to Fort Vancouver he made his way with a work party to Fort Langley, where, among other things, he was to cut up and prepare fish for export. However, on August 31, when he went down to the river to wash up after cleaning fish, he had a recurrence of his seizure disorder and wandered off in a fourteen-day episode of confusion and mayhem. During this time, stories abounded that he may have been done in by the Natives, as his clothes reappeared intact. Although somewhat skeptical of the story of murder, the Fort Langley managers prepared punitive action but, on the fourteenth day, Maniso emerged from the forest, a naked and starving walking skeleton. According to him, he had had a seizure and in the confusion had met Natives who robbed him of his clothes and generally maltreated him. Because of the potential for further damage, Maniso was sent back to the Sandwich Islands on the HBC vessel, *Vancouver.*

PS: HBCA Log of *Isabella; PPS:* McDonald, *Blessed Wilderness,* 82–85, 90–91; Maclachlan, *Fort Langley Journals,* 154–159

Manno [variation: **Mano**] (fl. 1844–1847)

Servant / HBC employee, b. ca. 1824, associated with:

barque *Toulon* (1844) servant
Fort Vancouver (1845–1847) laborer
barque *Columbia* (1847) passenger

A young Hawaiian named Mano worked as a servant on the barque *Toulon* traveling from the Columbia River to Honolulu, arriving on March 15, 1844. The barque tended to have one or more Hawaiian servants on its trips between the Pacific Northwest and Honolulu. The trip may have whetted his appetite for adventure. The same man, or another by the same name, joined the HBC from Oʻahu on May 7, 1845, for three years. He worked at Fort Vancouver as a laborer until July 6, 1847, at which point he returned to Oʻahu.

Manno had a wife who either came with him from the Islands or he encountered in the Pacific Northwest. She returned with him to Honolulu, arriving August 2, 1847.

PS: HBCA SandIsAB 3, YFSA 24–27, YFDS 18, HSA Passenger

Manoa (fl. 1858)

Occupation unknown, associated with:

British Columbia (1858)

Manoa was one of six Hawaiians to whom the governor of Oʻahu gave permission in May 1858 to proceed to the British Columbia gold rush. He, and likely also his wife, left Honolulu for Vancouver Island on the schooner *Alice* on May 19, 1858. They had deck passage. Manoa has not been traced further.

PS: HSA Passenger, Victoria

Manoa, Joe (fl. 1832–1850)

HBC employee, associated with:

brig *Lama* (1832–1833) seaman
Fort Simpson naval service (1833–1834) seaman
Fort Vancouver (1834–1836) middleman or laborer
steamer *Beaver* (1836–1837) middleman
Snake party (1837–1840) middleman
Fort Vancouver (1841–1842) middleman
Snake party (1842–1845) laborer, (1845–1846) goer and comer, (1846–1847) laborer
Fort Vancouver (1847–1849) laborer

Joe Manoa joined the service of the HBC in Oʻahu on September 5, 1832, and for the next eight years worked both on land and on various coastal vessels. He returned to Oʻahu on November 15, 1840, but reenlisted again and began receiving wages on July 9, 1841. His contract ended in 1850, but he received no wages for outfit 1849–1850, only accruing a small debt and a notation that he had done "nothing all the year." There was action on his account for the next two years, but his movements during these years have not been found.

PS: HBCA SMP 14, YFDS 5a–8, 11–12, 16, 20, YFSA 12–14, 19–20, 22–29, 31–32, FtVanSA 3–7

Manoui (fl. 1870)

Laborer, b. ca. 1843, associated with:

Port Gamble (1870) sawmill worker

At the time of the 1870 Census, Manoui was one of twenty-two Hawaiians working at Puget Mill at Port Gamble.

PS: 1870 U.S. Census, Washington Territory, Kitsap Co., Port Gamble

Manuhu (fl. 1859)

Seaman, associated with:

vessel *Koloa* (1859) seaman

Manuhu was one of five Hawaiians the Puget Mill Co. hired to man the *Koloa* leaving Honolulu for Puget Sound on April 13, 1859. The men returned on November 29, 1859, and were discharged February 11, 1860.

PS: HSA Seamen

Manuku (fl. 1859)

Laborer, associated with:

Port Gamble (1859) likely sawmill worker

On November 28, 1859, Manuku arrived back in Honolulu from Teekalet on the barque *Jenny Ford.* It is unclear how long, or if, he worked at the sawmill there.

PS: HSA Passenger

Mark (fl. 1860)

Laborer, b. ca. 1830, associated with:

Fort Vancouver area (1860) laborer

Mark was one of the many Hawaiians living in Kanaka Village in 1860. Like the others, he was not specifically employed by any one group and was likely a casual laborer.

PS: 1860 U.S. Census, Washington Territory, Clark Co.

Marks (fl. 1860)

Laborer, b. ca. 1820, associated with:

Fort Vancouver area (1860) laborer

Marks, along with several Hawaiians and their families, were living in the Fort Vancouver–Kanaka Village area in 1860. He may have been employed casually for what remained of the HBC interests in the area or for the nearby U.S. military post.

PS: 1860 U.S. Census, Washington Territory, Clark Co.

Markus, Harry [variation: **Henry Markus**] (fl. 1830–1831)

HBC employee, associated with:

Fort Vancouver general charges (1830–1831)
Fort Vancouver (1831) laborer
barque *Ganymede* (1831) passenger

Harry Markus joined the HBC in early 1830. He was discharged to Oʻahu on November 1, 1831, sailing on the *Ganymede.*

PS: HBCA FtVanSA 2, YFDS 4a–4b, YFSA 11

Marouna [variations: **Marrouna, Marruna, Morrouna**] (fl. 1817–1838)

NWC/HBC employee, b. ca. 1799, d. August 28, 1838, likely at Fort Vancouver, associated with:

ship *Columbia* (1817) passenger
Pacific slopes (1817–1821) employee
Columbia Department (1821–1823) laborer
Fort George [Astoria] (1823–1825) laborer
Columbia Department (1825–1826) laborer
Fort Vancouver (1826–1830) middleman, Indian trade (1830–1831) middleman
barque *Ganymede* (1831) passenger
Fort Vancouver Indian trade (1831–1836) middleman, laborer, sawmill worker

Fort George [Astoria] (1836–1837) middleman or laborer
Fort Vancouver (1838) laborer

Marouna joined the fur trade in 1817 at the age of eighteen, becoming one of the many Sandwich Islanders, almost all unnamed, who worked for the NWC. He joined the HBC at amalgamation, and on October 9, 1825, he together with **Harry Bell Noah, James Coah, Tourawhyheine,** and **Kaharrow,** confessed to having stolen blankets from the trade goods of the *William & Ann.* He was discharged to Oʻahu on November 1, 1831, sailing on the *Ganymede.* He soon returned to work at Fort Vancouver in the Indian trade and died at Fort Vancouver on August 22, 1838.

Marouna and an unidentified Native woman were the parents of **Mungo Marouna** (ca. 1827–?).

PS: HBCA YFSA 2–9, 11, 13–15, 18, FtGeo[Ast]AB 11–12, YFDS 2a, 3a–7, FtVanAB 10, SA 1–6, CB 9; *PPS:* Macdonald, *Blessed Wilderness,* 29

Marouna, Mungo [variation: **Mongo, Mevway**] (1827–1840s)

HBC employee, of mixed descent, b. ca. 1827 to Marrouna and an unnamed Native woman, associated with:

attached to Narcissa Whitman (1837–1841) child
Fort Vancouver (1841–1842) middleman, (1842–1843) laborer
Fort Nez Perces (1843–1845) laborer, (1845–1847) interpreter
Willamette (1847–1848) interpreter and guide

Mungo Marouna was born in about 1827 of Hawaiian father **Marouna** and an unidentified Native mother, at Fort Vancouver, where he appears to have spent much of the first eleven years of his life. A year before his father died, in August 1838, young Mongo was sent to the Waiilatpu mission and came under the care of Narcissa Whitman, who called him Mongo Mevway. When he was approximately of age in 1840, he was hired by the HBC and worked across the Columbia region until 1847, when he left the company. From 1847, he acted as an interpreter and guide, and on April 3, 1847, as a guide for Thomas Lowe's trip to York Factory. After the trip, he moved into the house of Charles Plante in the Willamette Valley, where he acted as an interpreter for the U.S. Army.

Mongo partnered early with an unnamed Native wife. Together they had Elisabeth (1843/46–1848).

PS: HBCA YFSA 20, 22, 24–27, FtVanSA 6-7, BCA PR-Lowe; *PPS:* Munnick, *St. Paul,* vol. 1; *SS: Transactions,* 108; Hulbert, *Whitman,* vol. 2: 237, 3: 158

Marro (fl. 1841–1850)

HBC employee, associated with:

Cowlitz farm (1841–1842) middleman, (1842–1844) laborer
Columbia Department (1845–1846) laborer
Cowlitz farm (1846–1850) laborer

Marro, from Oʻahu, joined the HBC in 1841. He worked at the Cowlitz farm until November 15, 1843, when he returned to Oʻahu. He reenlisted, reappearing in the Columbia in outfit 1845–1846 on a contract that ended in 1850. He may have stayed in the area, for there was movement on his accounts for the next two years.

PS: HBCA FtVanSA 6–7, YFSA 22–23, 25–32, YFDS 14

Marrow (fl. 1822–1823)

HBC employee, associated with:

Columbia Department (1822–1823) laborer

Marrow worked for the HBC around 1822 and, in outfit 1822–1823, returned to the Sandwich Islands.

PS: HBCA FtGeo[Ast]AB 10

Martin, Harry (fl. 1835–1837)

CRFTC/HBC employee, associated with:

ship *May Dacre* (1835) passenger
Fort William (1835) laborer
Forts Hall and William (1835–1836) laborer
Columbia Department (1836–1837) part-time HBC laborer

Harry Martin was one of thirty Hawaiians, six with wives in tow, who joined Nathaniel J. Wyeth's CRFTC in early 1835. He worked at both Forts William and Hall and in 1836–1837 did part-time work for the HBC, probably in the Fort Vancouver area. In outfit 1836–1837 he received half the wages of the laborer, indicating he was discharged partway through his employment. It is unclear precisely where he was working, whether in O'ahu or on the Northwest Coast.

PS: OHS FtHallAB, HBCA FtVanSA 3–4, YFDS 7, YFSA 16

Mataturay, John [variation: **Mariano Modetroy**] (fl. 1788–1790)

Maritime fur trade cabin boy, b. on Ni'ihau, d. December 3, 1790, on the west coast of Vancouver Island, associated with:

ship *Princess Royal* (1788–1789) servant
snow *Argonaut* (1789–1790) captain's servant
San Blas (1789–1790) prisoner
snow *Argonaut* (1790) captain's servant

John Mataturay got caught in the colonial struggle between Spain and Britain. Born the son of a Ni'ihau chief, John Mataturay appeared to voluntarily join Captain Charles Duncan of the *Princess Royal* on March 18, 1788, when the British ship stopped on the island on its way to the Northwest Coast. That October, Mataturay returned to Ni'ihau. He sailed on to Macao, where he joined another British ship, the *Argonaut,* as a servant to Captain James Colnett.

When the *Argonaut* reached the Northwest Coast, it was seized by the Spaniards, and Mataturay was taken with the crews of the *Argonaut* and *Princess Royal* to San Blas in New Spain [Mexico]. There the Sandwich Islander, who was not under regular contract, was singled out from the rest of the prisoners and became the subject of much correspondence between the viceroy of New Spain and Colnett. The Spanish claimed that Mataturay (Mariano Madetroy in the Spanish records), who made it all the way to Mexico City, had been taken by Colnett and the British under duress and so was to remain with the Spanish. This may have been a ploy to use the Islander to extend colonial claims to the Sandwich Islands. Mataturay was eventually released to Colnett and sailed north on the *Argonaut.* While the vessel was trading for furs on the east coast of Vancouver Island in December 1790, John Mataturay died of unstated causes.

PS: ArdeInd Martinez; *PPS:* "Spanish Balances" in Colnett, *Journal; SS:* Howay, "Hawaiian Islands"; Kuykendall, "Hawaiian"

Matte (fl. 1830–1836)

HBC employee, b. ca. 1799, associated with:

Fort Vancouver general charges (1830–1831)
Fort Simpson (1831–1834) middleman or laborer

Fort McLoughlin (1834–1836) middleman or laborer
steamer *Beaver* (1836) seaman

Matte joined the HBC from Oʻahu in April 1830 and worked in the northern posts of Fort Simpson and Fort McLoughlin and also on the steamer *Beaver*. He appears to have returned to Oʻahu in December 1836, although the records for 1837–1838 stated that he remained in the district.

PS: HBCA YFDS 4a–5b, 6–7, YFSA 11–16, FtVanSA 2–3

Mau (fl. 1858)

Occupation unknown, associated with:

Portland (1858)

Mau traveled from Honolulu for Portland on the schooner *San Diego* on July 13, 1858, perhaps enticed by the euphoria of the gold rush.

PS: HSA Passenger

Mauna (fl. 1862)

Occupation unknown, d. June 3, 1862, in Victoria area, associated with:

Victoria area (1862)

Nothing is known about Mauna, except for his death as an Anglican on June 3, 1862, in the Victoria area.

PS: BCA VS-CCC

Mayar (fl. 1866)

Farmer, b. ca. 1838, associated with:

Fraser Valley (1866) farmer

Described as born in the Sandwich Islands, Mayar was treated in the Royal Columbian Hospital in New Westminster on September 9, 1866, for a bowel obstruction. He was pronounced cured. He has not been subsequently traced.

Mayar was single at the time he was treated in hospital.

PS: BCA PR-RoyalCol

Meheula [variation: Miheula] (fl. 1845–1848)

HBC employee, associated with:

Fort Vancouver (1845–1848) laborer

Meheula joined the HBC from Oʻahu in 1845 and appears to have spent his time working at Fort Vancouver. He was likely, therefore, a resident of the adjacent Kanaka Village. He returned to Oʻahu, where he received his final HBC wages in July 1848.

PS: HBCA YFSA 25–29, SandIsAB 7

Mikapako [variations: Kikapako, Mikabako, Mikker Barkis] (fl. 1844–1849)

Servant / HBC employee, associated with:

Dr. I. L. Babcock (1844) servant
Fort Vancouver (1844–1845) laborer
barque *Vancouver* (1845) laborer
Fort Vancouver (1846–1849) laborer
barque *Columbia* (1849) laborer or passenger

On March 28, 1844, in Honolulu, "a native Hawaiian" named Mikapako agreed to accompany American medical doctor Ira Leonard Babcock, then on a brief visit to Hawaiʻi, to

Oregon for two years as a servant in exchange for his passage, food, lodging, $72 per year, and passage home. Mikapako signed the agreement with a sure hand, indicating he was literate. In November of that year, when Babcock prepared to depart the Oregon Territory with his family to take on a job with the U.S. Army, he struck an agreement with the HBC for Mikapako to transfer to the company. Mikabako began receiving HBC wages at Fort Vancouver on November 13, 1844. He worked on the barque *Vancouver* as well as at Fort Vancouver as a laborer until October 31, 1849, when he returned to O'ahu aboard the barque *Columbia*. He was paid his final HBC wages in Honolulu and from that point disappears from the records.

PS: HSA, 402-10-248, HBCA log of *Vancouver,* YFSA 24–30, YFDS 15, 20, SandIsAB 10; *PPS:* McLoughlin, *Business Correspondence,* 111, 120

Mikiloah (fl. 1841–1844)

HBC employee, associated with:

California estate (1841–1842) middleman, (1842–1844) laborer

Mikiloah, from O'ahu, began work with the HBC on July 9, 1841, at its California operations. His contract ended in 1844, at which point he was discharged in O'ahu, possibly as late as 1845.

PS: HBCA FtVanSA 6–7, YFDS 12, YFSA 22–25, SandIsAB 5

Moa (fl. 1825)

Maritime fur trade seaman, associated with:

brig *Convoy* (1825) seaman

Moa shipped aboard the brig *Convoy* at O'ahu after it arrived at that island on March 16, 1825, to unload cargo and take on supplies for the Northwest Coast. After sailing April 1 as a laborer, Moa and the vessel traded along the coast for a season, returning to Honolulu on November 2. It is not known whether he continued to sail with the *Convoy*.

PS: BCA PR-*Convoy; SS:* Howay, "List"

Moka (fl. 1862)

Cowboy, associated with:

Victoria (1862)

Moka, who described himself as a Hawaiian "vaquero" or cowboy, departed Victoria on the *Lady Young,* which reached Honolulu on September 9, 1862.

PS: HSA Passenger

Mokowhehe (fl. 1841–1846)

HBC employee, associated with:

Fort Vancouver (1841–1842) middleman or laborer
Fort Langley (1842–1843) middleman, (1843–1846) laborer

Mokowhehe joined the HBC from O'ahu in 1841 and began receiving wages on July 9 of that year. He worked at two forts in the Columbia area until November 30, 1846, when he returned to O'ahu.

PS: HBCA FtVanSA 6–7, YFDS 12, 17, YFSA 22–26

Moku (fl. 1837–1850)

HBC employee, d. ca. November 1850, likely in Snake Country, associated with:

Fort Vancouver (1837–1838) middleman
South party (1838–1839) middleman

Fort Vancouver (1839–1840) middleman
South party (1840–1842) middleman
Snake party (1842–1843) laborer
Fort Vancouver (1845–1847) laborer
Snake Country (1847–1850) laborer

Moku first joined the HBC in Oʻahu in July 1837 and began work at Fort Vancouver on August 10. He disappeared from the records in 1843 and likely returned to Oʻahu. He reenlisted on May 7, 1845, for three years. Moku died around the end of November 1850 and was probably buried in the Snake River area.

PS: HBCA SandIsAB 1, 3, YFSA 20, 22–23, 25–31, YFDS 8, 21, FtVanSA 4–7

Molaly, James [variation: **Molally**] (fl. 1850–1851)

HBC employee, b. ca. 1830, associated with:

Fort Vancouver (1850–1851) carpenter

James Molaly worked for the HBC at Fort Vancouver as a carpenter. His contract ended in 1851 and on November 1 of that year, he retired from the service. He remained in the area but has not been traced subsequent to 1851.

PS: HBCA YFSA 30–32, YFDS 22, FtVanSA 9, 1850 U.S. Census, Oregon, Clark Co.

Momuto, George (fl. 1831–1833)

HBC seaman, associated with:

brig *Cadboro* (1831) seaman
Naval Department (1831–1832) seaman
Fort Simpson naval service (1832–1833) seaman
brig *Dryad* (1833) passenger

George Momuto was engaged by the HBC on June 16, 1831, in Oʻahu as a seaman for work in coastal shipping. He worked until November 1, 1833, returning to Oʻahu as a passenger on the brig *Dryad.*

PS: HBCA SMP 14, YFSA 11–14, YFDS 4b–5b

Moo (fl. 1837–1844)

HBC employee, associated with:

Fort Vancouver (1837) middleman
Willamette mission (1837–1838) middleman
Fort Vancouver (1838–1840) middleman
Columbia Department (1841–1842) freeman
Fort Vancouver (1844) middleman

Moo signed on with the HBC in July 1837 in Oʻahu. He began work, likely at Fort Vancouver, on August 10, 1837, and, on November 12 was transferred to Jason Lee's Methodist mission in the Willamette Valley. He returned to Fort Vancouver the following outfit to work. His contract ended in 1840, and he appeared to be a freeman in 1841–1842 with no specific assignment. He briefly returned to Fort Vancouver, where he worked from July 12 to November 12, 1844. At that point he returned to Oʻahu.

PS: HBCA SandIsAB 1, FtVanSA 4–7, YFSA 17, YFDS 15

Moolah, J. (fl. 1850)

Raftsman, b. ca. 1824, associated with:

Oregon City (1850) raftsman

J. Moolah was living with **Susanna Moolah,** probably his wife, in Oregon City in 1850. Also in the house were **Cho, Calay,** and **Ki-o-ne,** also born in the Sandwich Islands.

PS: 1850 U.S. Census, Oregon, Clackamas Co.

Moolah, Susanna (fl. 1850)

Raftsman, b. ca. 1826, associated with:

Oregon City (1850) raftsman

Susanna Moolah was almost certainly the wife of **J. Moolah.** Like him, she had the occupation of raftsman.

PS: 1850 U.S. Census, Oregon, Clackamas Co.

Moreno, Thomas [variation: **Tom. Moreno**] (fl. 1832–1839)

HBC employee, b. ca. 1807, associated with:

Fort Vancouver (1832–1835) laborer
barque *Ganymede* (1835) passenger or crewman
Fort Vancouver general charges (1836) laborer
steamer *Beaver* (1836–1837) seaman
barque *Nereide* (1837–1838) middleman
Fort Vancouver (1838–1839) middleman
barque *Vancouver* (1839) passenger

Thomas Moreno signed on with the HBC in Oʻahu on September 6, 1832, and worked for the next half dozen years on coastal vessels. He went to Oʻahu on the *Ganymede* on October 3, 1835, and was reengaged at Oʻahu in January 1836. His contract came to an end in 1839, and he left on November 15, 1839, on the *Vancouver* for Oʻahu, where he was discharged.

PS: HBCA YFSA 12–15, 19, YFDS 5a–6, 10, FtVanSA 3–6, SMP 14

Morton, Benjamin (fl. 1868)

Seaman, b. ca. 1842, associated with:

Victoria area (1868)

Although Benjamin Morton had an anglicized name, his physical description in police records indicate that he was Hawaiian or of mixed descent, being born in the "Sandwich Islands." Roman Catholic by religion and having a "stout" build, Morton served six hours in a Victoria jail on October 12, 1868, for being drunk and disorderly. He then likely returned to his ship and sailed away.

PS: BCA Crt-Gaols

Moses [1] (fl. 1839)

HBC employee, associated with:

Fort Vancouver (1839) middleman
barque *Vancouver* (1839) passenger

Moses joined the HBC from Oʻahu in 1839 on a one-year contract. He worked for one outfit at Fort Vancouver and left on the *Vancouver* on November 16, 1839, for Oʻahu, where he was discharged.

PS: HBCA YFSA 19, FtVanSA 6, SMP 14

Moses [2] [variation: **Kanak Moses**] (fl. 1889–1891)

Farmer, b. ca. 1834, associated with:

Victoria (1889)

New Westminster (1889–1891) prisoner

Described as 5 feet, 3 inches tall, 174 pounds, and born in the Sandwich Islands, Moses was on October 8, 1889, in Victoria sentenced to two years' imprisonment in New Westminster Penitentiary for "maliciously wounding." By the time he was discharged on July 7, 1891, his weight had fallen to 136 pounds. He was illiterate both when he went into prison and when he was discharged. His record characterized him as intemperate. He has not been subsequently traced.

Moses was single at the time he was imprisoned.

PS: NAC Penitentiary

Moss, Joseph (fl. 1871)

Seaman, b. ca. 1835, associated with:

Victoria area (1871)

Joseph Moss, a seaman, was designated "Kanaka" in the police records of British Columbia. The slightly built, 5 foot, 2 inch, twenty-five-year-old Catholic Hawaiian had been caught selling "spirits to the Indians" in the Victoria area and, on December 28, 1871, was sentenced to three months in prison.

PS: BCA Crt-Gaols

Moumouto [variations: **Moumouton, Monmouton**] (fl. 1817–1851)

NWC/HBC employee, b. ca. 1797, associated with:

Columbia River area (1817–1823) laborer
Fort George [Astoria] (1823–1825) laborer
Columbia Department (1825–1826) sawyer
Fort Vancouver (1826–1835) sawyer, (1835–1837) middleman or laborer,
    (1837–1845) laborer, (1845–1847) sawyer
Willamette (1847–1848) freeman
Fort Vancouver (1848–1850) laborer

Moumouto was hired on by the NWC from the Hawaiian Islands in 1817. Early on he worked with the Fort George store but much of his time was spent at Fort Vancouver as a sawyer, and he probably lived in the fort's Kanaka Village. He retired in 1850 and disappeared from the records in 1851, for there was no movement on his account after that time. He may have drifted off to the Indian village of his wife as did other Hawaiians who did not continue employment with the company, after it moved its head of operations north to Fort Victoria.

Moumouton had one recorded wife, Marie (?–?), and three children Lalouise (ca. 1829–1845), Moise (1844–1844), and Jean Baptiste (1847–1848).

PS: HBCA YFSA 2–9, 11–15, 19–20, 22–32, FtGeo[Ast]AB 11–12, YFDS 2a, 3a–3b, 4b–7, 16–17, FtVanSA 1–7, 9; *PPS:* Munnick, *Vancouver,* vol. 2

Mowee [variations: **Maui, Mawē, Mowie**] (fl. 1844–1850)

HBC employee, d. late July 1850 at Fort Vancouver, associated with:

Cowlitz farm (1844–1850) laborer
Fort Vancouver (1850) laborer

Mowee, whose name may indicate he was from the island of Maui, joined the HBC from O'ahu in 1844. He worked at the Cowlitz farm until 1850, when he went to Fort Vancouver, possibly because of sickness. There, he died of unstated causes around the end of July, for he was paid for two months' work in outfit 1850–1851.

Mowee had one wife, an unnamed Native woman of the Fort Vancouver mission, and one child, Anne (1850–?).

PS: HBCA YFSA 24–31; *PPS:* Munnick, *Vancouver,* vol. 2; Robert, "Round Hand"

Mowray, A. (fl. 1856)

Laborer, associated with:

Fort Nisqually area (1856) laborer

A Hawaiian named A. Mowray was in 1856 working for a settler at Tlithlow near Fort Nisqually.

PS: HL FtNisTJ

Mowrey, John (fl. 1850)

Laborer, b. ca. 1826, associated with:

Oregon City resident (1850) sawyer

Little is known of John Mowrey, who was working in Oregon City as a sawyer in 1850. He was in the same household as **Tahuis Mowrey** and almost certainly her husband.

PS: 1850 U.S. Census, Oregon, Clackamas Co.

Mowrey, Tahuis (fl. 1850)

Occupation unknown, b. ca. 1830, associated with:

Oregon City (1850)

In 1850 Tahuis Mowrey was living in the same household in Oregon City as **John Mowrey,** almost certainly her husband.

PS: 1850 U.S. Census, Oregon, Clackamas Co.

Mu (fl. 1862)

Laborer, associated with:

Vancouver Island (1862)

Mu was one of eight laborers who left for Victoria on the *Constitution* on May 2, 1862. It is unclear where they were headed, but it may have been Puget Sound, if he is the **John Mu** who was working at Port Gamble in 1870.

PS: HSA Passenger

Mu, John (fl. 1870)

Laborer, b. ca. 1829, associated with:

Port Gamble (1870) sawmill worker

At the time of the 1870 Census, John Mu was one of eleven Hawaiians working at Puget Mill at Port Gamble. Living with him was his wife Mary (ca. 1841–?), also born in the Islands. He was likely **Mu,** who in 1862 left Honolulu for the Pacific Northwest.

PS: 1870 U.S. Census, Washington Territory, Kitsap Co., Port Gamble

Mu, Mary (fl. 1870)

Wife, b. ca. 1841, associated with:

Port Gamble (1870)

At the time of the 1870 Census, Mary Mu was living at Port Gamble with her husband **John Mu,** who was one of eleven Hawaiians working at Puget Mill at Port Gamble.

PS: 1870 U.S. Census, Washington Territory, Kitsap Co., Port Gamble

Mundon, Henry (fl. 1882–1907)

Farmer, of mixed descent b. ca. 1863, in Koloa, Kauaʻi, to James Mundon MacKenzie and Martha Kahilikia Kapule, d. December 19, 1907, in Victoria, associated with:

Moodyville (1882–1889) blacksmith
Salt Spring Island (1889–ca. 1895) farmer
Vancouver (1896–1901) boat builder
Thurlow Island (ca. 1902–1907) boat builder

According to a family history, Henry Mundon was born in Koloa, Kauaʻi, to James Mundon MacKenzie (1822–1900), an immigrant from Edinburgh who made his living as a blacksmith, and Martha Kahilikia Kapule (1835–1915), an indigenous Hawaiian woman. By 1882 Henry Mundon was working as a blacksmith in Moodyville on the north shore of Burrard Inlet. Moving to Salt Spring Island, he is said to have planted the first fruit trees at Isabella Point. Later he was a boat builder in Vancouver and on Thurlow Island. He died in 1907 of tuberculosis.

On January 3, 1883, Henry Mundon married a Haida woman named Lucy (?–?) at the Methodist mission in New Westminster. They were the parents of Robert Edward (1889–?) and, very likely, William Randall (ca. 1890–?). Henry Mundon and **William Newanna**'s daughter Sophie Tahouney (1858–1904), widow of **Louis Kallai**, were the parents of Mary (1890–1936), also known as Mamie and Melia. Mamie and her older half brother Dan are said to have been part of a popular Hawaiian music radio program out of Vancouver. On March 27, 1905, following Sophie's death, Henry Mundon married Mary Catherine Banzer Sullins.

PS: StEdC, BCA Hamilton, VS-MM; *SS:* Gonsalves, *Lahapa Kaleimakaliʻi;* Hansen, *Nawana*

Mytie (fl. 1835–1840)

HBC employee, associated with:

Fort Vancouver (1835–1836) laborer or middleman
Fort McLoughlin (1836–1837) middleman
Fort George (1837–1839) middleman
Fort Vancouver Indian trade (1839–1840) middleman

Mytie, from Oʻahu, joined the HBC at Fort Vancouver on November 1, 1835. He worked at coastal forts until November 15, 1840, when he returned to Oʻahu.

PS: HBCA YFSA 15, 19, YFDS 6–7, 11, FtVanSA 3–6

Naaco, George (fl. 1811–1814)

PFC/NWC employee, b. probably on Oʻahu, associated with:

ship *Tonquin* (1811) passenger
Fort Astoria (1811–1814) laborer
overland brigade (1814)

George Naaco joined the crew of the *Tonquin* as a laborer around February 21, 1811, when the vessel stopped at Oʻahu and took on a complement of twenty Sandwich Islanders. One month later, on March 22, the *Tonquin* arrived at the mouth of the Columbia and, on April 12, George was noted as helping to unload the vessel. In December of that year he was noted as gathering wood up the Cowlitz River and, on April 4, 1814, he joined the overland brigade heading for Fort William on the Great Lakes. Just how he got back to the Hawaiian Islands, or if he did so, is open to speculation.

PS: RosL *Astoria; PPS:* Franchère, *Journal*

Naau, John (fl. 1850)

Laborer, b. ca. 1825, associated with:

Oregon City (1850) laborer

Nothing is known of John Naau other than the Hawaiian-born man was working in Oregon City in 1850.

PS: 1850 U.S. Census, Oregon, Clackamas Co., Oregon City

Naeeve [variations: **Naeve, Nauve**] (fl. 1844–1845)

HBC/PSAC employee, d. July 15, 1845, at Cowlitz farm, associated with:

Fort Vancouver and Cowlitz farm (1844–1845) laborer

Nauve joined the HBC from Oʻahu in 1844 on a three-year contract. He worked for just over a year and died at Cowlitz farm on July 15, 1845.

PS: HBCA YFSA 24–27, YFDS 16

Nahalo, Jack (fl. 1870)

Laborer, b. ca. 1853, associated with:

Port Gamble (1870) sawmill worker

At the time of the 1870 Census, Jack Nahalo was one of twenty-two Hawaiians working at Puget Mill at Port Gamble.

PS: 1870 U.S. Census, Washington Territory, Kitsap Co., Port Gamble

Nahanee, Joe (fl. 1860s–1874)

Laborer, d. ca. 1874 at Burrard Inlet, associated with:

Burrard Inlet (1860s–1874)

According to oral tradition Nahanee was brought over by the HBC and worked at Fort Victoria. If so, he had another name at the time. In the 1860s Nahanee moved to Burrard Inlet and took up work in the boiler room of Hastings sawmill. He settled at Coal Harbour at what was known as Kanaka Ranch.

Nahanee and a Squamish woman named Mary See-em-ia (?–?), who already had a daughter by **Eihu**, were the parents of Lucy (ca. 1866–1933) and William (1872–1918). Nahanee descendants, who number in the hundreds, have become mainstays of the Squamish Nation in North Vancouver even while retaining pride in their Hawaiian heritage.

PS: VanA Nahanee

Naharou [variation: **Naharow**] (fl. 1840–1855)

HBC employee, associated with:

Fort Stikine (1840) middleman
Fort Langley (1840–1842) middleman, (1842–1843) laborer
Fort Vancouver (1843–1846) laborer
Snake party (1846–1848) laborer
Snake Country (1848–1850) laborer
Fort Vancouver (1850–1851) laborer
Snake Country (1851–1852) laborer, (1853–1855) laborer

Naharou joined the HBC from Oʻahu in 1840 and, after being first placed at Stikine, was sent to Langley, where he was needed more. He retired in 1844 and was paid off at the end of the year in Honolulu. This was a short break, for he was soon back at Vancouver and may have appeared in the 1850 Census with the surname of **Maharoui**. Naharou deserted in outfit 1852–1853 but likely rejoined again for, in outfit 1855, he retired and "left" the service.

No family has been traced.

PS: HBCA YFSA 20, 22–32, FtVanSA 6–7, 9–12, FtStikPJ 1, SandIsAB 3, FtVicDS 1, 1850 U.S. Census, Oregon Territory, Clark Co.

Naheeti, Peter (fl. 1853)

HBC employee, associated with:

ship *Pekin* (1853) seaman
ship *Mary Catherine* (1853) seaman

Peter, whose Hawaiian name was Naheeti, shipped aboard the HBC chartered vessel *Pekin* in Honolulu probably in the summer of 1853, sailed to the Northwest Coast, and arrived back in Honolulu September 27, 1853, on the *Mary Catherine*. He was given the final balance of his wages when he arrived back.

PS: HBCA SandIsLonIC 3

Nahiana (fl. 1858–1863)

Occupation unknown, associated with:

Vancouver Island (1858–1863)

Nahiani was one of fourteen Hawaiians departing Honolulu for Victoria on the schooner *Alice* on June 22, 1858, enticed by the euphoria of the gold rush. When his ship companion **Kahaleiwi** died in late 1862, it was Nahiana and **Kapoi** who administered the estate. Nahiana's signature suggests he was barely literate.

PS: HSA Passenger, Victoria

Naho [variation: **Naha**] (fl. 1848–1868)

Occupation unknown, associated with:

Victoria area (1848–1868)

Little is known of Naha, who lived in the Victoria area between 1848 and 1868. On September 20, 1852, Naho's son Frederick (ca. 1849–1868) was baptized.

PS: BCA VS-StAndC

Nahoa [variation: **Nehow**] (fl. 1845–1849)

HBC employee, associated with:

Fort Umpqua (1845–1847) laborer
Fort Vancouver Indian trade (1847–1849) laborer

Nahoa joined the HBC from Oʻahu on May 7, 1845, and was dispatched to Fort Umpqua as a laborer, being sent two years later to work in the Fort Vancouver Indian trade. He deserted in 1849, quite likely in the first part, as he received no wages in outfit 1849–1850, and probably headed to the California gold fields.

PS: HBCA SandIsAB 3, YFSA 24–29, YFDS 16–17

Nahoua [variations: **Nahona, Nahowa, Nahua, Nahor**] (fl. 1840–1864)

HBC/PSAC employee, associated with:

Fort Stikine (1840–1847) laborer and kitchen servant
Fort Nisqually outstation (1847–1849) shepherd

Fort Rupert (1850–1852) laborer
Fort Victoria (1852–1854) laborer
Belle Vue sheep farm (1854) laborer
Fort Victoria (1854–1857) laborer, (1857–1858) baker
Victoria area (1859–1864) restaurant worker

Nahoua joined the HBC from Oʻahu in 1840, and worked at Fort Stikine until November 10, 1847, at which point he returned to Oʻahu. After a few months on the Islands, he reenlisted again and began work for PSAC at Fort Nisqually on June 15, 1848, then at Forts Rupert and Victoria. At the San Juan sheep farm in 1854, he made lime and did a variety of jobs but after the clerk in charge had two shirts and four tobacco plugs stolen, Nahoua was forced to show his plugs; consequently, his feelings were hurt and he left in anger to continue work at Fort Victoria. He was there until October 1, 1858, and likely lived with his family on Kanaka Row. By 1862 he owned a property at 206 Humboldt Street, formerly Kanaka Row, valued at $1,200.

A Hawaiian recorded as Nahor, and almost certainly the same man, was repeatedly charged along with his Native wife Catch-hus or Kat-e-kah with morality offenses between 1859 and 1862. In 1859 they were fined £2 for supplying liquor to Indians. In May 1860 Nahor was convicted of "keeping a house of ill-fame" by virtue of his daughters, whom he said he could not control, calling out to strangers as they walked past their Kanaka Row dwelling. The situation became more complex after Kat-e-kah accused a Victoria police officer of promising her husband's release in exchange for sexual favors. Two years later Nahor was again charged with keeping "a house of ill fame."

Nahoua had one wife and between six and eight children, not all of whom made it past infancy. Nahoua took as a wife a Tsimshian woman, whose name was spelled Katsahls (?–?) at the time of his wedding. They had Hannah (?–bap. 1852–?), John (?–bap. 1852–?), James (?–bap. 1852–?), Louisa (?–bap. 1855–?), Harriet (?–bap. 1856–?), Cecilia (1857– 1858), Mary Ann (?–bap. 1859–?). The children were all baptized at Victoria as Anglicans.

PS: HBCA YFSA 20, 22–27, 30–32, FtVanSA 6–7, YFDS 18–19, FtVicSA 1–6, HL FtNisSA 5BCA VS-CCC, Crt-Magistrate, Assizes; *PPS:* McLoughlin, *Fort Vancouver Letters, 1839–44,* 358; *Victoria Gazette,* September 24, 1859; *Colonist,* August 11, 1860; *Government Gazette,* 1862, 1864; *SS:* Anderson, *Physical Structure,* 171

Nahouree [1] (fl. 1840–1843)

HBC employee, d. ca. 1843 possibly in the Snake Country, associated with:

Snake party (1840–1843) middleman

Nahouree joined the HBC from Oʻahu in 1840 and was sent to join the Snake party. His contract ended in 1843, at which point he appears to have died, possibly in the Snake Country.

PS: HBCA YFSA 20, 23, FtVanSA 6–7

Nahouree [2] (fl. 1860)

HBC employee, associated with:

Belle Vue sheep farm (1860) laborer

Nahouree, like several other Hawaiians in the Pacific Northwest, joined the HBC farming operations on the disputed San Juan Island. He could be one of several men going by the name of **Tamaree.**

PS: HBCA BelleVuePJ 2

Nahu [variations: **Nahua, Anahua, Naho, James Nahua**] (fl. 1851–1862)

HBC employee, possibly b. 1811, associated with:

Fort Langley (1858) occupation unknown

Nahu remains a shadowy figure who may have been employed by the HBC at Fort Langley in 1858. Oral tradition suggests his name was originally Nahua, Anahua, or Naho. He may be the James Nahua who died in New Westminster on May 13, 1862, age fifty-one. Nahu is reputed to have had three sons: Charles (ca. 1852–?), John (?–?), and Leon (ca. 1862–1913). By one account Leon's mother was a **Peeopeeoh** daughter from Fort Langley, by another born at Fort Vancouver. Leon's death certificate has him born on the north side of the Fraser River at Maple Ridge, where several former Fort Langley employees from the Hawaiian Islands took up land in 1860. The Nahu sons worked alongside each other in a Burrard Inlet sawmill during the early 1880s. John Nahu and a Musqueam woman named Mary were the parents of Catherine (1893–?) and Florence (ca. 1895–?). In 1881 young Leon was living at Fort Langley, but soon migrated to North Vancouver, where he worked in a sawmill and then as a longshoreman. Leon Nahu and Mary Agnes Haley (1867–1904), whose father **Haley** was also a Hawaiian, were the parents of Norman (1890–1953), Herbert (1891–1957), Agnes (1893–?), Ralph (1897–1950), and James (1902–1966).

PS: BCA VS-Deaths, 1881 and 1891 Canada Census, British Columbia, New Westminster, VST Coqualeetza; *SS:* Nelson, *Fort Langley,* 21

Nahua (fl. 1850)

HBC seaman, associated with:

barque *Cowlitz* (1850) seaman

Nahua shipped onboard the HBC vessel *Cowlitz* on February 3, 1850, at Honolulu and sailed to the Northwest Coast. The captain was unhappy with the performance of the Hawaiians and when the vessel arrived back in O'ahu in August, the Hawaiians rebelled, claiming their contract was up. However, Nahua and others returned to work until September 20, after which he disappears from the records.

PS: HBCA SandIsAB 10–11, Log of *Cowlitz* 8

Nahuaoleo (fl. 1843–1850)

PSAC employee, associated with:

Cowlitz farm (1843–1846) laborer

Nahuaoleo appeared on contract in the Columbia in outfit 1843–1844, working as a laborer on Cowlitz farm. His contract ended in 1846. In outfits 1847–1848, 1848–1849, and 1849–1850 he was listed but without any information, indicating that he wasn't working but might have remained in the area.

PS: HBCA YFSA 23–28, FtVanSA 8

Nakahene, Bob [variations: **Nakygohiny, Nakygooheny**] (fl. 1840–1841)

HBC employee, d. July 6, 1841, at Fort Simpson, associated with:

Fort Taku (1840–1841) middleman
Fort Simpson (1841) middleman

Nakahene joined the HBC from O'ahu in 1840 on a three-year contract and after reaching the Northwest Coast assisted in building Fort Taku in present-day Alaska. After the bulk of the construction was completed, he was sent to Fort Simpson, where he was noted in the journals as Bob, carrying on a variety of duties. Late in the spring of 1841 he became sick more frequently, and finally he was confined to bed. He died at Fort Simpson on July 6, 1841, of unknown causes with a simple notation "Bob the Kanaka died this afternoon." The next morning, an overcast morning when the wind was blowing moderately, Bob Nakahene was buried, likely on the knoll behind the fort.

PS: HBCA YFSA 20–21, FtVanSA 6–7, YFDS 12, FtSimp [N]PJ 6

Nakai [1] (fl. 1850)

HBC seaman, associated with:

barque *Cowlitz* (1850) seaman

Nakai shipped onboard the HBC vessel *Cowlitz* in February 3, 1850, at Honolulu and sailed to the Northwest Coast on a voyage on which the captain was unhappy with the performance of the Hawaiians. When the vessel returned to Hawai'i that summer, the Hawaiian crew rebelled but returned to the vessel to work a further month. Nakai finished his employment with the HBC on September 20 and goes off the records.

PS: HBCA SandIsAB 10–11, Log of *Cowlitz* 8

Nakai [2] (fl. 1879)

Laborer, associated with:

Port Gamble (1879) likely sawmill worker

On May 7, 1879, Nakai arrived back in Honolulu from Port Gamble on the *Camden*. It is unclear how long or if he worked at the sawmill there.

PS: HSA Passenger

Nakaululu (fl. 1860–1861)

Seaman or laborer, associated with:

Victoria (1861)

Nakaululu was one of four Hawaiians on the *Consort*, which was wrecked off northern Vancouver Island in late November 1860 en route from Honolulu to Puget Sound. The men, who got away in an Indian canoe, finally reached Victoria in mid-January, destitute and clothesless, to be rescued by the consul. Two were seamen and the other two contracted by a Puget Sound sawmill. Their subsequent activity is not known.

PS: HSA Victoria

Nakoko (fl. 1862)

Laborer, associated with:

Port Gamble (1862) sawmill worker

Nakoko was among seven men contracted in Honolulu on February 14, 1862, by the agent of Puget Mill Co. to work at its sawmill for $10 per month with a $20 advance. It is uncertain how long he did so.

PS: HSA Seamen

Nalehu (fl. 1862)

Laborer, associated with:

Vancouver Island (1862)

Nalehu was one of eight laborers who left for Victoria on the *Constitution* on May 2, 1862. It is unclear where they were headed.

PS: HSA Passenger

Namacoouroria [variations: **Namacooeroua, Nama eerooa**] (fl. 1840–1846)

HBC employee, associated with:

Fort Vancouver (1840–1841) middleman
Snake party (1841–1842) middleman, (1842–1845) laborer
Fort Vancouver general charges (1845–1846)

Namacoouroria first joined the HBC in July 1837 in Oʻahu and may have worked in Honolulu, as he didn't appear in Columbia accounts until 1840. Once on the Pacific slopes, he spent the majority of his time in Snake Country. He worked with the company until August 6, 1846, when he returned to Oʻahu.

PS: HBCA SandIsAB 1, YFSA 20, 22–26, FtVanSA 6–7, YFDS 17

Namahana [variation: **Namahama**] (fl. 1830–1834)

HBC employee, associated with:

Fort Vancouver general charges (1830–1831)
Fort Vancouver (1831–1834) laborer
brig *Eagle* (1834) passenger or seaman

Namahana joined the HBC in 1830. Described by Dr. William Fraser Tolmie as "slow in his motions as a sloth but quiet & docile," Namahana was his attendant in his surgery at Fort Vancouver in May 1833. Namahana worked in the Fort Vancouver area, probably as a laborer, until December 1, 1834, when, no doubt at the end of his contract, he was sent back to Oʻahu aboard the brig *Eagle*.

PS: HBCA FtVanSA 2–3, YFDS 4a–5c, YFSA 11–14, SandIsM, SMP 14, Tolmie, *Journals,* 173

Namakokyan [variation: **Namokokay**] (fl. 1815–1821)

NWC/HBC employee, associated with:

schooner *Columbia* (1815) crew member
Columbia Department (1821) laborer

Namakokyan appears to have worked for the NWC for a number of years and, in 1821, transferred to the HBC. Otherwise, nothing is known of him.

PS: HBCA NWCAB 5, 9

Namaurooa [variations: **Namaeeroua, Namaerooa**] (fl. 1837–1840)

HBC employee, associated with:

Fort Vancouver (1837) laborer
Willamette mission (1837–1838) middleman
steamer *Beaver* (1838–1839) middleman
Fort McLoughlin (1839–1840) middleman

Namaurooa, from Oʻahu, joined the HBC in 1837 and worked at Fort Vancouver from August 10 to November 13, 1837, whereupon he was transferred to the services of Methodist missionary Jason Lee. After helping Lee, he worked along the coast until November 15, 1840, the end of his contract, when he returned to Oʻahu.

PS: HBCA YFSA 17, 19–20, YFDS 8, 11, FtVanSA 4–6

Namhallow [variation: **Namahaloo**] (fl. 1844–1861)

HBC employee, associated with:

Fort Vancouver (1844–1847) laborer
New Caledonia (1847–1851) laborer

Fort Alexandria (1851–1852) laborer
New Caledonia (1852–1860) laborer
Western Department (1860–1861)

Namhallow joined the HBC from Oʻahu in 1844 and, after a stint at Fort Vancouver, worked in New Caledonia as a laborer for over a dozen years. His final contract ended in 1861, and for the next two years there was movement on his account; however, his further movements have not been traced nor has any family been located.

PS: HBCA YFSA 24–32, FtVicSA 1–10, BCA PR-FtAlex 1

Namotto (fl. 1844–1850)

HBC employee, associated with:

Fort Vancouver (1844–1845) laborer
steamer *Beaver* (1845–1846) laborer, (1846–1847) woodcutter
Fort Victoria (1848–1850) laborer
steamer *Beaver* (1850) woodcutter
Fort Vancouver (1850) laborer

Namotto joined the HBC in 1844 on a three-year contract, working as a laborer at Fort Vancouver and woodcutter on the *Beaver* until November 10, 1847, when he returned to Oʻahu. He reenlisted again in 1848, had a stint at Fort Victoria and another as a woodcutter on the *Beaver,* and, on June 19, 1850, deserted at Fort Victoria along with three non-Hawaiian fellow employees. He may have stayed in the area for a couple more years, for his account showed some movement, but he otherwise disappeared from the records.

PS: HBCA SandIsAB 7, YFSA 24–27, 30–32, YFDS 18–19

Nanamake (fl. 1811)

Occupation unknown, associated with:

Tonquin (1811)

According to John Papa Iʻi, a well-connected Hawaiian born in 1800, "a man belonging to the retinue of the heir of the kingdom" named as Nanamake, boarded the *Tonquin* when it was in Honolulu in the spring of 1811 with the intention of acquiring foreign clothing and goods and then going back home on the return voyage. If in fact Nanamake did so, he must have perished when the *Tonquin* was attacked off of Vancouver Island, for he does not appear in the records for Astoria.

PPS: Ii, *Fragments,* 87

Napahay, Aleck [variations: Napie, Napic, Napahy] (fl. 1839–1860)

HBC / PSAC employee, b. ca. 1820, associated with:

barque *Nereide* (1839) apprentice
Fort Vancouver (1839–1840) cabin boy and apprentice
schooner *Cadboro* (1840–1842) apprentice
Fort Nisqually (1842–1851) laborer, horse handler, and shepherd
Fort Vancouver (1851–1852) laborer
Fort Nisqually (1852–1860) casual laborer

Aleck Napahay joined the HBC from Oʻahu in 1839 on a one-year contract. He worked at various forts and on the schooner *Cadboro.* In the 1850 U.S. Census, he appeared as Napic, living in the same household as George Budabud (**Borabora**) and **Joe Tapou.** In March 1851, struck with paralysis on his left side and unable to work, he was taken from Nisqually by his friend **Kalama** to Vancouver to work but he obviously could not do so and was discharged in 1852. He remained in the vicinity and was repeatedly hired for short-term jobs such as carting goods to the various farms and to the nearby U.S. Army post at Steilacoom.

At least by 1848, Napahay had a wife who worked at Nisqually alongside the wives of **John Bull, Sam Arioha, Kahannui,** and **Cowie** whenever short-term jobs were to be had.

PS: HBCA SMP 14, YFSA 19–20, 22–32, FtVanSA 6–7, 9, FtNisCB; 1850 U.S. Census, Oregon Territory, Lewis Co., HL FtNisSA 2–3, 5–6, env, FtNisPJ 7, 12, FtNisB 6, 8, FtNisIA 5, FtNisIB 2–4, FtNisMJ

Napahē (fl. 1861–1862)

Laborer, associated with:

Port Gamble (1861–1862) sawmill worker

Napahē and five others were contracted in Honolulu on October 5, 1861, by the agent of Puget Mill Co. to work at its sawmill for $15 per month with a $15 advance. On November 15, 1862, Napahē left Teekalet on the barque *Jenny Ford* to return to Honolulu.

PS: HSA Passenger, Seamen

Napoua (fl. 1841–1847)

HBC employee, d. December 15, 1847, at Fort Vancouver, associated with:

Fort Vancouver (1841–1843) middleman, (1843–1847) laborer

Napoua joined the HBC from Oʻahu in 1841 and began receiving wages on July 1 of that year. He spent his entire career as a middleman and laborer at Fort Vancouver and died there on December 15, 1847, from the measles, as several of his fellow Sandwich Islanders did that winter. He was buried the following day at Fort Vancouver, and his salary was paid to his relatives in Hawaiʻi.

PS: HBCA FtVanSA 6–7, YFDS 12, 18, YFSA 22–27, SandIsAB 7; BCA PR-Lowe

Napu (fl. 1864–1865)

Occupation unknown, associated with:

Victoria area (1864–1865)

Napu appeared to live in the Victoria area in the 1860s. He was partnered with an unnamed Nisqually Native woman and together they had Alexander (?–bap. 1865–?).

PS: BCA VS-StAndC

Napuko, Henry [variation: **Harry Napuko**] (fl. 1834–1837)

HBC employee, associated with:

Fort Simpson (1834–1836) middleman or laborer
steamer *Beaver* (1836–1837) seaman
schooner *Cadboro* (1837) steward

Little is known of Henry or Harry Napuko, who joined the HBC from Oʻahu in 1834. On arriving on the Northwest Coast, he went from McLoughlin harbor to the old Nass site to likely participate in its dismantling prior to the post's move to the Tsimshian peninsula. After that he worked for a couple of years as a steward on coastal steamers. From that point on he wasn't specifically mentioned in the journals until he deserted, along with a non-Hawaiian fellow employee, at Monterey on October 1, 1837. He has not been traced after that.

PS: HBCA YFSA 14–15, YFDS 5c–7, FtSimp [N]PJ 3, FtVanSA 3–5, SMP 14

Naremarou [variation: François Xavier Naremarou] (fl. 1840–1844)

HBC employee, b. ca. 1814, d. August 21, 1844, at Fort Vancouver, associated with:

Fort Vancouver (1840–1842) middleman, (1842–1844) laborer

Naremarou joined the HBC from Oʻahu in 1840. After arriving on the Northwest Coast, he worked for the next four outfits at Fort Vancouver. His contract was to have ended in 1846, but he died of heart disease at Fort Vancouver hospital on August 21, 1844. While he was on his deathbed, Naremarou was baptized "François Xavier" by the Catholic priest, Modeste Demers.

PS: HBCA YFSA 20, 22–24, FtVanSA 6–7, YFDS 17, BCA PR-Lowe; *PPS:* Munnick, *Vancouver,* vol. 2

Narimma (fl. 1844–1851)

HBC employee, d. January 14, 1851, at Fort Simpson, associated with:

Fort Vancouver (1844–1845) laborer
Fort Nez Perces (1845–1847) laborer
Fort Stikine (1847–1849) laborer
Fort Rupert (1849–1850) laborer
Fort Simpson (1850–1851) laborer

Narimma, from Oʻahu, joined the HBC in 1844. He spent the majority of the next seven years working at coastal forts, his last assignment being Fort Simpson, where he died on January 14, 1851, of unspecified causes. He is most likely buried in the old, now overgrown hill cemetery behind the area where old Fort Simpson stood. He left a credit of £26.1.6 to his name.

PS: HBCA YFSA 24–31, YFDS 21, FtVicSA 1, BCA PR-Helmcken

Narkafoa (fl. 1837–1838)

HBC employee, associated with:

Columbia Department (1837–1838)

Nothing is known of Narkafoa, who made a brief appearance in HBC records in 1837–1838.

PS: HBCA FtVanSA 4

Narua (fl. 1837–1840)

HBC employee, associated with:

Fort Vancouver (1837–1838) middleman
Fort Simpson (1838–1840) middleman

Narua joined the HBC from Oʻahu in July 1837 and began work at Fort Vancouver on August 10 of that year. He worked there and at Fort Simpson until November 15, 1840, the end of his contract, when he returned to Oʻahu.

PS: HBCA SandIsAB 1, FtVanSA 4–6, YFDS 8, 11, YFSA 19–20

Nauka (fl. 1845–1849)

HBC employee, associated with:

Fort Vancouver (1845–1847) laborer
Snake Country (1847–1848) laborer
Fort Vancouver (1848–1849) laborer

Nauka joined the HBC from Oʻahu on May 7, 1845, for five years and worked as a laborer at Fort Vancouver and in the Snake Country. His obligation would have ended in 1850 but, on September 30, 1849, he deserted, probably for the gold fields of California. He has not been traced after that.

PS: HBCA SandIsAB 3, YFSA 25–29, YFDS 20

Naukana, L. (fl. 1865)

Laborer, associated with:

Port Madison, Washington (1865) sawmill worker

In October 1865 a Hawaiian signing himself as L. Naukana from Port Madison wrote to a Hawaiian-language newspaper in Honolulu with news from the Puget Sound sawmills.

SS: Naukana, "News"

Naukana, William [variations: **Naukanna, Lucamene, Lacamin, Lackaman, L'Gamine, Lagamin, Lickamean, William Manton, Nowkin, Louis Lagamine, Noukin**] (fl. 1845–1909)

HBC employee, farmer, b. ca. 1813, d. December 1909, on Salt Spring Island, associated with:

Fort Vancouver (1845–1846) laborer
New Caledonia (1846–1848) laborer
Fort Langley (1848–1849) laborer
New Caledonia (1849–1850) laborer
Thompson River (1850–1851) laborer
Fort Victoria (1851–1855) laborer
Belle Vue sheep farm (1857–1860) laborer
San Juan Island (1860–1870s) farmer
Portland and Salt Spring islands (1870s–1909) farmer

Naukana, according to HBC records, joined the HBC from Oʻahu in 1845 at about age thirty although, according to oral tradition, he is reputed to have come ten years earlier and to have been related to **John Cox**. According to the records, Naukana actively served with the HBC for ten years at interior and coastal posts and appears to have retired around 1855. In old age, Naukana recalled long HBC hunting expeditions through unsurveyed territory, being on the ship that surveyed the boundary line around the San Juan Islands with the United States, and having a personal relationship with HBC factor and Vancouver Island Governor James Douglas, for whom he sometimes served as interpreter. Around the time Naukana retired, he may have returned home where, according to oral tradition, he found that his family land had been appropriated for a plantation and so he returned to the Northwest Coast.

Once back on the Pacific slopes, Naukana settled on San Juan Island and obtained work on the HBC Belle Vue sheep farm under the name of L'Gamine until the end of his contract on October 28, 1860. Shortly after San Juan Island was awarded to the United States, Naukana and a large group of Hawaiians moved to Salt Spring Island. In 1875 Naukana and his good friend and son-in-law **John Pallao** preempted nearby Portland Island between them. There he grew vegetables, made his own tobacco, and, according to tradition, flew the flag of Hawaiʻi. According to oral tradition, he gave a piece of land for St. Paul's Catholic Church, constructed at Fulford Harbour. He appeared on British Columbia voters' lists under various versions of his surname from 1875 onward. William Naukana lived to a very old age of ninety-six and died in December 1909. He was buried at St. Paul's Catholic Church graveyard.

Naukana's family life is unclear. He had one or more Native wives and at least six children. William Naukana and an unnamed Kwantlen woman had Rosalie (?–bap. 1856–?), baptized at Fort Langley. Another daughter might have been Mary (?–?). He and Cecile (?–?), who was Lummi, were the parents of Francis (?–bap. 1866–ca. 1881) and Julia (ca. 1867–?). In 1870 Naukana and Cecile wed in a Catholic ceremony. His other children, according to record and oral tradition, were Sophie (1855–?), Cecilia (ca. 1860–1902), Annie (ca. 1863–?), Maryanne (1870–1903), and Matilda (1874–1943). Three of Naukana's daughters found Hawaiian husbands. Sophie wed her father's good friend John Pallao; Annie, **Kahananui;** and Cecilia, **George Napoleon Parker** and then a Filipino called Sufia Conoto.

PS: HBCA YFSA 25–32, FtVicSA 1–3, BelleVuePJ 2, BCA GR-Naturalization, VS-StandC, GR-Preemptions, PR-Hamilton, 1881, 1891, and 1901 Canada Census, British Columbia, Salt Spring; *PPS: Gulf Islands Cemeteries,* 43; British Columbia, *Sessional Papers,* voters' lists; SS: Hill, *Times Past;* Richardson, *Pig War Islands,* 160; Barman, "Naukana"

Naverharea, James (fl. 1850)

Laborer, b. ca. 1826, associated with:

Oregon City (1850) laborer

Little is known of James Naverharea other than he was working in Oregon City in 1850.

PS: 1850 U.S. Census, Oregon, Clackamas Co., Oregon City

Ned (fl. 1870)

Occupation unknown, associated with:

Victoria area (1870)

The court clerk may have been asleep in the Victoria courtroom when Ned was due to appear on January 19, 1870, to answer charges, for the entry is completely void of any information. Thus, the details of Ned, "a Kanaka," and his apparent crime, remain a mystery.

PS: BCA Crt-Gaols

Negro [variation: Neger, Nigre] (fl. 1834–1850)

CRFTC/HBC employee, d. ca. September 18, 1850, at Fort Vancouver, associated with:

ship *May Dacre* (1834) passenger
CRFTC brigade (1834) member
Fort Hall (1835–1837) laborer
Columbia Department (1837) laborer
Snake party (1837–1838) middleman
Snake party and Fort Vancouver (1838–1839) middleman
Fort Vancouver (1839–1842) middleman
Snake party (1842–1845) laborer, (1845–1846) goer and comer
Fort Vancouver (1846–1850) laborer

Negro was one of twenty men recruited for Nathaniel J. Wyeth's CRFTC in 1834 and among the dozen who deserted in November of the same year on the way to Fort Hall.

He returned to work there in the next year and remained until 1837, when he joined the HBC. He began work with the Snake party on July 31 of that year and the HBC settled his account with Wyeth that October. During most of the time with the Snake party he appeared to transport trappers to and from Fort Vancouver. He died around September 18, 1850, at Fort Vancouver of unspecified causes.

PS: OHS FtHallAB, CRFTCCB, HBCA FtVanSA 4–7, YFDS 8–9, 14, 16, 21, YFSA 19–20, 22–31; *PPS:* Wyeth, *Correspondence,* 235–239, 249–250

Nehanoui (fl. 1840–1844)

HBC employee, associated with:

Fort Taku (1840–1843) middleman
Fort Victoria (1843–1844) laborer

Nehanoui joined the HBC from O'ahu in 1840. He was first assigned to Fort Taku, which was being constructed on the Alaskan panhandle. After three outfits, he transferred to Fort Victoria. There he worked until November 23, 1844, when he returned to O'ahu.

PS: HBCA YFSA 20, 22–24, FtVanSA 6–7, YFDS 17

Nelu (fl. 1845–1846)

HBC employee, associated with:

Fort Vancouver (1845–1846) laborer
steamer *Beaver* (1846) laborer

Nelu joined the HBC from O'ahu on May 7, 1845, for three years. He worked at Fort Vancouver and on the *Beaver* until December 10, 1846, when he returned to O'ahu.

PS: HBCA SandIsAB 3, YFSA 25–26, YFDS 17

Nemanē [variations: Taylor, Neimane, Neemane, Nina, Havia] (fl. 1835–1845)

HBC/PSAC employee, d. July 10, 1845, likely at Cowlitz farm, associated with:

Fort Vancouver (1835–1837) laborer or middleman
attached to Dr. Marcus Whitman (1836–1838) laborer
Fort Vancouver (1838–1840) middleman
PSAC (1840–1841) laborer
barque *Vancouver* (1842–1843) laborer
Cowlitz farm (1843–1845) laborer

Nemanē from O'ahu, also known as Taylor, joined the HBC on November 1, 1835, at Fort Vancouver. The next September, he was assigned to work with missionary Dr. Marcus Whitman. From time to time he also assisted Whitman's colleague Henry Spalding. He was discharged in O'ahu in 1840. He reenlisted and died July 10, 1845, probably at the Cowlitz farm.

PS: HBCA YFSA 15, 19–20, 23–25, YFDS 6–7, FtVanSA 3–7, Hulbert, *Whitman,* 270

Neo (fl. 1845)

HBC employee, associated with:

Columbia Department general charges (1845)

Neo, from O'ahu, joined the HBC in 1845, appeared in the Columbia Department. He worked until December 10, 1845, at which point he returned to O'ahu, where he was paid his final HBC wages.

PS: HBCA YFSA 25, YFDS 16, SandIsAB 5

Newanna, William [variations: **Caboona, Nuana, Nawana, Onawon, Nohano**]
(fl. 1843–1900s)

HBC employee, b. ca. 1820, associated with:

Fort Vancouver (1843–1849) laborer
San Juan Island (ca. 1849–1874) farmer
Salt Spring Island (1874–1900s) farmer

Newanna joined the HBC from Oʻahu in 1843 and worked in Fort Vancouver until he deserted, probably for the gold fields of California, on October 10, 1849. In 1849–1853, the books carried outstanding balances, so he may have returned rather quickly, as some others did. Possibly around that time, he moved to San Juan Island, then in dispute between the United States and Canada. In 1874, after San Juan Island was awarded to the Americans, he moved to Salt Spring Island, where he preempted and settled on land at the tip of Isabella Point. There he raised a family and, according to author Beatrice Hamilton, brought the lively spirit of the luau to Salt Spring. He appeared on the British Columbia voters' list from 1875 onward.

William Nuana, as he became known, married a Native woman, Mary (ca. 1841–?), said to be from the San Juan Islands. They were the parents of Sophia (1858–1904) who married Hawaiians **Louis Kallai** and **Henry Mundon**, Kai (1862–?), Mary (ca. 1864–1961) who married Michael Erwin (1861–?) and William Lumley (1858–1911), Joseph (1867–1932) who had children with Emma Purser (1868–1952) and Delia Shepard (1867–1937), Daniel (ca. 1876–?), and Lena (ca. 1888–?). It seems likely the Nuanas were the parents of Joe Nuanna (ca. 1859–1874), who was convicted of a double murder occurring on San Juan Island in 1872 and hanged. Son Joseph changed his surname to Tahouney, becoming the progenitor of a large British Columbia family going by that name.

PS: HBCA FtVAnASA 8, YFSA 23–29, YFDS 20, Bio, 1870 U.S. Census, Washington Territory, San Juan Island, 1881 and 1901 Canada Census, British Columbia, Salt Spring; *PPS:* British Columbia, *Sessional Papers,* British Columbia voters' lists; *SS:* Koppel, *Kanaka,* 109; Hamilton, *Salt Spring,* 83

Niaupalu [variations: **Niapalau, Napalu, Nedpalu**] (fl. 1848–1851)

PSAC/HBC employee, associated with:

Fort Nisqually (1848–1850) laborer
Fort Vancouver (1850–1851) laborer

Niapalu joined the HBC in 1848 and began work at Fort Nisqually on June 15 of that year. There he did such jobs as thrashing oats and hauling firewood before transferring to Fort Vancouver sometime in 1850. He retired in 1851 and remained in the area but has not been traced further.

PS: HBCA SandIsAB 7, YFSA 28–32, YFDS 19, 22, FtVanSA 9, HL FtNisPJ 6

Nickaloa (fl. 1837–1842)

HBC employee, associated with:

Fort Vancouver (1837–1842) middleman, (1842) laborer

Nickaloa joined the HBC in July 1837 at Honolulu and began work at Fort Vancouver on August 10 of that year. He finished working with the company on June 24, 1842, at which point he returned to Oʻahu.

PS: HBCA SandIsAB 1, YFSA 17, 19–20, 22, YFDS 8, 13, FtVanSA 5–7

Noah, Harry Bell (fl. 1814–1831)

NWC/HBC employee, b. ca. 1795, d. September 30, 1831, likely at Fort Vancouver, associated with:

Columbia River area (1814–1821) laborer
Columbia Department (1821–1823) laborer
Fort George [Astoria] (1823–1825) middleman
Columbia Department (1825–1826)
Fort Vancouver (1826–1830) laborer, (1830–1831) middleman/laborer

Harry Bell Noah signed on with the NWC in 1814 and in 1821 transferred to the HBC, working the entire time in the Columbia area. Little is written of him except how he, together with **James Coah, Kaharrow, Tourawhyheine,** and **Marrouna,** confessed on October 9, 1825, to having stolen blankets from the trade goods of the *William & Ann*. He died of fever September 30, 1831. In 1833–1834, his family, probably in the Fort George area, was still being paid on the sundries account. Their names have not been traced.

PS: HBCA NWCAB 9, YFSA 1–9, 11, 13, FtGeo[Ast]AB 11–12, Log of *William & Ann* 1, YFDS 2a, 3a–4a, FtVanAB 10, SA 1–2, McDonald, *Blessed Wilderness,* 29

Nohiau (fl. 1834–1845)

HBC employee, associated with:

Fort Simpson (1834–1836) laborer
Fort Vancouver (1836–1837) laborer
barque *Nereide* (1837–1838) middleman
Fort Vancouver (1838–1844) middleman, (1844–1845) laborer

Little is known of Nohiau, who joined the HBC from Oʻahu in 1834. After his arrival at Fort Vancouver, he went north and was likely in on the dismantling of the old Fort Simpson Nass River site. He continued at the new site of Fort Simpson for two more years. After 1836, except for an outfit working on the barque *Nereide,* he was a laborer at Fort Vancouver, where he likely lived in Kanaka Village outside the palisades. His period of obligation ended in 1846, and he worked until December 10, 1845, at which point he returned to Oʻahu, where he received his final HBC wages.

PS: HBCA YFSA 14–15, 19–20, 22–25, YFDS 5c–12, 16, FtSimp[N]PJ 3, FtVan SA 3–7, SandIsAB 5

Nono (fl. 1840–1846)

HBC employee, d. ca. 1846 at Fort Stikine, associated with:

Fort Taku (1840–1843) middleman
Fort Stikine (1843–1846) laborer

From Oʻahu, Nono joined the HBC in 1840 and worked on the north coast at Forts Taku and Stikine. In outfit 1846–1847 he did not receive wages and had no specific location. He died at Fort Stikine, likely in 1846.

PS: HBCA YFSA 20, 22–27, FtVanSA 6–7

Noora (fl. 1860)

Laborer, b. ca. 1820, associated with:

Fort Vancouver area (1860) laborer

Noora was one of the many Hawaiians and their families living in the Kanaka Village area in 1860. As such, he may have worked for what remained of the HBC interests in the area or for the nearby U.S. military post. He could be any one of a number of former HBC employees with similar-sounding names.

PS: 1860 U.S. Census, Washington Territory, Clark Co.

Noowow (fl. 1839–1842)

HBC employee, associated with:

schooner *Cadboro* (1839–1842) steward

Noowow joined the HBC from Oʻahu in 1839 and worked as a steward aboard the *Cadboro* servicing coastal posts. His contract ended in 1843 but his last day of work was June 24, 1842, at which point he returned to Oʻahu.

PS: HBCA SMP 14, YFSA 19–20, 22, FtVanSA 6–7, YFDS 13

Nou, John (fl. 1870)

Laborer, b. ca. 1829, associated with:

Port Gamble (1870) sawmill worker

At the time of the 1870 Census, John Nou was one of 22 Hawaiians working at Puget Mill at Port Gamble.

PS: 1870 U.S. Census, Washington Territory, Kitsap Co., Port Gamble

Nouhee (fl. 1841–1849)

HBC/PSAC employee, associated with:

Fort Vancouver (1841–1842) middleman
Fort Nisqually (1842–1843) seaman
Fort Vancouver (1845–1849) laborer

Nouhee joined the HBC from Oʻahu in 1841. He worked at Forts Vancouver and Nisqually until October 31, 1843, at which point he returned to Oʻahu. He was reengaged, for he reappeared in the Columbia in outfit 1845–1846 with a contract that was eventually to end in 1851, but he deserted in 1849, probably in the first half, as he received no wages for outfit 1849–1850. He likely headed to the California gold fields.

PS: HBCA FtVanSA 6–7, YFSA 20, 22–23, 25–29, YFDS 14

Nūheana, Jack [variations: **Kanaka Jack, Jack Nihana**] (fl. 1858–1887)

Baker, b. ca. 1843 in Kohala to Hoēvah, associated with:

Victoria (1858–1859)
Port Townsend (1859–1887) baker and invalid

In 1858 Jack Nūheana left home and his father Hoēvah, recalled as a servant of King Kamehameha, at the age of fifteen for Victoria, likely attracted by the gold rush. The next spring, 1859, he moved across the border to Port Townsend and three years later became crippled when both hands were brushed in a machine while working in a bakery. In 1880 he was still working as a laborer in Port Townsend. Eventually he was no long able to support himself. Enjoying the sympathy of the community, he was able to go on public assistance and lodged in the county hospital.

Kanaka Jack, as he was known, was maintained as an invalid to 1886, for a total cost of $4,816.50. Then he decided he wanted to see his native land once more. So in May 1886 the county requested the Hawaiʻi consul at Port Townsend both to arrange a passage home, which he did a year later, and to pay the charges, which he refused to do on behalf of "His Majesty's Government."

PS: HSA PtTownsend, UBCSC Swan, 1880 U.S. Census, Washington Territory, Port Townsend

Nukai (fl. 1879)

Laborer, associated with:

Port Gamble (1879) sawmill worker

On May 7, 1879, Nukai left Port Gamble on the *Pawden* to return to Honolulu. It is unclear how long he worked at the sawmill there.

PS: HSA Passenger

Nyoray, Peter [variation: **Nyo-r-uy**] (fl. 1837–1844)

HBC employee, associated with:

barque *Nereide* (1837–1838) middleman
Fort Simpson (1838–1840) middleman
steamer *Beaver* (1840–1841) middleman
California estate (1841–1842) middleman, (1842–1844) laborer

Peter Nyoray, from Oʻahu, joined the HBC in 1837 and seemed to acquire the name Peter around 1841. It was soon dropped. He spent most of his time on coastal barques, with a stint in between at Fort Simpson. His contract ended in 1840 and, on November 15, 1840, he returned to Oʻahu. However, he must have rejoined, for he appears in 1841, beginning work on July 9 of that year and working on the HBC's California estate on a contract. He was discharged in Oʻahu in 1844.

PS: HBCA FtVanSA 4–7, YFSA 19–20, 22–25, YFDS 11–12

Ohia [variations: **Ohier, John Owyhee, John Oʻhea, Tahowia, Nawia**] (fl. 1840–1860s)

HBC/PSAC employee, b. Oʻahu, associated with:

barque *Columbia* (1840–1841) seaman
Fort Vancouver (1841–1842) middleman, (1842–1843) laborer
schooner *Cadboro* (1843) middleman
steamer *Beaver* (1843–1845) laborer
Fort Langley (1845–1846) laborer
Fort Nisqually outstation (1846) shepherd
Fort Langley (1846–1849) laborer, (1849–1851) cooper, (1851–1856) laborer
Fraser Valley (1857–1860s) farmer and laborer

Ohia joined the HBC from Oʻahu in 1840. In his sixteen years with the company, he spent considerable time at Fort Langley with interludes on coastal vessels and at Forts Vancouver and Nisqually. At Fort Langley he lived in the nearby Kanaka enclave and worked in the cooperage all year round making kegs, barrels, and vats for the salmon run. In 1852–1853, he only worked from November 23, 1852, and he appears to have retired around 1857; in outfit 1857–1860 he appeared on the sundries accounts with no further information.

Ohia and an unknown Kwantlen woman had Charles (?–bap. 1852–?) and Basile (?–bap. 1853–?), both baptized Catholic at Fort Langley. By 1858 Ohia was living in Fort Langley's Kanaka Village with **Peeopeeoh**'s daughter Algace Paiwa (ca. 1824–?). They had at least two children, Maria (?–bap. 1856–?), whose father the nearby Anglican cleric recorded as "Nawia of Wahu [Oʻahu]," and John (?–bap. 1859–?), whose father was recorded as "John Owyhee [Oʻahu]," a laborer in Kanaka Village.

In February 1860 Ohia, named as John O'hea, preempted land on the north bank of the Fraser River adjacent to claims being taken up about the same time by his father-in-law Peeopeeoh and brothers-in-law **Joseph Maayo** and **Peter Ohule**. He did not complete title and has not been traced further.

PS: HBCA Log of *Columbia* 4, SMP 14, YFSA 20, 22–32, YFDS 11, 13, FtVanSA 6–7, FtVicDS, SA 1–7, HL FtNisSA 3, BCA VS-StAndC; *SS:* Anderson, *Physical Structure;* Lugrin, *Pioneer Women,* 107; Laing, *Colonial Farm Settlers,* 98

Ohpoonuy [variations: **Ohpoonuay, Ohpoonuuy, Ohpooniuy**] (fl. 1836–1843)

HBC employee, associated with:

Fort Vancouver general charges (1836) laborer
South party (1836–1842) middleman, (1842–1843) laborer

Ohpoonuy was engaged by the HBC in Oʻahu in January 1836 and worked out of Fort Vancouver. His second contract, of four years, ended in 1843. After his last day of work, November 15, 1843, he returned to Oʻahu.

PS: HBCA YFSA 15, 19–20, 22–23, YFDS 6–7, 14, FtVansA 3–7

Ohule, Peter [variations: **Peter Ohulu, Peter Apnaut, Apnatih**] (fl. 1845–mid-1860s)

HBC employee, b. in Oʻahu, d. prior to 1867 in Fraser Valley, associated with:

Fort Vancouver (1845–1847) laborer
New Caledonia (1847–1848) district cook
Fort Langley (1848–1849) laborer
New Caledonia (1849–1850) cook
Fort Langley (1850–1851) laborer
Fort Victoria (1851–1853) laborer
Fort Langley (1853–1858) laborer
Fraser Valley area (1858–1860s) gold miner and farmer

Peter Ohule, described at his child's baptism as born in "Wahu," was hired on by the HBC in Oʻahu on May 7, 1845, and began work at Fort Vancouver on July 12 of that year. In 1846, he had deducted at the HBC Honolulu offices one barrel of salmon that may have been a family gift. He worked at a number of posts and, when at Fort Langley, acquired the first name of Peter. There, he lived in the nearby Kanaka Village and worked as a cooper alongside William Cromarty, **Ohia**, and **Joseph Maayo** making kegs, barrels, and vats used to salt salmon obtained from the salmon run.

Peter Ohule stayed in the area on retiring from the fur trade in 1858. During the Fraser River gold rush, he and his fellow Hawaiians panned for gold at what became known as Kanaka Bar. Ohule and the others were threatened with removal from Kanaka Ranch when it was thought that the site, known as Derby, would become the new capital of the mainland British colony of British Columbia. As soon as it became possible to preempt land in January 1860, Ohule, who now went by the surname of Apnaut, took up 160 acres on the north side of the Fraser River that later passed to his son George. A man by the name of Peter Ohule preempted land near Victoria on May 17, 1861. It's unclear if two men had the same name, or if he was geographically adventurous. This Peter Ohule, who wrote the letter himself in English, stated he had a house there.

Peter Ohule/Apnaut married Sophie (ca. 1830–?), a daughter of **Peeopeeoh**. They had a son George Peter (ca. 1854–1892) who was baptized at Fort Langley on June 29, 1856. He and a Native woman named Nancy (?–?) may have been the parents of Rosalie

(1864–?). Peter Ohule died prior to 1867, when Sophie, describing herself as a "Halfbreed Kanaka, widow of the late Apnatih," remarried. George Apnaut had two children by a granddaughter of fur trader Ovid Allard, Julia Hamburger (ca. 1862–), before she got the union annulled. He was well known for playing the violin at local dances and served on the Maple Ridge council in 1879. His descendants continue to live in British Columbia's Fraser Valley.

PS: HBCA SandIsAB 3, 5, YFSA 24–32, YFDS 16, 18, 20, FtVicSA 1–5, BCA GR-Pre-emption, VS-StAndC, OblH Fraser, PrivMS Kendrick 1, 2; *SS:* Lugrin, *Pioneer Women,* 107; Koppel, *Kanaka,* 85–86; Lang, *Colonial Farm Settlers,* 99; Waite, *Langley Story,* 102

Okaia [variations: **Ohaia, Kaʻiʻa**] (fl. 1840–1854)

HBC employee, d. ca. 1854 likely in or near Fort Victoria, associated with:

Fort Stikine (1840–1842) middleman, (1842–1843) laborer
Fort Victoria (1843–1848) laborer, (1850–1854) laborer

Okaia, a product of a missionary school in Oʻahu, where he learned to read and write biblical scriptures, joined the HBC in 1840 on a five-year contract. His first three years at his first posting, Fort Stikine, were probably rougher than he had anticipated. During his first winter he lost the large toe on his right foot due to frostbite. By April 20, 1842, some of the employees were in full rebellion against John McLoughlin Jr., who was in charge of the post. That evening, McLoughlin roused Okaia and others to arms to protect him against the ringleader Urbain Heroux and to shoot him on sight. Okaia was posted on the gallery with others, but Heroux managed to shoot and kill McLoughlin before Okaia and others could react. Taking the initiative in a still dangerous situation, Okaia and two other Hawaiians carried the body into the house, where they washed and dried it. One of the conspirators, Pierre Kanaguasse, had to be ejected from the room when he tried to tear off McLoughlin's vest and succeeded in throwing the body to the floor. The following year, Okaia transferred to a more peaceful Fort Victoria, where he worked until mid-November 1848 and then returned to Oʻahu. The visit or retirement was short, for he quickly reenlisted and returned to the Northwest Coast, where he continued working at Fort Victoria until 1854 when he died. He left a credit of £10.19.11 to his name.

PS: HBCA YFSA 20, 22–28, 30–32, FtVanSA 6–7, CB 30, YFDS 19, FtVicSA 1–2, FtStikPJ 2, SandIsAB 10

Okanaya, Owyhee (fl. 1824)

HBC employee, associated with:

Columbia Department (1824) laborer

Okanaya likely was an early HBC employee under a different name. He was deceased by 1842 when seventeen-year-old Marie Angelique (ca. 1825–?) got married at Fort Vancouver as the daughter of Okanaya and a Chinook woman.

PPS: Munnick, *Vancouver,* vol. 1

Olau (fl. 1840–1843)

HBC employee, associated with:

Fort Vancouver (1840–1842) middleman, (1842–1843) laborer

Olau joined the HBC in Oʻahu in 1840 on a three-year contract. He worked at Fort Vancouver until November 15, 1843, when he returned to Oʻahu.

PS: HBCA YFSA 20, 22–23, FtVanSA 6–7, YFDS 14

Olepau (fl. 1866)

Occupation unknown, associated with:

Victoria area (1866)

A Hawaiian identified as Olepau left Victoria for Honolulu, arriving May 11, 1866.

PS: HSA Passenger

Oll (fl. 1836–1843)

Occupation unknown, associated with:

Fort Vancouver area (1836–1843)

Little is known of the Hawaiian with the unusual name of Oll, who appeared in the Catholic Church (Fort) Vancouver records. In 1836 he partnered with an unidentified Native woman and had a son Louis (1836–?). He may have still been in the area in 1843 when their son was baptized.

PPS: Munnick, *Vancouver,* vol. 2

Omai (fl. 1840–1845)

HBC employee, associated with:

Fort Taku (1840–1841)

Fort McLoughlin (1841–1842) middleman, (1842–1843) laborer

Fort Victoria (1843–1845) laborer

Omai joined the HBC from O'ahu in 1840. He first worked along the north coast at Forts Taku and McLoughlin and at Fort Victoria from the time of its construction in 1943. Sometime thereafter he took ill, which was cause for concern in a letter exchanged between two HBC officials. "Omai who is the principal invalid having been confined to his house for three months in course of the past year, now appears to be perfectly recovered & is performing duty. Should he relapse into his usual infirm state, he shall be sent to Dr. Tolmie for medical advice" (Roderick Finlayson to John McLoughlin, January 11, 1845). As Omai's contract ended in 1846, he worked until December 31, 1845, when he returned to O'ahu, where he was paid off.

PS: HBCA YFSA 20, 22–25, FtVanSA 6–7, YFDS 16, SandIsAB 5, FtVicCB

Omi [variations: Omoi, Omai] (fl. 1801–1802)

Maritime fur trade seaman, associated with:

ship *Atahualpa* (1801–1802) seaman

Omi's experiences likely changed him. He probably joined the ship *Atahualpa* on its way to the Northwest Coast in late winter 1801. By the end of the first trading season he was busy making a cape of local bird feathers for his King Kamehameha back on the Islands. However, his behavior seemed to change, for he became somewhat aggressive toward the coastal Natives but nonetheless continued to do his work and occasionally was asked to dive for an object, such as a blunderbuss, which fell overboard. By July of the second trading season on the coast, he was getting anxious to return home. Evidence of a considerable change in personality was noted when he returned—he ignored the king's trading taboo, something that was punishable by death. He likely left the ship when it was in the Sandwich Islands and has not been subsequently traced.

PS: YU *Atahualpa,* CRMM *Atahualpa; SS:* Howay, "List"

Opeka (fl. 1865–1868)

HBC employee, associated with:

Fort Simpson (1865–1868) laborer

Opeka was one of the last Hawaiians to be taken on as a fully paid laborer on the HBC's servants' rolls. He may have landed by ship as there was no active recruiting at the time in the Islands for servants. Opeka spent his time at Fort Simpson and then disappeared from the records; he may have returned to Hawai'i.

PS: HBCA FtVicSA 13–16

Opunui [variations: **Opunui Maharoui, Opunoui, Opono**] (fl. 1840–1853)

HBC employee, b. ca. 1823, d. June 23, 1853, at Fort Vancouver, associated with:

Fort Taku (1840–1841) middleman
Fort Vancouver (1841–1844) middleman
steamer *Beaver* (1844–1845) laborer
Fort Vancouver (1845–1849) laborer, (1849–1851) farm laborer, (1851–1853) laborer

Opunui joined the HBC from O'ahu in 1840. After starting his career on the Alaska panhandle, and with one short break on the steamer *Beaver*, he spent the majority of his career at Fort Vancouver as a laborer. He worked until December 10, 1845, when he returned to O'ahu. He reengaged and returned to the Columbia. In 1850 almost certainly the same person, named as Opunui Maharoui, was living at Kanaka Village at Fort Vancouver with two other Hawaiians with the same surname, very possibly his brothers who came back with him. He was discharged on June 23, 1853, and died at Fort Vancouver that year.

Opunui had one wife, Marie, a Cascades woman (ca. 1830–1848), with whom he had Anne (1848–?). Marie died on September 8, 1848, at Fort Vancouver, probably from the lingering effects of childbirth.

PS: HBCA YFSA 20, 22–32, FtVanSA 6–7, 9–10, YFDS 16, FtVicDS 1, 1850 U.S. Census, Oregon, Clark Co.; *PPS:* Munnick, *Vancouver,* vol. 2

Oraroa [variation: **Oleloa**] (fl. 1859)

PSAC employee, associated with:

Fort Nisqually (1859) laborer

Sandwich Islander Oraroa went to work at Fort Nisqually on April 19, 1859, at a $10 monthly wage. He left on November 15, when he signed his name with a sure hand for his outstanding balance of $6.46.

Oraroa's purchases of a shawl and boys' blue hose in the spring of 1859 suggests a family.

PS: HL FtNisSA 14, FtNisbox 6

Orohuay [variations: **Oroohuay, Oroheeay, Ooroohuay**] (fl. 1830–1844)

HBC employee, b. ca. 1813, d. September 30, 1844, likely at Fort Vancouver, associated with:

Fort Vancouver general charges (1830–1831)
Fort Simpson (1831–1832) middleman
Fort Vancouver (1832–1837) middleman, laborer, and pigherd
barque *Nereide* (1837–1838) middleman
Fort Vancouver (1838–1840) middleman, (1842–1844) middleman

Orohuay joined the HBC in 1830 and returned to O'ahu in November 1840. He came back in 1842 and he was working on a new two-year contract when he died September 30, 1844, of unstated causes.

Orohuay was almost certainly the father of **Alexander Orohuay** (ca. 1833–?).

PS: HBCA FtVanSA 2–6, CB 9, YFDS 4a–7, 15, YFSA 11–15, 19–20, 22, 24

Orohuay, Alexander [variation: **Oroheeay**] (1833–1850s)

HBC apprentice cook, of mixed descent, b. ca. 1833 in Columbia District, associated with:

Fort Vancouver (1849–1851) apprentice, (1851–1852) apprentice cooper

Born in the Columbia District in 1833, Alexander Orohuay worked for the HBC as an apprentice cooper on a contract that ended in 1854. However, he was discharged on February 24, 1852, and has not been traced further.

Alexander Orohuay was almost certainly the son of **Oruhuay** and a Native woman.

PS: HBCA YFSA 29–31, YFDS 17, FtVanSA 9, 1850 U.S. Census, Oregon, Clark Co.

Oroora (fl. 1835–1846)

HBC employee, b. ca. 1811, associated with:

Fort Vancouver (1835–1836) laborer or middleman
Fort McLoughlin (1836–1837) middleman
Fort George [Astoria] (1837–1839) middleman
Fort Vancouver (1839–1840) middleman
Columbia Department (1840–1841) middleman
Fort Vancouver (1841–1843) middleman
Willamette (1844–1846) laborer
Fort Vancouver (1846) laborer

Oroora, from Oʻahu, joined the HBC at Fort Vancouver on November 1, 1835. He worked mostly at Fort Vancouver until November 10, 1842, at which point he returned to Oʻahu. He was reengaged and worked until August 6, 1846, when he again returned to Oʻahu.

PS: HBCA YFSA 15, 19–20, 22, 24–26, YFDS 6–7, 13, 17, FtVanSA 3–7

Orouku (fl. 1848–1849)

HBC employee, associated with:

Fort Vancouver (1848–1849) laborer

Orouku joined the HBC on June 1, 1848. He deserted in 1849, most likely in the first half, for in outfit 1849–1850, he received no wages. He probably headed south to the California gold rush.

PS: HBCA YFSA 28–29, YFDS 19

Ottehoh (fl. 1817–1839)

NWC/HBC employee, b. ca. 1798, associated with:

Columbia River area (1817–1823) laborer
Fort George [Astoria] (1823–1825) laborer
Columbia Department (1825–1826) laborer
Fort Vancouver (1826–1829) laborer, (1829–1831) scullion
barque *Ganymede* (1831) passenger
Fort Vancouver (1832–1833) middleman or laborer
Fort Simpson (1833–1834) middleman or laborer
Fort McLoughlin (1834–1835) middleman or laborer, (1835–1839) middleman
barque *Vancouver* (1839) passenger

Ottehoh joined the fur trade around 1817 from Oʻahu and worked almost continuously for over twenty years for the NWC and HBC. During this time he appears to have been, in part, a dishwasher. He was discharged from the Columbia on November 1, 1831, and returned to Oʻahu, sailing on the *Ganymede*. Less than a year later, on September 5, 1832, he was rehired in Oʻahu to work in the Columbia once again. He was finally discharged, likely in Oʻahu, on July 26, 1839.

No family has been located.

PS: HBCA YFSA 2–7, 9, 11–14, 19, FtGeo[Ast]AB 11–12, YFDS 2a, 3a–3b, 4b–7, 10, FtVanSA 1–6

Oui, Patrick (fl. 1812–1814)

PFC/NWC employee, associated with:

ship *Beaver* (1812) passenger
Fort George [Astoria] (1814) laborer

Just how the Hawaiian Patrick Oui secured a French name has not been traced but he probably arrived on the PFC vessel *Beaver* in May 1812. He was on record on April 4, 1814, as being prepared to work for the NWC through the summer at Fort George [Astoria]. NWC records are sketchy, so it is not surprising that no further information survives on Oui.

PPS: Henry, *Journal,* 711

Oulu (fl. 1839–1845)

HBC employee, associated with:

Fort Vancouver (1840–1843) middleman, (1844–1845) laborer

Oulu joined the HBC from Oʻahu in 1839. His contract ended in 1843 but his last day of work was November 10, 1842, at which point he returned to Oʻahu. However, he was reengaged on a contract that ended in 1846. He worked until December 10, 1845, again at Fort Vancouver, at which point he again returned to Oʻahu, where he received his final HBC wages.

PS: HBCA YFSA 20, 22, 24–25, FtVanSA 6–7, YFDS 13, 16, SandIsAB 5

Owhyeeman, Harry (fl. 1804–1805)

Maritime fur trade seaman, associated with:

ship *Atahualpa* (1803–1805) seaman

Harry Owhyeeman joined the crew of the *Atahualpa* probably on its stopover in 1803 on its way to the Northwest Coast. By January 1804, it was trading on the Northwest Coast, where the vessel wintered. The following spring, on June 12, 1805, in Millbanke Sound, two days after the local Natives had been ushered from the decks, the ship was attacked and the captain and eight of his men were killed. Harry was cut and stabbed over his whole body, and six days later there was fear that gangrene was going to set in. However, there is no record of Harry dying.

The *Atahualpa* fled to the Queen Charlotte Islands and four days later committed the bodies of the dead to the deep. The ship then went north to the south Prince of Wales Island, where it met the *Vancouver,* whose first mate assumed command of the *Atahualpa* and sailed the ship, in company with the *Vancouver, Juno,* and *Lydia,* to Newhitti. There, on June 30, all ships fired their cannons and hoisted their colors to half mast to honor the dead. The cargo of the *Atahualpa* was hoisted aboard the *Vancouver,* and the former departed immediately for Canton, arriving November 16, 1805. Harry likely disembarked at Hawaiʻi.

PS: YU Clinton; *SS:* Howay, "List"

Owtii (fl. 1844)

HBC employee, associated with:

Vancouver (1844) laborer

Owtii was likely hired by the HBC in Oʻahu in 1844. He worked at Fort Vancouver from July 12 to November 12, 1844, whereupon he returned to Oʻahu.

PS: HBCA YFSA 24, YFDS 15

Pa [variation: **Paa**] (fl. 1864–1865)

Laborer, associated with:

Alberni (1864–1865) sawmill worker

Pa was among five men contracted in Honolulu on August 24, 1864, by the agent of Alberni Mill Co. to work for $10 per month with a $20 advance. They departed Honolulu on September 1 on the *Alberni* and four of them arrived back in Honolulu on February 7, 1865, on the *Egoria*.

PS: HSA Seamen, Passenger

Paanui (fl. 1860–1861)

Seaman or laborer, associated with:

Victoria (1860–1861)

Paanui was one of four Hawaiians on the *Consort,* which was wrecked off northern Vancouver Island in late November 1860 en route from Honolulu to Puget Sound. The men, who got away in an Indian canoe, finally reached Victoria in mid-January, destitute and clothesless, to be rescued by the consul. Two were seamen and the other two contracted by a Puget Sound sawmill. Their subsequent activities are not known.

PS: HSA Victoria

Pa-ay-lay (fl. 1830–1850)

HBC/PSAC employee, associated with:

Fort Vancouver general charges (1830–1831)
Fort Simpson (1831–1833) laborer
Fort Vancouver Indian trade (1833–1836) middleman or laborer
South party (1836–1838) middleman
Cowlitz farm (1838–1840) middleman
PSAC (1840–1841) laborer
Fort Vancouver (1841–1842) middleman, (1842–1843) laborer
Fort Vancouver general charges (1843–1844) laborer
Fort Vancouver (1844–1845) laborer, (1845–1846) boute, (1846–1849) steersman
barque *Columbia* (1849) passenger
barque *Cowlitz* (1850) seaman

Pa-ay-lay joined the HBC from Oʻahu in 1830 and worked for it continuously for almost twenty years. After his arrival in the Columbia, he was taken north, where he participated in the construction of Fort Simpson on the Nass River. Afterward he worked at or around Fort Vancouver. His contract was to end in 1850, and he left for Oʻahu on October 31,

1849, aboard the barque *Columbia*. He was paid in Honolulu, but then rejoined the *Cowlitz* to sail back to the coast, perhaps because of a family he had formed there. He has not been traced further, nor has any family.

PS: HBCA FtVanSA 2–7, YFDS 4a–7, 16–20, YFSA 11–15, 19–20, 22–29, SandIsAB 10; *PPS:* Roberts, "Round Hand"

Pahah, Henry (fl. 1817)

Maritime fur trade seaman, associated with:

ship *Alert* (1817) seaman

Henry Pahah probably joined the Boston ship *Alert* around March, 1817, when it stopped at the Sandwich Islands on its way to the Russian settlements in present-day Alaska to trade for furs. On June 21, 1817, while the vessel was in the area of Kaiganee, Pahah was part of a minor revolt against the captain, apparently insulting him after the Sandwich Islander was told not to speak to certain men. When the captain ordered Pahah to be put in steerage, several other crew members stopped work in a show of support, and the situation was apparently resolved the same day. Pahah probably left the *Alert* when it returned to the Sandwich Islands in October 1817 on its way to Canton.

PS: ODHS *Alert*

Pahapalē (fl. 1838–1840)

Occupation unknown, associated with:

Fort Vancouver area (1838–1840)

Just when or how Pahapalē arrived on the Northwest Coast has not been traced, for he did not appear in fur trade records. By 1838 he was in the Fort Vancouver area and had partnered with a Native woman from the Cascades. Together they had Henriette (1839–1844); when Henriette died, she was an "orphan of an Owhyhe father and of an Indian mother," indicating that both parents may have been dead at this time.

PPS: Munnick, *Vancouver*, vols. 1–2

Pahas, Louis (fl. 1860)

Occupation unknown, b. ca. 1835, d. ca. August 12, 1860, associated with:

Victoria area (1860)

The twenty-five-year-old Hawaiian, Louis Pahas, appeared only once on the Catholic Church records when he was buried in Victoria on August 12, 1860. Nothing else is known about him.

PS: BCA VS-StAndC

Pahia, N. (fl. 1849)

Occupation unknown, b. possibly in Maui, associated with:

Victoria area / San Juan Island (1849)

N. Pahia did not appear to be associated with the fur trade although he was a friend of John Bull [3], who was probably living on San Juan Island at the same time. According to the church records Pahia was Hawaiian, a native of "Manhouis," which may be Maui. He partnered with a Native woman who died on October 27, 1849. Their child, Pierre Pahia (?–bap. 1849–?), was baptized the next day in Victoria.

PS: BCA VS-StAndC

Pahia, Peter [variation: **Pahai**] (fl. 1811–1814)

PFC/NWC employee, b. probably in Oʻahu, associated with:

ship *Tonquin* (1811) passenger
Fort Astoria (1811–1814) laborer

Peter Pahia joined the crew of the *Tonquin* as a laborer around February 21, 1811, when the vessel operated by the PFC stopped at Oʻahu and took on a complement of twenty Sandwich Islanders. One month later, on March 22, the *Tonquin* arrived at the mouth of the Columbia and, on April 12, Peter was noted as helping to unload the vessel. From that point on he did a variety of tasks, such as working on a December party that went up the Cowlitz River to gather timber. The following month he was trapping beaver. He is on record on April 4, 1814, as being prepared to work for the NWC through the summer at Fort George [Astoria]. He has not been subsequently traced.

PS: RosL *Astoria; PPS:* Henry, *Journal,* 711

Pahwack, Racoon (fl. 1817–1824)

NWC/HBC employee, b. ca. 1796, d. ca. 1824, associated with:

Columbia Department (1817–1822) laborer
Fort Okanagan (spring 1822) laborer
Columbia Department (1822–1824) laborer

Racoon Pahwack, who joined the fur trade in 1817 at just over twenty years of age, worked for the NWC and continued his employment with the HBC. Although he was recorded working in the spring of 1822 at the interior post of Okanagan, he may have been there for a longer period. In outfit 1824–1825 he received no wages and does not appear in outfit 1825–1826, indicating that he may have died in 1824. He was deceased by outfit 1826–1827.

PS: HBCA NWCAB 9, FtGeo [Ast]AB 4, YFSA 1–4, 6

Paka (fl. 1861)

Occupation unknown, associated with:

Victoria (1861)

Paka departed Honolulu for Victoria on the *Constitution* on February 22, 1861.

PS: HSA Passenger

Pakee [1] (fl. 1830–1840)

HBC employee, associated with:

Fort Vancouver general charges (1830–1831)
Fort Simpson (1831–1835) laborer
Columbia Department (1835–1836) laborer
Willamette Valley area (1836–1840)

Pakee joined the HBC from Oʻahu around 1830. After his arrival on the Northwest Coast, he headed north, where he was in on the construction of the first Fort Simpson Nass River site; he subsequently took part in its dismantling in 1834. At that time, in August 1834, he fell from the gallery, fracturing his skull. Dr. William Fraser Tolmie rushed to the fort on the brig *Dryad* with surgical instruments in hand, but he found that Pakee had only stunned himself severely and consequently left after a few days of observation. Pakee was brought to the new Simpson site on September 1, 1834, where he was to continue his work, but his injury may have been more severe than Tolmie diagnosed, for he received only partial wages for outfit 1834–1835. During that same outfit, the period of moving the fort, fellow Sandwich Islanders **Jemmy Mahoy** and **Jem Mamuka** were likewise disabled. Pakee worked in the Columbia until about 1836, at which point he appears to have settled down in the Willamette area.

Pakee and an unknown Chinook woman were the parents of Thomas (1829–1839), Rose (1837–?), and François (1840–?). **Thomas Pakee** died in 1839 at Methodist missionary Jason Lee's Willamette mission school. Perhaps for that reason, the next year they had their two younger children baptized Catholic by Father F. N. Banchet.

PS: HBCA FtVanSA 2, YFDS 4a–5c, YFSA 11–14, FtSimp [N]PJ 3; *PPS:* Tolmie, *Journals,* 290; *SS:* Lee and Frost, *Ten Years,* 169; Munnick, *St. Paul,* vol. 1

Pakee [2] [variations: **Parkee, Packee**] (fl. 1840–1865)

HBC employee, b. ca. 1819, associated with:

> Fort Vancouver (1840–1842) middleman
> Snake party (1842–1843) laborer
> Fort Nez Perces (1843–1845) laborer
> barque *Vancouver* (1845) seaman
> Fort Simpson (1845–1850) laborer
> brigantine *Mary Dare* (1850–1851) laborer
> Fort Victoria (1851–1852) laborer
> steamer *Beaver* (1852–1853) woodcutter
> Belle Vue sheep farm (1858–1859) laborer
> Nanaimo (1865)

Pakee joined the HBC in 1840 in Oʻahu. He worked at a variety of posts and on coastal shipping. In April 1850 he deserted with three other Hawaiians, but must have soon returned to work. In 1853 he joined the Victoria colonial militia, the Voltigeurs, and stayed with this force until it was disbanded in 1858, when he took employment at the San Juan Island sheep farm. He returned to Victoria and then Nanaimo where, on November 7, 1865, a gray-haired, 5 foot, 10 inch forty-six-year-old Hawaiian, Pakee, was sentenced to three months' hard labor for selling spirits to the Indians. At the time, Pakee could neither read nor write, nor did he profess any Western religion.

No family has been located.

PS: HBCA YFSA 20, 22–32, FtVanSA 6–7, Log of *Vancouver,* FtVicSA 1–2, BelleVuePJ 2, HL FtNisPJ 6, BCA Crt- Gaols; *SS:* Anderson, *Physical Structure*

Pakee, Thomas [variation: **Thomas Pekah**] (fl. 1829–1839)

Child, of mixed descent b. 1829, d. August 1839, associated with:

> Fort Vancouver (1829–1836) child
> Willamette mission (1836–1839) child convert

Thomas Pakee was born in 1829 to Hawaiian laborer **Pakee** [1] and a Chinook woman. Thomas was placed in Methodist missionary Jason Lee's school in December 1836. Three years later he died at Lee's Willamette mission of tuberculosis.

PPS: Lee and Frost, *Ten Years,* 169; Carey, "Mission Record Book"

Pakeeknaak, Thomas (fl. 1812–1814)

PFC/NWC employee, associated with:

> ship *Beaver* (1812) passenger
> Fort George [Astoria] (1812–1814) laborer

Thomas Pakeeknaak was brought to the Northwest Coast as a PFC laborer likely on the *Beaver.* He is on record, on April 4, 1814, as being prepared to work for the NWC through the summer at Fort George [formerly Astoria]. Just when, and if, he returned to the Hawaiian Islands has not been traced.

PPS: Henry, *Journal,* 711

Pakeokeo (fl. 1845–1849)

HBC employee, associated with:

Fort Nez Perces (1845–1848) laborer
Fort Vancouver (1848–1849) laborer
barque *Columbia* (1849) passenger

Pakeokeo joined the HBC from Oʻahu on May 7, 1845, and worked principally at Fort Nez Perces as a laborer. His contract was to have ended in 1850, but on October 31, 1849, he returned to Oʻahu aboard the barque *Columbia* and was paid his final wages.

PS: HBCA SandIsAB 3, 10, YFSA 25–29, YFDS 20

Paku (fl. 1858)

Occupation unknown, associated with:

British Columbia (1858)

Paku was one of six Hawaiians to whom the governor of Oʻahu gave permission in May 1858 to proceed to the British Columbia gold rush. He, and likely also his wife, left Honolulu for Vancouver Island on the schooner *Alice* on May 19, 1858. They had deck passage. Paku has not been traced further.

PS: HSA Passenger, Victoria

Paledin [variation: **Padulie**] (fl. 1850)

HBC seaman, associated with:

barque *Cowlitz* (1850) seaman

Paledin, whose name changed according to the recorder, shipped onboard the HBC vessel *Cowlitz* in February 1850 at Honolulu and sailed to the Northwest Coast on a voyage on which the captain was unhappy with the performance of the Hawaiians. Paledin and **Kula** both rebelled on August 27, as their contract was up, and did not return with the rest of the crew to the vessel. He has not been traced further.

PS: HBCA SandIsAB 10, Log of *Cowlitz* 8

Paleu (fl. 1864)

Laborer, associated with:

Port Gamble (1864) sawmill worker

Paleu and five others were contracted in Honolulu on May 27, 1864, by the agent of Puget Mill Co. to work at its sawmill for $10 per month with a $20 advance. It is unclear how long he worked there.

PS: HSA Seamen

Paleu, O. (fl. 1845)

Seaman, associated with:

brigantine *Bull* (1845)

O. Paleu was a "Kanaka" seaman on the brig *Bull* arriving in Honolulu on September 27, 1845, from the Columbia River.

PS: HSA Passenger

Pallao [variations: **Pallawu, Palao, Palew, Palow**] (fl. 1853–1860)

Occupation unknown, associated with:

Victoria area (1853–1860)

Pallao was in the Victoria area as early as 1853. In 1860 he was charged with smashing up a countryman's home on Kanaka Row (Humboldt Street) in Victoria.

Pallao partnered with Khesook (?–?), a Kwakuitl woman. Together they had Marguerite (1853–?), Jean (1854–?), and Ignace (1858–?).

PS: BCA VS-StAndC, *Colonist,* May 12, 1860

Pallao, John [variations: **Palua, Palow, Pellow, Palai, Pealou, Pallow, Herekario Pallao**] (fl. 1864–1907)

Farmer, b. ca. 1817, d. 1907 on Salt Spring Island, associated with:

Victoria area (1864–1874)
Portland Island (1875–1907) farmer

John Pallao first appears on record in 1873 when, already in his mid-fifties, he married countryman **William Naukana**'s daughter Sophie Lacamin (1855–?). He used the name of Herekario Pallao but was more commonly known as John Pallao. His earlier life is unknown, but he may be the **Pallao** living in the Victoria area from the 1850s. In 1875 John Pallao and his father-in-law William Naukana preempted Portland Island between them. John Pallao appeared on the British Columbia voters' list from 1875 onward. He died on Salt Spring Island in 1907.

John Pallao was the father of John (1865–1913), Louisa (?–bap. 1867–?), William Joseph (?–bap. 1871–?), Emma (ca. 1871–?), Rosa (?–bap. 1874–?), Rebecca (ca. 1876–1883), Lucy (?–?), William (1880–1903), Louis (1882–1883), Mary (ca. 1884–1895), Andrew (1886–1894), Pacidus (1887–?), and Louis (1891–?).

PS: BCA GR-Naturalization, VS StAndC, GR-Preemption, 1881 Canada Census, British Columbia, Salt Spring; *PPS: Gulf Islands Cemeteries,* 43

Pallow, William (fl. 1864–1901)

Farmer, b. ca. 1845, associated with:

Victoria (1864–1901) farmer

In 1901 William Pallow was a farmer living in North Victoria with his Indian wife Sophia (ca. 1865–?). Next door was his likely son John Pallow (1865–?), daughter-in-law Lydia (1875–?) of mixed English and Aboriginal descent, and their three young children.

PS: 1901 Canada Census, British Columbia, Victoria North

Palmer, John (fl. 1834)

CRFTC employee, d. December 1834 at Walla Walla, associated with:

ship *May Dacre* (1834) passenger
CRFTC brigade (1834) member

John Palmer was one of twenty men recruited for Nathaniel J. Wyeth's CRFTC in 1834 and among the dozen who deserted in November of the same year on the way to Fort Hall. He was reportedly killed soon after by Blackfeet Indians following a confrontation with them.

PS: OHS FtHallAB, CRFTCCB; *PPS:* Wyeth, *Correspondence,* 235–239, 249–250

Palupalu (fl. 1840–1843)

HBC/PSAC employee, associated with:

Fort Vancouver (1840–1841) middleman
Cowlitz farm (1841–1842) middleman, (1842–1843) laborer

Palupalu joined the HBC in 1840 from Oʻahu and began his work at Fort Vancouver on July 1 of that year. He worked there and the Cowlitz farm until November 15, 1843, when he returned to Oʻahu.

PS: HBCA YFSA 20, 22–23, YFDS 11, 14, FtVanSA 6–7

Panibaka (fl. 1846)

Occupation unknown, associated with:

Columbia area (1846)

Panibaka traveled to the Columbia River in April 1846 with "permission of the Governor," but it is unclear for what purpose. He may have been a returning HBC employee using another name for the trip than that by which he was employed.

PS: HSA Passenger

Paow, Dick (fl. 1811–1814)

PFC/NWC employee, associated with:

ship *Tonquin* (1811) passenger
Fort Astoria (1811–1814) laborer
ship *Isaac Todd* (1814) passenger

Dick Paow joined the crew of the *Tonquin* as a laborer around February 21, 1811, when the vessel operated by the PFC stopped at Oʻahu and took on a complement of twenty Sandwich Islanders. One month later, on March 22, the *Tonquin* arrived at the mouth of the Columbia and on April 12 Dick was noted as helping to unload the vessel. He did a variety of jobs but by 1813 was having bouts of both scurvy and, possibly, venereal disease. By May, he appears to have recovered and by November moved into a newly completed house along with three other Astoria men. He returned home in 1814.

PS: RosL Astoria; *PPS:* Henry, *Journal,* 711

Paparee, Jem [variation: **Gem Papara**] (fl. 1832–1849)

HBC employee, d. June 7, 1849, likely at Fort Vancouver, associated with:

Fort Simpson naval service (1832–1835) seaman
Snake party (1835–1838) middleman
Snake party and Fort Vancouver (1838–1839) middleman
South party (1839–1840) middleman
Columbia Department (1840–1841) middleman or laborer
barque *Cowlitz* (1841) working passenger
Fort Vancouver (1842–1849) laborer

Jem Paparee joined the HBC in Oʻahu on September 6, 1832, for work in the Columbia. After three years in coastal shipping, he became a member of various overland parties involved in transporting the members of the Snake parties to and from Fort Vancouver. In June 1841, he worked his passage back to Oʻahu on the *Cowlitz,* but returned to the coast and continued to work for the company. He died June 7, 1849, of unstated causes, likely at Fort Vancouver.

PS: HBCA YFDS 5a–7, 9, 20, YFSA 12–15, 19–20, 22–29, FtVanSA 3–6, FtSim[N]PJ 3, Log of *Cowlitz* 1

Paraou [variation: **Pareou**] (fl. 1840–1845)

HBC employee, associated with:

Fort Vancouver (1840–1842) middleman, (1842–1843) laborer, (1843–1845) freeman

Paraou joined the HBC from Oʻahu in 1840 and worked at Fort Vancouver. His contract expired in 1843, after which he appeared to work as a freeman. He had lost an arm, apparently while employed. Paraou worked until July 18, 1845, at which point he returned to Oʻahu, where he received an extra gratuity from the HBC.

PS: HBCA YFSA 20, 22–25, FtVanSA 6–7, SandIsAB 5

Parker, Annie (fl. 1890–1901)

Wife / widow, associated with:

Bowen Island (1890s)
North Vancouver (1901)

According to oral tradition Annie Parker set out with her husband **William** (?–late 1890s) from the Hawaiian Islands for British Columbia in 1890 in a 60-foot homemade sailing sloop. She was first mate and their children Napoleon (1879–?), Cecilia (1880–?), George (1886–?), John (1888–?), and William (1891–?) were deckhands. The family lived on Bowen Island during the 1890s. By the time of the 1901 Census Annie Parker was widowed and living with her children in North Vancouver. They were all Mormon, a faith the family likely brought with them from the Islands.

PS: 1901 Canada Census, British Columbia, North Vancouver; *SS:* "Last Rite"

Parker, George (fl. 1831–1837)

HBC employee, d. December 16, 1837, in San Francisco, associated with:

schooner *Cadboro* (1831) seaman
Naval Department (1831–1832) seaman
Fort Simpson naval service (1832–1833) seaman
brigantine *Dryad* (1833–1834) landsman
Fort Nez Perces (1834–1835) middleman or laborer
Fort Vancouver Indian trade (1835–1836) middleman or laborer
South party (1836–1837) middleman

George Parker, a Hawaiian with an anglicized name, was engaged by the HBC on June 16, 1831, in Oʻahu as a seaman to work on coastal shipping. It is not known how he got his name but, by 1812, at least one seaman by the name of Parker had been to the Islands. George worked on contract, although not always as a seaman, until 1837, after which he was a freeman. He died at San Francisco on December 16, 1837. Just why his name remained on the records is a bit of a mystery, but a possible answer is that the South party worked in isolation or that he had a family that was using his account.

PS: HBCA SMP 14, FtVanSA 3–5, YFSA 11–15, 18, YFDS 4b–7

Parker, George Napoleon (fl. 1875–1890)

Farmer, associated with:

Salt Spring Island (1875–1890) farmer

Hawaiian-born George Napoleon Parker and **William Naukana**'s daughter Cecilia had at least one son Johnny (?–1893). The family farmed for a time on Portland Island and also on Salt Spring Island at a location which became known as Kanaka Row, near to her sister Annie, married to **Kahananui.**

PS: StEdC, family recollections

Parker, Harry [1] [variation: **Harry**] (fl. 1834–1847)

CRFTC/HBC employee, associated with:

ship *May Dacre* (1834) passenger
CRFTC brigade (1834) member
HBC Snake party (1835) member
Forts William and Hall (1834–1837) laborer
Columbia Department (1837) laborer
barque *Columbia* (1847) passenger

Harry Parker was one of twenty men recruited for Nathaniel J. Wyeth's CRFTC in 1834. It is unclear from the surviving accounts whether or not he was among those who ran away later in the year. By the end of 1835 he was working at Fort Hall, where he remained until October 1837, when his account was settled by the HBC. Harry Parker must have remained in the Pacific Northwest, for in August 1847 he, or someone else with the same name, returned to Honolulu on the barque *Columbia.*

PS: OHS FtHallAB, CRFTCCB, HSA Passenger; *PPS:* Wyeth, *Correspondence,* 250; *SS:* Beidleman, "Fort Hall," 238

Parker, Harry [2] (fl. 1862)

Master mariner, associated with:

Victoria (1862)

Harry Parker, who described himself as Hawaiian, departed Victoria on the *Lady Young,* which reached Honolulu on September 9, 1862. He might be **Harry Parker** [1].

PS: HSA Passenger

Parker, William (fl. 1890s)

Fisherman, d. late 1890s, associated with:

Bowen Island (1890s)

According to oral tradition William Parker set out from the Hawaiian Islands for British Columbia in 1890 in a 60-foot homemade sailing sloop with his wife **Annie** (1853–?) as first mate and their children Napoleon (1879–?), Cecilia (1880–?), George (1886–?), John (1888–?), and William (1891–?) as deckhands.

William Parker, who identified himself as a Kanaka, was living with his family off of Bowen Island in their boat around 1893. It was to his house that Hawaiian **Tamaree** [5] went in 1896 and died the following year. William Parker claimed that he had known the seventy-two-year-old Tamaree for as long as he could remember, clearly from Island days.

By the time of the 1901 Census Annie Parker was widowed and living with her children in North Vancouver. They were all Mormon, a faith the family likely brought with them from the Islands.

PS: BCA Crt-Inquests, 1901 Canada Census, British Columbia, North Vancouver; *SS:* "Last Rite"

Patele (fl. 1841–1843)

HBC employee, associated with:

Fort Vancouver (1841–1842) middleman
schooner *Cadboro* (1843) laborer and middleman

Patele joined the HBC from Oʻahu in 1841 and began to receive wages on July 9 of that year. His contract ended in 1844, and he returned to Oʻahu on October 1, 1843.

PS: HBCA FtVanSA 6–7, YFDS 12, 14, YFSA 22–23

Pau [1] [variation: **Paii, Sam**] (fl. 1863–1864)

Laborer, associated with:

Alberni (1863–1864) sawmill worker

Pau and six other indigenous Hawaiians were contracted in Honolulu on September 23, 1863, by the agent of Alberni Mill Co. to work for $10 per month with a $20 advance. The same day they left for Victoria on the *Alberni*. On December 22, 1864, all of the men, except for **Kealili** who ran away, arrived back in Honolulu from Alberni on the ship *Buena Vista*. On the return list, Pau was called Sam, likely a first name he picked up in the Pacific Northwest.

PS: HSA Seamen, Passenger

Pau [2] (fl. 1864)

Occupation unknown, associated with:

Port Angeles, Washington (1864)

Pau and two other Hawaiians left for Port Angeles on the *N.S. Perkins* on October 25, 1864.

PS: HSA Passenger

Pau, Mary (fl. 1858–1865)

Wife, associated with:

Port Gamble (1858?–1865)

Mary Pau was the wife of longtime HBC employee **John Kau**, who settled at Port Gamble in the late 1850s. Their son was Pilipo (ca. 1859–?), for whom they gave a luau in 1865.

PS: HSA Passenger; *SS:* Naukana, "News"

Paulina (fl. 1862)

Laborer, associated with:

Port Gamble (1862) sawmill worker

Paulina was among seven men contracted in Honolulu on February 14, 1862, by the agent of Puget Mill Co. to work at its sawmill for $10 per month with a $20 advance. It is uncertain how long he did so.

PS: HSA Seamen

Paynee [variation: **Peney**] (fl. 1844–1848)

HBC employee, d. May 20, 1848, at Fort Vancouver, associated with:

Fort Vancouver (1844–1848) laborer

Paynee joined the HBC from Oʻahu in 1844 on a two-year contract and began work at Fort Vancouver on November 12, 1844. He appears to have worked temporarily on the schooner *Cadboro*, for while it was at Fort Vancouver on April 24, 1846, Paynee was sent on shore. On May 20, 1848, he died at Fort Vancouver of unspecified causes.

PS: HBCA YFSA 24–26, YFDS 10, 13, Log *Cadboro* 5

Peaennau, Joe [variations: **Pea-eannau, Pannau, Pranneau, Peannau**] (fl. 1836–1851)
HBC employee, associated with:

Fort Vancouver (1836–1837) middleman
Fort Langley (1837–1840) middleman
Fort McLoughlin (1840–1841) middleman
Fort Langley (1841–1842) middleman, (1842–1850) laborer
Fort Victoria (1850–1851) laborer

Joe Peaennau joined the HBC from Oʻahu in 1836. After working at a variety of coastal forts, mostly Fort Langley, over the next fifteen years, he appears to have retired in 1851, for in outfit 1851–1852 he was at Fort Victoria but he did not receive wages. He has not been traced further, nor has any family been located.

PS: HBCA YFDS 7, 22, YFSA 19–20, 22–32, FtVanSA 3–7, FtVicSA 1–2

Pedro (fl. 1860–1864)
Occupation unknown, associated with:

Victoria area (1864)

Hawaiian Pedro appeared in the Victoria Catholic records on February 26, 1864, when two of his children were baptized in the city. He had partnered with an unnamed Stikine woman and together they had Mary (1861–?) and Peter (1863–?). Given the cultural area of his wife, he may have been working for the Russians in the Alaska panhandle area.

PS: BCA VS-StAndC

Pee (fl. 1841–1844)
HBC employee, associated with:

Fort Vancouver (1841–1842) middleman, (1842–1844) laborer

Pee joined the HBC in Oʻahu in 1841 on a three-year contract. He began receiving wages on July 9, 1841, and for the next three and a half years worked at Fort Vancouver. His last day of work was November 23, 1844, at which point he returned to Oʻahu, where he received his final wages on December 31.

PS: HBCA FtVanSA 6–7, YFDS 12, YFSA 22–24, SandIsAB 5

Peeo (fl. 1844–1851)
HBC employee, associated with:

Fort Vancouver (1844–1847) laborer
barque *Columbia* (1847–1848) laborer
Fort Langley (1848–1851) laborer
brigantine *Mary Dare* (1851) passenger

Peeo, from Oʻahu, joined the HBC in 1844 on a three-year contract and for the next seven years worked from place to place. He retired on September 7, 1851, apparently remaining in the area, as his HBC account showed no movement.

PS: HBCA YFSA 24–31, YFDS 22, FtVicSA 1–2

Peeopeeoh [variations: **Maillot, Magno Pupu, Peeopeoh, Peo Peow, Peo Peo, Pion Pion, Peeoh Peeoh**] (fl. 1817–1860s)
NWC/HBC employee, b. ca. 1798, on the island of Hawaiʻi to Kanicheau and Klegina, associated with:

Columbia Department (1817–1823) laborer
Fort George [Astoria] (1823–1825) laborer

Columbia Department (1825–1826) sawyer
Fort Vancouver (1826–1827) sawyer
Fort Langley (1827–1837) sawyer, (1837–1842) middleman, (1842–1845) laborer,
(1845–1852) cooper
Fraser Valley (1850s–1860s)

According to his marriage certificate, Peeopeeoh was born on the island of Hawai'i to Kanicheau and Klegina. In 1817, nineteen-year-old Peeopeeoh, who was rumored to be related to King Kamehameha, joined the NWC. He later claimed to have gone as overseer or guardian of the sixty men with whom he arrived. His early movements have not been traced, as the Montreal company rarely named its Hawaiian employees.

After the amalgamation of 1821, Peeopeeoh, now a sawyer, continued on with the HBC and, in 1824, was part of an exploratory expedition seeking a suitable location at the mouth of the Fraser for a new trading post. In 1827, he helped construct Fort Langley, where he was to remain for the rest of his career. After Fort Langley was rebuilt upriver in 1840, Peeopeeoh and other Sandwich Islanders remained at the old Langley or Derby site, in an area collectively known as Kanaka Ranch, probably commuting the 3 miles each day to the new site. Peeopeeoh is said to have served as foreman of the other Hawaiians employed at the post. In 1852 he retired, but his name remained on the books until 1854.

In 1858 the Hawaiians were asked to move from the Derby site to make way for a proposed new capital of the British mainland colony of British Columbia, a request that Peeopeeoh vigorously protested to the government. At the beginning of 1860, as soon as it was legally possible to do so, Peeopeeoh and his sons and sons-in-law each preempted 160 acres across the Fraser River near the present-day community of Maple Ridge. The date of his death has not been traced.

Peeopeeoh appears to have had one wife, Catherine (?–?), who was Kwantlen and said to be a subchief's daughter. Their children were Algace or Paiwa (ca. 1824–?), who had children by **Ohia, Joseph Maayo** (ca. 1826–?), Sophie (ca. 1830–1916), who had children by **Peter Ohule** and New Brunswicker William Nelson, and **Henry** who acquired the surname of Pound (ca. 1835?–?).

PS: HBCA YFSA 2–9, 11–15, 19–20, 22–32, FtGeo[Ast]AB 11–12, YFDS 2a, 3a–3b, 4b, 5b–7, 16, FtVanAB 10, SA 1–6, FtVicSA 1, BCA VS-StAndC; *SS:* Laing, *Colonial Farm Settlers,* 99; Morton, *Fort Langley,* 288; Waite, *Langley Story,* 3–4; Jason Allard, *Daily World,* August 10, 1915

Peeopeeoh, Henry [variation: **Pound**] (1835–?)

Laborer, of mixed descent, b. ca. 1835 at Fort Langley to Peeopeeoh and Catherine, associated with:

Fort Langley area (1835–1860s)

Henry, son of longtime HBC employee Peeopeeoh, was born and raised, along with sisters Algace/Paiwa and Sophie and older brother **Joseph Maayo**, at the first site of Fort Langley. He likely worked for the HBC from time to time, although he does not appear on company records. By the mid-1850s numerous "free Kanakas" living at Kanaka Village, some of them retired employees, were hired as the need arose.

Henry and Margaret (?–?), likely a local Native woman, had at least two children, Bucie (?–bap. 1860–?) and John (?–bap.1860–?). At their baptisms in 1860, their father's surname was written as Pound, which may have represented the Anglican cleric's attempt to anglicize Peeopeeoh.

PS: BCA VS-StJohDiv; *SS:* Morton, *Fort Langley,* 288–289

Pēlāi (fl. 1853)

Occupation unknown, associated with:

Victoria area (1853)

Pēlāi is known only through his daughter Mary Ann (1853–?), who married Tahitian Noah Kamo in September 1867. Mary Ann's mother was Stahitl (?–?), a Kwantlen from near Fort Langley.

PS: BCA VS-StAndC

Peter [1] (fl. 1811)

Maritime fur trade seaman, d. March 24, 1811, near Cape Disappointment [Washington], associated with:

ship *Tonquin* (1811) seaman

Peter joined the crew of the *Tonquin* as a seaman in February 1811 when the vessel operated by the PFC stopped at Hawai'i. After arriving at the mouth of the Columbia on March 22, 1811, and after two days of efforts to establish a safe passage across the bar, the captain sent out Peter, fellow Sandwich Islander **Harry**, Stephen Weeks, Job Aiken, and John Coles in the pinnace to take soundings. When the small vessel filled with water, Aiken and Coles were lost but Weeks, Harry, and Peter stripped off their shirts and managed to right the pinnace, bailing it out with their hands. The cold, however, was too much for Peter, and he succumbed after the pinnace made it to shore. Weeks and Harry were rescued and on March 28, PFC clerks Gabriel Franchère and François Benjamin Pillet returned with six Sandwich Islanders who ceremoniously interred Peter's body at the beach.

PS: RosL *Astoria; PPS:* Franchère, *Journal,* 73–74

Peter [2] (fl. 1835–1837)

CRFTC employee, associated with:

ship *May Dacre* (1835) passenger
Fort Hall (1835–1837) laborer

Peter was one of thirty Hawaiians, six with wives in tow, who joined Nathaniel J. Wyeth's CRFTC in early 1835. He worked at Fort Hall until October 1837, when he returned home.

PS: OHS FtHallAB, CRFTCCB

Peter [3] [variations: **Pierre Jean, Peter Wahi**] (fl. 1837–1844)

HBC employee, associated with:

Fort Vancouver (1837–1838) middleman
Fort Nez Perces (1838–1839) middleman
barque *Vancouver* (1840) passenger
Fort Nez Perces (1840–1841) middleman
Fort Taku (1841–1843) middleman
Fort Victoria (1843–1844) middleman
Fort Vancouver (1844) middleman

Peter joined the HBC from O'ahu in 1837. At the end of his two-year contract, he returned to O'ahu on the *Vancouver*. He renewed his contract and worked at a variety of locations in the Columbia Department, from the Alaskan panhandle to the southern bend of the Columbia. His last day of work was November 12, 1844, at which point he returned to O'ahu and received his wages on Honolulu on December 31. He may have returned independently to the Columbia for, on April 27, 1845, at Fort Vancouver, a Pierre Jean all knew as Peter Wahi was baptized by the Catholic priests. He then disappeared from the records.

PS: HBCA YFSA 19–20, 22–24, YFDS 10, 15, FtVanSA 4–7, SMP 14, SandIsAB 3; *PPS:* Munnick, *Vancouver,* vol. 2

Peter [4] (fl. 1851–1852)

Occupation unknown, associated with:

Fort Victoria area (1851–1852)

A Hawaiian named only as Peter had his son Pierre (?–bap. 1852–?) baptized a Catholic on October 31, 1852, in Victoria.

PS: BCA VS-StAndC

Peter [5] (fl. 1853)

HBC employee, associated with:

ship *Pekin* (1853) seaman
ship *Mary Catherine* (1853) seaman

Peter shipped aboard the HBC chartered vessel *Pekin* in Honolulu, probably in the summer of 1853, sailed to the Northwest Coast, and arrived back in Honolulu September 27, 1853, on the *Mary Catherine*. He was given the final balance of his wages when he returned.

PS: HBCA SandIsLonIC 3

Peter [6] (fl. 1861)

Occupation unknown, associated with:

Victoria (1861)

Peter, who may be **Peter** [3], departed Honolulu for Victoria on the *Constitution* on February 22, 1861.

PS: HSA Passenger

Pibi (fl. 1872)

Seaman, b. 1841, associated with:

Victoria area (1872)

On August 12, 1872, in Victoria, Pibi, a thirty-one-year-old, 5 foot, 11 inch "Kanaka" seaman with gray hair, had a charge of assault against him dismissed as he was incapable of committing the offense. He could not read or write and was Catholic by faith.

PS: BCA Crt-Gaols

Pickard, Harry (fl. 1834)

CRFTC employee, d. December 1834 at Walla Walla, associated with:

ship *May Dacre* (1834) passenger
CRFTC brigade (1834) member

Harry Pickard was one of twenty men recruited for Nathaniel J. Wyeth's CRFTC in 1834 and among the dozen who deserted in November of the same year on the way to Fort

Hall. He was reportedly killed soon after by Blackfeet Indians following a confrontation with them.

PS: OHS FtHallAB, CRFTCCB; *PPS:* Wyeth, *Correspondence,* 235–239, 249–250

Pig (fl. 1835–1838)

CRFTC employee, associated with:

ship *May Dacre* (1835) passenger
Forts William and Hall (1835–1838)

Pig was one of thirty Hawaiians, six with wives in tow, who joined Nathaniel J. Wyeth's CRFTC in early 1835. He worked between Forts William and Hall until the end of 1837. Back at Oʻahu in March 1838, sporting a fine new suit of clothes, he was paid his outstanding balance of $206.68.

PS: OHS FtHallAB, CRFTCCB

Pipi (fl. 1862)

Laborer, associated with:

Vancouver Island (1862)

Pipi was one of eight laborers who left for Victoria on the *Constitution* on May 2, 1862. It is unclear where they were headed.

PS: HSA Passenger

Plomer, Harry [variation: **Henry Plomer**] (fl. 1830–1838)

HBC employee, possibly Hawaiian, associated with:

Columbia Department (1829–1830) seaman
Fort Vancouver (1830–1831) middleman
barque *Ganymede* (1831) passenger
Columbia Department (1838) laborer

Harry Plomer could possibly be a European who worked out of Hawaiʻi. He began work on coastal shipping with the HBC on February 1, 1830. He was discharged to Oʻahu on November 1, 1831, sailing in the *Ganymede.* He likely reappeared in the Columbia again in 1838, then apparently employed as a laborer.

Harry Plomer had one wife, a Native, Peggy (?–?) of unknown origin, and one recorded son, George (?–bap. 1838–?). His son was baptized Anglican in 1838 at Fort Vancouver, indicating the family was living there or nearby at the time.

PS: HBCA FtVanSA 2, YFDS 3b–4b, YFSA 9, 11, BCA VS-CCC

Ploughboy, Joe (fl. 1831–1849)

HBC employee, b. ca. 1812, associated with:

schooner *Cadboro* (1831) seaman
Naval Department (1831–1832) seaman
Fort Vancouver (1832–1833) laborer or middleman, (1833) sawmill worker,
   (1833–1837) laborer or middleman
barque *Nereide* (1837–1838) middleman
Fort Vancouver (1838–1840) middleman
South party (1840–1843) middleman
South party and California estate (1843–1844) middleman
California estate (1844–1846) laborer

Fort Vancouver (1846–1847) laborer
Snake Country (1847–1848) laborer
Fort Nez Perces (1848–1849) laborer
Fort Vancouver (1849) laborer

Joe Ploughboy enlisted with the HBC on June 16, 1831, in Oʻahu. He worked in a variety of places throughout the Columbia, including California, and, on September 5, 1849, the thirty-seven-year-old Sandwich Islander deserted, most likely for the gold fields of California.

PS: HBCA SMP 14, YFSA 11–15, 19–20, 22–29, YFDS 4a, 5a–7, 20, FtVanCB 9, SA 3–7

Poah, Paul [variations: **Pooao, Poak**] (fl. 1811–1823)

PFC / NWC / HBC employee, associated with:

ship *Tonquin* (1811) passenger
Fort Astoria (1811–1813) laborer
Fort George [Astoria] (1814) laborer
Columbia Department (1821–1823) milieu

Paul Poah became a twelve-year employee of the fur trade. He joined the crew of the *Tonquin* as a laborer around February 21, 1811, when the vessel stopped at Oʻahu and took on a complement of twenty Sandwich Islanders. One month later, on March 22, the *Tonquin* arrived at the mouth of the Columbia and, on April 12, Paul was noted as helping to unload the vessel. He stayed on shore, helped to construct the fort at Astoria, and, on October 12 of that year, sailed up the Columbia River on the maiden voyage of the newly constructed vessel *Dolly*. When the PFC was taken over by the NWC, Poah stayed on with the latter. He likely continued with the NWC in the area between 1814 and 1821, when he transferred to the HBC. His movements have not been traced after 1823, but he may have married and settled locally.

PS: RosL *Astoria*, HBCA NWCAB 9, YFSA 2; *PPS:* Henry, *Journal*, 711

Pookarakara, Bob [variation: **Packanakra**] (fl. 1811–1814)

PFC / NWC employee, associated with:

ship *Tonquin* (1811) passenger
Fort Astoria (1811–1814) laborer and hunter
overland brigade (1814)

Bob Pookarakara joined the crew of the *Tonquin* as a laborer around February 21, 1811, when the vessel stopped at Oʻahu. After his arrival, on March 22, he began working as a laborer but by the fall, when he went to winter at Young's Bay with an Iroquois hunter and his family, he appears to have become a hunter. On April 4, 1814, he left Astoria to travel overland with the brigade and likely arrived at Fort William by July of that year. He has not been traced further.

PS: RosL *Astoria*

Poonoroara (fl. 1844–1849)

HBC employee, associated with:

Fort Vancouver (1844–1849) laborer

Poornoroara joined the HBC from Oʻahu in 1844 and worked as a laborer at Fort Vancouver. He deserted in 1849, most likely at the beginning of the year, for in outfit 1849–1850 he received no wages.

PS: HBCA YFSA 24–29

Poopoo (fl. 1840–1843)

HBC/PSAC employee, associated with:

> Fort Vancouver (1840–1841) middleman
> Fort Nisqually (1841–1842) middleman, (1842–183) laborer
> Fort Vancouver (1843) laborer

Poopoo joined the HBC from Oʻahu in 1840 and began working at Fort Vancouver on July 14 of that year. He worked largely as a laborer at Forts Vancouver and Nisqually until November 15, 1843, when he returned to Oʻahu.

PS: HBCA YFSA 20, 22–23, YFDS 11, 14, FtVanSA 6–7, HL FtNisSA 2

Popoay (fl. 1830–1835)

HBC employee, associated with:

> Fort Vancouver general charges (1830–1831)
> Fort Simpson (1831–1832) laborer
> Fort Vancouver Indian trade (1832–1833) laborer
> Fort Simpson (1833–1834) laborer
> Fort McLoughlin (1834–1835) laborer
> barque *Ganymede* (1835) passenger

Popoay joined the HBC in April 1830. He worked intermittently on the north coast at Forts Simpson and McLoughlin and at Fort Vancouver. He is on record as leaving Fort Vancouver on the barque *Ganymede* on October 3, 1835, and being discharged in Oʻahu in 1835. He was paid his final HBC wage there.

PS: HBCA FtVanSA 2–3, YFDS 4a–6, YFSA 11–15, SandIsLonIC 1

Pora (fl. 1830–1832)

HBC employee, associated with:

> Fort Vancouver general charges (1830–1831)
> Fort Simpson (1831–1832) laborer
> Fort Vancouver (1832) laborer

Pora, from Oʻahu, joined the HBC in April 1830. He was discharged in Oʻahu on July 16, 1832.

PS: HBCA FtVanSA 2, YFDS 4a–4b, YFSA 11–12

Pouhow [variations: **Pouhou, Powhou, Powhow**] (fl. 1840–1846)

HBC employee, associated with:

> Fort Stikine (1840–1846) middleman

Pouhow may have attended missionary school in Oʻahu before joining the HBC in 1840, as he was able to read biblical scripture. After arriving at Fort Vancouver in April, he made his way to his first and only assignment, Fort Stikine, which he reached on the steamer *Beaver* on June 13. During the next six years, he appeared to spend the majority of his time in the saw pits.

On July 26, 1841, Pouhow was involved in a minor scuffle with a local Native who had consumed too much alcohol:

> It seems by report that it was the Indian that began to push him and on recovering he pretended to hit him but did not do so. The Indian immediately took up a piece of wood and struck Powhow with it. He then knocked around the Indian and gave

him a few clouts. The relations of the aggressor then came with guns to stop our work from going on and threatened to kill the first man they would see. (Fort Stikine journals, fo. 44)

Pouhow, who suffered no repercussions from the fray, was an exception in the servants' plot to kill the post manager, John McLoughlin Jr. Because from the fall through the spring the punitive beatings meted out by a sometimes drunken McLoughlin had grown progressively more severe, around Christmas time the servants plotted to kill him if he were not removed. All but Pouhow signed the agreement and on the evening of the murder the Hawaiians were called to arms by McLoughlin to protect him. It was for naught, for McLoughlin was murdered early that morning, on April 21, but Pouhow was the only servant not suspected of complicity. Pouhow helped to carry McLoughlin's body into a room and likely helped to wash and dry it. When murderer Pierre Kanaguasse tried to take McLoughlin's ring from the corpse, Pouhow took it from Kanaguasse and later gave it to McLoughlin's Indian wife. He also testified that he had seen young McLoughlin drunk only twice. As a reward for his noninvolvement, Pouhow continued to work uninterrupted at Stikine until December 10, 1846, at which point he returned to Oʻahu.

PS: HBCA YFSA 20, 22–26, FtVanSA 6–7, CB 29–31, YFDS 17, FtStikPJ 1–2; *PPS:* McLoughlin, *Fort Vancouver Letters, 1839–44*, 358

Pourere (fl. 1840)

HBC employee, associated with:

Fort Vancouver (1840) middleman

Pourere, from Oʻahu, joined the HBC on February 15, 1840, and is on record as working at Fort Vancouver until November 15 of that year. At that point he returned to Oʻahu.

PS: HBCA YFSA 20, FtVanSA 6, YFDS 11

Powhoken, Jack (fl. 1860)

Cook, b. ca. 1830, associated with:

Fort Vancouver area (1860) cook

Jack Powhoken, along with **J. Balia**, worked as a cook in 1860 for an HBC officer, three clerks, and a few other employees remaining at their nearly abandoned Fort Vancouver site. He wasn't listed as a contracted employee in HBC records, so may have been working casually.

PS: 1860 U.S. Census, Oregon, Clark Co.

Powlins (fl. 1822–1823)

HBC employee, associated with:

Columbia Department (1822–1823) laborer

Little is known about Powlins, who appeared once on the books in outfit 1822–1823 with a note that he had returned to the Islands. He appears to have worked only a short time in the Columbia area.

PS: HBCA FtGeo [Ast]AB 10

Powrowie, Jack [variations: **Powrowrie, Paraurriee**] (fl. 1811–1814)

PFC/NWC employee, b. probably on Oʻahu, associated with:

ship *Tonquin* (1811) passenger
Fort Astoria (1811–1814) laborer

Jack Powrowie came to the Columbia on March 22, 1811, on the *Tonquin* as a PFC laborer. On April 12, Jack Powrowie was noted as helping to unload the vessel and the following year was catching sturgeon as food for the trappers. He continued work with the NWC and, on April 4, 1814, he was prepared to work through the summer but later that month was sent to Fort George from Tongue Point very ill with venereal disease. He does not appear on record after that; however, he could be related to (or even the same as) **Joseph Powrowie.**

PS: RosL *Astoria; PPS:* Henry, *Journal,* 711, 722

Powrowie, Joseph (fl. 1821)

NWC/HBC employee, associated with:

Columbia Department (1821) laborer

Joseph Powrowie (who may be **Jack Powrowie**) was working for the NWC in 1821 when he joined the HBC. He may have worked for a short time for the HBC after that.

PS: HBCA NWCAB 9

Provero (fl. 1830–1833)

HBC employee, associated with:

schooner *Vancouver* (1830) seaman or laborer
schooner *Cadboro* (1831) seaman or laborer
Fort Vancouver general charges (1831–1832), Indian trade (1832–1833)
brigantine *Dryad* (1833) passenger

Provero joined the HBC in April 1830. He sailed on vessels supplying coastal posts and then worked on land in the Fort Vancouver area. At the end of his contract he was discharged and left the Columbia for Oʻahu on November 1, 1833, on the brig *Dryad.*

PS: HBCA SpMiscPap 14, FtVanSA 2, YFDS 4a–5b, YFSA 11–13

Puahili, Jim [variation: **Puahele**] (fl. 1834–1840)

HBC employee, associated with:

Fort Simpson (1834–1836) middleman or steersman
Fort Umpqua (1836–1837) middleman or steersman
Fort Vancouver (1837–1838) middleman
steamer *Beaver* (1838–1839) middleman, (1839–1840) middleman and woodcutter

Jim Puahili joined the HBC in 1834. He worked, possibly as a steersman, at Forts Simpson and Vancouver as well as a woodcutter on the HBC steamer *Beaver,* and was discharged at the end of his contract into retirement in Oʻahu on November 15, 1840.

PS: HBCA YFSA 14–15, 19–20, YFDS 5c–7, 11, FtVanSA 3–6, FtSimp[N]PJ 3

Pualoka (fl. 1866)

Seaman, associated with:

Victoria area (1866)

Nothing is known about Pualoka following his desertion from his vessel while docked in Victoria in April 1866.

PS: HSA Victoria

Puhelard, Pierre [variations: **Pollnharhre, Puhireho**] (fl. 1864–1866)

Occupation unknown, associated with:

Fort Langley area (1864–1866)

Little is known of Hawaiian Pierre Puhelard who appears to have resided in the Fort Langley/Derby area between 1864 and 1866.

Maria (ca. 1854–?), age ten, was baptized Catholic on October 31, 1864, as the daughter of Pierre Puhireho, "Kanaka," and Christina Walla-Walla (?–?). Puhelard, who was probably a friend of Tahitian **Noah Kamo**, appeared in the Catholic records again when his mixed descent wife Christine (?–?) died in Victoria on October 26, 1868, and was buried the next day. Their son Joseph (1866–1868), who had been born "on the Fraser River" on May 4, 1866, predeceased her on October 15.

PS: BCA VS-StAndC, OblH Fraser

Puili [variation: **Puilē**] (fl. 1844–1846)

HBC/PSAC employee, associated with:

Fort Vancouver (1844–1846) laborer
Fort Nisqually (1846) laborer

Puili, from Oʻahu, joined the HBC in 1844 on a three-year contract. He worked as a laborer at Forts Vancouver and Nisqually until November 30, 1846, when he returned to Oʻahu.

PS: HBCA YFSA 24–26, YFDS 17, HL FtNisSA env

Pulhelee, George [variations: **Pulhili, Pulaylay**] (fl. 1829–1833)

HBC employee, associated with:

Fort Vancouver general charges (1829–1831)
Fort Simpson (1831–1833) laborer
Fort Vancouver (1833) laborer

George Pulhelee joined the HBC probably in late 1829. He was taken north, where he helped to construct the original Fort Simpson [Nass]. He returned to Fort Vancouver in 1833 and left for Oʻahu at the end of his contract on November 3, 1833.

PS: HBCA FtVanSA 2, YFDS 4a–5b, YFSA 11–13

Punebaka (fl. 1840–1855)

HBC/PSAC employee, associated with:

Fort Vancouver (1840–1842) middleman, (1842–1843) laborer
Snake party (1843–1845) laborer, (1845) goer and comer
Cowlitz farm (1847–1849) laborer
steamer *Beaver* (1849–1850) woodcutter
Fort Simpson (1850–1852) laborer
Fort Victoria (1853–1855) laborer

Punebaka, from Oʻahu, joined the HBC in 1840 and worked at Fort Vancouver and as a goer and comer with the Snake party. As his contract ended in 1845, he worked until December 10 of that year, at which point he returned to Oʻahu. He reenlisted and, during the measles outbreak in the winter of 1847–1848, found himself looking after the other Sandwich Islanders who were ill at the Cowlitz farm. He became a woodcutter on the *Beaver* and then retired from the service at Fort Simpson on October 1, 1852. He appeared on the 1853–1855 Fort Victoria servants' abstracts without wages, although he was listed as a laborer, and between 1854 and 1858 he carried a debt of £13.9.8 indicating no movement on his account.

PS: HBCA YFSA 20, 22–25, 27–32, FtVanSA 6–7, YFDS 16, FtVicDS, SA 1–5; *PPS:* Roberts, "Round Hand"

Rad (fl. 1860)

Laborer, b. ca. 1840, associated with:

Fort Vancouver area (1860) laborer

Rad was one of the many Hawaiians living in the Kanaka Village–Fort Vancouver area in 1860. As such, he may have worked for what remained of the HBC interests in the area or for the nearby U.S. military post. If he was a former HBC employee, it was likely under a different name.

PS: 1860 U.S. Census, Washington Territory, Clark Co.

Rahilee, Columbia [variation: **Rahilu**] (fl. 1830–1831)

HBC employee, associated with:

Fort Vancouver general charges (1830–1831)
barque *Ganymede* (1831) passenger

Columbia Rahilee joined the HBC in 1830 and was discharged to Oʻahu on November 1, 1831, sailing on the *Ganymede*.

PS: HBCA FtVanSA 2, YFDS 4a, YFSA 11

Rappa, Moniday (fl. 1832–1839)

HBC employee, associated with:

Fort Simpson naval service (1832–1833) seaman
Fort Simpson (1833–1834) middleman or laborer
Fort McLoughlin (1834–1836) middleman or laborer
Fort Vancouver (1836–1838) middleman or laborer
barque *Nereide* (1838) landsman
barque *Vancouver* (1839) passenger

Moniday Rappa joined the HBC in Oʻahu on September 6, 1832, and worked principally at Forts Simpson and McLoughlin. He took passage back to Oʻahu on the *Vancouver* and landed there in December 1839. He may have continued to work at the Oʻahu establishment, for he is recorded as being discharged in 1840 at the end of his contract.

PS: HBCA YFDS 5a–7, 11, YFSA 12–15, 19, FtVanSA 3–6, SMP 14

Rattine [variation: **Ratline**] (fl. 1843–1847)

HBC employee, d. 1847 at Fort Vancouver, associated with:

Fort George [Astoria] (1843–1845) laborer
Fort Vancouver Indian trade (1845–1847) laborer

Rattine appeared in the Columbia area at Fort George in outfit 1843–1844 on a contract that ended in 1846. In outfit 1847–1848 he appears without wages and the notation that he died at Fort Vancouver around where he had mostly worked, meaning that he probably died in 1847.

PS: HBCA FtVanSA 8, YFSA 23–27, YFDS 16

Renomi (fl. 1854–1856)

Occupation unknown, associated with:

Victoria area (1855–1856)

Renomi, a Hawaiian with an unusual name, appeared in the Victoria area in 1855–1856. There he coupled with Tsassemaat (?–?), a Kwantlen woman, and together they had a son, Louis (ca. 1855–?). Because of his wife's cultural area, he may have spent some time at Derby.

PS: BCA VS-StAndC

Rhodes, Henry (fl. 1859–1878)

Hawai'i consul, b. 1824 in England, d. 1878 in Victoria, associated with:

Victoria (1859–1878) consul and businessman

Businessman Henry Rhodes served as Hawai'i consul in Victoria from 1859 to his death in 1878. He also ran a lumber business there. Born in England, he had earlier lived in the Islands and knew the language. He was the brother of Godfrey Rhodes, active in Islands politics.

Henry Rhodes and Sophia (1830–1899), who had been born in India of English descent, were the parents of Annie (1852–1920), Godfrey (1854–1882), and Harvey (ca. 1854–1895), all born in the Hawaiian Islands, and Sophie (1860–1902), Charles (1861–1912), and Martha (1869–1919), born in Victoria. In 1881 Harvey was living with his widowed mother and working as a bank clerk. Godfrey was living on his own in Victoria and working as a clerk. Two years later he was sentenced to one-month's hard labor in a Victoria jail for vagrancy. Sophie married George Walkem (1835–1908), who was premier of British Columbia, 1874–1876.

PS: HSA Victoria, 1881 Canada Census, British Columbia, Victoria; *PPS:* British Columbia, Superintendent of Police, *Annual Report,* 1883

Rice (fl. 1835–1838)

CRFTC employee, associated with:

ship *May Dacre* (1835) passenger
Forts William and Hall (1835–1838) laborer

Rice was among thirty Hawaiians, six with wives in tow, who joined Nathaniel J. Wyeth's CTFTC in early 1835. He spent the next three years at Fort Hall. He returned home in March 1838 sporting a fine new suit of clothes. There he was paid his outstanding balance of $190.69.

PS: OHS FtHallAB

Richard [1] (fl. 1810)

Maritime fur trade seaman, associated with:

brig *Albatross* (1810–1811) extra crew

Richard joined the Winship brothers' brig, *Albatross,* from the Sandwich Islands on April 2, 1810. The brig sailed to the Columbia River, arriving May 26, 1810. Upriver the crew attempted to establish a settlement of buildings and gardens near Oak Island, but they were soon flooded out, and the men were also unsuccessful at establishing anything farther down the river. The brig then sailed off to other locations and, for the next four years, sailed between the Northwest/California coast, the Sandwich Islands, and China. Just how long Richard stayed with the vessel as an extra crewman is uncertain.

PS: PrivMS *Albatross*

Richard [2] (fl. 1825)

Maritime fur trade seaman, associated with:

brig *Convoy* (1825) seaman

Richard [2] shipped aboard the brig *Convoy* at Oʻahu after it arrived there on March 16, 1825, to unload cargo and take on supplies for the Northwest Coast. After sailing April 1 as a laborer, Richard and the vessel traded for a season, returning to Honolulu on November 2. It is not known whether he continued to sail with the *Convoy*.

PSS: BCA PR-*Convoy; SS:* Howay, "List"

Robert (fl. 1825)

Maritime fur trade seaman, associated with:

brig *Convoy* (1825) seaman

Robert shipped aboard the *Convoy* at Oʻahu after it arrived at that island on March 16, 1825, to unload cargo and take on supplies for the Northwest Coast. After sailing April 1 as a laborer, Robert and the vessel traded for a season, returning to Honolulu November 2. It is not known whether he continued to sail with the *Convoy*.

PS: BCA PR-*Convoy; SS:* Howay, "List"

Roots, Jem [variation: **Gem Roots**] (fl. 1841–1844)

HBC/PSAC employee, associated with:

barque *Cowlitz* (1841) laborer
Cowlitz farm (1841–1842) middleman, (1842–1844) laborer

Jem Roots joined the HBC in Honolulu around July 15, 1841, under a three-year contract and sailed to the Northwest Coast on the *Cowlitz*. He spent the next three years until November 24, 1844, working as a laborer on the Cowlitz farm, at which time he returned to Oʻahu. He received his final wages there on December 31.

PS: HBCA Log of *Cowlitz* 1, FtVanSA 6–7, YFDS 12, 17, YFSA 22–25, SandIsAB 3, HL FtNisSA 2, FtNisB env

Ropeyarn, Jack [1] (fl. 1827)

Maritime fur trade laborer, associated with:

brig *Owhyhee* (1827) laborer or seaman

Jack Ropeyarn, from Oʻahu, joined the brig *Owhyhee* in January 1827, sailed to the Northwest Coast, and returned to Oʻahu in July, when he was discharged.

PS: CHS *Owhyhee*

Ropeyarn, Jack [2] (fl. 1836–1849)

HBC employee, associated with:

Fort Vancouver general charges (1836)
Fort Vancouver (1836–1837) middleman
attached to Dr. Marcus Whitman (1837–1838) middleman
Fort Vancouver (1838–1846) middleman and laborer, (1846–1848) cook
Willamette Falls (1848–1849) cook

Jack Ropeyarn, who may be the same as **Jack Ropeyarn** [1], joined the HBC in Oʻahu in January, 1836. In 1837–1838, he worked for the missionary Dr. Marcus Whitman. He retired before June 1, 1849, as he received no wages for outfit 1849–1850. Ropeyarn remained in the area but a family, if it existed, has not been traced.

PS: HBCA FtVanSA 3–7, YFDS 6–7, YFSA 15, 19–20, 22, 24–30, FtVicSA 1

Rora (fl. 1838–1839)

Laborer, d. Willamette mission, November 21, 1839, associated with:

Willamette mission (1838–1839) employee

A "brown Islander" named as Rora and described as "a faithful servant of the mission" was working at Jason Lee's Methodist mission on the Willamette for at least a year at the time of his death in November 1839. It is possible Rora was a nickname.

PPS: Baily, *Grains,* 191

Rowawa (fl. 1839)

HBC/PSAC employee, associated with:

Cowlitz farm (1839) middleman
barque *Vancouver* (1839) passenger

Rowawa was hired by the HBC in 1839 on a one-year contract, worked on the Cowlitz farm, and was sent back to O'ahu, leaving Fort Vancouver on November 15, 1839.

PS: HBCA YFSA 29, YFDS 10, SMP 14

Sam (fl. 1840–1844)

HBC employee, associated with:

Fort Taku (1840–1843) middleman
Fort Victoria (1843–1844) laborer

Sam joined the HBC from O'ahu in 1840 on a three-year contract. He was first assigned to Fort Taku, which was being constructed at the time. He worked on this northerly coastal fort on the Alaskan panhandle for three outfits before he was transferred to Fort Victoria. There he worked until November 23, 1844, at which point he returned to O'ahu and was given his final wages on December 31 in Honolulu.

PS: HBCA YFSA 20, 22–24, FtVanSA 6–7, SandIsAB 3

Samson (fl. 1844–1845)

Occupation unknown, associated with:

Fort Vancouver area (1844–1845)

Samson could be any number of Hawaiians listed here, including **Samuhumuhu,** who were in the area in the early 1840s. Samson partnered with a Native woman of the Dalles area and, by March 8, 1845, had a child Ignace (?-bap. 1845–?). The mother promised to raise the child Catholic even though she had not been baptized.

PPS: Munnick, *Vancouver,* vol. 2

Samuel [1] (fl. 1796–1797)

Maritime fur trade seaman, associated with:

brig *Sea Otter* (1795–1797) seaman

Samuel appears to have been in Boston when he joined the brig *Sea Otter* around October 1795 for its voyage to the Northwest Coast. After reaching the coast, the vessel traded in 1796 and wintered over into the next season when the captain, along with the steward and purser, were killed by Natives at Cushewa. Upon their death, the first mate took command, sailing the *Sea Otter* to Macao, where it arrived on November 30, 1797. Samuel, however, probably left the ship in the Sandwich Islands. If he stayed onboard for its return voyage to New England, he would have arrived back in Boston on July 21, 1798; however, this is unlikely.

PS: HUHL Lamb notes; *SS:* Howay, "List"

Samuel [2] (fl. 1825)

Maritime fur trade seaman, associated with:

brig *Convoy* (1825) seaman

Samuel shipped aboard the *Convoy* at O'ahu after it arrived at that island on March 16, 1825, to unload cargo and take on supplies for the Northwest Coast. After sailing April 1 as a laborer, Samuel and the vessel traded for a season on the Northwest Coast, returning to Honolulu November 2. It is not known whether he continued to sail with the *Convoy*.

PS: BCA PR-*Convoy; SS:* Howay, "List"

Samuel [3] (fl. 1861–1862)

Laborer, associated with:

Port Gamble (1861–1862) sawmill worker

Samuel and five others were contracted in Honolulu on October 5, 1861, by the agent of Puget Mill Co. to work at its sawmill for $15 per month with a $15 advance. On December 15, 1862, Samuel arrived back in Honolulu from Teekalet on the barque *Jenny Ford*.

PS: HSA Passenger, Seamen

Samuel [4] (fl. late nineteenth–early twentieth centuries)

Occupation unknown, associated with:

Tacoma area

Samuel was the surname adopted by a Hawaiian who did not want to be caught jumping ship in Tacoma, likely in the late nineteenth century. He spent his life in the area.

Samuel had several children by an unknown woman. He was determined his children would appreciate poi and retain the Hawaiian language, but a granddaughter lost her facility on being sent to Chemawa Residential School near Salem, Oregon.

PS: Sally Jo Moon, "Aloha Alive and Well in British Columbia," *Honolulu Star-Bulletin,* August 14, 1971

Samuel, Peter (fl. 1891)

Miner, b. ca. 1856, associated with:

Nanaimo (1891) coal miner

Born in the Sandwich Islands, as were both of his parents, Peter Samuel was in 1891 working as a coal miner in Wellington outside of Nanaimo. He could read and write.

PS: 1881 Canada Census, British Columbia, Nanaimo

Samuhumuhu (fl. 1840–1849)

HBC employee, associated with:

Fort Vancouver (1840–1843) middleman, (1843–1849) laborer

Samuhumuhu, from Oʻahu, joined the HBC in 1840. He spent his entire working career at Fort Vancouver until he deserted on July 20, 1849, likely for the gold fields of California. He has not been traced after that.

PS: HBCA YFSA 20, 22–29, FtVanSA 6–7, YFDS 20

Sharing [variation: **Shaving**] (fl. 1840–1845)

HBC employee, associated with:

Fort Nez Perces (1840–1843) middleman
Fort Vancouver general charges (1843–1844) laborer
steamer *Beaver* (1844–1845) laborer, (1845) woodcutter

Sharing joined the HBC from Oʻahu in 1840 and worked at Forts Nez Perces and Vancouver and as a woodcutter on the *Beaver*. As his contract ended in 1845, he worked until December 31, at which point he returned to Oʻahu, where he was paid off.

PS: HBCA YFSA 20, 22–25, FtVanSA 6–7, YFDS 16, SandIsAB 5

Smith, William (fl. 1856–1860)

Occupation unknown, associated with:

Oregon Territory (1856–1860)

Nothing is known about William Smith, a Hawaiian whose two sons by an unnamed Native woman, Paul (1857–?) and Andree (1859–?), were baptized by an itinerant Catholic priest in 1860.

PPS: Munnick, *Oregon City*

Spunyarn [1] (fl. 1815)

Maritime fur trade seaman, associated with:

schooner *Columbia* (1815) crew member

Spunyarn worked as a crew member on the NWC schooner *Columbia* when it was on the Northwest Coast trading for furs in 1815.

PS: HBCA NWCAB 5

Spunyarn [2] (fl. 1825)

Martime fur trade seaman, associated with:

brig *Convoy* (1825) seaman

Spunyarn shipped aboard the brig *Convoy* at Oʻahu after it arrived on March 16, 1825, to unload cargo and take on supplies for the Northwest Coast. After sailing April 1 as a laborer, Spunyarn and the vessel traded on the Northwest Coast for a season, returning to Honolulu November 2. It is not known whether he continued to sail with the *Convoy* and he has not been subsequently traced.

PS: BCA PR-*Convoy; SS:* Howay, "List"

Spunyarn [3] [variation: **Spunlure**] (fl. 1830–1853)

HBC employee, b. ca. 1807, d. ca. June 15, 1853, at Fort Vancouver, associated with:

Fort Vancouver general charges (1830–1831)
Fort Colvile (1831–1834) middleman or laborer
Fort Nez Perces (1834–1835) middleman or laborer
Snake party (1835–1839) middleman

Fort Vancouver (1839–1842) middleman, (1842–1843) laborer
Fort Vancouver (1843–1849) cooper, (1849–1850) laborer, (1849–1853) cooper

Spunyarn, who may be **Spunyarn** [2], joined the HBC from Oʻahu in 1830. He worked at various locations in the Columbia Department for a number of years until he became a cooper at Fort Vancouver in 1843. By 1851 he was the only full-fledged cooper left at Fort Vancouver, being paid £30 a year. His obviously non-Hawaiian name in English denotes cloth, a common trade item, but to the Catholic priests at Fort Vancouver it became "Spaniard" or "L'Espangol." He died and was buried on June 15, 1853, a time when many Hawaiians were dying at the fort from diseases brought up from the Isthmus of Panama by the U.S. Army.

Spunyarn had one named wife, Emilie (?–?), possibly more, and five children. The Spunyarn children were Olive (1840–?), François Xavier (ca. 1843–?), Catherine (1843–1843), Louis (ca. 1847–?), and Jean (ca. 1849–?).

PS: HBCA FtVanSA 2–6, 9–10, YFDS 4a–7, 11, 22, YFSA 11–15, 19–20, 22–32, 1850 U.S. Census, Oregon, Clark Co., FtHallAB; *PPS:* Munnick, *Vancouver,* vol. 2, *Oregon City*

Swain, Joseph (fl. 1831–1832)

Maritime fur trade seaman, d. March 29, 1832, at the mouth of the Nass River, associated with:

brig *Lama* (1831–1832) seaman

Joseph Swain likely joined the Boston brig *Lama* between March 11 and 29, 1831, when it was in Oʻahu on the way to the Northwest Coast. While the vessel was at Nass, Swain died from a long bout of illness. He was buried next day on the north side of the harbor. No relation to Spelman Swaine, who earlier visited the Islands, has been established.

PS: BCA PR-*Lama*

Swazey, Mrs. (fl. 1850)

Housewife and settler, possibly of mixed descent, b. ca. 1822, associated with:

Clatsop County (1850)

Nothing is known of Mrs. Swazey who was born on the Sandwich Islands and by 1850 had settled with her husband, who was a blacksmith from New York, in Clatsop County, Oregon. The time of her birth may indicate she was indigenous Hawaiian or of mixed descent.

PS: 1850 U.S. Census, Oregon, Clatsop Co., All Townships, HSA Passenger

Taeenui (fl. 1840–1845)

HBC/PSAC employee, associated with:

Fort Vancouver (1840–1841) middleman
Snake party (1841) middleman
Fort Nisqually (1841–1843) laborer and shepherd
Fort Vancouver (1843–1845) laborer

Taeenui joined the HBC from Oʻahu in 1840. He was assigned to the Snake party but was transferred to Fort Nisqually around the end of 1841. He worked as a shepherd and in April 1843 was billed for "1 ewe lamb left in the plains & devoured by the wolves." His contract ended in 1845, and he worked until July 18, 1845, at which point he returned to Oʻahu, where he was given a sum of money.

PS: HBCA YFSA 20, 22–25, YFDS 12, 16, FtVanSA 6–7, SandIsAB 5, HL FtNisSA 2, FtNisB env

Tahako (fl. 1840–1852)

HBC employee, associated with:

Fort Vancouver (1840–1842) middleman, (1842–1849) laborer
Thompson River (1849–1852) laborer

From Oʻahu, Tahako joined the HBC on a three-year contract in 1840 and for the next dozen years worked mostly at Fort Vancouver. In outfit 1851–1852 he was located at Thompson River but did not receive wages. He remained on the books for four more years, indicating that he may have still been in the area.

PS: HBCA YFSA 20, 22–32, FtVanSA 6–7, FtVicSA 1–2

Tahanoe (fl. 1830–1832)

HBC employee, associated with:

Fort Vancouver general charges (1830–1831)
Fort Simpson (1831–1832)

Tahanoe joined the HBC in April 1830. He was discharged to Oʻahu on July 16, 1832.

PS: HBCA FtVanSA 2, YFDS 4a–5a, YFSA 11–12

Tahaouni, Joseph (fl. 1873)

Occupation unknown, b. ca. 1833, associated with:

Victoria area (1873)

Joseph Tahaouni, so named, died a Catholic on July 22, 1873, in the Victoria area. He may be the same person as **Joseph Taharnai** or **Tahowna.**

PS: BCA VS-StAndC

Taharnai, Joseph (fl. 1850)

Laborer, b. 1823, associated with:

Fort Vancouver area (1850) laborer

Joseph Taharnai lived in Kanaka Village near Fort Vancouver in 1850 in the same house as **Likē.** It seems very likely they were brothers. He may be the same person as **Joseph Tahaouni.**

PS: 1850 U.S. Census, Oregon, Clark Co.

Tahayree (fl. 1840–1844)

HBC employee, associated with:

Fort Taku (1840–1842) middleman
Fort Vancouver (1842–1844) laborer

From Oʻahu, Tahayree joined the HBC in 1840 on a three-year contract. He was sent first to northerly Fort Taku and then to Fort Vancouver. At the end of his contract, he returned to Oʻahu.

PS: HBCA YFSA 20, 22–23, FtVanSA 6–7

Taheenou (fl. 1840–1846)

HBC employee, associated with:

Fort Stikine (1840–1841) middleman
Fort Langley (1841–1842) middleman, (1842–1846) laborer

Taheenou, from Oʻahu, joined the HBC in 1840. He worked at Forts Stikine and Langley until December 10, 1846, at which point he returned to Oʻahu.

PS: HBCA YFSA 20, 22–26, FtVanSA 6–7, YFDS 17

Taheerinai [variations: **Taherinai, Taheerina**] (fl. 1840–1850)
HBC employee, associated with:
Fort Vancouver (1840–1842) middleman, (1842–1850) laborer

Taheerinai, from Oʻahu, joined the HBC in 1840 on a three-year contract. He worked until November 15, 1843, at which point he returned to Oʻahu. He likely reenlisted right away and returned to Fort Vancouver. He deserted around November 1850 and has not been traced after that.

PS: HBCA YFSA 20, 22–30, FVASA 6–7, YFDS 14, 21

Tahenna [variation: **Tahanna**] (fl. 1844–1859)
HBC employee, associated with:
Fort Vancouver (1844–1845) laborer
Snake party (1845–1846) goer and comer
steamer *Beaver* (1846–1847) woodcutter
Fort Stikine (1847–1849) laborer
Fort Rupert (1849–1850) laborer
brigantine *Mary Dare* (1850–1851) laborer
steamer *Beaver* (1851–1852) woodcutter
Fort Simpson (1852–1859) laborer

Tahenna, from Oʻahu, joined the HBC in 1844 and spent the next fifteen years working at coastal forts and on vessels as a woodcutter. He was among a group of men seeking to return home in 1850, who were persuaded to stay on in the Pacific Northwest. He may have been literate in Hawaiian, for when he was recruited for missionary William Duncan's Men's Night School at Fort Simpson in 1857, it was noted he could not read and write in English, implying that he could in Hawaiian. On January 2, 1857, while in a fight with another HBC servant, he had a piece of his lip bitten off. His contract ended in 1859 and, on March 7 of that year, he sailed south to Victoria on the *Labouchere*. He has not been traced after that.

Tahenna appeared to have one wife, Cecile (?–?), of unknown origin, and one child Louis Auguste (?–bap. 1850–?), who was baptized Catholic on September 15, 1850.

PS: HBCA YFSA 24–32, YFDS 16, Log of *Beaver*, FtVicSA 1–7, FtSimp[N]PJ 7–8, BCA VS-StAndC, BCA PR-Helmcken, UBC Duncan

Tahia (fl. 1850–1851)
Occupation unknown, associated with:
Victoria area (1850–1851)

Nothing is known of Tahia other than his son Louis (?–bap. 1851–?), the product of Tahia and a Native wife, was baptized in the Victoria area on July 5, 1851.

PS: BCA VS-StAndC

Tahomeeraoo [variation: **Tymarow**] (fl. 1792)
Ship's companion, b. ca. 1776 on Niʻihau, associated with:
ship *Jenny* (1792) passenger
Nootka (1792) companion
ship *Discovery* (1792–1793) passenger

Tahomeeraoo, along with **Teheeopea,** joined the Bristol ship *Jenny* in the Sandwich Islands and traveled with the crew to Nootka, arriving there on October 12, 1792. On October 12, they were both taken aboard Captain George Vancouver's HMS *Discovery* and, with crew member and fellow Sandwich Islander **Kalehua** as chaperone, returned to the Islands.

PPS: Vancouver, *Voyage,* 688, 892–896

Tahoora (fl. 1822–1823)

HBC employee, associated with:

Columbia Department (1822–1823) laborer

Little is known of Tahoora, who was working in the Columbia area around 1822–1823. The records show he returned to his island at that time.

PS: HBCA FtGeo[Ast]AB 10

Tahouay [variations: Tahoway, Tahaouay] (fl. 1840–1852)

HBC employee, associated with:

Fort Taku (1840–1842) middleman, (1842–1843) laborer
Fort Stikine (1843–1849) laborer
Fort Rupert (1849–1850) laborer
Fort Simpson (1850–1852) laborer

Tahouay joined the HBC in 1840 from O'ahu. He worked at a variety of coastal forts until October 1, 1852, when he retired from Fort Simpson. He was on company books until 1856 and action on his account indicates that he may still have been in the area during that period.

Tahouay had a daughter, who died October 15, 1849, at Fort Rupert.

PS: HBCA YFSA 20, 22–32, FtVanSA 6–7, FtVicDS 1, SA 3, FtSimp[N]PJ 7, BCA PR-Helmcken

Tahouna, Paul (fl. 1870)

Occupation unknown, b. February 1, 1837, associated with:

San Juan/Victoria area (1870)

On December 19, 1870, a Hawaiian named as Paul Tahouna wed a woman named Mary (?–?) in a Catholic ceremony in Victoria.

PS: BCA VS-StAndC

Tahowna [variations: Tahaoune, Tahauni, Tahawini, Tahowia] (fl. 1844–1867)

HBC employee, associated with:

Fort Vancouver (1844–1846) laborer
Thompson River (1846–1849) laborer
Fort Alexandria (1849–1850) laborer
Fort Victoria (1851–1853) laborer
Victoria area (1853–1867)

Tahowna, from O'ahu, joined the HBC in 1844 on a three-year contract. He worked at both the interior and coast before retiring nine years later in 1853 and for the next four years carried on transactions with the HBC. From 1853 on, he may have spread his time between Fort Langley, where one of his children was baptized in 1853, and Victoria. Tahowna chose Salehexia / Tseleachei / Sara (ca. 1845–?), a Kwantlen woman, as his wife. Their recorded children were Basile (?–bap. 1853–?), Julie (ca. 1855–?), Sophia (ca. 1860–?), Mary (ca. 1864–?), and Joseph Edward (ca. 1867–?).

PS: HBCA YFSA 24–32, YFDS 21, FtVicSA 1–2; BCA VS-StAndC

Ta-i [variations: **Tai, Peter Tahi, Tēay**] (fl. 1830–1848)

HBC employee, d. ca. 1848 likely at Fort Langley, associated with:

Fort Langley (1830–1833)
Fort Nisqually (1833–1834)
Fort Langley (1834–1842) middleman or laborer, (1842–1848) laborer

Ta-i joined the HBC from O'ahu in April 1830. Other than assisting with the construction of Fort Nisqually in 1833–1834, he spent his entire career at Fort Langley until his death in 1848.

On September 4, 1841, at the Stellamaris mission at the mouth of the Columbia River, Eugene (1840–?) was baptized Catholic as a natural child of Tēay and of a Sauitch woman.

PS: HBCA FtVanSA 2–7, YFDS 4a–7, YFSA 11–15, 19–20, 22–29, HL FtNisPJ 1, FtNisB 1–2, *PPS:* Munnick, *Vancouver,* vol. 1

Tai-a-nui, Jem [variation: **Jim Tai-a-nui**] (fl. 1834–1836)

HBC employee, associated with:

Fort Simpson (1834–1836) middleman or laborer
Fort Vancouver (1836) middleman

Jim Tai-a-nui joined the HBC from O'ahu in 1834. At the end of his three-year contract and around December 1836, he returned to O'ahu. In 1837–1838, he appeared on the sundries account, indicating that he was possibly in the area at the time.

PS: HBCA FtSimp[N]PJ, YFSA 14–15, YFDS 5c–7, FtVanSA 3–4

Talao [variation: **Taluo**] (fl. 1837–1841)

HBC employee, associated with:

Snake party (1837–1841) middleman

Talao joined the HBC from O'ahu in 1837 and began work with the Snake party on July 31 of that year. He worked as a goer and comer for the trappers into the Snake River country until November 20, 1841, when he returned to O'ahu.

PS: HBCA FtVanSA 4–7, YFDS 8, 12, YFSA 19–21

Tamaherry (fl. 1844–1849)

HBC employee, associated with:

Willamette (1844–1846) laborer
Fort Vancouver (1846–1849) laborer

Tamaherry, from O'ahu, joined the HBC in 1844 and worked in the Willamette. In 1847–1849 he was employed by John McLoughlin, retired head of Fort Vancouver. Tamaherry retired in 1849, probably before outfit 1849–1850, as he received no wages for that outfit. He remained in the area.

PS: HBCA YFSA 24–29, YFDS 18–19

Tamaree [1] (fl. 1827)

Maritime fur trade seaman, associated with:

  brig *Owhyhee* (1827) seaman

Tamaree appears to have worked as a seaman on the brig *Owhyhee* when it traded on the Northwest Coast in 1827. When the vessel returned to Oʻahu in July 1827, he was discharged at his own request.

PS: CHS *Owhyhee; SS:* Howay, "List"

Tamaree [2] (fl. 1843)

PSAC employee, associated with:

  Fort Nisqually (1843) laborer

A man named Tamaree from the Sandwich Islands was employed at Fort Nisqually in 1843. He has not been traced further, but may be **Tamaree** [3].

PS: HL FtNisSA envelope

Tamaree [3] [variations: **Tamare, Tamaru, Tamau, Tamane**] (fl. 1851–1854)

HBC/PSAC employee, associated with:

  sloop *Georgiana* (1851–1852) cook
  Fort Nisqually (1852–1854) laborer

Tamare had a strong sense of adventure and self-interest. It is not known how he got to the coast but he was the cook on the *Georgiana,* when it sailed from Olympia to the Queen Charlotte Islands in November 1851 with a group of prospectors onboard. News of gold finds drew them north, but they had a very different adventure. After the sloop was shipwrecked off shore, the Haida took the men captive for ransom. Tamaree was one of three crew members selected to go by canoe to Fort Simpson to attempt to secure their release. Rescued two months later, Tamaree and the others returned to Puget Sound.

The Hawaiian named Tamaree who erected a dairy at the Tlithlow outreach Nisqually farm on June 8, 1852, was likely the same man. From December of that year, he appeared at Nisqually doing a variety of tasks from making paddles, squaring timber, and cutting firewood, to making carts, dipping rams in tobacco water, and thrashing wheat. On May 11, 1853, he was discharged for selling spirits to the Indians. He then began work for settler Charles Wren at Edgar's Lake, Muck, where he and **Kalama** stole three sheep; over the next few months they went on to kill a number of company's cattle. He returned September 19 and, with **Kupahi,** stole eighteen blankets and two sacks of sugar. Tamaree took fifty blankets with him to trade for horses and the rest he divided among the Hawaiians with whom he was working. He was tried at Steilacoom in November 1854. He has not been traced further, but may be **Tamaree** [4].

PS: HL FtNisPJ 8–10, FtNisSA 7–8; *SS:* Crooks, *Past Reflections,* 15–18

Tamaree [4] [variations: **Tamerea, Tomali, Tamara, Tamary, Thomara**] (fl. 1858–1870)

HBC employee, b. 1840, associated with:

  Belle Vue sheep farm (1858–1860) laborer
  Victoria (1869–1870)

By 1858, Tamaree, who may be **Tamaree** [2] and/or **Tamaree** [3], was found working at the HBC sheep farm on San Juan Island. In April 1860, he left for Victoria when his contract expired. He appeared to stay around for a number of years for, on July 3, 1869, a twenty-nine-year-old 5 foot, 7 inch Hawaiian of the same name was given the option of paying $10 or fourteen days in prison for assault. In May 1870, he was given the option of paying a fine or spending six hours in jail for being drunk and disorderly. Possibly the same person, a man named Tomali was the father of Maria Joanna (ca. 1859–?), born in 1859 and baptized on May 4, 1874, in Victoria.

PS: HBCA FtVicSA 7, BelleVuePJ 2, BCA VS-StAndC, Crt-Gaols

Tamaree [5] [variation: Tamree] (fl. 1896–1897)

Occupation unknown, b. ca. 1825, d. March 1897, on Bowen Island, associated with:

Steveston (1896)

Bowen Island (1896–1897)

Tamaree, probably one or more of the other Tamarees, was an old man of seventy-one years when he was at Steveston, British Columbia, in 1896, possibly working at or associating with workers in any of the twenty or so canneries there. He did not appear to have a family when, in August of that year, he joined his longtime friend **William Parker** on Bowen Island, British Columbia. Parker, who arrived in British Columbia in 1890, said at the inquest he had lived on Bowen Island for four years, but knew Tamaree for as long as he could remember, which means the relationship went back to the Islands. When Tamaree died in the spring of 1897, his body was taken in a rowboat by three men to Vancouver and presumably buried there.

PS: BCA Crt-Inquests, Gaols, HBCA FtVicSA 7, BelleVuePJ 2

Tamaree, Thomas [1] [variation: Komaree] (fl. 1881–1898)

Laborer, b. ca. 1828, associated with:

Portland Island (1881–1898)

An elderly Hawaiian named Thomas Tamaree worked for **William Naukana** and **John Palua** on Portland Island. He was naturalized in 1889 and on the provincial voters' lists listed as a "Kanaka." His friendship with the Naukanas and Paluas may have gone back to San Juan Island, where they lived prior to the island's being awarded to the United States in 1872. If so, he was likely **Tamaree [4]**.

PS: British Columbia GR-Naturalization, 1881 and 1891 Canada Census, British Columbia, Salt Spring; *PPS:* "Joe, His Full Confession," *Colonist,* March 13, 1874; British Columbia, *Sessional Papers,* voting lists

Tamaree, Thomas [2] (fl. 1873–1898)

Laborer, b. ca. 1837 in Honolulu, associated with:

North Vancouver (1881–1898) laborer

Thomas Tamaree worked variously as a logger, longshoreman, and millman at Moodyville in present-day North Vancouver from 1881 to 1898. He appeared on the British Columbia voting list from 1894.

Thomas Tamaree and an unnamed woman were the parents of George (ca. 1874–?), Matilda (ca. 1875–?), James (ca. 1877–?), and Elizabeth (1879–?). By 1891 Tamaree was widowed.

PS: 1881 and 1891 Canada Census, British Columbia, New Westminster; *PPS:* British Columbia directories, 1891–1898; British Columbia, *Sessional Papers,* voting lists

Tamaree, Thomas [3] [variation: Tamalee] (fl. 1846–1868)

Laborer, associated with:

Nanaimo (1865–1868) laborer

Thomas Tamaree lived in Nanaimo in the late 1860s. On December 4, 1868, after **Peter Kakua** killed his family in Nanaimo, Kakua went straight to fellow Hawaiian Tamaree and told him that he was going away because of what he had done. An incredulous Tamaree went to Kakua's house, discovered the bodies, and the following morning went to the local constable with the news. He essentially goes off record but may be one of the other Thomas Tamarees.

Thomas Tamaree married Jane Annie (?–?) in an Anglican ceremony at Nanaimo on August 26, 1866. At the time their daughter Jenny Culla Marlar (1866–?) was baptized in November 1866, Tamaree was working as a laborer. The couple had two older children, Lama (ca. 1847–1848) and **Thomas** (1849–1919).

PS: BCA Crt-Gaols, Kakua, VS-StPaul

Tamaree, Thomas [4] (1849–1919)

Occupation unknown, of mixed descent, b. 1849 in Victoria, d. March 26, 1919, in Wrangell, associated with:

> Victoria (1849–?)
> Wrangell (?–1919)

Born in Victoria in 1849 the son of **Thomas Tamaree** [3], Thomas Tamaree was, according to his obituary, the son and grandson of Hawaiians who worked in the fur trade. His mother was a member of the Shakes chiefly family of the Wrangell area. His parents settled in Victoria, where Tom and an older bother were born and raised. Following the death of Thomas's father, his mother returned to Wrangell. In about 1900, following his brother's death, Tom Tamaree moved to Wrangell with his wife to be nearer to his mother. Retrieving the Tlingit he knew as a child, he worked as an interpreter for the Salvation Army and Presbyterian Church.

Thomas Tamaree married in Victoria in the late 1870s. The couple had no children of their own, but adopted two children who predeceased them.

PS: "Tom Tamaree Passes Away At Age of 70," *Wrangell Sentinel,* March 27, 1919

Tamoree, George (fl. 1834–1835)

HBC employee, b. possibly on Oʻahu, associated with:

> Fort Vancouver (1834–1835) laborer
> barque *Ganymede* (1835) Dr. Gairdner's personal steward

George Tamoree first appeared on record in outfit 1834–1835 in the Columbia. He left Fort Vancouver for Oʻahu on the barque *Ganymede* on October 3, 1835, as personal student of the ailing HBC physician, Dr. Meredith Gairdner. Just how long he stayed with Gairdner is uncertain, but he is on record as being discharged in Oʻahu.

PS: HBCA YFSA 14–15, YFDS 5c–6, FtVanSA 3

Tamoree, Joe (fl. 1832–1837)

HBC employee, associated with:

> brig *Lama* (1832–1833) seaman
> Fort Simpson naval service (1833–1834) seaman
> Fort Simpson (1834–1835)
> Fort Vancouver Indian trade (1835–1836) middleman or laborer
> Fort Umpqua (1836–1837) middleman or laborer
> brig *Lama* (1837) seaman

Joe Tamoree joined the HBC in Oʻahu on September 6, 1832, for work in the Columbia and sailed to the Northwest Coast on the brig *Lama*. Around 1835, he broke from his sea-faring tradition and worked at Forts Vancouver and Umpqua. His contract ended in 1837, and he sailed to Oʻahu on the *Lama* and was discharged there on July 16, 1837.

PS: HBCA FtSimp[N]PJ 3, YFDS 5a–8, SMP 14, YFSA 12–15, 17, FtVanSA 3–5

Tanero [variation: **Tamero**] (fl. 1830–1835)

HBC employee, associated with:

schooner *Cadboro* (1830) seaman or laborer
Fort Vancouver general charges (1830–1831)
Fort Simpson (1831–1834) laborer
Fort McLoughlin (1834–1835) laborer
brig *Dryad* (1835) passenger

Tanero joined the HBC in April 1830. He worked at coastal forts and, on March 14, 1835, was discharged as a disabled person and returned to the Sandwich Islands aboard the *Dryad.*

PS: HBCA SMP 14, FtVansA 2, FtSimp[N]PJ 3, YFDS 4a–5c, YFSA 11–15

Taoutu [variations: **Taoutoo, Taeutoo**] (fl. 1837–1848)

HBC/PSAC employee, associated with:

Snake party (1837–1841) middleman
Cowlitz farm (1841–1842) middleman, (1842–1843) laborer
Fort Vancouver (1843–1844) laborer
Cowlitz farm (1844–1845) laborer
Fort Vancouver (1847–1848) laborer

Taoutu joined the HBC from Oʻahu in 1837 and began his work with the Snake party on July 31 of that year. During his four years in the Snake Country, he appeared to transport people and goods back and forth from Fort Vancouver. As his contract ended in 1845, he worked until December 11 of that year, when he returned to Oʻahu. He reenlisted and was in Fort Vancouver in 1847 but worked only until July 6 of that year, at which point he returned once more to Oʻahu. He reengaged again in 1848 but did not appear in further HBC records. His fate is unknown.

PS: HBCA FtVansA 4–7, YFDS 8, 11, 16, 18, YFSA 19–20, 22–25, 27, SandIsAB 5, 7

Tapou, Joe [variation: **Tapow**] (fl. 1840–1862)

HBC/PSAC employee, b. ca. 1820 to unknown father and Lohroh, associated with:

Fort Vancouver (1840) middleman
barque *Columbia* (1840–1841) seaman
Fort Nisqually outstations (1841–1842) laborer, (1842–1851) shepherd
Fort Nisqually (1851–1854) laborer and shepherd
Fort Nisqually outstations (1854–1856) laborer and shepherd, (1858–1862) shepherd

Joe Tapou joined the HBC in Oʻahu in 1840 under a three-year contract. He began his career as a seaman but spent the next fifteen years working on land as a shepherd at Fort Nisqually and its outstations of Tenalquot, Puyallup, and Tlithlow. Sometime in the early 1840s Tapou sent £5, or three and a half months' salary, to his mother Lohroh in Honolulu. In the 1850 U.S. Census, he was living in the same household as George Budabud (**Borabora**) and Napic (**Aleck Napahay**), being described as "dark Hawaiian, not black." Tapou was discharged briefly in 1855 and again the next year for being drunk, but returned in October 1858 to work for four more years. Later he reportedly worked for a nearby sawmill alongside his countrymen **Cowie** and **Keaveʻhaccow.**

Joe Tapou had an industrious Indian wife who in 1848–1849 traded moccasins to Fort Nisqually and who worked there at short-term jobs whenever possible. They had at least one child by 1853.

PS: HBCA Log of *Columbia* 4, SMP 14, YFSA 20, 22–32, YFDS 11, FtVanSA 6–7, 9–13, HL FtNisSA 1–3,5, 7–11, 13–14, env, FtNisPJ 7–11, 13, FtNisB 6–9, env, FtNisIB 2, FtNisTB 1, FtNisbox 6, FtNisMFJ, 1850 U.S Census, Oregon, Lewis Co.; *SS:* Anderson, *Physical Structure*

Tareaepou [variations: Terrapou, Teraeopau, Tereaepou, Taeeipow, Timothy Kliapoo] (fl. 1847–1859)

HBC employee, associated with:

Fort Langley (1847–1852) laborer
Derby (1852–1859) freeman

Tareaepou, from Oʻahu, began work with the HBC as a laborer at Fort Langley on August 19, 1847, and worked there through 1852. He may have remained at the nearby Kanaka enclave at Derby, working as a freeman.

On December 25, 1859, the Anglican cleric at Derby named Timothy Kliapoo and Tekoyah (?–?), likely a local Native woman, as the parents of Margaret (?-bap. 1859–?), whom he baptized. The cleric described Kliapoo as a "Kanaker" laborer living at Derby.

PS: HBCA YFSA 27–32, YFDS 18, FtVicSA 1–2, BCA VS-StJohDiv

Taroua (fl. 1844–1847)

HBC employee, associated with:

Fort Vancouver (1844–1847) laborer, Indian trade (1847) laborer

Taroua, from Oʻahu, joined the HBC in 1844 on a three-year contract. He worked at Fort Vancouver until October 15, 1847, at which point he returned to Oʻahu.

PS: HBCA YFSA 24–27, YFDS 18

Tarpaulin [variation: Taipaulin] (fl. 1843–1852)

HBC/PSAC employee, b. ca. 1820, associated with:

Cowlitz farm (1843–1847) laborer
Fort Victoria (1847–1848) laborer
Fort Vancouver (1848–1849) laborer
Columbia Department (1851–1852) laborer

Tarpaulin, from Oʻahu, appeared in the Columbia in outfit 1843–1844 with a contract that ended in 1846. He worked on the Cowlitz farm until November 10, 1847, when he returned to Oʻahu. He was engaged again at Oʻahu and began work at Fort Vancouver on October 1, 1848. He was not to work long, for on October 10, 1849, he deserted from Fort Vancouver. He may have gone to California, but likely stayed in the area or returned there, for he appeared in the U.S. Census of 1850 as well as in the Columbia records of 1851–1852. He became a freeman in 1852.

PS: HBCA YFSA 23–27, 31–32, YFDS 18–20, FtVanSA 8–9, 1850 U.S. Census, Oregon, Clark Co.

Tatooa (fl. 1837–1849)

HBC employee, associated with:

Snake party (1837–1841) middleman
Fort Vancouver (1844–1849) laborer

Tatooa joined the HBC from Oʻahu in 1837 and began work with the Snake party on July 31 of that year. He worked continually with a traveling party and was likely a goer and comer, transporting trappers in and out of the country from Fort Vancouver. He worked until November 20, 1841, at which point he returned to Oʻahu. He reengaged in 1844 and spent the next five years working at Fort Vancouver before he deserted, most likely for the gold fields of California.

PS: HBCA FtVanSA 4–7, YFDS 8, 12, YFSA 19–21, 24–29

Tatouira (fl. 1817–1826)

NWC/HBC employee, b. ca. 1798, d. ca. 1826 in the Columbia Department, associated with:

Columbia River area (1817–1822) laborer
Fort Nez Perces (spring 1822) laborer
Columbia Department (1822–26) laborer

Tatouira joined the fur trade around 1817 and was with the HBC in the Columbia District in the early 1820s. He was deceased by 1826.

PS: HBCA FtGeo [Ast]AB 4, YFSA 2–5

Tawai [variation: Towai] (fl. 1817–1845)

NWC/HBC employee, b. ca. 1788, associated with:

Columbia River area (1817–1823) laborer
Fort George [Astoria] (1823–1825) laborer
Columbia Department (1825–1826) laborer
Umpqua Snake expedition (1826–1827) laborer
Fort Vancouver (1827–1833) laborer or middleman, (1833–1839) pigherd,
    (1844–1845) middleman or laborer

Tawai joined the NWC in 1817 and became a laborer for the HBC from 1821. In October 1825 he was part of a group of Hawaiians accused of having stolen trade goods of the *William & Ann,* but denied any involvement. He is also mentioned on December 18, 1826, when he was sick and in need of medical attention. Tawai spent many years working under **John Cox** and with **Orohuay** as pigherds at the Fort Vancouver farm. His contract ended in 1842 but he worked until November 20, 1841, when he returned to Oʻahu. He was engaged again, for he appeared in the Columbia in 1844–1845. He worked until July 18, 1845, at which point he retired to Oʻahu.
    Tawai almost certainly was the father of **William Tawai.**

PS: HBCA YFSA 2–9, 11–15, 20–21, 24–25, FtGeo[Ast]AB 11–12, FtVanAB 10, SA 1–7, PJ4, CB 2, YFDS 3a–3b, 4b–7, 12, 16; *PPS:* Macdonald, *Blessed Wilderness,* 29

Tawai, William [variation: Tawaii, Touai] (1820s–1860)

HBC/PSAC employee, of mixed descent, probably d. ca. 1860 in British Columbia, associated with:

Fort Nisqually (1843) laborer
Fort Nisqually (1852–1853) shepherd
Fort Rupert (1854–1860) laborer
British Columbia (ca. 1860) gold miner

William Tawai, born on the Pacific slopes to a Hawaiian father, most likely **Tawai,** and a Native mother, appeared at Fort Nisqually in 1843 and again in March 1852. Although he was listed the second time as a shepherd, for the next fifteen months the one-armed

200-pound Tawai spent much of his time with the Natives working in the garden and the slaughter house, breaking in wild oxen, making paddles, and cleaning various buildings. By June 25 it was noted that he was "behaving shamefully, getting drunk with the Indians & staying out in the camp all night." For the next year, his drinking appeared to increase, and he finally deserted the post on June 13, 1853. It is possible he went north and is the Hawaiian recorded as Touai who worked at Fort Rupert, 1854–1860. A clerk at Fort Nisqually recalled Tawai drowning in the Fraser River during the British Columbia gold rush.

Tawai had an unnamed wife who apparently suffered greatly at the hands of her husband.

PS: HBCA FtVicSA 2–7, FtNis Huggins, Letters Outward, HL FtNisPJ 8–9, FtNisSA 7–8, env

Tayapapa [variation: Taiēpepe] (fl. 1840–1847)

HBC employee, d. December 12, 1847, at Fort Vancouver, associated with:

Columbia Department (1840–1841) middleman
Snake party (1841–1842) middleman, (1842–1843) laborer
Fort Vancouver (1843–1847) laborer

Tayapapa, from Oʻahu, joined the HBC in 1840 as a middleman and laborer. During his career, he worked in the Snake area and Fort Vancouver. He died at Fort Vancouver on December 13, 1847, of the measles, a disease that killed many of his fellow Sandwich Islanders at the time.

Tayapapa fathered a child, Joseph (1847–1848), by an unnamed Native woman.

PS: HBCA YFSA 20, 22–27, FtVanSA 6–7, YFDS 18, BCA PR-Lowe; *PPS:* Munnick, *Vancouver,* vol. 2

Tayba (fl. 1830–1833)

HBC employee, associated with:

Fort Vancouver general charges (1830–1831)
Fort Simpson (1831–1833) laborer
Fort Vancouver (1833) laborer

Tayba joined the HBC in April 1830. He was taken as a laborer to Fort Simpson [Nass], where he helped to construct the original fort on the Nass River site. At the end of his contract, likely 1833, he returned to Fort Vancouver and, on November 1, 1833, embarked on his return voyage to Oʻahu.

PS: HBCA FtVanSA 2, YFDS 4a–5b, YFSA 12–13

Teaheererey [variation: Teeaheererey] (fl. 1840–1849)

HBC/PSAC employee, associated with:

Fort Taku (1840–1841) middleman
Fort Langley (1841–1843) middleman
Cowlitz farm (1843–1847) laborer
Fort Vancouver (1847–1849) laborer
Fort Vancouver farm (1849)

Teaheererey, from Oʻahu, joined the HBC in 1840 on a three-year contract and began his career in northern Fort Taku. He worked along the coastal area, and finally at the Fort Vancouver farm, from which he deserted on September 10, 1849. He likely headed for the California gold fields. If he returned, he may be the same person given as **Tearhenard** in the 1850 Census.

PS: HBCA YFSA 20, 22–29, FtVanSA 6–7, YFDS 20, HL FtNisSA 2

Tearhenard (fl. 1850)

Cook, b. ca. 1820, associated with:

Fort Vancouver area (1850) cook

An "Owyhee" named as Tearhenard worked as a cook for the HBC chief factor, Peter Skene Ogden, at Fort Vancouver in 1850. He may be the same person as **Teaheererey.**

PS: 1850 U.S. Census, Oregon, Clark Co.

Teela (fl. 1836–1844)

HBC employee, associated with:

Fort Vancouver (1836–1838) middleman or laborer
Fort Umpqua (1838–1839) middleman
Fort Vancouver Indian trade (1839–1842) middleman
Fort Umpqua (1842–1844) laborer
Vancouver (1844) laborer

Teela joined the HBC in 1836 from Oʻahu and spent most of his time working in actual transactions with Native Americans. He worked until November 23, 1844, at which point he returned to Oʻahu and received his final wages at the Honolulu office on December 31.

PS: HBCA YFSA 19–20, 22–24, YFDS 7, 15, FtVanSA 3–7, SandIsAB 3

Teheeopea [variations: **Taheeopiah, Raheina**] (fl. 1792)

Ship's companion, b. ca. 1778 on Niʻihau, associated with:

ship *Jenny* (1792) passenger and ship's companion
Nootka (1792) visitor
HMS *Discovery* (1792–1793) passenger

Teheeopea, a young high-ranking woman from Niʻihau, along with an older relative **Tahomeeraoo,** and several other Hawaiian women, boarded the Bristol ship *Jenny* when it was in the Islands in 1792. When the ship was ready to sail, and apparently without the knowledge of the captain or the women's relatives, the two women were confined onboard and not discovered until the vessel was well under way. Not wishing to carry them farther after his arrival at Nootka on October 7, 1792, the captain of the *Jenny* transferred them to HMS *Discovery,* captained by George Vancouver, so they could return to their island and relatives. On October 12, with fellow Sandwich Islander **Kalehua** as chaperone, the two Hawaiians sailed off in the British naval vessel in safety and relative comfort. From that point of departure, however, Teheeopea insisted on being called Raheina and both exhibited a countenance and manners that charmed their hosts. This charm equally impressed their Spanish hosts at Monterey, where both women encountered domesticated animals they had never seen on Niʻihau and bravely rode horses for the first time. Both, however, became ill and did not fully recover until they arrived back at the Islands. As the island of Niʻihau had been abandoned because of a drought, the two had to be dropped at Kauaʻi in March 1793, and because they had broken the *kapu* (taboo) of eating alongside men, George Vancouver had to ensure that they would not be punished, by procuring for the women an estate on which they could live out their lives.

PPS: Vancouver, *Voyage,* 688, 892–896

Tekowē (fl. 1841–1846)

HBC/PSAC employee, associated with:

Cowlitz farm (1841–1842) middleman, (1842–1843) laborer
Fort Nisqually (1843–1844) laborer
Cowlitz farm (1844–1846) laborer

Tekowē joined the HBC from O'ahu in 1841 and began receiving wages on July 9 of that year. He spent the majority of his time as a farm laborer until November 30, 1846, when he returned to O'ahu.

PS: HBCA FtVanSA 6–7, YFDS 12, 17, YFSA 22–26, HL FtNisSA 2

Teogh, Cowlippi [variation: Teio] (fl. 1849–1880)

Laborer, b. ca. 1820, associated with:

Skamania, Washington (1880) laborer

Cowlippi Teogh was in 1880 working as a laborer at Skamania and living with his sons Charles (ca. 1850–ca. 1913), Alex (ca. 1851–1923), and John (ca. 1856–1995). Charles, a farmer, was married to an Indian woman named Cecilia (ca. 1850–?), with whom he had Frank (ca. 1868–?). Alex, who worked as a carpenter, was married to an Indian woman named Cascard (ca. 1854–?), and was the father of a daughter. John, whose wife was not in the household, was like his father a laborer.

PS: 1880 U.S. Census, Washington Territory, Skamania

Teouee [variation: Teowee] (fl. 1836–1839)

HBC employee, associated with:

Snake party (1837–1839) middleman
Fort Vancouver (1839) middleman
barque *Vancouver* (1839) passenger

Teouee joined the HBC in O'ahu in 1836 or 1837, beginning his work with the Snake party on July 31 of that year. He worked through his three-year contract and left for O'ahu on the *Vancouver* on November 15, 1839.

PS: HBCA FtVanSA 4–5, YFDS 8, YFSA 19, SMP 14

Teow, Isaac (fl. 1812–1814)

PFC/NWC employee, associated with:

Fort Astoria (1812–1814) laborer
Fort George [Astoria] (1814) laborer

Isaac Teow is on record on April 4, 1814, as being prepared to work for the NWC through the summer at Fort George [formerly Astoria]. He must have arrived on the *Beaver* in 1812 to work for the PFC at Fort Astoria.

PPS: Henry, *Journal,* 711

Terepoena [variation: Teupoena] (fl. 1840–1850)

HBC employee, associated with:

Fort Vancouver (1840–1842) middleman, (1842–1848) laborer
Fort Langley (1848–1849) laborer
Fort Vancouver (1849–1850) laborer

Terepoena joined the HBC from O'ahu in 1840. He worked at various posts, as needed, until 1850, at which point his HBC account remained static, indicating a probable return to Hawai'i.

PS: HBCA YFSA 20, 22–32, FtVanSA 6–7

Thomas, John (fl. 1840–1844)

HBC employee, associated with:

Fort Taku (1840–1843) middleman
Fort Victoria (1843–1844) middleman and laborer

John Thomas joined the HBC from O'ahu in 1840. He was first assigned to northerly coastal Fort Taku that was being constructed at the time. There he worked for three outfits until he was assigned to the new Fort Victoria in 1843. He worked at the Vancouver Island fort until November 23, 1844, when he returned to O'ahu. He received his final payout at the Honolulu office.

PS: HBCA YFSA 20, 22–24, FtVanSA 6–7, YFDS 15, SandIsAB 3

Thomokia (fl. 1852)

Occupation unknown, associated with:

Fort Victoria area (1852)

Little is known of Thomokia, who was identified as a Hawaiian in Victoria in 1852 although he could be **Thomas Keavē**. His wife's name has not been traced but they had a daughter, Marguerite (?–bap. 1852–?).

PS: BCA VS-StAndC

Ti (fl. 1862–1864)

Laborer, associated with:

Port Gamble (1862) sawmill worker
Alberni (1863–1864) sawmill worker

Ti was contracted in Honolulu on January 10, 1862, by the agent of Puget Mill Co. to work at its sawmill for $15 per month with a $15 advance. The same man, or another man with the same name, was contracted in Honolulu on September 23, 1863, by the agent of Alberni Mill Co., along with six others, to work for $10 per month with a $20 advance. The same day they left for Victoria on the *Alberni.* On December 22, 1864, all of the men, except for **Kealili** who ran away, arrived back in Honolulu from Alberni on the ship *Buena Vista.*

PS: HSA Seamen, Passenger

Tia (fl. 1865–1866)

Occupation unknown, associated with:

Fort Langley area (1865–1866)

Tia might be **Keea**. His daughter, Anselme (1866–?), was baptized on October 14, 1866, as the daughter of Tia, a Hawaiian living near Fort Langley, and Tselerontote (?–?) of Fort Langley.

PS: OblH Fraser

Tiainno (fl. 1839–1842)

HBC employee, associated with:

Fort Vancouver (1839–1842) middleman, (1842) laborer

Tiainno joined the HBC in Oʻahu in 1839. He worked at Fort Vancouver until June 24, 1842, at which point he returned to Oʻahu.

PS: HBCA YFSA 19–20, 22, FtVanSA 6–7, YFDS 13

Timeoy [variation: **Time-oy**] (fl. 1830–1849)

HBC employee, associated with:

Fort Vancouver general charges (1830–1831)
Fort Simpson (1831–1834) laborer
Fort McLoughlin (1834–1835) laborer
Fort Vancouver (1835) laborer
barque *Ganymede* (1835) passenger
Fort Umpqua (1836–1839) middleman
Fort Vancouver Indian trade (1839–1842) middleman
Fort Umpqua (1842–1846) laborer
Fort Vancouver Indian trade (1846–1848) laborer
Fort Vancouver (1848–1849) laborer

Timeoy, from Oʻahu joined the HBC in April 1830. He worked at coastal forts for the next four years and then left Fort Vancouver for Oʻahu on the barque *Ganymede* on October 3, 1835. Upon his arrival in Oʻahu, he was paid his final HBC wage. He engaged again in January 1836, and for the next thirteen years worked in the Fort Vancouver/Umpqua area. On August 31, 1849, he deserted, most likely for the gold fields of California.

PS: HBCA FtVanSA 2–7, YFDS 4a–6, YFSA 11–15, 20, 22–29, YFDS 6–7, 16–17, 20, SMP 14, SandIsLonIC 1

Tohem (fl. 1844)

HBC employee, associated with:

Fort Vancouver (1844) laborer

Tohem was likely hired by the HBC in Oʻahu in 1844. After he arrived on the coast, he worked at Fort Vancouver until November 12, 1844, at which point he returned back to Oʻahu.

PS: HBCA YFSA 24, YFDS 15

Tohoies (fl. 1809–1810)

Maritime fur trade seaman, d. June 17, 1810, associated with:

brig *Otter* (1809–1810) seaman

Tohoies was one of four Sandwich Islanders who were picked up by the *Otter* in the Islands in 1809 and brought to the Northwest Coast. Tohoies lasted less than one year on the vessel, dying of unstated causes on June 17, 1810.

PS: PEM *Otter*

Toholiēve [variation: **Toulaia**] (fl. 1842–1849)

Occupation unknown, d. 1849, associated with

Fort Vancouver area (1842–1849)

Little is known of Toholiēve, who also appears to be Toulaia, both of whom were in the Fort Vancouver area in the 1840s. He may have been the son of a Hawaiian father and unknown Native mother.

Toholiēve and an unnamed Native woman produced Catherine (1843–?). Toulaia and

Nancy Chinook (?–?) produced another Catherine (1849–?), implying that the first child may have died.

PPS: Munnick, *Vancouver,* vol. 2

Toi-o-foe (fl. 1830–1833)

HBC employee, associated with:

Fort Vancouver general charges (1830–1831)
brig *Dryad* (1831–1832) seaman
Fort Simpson naval service (1832–1833) seaman
schooner *Vancouver* (1833) cook
brig *Dryad* (1833) passenger

Toi-o-foe joined the HBC in April 1830. He worked on coastal vessels as a seaman and cook until November 1, 1833, when he returned to Oʻahu aboard the brig *Dryad.*

PS: HBCA FtVanSA 2, YFDS 4a–5b, YFSA 11–13, SMP 14

Tom [1] (fl. 1791–1792)

Maritime fur trade ship's cook, possibly Hawaiian, associated with:

ship *Columbia Rediviva* (1791–1792) green hand

Little is known of Tom who signed on as cook of the *Columbia,* which sailed from Boston on September 28, 1790. Tom and the *Columbia* arrived on the coast in June 1791 and traded that season. He sailed from the coast on October 3, 1792, and, after stopping at the Sandwich Islands and Canton, arrived in Boston July 25, 1793. He likely disembarked at Hawaiʻi.

PPS: Voyages of the Columbia, 447

Tom [2] (fl. 1836–1839)

HBC employee, associated with:

Fort Vancouver general charges (1836–1839)
barque *Vancouver* (1839) passenger

Tom was engaged by the HBC in Oʻahu in January 1836 on a three-year contract and worked at Fort Vancouver. He left for Oʻahu on the *Vancouver* on November 15, 1839.

PS: HBCA YFSA 15, 19, YFDS 6–7, FtVanSA 3–5, SMP 14

Tom, Boatswain (fl. 1812)

Maritime fur trade overseer, associated with:

ship *Beaver* (1812) overseer

By 1812, the "old experienced islander," Boatswain Tom had made several voyages to Europe and America. Possibly he was **Tom** [1] who sailed on the *Columbia Rediviva.* Boatswain Tom was given $15 a month to oversee the sixteen Hawaiians recruited on Oʻahu by the PFC who sailed to the mouth of the Columbia on the *Beaver* early in 1812. It is uncertain just how or when Boatswain Tom returned to the Hawaiian Islands.

PS: Cox, *Voyage,* 51

Tommo (fl. 1844–1863)

HBC employee, associated with:

Snake party (1844–1845) laborer, (1845–1846) goer and comer, (1846–1847) laborer
Fort Vancouver (1847–1848) laborer

Fort Nez Perces (1848–1849) laborer
Fort Vancouver (1849–1850) laborer
Columbia Department (1853) laborer
Victoria area (1863) interpreter

Tommo joined the HBC from Oʻahu in 1844 on a three-year contract. He was discharged on February 6, 1850, at which point he returned to Oʻahu. He returned to the Columbia, being back on the books in 1853 and noted as retiring that same year. He likely continued living in the area, fourteen years later, in May 1863, acting as an interpreter for the constabulary of Victoria. Tommo has not been traced after that, nor has any family been located.

PS: HBCA YFSA 24–30, YFDS 16, 20, FtVanSA 9–10, BCA Colonial

Tommy (fl. 1834–1835)

CRFTC employee, associated with:

ship *May Dacre* (1834) passenger
CRFTC brigade (1834) member
Forts William and Hall (1834–1835) laborer

Tommy was one of twenty men recruited for Nathaniel J. Wyeth's CRFTC in 1834. He along with **John Bull, Diblo,** and **Dido** reached Fort Hall just before Christmas. He remained until July 1835, when he may have gone to Fort William or died. He does not appear subsequently in the records.

PS: OHS FtHallAB; *PPS:* Beidleman, "Fort Hall," 238

Too, Toby (fl. 1811)

PFC employee, b. probably on Oʻahu, d. probably in July 1811 at Clayoquot Sound [Vancouver Island], associated with:

ship *Tonquin* (1811) crew
Fort Astoria (1811) temporary laborer

Toby Too joined the crew of the *Tonquin* as a laborer around February 21, 1811, when the vessel stopped at Oʻahu and took on a complement of twenty Sandwich Islanders. One month later, on March 22, the *Tonquin* arrived at the mouth of the Columbia and, on April 12, Toby was noted as helping to unload the vessel. As Toby did not appear in further Fort Astoria records, he likely stayed on as part of the crew when the vessel sailed on June 5 for Newitti. When the vessel anchored at Clayoquot Sound, it was attacked and Toby Too was killed along with the entire crew but one.

PS: RosL *Astoria; PPS:* Franchère, *Journal,* 73–74

Tooa (fl. 1837–1849)

HBC employee, d. July 7, 1849, at Fort Vancouver, associated with:

Willamette mission (1837–1838) middleman
Fort Vancouver (1838–1842) middleman, (1842–1849) laborer

Tooa joined the HBC in July 1837 from Oʻahu on a three-year contract and began his work at Fort Vancouver on August 10 of that year. On November 12, 1837, he was transferred to the service of missionary Jason Lee, where he appears to have worked for about a year before returning to Fort Vancouver. On July 7, 1849, he died at Fort Vancouver of unstated causes. He was likely buried in the fort's graveyard.

PS: HBCA SandIsAB 1, FtVanSA 4, 6–7, YFDS 8, 20, YFSA 17, 22–29

Tooharamokoo (fl. 1836–1837)

HBC employee, associated with:

Fort Vancouver (1836–1837) middleman or laborer

Tooharamokoo, from Oʻahu, was hired and discharged in outfit 1836–1837, having worked only six months at Fort Vancouver. A notation on the York Factory records said that he had "Gone to Woahu."

PS: HBCA FtVanSA 3, YFDS 7, YFSA 21

Toohareroa (fl. 1840–1849)

HBC employee, associated with:

Fort Vancouver (1840–1842) middleman, (1842–1845) laborer, (1846–1849) laborer

Toohareroa joined the HBC from Oʻahu in 1840. He worked at Fort Vancouver until December 10, 1845, at which time he returned to Oʻahu and, during August of that year, had part of his salary transferred to his mother. He reenlisted in 1846 and went back to work at Fort Vancouver. In 1849 he deserted, probably in the spring, and likely for the gold fields of California.

PS: HBCA YFSA 20, 22–25, 27–29, FtVanSA 6–7, YFDS 16, SandIsAB 5, HSA Passenger

Toopanehē [variations: **Kupanehe, Tupanehe**] (fl. 1840–1847)

HBC/PSAC employee, associated with:

Fort Nisqually (1840–1842) shepherd, (1842–1843) laborer
steamer *Beaver* (1843–1844) laborer
Columbia Department general charges and steamer *Beaver* (1844–1845) laborer and woodcutter
barque *Cowlitz* (1845) passenger
Fort Vancouver (1846–1847) laborer
barque *Columbia* (1847) passenger

Toopanehē joined the HBC in Oʻahu in 1840 on a three-year contract and worked first at Fort Nisqually and then on the *Beaver* as a laborer and woodcutter. He returned to Oʻahu in early 1845 but reengaged May 7 and returned in September on the *Cowlitz*. He worked in the Columbia until July 6, 1847, when he again returned to Oʻahu.

PS: HBCA YFSA 20, 22–24, 26–27, FtVanSA 6–7, YFDS 16, 18, SandIsAB 3, HL FtNisSA 1–2, env; HSA Passenger

Toouyoora [variations: **Toouyora, Toouyova**] (fl. 1830–1848)

HBC employee, d. January 2, 1848, at Fort Vancouver, associated with:

Fort Vancouver general charges (1830–1831)
Fort Simpson (1831–1834) laborer
Fort McLoughlin (1834–1836) laborer
Fort Vancouver (1836–1848) laborer

Toouyora, from Oʻahu, joined the HBC in April 1830. He worked for five years at the northern posts of Simpson and McLoughlin before being transferred to Fort Vancouver in 1936. He died at Fort Vancouver on January 2, 1848, in the middle of the measles epidemic, which killed several of his fellow Sandwich Islanders at the fort.

PS: HBCA FtVanSA 2–7, YFDS 4a–7, YFSA 11–15, 19–20, 22–27

Topa [variation: **Toopa**] (fl. 1845–1848)

HBC employee, associated with:

Fort Vancouver (1845) laborer
steamer *Beaver* (1846–1847) stoker, (1847–1848) woodcutter

Topa was hired by the HBC in Oʻahu on May 7, 1845. After arriving on the coast, he worked at Fort Vancouver until November 12, at which point he returned to Oʻahu. He was reengaged and appeared once again in the Columbia in outfit 1846–1847. He worked as a stoker and woodcutter on the *Beaver* until December 5, 1848, at which point he returned to Oʻahu for the last time, ending his career on the coast.

PS: HBCA YFSA 24, 26–28, YFDS 15, 19

Toro (fl. 1830–1850)

HBC employee, b. ca. 1815, associated with:

Fort Langley (1830–1831) laborer
Fort Simpson (1831–1834) laborer
Fort McLoughlin (1834–1835) laborer
Fort Vancouver (1835–1843) laborer or middleman
Fort Vancouver sawmills (1843–1844) laborer
Willamette (1844–1846) laborer
Fort Vancouver (1846–1847) laborer
Willamette (1847–1848) freeman
Fort Vancouver (1850) laborer

Toro joined the HBC from Oʻahu in April 1830 and worked at various locations along the coast. In outfit 1847–1848 he was noted as being a freeman in Willamette. He returned to work for the company and, on August 10, 1850, retired, remaining in the area.

Toro's family, if any, has not been traced.

PS: HBCA YFSA 11–15, 19–20, 22–27, 30–31, FtVanSA 2–7, 9, YFDS 4a–7, 19–20, 1850 U.S. Census, Oregon, Clark Co.

Touotoo (fl. 1846)

Occupation unknown, associated with:

Columbia area (1846)

Touotoo traveled to the Columbia River in April 1846 with "permission of the Governor," but it is unclear for what purpose. He may have been a returning HBC employee using another name for the trip.

PS: HSA Passenger

Touramano (fl. 1830–1832)

HBC employee, associated with:

Fort Vancouver general charges (1830–1831)
Fort Simpson (1831–1832)

Touramano joined the HBC in April 1830. He worked at Forts Vancouver and Simpson and was discharged to Oʻahu on July 16, 1832.

PS: HBCA FtVanSA 2, YFDS 4a–4b, YFSA 11–12

Tourawhyheine [variations: Tourawhyheene, Taureauathenie, Toureawanhie, Tuocoahina, Touracoahina] (fl. 1817–1847)

NWC/HBC employee, b. ca. 1801, associated with:

NWC (1817–1821) laborer
Columbia Department (1821–1823) laborer
Fort George [Astoria] (1823–1825) laborer
Fort Vancouver (1826) laborer
Umpqua Snake expedition (1826–1827) laborer
Thompson River (1827–1829) middleman
Fort Vancouver (1829–1930) middleman/laborer, Indian trade (1830–1834) middleman/laborer
brig *Eagle* (1834) seaman or passenger
Fort Vancouver Indian trade (1834–1835) laborer, general charges (1836) laborer or middleman
South party (1836–1837) middleman
Fort Vancouver (1837–1838) middleman
barque *Nereide* (1838–1839) landsman
barque *Vancouver* (1839) passenger
Fort Vancouver (1842–1843) laborer
Snake party (1843–1845) middleman
Fort Vancouver (1845–1847) laborer
barque *Columbia* (1847) passenger

Tourawhyheine joined the NWC in 1817 and worked for thirty years in the fur trade, almost all the time around Fort Vancouver. He transferred to the HBC on the amalgamation in 1821. He was one of the five Hawaiians who in October 1825 confessed to stealing blankets from the *William & Ann*'s trade goods. On Saturday, October 14, 1826, on an expedition to the Umpqua, he "lost his horse with his traps and other property." On Tuesday, February 13, 1827, he, along with two non-Hawaiian fellow employees, confirmed to the expedition leader that Ignace, a freeman on the expedition, had died at the hands of the Indians in retaliation from a gun accidentally going off. On December 1, 1834, he left for Oʻahu on the brig *Eagle* and did not receive wages in 1835. He reenlisted in Oʻahu in January 1836 and returned to the Columbia. He was eventually discharged in Oʻahu from the *Vancouver* around the end of November 1839, just after the end of his last contract, owing over £17 to the company. He reappeared again in outfit 1842–1843 and worked in both the Snake Country and Fort Vancouver until July 6, 1847, at which point he once again returned to Oʻahu.

PS: HBCA YFSA 2–9, 11–15, 19, 22–27, YFDS 2a, 3a–4a, 5a–7, 10, 18, FtGeo[Ast]AB 12, FtVanAB 10, SA 1–7, PJ 2, 4; HSA Passenger

Towello (fl. 1843–1845)

HBC employee, associated with:

Fort Vancouver (1843–1844) middleman
Cowlitz farm (1844–1845) middleman and laborer

Towello, from Oʻahu, appears to have been engaged at Fort Vancouver on August 8, 1843, on a contract that ended in 1845. For the next two outfits and until December 10, 1845, he worked as a farm laborer, at which point he returned to Oʻahu, where he received his final HBC wages.

PS: HBCA FtVanSA 8, YFSA 23–25, YFDS 14, 16, SandIsAB 5

Towhay [variation: **Touhay**] (fl. 1839–1844)

HBC employee, associated with:

Cowlitz farm (1839–1841) laborer and middleman
Fort Vancouver (1841–1842) middleman, (1842–1843) laborer
Fort Vancouver sawmills (1843–1844) middleman

Towhay joined the HBC in Oʻahu in 1839 on a three-year contract. He worked as a laborer, latterly in the Fort Vancouver sawmills, until November 23, 1844, at which time he returned to Oʻahu. He received his final wages at the Honolulu office on December 31, 1844.

PS: HBCA YFSA 19–20, 22–24, FtVanSA 6–7, YFDS 15, SandIsAB 3

Trask, James George (fl. 1861)

Laborer, of mixed descent, associated with:

Port Gamble (1861) sawmill worker

James George Trask, who was described as "half white," was contracted in Honolulu on February 18, 1861, by the agent of Puget Mill Co. to work at its sawmill for $15 per month with a $15 advance. It is uncertain how long he did so.

PS: HSA Seamen

Tshuna (fl. 1846–1849)

Occupation unknown, associated with:

Fort Vancouver area (1846–1849)

Tshuna (perhaps a Chinook Native pronunciation of Kahuna) was in the Fort Vancouver area in the late 1840s. Given the generic sense of his name, he could be any other number of people although no work or other record has been traced under Tshuna.

Tshuna partnered with an unnamed Chinook Native and had Henry (1847–?).

PPS: Munnick, *Vancouver,* vol. 2

Tsoo, Tom (fl. 1832–1836)

HBC seaman, possibly Chinese descent, associated with:

Fort Simpson naval service (1832–1833) seaman
Fort Vancouver (1833–1834) laborer
Columbia District (1834–1836) laborer

Tom Tsoo joined the HBC in Oʻahu on September 6, 1832, for work in the Columbia. In outfit 1834–1835, it was noted that he was disabled and as a result received only partial wages.

PS: HBCA YFDS 8–10, YFSA 12–15

Tuaha (fl. 1830–1845)

HBC employee, associated with:

schooner *Vancouver* (1830) seaman or laborer
Fort Vancouver general charges (1830–1831)
Fort Simpson (1831–1833) laborer
Fort Vancouver (1833–1834) middleman or laborer
brig *Lama* (1834) seaman
Fort Vancouver (1833–1845) middleman or laborer

Tuaha joined the HBC in April 1830. He was assigned to land work and probably one of the many Hawaiians living in Fort Vancouver's Kanaka Village. At one point he sailed down the coast as far as Monterey on the *Lama*. As his contract ended in 1845 he worked until December 10 of that year, at which point he returned to Oʻahu, where he received his final HBC wages.

PS: HBCA SMP 14, FtVanSA 2–6, YFDS 4a–7, 16, YFSA 11–15, 19–20, 22–25, Sand-IsAB 5

Tuana, Thomas [variation: Tuanna] (fl. 1811–1813)

PFC employee, b. probably on Oʻahu, associated with:

> ship *Tonquin* (1811) passenger
> Fort Astoria (1811–1813) laborer
> brig *Albatross* (1813) passenger

Thomas Tuana had a difficult two-year period in the fur trade, being laid up almost the entire time with venereal disease. Tuana joined the crew of the *Tonquin* as a laborer around February 21, 1811, when the Astor-owned vessel stopped at Oʻahu and took on a complement of twenty Sandwich Islanders. One month later, on March 22, the *Tonquin* arrived at the mouth of the Columbia and, on April 12, Thomas was noted as helping to unload the vessel. However, from that time on, he was sick almost continually and in 1812 was described as an "old invalid." Matters became so desperate that the officers in charge of Fort Astoria decided to try some folk medicine; that is, they killed and eviscerated a horse and put Tuana in the body of the still warm horse. All stopped work to witness this extraordinary event, but signs of improvement were apocryphal and did not materialize. In the spring of 1813, however, he was able to do some garden work. Eventually, on August 26, 1813, Thomas Tuana was sent back on the *Albatross* to the Sandwich Islands, a debilitated man.

PS: RosL *Astoria*

Tuarumaku, Jack [variations: Tueromoko, Tuarumaka] (fl. 1832–1836)

HBC employee, associated with:

> Fort Vancouver (1832–1834) middleman or laborer
> brig *Eagle* (1834) passenger or crew
> Fort Simpson (1834–1836) laborer or middleman
> Fort Vancouver (1836) middleman

Jack Tuarumaku was engaged by the HBC in Oʻahu on September 6, 1832. On December 1, 1834, he left for Oʻahu aboard the brig *Eagle* probably to visit his family. He reenlisted with the company in January 1836 and returned to the Columbia. He appears with wages on the 1836–1837 records with the notation that he had gone to Oʻahu, likely in December 1836. In 1837–1838 he appeared on the sundries account.

PS: HBCA YFSA 12–16, YFDS 5a–7, SMP 14, FtVanSA 3–4, FtSimp[N]PJ 3

Tuha (fl. 1846)

Occupation unknown, associated with:

> Columbia area (1846)

Tuha traveled to the Columbia River in April 1846 with "permission of the Governor," but it is unclear for what purpose. He may have been a returning HBC employee using another name for the trip.

PS: HSA Passenger

Tupui (fl. 1867)

Laborer, associated with:

Port Gamble (1867) sawmill worker

On May 29, 1867, Tupui left Honolulu to Teekalet on the barque *Kutusoff.* It is unclear how long he worked at the sawmill there.

PS: HSA Passenger

Tupy (fl. 1830–1833)

HBC employee, d. March 18, 1833, at Fort George [Astoria], associated with:

Fort Vancouver general charges (1830–1833)
Fort Simpson and Fort George [Astoria] (1833) middleman or laborer

Tupy joined the HBC in April 1830. He died at Fort George [former Astoria] March 18, 1833, of unstated causes.

PS: HBCA FtVanSA 2, YFDS 4a–5b, YFSA 11–13

Tuwia, Jack [variation: Tuwea] (fl. 1834)

HBC employee, associated with:

brig *Eagle* (1834) seaman or passenger
Fort Vancouver (1834) laborer

Jack Tuwia first appeared aboard the brig *Eagle* in 1834 as a HBC employee who was discharged at the Columbia River. He left Fort Vancouver for O'ahu on December 1, 1834, aboard the same vessel.

PS: HBCA YFSA 14, SandIsM 1, SMP 14

Tyah (fl. 1837–1838)

HBC employee, b. ca. 1814, d. September 20, 1838, at Fort Vancouver, associated with:

Fort Vancouver (1837–1838) middleman

Tyah joined the HBC from O'ahu in July 1837, beginning his work at Fort Vancouver on August 10 of that year. Before he was able to complete his three-year obligation, the twenty-four-year-old Sandwich Islander died at Fort Vancouver September 20, 1838, and was buried at the post the following day by Anglican minister Herbert Beaver.

PS: HBCA SandIsAB 1, FtVanSA 4–5, YFDS 8, YFSA 18; BCA VS-CCC

Ula Ula [variation: Ulla Ulla] (fl. 1841–1842)

HBC employee, d. 1842 at Fort Vancouver, associated with:

Fort Vancouver (1841–1842) middleman

Ula Ula joined the HBC from O'ahu in 1841 for three years and began receiving wages on July 9 of that year. Before he could complete his obligated period, he died at Fort Vancouver in 1842. His wages were paid to his relatives in Hawai'i.

PS: HBCA FtVanSA 6–7, YFDS 12, YFSA 22, SandIsAB 3

Ulii, Henry (fl. 1872)

Occupation unknown, associated with:

Victoria (1872)

Henry Ulii, who described himself as a Hawaiian, departed Honolulu for Victoria on the barque *Delaware,* which left Honolulu on July 1, 1872. He has not been located further.

PS: HSA Passenger

Ulu (fl. 1858–1859)

Laborer, associated with:

Port Gamble (1858–1859) sawmill worker

Ulu was one of six Hawaiians to whom the governor of Oʻahu gave permission in May 1858 to proceed to the Pacific Northwest. Ulu left Honolulu for Teekalet on May 8, 1858, on the barque *May Flower.* On March 21, 1859, he arrived back in Honolulu from Teekalet on the barque *Jenny Ford.*

PS: HSA Passenger, Victoria

Uluhua (fl. 1812)

Occupation unknown, associated with:

ship *Beaver* (1812) passenger

According to John Papa Ii, a well-connected Hawaiian born in 1800, "a man belonging to the retinue of the heir of the kingdom," by the name of Uluhua boarded the *Beaver* when it was in Honolulu in the spring of 1812 with the intention of acquiring foreign clothing and goods and then going back home on the return voyage. No other record names him.

PPS: Ii, *Fragments,* 87

Umi Umi (fl. 1844–1846)

HBC employee, associated with:

Fort Vancouver (1844–1846) laborer

Umi Umi, from Oʻahu, joined the HBC in 1844 on a three-year contract. He worked until November 30, 1846, at which point he returned to Oʻahu.

PS: HBCA YFSA 24–26, YFDS 17

Upahee (fl. 1830–1850)

HBC employee, associated with:

Fort Vancouver general charges (1830–1831)
Fort Simpson (1831–1832) laborer
Fort Vancouver (1832–1850) middleman or laborer

Upahee joined the HBC in April 1830. He spent the majority of his working career at Fort Vancouver before he became a freeman and retired in 1850.

PS: HBCA FtVanSA 2–7, 9, YFDS 4a–7, YFSA 11–15, 19–20, 22, 27–32

Upay (fl. 1844–1846)

HBC employee, associated with:

Fort Vancouver (1844–1846) laborer

Upay, from Oʻahu, joined the HBC in 1844 on a three-year contract. He worked at Fort Vancouver as a laborer until August 6, 1846, when he returned to Oʻahu.

PS: HBCA YFSA 24–26, YFDS 17

Waahela (fl. 1844–1850)

HBC employee, associated with:

Snake party (1844–1845) laborer
Fort Vancouver (1845–1846) laborer
Snake party (1846–1847) laborer

Snake Country (1847–1848) laborer
Fort Vancouver (1848–1850) laborer

Waahela, from Oʻahu, joined the HBC in 1844 and worked with the Snake party and at Fort Vancouver. Although his contract was to have ended in 1851, he deserted around the end of July 1850.

PS: HBCA YFSA 24–30, YFDS 21, FtVanSA 9

Wady (fl. 1860)

Laborer, b. ca. 1830, associated with:

Fort Vancouver area (1860) laborer

Wady was living with a group of Hawaiians and their families in the Fort Vancouver–Kanaka Village area in 1860. He may have worked for what remained of the HBC interests in the area or for the nearby U.S. military post.

PS: 1860 U.S. Census, Washington Territory, Clark Co.

Waha (fl. 1837–1840)

HBC employee, associated with:

Fort Vancouver (1837–1840) middleman

Waha joined the HBC at Oʻahu in July 1837 on a three-year contract and began his work at Fort Vancouver on August 10 of that year. He was discharged in outfit 1840–1841.

PS: HBCA SandIsAB 1, YFSA 19–20, YFDS 8, FtVanSA 4–5

Wahaila [variation: **Wahala**] (fl. 1856–1857)

PSAC employee, associated with:

Fort Nisqually outstation (1856–1857) shepherd

Little is known of Wahaila who was hired as a shepherd at a Fort Nisqually outstation in May 1856 and last appeared in the post's accounts in March 1857. He may be **Waahela** who deserted from Fort Vancouver in 1850.

PS: HL FtNisSA 11–12; *SS:* Anderson, *Physical Structure,* 183

Wahaloola (fl. 1844–1847)

HBC employee, associated with:

Fort Vancouver (1844–1845) laborer
Snake party (1845–1847) laborer
Snake Country (1847) laborer

Wahaloola, from Oʻahu, joined the HBC in 1844 on a three-year contract. He worked in the Snake Country until August 15, 1847, at which point he returned to Oʻahu.

PS: HBCA YFSA 24–27, YFDS 18

Wahapa [variation: **Mahapa**] (fl. 1863–1864)

Laborer, associated with:

Alberni (1863–1864) sawmill worker

Wahapa was among seven men contracted in Honolulu on September 23, 1863, by the agent of Alberni Mill Co. to work for $10 per month with a $20 advance. The same day they left for Victoria on the *Alberni.* On December 22, 1864, all of the men, except for **Kealili** who ran away, arrived back in Honolulu from Alberni on the ship *Buena Vista.*

PS: HSA Seamen, Passenger

Wahinahulu [variation: **Whyhanalalu**] (fl. 1850–1852)

HBC laborer, b. ca. 1826, associated with:

brigantine *Mary Dare* (1850) passenger

Fort Vancouver (1850–1852) laborer

Wahinahulu joined the HBC in Honolulu in 1850 for two years. He worked at Fort Vancouver, lived probably in the neighboring Kanaka Village, was discharged in 1852, and possibly made his way back to Oʻahu.

PS: HBCA SandIsAB 10, YFSA 30–32, FtVanSA 9, 1850 U.S. Census, Oregon, Clark Co.

Waiakanaloa [variations: **Waiakanalou, Waikanaloa**] (fl. 1845–1853)

HBC employee, d. September 2, 1853, at Fort Langley, associated with:

Fort Vancouver (1845–1847) laborer

Thompson River (1847–1848) laborer

New Caledonia (1848–1850) laborer

Fort Langley (1850–1853) laborer

Waiakanaloa joined the HBC from Oʻahu on May 7, 1845, and was dispatched to various locations. On September 2, 1853, while stationed at Fort Langley, he died, his death being reported to his friends in the Sandwich Islands. As there was no further movement on his account (he left a large credit of £21.1.6 that wasn't touched for five years), he may not have left a family in the area.

PS: HBCA SandIsAB 3, YFSA 25–26, 28–32, FtVicSA 1–6, FtLangCB 2

Waihaikia (fl. 1850)

HBC seaman, associated with:

barque *Cowlitz* (1850) seaman

Waihaikia served on the HBC vessel *Cowlitz* from February 3 to September 17, 1850, sailing from Oʻahu to the Northwest Coast and back again. On August 27, at Honolulu he and the other Hawaiian crew refused to work, claiming their contract was up but nonetheless returned to work for another month. He has not been traced further.

PS: HBCA SandIsAB 10–11, Log of *Cowlitz* 8

Wakanē, Jessie (fl. 1850–1851)

Wife, associated with

Point Chinook area (1848–1851)

Jessie Wakanē was one of the few named Hawaiian woman who made it to the Northwest Coast. By 1850, she had partnered with **Bill Louis Wawe** at Point Chinook and together they had a child, Marguerite (1851–?).

PPS: Munnick, *Vancouver,* vol. 2

Waʻkee (fl. 1880)

Laborer, b. ca. 1854, associated with:

Vashon Island (1880) sawmill worker

Waʻkee was in 1880 working in a sawmill on Vashon Island, Washington. He was single.

PS: 1880 U.S. Census, Washington Territory, Skamania

Walia (fl. 1849–1851)

HBC employee, associated with:

brigantine *Mary Dare* (1849) passenger
Fort Rupert (1849–1851) laborer

Walia appears to have joined the HBC in Honolulu and, on March 1849, sailed to Fort Victoria on the *Mary Dare*. He worked until 1851 at the coal mining post of Fort Rupert and then disappeared from the records.

PS: HBCA SandIsAB 9, YFSA 29–32, FtVicSA 1–6

Walla Walla, Tau (fl. 1846)

Servant, b. ca. 1811, associated with:

Columbia area (1846)

A Hawaiian female servant named as Tau Walla Walla left the Columbia River on the barque *Toulon* for Honolulu, arriving September 23, 1846. The barque tended to have one or more Hawaiian servants on its trips between the Pacific Northwest and Honolulu.

PS: HSA Passenger

Wasiaiva, Phillip (fl. 1870)

Laborer, b. ca. 1852, associated with:

Port Gamble (1870) sawmill worker

At the time of the 1870 Census, Phillip Wasiaiva was one of two dozen Hawaiians working at Puget Mill at Port Gamble. Also living in the household were Lizzie (ca. 1852–?), Siscilla (ca. 1860–?), Amanda (ca. 1866–?), Mary (ca. 1866–?), and Susan (ca. 1867–?), all born on the Islands.

PS: 1870 U.S. Census, Washington Territory, Kitsap Co., Port Gamble

Wavicareea [variations: **Wavickareea, Wavichareea**] (fl. 1830–1859)

HBC employee, associated with:

Fort Langley (1830–1831) middleman or laborer
brig *Dryad* (1831–1832) seaman or laborer
Fort Langley (1832–1842) middleman or laborer, (1842–1853) laborer
Fraser Valley (1850s)

Wavicareea, from O'ahu, joined the HBC in April 1830 and spent his entire career at Fort Langley with the exception of a short stint with the brig *Dryad*. He retired around 1853 and his name was carried on the books until 1859, although there appeared to be no transactions on his account.

Wavicareea had an unnamed Uiskwin woman as a wife, and two children, **Robert** (ca. 1835–?) and Adam (ca. 1836–?), both baptized Catholic in 1841.

PS: HBCA SMP 14, FtVanSA 2–7, YFDS 4a–6, YFSA 11–15, 19–20, 22–32, FtVicSA 1–6; *SS:* Laing, *Colonial Farm Settlers,* 103; Morton, *Fort Langley,* 270

Wavicareea, Robert [variations: **Wawakina, Winacarry, Wivacaria, Wivacarry, Yavicarea**] (fl. 1835–1890s)

HBC employee, of mixed descent, b. ca. 1835 at Fort Langley to Wavicareea and a "Uiskwin" woman, associated with:

Fort Langley (1853–1862) laborer
Fraser Valley (1860s–1895)

Robert Wavicareea, like his Sandwich Islander father **Wavicareea,** worked for the HBC at Fort Langley. There he appears to have worked as a cooper as well as doing other jobs such as salting fish. He retired from the HBC around 1862, although his name was carried on the books for two more years. In 1874, he preempted 160 acres at Port Haney and raised a family there. He eventually acquired 480 acres from others. He was still active in 1895.

Robert Wavicareea appears to have had one, possibly two wives, who were variously described as a Quytlen [Kwantlen?] and Marguerite (?–?), Sta-ei-els [Chehelis?] and a native of Kretsin [Katsey?], and nine recorded children. His children were Robert (?–bap. 1856–?), John (ca. 1856–?), Susan (ca. 1861–?), Blanche (ca. 1864–?), George (1867–?), Henry (ca. 1870–?), Lawrence Robert (1871–?), Lavinia (ca. 1872–?), and Frank (ca. 1875–?). The family was Catholic. They later adopted their father's first name of Robert as a surname.

PS: HBCA FtVicSA 1–11, BCA VS-StAndC, 1881 Canada Census, British Columbia, New Westminster North, OblH Fraser; *SS:* Laing, *Colonial Farm Settlers,* 100; Morton, *Fort Langley,* 270

Wawe, Louis Bill [variation: **Louis Bill**] (fl. 1847–1851)

Occupation unknown, b. ca. 1811, associated with:

    Point Chinook area (1847–1851)

It is not known how Louis Bill got to the Northwest Coast. By 1849, he was living at Point Chinook and had a daughter, Anne (1848–?) by an unnamed Native slave. In 1850 he was living with fellow Hawaiian **Jessie Wakanē,** and they had a daughter Marguerite (1851–?).

PPS: Munnick, *Stllamaris*

Whycanne (fl. 1822–1824)

HBC employee, associated with:

    Columbia Department (1822–1823) laborer
    Fort George [Astoria] (1823–1824) laborer

Whycanne worked for the HBC at Fort George from 1822 to 1824. Nothing else is known of him.

PS: HBCA YFSA 2–3, FtGeo [Ast]AB 11

Wiappeoo (fl. 1841)

HBC employee, associated with:

    Fort Vancouver general charges (1841) middleman

Wiappeoo, from Oʻahu, began work with the HBC on July 9, 1841 and labored as a middleman at Fort Vancouver until November 20, 1841, at which point he returned to the Sandwich Islands.

PS: HBCA FtVanSA 6–7, YFDS 12, YFSA 21

William [1] (fl. 1810)

Maritime fur trade seaman, associated with:

    brig *Albatross* (1810–1811) extra crew

On April 2, 1810, William along with **Richard** and **Corrina** joined the Winship brig *Albatross* on the Sandwich Islands. The brig sailed to the Columbia River, arriving May 26, 1810. Up river the crew attempted to construct a settlement of buildings and gardens but they were soon flooded out and were unsuccessful at establishing anything farther down the river. The brig then sailed off to other locations and for the next four years, sailed between the Northwest/California coast, the Sandwich Islands, and China. Just how long William stayed with the vessel is uncertain.

PS: PrivMS *Albatross*

William [2] (fl. 1830–1840)

HBC employee, associated with:

Fort Vancouver general charges (1830–1831)
Fort Simpson (1831–1834) laborer
Fort Vancouver (1834–1835) laborer
Fort Colvile (1835–1836) middleman, (1836–1837) servant
Snake party (1837–1838) middleman
Snake party and Fort Vancouver (1838–1839) middleman
Fort Vancouver general charges (1839–1840) middleman

William was hired by the HBC in 1830 from Oʻahu. After serving at Fort Simpson, he spent time at interior posts. In the middle 1830s he worked as a servant to the head of Fort Colvile, Archibald McDonald. In outfit 1838–1839 he was involved in transporting Snake party members to and from Fort Vancouver. He was discharged in Oʻahu in outfit 1840–1841.

PS: HBCA FtVanSA 2–6, YFDS 4a–7, YFSA 11–15, 19–20

Williams, Henry (fl. 1861)

PSAC employee, associated with:

Fort Nisqually (1861) laborer

A Kanaka identified as "Henry Williams," in quotation marks, purchased items at Fort Nisqually in May 1861. Nothing else is known about who he was.

PS: HL FtNisB 8

Williams, John (fl. 1870)

Laborer, b. ca. 1841, associated with:

Port Gamble (1870) sawmill worker

At the time of the 1870 Census, John Williams was one of 22 Hawaiians working at Puget Mill at Port Gamble. Also living in the household were Maggie (ca. 1856–?) and Aglook (ca. 1861–?), both born on the Islands.

PS: 1870 U.S. Census, Washington Territory, Kitsap Co., Port Gamble

Winee (fl. 1787) [variation: **Wynee**]

Maritime fur trade ship servant, d. February 5, 1788, at sea, associated with:

ship *Imperial Eagle* (1787) servant
snow *Felice Adventurer* (1788) passenger

Little is known of the early life of Winee, who may have been born on the Big Island of Hawaiʻi or resided or even born in Oʻahu. On May 24, 1787, she was one of several Sandwich Islanders who came onboard the *Imperial Eagle* upon its arrival there and expressed a desire to sail in the ship. Captain Charles William Barkley's seventeen-year-old wife chose her as a personal servant, and so Winee sailed off to the Northwest Coast. Winee so impressed Frances Barkley with her manners and general decorum that she agreed to take her on to Europe. However, after a season of trading on the Northwest Coast,

Winee's health appeared to deteriorate and, when the vessel sailed back to Canton, the Barkleys left her there so she could return to the Sandwich Islands on another vessel. Captain John Meares took Winee and the Kaua'i chief **Kaiana** aboard the *Felice Adventurer* on its way to the Sandwich Islands but, three weeks out, Winee died. Just before her death, she presented Kaiana, who had attended her, with a "plate looking-glass, and a basin and bottle of the finest China." To these gifts she added a gown, a hoop, a petticoat, and a cap for his wife; the rest of her property, consisting of a great variety of articles, she bequeathed to her family, "to be delivered to her mother and father." Winee's body was committed to the deep.

PS: UBC Howay, BCA PR-Barkley; *PPS:* Meares, *Voyages,* 27–29; *SS:* Howay, "List"; Hill, *Remarkable World,* 22; Nokes, *Almost a Hero,* 44

Woahii (fl. 1809–1810)

Maritime fur trade seaman, b. possibly on the island of Hawai'i, d. November 10, 1810, on Northwest Coast, associated with:

brigantine *Otter* (1809–1810) seaman

Woahii appeared to have a brief life in the fur trade. He likely signed on in the summer of 1809 with the Boston brig *Otter* in the Sandwich Islands on its way to the Northwest Coast. He was on the vessel when it wintered over in 1809–1810 and, on November 10, 1810, while it was still on the coast, died suddenly of unknown causes. He was buried at sea.

PS: PEM *Otter*

Woahoo (fl. 1845–1847)

HBC employee, associated with:

Fort Vancouver (1845–1847) laborer

Waohoo joined the HBC in 1845 in O'ahu on a three-year contract. He worked at Fort Vancouver until October 15, 1847, when he returned to O'ahu.

PS: HBCA YFSA 25–27, YFDS 18

Wood, Jack (fl. 1866)

Seaman, b. ca. 1842, associated with:

Victoria area (1866)

The physical description of Jack Wood, a twenty-four-year-old born in the Hawaiian Islands, would indicate that he was either Hawaiian or of mixed descent. While in Victoria on February 3, 1866, he was given the option of paying a fine or spending six hours in jail for being drunk and disorderly.

PS: BCA Crt-Gaols

GLOSSARY

Albatross [ship, fl. 1810–1815]: a 165-ton burthen Boston fur trading vessel under various ownerships that was sold to King Kamehameha in 1816

Alert [ship, fl. 1817]: a Boston vessel built in 1810; on the Northwest Coast for one season

Ann [brigantine, fl. 1819–1824]: a Massachusetts-built 204-ton vessel that ran furs to China and was sold on behalf of its Boston owners to the Russians in late 1823; it supplemented its crew with Hawaiians and paid them off with trade goods.

Argonaut [snow, fl. 1789–1791]: a Calcutta-built English vessel on the coast for two years

Atahualpa [ship, fl. 1800–1813]: a Maine-built 210-ton vessel on and off the coast for thirteen years, wrecked in Hawai'i in 1815

Beaver [ship, fl. 1812]: an Astor vessel, built in New York in 1805, on the coast for one season

Beaver [steamship, fl. 1836–1888]: an HBC vessel, built in 1835 in England, which went through various ownerships and was eventually wrecked at Vancouver, British Columbia, in 1888

Belle Vue farm [on San Juan Island, 1853–1862]: sheep farm operated by HBC

Boute: a fur trade term for the skilled positions of bowsman and steersman in a canoe or boat

Bull [brig, fl. 1845]: a Swedish freighter whose crew deserted in the Columbia River area

Cadboro [schooner, fl. 1827–1862]: a 71-ton vessel built in England for and sailed on the coast by the HBC until 1850, when it was sold to become a coal carrier; wrecked near Port Angeles, Washington, in 1862

California Establishment [fl. 1841–1849]: an HBC trading operation set up in Yerba Buena [San Francisco, on the west side of Montgomery Street between Sacramento and Clay streets]: to trade salmon and flower for hides, etc.; never profitable, it employed four Hawaiians and closed in 1849.

Chief Factor: the highest-ranking HBC commissioned officer, usually in charge of a district

Chief Trader: a second rank of HBC commissioned officer, often in charge of a larger post

Clerk: an HBC employee one step below an officer, who had clerical duties

Columbia [schooner, fl. 1814–1817]: a 185-ton NWC vessel running furs between the coast and China that was sold to King Kamehameha in 1818

Columbia [ship, fl. 1836–1849]: an English-built 308-ton HBC vessel used to transport furs out to London and goods back to the coast

Columbia Rediviva [ship, fl. 1788–1792]: a 212-ton vessel built in Massachusetts in 1773; on the coast for four years

Columbia River Fishing and Trading Company [1834–1837]: a New York and Boston based trading company set up by Nathaniel Wyeth to oppose the HBC in Oregon; it brought in thirty Hawaiians and built Forts Hall and William which were sold to the HBC in 1837.

Convoy [brig, fl. 1825–1836]: a 135-ton vessel owned by Boston interests that spent most of its lifetime running between the Northwest Coast, the Hawaiian Islands, and the California coast

Cowlitz [barque, fl. 1841–1850]: a 308-ton vessel built for the HBC in 1840 that sailed on the coast and between the Northwest Coast and England for a decade

Cowlitz farm [east end of Cowlitz prairie, Wash., fl. 1839–1857]: an HBC/PSAC operation, 5 miles by 2 miles on the east end of Cowlitz prairie, set up in 1839 to supply Forts Nisqually and Vancouver; about thirty Hawaiians were employed there at different times

Discovery, HMS [ship, fl. 1792–1794]: George Vancouver's British Royal Navy vessel of 340 tons that mapped the coast for three years

Dryad [brig, fl. 1826–1835]: a 240-ton HBC vessel built in 1825 in England that functioned both as a London supply ship and coastal trader until sold in 1836 in England

Eagle [brig, fl. 1828–1834]: a 193-ton HBC supply vessel built in England in 1824 that spent most of its time running supplies from London to the coast

Emma Rooke [schooner, fl. 1860]: vessel used to transport Hawaiian royalty to Victoria and San Francisco

Factor: term used liberally but inaccurately to describe anyone of responsibility at a post

Felice Adventurer [snow, 1788]: a nominally Portuguese, but English vessel used for a single season to trade and transport furs to China

Fort Alexandria [near Alexandria, B.C., fl. 1821–1865]: strategic Fraser River NWC/HBC post that served as a storage depot, supply fort, and staging post to Fort Kamloops/Thompson River; below the post, the river was impossible, necessitating movement of goods by overland pack-train; many Hawaiians passed through this post and several were stationed there

Fort Astoria/George [Astoria, Wash., fl. 1811–1846]: post of Astor's PFC, constructed in 1811 that was purchased by the NWC in 1813, renamed Fort George, and taken over by the HBC in 1821; after the upstream post of Fort Vancouver was constructed in 1825, it kept only a skeleton staff; many Hawaiians began their fur trade career at the post, which had two sites, the second lying in the middle of the present-day city

Fort Babine [aka Fort Kilmuars, 1822–1872; Babine, B.C.]: northern interior coast post founded in 1822 as a place to store dried salmon, which was shipped as far south as Fort Alexandria; only one Hawaiian is on record as having worked there, but others likely passed through

Fort Boise [near mouth of Boise River, fl. 1814–1855]: four posts set up at various times at which no Hawaiians were stationed but many of them passed through; in 1820, Donald MacKenzie founded a short-lived second trading post and it was during this time that three Hawaiians as part of his Snake party were killed on a nearby small river in southern Oregon, now called the Owhyhee River; in 1834, in order to compete with Nathaniel J. Wyeth's up-river **Fort Hall** set up earlier in the year, the HBC built a post a few miles from the mouth of the river

Fort Chilcotin [between Alexis Creek and Redstone, B.C., fl. 1829–1846]: outpost of Fort Alexandria visited by Hawaiians passing through the area

Fort Colvile [near Colville, Wash., fl. 1825–1871]: post constructed by the HBC in 1925 at the confluence of the Columbia and smaller rivers to replace Spokane House; at least seven Hawaiians worked there for extended periods and many others would have passed through

Fort Hall [near Fort Hall, Idaho, fl. 1834–1855]: post built by Nathaniel J. Wyeth in 1834 and purchased by John McLoughlin in 1837 to become part of the HBC realm; many Hawaiians worked there or passed through as part of any number of Snake parties

Fort Kamloops/Thompson River [Kamloops, B.C., fl. 1812–1872]: multipost site begun by the PFC in 1812 and abandoned the next year, used by the NWC from 1812, and taken over by the HBC in 1821; several Hawaiians were employed at the post

Fort Langley [Fort Langley, B.C., fl. 1827–1896]: post constructed by the HBC in 1827 that occupied three sites over time; the first down-river site was kept by the Hawaiians employed there as a permanent living area from where they boated to work 3 miles every day; more than thirty Hawaiians were stationed at Fort Langley, which is a National Historic Site

Fort McLoughlin [Bella Bella, B.C., fl. 1833–1843]: post constructed by the HBC to capture furs on the coast; local people, defending their trading control, attacked the post several times; after ten years, the HBC decided the same job could be carried out by its steamship *Beaver;* at least twenty-two Hawaiians worked at Fort McLoughlin

Fort Nez Perce/Walla Walla [at juncture of Walla Walla and Columbia rivers, Wash., fl. 1818–1855]: post built in 1818 by the NWC with the labor of thirty-two Hawaiians on the east bank of the Columbia River three-fourths of a mile north of the mouth of the Walla Walla River; many Hawaiians stayed there or passed through

Fort Nisqually and outstation farms [near Dupont, Wash., and on Nisqually bottoms, fl. 1833–1870]: post built at the end of Puget Sound by the HBC as a focal point for gathering furs, and as a terminus for the Cowlitz overland route from the Columbia River; shortly afterward it took on a major role, operating under the HBC subsidiary, the Puget Sound Agriculture Company, as an agricultural center; its outstation farms were Kull Kullee, Muck, Puyallup, Sastuc, Spaheuh, Steilacoom, Tenalquot, Tlithlow, Whyatchie, and Yelm; many Hawaiians worked there over time, some of them settling in the surrounding area; surviving buildings have been moved to the Fort Nisqually Living History Museum at Tacoma

Fort Okanagan [near Brewster, Wash., fl. 1811–1860]: post originally established in 1811 by the PFC to capture trade flowing south down the Okanagan River to the Columbia River; passed to NWC control two years later, it was taken over by the HBC in 1821 as an outstation of **Fort Kamloops/Thompson River;** unnamed Hawaiians worked there in the winter of 1813–1814, and others passed through traveling from and to Fort Vancouver

Fort Rupert [Beaver Harbor, B.C., fl. 1849–1880s]: HBC post constructed as a coal supply post for ships; about twenty Hawaiians worked at the post during its short life, and one stayed within the area

Fort Simpson [Nass]: [near Kincolith, B.C., then at Port Simpson LaxKw'Alaams, B.C., fl. 1831– 1954]: post founded on a rocky point at the mouth of the Nass River to capture the local fur trade and serve maritime interests, and moved west two years later to more accessible waters on the Tsimpsean Peninsula; after other coastal posts closed in 1841, it became the coastal transshipment point between Fort Vancouver and Sitka; rebuilt in 1859, the post closed in 1911, reopened in 1934, and finally, the remaining store closed in 1954; over fifty Hawaiians worked there for extended periods of time

Fort St. James/Stuart's Lake [four sites around Stuart's Lake, fl. 1806–1919]: an early palisaded fur trading fort that was the unconstituted capital of New Caledonia fur trade district covering much of the future province of British Columbia; only six Hawaiians can be traced as having worked out of the post, which has become a National Historic Site

Fort Stikine [Wrangel, Alaska, fl. 1839–1849]: post taken over by the HBC from the Russian American Fur Company by an agreement signed in 1839 and abandoned a decade later in favor of coastal vessels; twenty Hawaiians saw Fort Stikine as part of their contract

Fort Taku [at the head of Taku Harbor, near the Taku River, Alaska, fl. 1840–1843]: post established by the HBC in 1840 to trade with the Indians of Taku, Chilcat, and Cross Sound, and abandoned three years later due to access at low tide and unprofitability; sixteen Hawaiians worked here over the four years, a very high proportion considering the total was a little over thirty servants

Fort Umpqua/McKay's Fort [possibly five sites, the last one near Elkton, Ore., on the Umpqua River, 1820–1852]: a small post that did more to assert the presence of the HBC than carry on any substantial trade; during its years of operation, three Hawaiians were involved in expeditions to the area and about eight actually worked at the post

Fort Vancouver [Vancouver, Wash., fl. 1825–1860]: post built on the north bank of the Columbia River to replace Fort George/Astoria on the south bank as the main administration point of the Columbia Department until supplanted by Fort Victoria in 1846; most Hawaiians arriving in the Pacific Northwest were transshipped from Fort Vancouver; the village outside the palisades was called Kanaka Village because of the number of Hawaiians residing there; Fort Vancouver has been reconstructed as a National Historic Site

Fort Victoria [1843–1858: within Victoria, B.C.]: HBC post set up as an alternative to Fort Vancouver and to replace abandoned Forts McLoughlin and Taku; numerous Hawaiians worked there and some settled in the vicinity

Fort William [on Sauve Island, Ore., fl. 1834–1836]: post built in part by Hawaiian labor by Nathaniel J. Wyeth, who also constructed **Fort Hall** as part of his short-lived fishing and trading company

Freeman: Man free of company contracts who hired out to work

Ganymede [barque, fl. 1829–1836]: a 213-ton supply vessel first chartered, then owned by the HBC to send supplies from London to the coast

Hamilton [ship, fl. 1806–1822]: a Maine-built 233-ton vessel that traded on the coast four times over 18 years; it ran furs to China as well as Chinese goods to Boston for its Boston owners; in 1811, a Hawaiian woman accompanied the captain to the coast

Hazard [brig, fl. 1797–1808]: a 159-ton Boston trading vessel, notable for carrying the four-year-old George Prince Kaumuali'i to the Northwest Coast on his way to Boston to get an education

Honolulu agency [fl. 1834–1860]: an HBC operation (1834–1846 on the north side of Nu'uanu Street near King Street; 1834–1860 at the corner of Queen and Fort Street) set up to oversee the expediting of trade and the hiring of Hawaiians for the Columbia; Hawaiians who worked at site not included in book

Hope [brigantine, fl. 1791–1792]: a Boston trading vessel that ran furs to China over two trading seasons, losing $40,000 in the venture; it carried Kalehua to the coast after the Hawaiian had circumnavigated the globe on another vessel

Hudson's Bay Company [1670–present]: a British joint stock company given a royal charter for monopoly trade in territory around Hudson Bay; it expanded onto the Pacific slopes in 1821 when it amalgamated with the North West Company and was responsible for bringing hundreds of Hawaiians to the Pacific Northwest; it lost its monopoly rights when colonial governments took over; Canadian since 1970, its archives rest in Winnipeg, Manitoba

Imperial Eagle [ship, fl. 1787]: a 400-ton English vessel using an Austrian East India Company flag that spent one trading season on the Northwest Coast

Iphigenia Nubiana [snow, fl. 1788–1889]: a 200-ton British, nominally Portuguese flagged vessel that spent one or more trading seasons on the Northwest Coast

Jenny [schooner, fl. 1792–1794]: a 78-ton English vessel making two fur-trading trips to the coast

Kaighanee [early 1800s: southern Alaska]: location at the foot of the Alaska panhandle that became a regular stopping place for maritime fur trading vessels, many with Hawaiian crew

Labouchere [steam-driven sidewheeler, barque, fl. 1859–1866]: a 319-ton HBC vessel built in 1858 that was used for transport between Victoria and San Francisco

Lama [brigantine, fl. 1830–1838]: a 145-ton vessel built in New England in 1826 that was under American ownership before its purchase by the HBC

Margaret [ship, fl. 1792–1793]: a 161-ton Boston-built vessel that traded for one season on the coast

Mary Dare [brig, fl. 1849–1853]: an HBC purchased brig used for coastal trade

May Dacre [brig, fl. 1834]: a Maine-built 194-ton vessel used by its Boston owners to supply Wyeth's venture

Mercury [snow or bigantine, fl. 1795]: a Providence, Rhode Island vessel of 81 tons whose crew deserted ship in Hawai'i after a difficult voyage around Cape Horn and to Australia; the captain kidnapped several Hawaiians from Kaua'i and returned them after trading on the coast but was killed at sea afterwards on the return voyage to R.I.

Middleman: originally the middle position for paddlers in a canoe but later referring to a myriad of jobs, often that of laborer

Milieu: the same as middleman

Nereide [barque, fl. 1834–1839]: a 253-ton vessel built in India that served as an HBC supply ship and coastal trader

Newhitti: location just off the northern end of Vancouver Islands that became a regular stopping place for maritime fur trading vessels

Nootka [snow, fl. 1786–1787]: a 200-ton English trading vessel out of India that spent one season on the Northwest Coast

Nootka [Friendly Cove, Nootka Island, B.C.]: frequent stopping point for maritime fur trade vessels visited by, among others, Winee, the first Hawaiian on the coast

North West Company [1776–1821]: a Montreal based company of loose partnerships that exploited the land-based fur trade on the Pacific slopes from 1806–1821; largely French Canadian with Scottish managers, it nonetheless brought in Hawaiians as well as inherited a large number from the Pacific Fur Company which it took over in 1813

Otter [brig, fl. 1809–1811]: a 230-ton American vessel out of Boston that spent two trading seasons on the coast

Otter [steamer, fl. 1853–1890]: a 220-ton propeller-driven vessel built in 1852 in England for the HBC for coastal trading

Owhyhee [brig, fl. 1822–1830]: a 116-ton Boston vessel built in 1821 that served eight years on the coast

Pacific Fur Company [1810–1813]: a New York based John Jacob Astor company set up to exploit land-based fur trade in the Columbia River area. It was the first company to bring Hawaiians to the coast for the land-based fur trade.

Pearl [ship, fl. 1805–1809]: a 200-ton Boston vessel that spent two trips and three years on the coast

Pekin [ship, fl. 1851–1853?]: a HBC chartered supply vessel

Princess Royal [ship, fl. 1788–1889]: a 60-ton English trading vessel seized by the Spanish

Puget Sound Agriculture Company [1836–]: a HBC subsidiary company formed specifically to take over the agricultural operations of the HBC; it employed many Hawaiians at its various farms

Sea Otter [snow, fl. 1796–1797]: Boston-owned vessel that spent two trading seasons on the coast

Servant: a contracted employee of the HBC

Snake Party: term used for the fur trapping and trading parties that traveled throughout the rivers in the Snake River basin to trap and, later, when furs were depleted, often ran goods to **Forts Boise** and **Hall**

Steersman: skilled boatman in the stern of a canoe, responsible for guiding the vessel

Tonquin [ship, fl. 1811]: troubled 269-ton Astor vessel that was attacked and destroyed at Clayquot Sound, Vancouver Island, with a loss of all but one person

Vancouver [schooner, fl. 1826–1834]: a small 60-ton schooner built at Fort Vancouver by the HBC for coastal trade although it sometimes sailed to Hawai'i

Vancouver [barque, fl. 1839–1848]: a 400-ton supply vessel built in England for the HBC in 1838 and used as a London supply vessel until it was wrecked at the mouth of the Columbia in 1848

Volunteer [ship, fl. 1818–1829]: a 226-ton Connecticut-built, Boston-owned vessel that took on just one of the many unnamed Hawaiians who worked in the maritime fur trade

NOTES

PREFACE

1. Ralph Kuykendall's monumental three-volume history of the Hawaiian Islands between 1778 and 1893 (*The Hawaiian Kingdom* [Honolulu: University of Hawai'i Press, 1938–1967]) mentions departing Hawaiians, whatever their destination, only briefly and in passing, notably vol. 1: 85, 312–313; vol. 2: 138–139.

2. Terry Picard, "The Kanakas (Hawaiians of the North Shore)," *Kahtou: The Voice of B.C.'s First Nations* 13, no. 9 (September 2004): 1.

3. For a summary of scholarship in this area, see Edward D. Beechert, *Working in Hawaii: A Labor History* (Honolulu: University of Hawai'i Press, 1985), 1, 6–10.

4. Jason Allard, "Reminiscences," 10–11, in British Columbia Archives [BCA], EC A1 5A; Momilani Naughton, "Hawaiians in the Fur Trade: Cultural Influence on the Northwest Coast" (unpublished MA thesis, Department of Anthropology, Western Washington University, 1983), 37; "'Jumbo' Nahu," *Indian-Times* (Vancouver) 3, no. 2 (1957): 24; Rosemary Unger, conversation with Jean Barman, Victoria, June 27, 1990, based on research notes of Paul Roland.

5. Rona Tamiko Halualani, *In the Name of Hawaiians: Native Identities and Cultural Politics* (Minneapolis: University of Minnesota Press, 2002), 113.

6. Houston Wood, *Displacing Natives: The Rhetorical Production of Hawai'i* (Lanham, Md.: Rowman & Littlefield, 1999), 10; Eileen M. Root, *Hawaiian Names, English Names* (Kailua: Press Pacifica, 1987); Robert H. Stauffer, *Kahana: How the Land was Lost* (Honolulu: University of Hawai'i Press, 2004), 40; Titus Coan, *Life in Hawaii: An Autobiographic Sketch of Mission Life and Labors (1835–1881)* (New York: Anson D. F. Randolph & Co., 1882), 255.

7. William Ellis, *Narrative of a Tour Through Hawaii, or Owhyhee* (London: H. Faber and P. Jackson, 1828), 35; Mark Twain, Honolulu, April 1866, in Mark Twain, *Mark Twain's Letters from Hawaii*, ed. A. Grove Day (New York: Appleton-Century, 1966), 68.

8. Lists given in Naughton, "Hawaiians in the Fur Trade," 39–41; "St. Ann's Baptisms-Marriages, 1886–1896," held at St. Edward's Church, Duncan.

9. Charles Wilkes, *Narrative of the United States Exploring Expedition Covering the Years 1838, 1839, 1840, 1841, 1842*, vol. 4 (Philadelphia: Lea and Blanchard, 1845), 113; William Shaw, *Golden Dreams and Waking Realities; Being the Adventures of a Gold-Seeker in California and the Pacific Islands* (London: Smith, Elder and Co., 1851), 272.

10. Requirement set by the U.S. Congress in the Hawaiian Homelands Commission Act of 1920, and continued into the present day, for homesteading on public lands in the U.S.

Territory of Hawai'i, in *Loa'a Ka'Aina Ho'opulapula: Applying for Hawaiian Home Lands* (Honolulu: Department of Hawaiian Homelands, State of Hawai'i, 2000), 3.

11. Kekuni Blaisdell, "'Hawaiian' vs. 'Kanaka Maoli' as Metaphors," *Hawai'i Review* 13 (1989): 77–79; Jonathan Kay Kamakawiwo'ole Osorio, *Dismembering Lāhui: A History of the Hawaiian Nation to 1887* (Honolulu: University of Hawai'i Press, 2002), 2; Noenoe K. Silva, *Aloha Betrayed: Native Hawaiian Resistance to American Colonialism* (Durham: Duke University Press, 2004), 12.

12. David Chappell, *Double Ghosts: Oceanian Voyagers on Euroamerican Ships* (Armonk, N.Y.: M. E. Sharpe, 1997) and Bishop Museum web site http://www2.bishopmuseum.org/whaling/mainscreen.asp.

13. Harriet Duncan Munnick, ed., *Catholic Church Records of the Pacific Northwest*, 7 vols. (Portland: Binford & Mort, 1972–1987). A number of graduate theses have explored aspects of the topic, including Janice Duncan, "Minority without a Champion: The Kanaka Contribution to the Western United States, 1750–1900" (unpublished MA thesis, History, Portland State University, 1972); Susan Kardas, "The People Brought This and the Clatsop became Rich: A View of Nineteenth-Century Fur Trade Relationships on the Lower Columbia between Chinookan Speakers, Whites and Kanakas" (unpublished Ph.D. dissertation, Bryn Mawr College, 1971); M. Melia Lane, "The Migration of Hawaiians to Coastal British Columbia, 1810 to 1869" (unpublished MA thesis, Geography, University of Hawai'i, 1985); Naughton, "Hawaiians in the Fur Trade"; and Donnell J. Rogers, "Ku on the Columbia: Hawaiian Laborers in the Pacific Northwest Fur Industry" (unpublished MA thesis, Interdisciplinary Studies, Oregon State University, 1993). We have also benefited from earlier scholarship, including Ed Towse, "Some Hawaiians Abroad," *Papers of the Honolulu Historical Society* 11 (1904): 3–22; Guy Vernon Bennett, "Early Relations of the Sandwich Islands with the Old Oregon Territory," *Pacific Northwest Quarterly* 4, no. 2 (April 1913): 116–126; George Verne Blue, "Early Relations between Hawai'i and the Northwest Coast," Hawaiian Historical Society, *Annual Report*, 1925, 16–22; Robert Carleton Clark, "Hawaiians in Early Oregon," *Oregon Historical Quarterly* 35 (March 1934): 22–31; Harold Whitman Bradley, "The Hawaiian Islands and the Pacific Fur Trade, 1785–1813," *Pacific Northwest Quarterly* 30 (July 1939): 275–299; David Kittelson, "Hawaiians and Fur Traders," *Hawai'i Historical Review* 1, no. 2 (January 1961): 16–20; Richard A. Greer, "Wandering Kamaainas: Notes on Hawaiian Emigration Before 1848," *Journal of the West* 11 (April 1967): 221–225; Milton Bona, "Hawaiians Made Life 'More Bearable' at Fort Vancouver," *Clark County History* 8 (1972): 159–175; Tom Koppel, *Kanaka: The Untold Story of Hawaiian Pioneers in British Columbia and the Pacific Northwest* (Vancouver: Whitecap Books, 1995); and Jean Barman, "New Land, New Lives: Hawaiian Settlement in British Columbia," *Hawaiian Journal of History* 29 (1996): 1–32.

14. On the potential of Hawaiian-language newspapers, see Silva, *Aloha Betrayed*, 54–86; and Helen Geracimos Chapin, *Shaping History: The Role of Newspapers in Hawai'i* (Honolulu: University of Hawai'i Press, 1996).

CHAPTER I. LEAVING PARADISE

1. Estimates of the population at contact vary; for diverse perspectives, see Andrew F. Bushnell, "The 'Horror' Reconsidered: An Evaluation of the Historical Evidence for Population Decline in Hawai'i, 1778–1803," *Pacific Studies* 16 (September 1993): 115–161; Tom Dye, "Population Trends in Hawai'i before 1778," *Hawaiian Journal of History* 28 (1994):

1–20; Lilikalā Kameʻeleihiwa, *Native Land and Foreign Desires: Pehea Lā E Pono Ai?* (Honolulu: Bishop Museum Press, 1992); Robert C. Schmitt, *Historical Statistics of Hawaii* (Honolulu: University Press of Hawaiʻi, 1977); and David Stannard, *Before the Horror: The Population of Hawaiʻi on the Eve of Western Contact* (Honolulu: Social Science Research Institute, University of Hawaiʻi, 1989).

2. Juliette Montague Cooke to her brother Charles Montague, Honolulu, April 18, 1837, in Mary Atherton Richards, *Amos Starr Cooke and Juliette Montague Cooke* (Honolulu: Daughters of Hawaiʻi, 1987, orig. 1941), 122.

3. James Cook, *Captain Cook's Voyages of Discovery,* ed. John Barrow (London: Dent & Sons, 1906), 329.

4. Samuel S. Kamakau, "Hawaii Before Foreign Innovations," *Ka Nupepa Kaʻokoʻa,* January 4, 1868, translated in Samuel M. Kamakau, *Ruling Chiefs of Hawaii,* rev. ed. (Honolulu: Kamehameha Schools Press, 1992), 237.

5. Elizabeth Buck, *Paradise Remade: The Politics of Culture and History in Hawaiʻi* (Philadelphia: Temple University Press, 1993), 37; Kamakau, "Death of Kamhameha," *Ka Nupepa Kaʻokoʻa,* October 5, 1867, translated in his *Ruling Chiefs,* 201–202.

6. I. C. Campbell, "The Culture of Culture Contact: Refractions from Polynesia," *Journal of World History* 14, no. 1 (March 2003): 86; Camille de Roquefeuil, *Journal d'un voyage autour du monde pendant les années 1816, 1817, 1818, et 1819* (Paris: Ponthier, 1823), translated and reprinted in Mary Ellen Birkett, "Hawaiʻi in 1819: An Account by Camille de Roquefeuil," *Hawaiian Journal of History* 34 (2000): 81; Juri Mykkänen, *Inventing Politics: A New Political Anthropology of the Hawaiian Kingdom* (Honolulu: University of Hawaiʻi Press, 2003), 60.

7. Hiram Bingham, *A Residence of Twenty-One Years in the Sandwich Islands* (Hartford, Conn.: Hezekiah Huntington, 1847), 6; April 25, 1823, entry in Charles Samuel Stewart, *Private Journal of a Voyage to the Pacific Ocean and Residence at the Sandwich Islands in the Years 1822, 1823, 1824, and 1825* (New York: John P. Haven, 1828), 80; Sheldon Dibble, *A History of the Sandwich Islands* (Honolulu: Thrum, 1909, orig. 1843), 115; Patricia Grimshaw, *Paths of Duty: American Missionary Wives in Nineteenth-Century Hawaiʻi* (Honolulu: University of Hawaiʻi Press, 1989), 60.

8. Grimshaw, *Paths of Duty,* 60; Mykkänen, *Inventing Politics,* chapter 2, "The Politics of Virtue," 62–88; Juliette Montague Cooke, July 1837, in Richards, *Amos Starr Cooke,* 132; Stewart, *Private Journal,* 136–137.

9. "Mission at the Sandwich Islands," *Mission Herald* 20, no. 1 (January 1824): 110.

10. Sally Engle Merry, *Colonizing Hawaiʻi: The Cultural Power of Law* (Princeton: Princeton University Press, 2000), 6, also 101, 241.

11. Cited in Gavan Daws, *Shoal of Time: A History of the Hawaiian Islands* (Honolulu: University of Hawaiʻi Press, 1968), 90, also 97; Table 1, Robert C. Schmitt, "Religious Statistics of Hawaiʻi, 1825–1972," *Hawaiian Journal of History* 7 (1973): 42.

12. Alfred M. Bingham, "Sybil's Bones, a Chronicle of Three Hiram Binghams," *Hawaiian Journal of History* 9 (1975): 19; Edward Belcher, *Narrative of a Voyage Round the World* (London: H. Colburn, 1843), vol. 1: 62–63.

13. Auguste Bernard Duhaut-Cilly, reprinted in Alfons L. Korn, "Shadows of Destiny: A French Navigator's View of the Hawaiian Kingdom and its Government in 1828," *Hawaiian Journal of History* 17 (1983): 21–22.

14. Richard Charlton, "The Sandwich and Bonin Islands," London, August 11, 1832, reprinted in Hawaiian Historical Society, *Annual Report* 15 (1907): 38, 46–47; John A.

Hussey, ed., *The Voyage of the Raccoon: A 'Secret' Journal of a Visit to Oregon, California and Hawai'i, 1813–1814* (San Francisco: Book Club of California, 1958), 34; Belcher, *Narrative,* vol. 1: 272–273; Théodore-Adolphe Barrot, *Unless Haste Is Made: A French Skeptic's Account of the Sandwich Islands in 1836* (Kailua: Press Pacifica, 1978), 91.

15. Kame'eleihiwa, *Native Land and Foreign Desires;* David Malo, "On the Decrease of Population on the Hawaiian Islands," *Hawaiian Spectator* 2, no. 2 (April 1839): 125–126.

16. Hiram Bingham to his namesake son, quoted in Bingham, "Sybil's Bones," 16; Barbara Bennett Peterson, "Liliuokalani," in *American National Biography* (New York: Oxford University Press, 2000), on-line (www.anb.org). The students were Peter Young Kaeo, David Kalākaua (King Kalākaua, 1874–1891), James Kaliokalani, Victoria Kamamalu, Lot Kamehameha (King Kamehameha V, 1863–1872), Elizabeth Kekauiau, Moses Kekuaiwa, John Pitt Kinau, Alexander Liloliho (King Kamehameha IV, 1854–1863), Jane Loeau, William Charles Lunalilo (King Lunalilo, 1872–1874), Abigail Maheha, Lydia Makaeha (Queen Liliuokalani, 1891–1893), Polly, Bernice Pauahi, and Emma Rooke (wife of King Kamehameha IV), as listed in Richards, *Amos Starr Cooke,* 389–390. Richards gives an excellent insider view of the school. For another sympathetic but also critical perspective, see Linda K. Menton, "A Christian and 'Civilized' Education: The Hawaiian Chiefs' Children's School, 1839–50," *History of Education Quarterly* 32, no. 2 (Summer 1992): 213–242.

17. Silva, *Aloha Betrayed,* 40; Marion Kelly, "Land Tenure in Hawai'i," *Amerasia Journal* 7, no. 2 (1980): 57; Kamakau, "A Constitutional Monarchy," *Ka Nupepa Ka'oko'a,* May 20, 1869, translated in his *Ruling Chiefs,* 376.

18. Stauffer, *Kahana,* esp. 15–16, 31, 35–36; also Kelly, "Land Tenure," 64; Kame'eleihiwa, *Native Land,* 296; Kamakau, "Legislative Problems," *Ka Nupepa Ka'oko'a,* September 9, 1869, translated in his *Ruling Chiefs,* 404.

19. Kelly, "Land Tenure," 66; "Census of the Islands," *The Friend,* November 15, 1849; A. V. Vyshesalavtsev, reprinted in Ella L. Wiswell, "A Russian Traveler's Impressions of Hawai'i and Tahiti, 1859–1860," *Hawaiian Journal of History* 17 (1983): 91; Caroline Ralston, "Hawai'i 1778–1854: Some Aspects of *Maka'ainana* Response to Rapid Cultural Change," *Journal of Pacific History* 19, nos. 1–2 (January–April 1984): 22.

20. Kamakau, "Legislative Problems," 403–404; Ralston, "Hawai'i 1778–1854," 24, 29; Patrick V. Kirch and Marshall Sahlins, *Anahulu: The Anthropology of History in the Kingdom of Hawai'i,* vol. 2 (Chicago: University of Chicago Press, 1992), 2.

21. Ralston, "Hawai'i 1778–1854," 37, 38–39; Merry, *Colonizing Hawai'i,* 13; Silva, *Aloha Betrayed,* esp. 35–43.

22. Ralph S. Kuykendall, "American Interests and American Influence in Hawai'i in 1842," Hawai'i Historical Society, *Report,* 1930, 50; Amos Starr Cooke to Fanny Montague, February 25, 1850, in Richards, *Amos Starr Cooke,* 384; Daws, *Shoal of Time,* 128.

23. Amos Starr Cooke to his brother-in-law Mr. Seeley, July 6, 1849, in Richards, *Amos Starr Cooke,* 374; Daws, *Shoal of Time,* 147.

24. Amos Starr Cooke to his sister Mrs. Seeley, November 14, 1850, in Richards, *Amos Starr Cooke,* 396; Rufus Anderson, *The Hawaiian Islands: Their Progress and Condition under Missionary Labors* (Boston: Gould and Lincoln, 1865), 32; Laura Fish Judd, *Honolulu: Sketches of Life in the Hawaiian Islands from 1828 to 1861* (Chicago: Lakeside Press, 1966), 330; Beechert, *Working in Hawaii,* 40–41.

25. William Little Lee to Joel Turrill, October 11, 1851, cited in Merry, *Colonizing Hawai'i,* 5; Amos Starr Cooke to his mother-in-law, January 6, 1849, in Richards, *Amos Starr Cooke,* 360.

26. Noenoe K. Silva, "*He Kānāwai E Ho'opau I Na Hula Kuolo Hawai'i:* The Political Economy of Banning the Hula," *Hawaiian Historical Review* 34 (2000): 46; Osorio, *Dismembering Lāhui,* 3; Haunani-Kay Trask, *From a Native Daughter: Colonialism and Sovereignty in Hawai'i,* rev. ed. (Honolulu: University of Hawai'i Press, 1999), 6.

27. Romanzo Adams, *Interracial Marriage in Hawai'i* (New York: Macmillan, 1937), 8; Rona Tamiko Halualani, *In the Name of Hawaiians: Native Identities and Cultural Politics* (Minneapolis: University of Minnesota Press, 2002), 7.

28. Malo, "On the Decrease," 127–128.

29. Caroline Ralston, *Grass Huts and Warehouses: Pacific Beach Communities of the Nineteenth Century* (Canberra: Australian National University Press, 1977); "Native Seamen," *The Friend,* September 4, 1844, 79. Numbers in whaling come from Susan Lebo, Cultural Studies Division, Bishop Museum, Honolulu, and its web site http://www2.bishopmuseum.org/whaling/mainscreen.asp.

30. Jimmy M. Skaggs, *The Great Guano Rush: Entrepreneurs and American Overseas Expansion* (New York: St. Martin's Press, 1994), 72–73.

31. Kamakau, "A Constitutional Monarchy," 372, 378.

32. Kamakau, "Hawaii Before Foreign Innovations," 235, and "Legislative Problems," 404; John Papa I'i, *Fragments of Hawaiian History* (Honolulu: Bishop Museum Press, 1959), 127; Keme'ileihiwa, *Native Land,* 322.

33. C. Axel Egerström, *Borta är bra, men hemma är bäst* (Stockholm: Bonnier, 1859), translated and reprinted in "Hawai'i in 1855," *Hawaiian Journal of History* 9 (1975), 43; George Hu'eu Sanford Kanahele, *Kū Kanaka, Stand Tall: A Search for Hawaiian Values* (Honolulu: University of Hawai'i Press and Waiaha Foundation, 1986), 28.

CHAPTER 2. MARITIME SOJOURNERS

1. F. W. Howay, "A List of Trading Vessels in Maritime Fur Trade," Royal Society of Canada, *Transactions,* section II (1930): 111–134, (1931): 117–149; (1932): 43–86; (1933): 11–49; (1934): 119–147.

2. John Meares to Robert Funter, Friendly Cove, Nootka Sound, September 10, 1788, in James Colnett, *The Journals of Captain James Colnett* (Toronto: Champlain Society, 1940), 38.

3. Halualani, *In the Name,* 49.

4. Quoted in Beth Hill, *The Remarkable World of Frances Barkley: 1769–1845* (Sidney, British Columbia: Gray's Publishing, 1978), 22; John Meares, *Voyages Made in the Years 1788 and 1789, from China to the North West Coast of America* (London: Logographic Press, 1790), 28.

5. J. T. Walbran, "The Cruise of the Imperial Eagle," *Colonist,* March 3, 1901; Meares, *Voyages,* 29; also Frederick W. Howay, "The Story of Winee," typescript in Frederick W. Howay Papers, University of British Columbia Special Collections, Box 28, "Hawaiian Island Misc. Files."

6. Meares, *Voyages,* 4, 7. Ka'iana's story is told in David G. Miller, "Ka'iana, the Once Famous 'Prince of Kaua'i,'" *Hawaiian Journal of History* 22 (1988): 1–19.

7. Meares, *Voyages,* xxxix, 6–7; Kepelino, *Kepelino's Traditions of Hawaii,* ed. Martha Warren Beckwith (Bernice P. Bishop Museum, Bulletin 95, Honolulu, 1932), 134.

8. Meares, *Voyages,* 27–29.

9. Ibid., 208, 210.

10. Ibid., 335, 342.

11. Ibid., 279.

12. Colnett, *Journal*, 105, 41.

13. Cited in Albert Pierce Taylor, ed., *The Hawaiian Islands* (Honolulu: Archives of Hawai'i Commission, 1930), 17.

14. Colnett, *Journal*, 103; Colnett to El Conde de Revilla Gigedo, Mexico, May 3, 1790, in Colnett, *Journal*, 109.

15. Ibid., 106, 117. We are grateful to the manuscript reader for University of Hawai'i Press for correcting Colnett's mistakes in grammar; his first question reads in the original: "Oe No Ho No ho Padree or Tehuna?"

16. Ibid., 118.

17. Ibid., 198.

18. *New England Magazine*, June 1792, 479, cited in Taylor, *Hawaiian Islands*, 14.

19. June 14, 15, 1891, entries, journal of John Hoskins in Frederic W. Howay, ed., *Voyages of the "Columbia" to the Northwest Coast 1787–1790 and 1790–1793* (Boston: Massachusetts Historical Society, 1941), 185–186.

20. February 1792, entry, journal of John Hoskins in Howay, *Voyages*, 271.

21. October 2, 1892, entry, journal of John Boit in Howay, *Voyages*, 418–419.

22. Joseph Ingraham, *The Log of the Brig Hope* (Honolulu: Hawaiian Historical Society, 1918), 12.

23. George Vancouver, *A Voyage of Discovery to the North Pacific Ocean and Round the World 1791–1795*, vol. 2 (London: Hakluyt Society, 1984), 449–451.

24. Vancouver, *Voyage*, vol. 2: 454.

25. Ibid., vol. 3: 893.

26. Ii, *Fragments*, 87; Vancouver, *Voyage*, vol. 2: 689.

27. Vancouver, *Voyage*, vol. 3: 894.

28. Archibald Menzies, "Menzies' California Journal," *California Historical Society Quarterly* 2, no. 4 (January 1924): 271–272, 283–284.

29. Vancouver, *Voyage*, vol. 3: 894.

30. Ibid., vol. 3: 799.

31. March 29, 1793, entry in Archibald Menzies' journal, in Vancouver, *Voyage*, vol. 2: 894–895, 895 n 1.

32. Vancouver, *Voyage*, vol. 3: 1198, also 1198 n 1.

33. Meares, *Voyages*, 210.

34. "Commercial Journal—Copies of Letters, and accts of Ship Rubys Voyage to N. W. Coast of America and China, 1794.5.6. by Chas Bishop, Commander," BCA Ships' logs, 119.

35. Information not specifically cited can be found in the relevant biographies.

36. George Simpson, in *Part of Dispatch from George Simpson . . . 1829*, ed. E. E. Rich (London: Champlain Society for the Hudson's Bay Record Society, 1947), 103.

37. March 12, 1805, entry in F. W. Howay, "The Ship Pearl in Hawai'i in 1805 and 1806," Hawaiian Historical Society, *Report*, 1937, 42; Stephen Reynolds, *The Voyage of the New Hazard to the Northwest Coast, Hawai'i and China, 1810–1813*, ed. F. W. Howay (Salem, Ore.: Ye Galleon Press, 1970), 14, 18, 22, 23, 26, 32, 33–34, 39–40, 46.

38. F. W. Howay, "The Brig Owhyhee in the Columbia, 1829–30," *Oregon Historical Quarterly* 35, no. 1 (March 1934): 12, 14, 16–17.

39. John C. Jones to Secretary of State Adams, O'ahu, December 31, 1821, cited in Harold Whitman Bradley, "The Hawaiian Islands and the Pacific Fur Trade, 1785–1813," *Pacific North-*

west Quarterly 30 (July 1939): 294; Bryan and Sturgies to Capt. James Hale, August 31, 1818, cited in Kuykendall, *Hawaiian Kingdom 1778–1854,* 88; Roquefeuil, *Journal,* 80.

40. Theodore Morgan, *Hawaii: A Century of Economic Change, 1778–1876* (Cambridge, Mass.: Harvard University Press, 1948), 103–105; also Beechert, *Working in Hawaii,* 8.

41. Richard Pierce, *Russian America: A Biographical Dictionary* (Kingston, Ont., and Fairbanks, Alaska: Limestone Press, 1990), 388–389; April 23, 1811, entry in Reynolds, *Voyage,* 15.

42. Roquefeuil, *Journal,* 80.

CHAPTER 3. THE ASTORIA ADVENTURE

1. Log of *Albatross,* privately held; also Briton C. Busch and Barry M. Gough, *Fur Traders from New England: The Boston Men in the North Pacific, 1787–1800* (Spokane: Arthur H. Clark, 1997).

2. James P. Ronda, *Astoria & Empire* (Lincoln: University of Nebraska Press, 1990), 58.

3. Gabriel Franchère, *Journal of a Voyage on the North West Coast of North America during the Years 1811, 1812, 1813 and 1814* (Toronto: Champlain Society, 1969), 59; Alexander Ross, *Adventures of the First Settlers on the Columbia River* (London: Smith, Elder & Co., 1849), 44.

4. Alexander Ross, *The Fur Hunters of the Far West,* ed. Kenneth A. Spaulding (Norman: University of Oklahoma Press, 1956), 194.

5. Franchère, *Journal,* 67–68; Ross, *Adventures,* 49–50.

6. Washington Irving, *Astoria or Anecdotes of an Enterprise Beyond the Rocky Mountains,* ed. Edgeley W. Todd (Norman: University of Oklahoma Press, 1964), 72; Franchère, *Journal,* 70; also February 11, 1811, entry in Duncan McDougall, *Annals of Astoria: The Headquarters Log of the Pacific Fur Company on the Columbia River, 1811–1813,* ed. Robert F. Jones (New York: Fordham University Press, 1999), 3.

7. Ii, *Fragments,* 87.

8. Ibid.; Ross Cox, *Adventures on the Columbia River* (New York: J. & J. Harper, 1832), 50–51.

9. Cox, *Adventures,* 51.

10. Ross, *Adventures,* 50; Cox, *Adventures,* 51.

11. Ii, *Fragments,* 87.

12. March 24, 1811, entry in McDougall, *Annals,* 4. Post journal entries are not footnoted where identified by date.

13. Stephen Weeks, quoted in Ross, *Adventures,* 63–64.

14. Weeks, accounts in Ross, *Adventures,* 64, and McDougall, *Annals,* 5; Franchère, *Journal,* 74.

15. April 12, 1811, entry in McDougall, *Annals,* 10.

16. Franchère, *Journal,* 75.

17. Alfred Seton, *Astorian Adventure: The Journal of Alfred Seton 1811–1815,* ed. Robert F. Jones (New York: Fordham University Press, 1993), 124.

18. Ross, *Adventures,* 114.

19. David Thompson, *David Thompson's Narrative,* ed. Richard Glover (Toronto: Champlain Society, 1962), 365–366.

20. Thompson, *Narrative,* 369; David Thompson, *Columbia Journals,* ed. Barbara Belyea (Montreal and Kingston: McGill-Queen's University Press, 1994), 173.

21. Thompson, *Narrative,* 381.

22. Franchère, *Journal,* 68.

23. Ibid., 59, 64.

24. Ibid., 66; Ross, *Adventures,* 45.

25. Cox, *Adventures,* 79.

26. Franchère, *Journal,* 89–90; Cox, *Adventures,* 91.

27. Ross, *Adventures,* 74.

28. Ross, *Fur Hunters,* 194.

29. James Ronda suggests in *Astoria & Empire* that the Hawaiians were most likely to become infected ("As early as July 1811, McDougall found that several of the Hawaiians had venereal diseases" [227–228]). The inference left is that they were the most likely to engage in sexual relations with local women contaminated by earlier newcomers. McDougall's post journal tells a different story. The initial entry refers to venereal disease more generally being present only from February 8, 1813, and relates it with non-Hawaiians. "Three of our men beside Tuanna are now ill of the Venereal. Viz. Little Milligan & LaPierre." Richard Milligan was the tailor, Joseph LaPierre a laborer. The post journal observed four days later how "more or less of our number are continually afflicted with it." A subsequent entry, on July 9, ran: "J. Lapierre & Tuanna laid up with the Venereal, both making use of Mercury. One other S. Islander also slightly affected with the same disease, making 3 men sick."

30. McDougall, *Annals,* 132–133, 133n.

31. John McDonald of Garth, "Autobiographical Note," in L. R. Masson, *Les Bourgeois de la Compagnie du Nord-Ouest,* vol. 2 (New York: Antiquarian Press, 1960), 44–45.

32. Cox, *Adventures,* 108.

33. Franchère, *Journal,* 123.

34. Seton, *Astorian Adventure,* 124.

35. Elliott Coues, ed., *New Light on the Early History of the Greater Northwest: The Manuscript Journals of Alexander Henry and of David Thompson,* vol. 2 (Minneapolis: Ross & Haines, orig. 1897, 1965), 756.

36. Seton, *Astorian Adventure,* 134.

37. Joseph McGillivray to Ross Cox, Oakinagan, February 1814, in Cox, *Adventures,* 130.

38. Franchère, *Journal,* 145; Coues, *New Light,* vol. 2: 843.

39. Peter Corney, *Voyages in the Northern Pacific* (Honolulu: Thomas G. Thrum, 1896, reprinted from *London Literary Gazette,* 1821, and reprinted Fairfield, Wash.: Ye Galleon Press, 1965), 114.

CHAPTER 4. IN THE SERVICE OF THE HUDSON'S BAY COMPANY

1. Samuel Elliot Morison, "Boston Traders in Hawaiian Islands," *Proceedings of the Massachusetts Historical Society* 54 (October 1920–June 1921): 23.

2. Corney, *Voyages,* 113.

3. Cox, *Adventures,* 173, 176.

4. Ibid., 183–184.

5. Ibid., 221; Donald Mackenzie to Ross Cox, Spokane House, February 12, 1817, in Cox, *Adventures,* 220.

6. Cox, *Adventures,* 236, 289.

7. Corney, *Voyages,* 155.

8. Ibid., 159, 162; "Oldest Native Lives at Derby," *Vancouver World,* August 10, 1915; Ii, *Fragments,* 127.

9. Corney, *Voyages,* 218.

10. Ibid., 222.

11. Ross, *Fur Hunters,* 121; James Keith to Frederick Hickey, Fort George, October 7, 1818, in Katharine B. Judson, "British Side of the Restoration of Fort Astoria—II," *Oregon Historical Quarterly* 20, no. 4 (December 1919): 322; February 17, March 24, 1826, entries in *Peter Skene Ogden's Snake Country Journals 1824–25 and 1825–26,* ed. E. E. Rich (London: Hudson's Bay Record Society, 1950), 129–130, 146.

12. Ross, *Fur Hunters,* 193–194.

13. Ibid.

14. Cox, *Adventures,* 177–178; Corney, *Voyages,* 87–88.

15. Journal, 1824–1825, in George Simpson, *Fur Trade and Empire: George Simpson's [1824–5] Journal,* ed. Frederick Merk (Cambridge, Mass.: Harvard University Press, 1968), 91.

16. Ibid.

17. Ibid.; Robert Dampier, May 1825, in Robert Dampier, *To the Sandwich Islands on H.M.S. Blonde* (Honolulu: University Press of Hawai'i, 1971), 47.

18. Journal, 1824–1825, in Simpson, *Fur Trade and Empire,* 91.

19. March 21, 22, 1825, entries in John Work, "The Journal of John Work March 21–May 14, 1825," ed. Nellie B. Pipes, *Oregon Historical Quarterly* 45, no. 2 (June 1944): 140–141.

20. November 30, 1824, entry in John Work, "Journal of John Work, November and December 1824," *Washington Historical Quarterly* 3, no. 3 (July 1912): 208; John McLoughlin to HBC Governor and Committee, Fort Vancouver, July 6, 1827, Hudson's Bay Company Archives [HBCA], Fort Vancouver Correspondence Book [FtVanCB] B.223/b/3, fo. 6d.

21. Entries in Morag Maclachlan, *The Fort Langley Journals, 1827–30* (Vancouver: UBC Press, 1998), 31–41, also August 10, 1827 (31), October 23, 25, 30 (43–44), November 5 (44). Journal entries dated in the text are not separately footnoted.

22. October 4, 1827, entry in Maclachlan, *Fort Langley Journals,* 40.

23. Simpson, in *Part of Dispatch,* 84.

24. McLoughlin to HBC Governor and Committee, Fort Vancouver, October 6, 1825, in John McLoughlin, *The Letters of John McLoughlin, 1825–28,* ed. E. E. Rich (London: Hudson's Bay Record Society, 1941), 2.

25. Simpson, in *Part of Dispatch,* 86, 106.

26. Simpson, in ibid., 109.

27. McLoughlin to Charlton, Fort Vancouver, August 4, 1829; and McLoughlin to HBC Governor and Committee, Fort Vancouver, August 5, 1829, in John McLoughlin, *Letters of Dr. John McLoughlin Written at Fort Vancouver 1829–1832,* ed. Burt Brown Barker (Portland: Oregon Historical Society, 1948), 27, 36.

28. McLoughlin to Richard Charlton, Fort Vancouver, August 4, 1829, in McLoughlin, *Letters, 1829–1832,* 27; Charlton to Kamehameha III, British Consulate, Honolulu, January 22, 28, 1834, Hawai'i State Archives [HSA], 402-3-47.

29. Herbert Beaver to Aboriginal Protection Society of London, 1842, in Herbert Beaver, "Indian Conditions in 1836–38," ed. Nellie B. Pipes, *Oregon Historical Quarterly* 32 (1931): 340; Edith I. Burley, *Servants of the Honourable Company* (Toronto: Oxford, 1997), 58.

30. McLoughlin to Charlton, Fort Vancouver, October 27, 1831, in McLoughlin, *Letters, 1829–1832,* 226, 229.

31. McLoughlin to HBC Governor and Committee, Fort Vancouver, November 20, 1844, HBCA FtVanCB 1843–1844, B.223/b/31, fo. 200d.

32. McLoughlin to HBC Governor and Board, Fort Vancouver, October 11, 1830, in McLoughlin, *Letters, 1829–1832,* 139–140.

33. McLoughlin to Charlton, Fort Vancouver, October 19, 1831, 230.

34. Hall J. Kelley, *A Geographical Sketch of that Part of North America called Oregon* (Boston: J. Howe, 1830), reprinted in Fred Wilbur Powell, ed., *Hall J. Kelley on Oregon* (Princeton: Princeton University Press, 1932), 62–63; Nathaniel Wyeth to Jacob Wyeth, December 8, 1831, in Nathaniel J. Wyeth, *The Correspondence and Journals of Captain Nathaniel J. Wyeth 1831–6,* ed. F. G. Young (Eugene: University Press, 1899), 11.

35. Nathaniel J. Wyeth to Captain Lambert, January 1, 1834, Fort Hall copy book, Oregon Historical Society; September 15, 1834, entry in Wyeth, *Correspondence,* 233; September 25, 16, entries in John Kirk Townsend, *Narrative of a Journey Across the Rocky Mountains to the Columbia River* (Philadelphia: Perkins, 1839), 172–173, 169.

36. September 16, 1834, and November 21, 1835, entries in Townsend, *Narrative,* 169, 263.

37. November 25, 1834, entry in Townsend, *Narrative,* 179; Wyeth, *Correspondence,* 234–235. In a letter written on April 3, 1835, Wyeth put the number of runaways at 13 (148).

38. March 26, May 20, 1835, entries in Townsend, *Narrative,* 215, 219–220.

39. June 11, 1835, entry in Townsend, *Narrative,* 224–225.

40. Samuel Parker, *Journal of an Exploring Expedition Beyond the Rocky Mountains* (Minneapolis: Ross & Haines, 1967, orig. 1838), 156, 142.

41. Fort Hall accounts, 1834–1837, consisting of two ledgers and a journal in Oregon Historical Society.

42. James Douglas to HBC Governor and Committee, Fort Vancouver, October 18, 1838, HBCA FtVanCB 1838, B.223/b.20, fos. 10–10d.

43. Andrew Dominique Pambrun, *Sixty Years on the Frontier in the Pacific Northwest* (Fairfield, Wash.: Ye Galleon Press, 1978), 28.

44. Memorial in William Slacum, "Document: Slacum's Report on Oregon, 1836–7," *Oregon Historical Quarterly* 13 (1912): 185; Thomas J. Farnham, *An 1839 Wagon Train Journal* (New York: Greeley and McElrath, 1843), 98; July 28, 1841, entry, George Thornton Emmons, "Extracts from the Emmons Journal," *Oregon Historical Quarterly* 26 (1925): 268.

45. Simpson, in *Part of Dispatch,* 79; Simpson to Captain Amelius Simpson, "Cadboro," October 1828, in Simpson, *Fur Trade and Empire,* 298.

46. Sereno Edwards Bishop, *Reminiscences of Old Hawaii* (Honolulu: Hawaiian Gazette, 1916), 29; Wilkes, *Narrative,* vol. 5: 123, vol. 3: 373.

47. John Ball, *Autobiography* (Glendale, Calif.: Arthur H. Clark Co., 1925), 107; Wilkes, *Narrative,* vol. 3: 386.

48. Ball, *Autobiography,* 107; Wilkes, *Narrative,* vol. 3: 386.

49. Agreement between Kekuanoa and G. Pelly, Honolulu, February 11, 1840, original in Hawaiian with translation in English, HSA, 402-5-120.

50. Beaver to Aboriginal Protection Society of London, 1842, 341; Wilkes, *Narrative,* vol. 4: 339–340; Passenger Manifest, April 30, 1846, HSA, 82.

51. J. S. Helmcken, June 27 and July 10, 1850, entries; Helmcken to Richard Blanshard, Fort Rupert, July 2, 1850, and George Blenkinsop to Helmcken, Fort Rupert, June 28, 1850, all in Helmcken, Fort Rupert Letters.

52. Richard Somerset Mackie, *Trading Beyond the Mountains: The British Fur Trade on the Pacific 1793–1843* (Vancouver: UBC Press, 1997).

53. Douglas to HBC Governor and Committee, Fort Vancouver, October 14, 1839, HBCA FtVanCB 1839, B.223/b/23, fo. 3d.

54. June 13, 1840, entry in Stikine Post Journal, 1840–42, fos. 6-7, HBCA, B.209/z/1. fo. 1.

55. Simpson to HBC Governors, Fort Vancouver, November 25, 1841, in George Simpson, *London Correspondence Inward from Sir George Simpson,* ed. Glyndwr Williams (London: Hudson's Bay Record Society, 1973), 74-75, 95-96.

56. HBC Governor and Committee to McLoughlin, London, December 31, 1839, in John McLoughlin, *The Letters of John McLoughlin from Fort Vancouver, 1839–44,* ed. E. E. Rich (London: Hudson's Bay Record Society, 1943), 19n; McLoughlin to HBC Governor and Committee, Fort Vancouver, November 18, 1843, HBCA FtVanCB 1842–1843, B.223/b/30, fo. 91d.

57. Francis A. Chamberlain, testimony in *In the Supreme Court of Oregon Territory, January Term, A.D. 1889, The Corporation of the Catholic Bishop of Nesqually, in the Territory of Washington, v. John Gibbon, T.M. Anderson, and R.T. Yeatman* (no publishing data), 197, 212.

58. Simpson to McLoughlin, Honolulu, March 1, 1842, in McLoughlin, *Letters, 1839–44,* 271; McLoughlin to Simpson, Honolulu, March 1, 1842, HBCA FtVanCB 1842–1843, B.223/b/29, fos. 69-69d.

59. Simpson to McLoughlin, Red River Settlement, June 21, 1843, in McLoughlin, *Letters, 1839–44,* 157n; McLoughlin to HBC Governor and Committee, Fort Vancouver, November 18, 1843, fo. 80d; January 11, 1835, entry in Townsend, *Narrative,* 199.

60. Jean Baptiste Bolduc to "Mr. T.," Honolulu, August 5, 1842, in *Notices & Voyages of the Famed Quebec Mission to the Pacific Northwest* (Portland: Oregon Historical Society, 1956), 133; "Native Seamen," *The Friend,* September 4, 1844, 79.

61. George Simpson, *Narrative of a Journey Round the World, During the Years 1841 and 1842* (London: Henry Colburn, 1847), vol. 1: 257; Simpson to HBC Governors, Honolulu, March 1, 1842, in Simpson, *London Correspondence,* 130.

62. Simpson, *Narrative,* vol. 2: 14-15.

63. Ibid., vol. 2: 53; Simpson to McLoughlin, Honolulu, March 1, 1842, 271.

64. McLoughlin to HBC Governor and Committee, Fort Vancouver, November 18, December 4, 1843, HBCA FtVanCB 1842–1843, B.223/b/30, fos. 83, 89, 159; McLoughlin to Simpson, March 20, 1844, in John McLoughlin, "Documentary," ed. Katherine B. Judson, *Oregon Historical Quarterly* 17 (1916): 227.

65. McLoughlin to HBC Governor and Committee, Fort Vancouver, November 20, 1844; Marcel Bernier, testimony in *In the Supreme Court,* 188.

66. "Decrease of Polynesian Races," *The Friend,* March 1, 1849, 20; William Little Lee to Catherine Lee, Honolulu, September 28, 1849, in Barbara E. Dunn, "William Little Lee and Catherine Lee: Letters from Hawai'i 1848–1855," *Hawaiian Journal of History* 38 (2004): 73; "Instructions to the Captain of the Port for discharging native seamen," approved by Privy Council, November 27, 1849, HSA, 402-27-550.

67. E. Huggins, undated memo, FN, Box 6.

68. Roderick Finlayson to Hamilton Moffat, Victoria, September 17, 1864, Fort Victoria Correspondence Book, 1864–1866, HBCA, B.226/b/28, fo. 60d.

CHAPTER 5. MAKING A LIFE IN THE FUR TRADE

1. March 28, 1833, entry in William Fraser Tolmie, *The Journals of William Fraser Tolmie: Physician and Fur Trader,* ed. R. G. Large (Vancouver: Mitchell Press, 1963), 133.

2. May 6, 1833, entry in Tolmie, *Journals,* 173.

3. May 19, 22, 25, 26, 1833, entries in Tolmie, *Journals,* 181, 183, 186, 189, 191.

4. May 26, 1833, entry in Tolmie, *Journals,* 191.

5. McLoughlin to HBC Governor and Committee, Fort Vancouver, July 6, 1827, HBCA FtVanCB 1827–1828, B.223/b/3, fo. 6d; Ross, *Fur Hunters,* 196; McLoughlin to Simpson, Fort Vancouver, s.d. [March 1830], in McLoughlin, *Letters, 1829–1832,* 83; Helmcken to R. Brown, Fort Rupert, July 10, 1850, in Helmcken, Fort Rupert Letters.

6. March 5–6, May 11, 1846, entries in Alexandre Latte, "Alexander Latte's Fort George Journal, 1846," *Oregon Historical Quarterly* 64, no. 2 (September 1963): 211, 226.

7. Edward Huggins to Eva Emory Dye, South Tacoma, Washington, September 12, 1904, in "Letters Outward: The Letters of Edward Huggins 1862–1907," typescript in Fort Nisqually Historic Site Archives [FNHSA], Tacoma; McLoughlin to HBC Governor and Committee, Fort Vancouver, November 20, 1844, HBCA FtVanCB 1842–1843, B.223/b/30, fo. 223d.

8. Helmcken to Blanshard, Fort Rupert, July 2, 1850, and Helmcken to R. Brown, Fort Rupert, July 10, 1850, in Helmcken, Fort Rupert Letters.

9. Beaver to HBC Governors, Fort Vancouver, October 2, 1838, HBCA FtVanCB 1838, B.223/b/20, fos. 55–55d; McLoughlin to Simpson, Fort Vancouver, s.d. [March 1830], in McLoughlin, *Letters, 1829–1832,* 83.

10. Wilkes, *Narrative,* vol. 4: 329, 433; Horatio Hale, *Ethnography and Philology* (Philadelphia: Lea and Blanchard, 1846), 644.

11. Hale, *Ethnography,* 644; Simpson, *Narrative,* vol. 1: 177.

12. Statement of John O'Brien, June 2, 1845, enclosed in McLoughlin to J. H. Pelly, Oregon City, July 12, 1846, in John McLoughlin, *The Letters of John McLoughlin, 1844–46,* ed. E. E. Rich (London: Hudson's Bay Record Society, 1943), 173; McLoughlin to HBC Governor and Committee, Fort Vancouver, November 10, 1844, HBCA FtVanCB 1843–1844, B.223/b/31, fo. 28d.

13. McLoughlin to HBC Governor and Committee, Fort Vancouver, November 10, 1844, HBCA FtVanCB 1843–1844, B.223/b/31, fo. 28d; same to same, November 15, 1843, HBCA FtVanCB 1842–43, B.223/b/30, fo. 65.

14. McLoughlin to HBC Governor and Committee, Fort Vancouver, June 24, 1842, HBCA FtVanCB 1842–1843, B.223/b/29, fos. 6d, 13; Simpson to HBC Governor and Committee, London, January 5, 1843, HBCA FtVanCB 1842–1843, B.223/b/29, fo. 25.

15. McLoughlin to HBC Governor and Committee, Fort Vancouver, November 20, 1844, HBCA FtVanCB 1843–1844, B.223/b/31, fo. 203.

16. McLoughlin to HBC Governor and Committee, Fort Vancouver, November 15, 1843, HBCA FtVanCB 1842–1843, B.223/b/30, fos. 65–65d; C. O. Ermatinger, "The Columbia River under Hudson's Bay Company Rule," *Washington Historical Quarterly* 5, no. 2 (April 1914): 200.

17. Richard H. Dillon, *Siskiyou Trail: The Hudson's Bay Company Route to California* (New York: McGraw-Hill, 1975), 226.

18. May 1825, entry in Dampier, *To the Sandwich Islands,* 46; Simpson, *Narrative,* vol. 2: 61–62.

19. Paul Kane, *Wanderings of an Artist* (Edmonton: Hurtig, 1968, orig. 1859), 179.

20. Edward Huggins, "Reminiscences of Puget Sound," 139–140, typescript, FNHSA.

21. Edward Huggins to Frank B. Cole, Steilacoom, Washington, October 20, 1901, in "Letters Outward."

22. January 1–3, 1835, entries in Tolmie, *Journals,* 300.

23. McLoughlin to Simpson, Vancouver, February 1, 1844, HBCA FtVanCB 1843–1844, B.223/b/31, fos. 168d, 180d.

24. Ross, *Fur Hunters,* 61–62.

25. Wyeth, *Correspondence,* 235–237.

26. Alexander Simpson to HBC Governor and Committee, *Columbia* at Sea, October 1, 1840, HBCA FtVanCB 1840–1841, B.223/b/28, fo. 38d; Beaver to HBC Governors, Fort Vancouver, March 19, 1838, in Herbert Beaver, *Reports and Letters of Herbert Beaver, 1836–1838,* ed. Thomas E. Jessett (Portland: Champoeg Press, 1959), 86.

27. May 17, July 2, 21, 29, 1826, entries, A. R. McLeod, journal, HBCA FtVanPJ 1826, B.223/a/2, fos. 5, 13d, 17d, 20.

28. October 14, November 4, 1826, entries, A. R. McLeod, journal, HBCA FtVanPJ 1826–1827, B.223/a/4, fos. 4d, 7d.

29. Wilkes, *Narrative,* vol. 4: 329; Peter W. Crawford, testimony in *In the Supreme Court,* 134.

30. Fort Nisqually entries come from post journals, Huntington Library, Fort Nisqually, FN 1234, vols. 1–16. The journals to September, 27, 1859, are transcribed in George Dickey, ed., *The Journal of Occurrences at Fort Nisqually* (Tacoma: Fort Nisqually Association, 1989).

31. Archibald McDonald to HBC officials, Fort Langley, February 10, 1831, in Archibald McDonald, *This Blessed Wilderness: Archibald McDonald's Letters from the Columbia, 1822–44,* ed. Jean Murray Cole (Vancouver: UBC Press, 2001), 87; February 25, 1830, report, in Maclachlan, *Fort Langley Journals,* 221–222.

32. McLoughlin to James Birnie, Fort Vancouver, October 6, 1830 [1829]; McLoughlin to Francis Heron, Fort Vancouver, September 9, 1831; McLoughlin to P. S. Ogden, Fort Vancouver, August 14, 1831, in McLoughlin, *Letters, 1829–1832,* 60, 213, 208.

33. McLoughlin to A. R. McLeod, March 20 [1831]; McLoughlin list [June 1831], in McLoughlin, *Letters, 1829–1832,* 194, 202.

34. August 31, 1830, entry in Maclachlan, *Fort Langley Journals,* 154.

35. August 31, 1830, entry in Maclachlan, *Fort Langley Journals,* 155; Archibald McDonald to Captain William Ryan, Fort Langley, September 13, 1830, in McDonald, *Blessed Wilderness,* 82.

36. September 13, 1830, entry in Maclachlan, *Fort Langley Journals,* 157; McDonald to Captain William Ryan, Fort Langley, September 13, 1830, in McDonald, *Blessed Wilderness,* 82.

37. McDonald to McLoughlin, Fort Langley, September 20, 1830, in McDonald, *Blessed Wilderness,* 82–84; September 13, 1830, entry in Maclachlan, *Fort Langley Journals,* 157–158.

38. September 15, 1830, entry in Maclachlan, *Fort Langley Journals,* 158; McDonald to Edward Ermatinger, Fort Langley, February 20, 1831; McDonald to McLoughlin, Fort Langley, September 20, 1830, in McDonald, *Blessed Wilderness,* 90, 85.

39. John Minto, "Reminiscences of Experiences on the Oregon Trail in 1844," *Oregon Historical Quarterly* 2, no. 3 (September 1901): 234.

40. Wilkes, *Narrative,* vol. 4: 329–330.

41. March 11, June 8, 1829, entries in Maclachlan, *Fort Langley Journals,* 115; Juliette

Montague Cooke to her aunt Sally Smith, Honolulu, November 18, 1839, in Richards, *Amos Starr Cooke*, 189; Alexander Spoehr, "Fur Traders in Hawai'i : The Hudson's Bay Company in Honolulu, 1829–1861," *Hawaiian Journal of History* 20 (1986): 50.

42. January 11, 1835, entry in Townsend, *Narrative*, 199.

43. Douglas to Archibald Barclay, Fort Victoria, November 16, 1860, in Hartwell Bowsfield, ed., *Fort Victoria Letters 1846–1851* (Winnipeg: Hudson's Bay Record Society, 1979), 131; July 28, 1841, entry in Emmons, "Extracts," 268; Simpson, *Narrative*, vol. 1: 246; Simpson to HBC Governors, Fort Vancouver, November 25, 1841, in Simpson, *London Correspondence*, 94.

44. Wilkes, *Narrative*, vol. 4: 329.

45. George B. Roberts to Mrs. F. F. Victor, Cathlamet, Washington, November 28, 1878, in George B. Roberts, "The Round Hand of George B. Roberts: The Cowlitz Farm Journal, 1847–51," *Oregon Historical Quarterly* 63, nos. 2–3 (June–September 1962): 197.

46. Roberts to Victor, Cathlamet, Washington, November 28, 1878; Andrew Muir, May 22, 1850, entry, diary, BCA, E/B/M91/A.

47. Parker, *Journal*, 140; September 16, 1834, entry in Townsend, *Narrative*, 171–172; Memorial in Slacum, "Document," 185; Bernier, testimony, 188.

48. Ball, *Autobiography*, 91; Crawford, testimony, 131.

49. September 16, 1834, entry in Townsend, *Narrative*, 172; Kane, *Wanderings*, 117; Hale, *Ethnography*, 644.

50. Chamberlain, testimony, 197; July 25, 1841, entry in Emmons, "Extracts," 266.

51. Adams, *Interracial Marriage*, 63.

52. Roberts to Victor, Cathlamet, Washington, November 28, 1878, 193; John McLoughlin to HBC Governor and Committee, Fort Vancouver, November 20, 1844, HBCA FtVanCB 1843–1844, B.223/b/31, fo. 201d; McLoughlin to HBC Governor and Committee, Fort Vancouver, July 7, 1842, HBCA FtVanCB 1842–1843, B.223/b/29, fo. 29.

53. Journal, 1824–1825, in Simpson, *Fur Trade and Empire*, 108.

54. Archibald McDonald to Henry Hanwell, Fort Vancouver, October 19, 1825, in McDonald, *Blessed Wilderness*, 29.

55. February 28, March 3, 1829, entries in Maclachlan, *Fort Langley Journals*, 99.

56. March 7, 1829, entry and February 25, 1830, report in Maclachlan, *Fort Langley Journals*, 100, 222; Notice no. 5, January 1843, cited in *Notices*, 104.

57. Jason O. Allard, "Christmas at Fort Langley, Gay Time in Olden Days," *Province*, October 25, 1924.

58. Beaver to HBC Governors, Fort Vancouver, October 2, 1838, HBCA FtVanCB 1838 B.223/b/20, fo. 55d; December 21, 1847, entry in Roberts, "Round Hand," 139; Crawford, testimony, 133; Marcus Whitman to David Greene, Wieleipoo, March 12, 1838, in Archer Butler Hulbert and Dorothy Printup Hulbert, eds., *Marcus Whitman, Crusader*, vol. 1 (Denver: Stewart Commission of Colorado College and Denver Public Library, 1936), 298.

59. January 14, 1845, entry in Fort Nisqually, Servants' Accounts, Huntington Library [HL], FN 1239, vol. 4; Parker, *Journal*, 170.

60. Simpson, *Narrative*, vol. 1: 246; "Tlithlow Journal 1851," typescript, FNHSA.

61. Wilkes, *Narrative*, vol. 4: 330.

62. Ibid.

63. Kirch and Sahlins, *Anahulu*, 179–182.

64. January 19, 1834, entry in Tolmie, *Journals*, 263.

65. Roquefeuil, *Journal,* 80.

66. December 16–17, 1847, entries in Roberts, "Round Hand," 138.

67. December 17, 29, 1847, and January 29, 30, 1848, entries in Roberts, "Round Hand," 138, 141–142; Douglas to Governor and Committee, Fort Victoria, December 5, 1848, HBCA FtVanCB 1847–1849, B.223/b/38, fo. 62d.

68. September 12, 1835, entry in John Work, "The Journal of John Work, 1835," ed. Henry Drummond Dee, pt. 5, *British Columbia Historical Quarterly* 9, no. 2 (April 1945): 130.

69. September 22, 1835, entry in Work, "Journal, 1835," 134.

70. May 6, 1833, entry in Tolmie, *Journals,* 173; Napoleon M'Gillvray, Bernier, Crawford, Sarah Jane Anderson, testimonies in *In the Supreme Court,* 101, 186,

CHAPTER 6. HAWAIIANS IN THE MISSIONARY ADVANCE

1. Obookiah continues to inspire, as indicated by the brochure available to visitors to Poʻokela Church at Makawao on the south Maui coast. *History of Poʻokela Church* (Makawao: Poʻokela Church, 2002) devotes its first half page to Obookiah's story as the impetus to its missionary founder, Jonathan Green, being "moved to come to the islands" (1) and in 1843 establish Poʻokela Church.

2. Jonathan S. Green, *Journal of a Tour to the North West Coast of America in the Year 1829* (New York: C. F. Heartman, 1915), 16–17.

3. Clifford Merrill Drury, *Marcus Whitman, M.D. Pioneer and Martyr* (Caldwell, Idaho: Caxton, 1937), 204; Narcissa Whitman to Rev. and Mrs. Leverett Hull, October 25, 1836, in Hulbert and Hulbert, *Marcus Whitman,* vol. 1: 245; Lowell Smith to Methodist Episcopal Mission, Oregon Territory, Honolulu, January, 29, 1840, Hawaiian Mission Children's Society Library [HMCSL], Oregon Mission files [OMF].

4. John Stensgair, testimony in *In the Supreme Court,* 64.

5. Parker, *Journal,* 141; D. Lee and J. H. Frost, *Ten Years in Oregon* (New York: The Authors, 1844), 280.

6. May 5, 1839, entry in Henry Spalding, diary, in Clifford Merrill Drury, ed., *The Diaries and Letters of Henry H. Spalding and Asa Bowen Smith relating to the Nez Perces Mission 1838–1842* (Glendale, Calif.: Arthur H. Clark, 1958), 262; Chamberlain, testimony, 212.

7. Henry Perkins to his wife Elvira, March 25, 1838, reproduced in Robert Boyd, *People of the Dalles: The Indians of Wascopam Mission* (Lincoln: University of Nebraska Press, 1996), 227–228.

8. Charles Henry Carey, ed., "The Mission Record Book of the Methodist Episcopal Church, Willamette Station, Oregon Territory, North America, Commenced 1834," *Oregon Historical Quarterly* 23 (1922): 242. On the Japanese men, see September 24, 1834, entry in Cyrus Shepard, *Diary of Cyrus Shepard, March 4, 1834–December 20, 1835* (Vancouver, Wash.: Clark County Genealogical Society, 1969), 67.

9. Lee and Frost, *Ten Years,* 169–170.

10. Margaret Jewett Bailey, *The Grains or Passages in the Life of Ruth Rover, with Occasional Pictures of Oregon, Natural and Moral* (Corvallis: Oregon State University Press, 1985), 191; Lee and Frost, *Ten Years,* 256.

11. Wilkes, *Narrative,* vol. 4: 350–353.

12. Gustavus Hines to Corresponding Secretary, Missionary Society, Methodist Episco-

pal Church, Willamette River, March 15, 1843, in Gustavus Hines, "A Document of Mission History, 1833–43," ed. Robert Mouton Gatke, *Oregon Historical Quarterly* 36 (1935): 175, 181; L. H. Judson to Amos S. Cooke, Fort Vancouver, August 6, 1843, HMCSL, OMF.

13. Robert J. Loewenberg, *Equality on the Oregon Frontier: Jason Lee and the Methodist Mission 1834–43* (Seattle: University of Washington Press, 1976), 64; contract with Gustavus Hines, Honolulu, March 27, 1844, and memo at end, Honolulu, October 9, 1845, HSA, 402-10-248.

14. February 4, 1845, entry in George Gary, "Diary of Rev. George Gary," ed. Charles Henry Carey, *Oregon Historical Quarterly* 24, no. 3 (September 1923): 272; October 23, December 2, 4, 1844, entries in Gary, "Diary of Rev. George Gary," ed. Charles Henry Carey, *Oregon Historical Quarterly* 24, no. 1 (March 1923): 174, 176, 179, 180.

15. September 16, 1836, entry, journal, in Narcissa Whitman, *Letters* (Fairfield, Wash.: Ye Galleon Press, 1986), 38; Narcissa Whitman to Rev. and Mrs. Leverett Hull, October 25, 1836, vol. 1: 243; Spalding to Levi Chamberlain, Clear Water River, January 9, 1840, HMCSL, OMF.

16. Lee and Frost, *Ten Years,* 221; Marcus Whitman to Samuel Parker, [Fort] Vancouver, September 18, 1836, in Hulbert and Hulbert, *Marcus Whitman,* vol. 1: 232.

17. Marcus Whitman, Henry Spalding, and Henry Gray to Hiram Bingham, Vancouver, September 19, 1836, HMCSL, OMF.

18. December 26, 1836, entry, journal, in Whitman, *Letters,* 46.

19. Marcus Whitman to Greene, Wailalatpu, October 22, 1839, in Hulbert and Hulbert, *Marcus Whitman,* vol. 2: 159; May 2, 1837, entry in diary letter of Narcissa Whitman to family, Wi-el-et-poo, March 30, 1837, in Whitman, *Letters,* 48; Marcus Whitman to Greene, Wieletpoo, March 12, 1838, vol. 1: 292, 294.

20. May 2, 1837, entry in diary letter of Narcissa Whitman to family, Wi-el-et-poo, March 30, 1837, in Whitman, *Letters,* 48.

21. May 2, 3, 1837, entries in diary letter of Narcissa Whitman to family, Wi-el-et-poo, March 30, 1837, 48, 50.

22. Narcissa Whitman to her family, Wieletpoo, May 2, 1837, in T. C. Elliott, "The Coming of the White Women, 1836," *Oregon Historical Quarterly* 38, no. 1 (March 1937): 57; May 2, 1837, entry in diary letter of Narcissa Whitman to family, Wi-el-et-poo, March 30, 1837.

23. Marcus Whitman to Greene, Wieleipoo, March 12, 1838, vol. 1: 299.

24. Narcissa Whitman to her sister Jane, Wieletpoo, September 18, 1838, in Whitman, *Letters,* 62.

25. Marcus Whitman to Greene, Wieleipoo, March 12, 1838, vol. 1: 298; Marcus Whitman to Levi Chamberlain, Willitpuo, October 16, 1837, HMCSL, OMF; Narcissa Whitman to mother, Waiilatpoo, October 9, 1940, in Whitman, *Letters,* 98.

26. Marcus Whitman to Levi Chamberlain, Willitpuo, October 16, 1837; Narcissa Whitman to Mrs. Parker, Wieletpoo, October 3, 1838, in Whitman, *Letters,* 70; Drury, *Marcus Whitman,* 208; September 24, 1839, entry in Thomas Jefferson Farnham, *Travels in the Great Western Prairies* (Cleveland: A. H. Clark, 1906), 137.

27. Marcus Whitman, report to American Board, Lapwai, July 6, 1840, in Hulbert and Hulbert, *Marcus Whitman,* vol. 2: 178; Narcissa Whitman to her mother, Waiilatpu, October 9, 1940.

28. Minutes, Presbyterian Synod of Washington, August 18, 1838, in Clifford Merrill Drury, *Henry Harmon Spalding* (Caldwell, Idaho: Caxton, 1936), 188.

29. Narcissa Whitman to Lyman Judson, Wieletpoo, September 29, 1838, in Hulbert and Hulbert, *Marcus Whitman*, vol. 1: 323.

30. Myron Eells, *Father Eells* (Boston: Congregational Sunday-School and Publishing Society, 1894), 87.

31. Narcissa Whitman to her sister, Weiletpoo, June 25, 1839, in Whitman, *Letters*, 9.

32. Marcus Whitman to his brother, May 1841, cited in Myron Eells, *Marcus Whitman: Pathfinder and Patriot* (Seattle: Alice Harriman Co., 1909), 118; Marcus Whitman to Greene, Waiilatpu, October 15, 1840, in Hulbert and Hulbert, *Marcus Whitman*, vol. 2: 190–191.

33. Narcissa Whitman to her mother, Waiilatpu, October 9, 1940.

34. Narcissa Whitman to Marcus Whitman, Wieletpoo, October 4, 1842, in Whitman, *Letters*, 143; Marcus Whitman to Greene, Waiilatpu, November 11, 1841, in Hulbert and Hulbert, *Marcus Whitman*, vol. 2: 237.

35. Alexander Simpson to HBC Governor and Committee, *Columbia* at Sea, October 1, 1840, HBCA FtVanCB, 1840–1841, B.223/b/28, fo. 35d.

36. Narcissa Whitman to Marcus Whitman, Wieletpoo, October 4, 1842.

37. Narcissa Whitman to Marcus Whitman, Wieletpoo, October 4, 1842, 142, 144; Marcus Whitman to Elkanah Walker, Waiilatpu, March 20, 1845, in Hulbert and Hulbert, *Marcus Whitman*, vol. 3: 160.

38. Narcissa Whitman to her mother, Wieletpoo, May 2, 1840, in Whitman, *Letters*, 93, 94.

39. Munnick, *St. Paul, Oregon,* in *Catholic Church Records,* vol. 1, 171–173.

40. Narcissa Whitman to family, Wi-el-et-poo, March 30, 1837, in Whitman, *Letters,* 48; and Marcus Whitman to Greene, Wieleipoo, March 12, 1838, vol. 1: 298; Drury, *Spalding,* 185n, 187.

41. Asa B. Smith to Greene, Kamiah, Oregon Territory, September 3, 1840, in Drury, *Diaries,* 173–174.

42. Hiram Bingham to McLoughlin, Honolulu, February 22, 1840, HMCSL, OMF.

43. Bingham to McLoughlin, Honolulu, February 22, 1840; William Gray to Levi Chamberlain, Willamette, July 31, 1843, HMCSL, OMF.

44. Gray to Chamberlain, Willamette, July 31, 1843.

45. Asa B. Smith to Prudential Committee of the American Board of Commissioners for Foreign Missions, Wieletpoo, Oregon Territory, April 29, 1839; September 21, 1839, entry in Spalding, diary, in Drury, *Diaries,* 97–98, 276.

46. Asa B. Smith to Greene, Kamiah, Oregon Territory, August 31, 1840, in Drury, *Diaries,* 152.

47. Asa B. Smith to Greene, Kamiah, Oregon Territory, August 31, 1840.

48. Asa B. Smith to Elkanah Walker, Kamiah, Oregon Territory, October 12, 1840, Drury, *Diaries,* 192.

49. October 12, 13 [sic 14] 1840 entries in Asa Smith, diary, in Drury, *Diaries,* 197.

50. L. H. Judson to Amos S. Cooke, Fort Vancouver, August 6, 1843, HMCSL, OMF.

51. Simpson to HBC Governors, Fort Vancouver, November 25, 1841, in Simpson, *London Correspondence,* 79.

52. Beaver to Narcissa Whitman and Eliza Spalding, Fort Vancouver, October 1, 1836, HBCA FtVanCB 1836, B.223/b/13, fo. 10d.

53. Beaver to HBC Governors, Fort Vancouver, November 10, 1836, in Beaver, *Reports,* 2.

54. Douglas to HBC Governors, Fort Vancouver, October 5, 1838, HBCA FtVanCB 1837–1838, B.223/b/21, fo. 5.

55. Beaver to HBC Governors, Fort Vancouver, October 2, 1838, HBCA FtVanCB 1838 B.223/b/20, fo. 55d; Beaver to Aboriginal Protection Society of London, 1842, 341.

56. Beaver to HBC Governors, Fort Vancouver, October 2, 1838, fos. 55d, 57; Douglas to HBC Governors, Fort Vancouver, October 5, 1838, HBCA FtVanCB 1837–1838 B.223/b/21, fo. 10.

57. Beaver to HBC Governors, Fort Vancouver, October 2, 1838, fos. 55d–56.

58. Beaver to Aboriginal Protection Society of London, 1842, 340–341.

59. Narcissa Whitman to Rev. and Mrs. Leverett Hull, October 25, 1836, vol. 1: 246.

60. Alanson Beers to Levi Chamberlain, Willamette, November 12, 1838, HMCSL, OMF.

61. Henry Spalding to Levi Chamberlain, Clear Water, October 7, 1839, HMCSL, OMF.

62. Narcissa Whitman to Mr. and Mrs. Allen, Waiilatpu, August 23, 1842, in Whitman, *Letters,* 136.

63. Jean Baptiste Bolduc to "Mr. T.," Honolulu, August 5, 1842, in *Notices,* 133.

64. April 9, 1839, entry in Fort Nisqually, Post Journal, FN 1234, vol. 4.

65. Munnick, *Vancouver,* in *Catholic Church Records,* vol. 1, 19–20.

66. M'Gillvray, testimony, 100.

67. Stensgair, testimony, 63.

68. Bernier, testimony, 185.

69. Munnick, *St. Paul, Oregon,* vol. 1, 103–105, 32–34.

70. Chamberlain, testimony, 193.

71. A. F. Waller to Amos S. Cooke, Willamette Falls, August 25, 1842, HMCSL, OMF.

72. McLoughlin to HBC agent in Honolulu, July 1, 1844, cited in George H. Atkinson, "Diary of Rev. George H. Atkinson, D.D. 1847–1858," ed. E. Ruth Rockwood, *Oregon Historical Quarterly* 40, no. 2 (June 1939): 181n.

73. These and the following quotes from Kaulehelehe's correspondence are taken from Yvonne Mearns Klan, "Kanaka William," *Beaver* 38 (Spring 1979): 40–41.

74. Douglas to HBC agent in Honolulu, January 9, 1845, cited in Atkinson, "Diary," 181n.

75. June 19, 1848, entry in Atkinson, "Diary," 181.

76. Stensgair, testimony, 64.

77. Elkanah Walker to Levi Chamberlain, Thimakain, September 6, 1842, HMCSL, OMF.

78. Neil M. Howison, "Report of Lieutenant Neil M. Howison on Oregon, 1846," *Oregon Historical Quarterly* 14, no. 1 (March 1913): 44.

CHAPTER 7. BOUNDARY MAKING

1. Narcissa Whitman to her mother, Wieletpoo, May 2, 1940, and to her brother Galusha, Shawnee Mission, May 28, 1843, in Whitman, *Letters,* 93, 161; McLoughlin to HBC Governor and Committee, Fort Vancouver, November 20, 1844, HBCA FtVanCB 1843–1844, B.223/b/31, fo. 225d; June 15, 1848, entry in Atkinson, "Diary," 177.

2. Douglas to HBC Governor and Committee, Fort Vancouver, October 18, 1838, fos. 6, 7; Howison, "Report," 23.

3. Douglas to HBC Governor and Committee, Fort Vancouver, October 18, 1838, fo. 7.

4. July 29–30, 1841, entry in Emmons, "Extracts," 269; Minto, "Reminiscences," 234; Howison, "Report," 10, 30.

5. Wilkes, *Narrative*, vol. 4: 359; William H. Gray, testimony in *In the Supreme Court*, 52.

6. Douglas to Simpson, Fort Vancouver, March 18, 1838, HBCA FtVanCB 1838, B.223/b/20, fo. 68; Senate Documents, 25th Congress, 2nd Session, vol. 5, document no. 470, June 6, 1838, cited in Guy Vernon Bennett, "Early Relations of the Sandwich Islands to the Old Oregon Territory," *Washington Historical Quarterly* 4, no. 2 (April 1913): 125.

7. Shepard, *Diary*, 80; Huggins, "Reminiscences," 173.

8. Ball, *Autobiography*, 90.

9. Simpson, *Narrative*, vol. 2: 50.

10. Nathaniel Wyeth to Leonard Wyeth, Columbia River, October 6, 1834, in Wyeth, *Correspondence*, 145–146; Narcissa Whitman to her mother, Mrs. H.K.W. Perkins, Wieletpoo, May 2, 1840, 93; Gustavus Hines to Corresponding Secretary, Missionary Society, Methodist Episcopal Church, Willamette River, March 15, 1843, in Hines, "Document," 176.

11. Drury, *Marcus Whitman*, 214; Narcissa Whitman to her sister Jane, Wieletpoo, October 1, 1841, in Whitman, *Letters*, 129; McLoughlin to HBC Governor and Committee, Fort Vancouver, March 28, 1845, in McLoughlin, *Letters, 1844–46*, 73.

12. "An act in regard to Slavery and free Negroes and Mulattoes," in Oregon Provisional Government, Copy of the Oregon Laws, HBCA FtVanCB 1843–1844, B.223/b/31, fos. 49-49d.

13. Samuel Chenery Damon, "Lower Oregon.—Population," *The Friend*, October 1, 1849, 51; Richard White, *"It's Your Misfortune and None of My Own": A History of the American West* (Norman: University of Oklahoma Press, 1991), 322; 1850 U.S. Census, Lewis County, Oregon.

14. Samuel R. Thurston, debate, House of Representatives, May 28, 1850, *Congressional Globe*, May 30, 1850, 10759, column 2. For the entire debate, see 1075–1080, 1090–1096.

15. Thurston, debate May 28, 1850, 10759, column 3.

16. Debate, May 30, 1850, 1078, column 3, and 1093, columns 1–2.

17. Among other sources, Anna Sloan Walker, "History of the Liquor Laws of the State of Washington," *Washington Historical Quarterly* 5, no. 2 (April 1914): 117; F. G. Young, "The Financial History of the State of Oregon," *Oregon Historical Quarterly* 10, no. 3 (September 1909): 283.

18. Anderson, testimony, 148; June 19, 1848, entry in Atkinson, "Diary," 185; Francis N. Blanchet, deposition in *In the Supreme Court*, 223.

19. Damon, "Lower Oregon," 51; June 19, 1848, entry in Atkinson, "Diary," 184.

20. E. Huggins in "Receipts, etc. of Sandwich Islanders employed at Fort Nisqually," HL, FN Box 6; composite May 7–June 1, 1851, entry in Tlithlow Journal, HL, FN 1235.

21. Joseph Thomas Heath, *Memoirs of Nisqually* (Fairfield, Wash.: Ye Galleon Press, 1979), 90.

22. Huggins, "Reminiscences," 154.

23. Huggins, undated note, HL, FN box 6.

24. November 24–25, December 9, 1847, and February 2, 7, 1848, entries in Roberts, "Round Hand," 134, 137, 142–143.

25. Muck farm journal, HL, FN 1236.

26. Edward Huggins to Clarence B. Bagley, South Tacoma, Wash., April 26, 1904, in

"Letters Outward"; J. Jaquith to Edward Huggins, Steilacoom, April 6, 1857, HL, FN Box 10.

27. October 31, 1857, entry in Fort Nisqually, Servants' Accounts, HL, FN 1239, vol. 12.

28. November 1, 1856, entry in Fort Langley, Servants' Accounts, HL, FN 1239, vol. 11; October 31, 1857, entry, vol. 12.

29. February 1, March 2, 17, April 4, 1856, entries, Fort Nisqually, Servants' Accounts, HL, FN 1239, vol. 11.

30. Kamakau, "Legislative Problems," 404.

31. Ibid. The story of Naukana is recounted in Beatrice Hamilton, *Salt Spring Island* (Vancouver: Mitchell Press, 1969), 77–78, whose father heard it from Naukana.

32. Kamakau, "Death of Kamehameha III," 416.

33. Simpson, *Narrative,* vol. 2: 48.

34. "Native Seamen," 79; Egerström, *Borta är bra,* 52; Coan, *Life in Hawaii,* 58.

35. Kane, *Wanderings,* 181–182.

36. Damon, "Lower Oregon," 51.

37. Erwin G. Gudde, *Sutter's Own Story* (New York: Putnam's, 1936), 34, 48.

38. Frank Soulé, John Gihon, and James Nisbet, *Annals of San Francisco* (New York; Appleton, 1854), 176–178; Passenger Manifests, HSA, 88; Amos Starr Cooke to Charles Montague, September 20, 1851, in Richards, *Amos Starr Cooke,* 405.

39. Samuel Chenery Damon, "Kanaka Diggings," *The Friend,* December 1, 1849, 83; Damon, "Hawaiians in California," *The Friend,* February 2, 1863, 10.

40. "An Act to Prohibit Natives from Leaving the Islands," July 2, 1850, reproduced in David W. Forbes, *An Act to Prohibit Hawaiians from Emigrating to California "Where They May Die in Misery"* (San Francisco: Paul Markham Kahn, 1986), n.p.; Morgan, *Hawai'i,* 107, 193.

41. "An Act," n.p ; "Na Luina Hawai'i," *Ka Nupepa Ka'oko'a,* December 10, 1869. We are grateful to Susan Lebo of the Bishop Museum for making available the article and its translation.

42. Damon, "Kanaka Diggings," 82. First published in *Overland Quarterly* in August 1869, the Harte story has been repeatedly reprinted.

43. Lowell Smith, *Ka Hae Hawai'i,* December 1858–January 1859, reproduced and translated in Charles Kenn, "A Visit to California Gold Fields," Hawaiian Historical Society, *Annual Report* 74 (1965): 14; J. F. Pogue, "Hawaiian Settlements in California," *The Friend,* August 1868, 69.

44. The mining fee was enacted in Jackson County, the trade restriction in both Jackson and Josephine counties. Young, "Financial History," 182.

45. W. W. Fidler, "Kanaka Flat," *Bonville's Western Weekly,* March 1909, 71; cited in Verne Blue, "Mining Laws of Jackson County, 1860–1876," *Oregon Historical Quarterly* 23, no. 2 (June 1922): 139n. We are grateful to Carol Harbison-Samuelson of the Southern Oregon Historical Research Library for locating materials relating to the southern Oregon gold rushes.

46. "Killed," *Oregon Sentinel* (Jacksonville), April 6, 1867; Fidler, "Kanaka Flat," 71–72.

47. Marriage registration and Jacksonville road taxes paid 1867, Southern Oregon Historical Society Research Library; "Here and There," *Democratic Times* (Jacksonville, Ore.), May 11, 1888; Marjorie O'Harra, "From The Desk," *Medford Mail Tribune,* March 22, 1867.

48. George Moore, November 18–19, 1851, entries, log reproduced in "Public Meeting,"

Oregonion, March 6, 1852; Samuel D. Howe, "The Early History," *Washington Standard,* May 23, 1868.

49. E. E. Dye, interview, cited in Erwin F. Lange, "Oregon City Private Schools, 1843–59," *Oregon Historical Quarterly* 37, no. 4 (December 1936): 309; Anson Sterling Cone, "Reminiscences," *Oregon Historical Quarterly* 4, no. 3 (September 1903): 255.

50. Howison, "Report," 23; "John McLoughlin's Bond with Dr. Ira Leonard Babcock," November 11, 1844; and McLoughlin to Peter Skene Ogden and Douglas, Oregon City, June 2, July 16, September 26, 1847, in John McLoughlin, *John McLoughlin's Business Correspondence, 1847–48,* ed. William P. Sampson (Seattle: University of Washington Press, 1973), 111, 27, 29, 55.

51. Mrs. E. E. Dye, interview, cited in Lange, "Oregon City Private Schools," 309; Munnick, *Oregon City,* in *Catholic Church Records,* vol. 1, 30–31.

52. McLoughlin, *Business Correspondence,* 79n; contracts with I. L. Babcock, William Bailey, and Gustavus Hines, Honolulu, March 27, 1844, HSA, 402-10-248; John Minto, "From Youth to Old Age as an American," *Oregon Historical Quarterly* 9, no. 1 (March 1908): 128.

53. Howison, "Report," 27; Edward Huggins to Clarence B. Bagley, Steilacoom, Wash., September 3, 1903, in "Letters Outward"; McLoughlin, *Business Correspondence,* 112n; Lucile McDonald, *Swan Among the Indians: Life of James G. Swan, 1818–1900* (Portland: Binfords & Mort, 1972), 56 and 58.

54. Native Seamen, Seamen's Records, HSA, 88-1-3; Passenger Manifests, HSA, 82, 1853–1880; Henry Rhodes to Robert Wyllie, Victoria, January 11, 1861, and April 16, 1867, HSA, 404-46, 740/743.

55. Edwin T. Coman Jr. and Helen M. Gibbs, *Time, Tide and Timber: A Century of Pope & Talbot* (Stanford: Stanford University Press, 1949); Jan Eakins, "Port Gamble: Managing Cultural Diversity on Puget Sound," *CRM* [Cultural Resource Management] 8 (1999): 23–27; Thomas Miller, *A Genealogical Glimpse of Historical Port Gamble* (Port Gamble: privately printed, n.d.).

56. "News on the events held by the Hawaiians in Port Gamble," *Ka Nupepa Ka'oko'a,* November 14, 1865, reproduced in the original Hawaiian in Naughton, "Hawaiians in the Fur Trade," 86. We are grateful to Jennifer Jane Leilani Basham for the translation.

57. "Arioha or Sam" entry for Outfit 1867 in Fort Nisqually, Servants' Accounts, HL, FN 1239, vol. 11; W. P. Bonney, *History of Pierce County Washington,* vol. 1 (Chicago: Pioneer Historical Publishing Co., 1927), 404; *Choir's Pioneer Directory of the City of Seattle and King Country* (Pottsville, Pa.: Miners' Journal Room, 1878), 114.

58. Howison, "Report," 8; H. Rhodes to Minister of Foreign Affairs, April 6, 1866, HSA, 404-33-527; James G. Swan to Minister of Foreign Affairs, January 7, 1885, HSA, 404-33-527.

59. John McCracken to J. M. Kapena, Minister of Foreign Affairs, Portland, August 6, 1879, and May 26, 1880, and enclosures, HSA, 404-33-540.

60. James G. Swan to Minister of Foreign Affairs, May 15, August 13, September 27, 1886, HSA, 404-33-528; miscellaneous bills, James Swan fonds, University of British Columbia, Special Collections, Box 10, Hawaiian Consulate files.

61. George R. Carter to George C. Potter, Secretary, Foreign Department, Seattle, April 10, May 8, 1894, HSA, 404-41-649; Potter to Carter, Honolulu, April 26, June 12, 1894, HSA, 410-73.

62. O'Harra, "From The Desk."

63. Fidler, "Kanaka Flat," 72; George Verne Blue, "A Hudson's Bay Company Contract for Hawaiian Labor," *Oregon Historical Quarterly* 25, no. 1 (March 1924): 73, 74, 74n4; Duncan, "Minority," 7.

CHAPTER 8. NORTH OF THE 49TH PARALLEL

1. Douglas to Donald Ross, November 27, 1849, cited in Margaret Ormsby, introduction to Bowsfield, *Fort Victoria Letters*, xxii; John Sebastian Helmcken, *The Reminiscences of Doctor John Sebastian Helmcken*, ed. Dorothy Blakey Smith (Vancouver: UBC Press, 1975), 283. On the history of British Columbia, see Jean Barman, *The West beyond the West: A History of British Columbia*, rev. ed. (Toronto: University of Toronto Press, 1996).

2. Helmcken, *Reminiscences*, 128; Douglas to Blanshard, Fort Victoria, August 5, 1850, typescript, FNHSA.

3. Helmcken, *Reminiscences*, 304, 307, 317.

4. Joseph William McKay to Douglas, Wentuhuysen Inlet, September 16, 1852, in Nanaimo Correspondence, BCA, A/C/20.1/N15; Mark Bate, "The Men Who Helped to Build Nanaimo," *Nanaimo Free Press*, March 23, 1907.

5. Interview with Jack and Paul Roland, typescript, BCA, tape collection.

6. Douglas to Archibald Barclay, Fort Victoria, April 16, 1851, in Bowsfield, *Fort Victoria Letters*, 174.

7. R. P. Rithet to Minister of Foreign Relations, September 5, 1879, HSA, 404-46-746.

8. Robert Wyllie to William G. Dunlap, Honolulu, May 7, 1858, HSA, 404-30-472; also governor of O'ahu to Wyllie, May 12–14, 1858, HSA, 15, local officials 1858: May. We are grateful to HSA archivist Jason Achiu for translating the governor's letters from Hawaiian into English for us.

9. Henry Rhodes to Robert Wyllie, Minister of Foreign Relations, Victoria, September 25, 1860, HSA, 404-46-739; "Arrival of Prince Kamehameha and Suite" and "Sandwich Islands," *Colonist*, September 19, 1860; "Prince Kamehameha and Suite," *Colonist*, September 21, 1860; "Departure of Distinguished Visitors," *Colonist*, September 25, 1860.

10. Loretta Roland, conversation with Jean Barman, Fulford Harbour, Salt Spring Island, February 24, 1991.

11. Ralston, *Grass Huts*.

12. Douglas to James Murray Yale, July 1, 1857, cited in Jamie Morton, *Fort Langley: An Overview of the Operations of a Diversified Fur Trade Post 1848 to 1858 and The Physical Context in 1858* (Ottawa: Microfiche Report Series, Canadian Parks Service, Environment Canada, 1980), 159.

13. Morton, *Fort Langley*, 258; January 1859, entries in Arthur Thomas Bushby, "The Journal of Arthur Thomas Bushby, 1858–1859," ed. Dorothy Blakey Smith, *British Columbia Historical Quarterly* 21 (1957–1958): 127; Richard Moody to Douglas, April 1, 1859, BCA, Land and Works Department, GR2900, vol. 1.

14. "Letter from Langley," *Weekly Gazette* (Victoria), April 16, 1859, cited in Morton, *Fort Langley*, 288; Moody to Douglas, April 1, 1859.

15. Lucile S. McDonald, *Making History: The People Who Shaped the San Juan Islands* (Friday Harbor, Wash.: Harbor Press, 1990); Bonney, *History of Pierce County*, 254.

16. Lila Hannah Firth, "Early Life on San Juan Island," typescript, San Juan Library, Friday Harbor, Wash.

17. McDonald, *Making History*, 72; Firth, "Early Life."

18. C. A. Bayley, "Early Life on Vancouver Island," manuscript in Bancroft Library, University of California at Berkeley, MSS P-C 3.

19. Northwest Washington historian Howard Buswell interviewed Charles Kahana on February 12, April 17, May 21, June 4, 1946, March 12, 1948, and April 11, 1956. Center for Pacific Northwest Studies, Buswell Collection, Series 1, Box 4/34.

20. Announcement in *Victoria Gazette,* September 16, 1858; Henry Rhodes to Robert C. Wyllie, Victoria, August 19, 1864, HSA, 404-46-742.

21. Cited in John A. Hussey, *The History of Fort Vancouver and its Physical Structure* (Tacoma: Washington State Historical Society, 1957), 108.

22. William Kaulehelehe to H. M. Whitney, Victoria, March 20, 1865, to S. H. Kulika, Victoria, April 27, 1865, and to L. H. Gulick, Victoria, December 4, 1865, HMCSL, Kaulehelehe file; Henry Rhodes to Robert Wyllie, Victoria, August 18, 1863, and account of estate signed by Nahiana and Kapoi, Victoria, August 19, 1863, HSA, 404-46-741; Henry Rhodes, Memorandum, Victoria, November 19, 1866, HSA, 404-46-743.

23. "A Kanaka Row," *Colonist* (Victoria), May 12, 1860.

24. May 28, 1860, session, Court records, Victoria, BCA, GR419, Box 1, File 1860/69.

25. "Demands Enquiry," *Evening Express,* June 27, 1864; British Columbia, GR1327, June 27, 1864; "Inquest," *Daily Chronicle,* June 28, 1864.

26. Godfrey Rhodes, notes, part of extensive correspondence with Ministry of Foreign Relations, 1869, HSA, 404-46-744.

27. Peter Kakua, statement, March 5, 1869, enclosed in Henry Rhodes to Minister of Foreign Relations, May 18, 1869, HSA, 404-46-744. The case is graphically described in W. J. Illerbrun, "'Kanaka Pete,'" *Hawaiian Journal of History* 6 (1972): 156–166.

28. Church records, St. Andrew's Catholic Cathedral, Victoria, 1849–1934, BCA, Add. Ms. 1.

29. December 20, 1870 in Church records, St. Andrew's Cathedral.

30. Archibald Fleming, interview in *Told by the Pioneers: Tales of Frontier Life as Told by Those Who Remember The Days of the Territory and Early Statehood of Washington* (Washington Pioneer Project), vol. 3 (1938), 52.

31. Firth, "Early Life."

32. Ibid.; "Police Court," *Colonist,* June 18, 1873; also May 17, June 7, 17–19, 21, and 25, October 10, 25, and 29, 1873, and March 7, 1874.

33. Firth, "Early Life."

34. Interview with Miss B. Hamilton, Mrs. Ina Hamilton, Mrs. A. Mabel Davis, 1965, tape no. 800, BCA; interview with Jack and Paul Roland.

35. Interview with Hamilton, Hamilton, and Davis; W. F. Tolmie to Henry Fry, J.P., Cloverdale, Victoria District, June 8, 1885, BCA.

36. File notes, West Coast preemptions, BCA, GR766, Box 8, File 1082.

37. Bea Hamilton, *Salt Spring Island* (Vancouver: Mitchell Press, 1969), 144.

38. Interview with Hamilton, Hamilton, and Davis.

39. Interview with Jack and Paul Roland; interview with Hamilton, Hamilton, and Davis.

40. File notes, West Coast preemptions.

41. Alice Crakanthorp, interviews with J. S. Matthews, Vancouver, March 21, 28, 1935; Walter Keamo, interview with Matthews, Vancouver, April 18, 1952; Elizabeth Walker, interview with Matthews, April 22, 1940, City of Vancouver Archives [CVA], Add. Ms. 54.

42. Royal Columbian Hospital, New Westminster, Register, 1862–1901, BCA, microfilm 95A.

43. Johan Adrian Jacobsen, *Alaskan Voyage 1881–1883: An Expedition to the Northwest Coast of America* (Chicago: University of Chicago Press, 1977), 33.

44. Interview with Hamilton, Hamilton, and Davis.

45. Rosemary Unger, conversation with Jean Barman, Victoria, June 27, 1990, based on research notes of Paul Roland.

46. Interview with Jack and Paul Roland; St. Ann's Baptisms-Marriages, 1859–1885, held at St. Eugene's Church, Duncan; "Plan of Graves in graveyard beside the church," courtesy of Rosemary Tahouney Unger. A good visual comparison is with Keawala'i Congregational Church at Makena, Mau'i, erected in 1855.

47. Interview with Hamilton, Hamilton, and Davis.

48. Interview with Jack and Paul Roland.

49. Rosemary Unger conversation with Jean Barman; McMinn, "Portland Island," typescript in Salt Spring Archives.

50. "Coqualeetza Industrial School, Admissions and Discharges," United Church Archives, Vancouver School of Theology.

51. See Hamilton, *Salt Spring Island,* 81.

52. Rev. Robert James Roberts, Diary, BCA, A/E/R54/R54A.

53. Henry, Barneby, *Life And Labour In The Far, Far West: Being Notes of a Tour in The Western States, British Columbia, Manitoba, and The North-west Territory* (London: Cassell & Company, Ltd, 1884), 144. We are grateful to Brad Morrison for this reference.

54. Walker, interview.

55. "St. Mary's Mission School, Mission City, B.C., 1862–1950," typescript in Sisters of St. Ann, Victoria, Archives, RGII, S. 55, Box 55-1, p8.

56. File notes, West Coast preemptions.

57. Photos courtesy of Rosemary Unger, Ken Seeley, Karey Litton, and BCA. For comparable photos from California, see Kenn, "Sutter's Hawaiians," 4–5.

58. Petition to A. Haslam, Salt Spring Island, July 1, 1895, National Archives of Canada, R63, Post Office, 1895-367, reel C-7231.

59. Adams, *Interracial Marriage,* 8; S. E. Bishop, "Why are the Hawaiians Dying Out?" *The Friend,* March 1889, 18–20; April 1889, 26–27.

60. William Fremont Blackman, *The Making of Hawaii: A Study in Social Evolution* (New York: Macmillan, 1899), 88, 99, 209.

CHAPTER 9. MOVING ACROSS THE GENERATIONS

1. *History of the Pacific Northwest: Oregon and Washington,* vol. 1 (Portland: North Pacific History Company, 1889), 589.

2. Edward Huggins to Clarence B. Bagley, Steilacoom, Washington, May 18, 1904, in "Letters Outward."

3. Huggins to Bagley, Steilacoom, Washington, May 18, 1904.

4. Ibid.

5. William Burton Crickmer, "Story of the planting of the English Church in Columbia," *Christian Advocate and Review,* s.d., 780, in Vancouver Public Library.

6. James Nahanee, conversation with Jean Barman, Burnaby, January 7, 2003.

7. On the Friday family, see Bryce Wood, *San Juan Island: Coastal Place Names and Cartographic Nomenclature* (Tacoma: Washington State Historical Society, 1980), 94.

8. Naughton, "Hawaiians in the Fur Trade," 32, 36–37, 55.

9. Charles Kahana, interviews with Howard Buswell.

10. Robert Emmett Hawley, *Skqee Mus or Pioneer Days on the Nooksack* (Bellingham, Wash.: Whatcom Museum of History and Art, 1945), 27, 78, 177.

11. Roree Wright (Oehlman), conversation with Jean Barman, Vancouver, March 20, 1993; Alan Morley, "Romance of Vancouver," *Sun,* May 7, 1940.

12. Alice Crakenthorp, interview with J. S. Matthews, Vancouver, April 22, 1937, CVA; John Warren Bell, "Apologia," ms, CVA, Add. Ms. 144, file 3; Morley, "Romance of Vancouver."

13. Church records, St. Andrew's Cathedral.

14. Pre-confederation marriage records, 1859–1872, BCA, GR-3044; Violet Bell, conversation with Jean Barman, Victoria, April 22, 1991.

15. Jean Barman, *Stanley Park's Secret: The Forgotten Families of Whoi Whoi, Kanaka Ranch and Brockton Point* (Madeira Park, B.C.: Harbour, 2005); Louis Cordocedo, conversation with Jean Barman, North Vancouver, June 29, 1993.

16. Hamilton, *Salt Spring Island,* 145. On Maria Mahoi's life and family, see Jean Barman, *Maria Mahoi of the Islands* (Vancouver: New Star, 2004).

17. Loretta Roland, conversation with Jean Barman.

18. Munnick, *Vancouver,* vol. 2, 141, A-16.

19. Bea Shepard, Vina Segalerba, and Rosemary Unger, conversation with Jean Barman, Victoria, June 27, 1990.

20. Interview with Jack and Paul Roland.

21. Jennie Mulcahy to her brother Tommy Tamaree, Juneau, February 11, 1891, in family possession.

22. Vi Johnston, conversation with Jean Barman and Bruce Watson, New Westminster, British Columbia, September 23, 1994.

23. Bea Hamilton, *Salt Spring Island,* 82n, 84–85.

24. Bea Hamilton's father heard the story both from Alfred Cooke and from William Naukana's grandson Peter Roland. Hamilton, *Salt Spring Island,* 81–82.

25. Rosemary Unger, conversation with Jean Barman, based on information from her mother Sophie Roland, daughter of Naukana's youngest daughter Matilda; Nick Stevens, conversation with Imbert Orchard, ca. 1965, British Columbia Archives, tape no. 735.

26. Loretta Roland, conversation with Jean Barman.

27. Sally Jo Moon, "Aloha Alive and Well in British Columbia," *Honolulu Star-Bulletin,* August 14, 1971. We are grateful to Rosemary Unger for sharing this article with us.

28. Norman Schlesser, "Kanakas in the Oregon Country," *Umpqua Trapper* (Douglas County Historical Society) 8, no. 1 (Spring 1972): 12–13, and his example of Makaine Owyhee family, 6, 8, and 11; Naughton, "Hawaiians in the Fur Trade," 74; Munnick, *Vancouver,* A-61; "Hawaiian Pioneers?" Washington Country Historical Society (Hillsboro, Ore.), *Express,* March 1981, 6.

29. Theresa Gibson, conversation with Susan Garcia and Jean Barman, Richmond, June 13, 2004.

30. James Robert Anderson, "Notes and Comments on Early Days and Events in British Columbia, Washington and Oregon," 1925, 171, in BCA, Add. Ms. 1912, Box 9/18.

31. 1901 Canada Census, British Columbia, Victoria North, Portland, household 33.

32. Clellan S. Ford, *Smoke From Their Fires: The Life of a Kwakiutl Chief* (New Haven: Yale University Press, 1941), 202.

33. Dale Seeley, conversation with Jean Barman, Campbell River, July 22, 1992; Loretta Roland, conversation with Jean Barman; Stanley and Pauline Harris, conversation with Jean Barman, Ladner, British Columbia, March 10, 1991.

34. Lloyd Kendrick, conversation with Jean Barman, Ruby Creek, British Columbia, March 10, 1999; Kendrick, interview with Jack Montgomery, June 1993, transcript in authors' possession.

35. Mary Cooke, "Hawaiian Colony Found in Canada," *Honolulu Advertiser,* June 29 1971. We are grateful to Rosemary Unger for sharing this article with us.

36. Cooke, "Hawaiian Colony"; Moon, "Aloha Alive and Well"; Bea Hamilton, "Dreams Come True," *Colonist,* October 31, 1971.

37. On the Hawaiian Islands, Adams, *Interracial Marriage,* 8.

38. Maurice Nahanee, "Nahanee's Notebook," *Kahtou News* (Vancouver), August 1, 1992.

39. See Paul Spickard, Joanne L. Rondilla, and Debbie Hippolite Wright, eds., *Pacific Diaspora: Island Peoples in the United States and Across the Pacific* (Honolulu: University of Hawai'i Press, 2002).

40. Picard, "The Kanakas," 1.

SOURCES

[*Note:* Codes used in biographies are in square brackets.]

ARCHIVAL SOURCES

Primary Archival Sources

Archivo de Indias, Seville, Spain [ArdeInd]
Copy of Martinez's September 26, 1789, San Lorenzo de Nutka report, Mexico, 1529, Expediente 1789 [Martinez]

British Columbia Archives, Victoria, British Columbia [BCA]
Government Records [GR-]
Colonial correspondence outward, GR2900 [Colonial]
Preemption records for West Coast land, 1861–1886, GR766 [Preemption]
Naturalization records for Victoria, 1859–1963, GR1865 [Naturalization]
Court Records [Crt-]
Court of Assizes, GR419, box 1, file 1860/69 [Assizes]
Inspector of Gaols, 1859–1914, GR0308 [Gaols]
Magistrates charge book entries, GR848 [Magistrate]
Victoria County Court, Naturalization Papers, 1867, GR1554 [Naturalization]
Police Department charge book, New Westminster, GR1372/1410 [NewWest]
Victoria special sessions, petty sessions and licensing court, minute book, G88–106 [Petty]
Vancouver Island, Police and Prisons Department, 1858–1859, GR848 [Prisons]
Att. Gen., Peter Kakua Murder Documents [Kakua]
Inquests, GR1327 [Inquests]
Vital Statistics [VS-]
Vancouver Island Colonial Secretary, Death records, C/AA/30.1/1 [Deaths]
Division of Vital Statistics, Registration of Births, Deaths, and Marriages, GR2951 [BCVS]
Christ Church Anglican Cathedral, Victoria, A834 [CCCath]

Methodist mission, New Westminster, Reel A48A [MM]
St. Andrew's Catholic Cathedral, Victoria, Microfilm Reel 1A [StAndC]
St. John the Divine Anglican Church, Derby, Reel 25A [StJohDiv]
St. Paul's Anglican Church, Nanaimo [StPaul]
Ross Bay Cemetery Records, 1871–1881 [RossBayCem]
Private Records [PR-18]

> Allard, Jason Allard, "Reminiscences," EC A1 5A
> Anderson, James Robert, "Notes and Comments on Early Days and Events," 1925, Add. Ms.1912, Box 9/18 [Anderson]
> Anonymous, "Journal of a Voyage kept on Brig *Lama*, 1830–32" [*Lama*]
> Barkley, Frances, "Reminiscences" [Barkley]
> Fort Alexandria, Post Journal, 1850–1851, A/C/20/Al2 [FtAlex]
> Hamilton, Bea, Ina Hamilton, and A. Mabel Davis, interview, 1965, tape no. 800 [Hamilton]
> Helmcken, John S., Letters from Fort Rupert, C/A/a/40.3/R3 [Helmcken]
> Lowe, Thomas, Private Journal kept at Fort Vancouver, 1843–1850, E/F/L 95A [Lowe]
> McNeill, William H., "Journal of a Voyage to the N. W. Coast of North America kept on Board Brig *Convoy*, April 1, 1825–Oct. 18, 1825," Ms AB20.5 C762 [*Convoy*]
> Morison, Charles Frederic, Reminiscences of the Early Days of British Columbia, 1862–1876 [Morison]
> Nanaimo Correspondence, A/C/20.1/N15 [Nanaimo]
> Roberts, Rev. Robert James, Diary, A/E/R54/R54A
> Roland, Jack and Paul, interview, tape, n.d.
> Royal Columbian Hospital, New Westminster, Register, 1862–1901 [RoyalCol]
> Stevens, Nick, conversation with Imbert Orchard, ca. 1965, tape no. 735
> Tolmie, Simon Fraser, to Henry Fry, J.P., June 8, 1885, M552 [Tolmie]

California Historical Society, San Francisco [CHS]
Anonymous, "Journal of a Voyage in the Brig *Owhyhee* from Oahu to & from the Northwest Coast," Ms 091 J8 [*Owhyhee*]

City of Vancouver Archives, Vancouver [VanA]
Bell, John Warren, "Apologia," Ms., CVA, Add. Ms. 144, file 3
Crakenthorp, Alice, interviews with J. S. Matthews, April 22, 1937, Add. Ms. 54
Keamo, Walter, interview with J. S. Matthews, April 18, 1952, Add. Ms. 54 [Keamo]
Pamphlet, Frederick William, interview with J. S. Matthews, May 6, 1938, Add. Ms. 54 [Pamphlet]
Walker, Elizabeth, interview with J. S. Matthews, April 22, 1940, Add. Ms. 54 [Walker]

Columbia River Maritime Museum, Astoria, Oregon [CRMM]
Haskin, Ralph, Journal of the *Atahualpa*, 1802–1803 [*Atahualpa*]

Detroit Library [DetL]
Dorr, Ebenezer, "Logbook of the *Hope,* Sept. 14, 1791–Mar. 2, 1792," Burton Historical Collection, Ebenezer Dorr Papers [*Hope*]

Fort Nisqually Historic Site Archives, Tacoma [FtNis]
"Letters Outward: The Letters of Edward Huggins 1862–1907" [Huggins]

"Journal of Occurrences on Puget's Sound Agricultural Coy's Farm at Muck 1858," unpaginated typescript [Muck]

Huggins, Edward, "Reminiscences of Puget Sound," typescript [Reminiscences]

"Tlithlow Journal 1851," unpaginated typescript [Tlithlow]

Harvard University, Houghton Library, Cambridge, Massachusetts [HUHL]

Lamb, Horatio Appleton, "Notes on Trade with the Northwest Coast, 1790–1810," Ms. AMW 65 [Lamb]

Hawai'i State Archives, Honolulu [HSA]

Government correspondence, 402, 410 [Government]

Customs

Honolulu Harbormaster, Seamen's records, 88, vol. 113, 7–8 [Seamen]

Passenger Arrivals and Departures, 82 [Passenger]

Foreign Office and Executive [F.O. & Ex.]

General, 402

Hawaiian Officials Abroad

Consul at Port Townsend, 404/33/526-536 [PtTownsend]

Consul at Portland, 404/33/537-542

Consul at Seattle, 404/41/649-650

Consul at Victoria, 404/46/738-747 [Victoria]

Cartwright, Bruce, Biographical Information about "Haole Families" [Cartwright]

Hawaiian Historical Society, Honolulu [HHS]

Stephen Reynolds, Journal, November 1823–August 1855 (transcript, original in Peabody Museum of Salem, Mass.) [Reynolds]

Hawaiian Mission Children's Society Library, Honolulu [HMCS]

Oregon mission files [OrMission]

Hudson's Bay Company Archives, Winnipeg [HBCA]

North West Company [NWC]

Account Books [AB]

[1815–1817] F.4/17 (Crew of the *Columbia*, etc.) [5]

[1821] F.4/46 (List of NWC 1821 Transfers to HBC) [9]

York Factory [YF]

Abstracts of Servants' Accounts 1–33 [SA]

[1821–1822] B.239/g/1 [1]

[1822–1823] B.239/g/2 [2]

[1823–1824] B.239/g/3 [3]

[1824–1825] B.239/g/4 [4]

[1825–1826] B.239/g/5 [5]

[1826–1827] B.239/g/6 [6]

[1827–1828] B.239/g/7 [7]

[1828–1829] B.239/g/8 [8]

[1829–1830] B.239/g/9 [9]

[1830–1831] B.239/g/10 [10]

[1831–1832] B.239/g/11 [11]

[1832–1833] B.239/g/12 [12]

[1833–1834] B.239/g/13 [13]

[1834–1835] B.239/g/14 [14]
[1835–1836] B.239/g/15 [15]
[1836–1837] B.239/g/16 [16]
[1837–1838] B.239/g/17 [17]
[1838–1839] B.239/g/18 [18]
[1839–1840] B.239/g/19 [19]
[1840–1841] B.239/g/20 [20]
[1841–1842] B.239/g/21 [21]
[1842–1843] B.239/g/22 [22]
[1843–1844] B.239/g/23 [23]
[1844–1845] B.239/g/24 [24]
[1845–1846] B.239/g/25 [25]
[1846–1847] B.239/g/26 [26]
[1847–1848] B.239/g/27 [27]
[1848–1849] B.239/g/28 [28]
[1849–1850] B.239/g/29 [29]
[1850–1851] B.239/g/30 [30]
[1851–1852] B.239/g/31 [31]
[1852–1853] B.239/g/32 [32]
[1853–1854] B.239/g/33 [33]
District Statements 1a–23 [DS]
[1823–1824] B.239/l/1a [1a]
[1825–1826] B.239/l/1b [1b]
[1826–1827] B.239/l/2a [2a]
[1827–1828] B.239/l/2b [2b]
[1828–1829] B.239/l/3a [3a]
[1829–1830] B.239/l/3b [3b]
[1830–1831] B.239/l/4a [4a]
[1831–1832] B.239/l/4b [4b]
[1832–1833] B.239/l/5a [5a]
[1833–1834] B.239/l/5b [5b]
[1834–1835] B.239/l/5c [5c]
[1835–1836] B.239/l/6 [6]
[1836–1837] B.239/l/7 [7]
[1837–1838] B.239/l/8 [8]
[1838–1839] B.239/l/9 [9]
[1839–1840] B.239/l/10 [10]
[1840–1841] B.239/l/11 [11]
[1841–1842] B.239/l/12 [12]
[1842–1843] B.239/l/13 [13]
[1843–1844] B.239/l/14 [14]
[1844–1845] B.239/l/15 [15]
[1845–1846] B.239/l/16 [16]
[1846–1847] B.239/l/17 [17]
[1847–1848] B.239/l/18 [18]
[1848–1849] B.239/l/19 [19]
[1849–1850] B.239/l/20 [20]

[1850–1851] B.239/l/21 [21]
[1851–1852] B.239/l/22 [22]
[1852–1853] B.239/l/23 [23]
Belle Vue Farm [BelleVue]
   Post Journals [PJ]
      [1854–1855] B.15/a/1 [1]
      [1858–1862] B.15/a/2 [2]
   Account Book [1853–1858] B.15/d/1 [AB]
Fort Alexandria [New Caledonia] [FtAlex]
   Post Journals [PJ]
      [1833–1834] B.5/a/3 [1]
      [1845–1848] B.5/a/7 [7]
   Account Book [1829–1832] B.5/d/1 [AB]
Fort George [Columbia River/Astoria] [FtGeo [Ast]]
   Account Books [AB]
      [1820–1822] B.76/d/4 [4]
      [1822–1823] B.76/d/10 [10]
      [1823–1824] B.76/d/11 [11]
      [1824–1825] B.76/d/12 [12]
Fort Langley [FtLang]
   Post Journals [PJ]
      [1827–1828] B.113/a/1 [1]
      [1828–1829] B.113/a/2 [2]
      [1829–1830] B.113/a/3 [3]
   Correspondence Book [1844–1870] B.113/c/1 (inward) [CB]
Fort Nisqually [FtNis]
   Correspondence [1850–1852] (outward) B.151/b/1 [CO]
   For other records, see Huntington Library
Fort Rupert [FtRup]
   Post Journal [1849–1850] B.185.a/1 [PJ]
Fort St. James [FtStJms]
   Reports on District [1824–1825] B.188/e/3 [RD]
   List of Servants [1824–1825] B.188/f/1 [LS]
   Correspondence [1828–1829] B.188/b/6 [CB]
Fort Simpson [Nass] [FtSimp [N]]
   Post Journals [PJ]
      [1834–1838] B.201/a/3 [3]
      [1838–1840] B.201/a/4 [4]
      [1852–1853] B.201/a/7 [7]
      [1855–1859] B.201/a/8 [8]
Fort Stikine [FtStik]
   Post Journals [PJ]
      [1840] B.209/a/1 [1]
      [1841] B.209/a/2 [2]
      [1842] B.209/a/3 [3]
Fort Vancouver [Columbia] [FtVan]
   Post Journals [PJ]

[1826] B.223/a/2 (A. R. McLeod's journal south of Columbia, May 5–August 17, 1826) [2]

[1826–1827] B.223/a/4 (Alexander Roderick McLeod's south expedition to the Umpqua, September 15, 1826–March 13, 1827) [4]

Account Books [AB]

[1827–1828] B.223/d/10 [10]

[1828–1829] B.223/d/19 [19]

[1830] B.223/d/28 [28]

Abstracts of Servants' Accounts [SA]

[1827–1828] B.223/g/1 [1]

[1830–1831] B.223/g/2 [2]

[1836–1837] B.223/g/3 [3]

[1837–1838] B.223/g/4 [4]

[1838–1839] B.223/g/5 [5]

[1841–1842] B.223/g/6 [6]

[1842–1843] B.223/g/7 [7]

[1843–1844] B.223/g/8 [8]

[1853–1854] B.223/g/9 [9]

[1854–1855] B.223/g/10 [10]

[1855–1856] B.223/g/11 [11]

[1856–1857] B.223/g/12 [12]

[1857–1858] B.223/g/13 [13]

[1858–1859] B.223/g/14 [14]

Correspondence Books [CB]

[1826] B.223/b/2 [2]

[1827–1828] B.223/b/3 [3]

[1832–1833] B.223/b/8 [8]

[1833–1834] B.223/b/9 [9]

[1836–1837] B.223/b/15 [15]

[1842–1843] B.223/b/29 [29]

[1842–1843] B.223/b/30 [30]

[1843–1844] B.223/b/31 [31]

Fort Victoria [FtVic]

Abstracts of Servants' Accounts [SA]

[1853–1854] B.226/g/1 [1]

[1854–1855] B.226/g/2 [2]

[1855–1856] B.226/g/3 [3]

[1856–1857] B.226/g/4 [4]

[1857–1858] B.226/g/5 [5]

[1858–1859] B.226/g/6 [6]

[1859–1860] B.226/g/7 [7]

[1860–1861] B.226/g/8 [8]

[1861–1862] B.226/g/9 [9]

[1862–1863] B.226/g/10 [10]

[1863–1864] B.226/g/11 [11]

[1864–1865] B.226/g/12 [12]

[1865–1866] B.226/g/13 [13]

[1866–1867] B.226/g/14 [14]
[1867–1868] B.226/g/15 [15]
[1868–1869] B.226/g/16 [16]
District Statements [1852–1853] B.226/l/1 [DS]
Correspondence Books [1844–1845] B.226/l/1 [CB]
Puget Sound Agricultural Company [PSAC]
Account Books [AB]
[1844–1909] 8-39 [39]
[1855–1859] F.15/38 [38]
Miscellaneous Papers [1840–1910] F.26/1 [Mis]
Sandwich Islands [SandIs]
Account Books [AB]
[1836–1837] B.191/d/1 (George Pelly's Woahoo Accounts) [1]
[1844–1845] B.191/d/3 [3]
[1845–1846] B.191/d/5 [5]
[1846–1847] B.191/d/6 [6]
[1847–1848] B.191/d/7 [7]
[1848–1849] B.191/d/9 [9]
[1849–1850] B.191/d/10 [10]
[1850–1851] B.191/d/11 [11]
Miscellaneous Items [1834–1867] B.191/z/1 [M]
Correspondence Inward [1844–1861] B.191/c/1 [CI]
London Inward Correspondence [LonIC]
[1835–1840] A.11/61 [1]
[1843–1852] A.11/62 [2]
[1853–1861] A.11/63 [3]
Ships' Logs [Log of]
Beaver [1850–1852] C.1/208 [*Beaver*]
Columbia [1839–1842] C.1/246 [*Columbia 4*]
Columbia [1845–1848] C.1/250 [*Columbia 9*]
Cowlitz [1840–1842] C.1/257 [*Cowlitz 1*]
Cowlitz [1849–1851] C.1/265 [*Cowlitz 8*]
Isabella [1829–1830] C.1/355 [*Isabella*]
Otter [1852–1861] C.1/625 [*Otter*]
Vancouver [1844–1847] C.1/1065 [*Vancouver*]
William & Ann [1824–1825] C.1/1066 [*William & Ann*]
Ship's Miscellaneous Papers [SMP]
[1851] C.7/175 *(Princess Royal)* [13]
[1828–1841] C.7/177 *(Beaver, Cadboro, Columbia, Dryad, Eagle, Ganymede, Lama, Nereide, Sumatra, Vancouver 2, Vancouver 3)* [14]
Compiled biographies of officers and servants [Bio]
Miscellaneous Items [1834–1867] B.191/z/1 (Sandwich Islands) [MiscI]
Huntington Library, San Marino, California [HL]
Fort Nisqually [FtNis]
Post Journals [PJ]
[1833–1835] FN 1234/v. 1 [1]
[1835–1836] FN 1234/v. 2 [2]

[1836–1837] FN 1234/v. 3 [3]
[1837–1839] FN 1234/v. 4 [4]
[1846–1847] FN 1234/v. 5 [5]
[1849–1850] FN 1234/v. 6 [6]
[1850–1851] FN 1234/v. 7 [7]
[1851–1852] FN 1234/v. 8 [8]
[1852–1854] FN 1234/v. 9 [9]
[1854–1856] FN 1234/v. 10 [10]
[1856–1857] FN 1234/v. 11 [11]
[1857–1859] FN 1234/v. 12 [12]
[1860–1861] FN 1234/v. 13 [13]
[1861–1863] FN 1234/v. 14 [14]
[1863–1867] FN 1234/v. 15 [15]
[1867–1870] FN 1234/v. 16 [16]
Correspondence Books [CB]
[1855–1858] FM 1231 [1]
[1858–1865] FN 1232 [2]
Letter Press Copy Book [1863–1867] FN 1233 [LP]
Transfer Books [TB]
[1854] FN 1243/v. 1 [1]
[1858] FN 1243/v. 2 [2]
[1859–1860] FN 1243/v. 3 [3]
[1861–1870] FN 1243/v. 4 [4]
Abstracts of Servants' Accounts [SA]
[1841–1842] FN 1239/v. 1 [1]
[1843] FN 1239/v. 2 [2]
[1845] FN 1239/v. 3 [3]
[1846] FN 1239/v. 4 [4]
[1847] FN 1239/v. 5 [5]
[1851] FN 1239/v. 6 [6]
[1853] FN 1239/v. 7 [7]
[1853 balances] FN 1239/v. 8 [8]
[1854] FN 1239/v. 9 [9]
[1855] FN 1239/v. 10 [10]
[1856] FN 1239/v. 11 [11]
[1857] FN 1239/v. 12 [12]
[1858] FN 1239/v. 13 [13]
[1859] FN 1239/v. 14 [14]
[1867] FN 1239/v. 15 [15]
[1848–1869] FN 1239/envelope [Env]
Account Books [AB]
Cowlitz farm [1852–1857] FN 1250 [Cow]
Fur Trade Book [FT]
[1868–1874] FN 1244/v. 4 [4]
Indian Accounts [IA]
[1842] FN 1242/v. 1 [1]
[1849] FN 1242/v. 2 [2]
[1850–1851] FN 1242/v. 3 [3]

[1851] FN 1242/v. 4 [4]
[1853] FN 1242/v. 5 [5]
[1857] FN 1242/v. 6 [6]
[Undated] FM 1242/envelope [Env]
Blotters [B]
[1834] FN 1247/v. 1 [1]
[1838] FN 1247/v. 2 [2]
[1844] FN 1247/v. 3 [3]
[1845] FN 1247/v. 4 [4]
[1846] FN 1247/v. 5 [5]
[1848] FN 1247/v. 6 [6]
[1848–1849] FN 1247/v. 7 [7]
[1860–1861] FN 1247/v. 8 [8]
[1862–1863] FN 1247/v. 9 [9]
[1863–1865] FN 1247/v. 10 [10]
[1865–1868] FN 1247/v. 11 [11]
[1868–1872] FN 1247/v. 12 [12]
[1843] FN 1247/envelope [Env]
Indian Blotters [IB]
[1847] FN 1241/v. 1 [1]
[1849–1851] FN 1241/v. 2 [2]
[1850–1851] FN 1241/v. 3 [3]
[1850–1852] FN 1241/v. 4 [4]
[1853] FN 1241/v. 5 [5]
[1857] FN 1241/v. 6 [6]
[Various dates] FM 1241/envelope [Env]
Map [1857] FN 1852/map 10 [M]
Loose Papers and Correspondence [Box]
[1840–1850] FN Box 1 [1]
[1850–1851] FN Box 2 [2]
[1851–1852] FN Box 3 [3]
[1852–1853] FN Box 4 [4]
[1854] FN Box 5 [5]
[1854] FN Box 6 [6]
[1855] FN Box 7 [7]
[1855–1856] FN Box 8 [8]
[1856–1857] FN Box 9 [9]
[1857] FN Box 10 [10]
[1858] FN Box 11 [11]
[1859] FN Box 12 [12]
[1859–1860] FN Box 13 [13]
[1860–1861] FN Box 14 [14]
[1861–1862] FN Box 15 [15]
[1863] FN Box 16 [16]
[1863–1864] FN Box 17 [17]
[1865] FN Box 18 [18]
[1866] FN Box 19 [19]
[1867] FN Box 20 [20]

[1868–1869] FN Box 21 [21]
[1870–1901] FN Box 22 [22]
Muck Farm Journal [1858–1859] FN 1236 [MFJ]
Tlithlow Journal [1851, 1856–1857] FN 1235 [TJ]

Massachusetts Historical Society, Boston [MHS]
Extracts from the Log *Margaret,* 1791–1894 [*Margaret*]
Anonymous, "Logbook of the Ship *Pearl,* 1804–1808" [*Pearl*]

National Archives of Canada [NAC]
New Westminster Penitentiary, Register of inmates and Educational register,
RG 73, vol. 277 (in Regional Depository, Burnaby, BC) [Penitentiary]
Post Office records, R63

Oblate House, Vancouver [OblH]
Alert Bay, Fort Rupert baptismal, marriage, death records [Alert]
Fraser Valley baptismal, marriage, death records [Fraser]

Old Dartmouth Historical Society and Whaling Museum, New Bedford,
Massachusetts [ODHS]
Leonard, Spencer, "Ship *Alert* Log Book of Boston Lemuel Porter Esq.," Ms. 477
[Alert]

Oregon Historical Society, Portland [OHS]
Account Books of Fort Hall, July 31–August 1837, MS 1198 [FtHallAB]
Columbia River Fishing and Trading Company Correspondence Book [CRFTCCB]

Peabody Essex Museum, Salem, Massachusetts [PEM]
Kemp, Robert, Journal of the *Otter,* 1809–1811 [*Otter*]

Rosenbach Library, Philadelphia [RosL]
McDougall, Duncan, *Astoria* Journal, 1811–1813 [*Astoria*]

St. Edward's Church, Duncan, British Columbia [StEdC]
St. Ann's Baptisms-Marriages, 1886–1896

St. Elizabeth's Church, Sidney, British Columbia [StElizC]
Assumption Baptisms-Marriages

Salt Spring Archives, Ganges, British Columbia [SSA]
McMinn, Diane, "Portland Island," typescript

San Juan Library, Friday Harbor, Washington
Firth, Lila Hannah, "Early Life on San Juan Island," transcript

Sisters of St. Ann Archives, Victoria
"St. Mary's Mission School, Mission City, BC, 1862–1950," typescript

South Oregon Historical Society, Medford [SOHS]
Various manuscript materials

University of British Columbia Library, Special Collections, Vancouver [UBC]
William Duncan Papers, Community Education Registers, 1857–1860 [Duncan]
Frederick W. Howay Papers, Hawaiian Island Files, Box 10 [Howay]
James Swan Papers, Hawaiian Consulate Files, Box 10 [Swan]

University of California at Berkeley, Bancroft Library, Berkeley, California
Bayley, C. A., "Early Life on Vancouver Island," Mss. P-18C3

University of Western Washington, Center for Pacific Studies, Bellingham [UWW]
Jeffcott Collection, Series 1, Box 1/8 [Jeffcott]
Buswell Collection, Series 1, Boxes 4/24 and 5/31 [Buswell]

Vancouver School of Theology, United Church Archives, Vancouver [VST]
Coqualeetza Industrial School, Admissions and Discharges [Coqualeetza]

Yale University, Beinecke Library, New Haven, Connecticut [YU]
Haskins, Ralph, "Journal of a Fur Trading Voyage from Boston to the Northwest Coast of America in the Ship *Atahualpa,* 1800–03," Western Americana, Ms. s-126 [*Atahualpa*]
Clinton, Ebenezer, "Journal of ships *Vancouver* and *Atahualpa,* 1804–06," Western Americana, Ms. 92 [Clinton]

Private Collections [PrivMS]
Cordocedo, Louis, conversation with Jean Barman, North Vancouver, June 29, 1993
Gale, William A., "A Journal Kept on Board the Ship *Albatross,* Nathan Winship, *Albatross* Commander, On a Voyage from Boston to the Northwest Coast of America and China in the Years 1809, 10, 11, 12"
Gibson, Theresa, conversation with Susan Garcia and Jean Barman, Richmond, June 13, 2004
Harris, Stanley and Pauline, conversation with Jean Barman, Ladner, March 10, 1991
Huson, Elizabeth, interview with Dorothy Myers, Vancouver, August 1971 [Huson]
Jackson, John C., research on Cawaniah family and conversation, March 13, 2004
Johnston, Vi, conversation with Jean Barman and Bruce Watson, New Westminster, September 23, 1994 [Johnston]
Kamano family bible [Kamano]
Kendrick, Lloyd, interview with Jack Montgomery, Maple Ridge, June 1993 [Kendrick 1]
Kendrick, Lloyd, conversation with Jean Barman, Ruby Creek, March 10, 1999 [Kendrick 2]
Mulcahy, Jennie, to her brother Tommy Tamaree, Juneau, February 11, 1891, in family possession
Myers, Carey, conversations with Jean Barman and Bruce Watson, various dates up to January 28, 2005 [Myers]
Nahanee, James, conversation with Jean Barman, North Vancouver, January 7, 2003
Roland, Loretta, conversation with Jean Barman, Fulford Harbour, February 24, 1991
Seeley, Ken and Dale, conversation with Jean Barman, Campbell River, July 22, 1992
Shepard, Bea, Vina Shepard, and Rosemary Unger, conversation with Jean Barman, Victoria, June 27, 1990
Unger, Rosemary Tahouney, "Plan of Graves in graveyard beside the church"
Wright (Oehlman), Roree, conversations with Jean Barman, Vancouver, March 20, 1993, Island of Hawai'i, December 11, 2005

Various Locations
1850–1880 U.S. Manuscript Censuses [1850–1880 U.S. Census]
1881–1901 Canada Manuscript Censuses [1881–1901 Canada Census]

Primary Printed Sources

Allard, Jason O. "Christmas at Fort Langley, Gay Time in Olden Days." *Province,* October 25, 1924.

Anderson, Rufus. *The Hawaiian Islands: Their Progress and Condition under Missionary Labors.* Boston: Gould and Lincoln, 1865.

———. *A History of the Sandwich Islands Mission.* Boston: Boston Congregational Publishing Society, 1870.

Atkinson, George H. "The Diary of Rev. George H. Atkinson, D. D., 1847–1858." Edited by E. Ruth Rockwood. *Oregon Historical Quarterly* 40–41 (1939).

Bailey, Margaret Jewett. *The Grains or Passages in the Life of Ruth Rover, with Occasional Pictures of Oregon, Natural and Moral.* Corvallis: Oregon State University Press, 1985.

Ball, John. *Autobiography.* Glendale, Calif.: Arthur H. Clark, 1925.

Barneby, Henry. *Life and Labour in the Far, Far West: Being Notes of a Tour in the Western States, British Columbia, Manitoba, and the North-west Territory.* London: Cassell, 1884.

Barrot, Théodore-Adolphe. *Unless Haste Is Made: A French Skeptic's Account of the Sandwich Islands in 1836.* Kailua: Press Pacifica, 1978.

Bate, Mark. "Reminiscences of Early Nanaimo Days." *Nanaimo Free Press,* February–May 1907.

Beaver, Herbert. "Indian Conditions in 1836–38." Edited by Nellie Pipes. *Oregon Historical Quarterly* 24 (1923).

———. *Reports and Letters of Herbert Beaver, 1836–1838.* Edited by Thomas E. Jessett. Portland: Champoeg Press, 1959.

Belcher, Edward. *Narrative of a Voyage Round the World.* Vol. 1. London: H. Colburn, 1843.

Bennett, Guy Vernon. "Early Relations of the Sandwich Islands to the Old Oregon Territory." *Washington Historical Quarterly* 4, no. 2 (April 1913).

Bingham, Hiram. *A Residence of Twenty-One Years in the Sandwich Islands.* Hartford, Conn.: Hezekiah Huntington, 1847.

Bishop, Sereno Edwards. *Reminiscences of Old Hawaii.* Honolulu: Hawaiian Gazette, 1916.

———. "Why are the Hawaiians Dying Out?" *The Friend,* March 1889, 18–20; April 1889, 26–27.

Blackman, William Fremont. *The Making of Hawaii, A Study in Social Evolution.* London: Macmillan, 1899.

Blue, George Verne. "A Hudson's Bay Company Contract for Hawaiian Labor." *Oregon Historical Quarterly* 25, no. 1 (March 1924).

Boelen, Jacobus. *A Merchant's Perspective: Captain Jacobus Boelen's Narrative of his Visit to Hawaii'i in 1828.* Translated by Frank J. A. Broeze. Honolulu: Hawaiian Historical Society, 1988.

Bonney, W. P. *History of Pierce County Washington.* Vol. 1. Chicago: Pioneer Historical Publishing Company, 1927.

Bowsfield, Hartwell, ed. *Fort Victoria Letters, 1846–1851.* Winnipeg: Hudson's Bay Society, 1979.

British Columbia, Superintendent of Police, *Annual Report,* 1881, 1882, 1894.

British Columbia Gulf Island Cemeteries. Richmond: BC Genealogical Society, 1989.

Bushby, Arthur T. "The Journal of Arthur Thomas Bushby, 1858–1859." Edited by Dorothy Blakey Smith. *British Columbia Historical Quarterly* 21 (1957–1958).

Carey, Charles Henry, ed. "The Mission Record Book of the Methodist Episcopal Church, Willamette Station, Oregon Territory, North America, Commenced 1834." *Oregon Historical Quarterly* 23, no. 3 (1922).

"Census of the Islands." *The Friend,* November 15, 1849.

Charlton, Richard. "The Sandwich and Bonin Islands," London, August 11, 1832. Reprinted in Hawaiian Historical Society, *Annual Report* 15 (1907).

Choir's Pioneer Directory of the City of Seattle and King County. Pottsville, Pa.: Miners' Journal Book, 1878.

Coan, Titus. *Life in Hawaii: An Autobiographic Sketch of Mission Life and Labors (1835–1881).* New York: Anson D. F. Randolph & Co., 1882.

Colnett, James. *The Journal of Captain James Colnett aboard the "Argonaut" from April 26, 1789, to Nov. 3, 1791.* Edited by F. W. Howay. Toronto: Champlain Society, 1940.

Colonist. Victoria, British Columbia.

Cone, Anson Sterling. "Reminiscences." *Oregon Historical Quarterly* 4, no. 3 (September 1903).

Cook, James. *Captain Cook's Voyages of Discovery.* Edited by John Barrow. London: Dent & Sons, 1906.

Corney, Peter. *Voyages in the Northern Pacific.* Honolulu: Thos. G. Thrum, 1896. Reprinted from *London Literary Gazette,* 1821, and reprinted Fairfield, Wash.: Ye Galleon Press, 1965.

Coues, Elliot, ed. *New Light on the Early History of the Greater Northwest: The Manuscript Journals of Alexander Henry and of David Thompson.* 2 vols. Minneapolis: Ross & Haines, 1965, orig. 1897.

Cox, Ross. *Adventures on the Columbia River, Including the Narrative of a Residence of Six Years' on the West Side of the Rocky Mountains among Various Tribes of Indians Hitherto Unknown: Together with A Journey Across the American Continent.* New York: J. & J. Harper, 1832.

Damon, Samuel Chenery. "Hawaiians in California." *The Friend,* February 2, 1863, 10.

———. "Kanaka Diggings." *The Friend,* December 1, 1849, 83.

———. "Lower Oregon—Population." *The Friend,* October 1, 1849, 51.

Dampier, Robert. *To the Sandwich Islands on H.M.S. Blonde.* Honolulu: University Press of Hawai'i, 1971.

Dibble, Sheldon. *A History of the Sandwich Islands.* Honolulu: Thrum, 1909, orig. 1843.

Dickey, George, ed. *The Journal of Occurrences at Fort Nisqually, May 30, 1833–September 27, 1859.* Tacoma, Wash.: Fort Nisqually Association, 1989.

Drury, Clifford Merrill. *The Diaries and Letters of Henry H. Spalding and Asa Bowen Smith relating to the Nez Perce Mission 1838–1842.* Glendale, Calif.: Arthur H. Clark, 1938.

Duhaut-Cilly, Auguste Bernard. "Shadows of Destiny: A French Navigator's View of the Hawaiian Kingdom and its Government in 1828." Edited by Alfons L. Korn. *Hawaiian Journal of History* 17 (1983).

Dunn, Barbara E. "William Little Lee and Catherine Lee: Letters from Hawai'i 1848–1855." *Hawaiian Journal of History* 38 (2004).

Egerström, C. Axel. *Borta är bra, men hemma är bäst.* Stockholm: Bonnier, 1859. Translated and reprinted in "Hawaii in 1855," *Hawaiian Journal of History* 9 (1975).

Ellis, William. *Narrative of a Tour Through Hawaii, or Owhyhee.* London: H. Faber and P. Jackson, 1828.

Emmons, George Thornton. "Extracts from the Emmons Journal." *Oregon Historical Quarterly* 64, no. 3 (September 1963).

Farnham, Thomas J. *Travels in the Great Western Prairies, the Anahuac and Rocky Mountains and the Oregon Territory.* Cleveland: A. H. Clark, 1906, orig. 1843.

————. *An 1839 Wagon Train Journal.* New York: Greeley and McElrath, 1843.

Fidler, W. W. "Kanaka Flat." *Bonville's Western Weekly,* March 1909, 71.

Forbes, David W. *An Act to Prohibit Hawaiians from Emigrating to California "Where they May Die in Misery."* San Francisco: Paul Markham Kahn, 1986.

Franchère, Gabriel. *Journal of a Voyage on the North West Coast of North America During the Years 1811, 1812, 1813, and 1814.* Edited by W. Kaye Lamb. Toronto: Champlain Society, 1969.

Gary, George. "Diary of Rev. George Gary." Edited by Charles Henry Carey. *Oregon Historical Quarterly* 24, nos. 1–3 (March–September 1923).

Government Gazette. Victoria.

Green, Jonathan S. *Journal of a Tour to the North West Coast of America in the Year 1829.* New York: C. F. Heartman, 1915.

Hale, Horatio. *Ethnography and Philology.* Philadelphia: Lea and Blanchard, 1846.

Harte, Bret. "The Luck of Roaring Camp." *Overland Monthly,* August 1868.

Hawley, Robert Emmett. *Skqee Mus or Pioneer Days on the Nooksack.* Bellingham, Wash.: Whatcom Museum of History and Art, 1945.

Heath, Joseph Thomas. *Memoirs of Nisqually.* Fairfield, Wash.: Ye Galleon Press, 1979.

Helmcken, John S. *The Reminiscences of Doctor John Sebastian Helmcken.* Edited by Dorothy Blakey Smith. Vancouver: UBC Press, 1975.

Henry, Alexander, Jr. *The Journal of Alexander Henry the Younger, 1799–1814.* Vol. 2. Toronto: Champlain Society, 1992.

"Here and There." *Democratic Times,* May 11, 1888.

Hines, Gustavus. "A Document of Mission History, 1833–43." Edited by Robert Mouton Gatke. *Oregon Historical Quarterly* 36 (1935).

Howay, Frederic W., ed. "The Brig Owhyhee in the Columbia, 1829–30." *Oregon Historical Quarterly* 35, no. 1 (March 1934).

————. "The Ship Pearl in Hawaii in 1805 and 1806." *Hawaiian Historical Society,* Report, 1937.

————. *Voyages of the "Columbia" to the Northwest Coast 1787–1790 and 1790–1793.* Boston: Massachusetts Historical Society, 1941.

Howe, Samuel D. "The Early History." *Washington Standard,* May 23, 1868.

Howison, Neil M. "Report of Lieutenant Neil M. Howison on Oregon, 1846." *Oregon Historical Quarterly* 14, no. 1 (March 1913).

Hulbert, Archer Butler, and Dorothy Printup, eds. *Marcus Whitman, Crusader.* Vols. 1–3. Denver: Stewart Commission of Colorado College and Denver Public Library, 1938–1941.

————. *The Oregon Crusade: Across Land and Sea to Oregon.* Vol. 5 of *Overland to the Pacific.* Denver: Stewart Commission of Colorado College and Denver Public Library, 1935.

Hussey, John A., ed. *The Voyage of the Raccoon: A "Secret" Journal of a Visit to Oregon, California and Hawaii, 1813–1814.* San Francisco: Book Club of California, 1958.

Ii, John Papa. *Fragments of Hawaiian History.* Honolulu: Bishop Museum Press, 1959.

In the Supreme Court of Washington Territory. January Term, A. D. 1889. *The Corporation of the Catholic Bishop of Nesqually, in the Territory of Washington, Plaintiff and Appellant, v. John Gibbon, T. M. Anderson and R. T. Yeatman, Defendants and Appellees. Brief on Behalf of the Appellees, and the United States of America, the Real party in Interest.* No publishing data (copy in Kent State University Library).

Ingraham, Joseph. *The Log of the Brig Hope.* Honolulu: Hawaiian Historical Society, 1918.

Irving, Washington. *Astoria or Anecdotes of an Enterprise Beyond the Rocky Mountains.* Edited by Edgeley W. Todd. Norman: University of Oklahoma Press, 1964.

Jacobsen, Johan Adrian. *Alaskan Voyage 1881–1883: An Expedition to the Northwest Coast of America.* Chicago: University of Chicago Press, 1977.

Judd, Laura Fish. *Honolulu: Sketches of Life in the Hawaiian Islands from 1828 to 1861.* Chicago: Lakeside Press, 1966.

Kamakau, Samuel Mānaiakalani. *Ka Po'e Kahiko: The People of Old.* Translated by Mary Kawena Pukui. Honolulu: Bishop Museum Press, 1964.

———. *Ruling Chiefs of Hawaii.* Rev. ed. Honolulu: Kamehameha Schools Press, 1992.

———. *Tales and Traditions of the People of Old: Nā Mo'olelo a ka Po'e Kahiko.* Translated by Mary Kawena Pukui. Honolulu: Bishop Museum Press, 1991.

———. *The Works of the People of Old: Nā Hana a ka Po'e Kahiko.* Translated by Mary Kawena Pukui, edited by Dorothy B. Barrère. Honolulu: Bishop Museum Press, 1976.

Kane, Paul, *Wanderings of an Artist.* Edmonton: Hurtig, 1968, orig. 1859.

Kelley, Hall J. *A Geographical Sketch of that Part of North America called Oregon.* Boston: J. Howa, 1830. Reprinted as *Hall J. Kelley on Oregon.* Edited by Fred Wilbur Powell. Princeton: Princeton University Press, 1932.

Kenn, Charles. "A Visit to California Gold Fields." Hawaiian Historical Society, *Annual Report* 74 (1965).

Kepelino. *Kepelino's Traditions of Hawaii.* Edited by Martha Warren Beckwith. Bernice P. Bishop Museum, Bulletin 95, Honolulu, 1932.

"Killed." *Oregon Sentinel,* April 6, 1867.

Lattie, Alexander. "Alexander Lattie's Fort George Journal, 1846." *Oregon Historical Quarterly* 64, no. 2 (September 1963).

Lee, D., and J. H. Frost. *Ten Years in Oregon.* New York: The Authors, 1844.

Loa'a Ka 'Aina Ho'opulapula: Applying for Hawaiian Homelands. Honolulu: Department of Hawaiian Homelands, State of Hawai'i, 2000.

McDonald, Archibald. *This Blessed Wilderness: Archibald McDonald's Letters from the Columbia, 1822–44.* Edited by Jean Murray Cole. Vancouver: UBC Press, 2001.

McDougall, Duncan. *Annals of Astoria: The Headquarters Log of the Pacific Fur Company on the Columbia River, 1811–15.* Edited by Robert F. Jones. New York: Fordham University Press, 1999.

McKenney's Pacific Coast Directory for 1883–84. San Francisco.

McLoughlin, John. "Documentary." Edited by Katharine B. Judson. *Oregon Historical Quarterly* 17 (1916).

———. *John McLoughlin's Business Correspondence, 1847–48.* Edited by William R. Sampson. Seattle: University of Washington Press, 1973.

———. *The Letters of John McLoughlin, 1825–28.* Edited by E. E. Rich. London: Hudson's Bay Record Society, 1941.

————. *Letters of Dr. John McLoughlin Written at Fort Vancouver, 1829–1832.* Edited by Burt Barker. Portland: Binford & Mort for the Oregon Historical Society, 1948.

————. *The Letters of John McLoughlin from Fort Vancouver, 1839–44.* Edited by E. E. Rich. Winnipeg: Hudson's Bay Society, 1943.

Maclachlan, Morag, ed. *Fort Langley Journals, 1827–30.* Vancouver: UBC Press, 1998.

Malo, David. *Hawaiian Antiquities: Mo'olelo Hawaii.* Honolulu: Hawaiian Gazette, 1903.

————. "On the Decrease of Population on the Hawaiian Islands." *Hawaiian Spectator* 2, no. 2 (April 1839).

Meares, John. *Voyages Made in the Years 1788 and 1789 from China to the North West Coast of America.* London: Topographical Press, 1790.

Menzies, Archibald. "Menzies' California Journal." *California Historical Society Quarterly* 2, no. 4 (January 1824).

Minto, John. "From Youth to Old Age as an American." *Oregon Historical Quarterly* 9, no. 1 (March 1908).

————. "Reminiscences of Experiences on the Oregon Trail in 1844." *Oregon Historical Quarterly* 2, no. 3 (September 1901).

Moore, George. "Public Meeting." *Oregonian,* March 6, 1852.

Munnick, Harriet Duncan, ed. *Catholic Church Records of the Pacific Northwest: Vancouver.* 2 vols. St. Paul, Ore.: French Prairie Press, 1972; *Stellamaris Mission.* St. Paul, Ore.: French Prairie Press, 1972; *St. Paul.* 3 vols. Portland: Binford & Mort, 1979; *Oregon City.* Portland: Binford & Mort, 1984.

"Native Seamen." *The Friend,* September 4, 1844, 79.

Naukana, L. "News on the events held by the Hawaiians in Port Gamble." *Ka Nupepa Kuokoa,* November 14, 1865.

Notices & Voyages of the famed Quebec Mission to the Pacific Northwest. Portland: Oregon Historical Society, 1956.

Ogden, Peter S. *Peter Skene Ogden's Snake Country Journals 1824–25 and 1825–26.* Edited by E. E. Rich. London: Hudson's Bay Record Society, 1950.

O'Harra, Marjorie. "From the Desk." *Medford Mail Tribune,* March 22, 1867.

Pambrun, Andrew Dominique. *Sixty Years on the Frontier in the Pacific Northwest.* Fairfield, Wash.: Ye Galleon Press, 1978.

Parker, Samuel. *Journal of an Exploring Expedition Beyond the Rocky Mountains.* Minneapolis: Ross & Haines, 1967, orig. 1838.

Pogue, J. F. "Hawaiian Settlements in California." *The Friend,* August 1868, 69.

Portlock, Nathaniel. *A Voyage Round the World; But More Particularly to the North-west Coast of America: Performed in 1785, 1786, 1787, and 1788.* London: Stockdale and Goulding, 1789.

Reynolds, Stephen. *The Voyage of the New Hazard to the Northwest Coast, Hawaii and China, 1810–1813.* Edited by F. W. Howay. Salem, Ore.: Ye Galleon Press, 1970.

Roberts, George B. "The Round Hand of George B. Roberts, The Cowlitz Farm Journal." Edited by Thomas Vaughan. *Oregon Historical Quarterly* 63 (June–September 1962).

Roquefeuil, Camille de. *Journal d'un voyage autour du monde pendant les années 1816, 1817, 1818, et 1819.* Paris: Ponthier, 1823. Translated and reprinted in Mary

Ellen Birkett. "Hawai'i in 1819: An Account by Camille de Roquefeuil." *Hawaiian Journal of History* 34 (2000).

Ross, Alexander. *Adventures of the First Settlers on the Oregon or Columbia River, 1810–1813.* London: Smith, Elder & Co., 1849.

———. *The Fur Hunters of the Far West.* Edited by Kenneth A. Spaulding. Norman: University of Oklahoma Press, 1956.

Sandwich Island Gazette. Honolulu.

Seton, Alfred. *Astorian Adventure: The Journal of Alfred Seton, 1811–1815.* Edited by Robert F. Jones. New York: Fordham University Press, 1993.

Shaw, William. *Golden Dreams and Waking Realities; Being the Adventures of a Gold-Seeker in California and the Pacific Islands.* London: Smith, Elder and Co., 1851.

Shepard, Cyrus. *Diary of Cyrus Shepard, March 4, 1834–December 20, 1835.* Compiled by Gerry Gilman. Vancouver, Wash.: Clark County Genealogical Society, 1969.

Simpson, George. *Fur Trade and Empire, George Simpson's Journal, 1824–25.* Edited by Frederick Merk. Cambridge, Mass.: Harvard University Press, 1968.

———. *London Correspondence Inward.* Edited by Glyndwr Williams. Winnipeg: Hudson's Bay Society, 1973.

———. *Narrative of a Journey Round the World, During the Years 1841 and 1842.* London: Henry Colburn, 1847.

———. *Part of Dispatch from George Simpson . . . 1829.* Edited by E. E. Rich. Winnipeg: Hudson's Bay Society, 1947.

Slacum, William A. "Document: Slacum's Report on Oregon, 1836–37." *Oregon Historical Quarterly* 34 (1935).

Soule, Frank, et al. *Annals of San Francisco.* New York: Appleton, 1854.

Stewart, Charles Samuel. *Private Journal of a Voyage to the Pacific Ocean and Residence at the Sandwich Islands in the years 1822, 1823, 1824, and 1825.* New York: John P. Haven, 1828.

Thompson, David. *David Thompson's Narrative, 1784–1812.* Edited by Richard Glover. Toronto: Champlain Society, 1962.

———. *Columbia Journals.* Edited by Barbara Belyea. Montreal and Kingston: McGill-Queen's University Press, 1994.

Told by the Pioneers: Tales of Frontier Life As Told By Those Who Remember The Days of the Territory and Early Statehood of Washington. Vol. 3. Olympia: Washington Pioneers Project, 1938.

Tolmie, William Fraser. *The Journals of William Fraser Tolmie: Physician and Fur Trader.* Vancouver: Mitchell Press, 1963.

Townsend, John Kirk. *Narrative of a Journey Across the Rocky Mountains to the Columbia River.* Philadelphia: Henry Perkins, 1839.

Twain, Mark. *Mark Twain's Letters from Hawaii.* Edited by A. Grove Day. New York: Appleton-Century, 1966.

Vancouver, George. *A Voyage of Discovery to the North Pacific Ocean and round the World, 1791–1795.* Edited by W. Kaye Lamb. London: Hakluyt Society, 1984.

Vancouver Sun. Vancouver.

Vancouver World. Vancouver.

Varigny, Charles de. *Fourteen Years in the Sandwich Islands 1855–1868.* Translated by Alfons L. Korn. Honolulu: University Press of Hawai'i, 1981.

Whitman, Narcissa. *Letters.* Fairfield, Wash.: Ye Galleon Press, 1986.

Wilkes, Charles. *Narrative of the United States Exploring Expedition during the Years 1838, 1839, 1840, 1841, 1842.* 5 vols. Philadelphia: Lea and Blanchard, 1845.

Wiswell, Ella L. "A Russian Traveler's Impressions of Hawaii and Tahiti, 1859–1860." *Hawaiian Journal of History* 17 (1983).

Work, John. "The Journal of John Work, March 21–May 14, 1825." Edited by Nellie B. Pipes. *Oregon Historical Quarterly* 45, no. 2 (June 1944).

———. "Journal of John Work, November and December 1824." *Washington Historical Quarterly* 3, no. 3 (July 1912).

———. "The Journal of John Work, 1835." Edited by Henry Drummond Dee. Pt. 5. *British Columbia Historical Quarterly* 9, no. 2 (April 1945).

Wyeth, N. J. *The Correspondence and Journals of Captain Nathaniel J. Wyeth, 1831–36.* Edited by F. G. Young. Eugene: University Press, 1899.

Secondary Sources

Adams, Romanzo. *Interracial Marriage in Hawaii.* New York: Macmillan, 1937.

Anderson, Steven A. *The Physical Structure of Fort Nisqually.* Tacoma: Metropolitan Park District of Tacoma, 1988.

Barbeau, Marius. *Totem Poles.* Vol. 2. Ottawa: National Museum, 1964, orig. 1950.

Barman, Jean. *Maria Mahoi of the Islands.* Vancouver: New Star, 2004.

———. "Family Life at Fort Langley." *British Columbia Historical News* 32, no. 4 (Fall 1999): 16–23.

———. "New Land, New Lives: Hawaiian Settlement in British Columbia." *Hawaiian Journal of History* 29 (1996): 1–32.

———. *Stanley Park's Secret: The Forgotten Families of Whoi Whoi, Kanaka Ranch, and Brockton Point.* Madeira Park, B.C.: Harbour, 2005.

———. *The West beyond the West: A History of British Columbia.* Rev. ed. Toronto: University of Toronto Press, 1996.

———. "William Naukana." In *Dictionary of Canadian Biography.* Vol. 13 (1994): 761–762.

Beechert, Edward D. *Working in Hawaii: A Labor History.* Honolulu: University of Hawai'i Press, 1985.

Beidleman, Richard G. "Nathaniel Wyeth's Fort Hall." *Oregon Historical Quarterly* 58 (1957): 196–250.

Bennett, Guy Vernon. "Early Relations of the Sandwich Islands with the Old Oregon Territory." *Pacific Northwest Quarterly* 4, no. 2 (April 1913): 116–126.

Bingham, Alfred M. "Sybil's Bones, a Chronicle of Three Hiram Binghams." *Hawaiian Journal of History* 9 (1975).

Blaisdell, Kekuni. "'Hawaiian' vs. 'Kanaka Maoli' as Metaphors." *Hawaii Review* 13 (1889).

Blue, George Verne. "Early Relations between Hawaii and the Northwest Coast." Hawaiian Historical Society, *Annual Report,* 1925, 16–22.

———. "Mining Laws of Jackson County, 1860–1876." *Oregon Historical Quarterly* 23, no. 2 (June 1922).

Bona, Milton. "Hawaiians Made Life 'More Bearable' at Fort Vancouver." *Clark County History* 8 (1972): 159–175.

Boyd, Robert. *People of the Dalles, The Indians of Wascopam Mission.* Lincoln: University of Nebraska Press, 1996.

Bradley, Harold Whitman. *The American Frontier in Hawaii, The Pioneers, 1789–1843.* Gloucester, Mass.: Peter Smith, 1968.

———. "The Hawaiian Islands and the Pacific Fur Trade, 1785–1813." *Pacific Northwest Quarterly* 30 (July 1939): 275–299.

British Columbia Gulf Islands Cemeteries. Richmond: BC Genealogical Society, 1989.

Buck, Elizabeth. *Paradise Remade: The Politics of Culture and History in Hawai'i.* Philadelphia: Temple University Press, 1993.

Burley, Edith I. *Servants of the Honourable Company.* Toronto: Oxford, 1997.

Busch, C., and Barry M. Gough. *Fur Traders from New England: The Boston Men in the North Pacific, 1787–1800.* Spokane: Arthur H. Clark, 1997.

Bushnell, Andrew F. "The 'Horror' Reconsidered: An Evaluation of the Historical Evidence for Population Decline in Hawai'i, 1778–1803." *Pacific Studies* 16 (1993).

Campbell, I. C. "The Culture of Culture Contact: Refractions from Polynesia." *Journal of World History* 14, no. 1 (March 2003).

Chapin, Helen Geracimos. *Shaping History: The Role of Newspapers in Hawai'i.* Honolulu: University of Hawai'i Press, 1996.

Chappell, David A. *Double Ghosts: Oceanian Voyagers on Euroamerican Ships.* New York: M. E. Sharpe, 1997.

Clark, Robert Carleton. "Hawaiians in Early Oregon." *Oregon Historical Quarterly* 35 (March 1934).

Coman, Edwin T., Jr., and Helen M. Gibbs. *Time, Tide and Timber: A Century of Pope & Talbot.* Stanford: Stanford University Press, 1949.

Cooke, Mary. "Hawaiian Colony Found in Canada." *Honolulu Advertiser,* June 19, 1971.

Crickmer, William Burton. "Story of the Planting of the English Church in Columbia." *Christian Advocate and Review,* s.d. (copy in Vancouver Public Library).

Daws, Gavan. *Shoal of Time: A History of the Hawaiian Islands.* Honolulu: University of Hawai'i Press, 1968.

Dillon, Richard H. *Siskiyou Trail: The Hudson's Bay Company Route to California.* New York: McGraw-Hill, 1975.

Drury, Clifford Merrill. *Henry Harmon Spalding.* Caldwell, Idaho: Caxton Printers, Ltd, 1936.

———. *Marcus Whitman, M.D., Pioneer and Martyr.* Caldwell, Idaho: Caxton Printers, Ltd, 1937.

Duncan, Janice K. "Minority Without a Champion: The Kanaka Contribution to the Western United States, 1750–1900." Unpublished MA thesis, History, Portland State University, 1972.

Dye, Tom. "Population Trends in Hawai'i before 1778." *Hawaiian Journal of History* 28 (1994).

Eakins, Jan. "Port Gamble: Managing Cultural Diversity on Puget Sound." *CRM* [*Cultural Resource Management*] 8 (1999).

Eells, Myron. *Marcus Whitman, Pathfinder and Patriot.* Seattle: Alice Harriman Company, 1909.

———. *Father Eells.* Boston: Congregational Sunday-School and Publishing Society, 1894.

Elliott, T. C. "The Coming of the White Women, 1836." *Oregon Historical Quarterly* 38, no. 1 (March 1937).

Ermatinger, C. O. "The Columbia River under Hudson's Bay Company Rule." *Oregon Historical Quarterly* 5, no. 2 (April 1914).

Fidler, W. W. "Kanaka Flat." *Bonneville's Western Weekly,* March 1909.

Ford, Clellan S. *Smoke From Their Fires: The Life of a Kwakiutl Chief.* New Haven: Yale University Press, 1941.

Gonsalves, Puanani Mundon. *Lahapa Kaleimakali'i.* N.p.: September 1997. Copy courtesy of Gil Garrison.

Greer, Richard A. "Wandering Kamaainas: Notes on Hawaiian Emigration Before 1848." *Journal of the West* 11 (April 1967): 221–225.

Grimshaw, Patricia. *Paths of Duty: American Missionary Wives in Nineteenth-Century Hawaii.* Honolulu: University of Hawai'i Press, 1989.

Gudde, Erwin G. *Sutter's Own Story.* New York: Putman's 1936.

Halualani, Rona Tamiko. *In the Name of Hawaiians: Native Identities and Cultural Politics.* Minneapolis: University of Minnesota Press, 2002.

Hamilton, Beatrice. "Dreams Come True." *Colonist,* October 31, 1971.

———. *Salt Spring Island.* Vancouver: Mitchell Press, 1969.

Handy, E. S. Craighill, and Elizabeth Green Handy. *Native Planters in Old Hawaii: Their Life, Lore, and Environment.* Bernice P. Bishop Museum Bulletin 233, Honolulu, 1972.

———, and Mary Kawena Pukui. *The Polynesian Family System in Ka'u, Hawai'i.* Wellington: Polynesian Society, 1958.

Hanson, Wade R. *Nawana.* Bellingham, Wash., n.d. Courtesy of Gil Garrison.

"Hawaiian Pioneers?" Washington Country Historical Society, *Express,* March 1981.

Herman, R.D.K. "Coin of the Realm: The Political Economy of 'Indolence' in the Hawaiian Islands." *History and Anthropology* 11, nos. 2–3 (1999).

Hill, Beth. *The Remarkable World of Frances Barkley: 1769–1845.* Sidney: Gray's Publishing, 1978.

———. *Times Past: Salt Spring Island Houses and History before the Turn of the Century.* Ganges: Community Arts Council, 1983.

History of the Pacific Northwest: Oregon and Washington. Vol. 1. Portland: North Pacific History Company, 1889.

History of Po'okela Church. Makawao, Hawai'i: Po'okela Church, 2002.

Howay, Frederick William. "A List of Trading Vessels in Maritime Fur Trade, 1785–1794." *Transactions of the Royal Society of Canada,* Section II, 1930.

Hussey, John A. *The History of Fort Vancouver and its Physical Structure.* Tacoma: Washington State Historical Society, 1957.

Illberbrun, W. J. "Kanaka Peter." *Hawaiian Journal of History* 6 (1972): 156–166.

Judson, Katharine B. "The British Side of the Restoration of Fort Astoria." *Oregon Historical Quarterly* 20, no. 4 (December 1919).

Kame'eleihiwa, Lilikalā. *Native Land and Foreign Desires: Pehea Lā Pono Ai?* Honolulu: Bishop Museum Press, 1992.

Kanahele, George Hu'eu Sanford. *Kū Kanaka, Stand Tall: A Search for Hawaiian Values.* Honolulu: University of Hawai'i Press and Haiaha Foundation, 1986.

Kardas, Susan. "The People Brought This and the Clatsop became Rich: A View of Nineteenth Century Fur Trade Relationships on the Lower Columbia between Chinookan Speakers, Whites and Kanakas." Unpublished Ph.D. dissertation, Bryn Mawr College, 1971.

Kelly, Marion. "Land Tenure in Hawaii." *Amerasia Journal* 7, no. 2 (1980): 57–73.

Kirch, Patrick V., and Marshall Sahlins. *Anahulu: The Anthropology of History in the Kingdom of Hawaii.* Vol. 2. Chicago: University of Chicago Press, 1992.

Kittleson, David. "Hawaiians and Fur Traders." *Hawaii Historical Review* 1, no. 2 (January 1961): 16–20.

Klan, Yvonne Mearns. "Kanaka William." *Beaver* 38 (Spring 1979).

Koppel, Tom. *Kanaka: The Untold Story of Hawaiian Pioneers in British Columbia and the Pacific Northwest.* Vancouver: Whitecap Books, 1995.

Kuykendall, Ralph. S. "American Interests and American Influence in Hawaii in 1842." Hawaii Historical Society, *Report,* 1930.

——. *The Hawaiian Kingdom.* 3 vols. Honolulu: University of Hawai'i Press, 1938, 1953, 1967.

Laing, F. W. *Colonial Farm Settlers on the Mainland of British Columbia, 1858–1871.* Victoria, 1939.

Lane, M. Melia. "The Migration of Hawaiians to Coastal British Columbia, 1810 to 1869." Unpublished MA thesis, Geography, University of Hawai'i, 1985.

Lange, Erwin F. "Oregon City Private Schools, 1843–59." *Oregon Historical Quarterly* 37, no. 4 (December 1936).

Large, R. Geddes. *The Skeena, River of Destiny.* Vancouver: Mitchell Press, 1957.

"Last Rite Conducted for 'Jumbo Nahu.'" *Vancouver Sun,* January 3, 1957.

Loewenberg, Robert J. *Equality on the Oregon Frontier: Jason Lee and the Methodist Mission, 1834–43.* Seattle: University of Washington Press, 1976.

Lugrin, N. de Bertrand. *Pioneer Women of Vancouver Islands, 1843–1866.* Victoria: Women's Canadian Club of Vancouver Island, 1928.

McDonald, Lucile S. *Making History: The People Who Shaped the San Juan Islands.* Friday Harbor, Wash.: Harbor Press, 1990.

——. *Swan Among the Indians: Life of James G. Swan, 1818–1900.* Portland: Binfords & Mort, 1972.

Mackie, Richard Somerset. *Trading Beyond the Mountains: The British Fur Trade on the Pacific 1793–1843.* Vancouver: UBC Press, 1997.

Mallandaine, E. *First Victoria Directory, 1860, 1870.*

Masson, L. R. *Les Bourgeois de la Compagnie du Nord-Ouest.* Vol. 2. New York: Antiquarian Press, 1960.

Menton, Linda. K. "A Christian and 'Civilized' Education: The Hawaiian Chiefs' Children's School, 1839–50." *History of Education Quarterly* 32, no. 2 (Summer 1992): 213–242.

Merry, Sally Engle. *Colonizing Hawai'i: The Cultural Power of Law.* Princeton: Princeton University Press, 2000.

Miller, Charles A. *Valley of the Stave.* North Vancouver: Hancock, 1981.

Miller, David G. "Ka'iana, the Once Famous 'Prince of Kaua'i.'" *Hawaiian Journal of History* 22 (1988): 1–19.

Miller, Thomas. *A Genealogical Glimpse of Historical Port Gamble.* Port Gamble: privately printed, n.d.

Moon, Sally Jo. "Aloha Alive and Well in British Columbia." *Honolulu Star-Bulletin,* August 14, 1971.

Morgan, Theodore. *Hawaii: A Century of Economic Change, 1778–1876.* Cambridge, Mass.: Harvard University Press, 1948.

Morison, Samuel Elliot. "Boston Traders in the Hawaiian Islands." *Proceedings of the Massachusetts Historical Society* 54 (October 1920–June 1921).

Morley, Alan. "Romance of Vancouver." *Sun* (Vancouver), May 7, 1940.

Morton, Jamie. *Fort Langley, An Overview of the Operations of a Diversified Fur Trade Post, 1848–1858 and the Physical Context in 1858.* Ottawa: Parks Canada, 1980.

Mykkänen, Juri. *Inventing Politics: A New Political Anthropology of the Hawaiian Kingdom.* Honolulu: University of Hawai'i Press, 2003.

Nahanee, Maurice. "Nahanee's Notebook." *Kahtou News,* August 1, 1992.

Naughton, Momilani. "Hawaiians in the Fur Trade: Cultural Influence on the Northwest Coast." Unpublished MA thesis, Anthropology, Western Washington University, 1983.

Nelson, Denys. *Fort Langley 1827–1927: A Century of Settlement in the Valley of the Lower Fraser River.* Vancouver: Art, Historical and Scientific Association, 1927.

Nicholls, Margaret. "Kamano—A Kanaka." *BC Historical News* 12 (December 1991).

Nokes, Richard J. *Almost a Hero: The Voyages of John Meares, R.N., to China, Hawaii and the Northwest Coast.* Pullman: Washington State University Press, 1998.

Osorio, Jonathan Kay Kamakawiwoʻole. *Dismembering Lāhui: A History of the Hawaiian Nation to 1887.* Honolulu: University of Hawai'i Press, 2002.

Peterson, Barbara Bennett. "Liliuokalani." In *American National Biography.* New York: Oxford University Press, 2000, on-line (www.anb.org).

Picard, Terry. "The Kanakas (Hawaiians of the North Shore)." *Kahtou: The Voice of B.C.'s First Nations* 13, no. 9 (September 2004).

Pierce, Richard. *Russian America: A Biographical Dictionary.* Kingston, Ont., and Fairbanks, Alaska: Limestone Press, 1990.

Ralston, Caroline. *Grass Huts and Warehouses: Pacific Beach Communities of the Nineteenth Century.* Canberra: Australian National University Press, 1977.

———. "Hawaii 1778–1854: Some Aspects of Makaʻainana Response to Rapid Cultural Change." *Journal of Pacific History* 19, nos. 1–2 (January–April 1984).

Richards, Mary Atherton. *Amos Starr Cooke and Juliette Montague Cooke.* Honolulu: Daughters of Hawaii, 1987, orig. 1941.

Richardson, David. *Pig War Islands.* Eastsound, Wash.: Orcas Publishing Company, 1971.

Rogers, Donnel J. "Ku on the Columbia: Hawaiian Laborers in the Pacific Northwest Fur Industry." Unpublished MA thesis, Interdisciplinary Studies, Oregon State University, 1993.

Ronda, James P. *Astoria & Empire.* Lincoln: University of Nebraska Press, 1990.

Root, Eileen M. *Hawaiian Names, English Names.* Kailua: Press Pacifica, 1987.

Royal Lineage. Honolulu: Bishop Museum Press, 2001.

Schlesser, Norman. "Kanakas in the Oregon Country." *Umpqua Trapper* 8, no. 1 (Spring 1972).

Schmitt, Robert C. *Demographic Statistics of Hawaii: 1778–1985.* Honolulu: University of Hawai'i Press, 1968.

———. *Historical Statistics of Hawaii.* Honolulu: University Press of Hawai'i, 1977.

———. "Religious Statistics of Hawaii, 1825–1972." *Hawaiian Journal of History* 7 (1973).

Silva, Noenoe K. *Aloha Betrayed: Native Hawaiian Resistance to American Colonialism.* Durham: Duke University Press, 2004.

———. "*He Kānāwai E Hoʻopau I Na Hula Kuolo Hawaiʻi:* The Political Economy of Banning the Hula." *Hawaiian Historical Review* 34 (2000).

Skaggs, Jimmy M. *The Great Guano Rush: Entrepreneurs and American Overseas Expansion.* New York: St. Martin's Press, 1994.

Spickard, Paul, Joanne L. Rondilla, and Debbie Hippolite Wright, eds. *Pacific Diaspora: Island Peoples in the United States and Across the Pacific.* Honolulu: University of Hawaiʻi Press, 2002.

Spoehr, Alexander. "Fur Traders in Hawaii: The Hudson's Bay Company in Honolulu, 1829–1861." *Hawaiian Journal of History* 20 (1986): 27–66.

Stannard, David. *Before the Horror: The Population of Hawaiʻi on the Eve of Western Contact.* Honolulu: Social Science Research Institute, University of Hawaiʻi, 1989.

Stauffer, Robert H. *Kahana: How the Land was Lost.* Honolulu: University of Hawaiʻi Press, 2004.

Taylor, Albert Pierce, ed. *The Hawaiian Islands.* Honolulu: Archives of Hawaii Commission, 1930.

Towse, Ed. "Some Hawaiians Abroad." *Papers of the Honolulu Historical Society* 11 (1904).

Trask, Haunani-Kay. *From a Native Daughter: Colonialism and Sovereignty in Hawaiʻi.* Rev. ed. Honolulu: University of Hawaiʻi Press, 1999.

Waite, Donald E. *The Langley Story Illustrated: An Early History of the Municipality of Langley.* Altona, Manitoba: Friesen, 1977.

Walker, Anna Sloan. "History of the Liquor Laws of the State of Washington." *Washington Historical Quarterly* 5, no. 2 (April 1914).

Wallace, Lee. *Sexual Encounters: Pacific Texts, Modern Sexualities.* Ithaca: Cornell University Press, 2003.

White, Richard. *"It's Your Misfortune and None of My Own": A History of the American West.* Norman: University of Oklahoma Press, 1991.

Wood, Bryce. *San Juan Island: Coastal Place Names and Cartographic Nomenclature.* Tacoma: Washington State Historical Society, 1980.

Wood, Houston. *Displacing Natives, The Rhetorical Production of Hawaiʻi.* Lanham, Md.: Rowman & Littlefield, 1999.

Young, F. G. "The Financial History of the State of Oregon." *Oregon Historical Quarterly* 10, no. 3 (September 1909).

General Index

Biographies are not indexed by subject but by name in the Names Index.
References to Hawaiians are to indigenous Hawaiians.

Index of Hawaiians in the Pacific Northwest

This index is organized by name, meaning persons sharing the same name are indexed together.

ABOUT THE AUTHORS

Jean Barman writes about British Columbia history. A fellow of the Royal Society of Canada, she is the author of, among other books, *The West beyond the West: A History of British Columbia* (University of Toronto Press). Bruce Watson is completing a biographical dictionary of the fur trade in the Pacific Northwest. In 2000 the authors, both of whom live in Vancouver, received the Charles Gates Memorial Award for best article published in *Pacific Northwest Quarterly* from the Washington State Historical Society.

Production Notes for Barman and Watson / Leaving Paradise:
Indigenous Hawaiians in the Pacific Northwest, 1787–1898

Cover and interior designed by Liz Demeter
in Garamond with display text in Dearest Script

Composition by Josie Herr

Printing and binding by The Maple-Vail Book
Manufacturing Group.

Printed on 50# Text White Opaque II, 606 ppi